1980.
10⁻

THE SEED OF THE WOMAN

The Seed of
the Woman

ARTHUR C. CUSTANCE

DOORWAY PUBLICATIONS
Box 291, Brockville, Ontario, K6V 5V5

Other Books by the Author

Without Form and Void (1970)
Noah and his Three Sons (1975)
Genesis and Fossil Man (1975)
Man in Adam and in Christ (1976)
Evolution or Creation (1976)
The Virgin Birth and the Incarnation (1977)
Time and Eternity (1977)
Hidden Things of God's Revelation (1977)
Science and Faith (1978)
The Flood: Local or Global (1979)
The Sovereignty of Grace (1979)
The Mysterious Matter of Mind (1980)
Indexes of the Doorway Papers (1980)

ISBN 0-919857-00-0

SUBSCRIBERS

Dr. & Mrs. Charles W. Asbell
Mr. & Mrs. Robert L. Asbell
Miss Anne Beams
Mr. Richard D. Boutros
Dr. Brian Bull
Mr. Raymond M. Caldwell
Mrs. Elsie Carr
Dr. & Mrs. Elihu Carranza
Mr. F. J. Cottrell
Mr. & Mrs. Clarence B. Cree
Miss Peggy Foster
Professor Wayne Frair
Mr. Gerald L. Gooden
Mr. & Mrs. C. H. Halvorson
Mr. Kenneth F. Hensley
Mr. & Mrs. Richard Hesselbarth

Mr. Stanley M. Hoersch
Dr. John R. Howitt
Mr. & Mrs. Glenn I. Kirkland
Mr. & Mrs. Hal J. Lochrie
Mrs. William W. McCall
Mrs. Eileen Powers
Mr. & Mrs. Everett W. Purcell
Mr. & Mrs. David F. Rice
Mr. William E. Rooks
Mr. & Mrs. Robert Ryan
Mr. & Mrs. Daniel F. Searle
Mr. & Mrs. Theodore R. Smith
Mr. Cornelius A. van der Gugten
Miss Evelyn White
Mr. Eric Jon Thomas
Mr. Douglas Yowell

Discovery Foundation Inc., Palo Alto (Dr. Ray C. Stedman)

While these generous friends made the publication of this volume possible, they are not to be held responsible in any way for its content. I am sure there are points in the broad sweep of its thesis with which they would individually find themselves in disagreement. But without them it would never have been published and I am deeply grateful for their help, often at considerable sacrifice to themselves.

Acknowledgement.

To Evelyn May White, the final appearance of this volume in print may be her sufficient reward. But I want to acknowledge explicitly her contribution towards its completion, a contribution that is quite beyond any true accounting.

For her remarkable level-headedness under pressure, her unfailing confidence and good nature under provocation, her perceptive criticism, and her total dedication.... I can only say — Thank you with all my heart.

To which I should add, that without any previous experience, she set the whole manuscript in camera-ready form, using an Electronic Composer: And did a magnificent job.

Arthur C. Custance.

TABLE OF CONTENTS

PART IV: TRIUMPH OVER DEATH

APPENDIXES

LIST OF TABLES

LIST OF FIGURES

NOTE REGARDING DOCUMENTATION

A dual system of notations and references has been adopted. Those works which are readily available to the average reader or are likely to be quite familiar have been put as footnotes, using symbols to indicate where they belong.

When the documentation is likely to be unfamiliar or is of a technical or scientific nature, they will be found at the end of the volume and are indicated by call numbers in the text. The reader who wishes only to follow the basic thesis of the book without reference to these somewhat extended notes and documentations, may ignore the call numbers.

Gen. 3:15
*Her seed
shall bruise
(Satan's) head.*

Gal. 3:16
That seed is Christ.

John 12:24
Except a seed . . . die, it abideth alone.

INTRODUCTION

And now . . . .
lest he live for ever . . . .
God drove the man
from the Garden.
Genesis 3:22-24

Was there once such a Garden where man lived and might never have died, a substantive basis for all those Shangri-las where people scarcely ever grew old — only, in this Garden, they would never have grown old at all?

Is it conceivable that man could have lived on and on endlessly, for hundreds of years, even for thousands of years — perhaps, indeed, even for ever? Is not death inevitable as the appropriate and expected end for every thing that lives — not only for animals but for man as well? Is not dying automatically part and parcel of the price of living? Is not every living thing destined to die?

Research in the Life Sciences has been modifying our opinion on these matters quite fundamentally. It is now clear that innumerable living things actually never do die. They simply divide into two and go merrily on their way, multiplying indefinitely but leaving no dead behind — barring accidents. Such forms of life actually far outnumber those that are *mortal*! It is quite true that they are tiny organisms and might not be thought to have any kind of "real life" experience: but this is not so. Small though they are, those who have investigated them have concluded that in their own way they experience many of the reactions which we attribute to higher organisms with intelligence, e.g., dogs*. Life is by no means wedded to death. Although all living

---

* This statement was made by H. S. Jennings, one of the first to observe the actions of amoeba for hours on end. He reported his observations in fascinating detail in *Behaviour of the Lower Organisms*, Columbia Univ. Biological Series X, Col. Univ. Press, 1915, xvi & 366 pp.

things are clearly capable of being killed in one way or another, remarkably few classes of organisms are actually subject to 'natural' death.

It should be realized that animals experience death for many reasons. They are subject to predators, to accident, to disease, to starvation, to dehydration, even to the very effects of their bulk which (if they grow large enough) can immobilize them and reduce their chances of getting food or defending themselves. So they die. But the important point is that they do not die for *inherent* reasons. Thus for billions of living, growing creatures, death is not the 'expected end' and almost certainly never was. Living tissue that is functionally immortal is not a poet's dream but a biological reality. Granted the fact of the *creation* of life, it is mortality, not immortality, that needs accounting for.

To many people unacquainted with the literature of modern research in this area, this is a new thought. To the biologist, it is not. Immortality — and I am speaking of *physical*, not spiritual, immortality — is commonplace among living things whether plant or animal, and the Bible assures us that man, although he is a far more complex organism, was a candidate for this kind of immortality. Placed in a special environment, in a real honest-to-goodness garden, planted with real honest-to-goodness trees bearing real honest-to-goodness edible fruits and edible leaves, he was so constituted that he could have lived for ever. He was provided with the means of either maintaining this immortal constitution or destroying it. For man as created, mortality was only a contingent possiblity: it was by no means inevitable. When man disobeyed and ate the forbidden fruit he did not merely *shorten* his life: he introduced death into it *as something entirely foreign to its original design.*

The more we examine the evidence in the light of what we know, the more certain we can be that biblical commentators of former times (both Jewish and Christian) were perfectly correct in their understanding of the constitution of the first parents of the human race. Adam and Eve and their descendants (you and I) might very well have still been enjoying physical immortality if certain tragic circumstances had not intervened to change everything. Scripture has been telling us about this potential physical immortality for thousands of years: and now science is just beginning to acknowledge not only that such a concept is valid, but that it might yet be again true in the future.

Now the fact that the great majority of living things never do die naturally but for the most part come to an end by accident, indicates two rather obvious but very important circumstances regarding the nature of life in such organisms.

First: they CAN die, for otherwise they could not be killed. But, secondly, they do not *need* to die, for they can actually go on living indefinitely.   We thus have an important distinction to note regarding the meaning of the term *physical immortality* as applied to any organism — including Adam and Eve as created.

In the light of modern research, physical immortality means that a living creature *will not die unless it is killed.*   It does not mean that it cannot be put to death but only that death is not an inherent condition of its life.   Death overtakes it, happens *to* it.   By avoiding accident successfully, it is quite capable of living on for ever.

And this, I believe, was precisely the position of man when he was first created.   Adam need never have died: but he did die in due course because he introduced a poison into his body through the agency of the forbidden fruit with fatal consequences to himself and to the bodies of all his descendants (including you and me), besides perverting his spirit with equally fatal consequences for his relationship with God.   He might, even after his disastrous disobedience, have partaken of the healing leaves of the *Tree of Life* and recovered his physical well-being . . . . though not his spiritual well-being.   And physical immortality in such a state would have been condemnation to everlasting defeat and disappointment from which there could be virtually no escape except by some kind of suicide.   It is almost certain that it was for this reason, God drove the man out of the Garden and excluded him rigidly from the Tree of Life.

From this graphic record of the events that transpired in Eden, events that seem almost childishly naive, arose a situation for mankind which called forth the working out of a plan of redemption made possible only because the laws of nature had been designed to accomodate it.   Though divine intervention marks every step of the plan, at no point was the natural order violated.   The natural order was merely put by the Creator to a higher service.   And we now have many new insights into the physiological whys and wherefores of the steps by which man's redemption was to be made possible.

Why Eve was taken out of Adam and not made a separate creation: why death was both a penalty and a remedy, and *how* this penalty was made the basis of the remedy: why the virgin conception was essential to the vicarious death of the Redeemer and how that death was *physiologically* unique: and finally, why his resurrected body had not seen corruption though entombed under conditions of burial very similar to those of Lazarus: — all these were part and parcel of the plan of redemption.   Such, then, is the subject matter of this volume which is a study of some of the biological factors in the plan of redemption which are seldom treated as a connected chain of events.

Is it all fantasy?   I think not.   I believe it is sober history.   This is a new approach to the study of the Articles of the old Faith which in the light of modern research proves itself to be indeed a Faith needing no apology.

Here, in fact, is the meeting place of Science and Theology. To the theologian, much of science seems highly speculative. To the scientist, theology often seems speculative to the point of being irrelevant to the facts. In each branch of inquiry, a problem has been created because of ignorance of the data, method, motivation, and philosophy of the other. Theology is based on the strictest form of logic applied to revelation. The scientist applies his logic just as rigidly, but to the data of experiment and observation. Neither side always respects these pre-requisites, and many contradictory conclusions result through misinterpretation of the meaning of the data.

But it seems time now to attempt some kind of joining — and as in all such "weddings" there will continue to be quarrels. But the marriage could have tremendous possibilities. Such weddings have been tried in recent years by *groups* of people, and proved disappointing failures. Perhaps a one-man effort to form such a union might have a better chance of success. This volume has at least a certain inner harmony which may help towards achieving a more fruitful partnership.

An established fact is as sacred as a revealed truth.

PART I

**THE INTRUSION
OF DEATH**

When Adam ate the forbidden fruit, he did not merely shorten his life and thus die prematurely.

He introduced into human existence an entirely new and foreign element: DEATH — both spiritual *and physical.*

Chapter 1

'NATURAL' DEATH: A MEDICAL FACT OR LEGAL FICTION?

By one man
sin entered into the world,
and death by sin;
and so death passed upon all men.
Romans 5:12

We all know that we must die, sometime. This is a fact of life. Man is, in short, a mortal creature.

The Greeks, with tongue in cheek and with considerable subtlety of thought, held that the ideal was to die young but to postpone dying as long as possible! It is indeed hard to know whether a short life of youthful health is to be preferred to a long life with the accompanying ills of old age. Given the choice, most of us would settle for the latter. There may be, however, something to be said even for failing health, for as Sir Charles Tennyson (grandson of the famous poet) remarked in an interview recently, "the surest recipe for a long life is never to feel really well"! [1] * There could be some sound medical sense in this, though the difficulty lies in defining how much ill health one ought to be prepared to "enjoy" with this in view. It is a paradox that we wish for long life while fearing the process of growing old which inevitably goes with it. The Greeks certainly hit upon the ideal, but how difficult it is to achieve.

---

* Call numbers lead to references and comments on scientific and theological matters. Footnotes give documentation to sources likely to be available to the ordinary reader.

What we are increasingly finding out from biological and medical research is that both senescence and even death itself almost certainly form no essential part of the process of being alive, that natural death is unknown to vast numbers of living things, that functioning protoplasm *per se* is in no way naturally subject to death.   For animals below man, death seems to be a statistical probability rather than a biological necessity.

Physical immortality now emerges as a perfectly valid concept, and the phenomenon of death appears rather as an intrusion, something foreign to life — *even for man himself.** It is true that man now dies inevitably.   Yet the evidence increasingly supports the view that death is no more "natural" for him than it is for millions of lower forms of life which simply go on living for ever if they are not killed. In man, death is more like a disease than a consequence of having lived.

The anthropologist Gy. Acsadi and the demographer J. Nemeskeri, both of the Hungarian Academy of Sciences of Budapest, recently pooled their energies and their information to produce what must surely be the most thorough analysis of the factors governing human mortality ever undertaken.   Their conclusion is summed up quite early in their text with the words: 2

> Although 50 million people died every year in the last decade, biological death could not once be ascertained. *Using adequate standards, examination always established some disease, injury or poisoning as the cause of death* (emphasis mine).
> According to the present state of our knowledge, people die of diseases and of pathological processes.   The possibility of long human life without pathological signs and whether human death of a purely biological character without pathological changes is at all conceivable, is still an open question.   It would, however, be of some interest to study the extraordinary life spans of certain people, possibly achieved by the interaction of exceptionally favourable circumstances.

These two authorities, in spite of their admission that "it would be of interest" to study the life histories of some very long-lived individuals, do not by their own confession have much confidence in the many reports now available (quite apart from the records in Genesis)

---

* Herman Bavinck commented: "Men of science are by no means in agreement about the causes and nature of death.   Over against those that see in death a natural and necessary end of life there are many who find death an even greater riddle than life, and who roundly declare that there is not a single reason why living beings should from some inner necessity have to die".   [*Our Reasonable Faith*, tr. Henry Zylstra, Grand Rapids, Baker, 1956, p.258].

of such people!   They say, "Many examples of longevity have been recorded in literature but there is little value in the reports".[3]   We shall consider scores of records of long-lived individuals in a later chapter, but for the moment it is enough to note that Acsadi and Nemeskeri would virtually exclude the reality of *natural* death for man altogether.   Man always dies from accident or disease: natural death is more legal fiction than medical fact.

But surely one may ask, Even if a man does not die of either accident or disease, may he not die simply of old age?   Well, even this is surprisingly difficult to establish, as we shall see.   The evidence available from many lines of research at the present moment agrees in this that there really is, as Acsadi and Nemeskeri are saying in so many words, no known case of a human being dying a natural death.   In short, he is really always "killed" *by something,* and usually the death certificate will specify what that something was.

They are not alone in this conclusion.   Some years ago, in 1938, an editorial in the medical journal *Lancet* under the title "Old Age in Mind and Body" took notice of the visit to England of one of the world's most renowned pathologists, Dr. Ludwig Aschoff, who had completed a series of critical review articles in *Medizinische Klinik* on the morbid anatomy of old age.   The editorial notes:[4]

> It is easy to adopt the sophism that it is life that consumes the body, and that natural death marks the exhaustion of a store of energy; but this explains nothing since it is not necessarily those who live strenuous lives who die young. . . .
>
> In Dr. Aschoff's long experience (he is now 71 years of age) he has never found a case of purely natural death: autopsy has always revealed some pathological process as a cause.
>
> Sometimes, however, he has noted that disease may be less distressing in its effects on the aged and he recalls the "unexpected" death at the age of 97 of a colleague only two days after he himself had seen and talked with him.   Here Aschoff expected to find a case of natural death, for there had been no sign of illness, but at autopsy a severe lobar pneumonia of 4 or 5 days standing was found together with numerous metastases of a malignant tumour of the thyroid.   This old physician who was well qualified to appreciate his physical state, had suffered little discomfort and had apparently been unaware of his condition.

More recently Dr. Hans Selye of Montreal, probably the world's leading authority on human stress, asserted that in all his autopsies he has never yet seen a man who died simply of old age, nor does he think anyone ever has.[5]   Dr. George W. Casarett, radiation pathologist at the University of Rochester School of Medicine and Dentistry at the time of writing, was reported in *Science News Letter* as saying that he knew of no evidence indicating the existence of a "built-in time clock".[6]   Aging is a "pathological consequence".   From a philosophical point of view "man could be a potentially immortal animal".*

It is necessary to pause for a moment to consider what is meant here by the term "natural" death as used by Aschoff.   He meant death as a result simply of the passage of years in the absence of disease or accident as a cause.   If *life* is a fixed and measured quantity having a precise end as it has a precise beginning and having a limited power to sustain itself, then, when a man exhausts this limited supply of energy, he dies naturally, expectedly, inevitably.   What is becoming clearer increasingly as a result of research into life processes is that there is no such limitation.   A living thing does not *age* in the accepted sense, in the sense that a car does, or a pair of shoes.   It is apparently capable of unending renewal of its own energies.   Life, once initiated, will continue indefinitely.   A living thing must have its life terminated for it by some mechanism not inherent in the livingness of the thing itself.   We shall see plenty of evidence of this subsequently.

Thus when a man dies, he really dies because something *kills* him. He is, in fact, put to death.   It may be by some disease, or it may be by a defect, or injury, or accident.   The cause of death is foreign to the phenomenon of life.   Death is strictly not "natural" to man so far as the medical evidence goes.

Yet, commonly speaking, medical literature in general and death certificates in particular use the term "natural death" while really they mean something quite alien to nature in the sense that disease is alien. For example, a recent article on some factors in sudden death due to heart failure while driving a car is titled, "Natural Death at the Wheel".[7]   This article is illustrated from twelve cases.   All of them describe serious accidents resulting from the sudden "natural" death of the driver at the wheel.   And every single case reveals that the sudden death was *not* natural at all.   All the deceased had heart failure as a result of some pathological condition of long standing.   Such things as severe coronary arteriosclerosis, acute myocardial infarction, massive subarachnoid hemorrhage caused by rupture of a congenital aneurysm, and so on.   It is perhaps useful to employ the word *natural* here to distinguish these deaths from poisonings, drownings, and such like accidents, but one can hardly speak of a diseased heart

---

* C. F. von Weizsacker, an internationally known biochemist, observed: "I see no biochemical reason why individuals should not be possible who would stay alive indefinitely, if not killed by force".   [*Relevance of Science*, London, Collins, 1964, p.134].

as a natural heart or a death by disease as a natural death if one wishes to be precise.

It is true that medical literature often employs the term *natural death* and the meaning is clear enough in the context, but in point of fact such types of death are really anything but natural.   They are pathological.   Aschoff used the term in a more precise sense, and his conclusion is fully corroborated by Selye and Acsadi and many others in the field.   No man ever dies a strictly natural death simply marking the termination of his own little allotment of life energy.   Man dies, slain by some intrinsic defect which undermines the vitality of his cells, yet which is still unidentified except in so far as the Bible tells us that death gained entrance in the first place (Rom.5:12) through the eating of a forbidden fruit (Gen.2:17).

Professor H. S. Simms of Columbia University in 1947 was reported to have expressed the view that "there is at the present time no proof for or against the possibility that we can some day extend our active life an extra one hundred or two hundred years with retention of youthful health, intelligence, and appearance".[8]   In a more popular vein, Simms was prepared to go much further by saying that if the human body could retain throughout life the ability to resist disease and to repair breakdown which it possesses at the age of ten, "man would have a life expectancy of 800 years and some individuals might survive 22,000 years"![9]

Twenty-two thousand years seems rather an exaggeration, but it at least points up a notable fact of life that is increasingly emerging from gerontological research, which is that we do not appear to have any *built-in* limitations against achieving immortality, but only *acquired* ones, acquired by inheritance or by experience from birth or perhaps even from the time of actual conception.   Dr. Selye said:[10]

> When a living cell is nourished, washed and sheltered in a test-tube, it neither decays nor dies; it divides and it endures.[11]   It defeats death.
>
> Biologists were familiar with this technical form of immortality when I was a medical student thirty years ago.   Cell tissue from rats and chicks born at about that time is alive and healthy in laboratory tubes today.   On the human scale of life, this tissue would be nearly a thousand years old.   No one knows how far man can prolong his life.

If medical research should ever find ways of doing for whole organisms what can even now be done for some tissues, then the world will be a different place entirely!   Millions of people will live on year after year, century after century, accumulating wealth and experience and, hopefully, wisdom as well.   The very fact of an enormously expanded time for the gathering of knowledge by each individual would certainly accelerate man's mastery over the forces of Nature — if he does not simply destroy himself in the process.   There is a sense in which we are witnessing this process of acceleration even today simply by the perfection of alternative means for rapid communication and dissemination of knowledge on a large scale.   In the pre-Flood days of Noah, longevity enormously multiplied man's capacity for much the same reasons, but sadly increased his wickedness to a crucial point at the same time.

In terms of his physical being, man might well turn out to be almost a different kind of creature.   Dr. V. Korenchevsky of the Gerontological Research Unit, Oxford, in an address to a group organized for the first time specifically to do research on aging, held in July, 1946, at the Imperial College in London, remarked:[12]

> The aim is not only a longer life but a stronger one — to add life to years, not just years to life — not only prevention of the premature appearance of senile decay but also elimination of those pathological features which are not necessarily associated with normal old age, since they are not present in some rare cases of less pronounced pathological ageing.
> As ageing starts very early, actually with the *normal* process almost the whole of the span of human life will be changed, and therefore in some distant future man will probably become in some respects a different creature.

Similarly, Professor J. B. S. Haldane, looking forward to the same prospect, foresaw that "man would develop slowly, continuing to learn up to maturity at 40 [sic!], then living several centuries. . . . He would be of high general intelligence by our standards, and most individuals would have some special aptitude to the degree we call genius".[13]

That *cells* need never die has been known for a long time — ever since microscopes allowed man to study the life cycle of unicellular creatures like the amoeba.   These creatures have a life "cycle" only in the sense that they grow into two.   They do not have a life cycle in the sense that they are born, mature, grow old and die.   For they never die at all in the ordinary sense: that is to say, they are not subject to *natural* death.   They only die accidentally.   At maturity they divide into two so-called daughter-cells, passing on all their substance and leaving no corpse.   It may be true that the original amoeba "disappears", but this is no more *death* than that the boy in becoming a man "dies" in so doing.   The daughter-cells in turn mature to repeat the dividing process, and so on *ad infinitum*.   They are, in the strictest sense, immortal.

Amoeba are by no means the only unicellular organisms which enjoy immortality. Paramecia do also. One well known experiment conducted by L. L. Woodruff of Yale reveals what the potential of life is in this respect. In 1943 a culture of single-celled paramecia had completed its 37th year of continuous growth during which time it had passed through 20,000 generations.[14] If all the individuals produced had been allowed to live they would have covered the entire surface of the earth. It was estimated by Professor George A. Dorsey that at the time of the 10,000[th] generation, if each generation had equalled a human generation, Woodruff's original single paramecium would now be well over a quarter of a million years old; yet as he points out, "it remains eternally young and shows no loss of virility"![15]

And this brings us to an important matter of definition. By "immortality" biologists mean *physical* immortality, of course, not *spiritual* immortality. Moreover, they do not mean that an animal possessing immortality cannot die: they mean only that it NEED not die. Such creatures may be killed by poisoning, or dehydration, or starvation, or crushing, and so forth. But inherently and by nature they are quite capable of living on for ever and ever. This is what is meant in the present context and throughout the rest of this volume by the term *immortality*. The point is a very important one, both by reason of what it does mean and of what it does not mean. It does not mean they are beyond the power of death; and this is most fortunate for otherwise the surface of the earth would soon be yards deep in living tissue.

Augustine, writing in the early part of the fifth century A.D., observed of Adam when he was first created that "it was not impossible for him to die but it was possible for him not to die". Or as he put it in the original, *non imposse mori sed posse non mori.** His statement is precisely correct as a definition of immortality when used by biologists. It was not impossible for Adam to die, for by an act of disobedience in eating a forbidden fruit he evidently introduced into his body some toxic agent which upset its originally perfect balance and initiated, that day, a process of dying which was only completed centuries later. As we shall see, there are excellent reasons for believing that the Genesis record intends us to understand that if he had not disobeyed he would not have become subject to physical death. And Augustine's profound insight into Adam's position exactly expresses what the modern biologist means when he speaks of an animal as being immortal.

---

* Augustine: *De Genesi ad Litteram*, Bk.I, 25, note 35.

Now it is not merely that certain single-celled creatures have the gift of immortality, but even tissues composed of thousands of cells enjoy the same immortality if they are protected adequately. At the Rockefeller Institute in 1912 Alexis Carrel removed a bit of heart tissue and immersed it in a nutrient solution of food stuffs extracted from embryos. Trimmed back to size every so often and regularly provided with fresh nutrients, this tissue lived and grew until the experiment was terminated in 1946, forty-three years later. A chicken hatched in 1912 would have been dead by 1928 almost certainly, yet there is no reason to suppose that this little segment of heart tissue would ever have died if the equipment which sustained it in the laboratory had not failed and brought the experiment to an end.

Whole organisms of quite complex structure and of large size may very well enjoy a similar immortality. Professor Raymond Pearl in his book *The Biology of Death* had no hesitation in asserting that "natural death is not the inevitable penalty of life".[16] Even highly specialized cells are, he pointed out, "essentially immortal". And Professor H. J. Muller of the Department of Zoology, Indiana University, is perhaps even more explicit. He says, "Natural death is not the expression of an inherent principle of (functioning) protoplasm".[17] Similarly, T. Dobzhansky observed: "Life carries the potentiality of endless self-replication, but the realization of this potentiality is restricted by the resistence of the environment". [18]

Dr. Paul A. Zahl, Associate Director of the Haskins Laboratories in New York City at the time of writing, said:[19]

> Senescence and death are by no means universal biological phenomena . . . . Perennial organisms, for example, are not in fact subject to senescence and never wear down to natural expiration. This condition prevails presumably, because the body tissues of such organisms have not been specialized to the point where they have wholly lost their reproductive capacity . . . . Among organisms of this class, life can be stopped (as it most often is) only by accident, attack by preying organisms, or severe environmental adversity.

He concluded subsequently: "We may infer from the absence of inevitable death among the lower organisms that *there is nothing in the fundamental nature of protoplasm that demands a wearing out* (emphasis mine). A man is protoplasm; a sequoia is protoplasm. One has a death-determined cycle; the other does not. A man is a mammal; so is a mouse. Yet one lives thirty times longer than the other".[20] But as Zahl has just finished demonstrating, size really has nothing to do with it. The rotifer lives only a few days; an amoeba, which is smaller, lives for ever . . . . An elephant (dying between 55 and 60 years of age), which is about sixty times the weight of a man, is not as long lived as a man, while some fish, though lighter than man, may live much longer.   A sturgeon caught in Lake of the Woods (Ontario, Canada) in 1954 was estimated by the Department of Lands and Forests to be 152 years old.   This estimate was subsequently confirmed by microscopic analysis.[21]

Now some of the living things which enjoy immortality, to which Zahl makes reference, belong within the plant kingdom, e.g., the sequoia.   In 1938 Sir Julian Huxley published a series of short essays, one of which was titled "The Meaning of Death".   In this essay he explored briefly the question of whether death is in any sense natural for living things.   With respect to plant life, he wrote:[22]

> We have records of trees of vast age and size, whose death seems only to have been due to accident, that is to say, to something in the external world and not in the tree itself, and therefore something that could be avoided . . . .   There is nothing inherent in the tree itself which causes its death, merely the long-continued shocks and buffets of the world, preventable things one and all; by which I mean that if one could shelter the tree from storms, keep off its active enemies, and provide it with a reasonable amount of food, water and air, we must suppose that it would go on living forever.

He then speaks of one particular tree in the Calcutta Botannical Gardens which has been sheltered artificially from at least some of these active enemies, and which shows every sign of continuing indefinitely.   On this he comments:[23]

> Thus we have persuaded ourselves that a single individual can in some cases go on living indefinitely, and two pertinent questions arise and demand an answer.
> First, if functioning protoplasm is not, necessarily, subject to death, why did death appear?   And secondly, granted that death must come for mankind, would it be possible in ourselves for instance to postpone its coming . . . for a short space, for a long space, or even for ever?

So we are in effect on the edge of a whole new concept of what life is and of what death is.   It is true that immortality appears to be reserved for lower forms of animal life and for plants, but the reasons for this limitation are being actively explored at the present time and there is no evidence to support the view that the basic nature of *life* in the higher organisms is in any fundamental way different.   The programming of death into life below man by the Creator appears to be a deliberate arrangement for reasons which are becoming increasingly clear to biologists.   Moreover, even now there are grounds for believing that some of the *higher* forms of life are only subject to death by accident. This is probably true, for example, of fishes which may or may not have a pre-determined life span but which actually fail to achieve greater longevity only because the longer they live the greater are their chances of succumbing to predators.   Sir Edwin Ray Lancaster, over eighty years ago, said, "Fish are not known to get feeble as they grow old and many fish are known not to get feebler". [24] Sir Peter Medawar comments on this acute observation:[25]

> Fish *may* be potentially immortal in the sense that they do not undergo an innate deterioration with ageing, and yet the naturalists who ought to know about it simply can't be sure! Whether animals *can*, or cannot, reveal an innate deterioration with age is almost literally a domestic problem; the fact is that under the exactions of natural life they do not do so. *They simply do not live that long.* (Emphasis his).

Many authorities support the view that fishes never die of old age, indeed do not age at all in the sense in which ageing is applied to man. Dr. G. P. Bidder, in his Linnean Lecture on Ageing in 1932, argued that fish continue to grow without limit and never undergo senescence nor suffer natural death.   He stated that he could not remember any evidence of any marine animal dying a natural death. [26]

Lincoln Barnett observed more recently:[27]

> Some biologists believe that for aquatic animals, liberated from the destructive power of gravity by the dense medium in which they dwell, growth, though it may slacken almost to cessation, never halts entirely.   So long as they escape — or are protected — from the primitive dangers of the sea, fish may therefore continue to grow by simple enlargement year after year.   And so long as they continue to grow, according to this theory, they do not grow old.   For them there is no old age, only the violent death that lurks everywhere in the world of water.

It may be observed that salmon age and die as part of the breeding cycle.   This has the appearance of natural death in the sense that it is natural enough for the salmon.   However, it may also be noted that a number of organisms which suffer death as a result of the activity of reproduction, do not die if this particular activity is prevented. This is apparently true of certain simple forms of life which have developed a mode of sexual reproduction; for example, the *Infusoria*. They normally multiply by a process of union with a mate which is called *conjugation* which seems to be in some way responsible for their subsequent dying.   Sir Julian Huxley notes that if by feeding them on a special diet they can be induced to multiply without conjugation (an alternative method of reproduction of which they are capable), death is obviated.   As he says, "Experiments of this nature (discontinued only after hundreds of generations when it seemed clear they might go on forever) seemed to show that functioning protoplasm is not in itself mortal, but that the cause of death is to be found in the external conditions; for by altering these, death may be put off, it would seem, indefinitely".[28]   Something of this kind could conceivably be true of salmon who otherwise provide us with a notable exception to what is observed elsewhere in marine life.

So fish do die but, with the one notable exception which may not actually be an exception, fish do not appear to die a natural death. They become prey to predation or disease or accident of some kind. And as for land animals, both birds and mammals, Bidder put forward the theory that they die because of size limitations.   If their cells went on multiplying without hindrance, their size would increase to the point where the animal could not navigate either on wings or feet. The limitations upon life on land or in the air have been thoroughly and intriguingly explored by a number of zoologists.   The consequence is that the animal must collapse, as it were, by the very encumbrance of its own size.[29] Where such animals (mammals included) are not embarrassed by the fact of weight per se, size limitations do not place the same constraints upon their continuance and accordingly they may live a lot longer. . . .   Only accident and perhaps some functional limitations of a physiological nature operate here. Marine animals, like whales, fall within this category.   The elephant, on land, may reach a weight of five tons and live possibly 55 or 60 years; whereas the whale reaching a weight of up to one hundred and fifty tons, or thirty times as much, may live between 65 and 70 years.

There is a principle here that life is always associated with growth and that so long as an organism is growing it is not subject to natural death.

It is quite conceivable that man himself, if he were to live on and on, might for the same reason be far larger in stature, if not giant in size . . . . a fact which could shed light on certain statements in the early chapters of Genesis respecting the size of men at the time of the Flood and shortly after (Gen.6:4).   It does seem, however, that there must be some limitations for man on account of his upright posture, as ably pointed out by F. W. Went.[30] It is conceivable that the growth factor in man might be asymptotic, i.e., steadily slowing up with age but continuous nevertheless.   As Alex Comfort has pointed out, "all, or almost all, organisms grow more slowly the larger they get".[31] The consequences of such growth for man, if Adam had not lost for us our physical immortality, are explored in a later chapter.

Even yet, man contains within himself some at least of the seeds of his pristine condition of immortality.   Dr. Kenneth Walker has stated this fact very effectively:[32]

> In the "theory of the continuity of the germplasm" pub-
> lished in 1885, Weismann showed that at a very early period
> the fertilized ovum (which later becomes the embryo) sep-
> arates into two parts, a somatic part and what Weismann called
> the propagative part.   The somatic half grows into the body
> of the individual, while the propagative half forms only the
> germinal epithelium or reproductive glands.   A clear and very
> early division is therefore made between the cells which are to
> form the body and those highly specialized cells which become
> the sex glands and eventually give rise to the next generation.
> A man's body is doomed to die, but in a way, his reproductive
> cells are immortal . . . .

Although Weismann was writing so many years ago, and although
certain of his conclusions are now considered questionable, his concept of the immortality of the germ plasm has stood the test of time.
Weismann wrote: [33]

> "Death", i.e., the end of life, is by no means, as is usually
> assumed, an attribute of all organisms.   An immense number
> of protozoa do not die, although they are easily destroyed,
> being killed by heat, poisons, etc.   As long, however, as the
> conditions which are necessary for their life are fulfilled they
> continue to live, and they thus carry the potentiality of unend-
> ing life in themselves . . . .   Death is not an essential attribute
> of living matter.

Subsequently Weismann developed his theme in the following
way, allowing for some editing on my part: "Death is not, as has
hitherto been assumed, an inevitable phenomenon essential to the
very nature of life itself.   Protozoa (the very lowest unicellular forms
of life) are immortal.   Metazoa (more complex than protozoa) have
lost this power . . . . in some of their cells, but not in all.   The immortality of the protozoan organism has merely passed over to the ova
or spermatozoa: the other cells (body cells) will die, and since the
body of the individual is chiefly composed of them, it will die also".[34]

Some pages later, after exploring the implication of what he calls
"this division of labour", he observed: "This limitation (the surrender
of immortality of the whole organism) went hand in hand with the
differentiation of the cells of the organism into reproductive and somatic cells".[35]

I have already noted that Weismann's views, so lucidly expressed
throughout his writings, have been challenged at one or two points in
modern times.   It may be well to state very briefly where the current
disagreement exists.   Weismann believed that all somatic or body
cells had fully surrendered their immortality.   It is now known that

in certain forms of life below man, body cells have not entirely lost their immortality, as we have already seen in the case of Alexis Carrel's chicken tissue culture.   Even so, such cell cultures are highly artificial and would certainly not retain their immortality under natural conditions.   There are one or two other rather complex aspects of current embryological doctrine which demonstrate Weismann to have been in error but they do not significantly challenge what has been quoted above and are rather too involved to introduce at this point.

The substance of Weismann's view is simply that when the organization of the cells in more complex animal forms involved a division of labour, certain of these cells retained their original immortality but the majority of them did not.   The loss of immortality by the majority of the cells in the animal led inevitably to the death of the animal as a whole.   As a consequence most of the higher organisms are mortal, though some of their tissues can be shown under appropriate conditions of culture to be capable of living on almost indefinitely. It is the animal as a whole which has surrendered its immortality.   The reason why this surrender has been built-in by the Creator will be considered subsequently in Chapter 8.

In man, the situation is more complex.   Some intrusive factor appears to be resident in the somatic or body cells which act upon the whole organism like a fatal disease.   There are those who believe that this fatal disease or mortogenic* factor will one day be identified and that, when it is, human life will be enormously extended, the individual then becoming subject to death only by accident.

Formerly, it was customary to ask with Job, "If a man die, shall he live again?" (Job 14:14).   Today, in the light of current knowledge, the question is being rephrased to read: "If a man lives, why should he ever die?"   About all we can agree upon is that the great majority of living things (in terms of numbers of individuals) are not subject to death at all except by being killed, and of those animals below man which do appear to have a limited life span, the limitations are still for the most part due to external factors.   Only man seems to have the limitations within himself, so that even barring fatal accidents, death would still occur for pathological reasons.

❦

---

* Mortogenic = "death generating".

Chapter 2

DEATH: EVENT OR PROCESS?

But of the tree of knowledge of good and evil
thou shalt not eat of it:
for in the day thou eatest thereof
dying thou shalt die.
Genesis 2:17

Because of the importance to the living of transplanted organs from the recently dead, one of the great problems today is that of establishing when death has really occurred.   What *is* death by definition, a process or an event?   By what criteria is death to be certified in any particular case — especially when the living are waiting to benefit from it?

The situation is viewed differently by the biologist, the medical man, and the legal authority.   The biologist may say that the problem is so complex that a facetious answer is about the best that one can give at the present: the difference between a live body and a dead one is that a competent physicist could predict what would happen if you kick a corpse but not if you kick a live body!   This is another way of saying that the living are distinguishable from the non-living chiefly because they are unpredictably reactive.

Even the medical people have in the past adopted the same basic principle in so far as they view the absence of responsiveness or reactivity to various stimuli as the most convincing evidence of real death. This is valid up to a point, but recent resuscitative techniques have seriously challenged it.

As a result of a legal dispute involving an inheritance, it became necessary quite recently to determine precisely which of two men, who had both been killed in an accident together, had actually died first.   The Harvard Medical School set up an *ad hoc* Committee to establish a definition of death suitable for such emergencies.   They published their report under the heading, "A Definition of Irreversible Coma".[36]   Their basic conclusion at the time (1968) was that four criteria may be used, which are as follows:

> 1. *Total unresponsitivity,* i.e., total unawareness of extern-ally applied stimuli, even when painful, by vocal or other response, including groans, or withdrawal of limb, or quicken-ing of respiration.

> 2. *No movement or breathing* over a period of at least one hour.   Artificial respiration to be cut off to see whether any attempt at breathing would be made within a period of three minutes.

> 3. *No reflexes:* the pupil fixed, dilated, and unresponsive to a light source.   Since the establishment of a fixed dilated pupil is clearcut in clinical practice, it was felt that there should be no uncertainty in such a case.

> 4. *Flat encephalogram* for 24 hours with no measurable change.

> NOTE: in each case the assumption is made that there is no evid-ence of hypothermia (temperature below 90° F. or 32.2° C.) or the use of central nervous system depressants such as barbiturates.

In the light of these criteria it is interesting to note that legal opinion was at that time committed to the definition of death as given in Black's *Law Dictionary,* which reads: "Death occurs pre-cisely when life ceases and does not occur until the heart stops beating and respirations ends.   Death is not a continuous event but an event which takes place at a precise time."   Undoubtedly, this legal posit-ion will have to be modified, for measures are now possible for the revival of the "dead" under circumstances which blur the issues in very embarrassing ways.   Indeed, as Professor F. Camps said (in re-viewing a book entitled *The Chemistry of Death* by W. E. D. Evans), "It would now appear to be possible to die several times on the basis of medical evidence".[37]   The pertinence of this remark and the serious nature of the problem will be seen from the following illust-rations.

In 1962 there appeared in *World-Wide Abstracts from General Medicine* a report by a Dr. E. Doskaoh from India of a case of resuscitation under rather extraordinary circumstances.[38]   A young man in the northern part of that country was apparently thrown from a tractor in the middle of winter during a severe snowstorm, with only minor injuries which nevertheless brought about his collapse. He was found later in the field, manifestly dead, his whole body covered with hoar frost and his limbs "ringing like wood when struck with a percussion hammer". A film of ice covered his wide open eyes, and no breathing, heart beat, or pulse could be detected. He was taken to a local hospital and treated with heaters, rubbed with alcohol and bathed in hot water. Heart massage and artificial respiration were started and 150 ml. of blood was injected intra-arterially, and glucose and alcohol intravenously. After forty minutes of artificial respiration, signs of spontaneous breathing became evident. Five minutes later a faint pulse could be felt.

One hour and fifty minutes after the start of resuscitation, the man was clearly alive, although remaining unconscious for some time. Upon the return of consciousness, he was able to describe how the accident had occurred. He later developed pneumonia and showed some signs of mental disorder, from both of which he recovered. The terminal two phalanges had to be amputated from four fingers of his right hand and three of his left. No mention is made of any other operation being required. One year later the man was able to return to work.

The Russians have had somewhat similar experiences with frozen men. V. A. Negovsky and V. I. Soboleva have reported the case of a tractor driver named Vladimir Kharin, on a farm in Tselinny Territory, who was caught in a snowstorm when his tractor stalled.[39] For two hours he tried to get it working again until with hands numb his strength gave way. The engine refused to start and Kharin began to walk on foot back to the state farm which was some ten miles away. His last thought before losing consciousness was that he was only twenty-three, had a wife and daughter, and very much wanted to live. After he had lain in the snow for about three hours, he was found by a crew of workmen from the Yaroslavsky State Farm in the Aktyubinsk Region. He appeared to be dead, his frozen fists were tightly clenched, his still body sounded hollow and wooden upon the floor of the truck where he was laid, and his eyes, covered with a film of ice, were glassy.

He was taken to a hospital and examination showed that both heart and respiration had stopped and his pupils did not react to light. His skin, instead of the usual corpse-like pallor, was bluish-purple in colour. It thus seemed that he might still be in a state of clinical rather than biological death. An attempt was made to save him.

The heroic measures taken are then described. After forty minutes he began to revive, his skin became warm and his pulse could just be detected. Consciousness returned twelve hours after the patient had been admitted to the hospital and he was able to answer questions.

Several months later Kharin recovered sufficiently to return to his job.

It will be noted in both these cases that most of the accepted signs of death were manifested.   It will also occur to a knowledgeable reader that some brain damage might have been expected.   However, the situation was such that both men were undoubtedly in a state of deep hypothermia, a circumstance which protected their central nervous systems from damage due to lack of oxygen.   If we were guided by the four criteria listed in the Harvard Medical School Committee Report, we would have to say that both these men were indeed *clinically* and *legally* dead — but they were clearly not *biologically* dead.

A classic example of a man who "died" several times and finally recovered from the ordeal is the case of the Soviet theoretical physicist, Dr. Leo Davidovich Landau.[40]   This renowned teacher with an international reputation, on the morning of January 7, 1962, was involved in a car accident in which he was so badly injured that the medical report refers to his condition as being "simply appalling".   He was rushed to a hospital in Moscow still breathing but terribly injured. Examination revealed a fractured skull, nine fractured ribs — some of which had pierced the membrane enveloping the lung, the left lung had collapsed, on the right side blood had accumulated in the pleural cavity and that lung was also partially collapsed.   Three pelvic bones were broken as well as the left leg, and shattered bone had perforated an unknown number of internal organs.   In spite of tremendous efforts made to keep him alive, Dr. Landau died literally time after time, being again and again revived by the taking of extraordinary measures in which a team, composed of the very best brains that Europe and America could provide, co-operated.   Time after time his breathing and pulse stopped and he was, to all intents and purposes, clinically dead.   Yet eleven months later Dr. Landau was well enough to walk to a brief ceremony in a hospital conference room to receive the Nobel Prize for Physics.

Until very recently, it was such instances as these that had driven specialists to conclude that the only safe criterion of real death is the total absence of any electroencephalographic signal for a period of twenty-four hours, assuming there is no evidence of severe hypothermia (from cold exposure) or the use of depressant drugs.   This has been referred to more simply as "electrocerebral silence".   However, even this criterion has recently been shown not to be dependable.   Under the title, "Death Needs Better Definition",[41]   two cases have recently been reported from Israel which seriously challenge the usefulness of electrocerebral silence as absolute proof of death, although the report does admit that in probably 99.9% of cases it would be adequate. The first exceptional case reported is that of a fifteen year old boy

who fell into a deep cave while on a hike.   On admission to the hospital, he was in a profound coma, a condition which technically means
a total absence of reactivity to any stimuli.   His pupils were widely
dilated and did not respond to light.   Nor did he react to painful
stimuli in any way.   Shortly after admission he stopped breathing
and artificial respiration was begun.   The electroencephalograph
(EEG) reading of the electrical activity of the brain was completely
flat.   He therefore had fulfilled the four conditions of true death
according to the Harvard Committee Study.

Nevertheless, he was kept on artificial respiration in order to maintain a pulse and on drugs to keep the blood pressure up, although
throughout this period the EEG reading was flat.   The report continues: "Then his condition began to improve, spontaneous respiration
was regained and the EEG changed.   After a further week he was
conscious, and two months after the accident the boy was physically
and mentally in an excellent condition with a normal EEG".   He has
since been reported as being "completely recovered" and "absolutely
normal".

A second case is reported of a fourteen year old girl wounded in
the head by a shell fragment during the Six Day War in Israel, although in this case the sole evidence of death was a completely flat
EEG recording.   This girl was still breathing spontaneously and her
blood pressure was normal so that she was "alive" according to the
Harvard criteria, in spite of the electrocerebral silence.

As the report states, it becomes exceedingly difficult to define
death in circumstances such as these.   Had the heroic measures not
been taken and sustained for an exceptionally long time in the case of
the young boy, it is probable that he would never have given any signs
that life still lingered in his body and therefore he would have been
considered dead; and to all intents and purposes he *was* dead.[42]   It is
the opinion of some medical authorities that an individual kept alive
solely by artificial means but without consciousness is not really a
"person" but is merely a "heart-lung" preparation.

A further complicating factor which is becoming increasingly
apparent is that a body does not die at the same time everywhere.
Some parts of the body may die while other parts remain alive.   This
is the difference between *necrosis,* which is death of tissue, and *death*
which commonly applies to the decease of the whole organism.   It
is usually the necrosis of some vital tissue which brings about the
death of the whole.   Experiments with animals have shown that even
after the death of the whole, many tissues can be kept alive when isolated from the body.   The heart of a frog can be kept beating long
after the frog has died as a result of its removal.   A human heart can
be kept alive and will record characteristic electrocardiograph (ECG)

waves for sometime after its former owner has ceased to live.[43] Such a preparation was maintained by a group of surgeons at the University of Amsterdam and continued to beat on the laboratory bench for six hours, during which time hundreds of measurements were made of the electrical activity accompanying each cardiac contraction. Dr. Harold Hillman in the Department of Physiology at the University of Surrey, observed that an excised perfused kidney can go on producing urine, and even an excised udder will continue to give milk.[44]

It is therefore quite proper to speak of three kinds of physical death: clinical, biological, and cellular. *Clinical* death occurs first: confirmed by cessation of pulse and breathing. Thereafter, sooner or later, there follows biological death which has been defined by Dr. A. S. Parkes as "the state from which resuscitation of the body as a whole by currently known means is impossible".[45] Thus a man is clinically dead when normal means of detecting the four signals of life produce no measurable response. But heroic measures could, in some cases, probably resuscitate some individuals who have been pronounced clinically dead. When ever such measures fail, it may be assumed that life has indeed fled and the individual is now *biologically* dead. Nevertheless, he is not wholly dead, for his hair may continue to grow and a very large proportion of other tissues are capable of being kept alive by cultivation in the laboratory.[46] In fact, Professor Robert C. W. Ettinger holds that as much as 95% of body tissue is still viable, including brain tissue.[47]

So certain is Ettinger that the body can in many cases be revived successfully after death due to some fatal disease (provided that it is protected against putrefaction by immediate freezing) that he abandoned his university career and established a company which undertakes to preserve the recently dead by freezing, with a view to making it possible that if a cure for their fatal disease should be found, they may be restored to life. They would then be provided with curative treatment in the hopes of complete recovery. The idea is not perhaps very realistic in view of the problems that will be created for any who do so recover, when they find that their world is no longer recognizable, or simply treats them as though they were still dead. But it does, however, point up the difficulties of defining in any simple way when a man really is dead in the eyes of the law.

Finally, to revert to the third type of death, we have *cellular* death where even the tissues have begun to suffer general putrefaction, the final evidence of the total disorganization of life. It is apparent from all this that the legal opinion as set forth in Black's *Dictionary* is really no longer adequate. It is as difficult to assign a moment of cessation of person-hood during the process of dying as it is to establish a moment of achievement of the status of person-hood during foetal development.

In scientific circles there is considerable difference of opinion as to whether death is a process or an event, as witnessed by two recent contributions (and the attendant correspondence) to *Science* by Professor Robert S. Morison and Dr. Leon R. Kass.[48] Morison's view is that the simple facts of the case strongly favour the "process" concept and that to choose any particular criterion of death in order to make it an event and to favour this above other equally real evidences of continued life, is quite arbitrary. The *only* single decisive terminal event that could conceivably be taken as conclusive, he holds, would be when "some spirit or essence associated with life has left the body and gone to a better world".[49]

I am not sure that Morison is serious here, but apart from the optimism implicit in the journey "to a better world", I think the departure of the spirit really *is* the one crucial terminal event, even as I hold that the giving of a spirit by God (Eccl.12:7) is the one crucial initiating event that converts the mere organism into a "person".

Accordingly, I propose that the physical death of a person really involves two factors. The first is the departure of the spirit back to God who gave it (an *event*) which presumably would be followed at once by complete electrocerebral silence indicating the total absence of consciousness: and the second would be the progressive breakdown (a *process*) of all functions of the body unless artificial means are used to prevent it. Where artificial means are used and recovery of true consciousness follows (beyond mere reflex activity) I would presume that the spirit has returned. This is the kind of revival recorded on a number of occasions in the Bible, and would apply in the cases of Dr. Landau and the two Israeli children. Those who have been *clinically* dead can obviously recover their personal identity when they are resuscitated. Presumably such recovery is only possible because God has been pleased to return the spirit to the revitalized body, thus reconstituting the whole person again. This must surely have happened in the case of the widow of Nain's son (Luke 7:11-15) and of Lazarus (John 11), and of all others who were truly dead and yet were brought back to life by the Lord.* Indeed, Luke 8:55 tells us, in the case of a young girl brought back to life, that "her *spirit* came again and she immediately rose up". Moreover, in these three cases at least, there is no indication that the individual suffered any change in identity. Any brain damage that might have been done must have been miraculously repaired, or never occurred.

It does not seem to me that merely to restore the functions of the

---

* See also the two cases in the Old Testament: 2 Kings 4:18-37 and 13:20.

organism is the undoing of "death" in the human case, unless there is
a return of consciousness as evidence of the presence of the spirit once
again.   Even reactivity to physical stimuli is not by itself a sufficient
evidence that consciousness has returned, for anencephalic children (in
whom there is no brain wherein consciousness in the ordinary sense
could be seated) will respond to environmental stimuli.   Similarly,
animals without brains can perform many functions of life such as
landing on their feet when dropped in an upside down position,[50] flying and perching, [51] running on a treadmill, [52] and even raising their
young . . . . all entirely without "consciousness".[53] For this reason, let
me repeat, I do not believe that mere restoration of bodily functions
can be equated with the undoing of death in the human case.

There is a wide measure of agreement among theologians that man
is a dichotomy of spirit and body.   Both constitutents must be
present for the organism to be a person.   The "soul" or the "person"
emerges as a result of the presence of a spirit which comes directly
from God within a body which is derived from the parents.   The body
without the spirit is a mere corpse (James 2:26).   When the spirit returns to the body, the person as such is reconstituted (Luke 8:55).
This indicates that man experiences two kinds of death.   One is
the departure of his spirit from his body, and the other is the cessation
of the electrochemical processes which in an organized way prevent
the body from disintegration.   The divergence of opinion on the
question of whether death is an event or a process could therefore
result from the fact that man has two kinds of life and therefore two
kinds of death.   He may die as a *person* and he may die as an
organism.   The spirit is given at some specific point in time near the
beginning of existence, and taken away at some specific point in time
at the end.   It is therefore perfectly proper to speak of death as an
event in this connection, especially since the law is primarily concerned with the rights of persons as such.
But *biologically* the death of the organism, which is the chief
point of interest at the present moment, is almost certainly a process,
and is presented as such in Genesis.   Genesis 2:7 records that Adam
was warned of the consequences of eating the forbidden fruit when he
was told that "in the day thou eatest thereof thou shalt surely die".
The original Hebrew here is interesting and literally reads "dying thou
shalt die".   There is some question as to the precise meaning of this
phrase but it would be quite appropriate to render it "in the day thou
eatest thereof, thou art a dying man".   He did not die that day but
he became that day a dying creature, a *mortal* man.   Although he
survived another 930 years, he was already under sentence of death.
Prior to this he was not subject to natural death: he had enjoyed a

physical immortality which was contingent on his preserving it by not eating the forbidden fruit.

He lost this privileged condition, and by disobeying a seemingly simple prohibition, introduced some mortogenic factor into his body, as Eve had also already done shortly before; and by natural generation this acquired character — mortality — was passed on to all his descendants, and so "death passed upon all men" (Rom.5:12).   How such an acquired character could be inherited is the subject of later chapters in this work.

Considering man merely from the biological point of view as an organism with an inherited condition of mortality that was not originally intended for him, the question arises, If this condition is passed on from generation to generation, at what point in development does the process of dying actually begin in the life of an individual?   Dr. George Wakerlin in the *Journal of the American Medical Association* pointed out that "the various structures and functions of the human being reach their acme and begin to decline at different times in the life span".   He observed:[54]

> Aging begins with birth (or possibly with conception) in terms of growth, with birth in relation to arterial elasticity, at ten years of age in terms of acuity of hearing, at fifteen years of age in relation to antibody production and at twenty-five years in terms of neuromuscular function.   Such data suggest that aging may be a multicentric phenomenon in man.

It thus appears that in man the process of dying begins very early in life, if not from the very moment of conception.   It is this implication that Kass objected to, if dying is admitted to be a process and not an event.   In his words, it is tantamount to saying that "dying (is) synonymous with living".[55]   Maybe it *is*, for man! Indeed, Sir Peter Medawar shows that we are actually dying in some cells of the body more *rapidly* when we are young than when we are old. As he put it, "We are all moving towards our graves, but none so fast as they who have farthest to go". [56]   Some years ago, the German evangelical scholar, Erich Sauer, wrote:[57]

> At the moment of the (fall), spiritual death entered and with it also, under divine judgment, freedom from bodily death was forfeited . . . .
> Forthwith "life" is merely a gradual dying and birth is the beginning of death.

It is remarkable how the Scriptures can direct a man's thinking along the right paths even when those paths are outside his normal range of competence.   I suspect that in the light of today's knowledge, Sauer might even have said "*conception* is the beginning of death"; for it is at the time of conception that the immortality of the seed — or more precisely, of the body which is to house it — begins to be surrendered.   So that Psalm 51:5 is perhaps more literally true than we have customarily allowed: "Behold, I was shapen in iniquity, and in sin did my mother conceive me".   This is not because the act of procreation is sinful in itself but because it marks the point of entry into the stream of human life (as it is conveyed from germ plasm to germ plasm) of that particular form of poison which was introduced from the forbidden fruit and which in Romans 5:12 is termed SIN and to which is attributed the entrance of death.   Thus mortality is passed on by inheritance from generation to generation, and if we are permitted to take this passage literally, it is passed on *through the male seed,* "by man", and not through the seed of the woman.   Treatment of this point will be undertaken in Chapter 5 of Part II.

In all this discussion, I think it is also important — in the interests of precision in the use of terminology — to recognize the difference between *ageing* and *senescence.*   We age the moment we begin the process of living, since each day makes us one day older.   In itself, ageing means no more than adding years to our past, and hopefully it can be equated with the concept of maturing.   The rose in full bloom is older (more aged, in this sense) than the bud which it formerly was, both bud and bloom being perfect at each stage.   Senescence and senility have a sadder note to them, for they imply some measure of declining vitality and of decay both mental and physical.   But when reading the scientific literature, it is well to determine what the writer means when he speaks of ageing, for he may not be intending senescence.   I think both Wakerlin and Medawar wished to convey something of senescence and death in their use of the word *ageing.* Of course, to grow at all is to grow older and therefore to age, but to grow older, as the amoeba or paramecium does, in no way involves them in senescence provided that they divide once they have reached a certain size.   The process of division renews their vitality entirely and they escape death altogether.   Professor Bradley T. Scheer makes this observation regarding senescence:[58]

> The problem of aging may be segregated under two headings — senescence and death.   It is ordinarily considered that the two are related and that death is a consequence of senescence.   This has not been proved, however, and there are all about us instances of senile individuals who do not die and dead individuals who never became senile.

The point he makes is a useful one — and certainly true.   Nor can *age* be linked with senescence in chronological terms, for there is a disease of tragic nature in which the expected life span of the individual is "compressed", during which time the subject passes rapidly through childhood, adolescence, manhood, senility and death: and all within the space of a few years.   The disease is known as *progeria.*

Progeria is a peculiarly sad disease for those who are afflicted with it, for they see their lives racing by while their contemporaries slowly mature with what must appear to them "all the time in the world" to enjoy life.   It seems to me that we would all feel this if we found ourselves living alongside of Adam or Methusaleh . . . . It is not known what causes the disease but it is perhaps worth remembering that we might not recognize it as a disease at all if it equally afflicted *all* of us.   The fact is that, for all we know, we who live only three score years and ten may be suffering a form of progeria relative to the biblical patriarchs whose lives spanned ten times as many years and who evidently matured with corresponding slowness, since the time from birth to maturity was even then about one-sixth of the expected life span,[59] as it still is today both for man and many creatures below him.   Adam, for example, died at the age of 930 years, but did not give birth to his first son till he was 130 years of age (Gen.5:3-5).

In order to give some force to what is implied above, it may be useful to illustrate what happens to those who suffer from progeria at the present time.   In 1962 an eleven year old boy in California died of "old age",[60] resembling a wizened old man, his skin rough and wrinkled, only a few hairs on his head, the veins of his scalp protruding.   His teeth had "long since" been replaced by false teeth, his voice was high and feeble and he was afflicted with arteriosclerosis.   He had already suffered two heart attacks.   Yet the first eighteen months of his life had been quite normal and he had been a bright and cheerful child.   A photograph of him taken when he was seven years old fills one with sadness.   And there are 52 known cases at the present moment.

In 1967 there was a report from New Brunswick (Canada) of an eleven year old child who had already aged to the condition of a ninety-five year old.[61]   And this unhappy boy's sister, who was then two years younger than himself, was equally afflicted and already showed all the characteristics of an eighty year old woman at the time. In 1970 the *San Francisco Chronicle*[62] reported the case of a young girl of fourteen who had died suddenly and quite unexpectedly, and whose autopsy showed that she had actually succumbed to arteriosclerosis such as would normally be found in a seventy-five year old woman.

Recently there was reported a case from San Diego of a "little old lady", Penny Vantine, who at only five years of age was already an old woman (*Toronto Star,* 9 July, 1979).   Weighing barely nine pounds and only twenty-nine inches in height, her appearance and constitution was already that of an eighty year old. It was reported by her doctors that she was ageing at the rate of fifteen to twenty years every twelve months.

Imagine what this unfortunate child must think as she looks up at the nurse holding her, "This person is already forty, or eight times as old as I am . . . ." Were I to experience such a thought, being now seventy, what would my feelings of awe be to think of my nurse as already 560 years old and obviously still quite young! There really is no way in which we can know whether we, too, in our apparent normal state of being, are not afflicted with progeria or some such disease as Cockayne's Syndrome which afflicts little Penny Vantine.

It is well to ponder what this signifies. We have no way of knowing whether we might not in fact be living — all of us — at a tremendously accelerated rate relative to what men lived in pre-Flood times. Their rate of living, slow as it might seem today, may actually have been much more nearly what was intended as normal for the whole human race. But the rate of living of Adam and Eve before the Fall may have been even more leisurely. Even after the Fall, Adam's "childhood" still lasted around a hundred years; our childhood lasts perhaps fifteen; these four sad victims of progeria had a childhood of little more than a year.

Consider for a moment what the consequences would be if at some time in the future the normal life span of man was reduced to ten or twelve years, as though the world had become a progeriac world. There would be no Michelangelo to paint a Sistine Chapel, for no man would live long enough to complete the task. And perhaps there would be no one even to build a Sistine Chapel because, if the only people alive were little people with the stature and strength of an eight or ten year old, no one would have sufficient energy to erect anything more than small structures involving comparatively light materials. It is conceivable that some compensation would result from the development of refined machines representing a kind of building automation, but it is difficult to see how the fan tracery of a Gothic cathedral ceiling, for example, could be handled mechanically. The human hand has a dexterity that is not likely to be replaced by machinery where art is concerned. The time available, the energy required, and the necessary experience of life would all be drastically curtailed in a progeriac world.

There is one other factor of great significance in this shortened life span experience. It takes a certain amount of time to accumulate knowledge whether by reading or by visual means. It is true that speed reading might compensate a little but surely not sufficiently to allow an educational process which would be limited to a period between the ages of, say, seven and ten to compensate for a formal educational process that may today well occupy the period from seven years of age to twenty-seven in the pursuit of some higher degrees. The accomplishments of today would surely be severely curtailed.

However, consider the converse course of events.   Suppose that we lived in pre-Flood days and had ten times the number of years that we now have in which to accumulate knowledge and skill by study and experience.   How rapidly would civilization develop!   If we look upon a progeriac world as a world of little people when compared with our own adult world, would we not be required to look upon a super-super-centenarian world as a world of very much "larger" people compared with ourselves, indeed a world of giants?   Maybe there were "giants in the earth in those days" (Gen.6:4) for this very reason.   In short, it would be a very different world, but not an abnormal one.   It is *our* world that is abnormal by their standards, just as a progeriac world would be abnormal by ours.

There really is nothing impossible in this hypothetical situation. We are merely judging the old world by the wrong standards; and the progeriac world looking back upon ours might smile at any idea that there were "giants in the earth" in our day except that they might look upon our buildings and wonder at the size of things as we in fact wonder today at the enormity of some of the structures of antiquity.

Certainly there is nothing unreasonable about these very ancient records of unusual longevity in the early chapters of Genesis.   They have not been taken seriously enough, either by those in the Life Sciences (which is a pity) nor even by Christians (which is a tragedy). From these records we may learn a great deal about the *potential* life span of man, as well as about the origin of death as it relates specifically to man by contrast with other species.

As we have already noted, death for man comes as a tragedy, a violent rending asunder of his being in a way that does not seem equally true in the animal world.   It all began with an event which theologians associate with original sin.   By an act of disobedience Adam introduced to all his descendants an inheritable disease in the form of a transmissible agent of death both biological and spiritual. Its *biological* effects can be explored as one would explore the effects of any other genetically determined pathological condition.   The very concept of an acquired mortogenic factor which can be passed on by inheritance has particular significance for the geneticist. And the fact that Adam and Eve acquired mortality which was then inherited by their descendants is just such a case, as Sir Gavin de Beer was astute enough to recognize.[63] Yet, to my knowledge, no Christian writer with a background in genetics seems to have recognized its implications.

So I propose to examine the evidence that men did indeed live to such extraordinary ages, that these ancient records are indeed sober history, and that the very figures given to us can be usefully analyzed to show us a pattern of decline that strikingly accords with what we now know from genetics about the effect over successive generations wherever an inheritable disease is involved.

Death has been imposed upon man as a penalty.   At first its effects were delayed, but after the Flood those effects were greatly accelerated for reasons now understood in part.   Today we die at an age which to them would have seemed comparable to the death of a mere infant.   While we may expect to live for three score and ten, they did not even reach the child-bearing stage till they were one hundred and thirty years old or thereabouts!

This death of which we speak involves the separation of two components, and takes place when the spirit leaves the body irretrievably.   The departure of the spirit is best described as an event.   The dissolution of the body is best described as a process.   Death is therefore both event *and* process.

Chapter 3

MODERN METHUSELAHS

And the Lord said,
My spirit shall not always abide in man
for that he also is flesh:
yet his days shall be an hundred and twenty years.
Genesis 6:3

Living things often exhibit an amazing viability. Some organisms are remarkably difficult to kill! Let us consider first, briefly, some of the factors that govern the longevity of *any* form of life — whether plant or animal.

We have already noted that animals are viable as long as they grow: continued growth means continued vitality. But warm-blooded animals cannot go on growing indefinitely since ultimately they become too large: certain functional and structural limitations bring about their demise in due time for reasons which really have nothing to do with the fact of their age per se.

There is, however, one way in which growth of a simple organism can be continued indefinitely without undue enlargement, and this is by dividing into two when size reaches a certain point. For example, unicellular animals simply divide into two organisms as soon as they reach a critical size, and they thus renew their lease on life without ever getting too bulky yet always continuing the process of growing. But if an elephant were to continue to grow indefinitely it would be immobilized in due time by its sheer mass. It is doomed not merely by the likelihood of fatal injury due to accident or disease (which increases with the increase of years), but its size is thus determined by reason of the fact that a free-standing organism cannot sustain its own weight beyond the strength limitations of the materials out of which its limbs and backbone are constructed.[64]

The average life span of each species is more or less predetermined by its susceptibility to fatal accident. In the case of marine animals, the life span is extended somewhat (in whales for example, in spite of their enormously increased size) simply because of the fact that the animal's bulk, being immersed in a weight-supporting medium like water, places less strain upon its structure and on its energy resources. But even here there are limitations not only for physiological reasons but also because the animal is mobile in three dimensions (as opposed to the two dimensional mobility of land animals) and it therefore exposes itself to an increased range of hazards. It is in danger not merely on its own ground level, but from above and below as well.

In the case of plants we find the effects of the hazards of life are somewhat reduced. In the first place, if mobility contributes to the range of hazards, immobility may reduce that range. In the second place, immobility reduces the physiological need for a sophisticated central nervous system and the complex musculature required for locomtion. The whole life support system is enormously simplified. Thus plants such as trees need none of these structural complexities. Moreover, they can distibute their weight more effectively on the ground by spreading their base root system adequately or by thrusting into the earth deep tap roots to serve as anchors, thus decreasing the risk of injury by upset. Their fibre structure also contributes to their greater resistance to damage. For these reasons trees are almost certainly among the longest living organisms we know.

Here are some average ages among trees noted for their longevity:

SPECIES	AGE
Elm	335 years
Ivy	450
Palm	650
Lime	1100
Oak	1200
Yew	2800
Sequoia	4000
Baobab and Bristlecone	5000 and up
Japanese Cedar	7200 (by C_{14})[65]

It is difficult to think of a single organism surviving 7000 years or more, but there are possibly circumstances under which living things may survive even longer than this. Since one important contributing factor in long life is slowness of growth, it follows that almost any living thing can be forced, by cooling or underfeeding or reducing its access to light or water, to slow up its metabolism until it almost stops altogether.   Dormancy thus becomes another key to longevity.[66]

Seeds may be dormant for tremendous periods of time and yet retain their viability, as proven by their subsequent germination after centuries of apparent lifelessness.   Some years ago the magazine *Think* published a photograph of a bean sprout flourishing in the warm Egyptian sunshine which had germinated from a seed taken from the tomb of Tutankhamen (14th century B.C.).[67]   There may be some question as to whether this particular bean really was from the ancient monarch's tomb, but since that time there are a number of other fairly well authenticated instances of recovery from great periods of dormancy.   In 1965 J. T. Bonner, in commenting on the above reputed revival of a seed, remarked,[68]

> Although the extent of seed longevity has been greatly exaggerated, there are known cases of seeds being stored successfully over 3000 years.   This means that for this great period the embryo remained in what amounts to suspended animation.

Professor H. Godwin of the Department of Botany (Cambridge) refers to seeds of *Nelumbium* collected in 1705 and kept in the Hans Sloane Collection at the British Museum until 1942 when they were revived successfully.[69]   Godwin also refers to seeds of the same plant received from a drained lake in Southern Manchuria which were believed to have an age of several thousand years.   These, too, were still viable.   It is true that in the last instance radiocarbon dating did not support such an age, but Godwin refers to a radiocarbon dating of a canoe at Henisgawa, near Tokyo, which established an age of over 3000 years for some viable seeds of water lily found in association with it.   He mentions several other similar examples but feels that in every case the date reckoning is not unequivocal.   However, in 1969 a report from La Plata in Argentina records the germination of seeds estimated to be about 550 years old by scientists from the National Univerity.   These seeds were discovered while excavating a tomb where a necklace was found made out of nuts of *Juglands arcticus*. [70] Inside each nut was a seed and these seeds, being sown in sterile conditions in a highly nutritious medium, germinated almost immediately, sprouted, formed roots, and then formed leaves by the tenth day.   There is little doubt about these particular seeds.   In 1967 a Dr. Michael Black had reported the germination of the seeds *Lupinus arcticus* found in the Yukon in a rodent burrow beneath overlying "muck" which had been frozen during the last glaciation, which accredits to them a hoary age in excess of 10,000 years.[71]   These seeds also germinated.

Again, it should be said that although a supporting radiocarbon date of 14,860 to 14,840 years is given by the investigators, it is not absolutely certain that the seeds themselves were not intrusions.   It hardly seems possible that every single instance of a truly ancient seed that germinates should be an intrusion, though it is proper to exercise caution.

Contrary to popular opinion, what is alive may be remarkably difficult to kill.   Life has amazing power to maintain itself.[72]

We now turn to the evidence of unusual longevity for man himself, as reflected in the traditions of antiquity but now increasingly in the records of more recent times.   For as will be seen, there are still a significant number of individuals who reach an extraordinary old age — even if a small percentage of them prove to be fictitious as to the age achieved.   From the earliest times right up to the present day there have been stories of men who lived to such great ages so far beyond our expectations as to seem little more than "old wives' tales".

Some of the very oldest records, of course, speak of life spans extending over many centuries and therefore far exceeding even the antiquarians of our own times.   And we might therefore feel that they really are entirely legendary.   But in recent years Archaeology has been consistently confirming many ancient traditions and unexpectedly demonstrating their entire trustworthinesss, not merely in the broad scope of their observations but even in their more precise details.   There is a growing respect among archaeologists not only for the early records of Scripture itself but for the writings of secular historians as well.   It has been either our ignorance of the past or our failure to interpret these records correctly that has hitherto contributed to our scepticism.

It is well to remember this when questioning the hearsay of longevity of individuals in an illiterate or only semi-literate society where written records such as birth certificates are virtually absent, for in such societies every one is tied in and involved deeply in all kinds of personal relationships which are of particular importance to the whole community and therefore not likely to be easily forgotten.   If a man lives for 150 years or so, he will have a tremendous number of relatives who don't forget, even though there may be not one scrap of paper to prove a word any of them has to say.   The network of testimony is hard to discount.

With particular reference to the great ages achieved by individuals in the early days of human history, such as have been recorded by men like Hesiod and others, we may note that Josephus appeals to them as supporting evidence for the veracity of the early chapters of Genesis; and Josephus, like other ancient historians, has been proving himself to be a more careful recorder than was formerly believed.

In his *Antiquities of the Jews* Josephus wrote:[73]

> Now I have for witnesses to what I have said, all those that
> have written Antiquities, both among the Greeks and barbar-
> ians; for even Manetho who wrote the Egyptian History, and
> Berosus who collected the Chaldean Monuments, and Mochus,
> and Hestiaeus, and besides these, Hieronymus, the Egyptian,
> and those who composed the Phoenician history, agree to
> what I here say.   Hesiod also, and Hecataeus, Hellanicus, and
> Acusilaus; and besides Ephorus and Nicolaus relate that the
> ancients lived a thousand years.

In his book, *The Beginnings of History,* Francois Lenormant
points out that Hesiod records in this connection that, in the Silver
Age which immediately followed the Golden Age of man's unfallen
estate, men remained for a hundred years with their mothers in a
state of childhood.[74]   Hellanicus, speaking of a time somewhat later,
related that the Epaeans who had been forced by the tyranny of
Salmonaeus to emigrate from Elis and to settle in Aetolia lived 200
years for several successive generations; one of them, according to
Damastes of Signaeum, even attained 300 years.   Pliny and Valerius
Maximus have collected a certain number of similar cases from various
quarters.   They do not all belong to Greece.   They show that the
Illyrians, for instance, on the authority of Cornelius Alexander,
counted as their ancestor Dathon or Dadon, who lived 500 years in
good health.   According to *The Periplus* of Xenophon (of Lamp-
sacus), the Thyians headed their royal list with a prince who lived 600
years, a period eclipsed only by the 800 years of his son's life span.
As Lenormant concluded, "All these are just so many witnesses to the
belief, common to all nations, in an extreme longevity among the
earliest ancestors of the human race".[75]

In one of his studies of antiquity, the great classical scholar George
Rawlinson observed:[76]

> There is a large amount of consentient tradition to the
> effect that the life of man was originally far more prolonged
> than it is at present extending to at least several hundreds of
> years.   The Babylonians, Egyptians, and the Chinese all
> exaggerated these into hundreds of thousands of years.   The
> Greeks and Romans with more moderation limited human life
> within a hundred to eight hundred years.   The Hindus still
> further shortened it . . . .   Their books taught that in the first
> ages of the world man was free from diseases and lived origin-
> ally 400 years.   In the second, the term of life was reduced
> from 400 to 300.   In the third, it became 200 years.
>   So strange did the fact first appear to the Chinese that an
> Emperor who wrote a medical work [I presume the reference
> is to the Yellow Emperor's Classic work **Internal Medicine,**
> dated c.2600 B.C., and in which, incidentally, the circulation

of the blood was specifically spelled out. ACC] proposed an
inquiry into the reasons why the ancestors attained to so much
more advanced an age than the moderns.

Joseph Needham,[77] the author of the most comprehensive study
of Chinese civilization and technology to be undertaken by a European, and a co-worker Lu Gwei-Djen, published a paper which dealt in
part with the supposed causes underlying the substantial ages (100 to
200 years) reached by certain notable Chinese of the Middle Ages who
apparently displayed little evidence of senescence either in mind or
body.   The Chinese attributed it largely to the use of urine as a medicine.   For example:[78]

> Early in the fourteenth century A.D., Chu Chen-Heng tells
> us that he once attended an old woman over eighty years of
> age who gave the appearance of being only forty.   In reply to
> his questioning she explained why she had had such good
> health and suffered no illnesses.   Once when she had been ill
> she had been instructed to take human urine, and this she had
> done for several decades.   Who could maintain, therefore,
> says Chu Chen-Heng, the old belief that the property of urine
> is algorific [causing a fall in body temperature] and that it
> could not be taken for a long time?

It is conceivable that continued use of this treatment might indeed
cause a chronic depression of body temperature which would actually
contribute to the prolonging of life (and youthfulness) in the same
way that cooling laboratory animals has been found to extend their
life by slowing up metabolic activity.

Several common ideas appear repeatedly in these ancient traditions.   For one thing, people are said to have retained their vigour and
health.   They did not linger on in a state of senility.   As we shall see,
there is some evidence (in some of the exceptionally aged individuals)
of a partial recovery of youth — witnessed, for example, by the return
of hair colour and the "cutting" of a third set of teeth.   Another fact
upon which all the ancient authorities agree is that the nearer a man
was to the Golden Age of sinlessness, the longer he lived.   The course
of history in this respect has not been progressive in nature but degenerative.   At this point, of course, tradition and the earliest written
records stand in direct opposition to current evolutionary doctrine.

We have a few witnesses to the achievement of a hoary enough old
age even in the past seven or eight hundred years. Marco Polo wrote a
record of his travels in the Kingdom of Ghengis Khan towards the end
of the thirteenth century and his observations have proved remarkably
dependable and sober-minded wherever they could be checked, in
spite of the opportunities he had to observe so many entirely new and
strange things (such as the use of fireproof clothing woven out of

asbestos fibres, for example!).   At one place he mentions the Yogi,
a "class of people who are indeed properly Brahmins,, but they form a
religious order devoted to idols.   They are extremely long-lived, every
one of them living from 150 to 200 years.   They eat very little, but
what they do eat, is good".[79]   In view of what has been said previously about the reduction of food intake in connection with dormancy
in animals and the consequent extension of life, his remark about
their meagre fare, which is obviously a casual aside, has added significance.   I do not recall any reference in Marco Polo's writings to the
sad effects of over-indulgence, but there is a very ancient proverb,
undoubtedly borne of experience, which says, "Man does not die: he
kills himself and he digs his grave with his teeth".

Of course, we are so far from the starting point of man now that
we cannot expect, perhaps, to find any further instances of people
living to four or five hundred years, but there really is no reason to
doubt that there are many modern "ancients" who are very old,
certainly over 120 and probably quite a number over 150 years of age.

In modern times we read of certain areas of the world, such as
Azerbaijan and Abkhasia in USSR, Hunza in Kashmir, Vilcabamba in
Ecuador, and other Shangri-las, where ordinary men and women live
in health and vigour to ages that make us seem to die as mere children
with our three score and ten years.   That the extraordinary ages
achieved by these people, not infrequently in excess of 130 years or
more, are genuine (contrary to the scepticism of Acsadi and Nemeskeri) seems now reasonably well established.   A review recently
appeared in the *Royal Anthropological Institute News* of a book by
David Davies, *The Centenarians of the Andes*.   In this review,
O. Harris notes: [80]

> Dr. Davies' book gives an account of a remarkable number
> of centenarians living in a crescent of villages round Vilcabam-
> ba in southern Ecuador.   The interest of these people is
> considerable: because of the meticulous recording of births
> and deaths by the Catholic Church, there is documentary evid-
> ence of their ages which is not available in the other two zones
> where comparable numbers of centenarians are known to
> exist — namely, the Abkasians to the east of the Black Sea,
> and the Hunzas in North Kashmir/southwest China.

From one of these areas (Abkhasia in the Georgian Soviet Union)
Alexander Leaf reports his investigation of ages where no such metic-
ulous recording of births is available.   He writes:[81]

> There is no baptismal record for Khfaf Lasuria.   So as I
> talked to her, I kept doing mental arithmetic.   I have said
> that she is more than 130; I should have said "at least".
> According to her account, her father lived to be 100 and her

mother 101 or 102.   She had seven sisters and three brothers,
and is the only survivor.   Her son, who was born when she
was 52, is now 82 (arithmetic: 82 + 52 = 134).   She was
married a second time at age 50, at the time of the Turkish
war — which ended 94 years ago in 1878 (50 + 94 = 144).
When she was 20, her first husband almost left home to fight
in the Crimean War of 1853-56 (118 + 20 = 138).   She started
smoking in 1910 when her younger brother died at the age of
60;   he was some ten years younger than she (60 + 10 + 62 =
132).   Her second husband, who was two years younger than
she, died 28 to 30 years ago, when he was more than 100
(100 + 29 + 2 = 131).

My interview was conducted in such a way that it would
have been difficult for each of these assessments to come out
in such fair agreement unless a common thread of reality linked them.   Mrs. Lasuria believes she is 141 years old; thus I
would accept some age between 131 and 141.

Our reactions to these reports are apt to be ambivalent.   There
are few who would not want to extend their lives by scores of
years — when they are in life's prime and not facing the limitations of
the older folk.   When we reach senior years we begin to have second
thoughts about going on for too long in such a condition.   But these
supercentenarians seem not merely to have added years to life but life
to years.   Yet even here there comes a time apparently when the
desire to go on living decreases with the gradual decline in energy.
One centenarian from Vilcabamba who is still active at a modest 120
years, nevertheless said somewhat cynically to an interviewer, "Who
wants to live to be 120?"

It is interesting that such people not infrequently seem to die by
an almost deliberate loosening of their hold on life.   A note in the
San Francisco Chronicle (Saturday, 12 July, 1975) reported:

> Of those people who live to be at least 100 years old,
> medical experts have found a remarkably high proportion of
> them die by decision.   In other words, they simply decide on
> a time to go, then go.   Studies have turned up an unusually
> large number of people in that age bracket who predicted the
> week or even the day they would die.

It is true that statistics show we are improving our chances a little.
But it is our chances of reaching 70 or so that are improved, not our
chances of reaching 100 or 200.   More babies and children are being
saved from an early death and thus the mean for the population is
raised, but the potential life span for man as a whole seems to have
remained pretty much the same.

The point is important because the often reported finding that the
average age is now greatly improved does not mean that people will
steadily achieve longer and longer lives until we become like the patri-

archs of Genesis.   It is possible that we shall indeed so become, but not because the present trend is leading that way.   As Professor A. S. Warthin in a United States Census Report put it, "the increase in the average longevity is due to the saving of life through the prevention of extrinsic pathological death in the earlier decades of life, but there has been no extension of the normal or biologic life limit".[82]   This was written fifty years ago but it also reflects the present position quite faithfully except that one might add the further factor of the reduction of some diseases of *old age* as well.   Raymond Pearl has stated the case this way: "In 1890 only 72% of boy babies got a foothold on the ten year rung; now 91% do . . . .   The *span* of human life has *not* been lengthened" (his emphasis). [83]

It may be useful to note in passing what this average age improvement signifies in the long term.   Acsadi and Nemeskeri give the following figures for the average ages attained from Graeco-Roman times to the present, based on skeletal remains.[84]

Greek and Roman times	c. 28 years
Middle Ages	25-35 years
17th and 18th centuries	25-35 years

The census published by the Registrar-general of England and Wales for the period from 1838 - 1854 gave an average age of 40 for males and 42 for females; and a subsequent census for 1937 showed the average age for males to be 60 and for females 64.   It should be noted that these ages are *averages* and not maxima attainable, for as will be seen from the tabulation below, there were exceptional individuals living to very much greater ages throughout these periods. The Soviet Census of 1959 listed 5600 centenarians, among whom were 578 people over 120 years of age.[85]   Perhaps some of these are mistakenly recorded, but certainly not every one of them.   Acsadi and Nemeskeri give some figures for centenarians in Hungary as follows:

In 1910 in a population of 7,612,000 there were 122 centenarians.
In 1960 in a population of 9,961,000 there were 67 centenarians.

However, they say that of the 67 individuals listed for 1960, fifty-three were found to have been recorded erroneously and only fourteen were considered validated.   Taking all their data for European countries — and this data is actually very substantial — they conclude on the basis of the available figures: "It is more or less generally accepted that man's maximum length of life can be counted at present to be 110 plus or minus 10 years".   This is an interesting observation to appear in what is probably the most exhaustive study of human mortality in recent years, for it in effect sets the probable top figure (for all but a few exceptional and numerically small scattered populations) at 120 years.   This figure has special significance in the light of a statement made in Genesis 6:3, which we shall have occasion to look at more closely in a later chapter.   The following Tabulation indicates the kind of evidence that exists for extreme longevity in comparatively recent and modern times.

TABLE 1

The following individuals have achieved longevity in excess of 100 years.   The names are in chronological order by age.   Further details are given in Appendix I.

Maude Tull	103 in 1975	Los Angeles, USA
Isabel Mendieta	103 in 1973	Vilcabamba
Anna Schwab	104 in 1972	Ohio, USA
Micaela Quezada	104 in 1976	Vilcabamba
John Walker	104 in 1969	Ontario, Can.
Frances Johnson	107, d.1832	Jamaica
Robert Thomas	107, d. 1821	Fairfax Co., USA
Emma Mills	108 in 1973	Ontario, Can.
Mary Holoboff	108, d. 1942	British Columbia, Can.
Thomas Robinson	110, d.1970	Ontario, Can.
Elizabeth Lambe	110, d. 1830	West Indies
Astana Shlarba	110 in 1966	Georgia, USSR
Jim Ho	111 in 1976	Prince Edward Island, Can.
Spencer Church	111 in 1961	Ontario, Can.
Ada Roe	111, d. 1970	England
John Turner	111, d. 1968	England
Caesar Paul	112 in 1975	Ontario, Can.
Mittelstedt	112, d. 1792	Prussia
Francis Hongo	113, d. 1702	Venice
Arma Darendonian	113, d. 1972	France
Annie Firlotte	113 in 1954	New Brunswick, Can.
Gabriel Sanchez	113 in 1976	Vilcabamba
Amina Orujeva	114 in 1967	Azerbaijan, USSR
Zibeida Sheidayeva	114 in 1974	Azerbaijan, USSR
Teb Sharmat	115 in 1966	Abkhasia, USSR
Murtee, Johnny,	115, d.1976	Australia
Walter Williams	117, d. 1959	Texas, USA
Mary Mills	118, d.1805	West Indies
Mr. C. Cotterel	120, d. 1760?	Philadelphia, USA
Jane Morgan	120, d. 1830	Jamaica
Mary Goodsall	120, d.1820	Jamaica
Mrs. Gray	121, d. 1770	Kent, England
Charles Layne	121, d. 1821	Virginia, USA
Rev. Toby Crosby	122, d. 1976	Florida, USA
Sabir Kurbonadaov	122 in 1973	Tajik Republic, USSR
John Gilley	123, d. 1813	Maine, USA
Noah Raby	123, d. 1895	New Jersey, USA
Demetrius Liondos	123 in 1970	Greece

Thomas Wishart	124, d. 1760	Dumfries, Scotland
Francisco Rubio	124, d. 1943	Mexico
Attila, the Hun	124, d. 453?	Germany
Sylvester Magee	126 in 1967	Missouri, USA
Mary Yates	127, d. 1776	England
Miguel Carpio	127 in 1976	Vilcabamba
Eglebert Hoff	128, d. 1764	New York, USA
Ephriam Zithundu Zulu	130, d. 1975	South Africa
Margaret Darby	130, d. 1821	Jamaica
Francis Peat	130, d. 1830	Jamaica
Ramonotowane Seran	130, d. 1945	Bechuanaland, Africa
Balakishi Orujeva	130 in 1967	Azerbaijan, USSR
Peter Garden	131, d. 1775	Edinburgh, Scotland
Mathayo Achungo	132, d. 1976	Kenya, Africa
Gabriel Erazo	132 in 1976	Vilcabamba
Charlie Smith	133 in 1976	Florida, USA
Henry Francisco	134, d. 1820	New York, USA
Beim Mekraliyeva	134 in 1966	Azerbaijan, USSR
Anton Pilya	135, d. 1965	Georgia, USSR
Nicholas Petours	137, d. 1775?	Germany
Juan Moroygota	138 in 1828	Columbia, South America
Gentleman	140 in 1838	South America
Lasuria Khfaf	140 in 1974	Azerbaijan, USSR
Medzhig Agayev	140 in 1976	Azerbaijan, USSR
William Hotchkiss	140, d. 1895	St. Louis, USA
Jose David	142 in 1973	Vilcabama
Hilario Pari	143, d. 1807?	Lima, Peru
Jean Effingham	144, d. 1757	Cornwall, England
Countess of Desmond	145, d. 1619	England
Joseph Bam	146, d. 1821	Jamaica
Bridget Devine	147, d. 1845	England
Catherine Hiatt	150, d. 1831	Jamaica
Unnamed Lady	150, d. 1894	France
C. Jacobsen Drakenberg	150, d. 1772	Denmark
Mahmoud Nivazov	150 in 1959	Azerbaijan, USSR
Judith Crawford	151, d. 1829	Jamaica
G. Stanley	151, d. 1719	England
Thomas Parr	152, d. 1635	England
Thomas Newman	153, d. 1542	England
Asmar Salakhova	154 in 1966	Soviet Armenia
Iwan Yorath	156, d. 1621	Wales
A Peasant	157, d. 1800?	Poland
Sampson Skakoragaro	158 in 1969	Tanzania, Africa
Robert Lynch	160, d. 1830	Jamaica
Joseph Surrington	160, d.?	Norway
Zaro Aga	164, d. 1932	USA
Sarah Desson Rovin	164, d. 1741	England
Jonas Warren	167, d. 1787	Ireland
Shirali Mislimov	168, d. 1973	Azerbaijan, USSR
Ali Ashraf Husseini	168 in 1976	Iran
Javier Pereira	169, d. 1958	Columbia, S.A.
Henry Jenkins	169, d. 1670	England
John Rovin	172, d. 1741	England

John Gower	172, d. ?	England
Jean Korin	172, d. ?	Hungary
A Negress	174 in 1775	South America
Baba Harainsingh	176 in 1952	India
Elizabeth Yorath	177, d. 1668	England
Kentigren	185, d. 600	Scotland
Peter Torton	185, d. 1724	England
Petrarsh Zartan	187, d. 1724	Hungary
Gentleman	192, d. 1895?	Vera Cruz, Mexico
Gentleman	207, d. 1500?	England
Li Chang-Yun	256, d. 1933	China

Concluding Remarks.

In certain areas of the world where life is less hectic, where social ties are far more personal, where the family is strongly integrated, where age is respected rather than feared, where the work ethic is still honoured by all alike, where the routine of daily life is comparatively simple and unhurried, where diet is stable and uncomplicated, and where the climate is neither too hot nor too cold — there we find pockets of "super-centenarians", as they have been called.

Some areas do seem more favourable. Pliny records from a census of 76 A.D. in the days of Emperor Vespasian that there were living in the valley between the Apennines and the Po River 124 persons over the age of 100, two of whom were 135, four were 137, and three were 140. In 1864 the census for the town of Pilagum in Ecuador, lying 11,000 feet above sea level with a population of about 2000, reported a hundred over 70 years of age, thirty above 90, five above 100, and one at 115.[87] Today these favoured pockets persist.

It will be noted, too, from the augmented data of Appendix I that hard work does not shorten life, and the "wear and tear" theory of ageing is therefore not borne out. The stress factor, surprisingly, is also probably small. As a matter of interest and possibly having a bearing on the advantages of a life of hard work as opposed to a life of comparative ease, it is interesting to note that in the 1835 census of the black and white populations of the State of New Jersey, it was found that only two individuals of the *white* population had attained the age of 100 in a total of 320,800 people whereas eleven *blacks* had reached an age of 100 or over in a population of only 20,000 people.[88] The vitality of the latter (hard-worked though they probably were) exceeded that of the whites by a factor of 75 times, though the environmental conditions were approximately the same for both. Professor Raymond Pearl found that animals in captivity which are worked hard, such as elephants for which records are available in India, far outlived their fellows in the wild state.[89]

There is no evidence that in these pockets of very long-lived people any special effort was made by the inhabitants to adjust their diet in order to enhance life except that the people of Vilcabamba preferred the local river water to the water from the wells which the government had undertaken to drill for them.   There is some evidence of a low food intake (1700 calories per day in Vilcabamba as opposed to 3500 in Britain) and certainly they do not seem to over-eat, though they do not refuse sweet things at all.   Some drink considerable wine, but the alcoholic content may not be high.   Quite a number are heavy smokers (40 to 60 cigarettes a day)![90]

In a few cases we meet with the strange phenomenon of rejuvenation — darkening of gray hair and recovery of teeth, for example. Baba Harainsingh of India had grown a complete new set of teeth and his hair was recovering its original colour by the time he was 176 years old.   Hufeland, writing in 1870, gives the instance of a magistrate on the Continent who had lost all his teeth and at the age of 116 eight new ones appeared.   At the end of six months these dropped out but were replaced again.   This process was repeated so that in all he acquired — and lost — without pain, 150 teeth by the time of his death four years later in 1791.   There was also a woman by the name of Helen Gray who acquired another set of teeth a few years before her death at age 105.[91]

There is little or no evidence of the diseases of old age common to our society (arterial or otherwise) in some of the oldest people listed. "Old Parr" who died at the age of 152 less than a year after being presented to the King, was autopsied by the famous Dr. William Harvey who found that the internal organs were in a most perfect state and that the cartilages were not even ossified.   No natural cause of death could be found and the general impression was that he died (was "killed") from being over-fed and too well treated in London. [92] Recently, Mislimov was declared to be medically "in perfect health" at 166 with a blood pressure of 120/75 and a pulse of 72 after climbing three flights of stairs!   An autopsy of Zaro Aga at 164 showed that all his glands and organs were still without evidence of disease. Where there is available information, it appears that most of these very old people die quite peacefully in their sleep.   Occasionally there are sufferers from arthritis, but on the whole they remain active almost to the end.   One ancient worthy of a mere 99 years, Abkha Suleiman, complained that he was finding it difficult to climb trees any longer!

There is clear evidence of a genetic factor.[93]   There is the case of John Moore who died in 1805 at the age of 107.[94]   His father died at the age of 105 and his grandfather at 115.   An aged mother gives a better chance of longevity than an aged father, and daughters have a better chance than sons, although Acsadi and Nemeskeri show that this is a comparatively modern phenomenon.[95]   The reasons are not clear.   This circumstance is to be noted in the case of Joseph Joachim de Prado, of good family, a strong active man living in the district of Campinos, who was 107 in 1886.   His mother had died, by accident, at 112, while his maternal grandmother died at 122 years of age.[96]   A modern example is that of the head of the familiar Five & Ten Chain Stores, Sebastian S. Kresge, who had reached the age of 91 in 1958 in excellent health, his mother having died at the age of 103 and his grandmother at 101 years of age.[97]

It will be noted that one oldster was still able to sire a child at 136 years of age, namely, Sampson Skakoragaro who fathered his youngest son at that time.   Robert Plot, an Oxford historian of 1686, reported that John Best of the parish of Horton at age 104 married a woman of 56 and begat a son.

There is evidence that non-whites (blacks, Chinese, etc.) are often longer-lived than whites, only it is well to point out that the people of Vilcabamba are of *Spanish* origin.   But there are an unusual number of black "ancients", many of whom were slaves.   In many cases these long-lived people are said to have died as a result of accident or disease, not infrequently from influenza caught from visiting outsiders. It makes one cringe to learn that scientific types are making plans to go into these areas to investigate the causes of their longevity!

And finally, the idea that when people reach the age of, say, 95, they quickly skip to a claimed 100 years, is not borne out by those who are still alive.   The Abkhasians do not believe a man is really very old until he is considerably more than 100, and do not particularly want to be thought of as old in any case.   They actually tend to minimize their ages and feel quite able to marry, and are anxious to be married, until they are considered too old by others.   One aged fellow who was about to marry insisted he was only 95.   But when it was pointed out that he already had a daughter aged 81, he became very angry and refused to discuss it.   It turned out that he was probably 108 or more!   The point is an important one because we generally assume that up to a certain unspecified age everyone pretends they are not as old as they are, and then when they reach this unspecified age they suddenly begin to claim the honour of being *older* than they are.   It seems that we can think of this as applying to others whom we suppose will be anxious to be thought very ancient, whereas the very ancient individual continues to think of himself as quite youthful still.

I think that it is time to take a second look at the possibility that man may very well have survived for centuries in former days. Biology knows nothing that renders this unlikely, and careful analysis of the records of longevity in the early chapters of Genesis only serves to increase our respect for the figures which are given there, the implications of which if projected backwards to man's *unfallen* state have tremendous theological significance.   In the next chapter these figures are examined.

Chapter 4

LONGEVITY IN ANTIQUITY

And Adam lived an hundred and thirty years,
and begat a son . . . .
The days of Adam after he had begotten (a son)
were eight hundred years . . . .
and all the days that Adam lived were
nine hundred and thirty years:
and he died.
Genesis 5:3-5

The fifth chapter of Genesis contains a list of names of ten individuals whose lives spanned the period from Adam to Noah. We are also told their ages at the birth of their first son and at the time of their death. This arrangement in Genesis is unique and is not found in any of the other parallel lists thus far discovered from antiquity. It is unique in that it allows us to extract information of great value which cannot be extracted from any of the Sumerian, Babylonian, Assyrian or Egyptian King Lists that are roughly comparable in objective.

The biblical arrangement makes it possible to calculate precisely the interval between the creation of Adam and the Deluge which occurred when Noah was 600 years old (Gen.7:11). It also allows us to obtain some idea of the rate of maturing at a time when men lived far longer than they do today, since we can compare the time to the birth of the first son in proportion to the total life span of each individual. We can also calculate the average life span for this period of history as a measure of the vitality of man when the human race was still in its infancy.

The King Lists of antiquity do not provide information of this sort: they are concerned rather with the lengths of *reign,* not lengths of life.   Nor do they provide us with the age of the father at the time of the birth of his son.   Superficially, the King Lists appear to be quite comparable, except for their gross exaggeration of the time periods involved.   However, there are certain discrepancies but, as we shall see, these discrepancies (particularly with respect to the number of names listed and the actual names themselves) find their most reasonable explanation in the light of the genealogy provided in Genesis 5.

The data from Genesis 5 may be tabulated as follows:

TABLE II

NAME	TIME TO MATURITY	TOTAL AGE
Adam	130	930
Seth	105	912
Enos	90	905
Cainan	70	910
Mahaleel	65	895
Jared	162	962
Enoch	65	(365)
Methuselah	187	969
Lamech	182	777
Noah	500	950

From the above we learn (a) that the average life span (exclusive of Enoch who "was translated that he should not see death", Hebrews 11:5) was 912 years; and (b) that the average age to maturity is 166 years if Noah is included.   However, Genesis 5:32 (which gives Noah's age at the time of the birth of all *three* sons) seems to introduce a complication.   Therefore, it is perhaps safer to exclude Noah from this computation.   If we omit the figures for Noah, the average age to maturity is found to be 128 years.

Taking this average time to maturity of 128 years, we note that it works out at approximately one seventh of the total average life span of 912 years.   The proportion is most reasonable in the light of the fact that although other mammalian species show a fairly wide variation, in most higher animals growth to maturity relative to duration of life is in the proportion of one-sixth, for such creatures as rabbits, dogs, horses, camels and elephants.[98]   It may also be remembered that Hesiod spoke of the tradition that men were still children at 100 years in the so-called Silver Age: and Isaiah (65:20) looked forward to a return of this situation in the Golden Age yet to come when anyone dying at 100 years of age would be considered still only a child.   It may further be recalled that Simms, Selye, and Huxley are now willing to admit that for man to be capable of living a thousand years no longer seems so absurd as it did even fifty years ago.[99]

But in their book on the history of human mortality, Acsadi and Nemeskeri dismiss the Genesis account as of little substantial worth because they cannot accept the possibility that man once lived so very much longer than he does now.   So they attempt to explain the figures away by saying:[100]

> Observations over many centuries show evidence of the fact that individual spans of life may vary from the normal both by their brevity and their exceptional length.   Indeed many examples of longevity have been recorded in literature but there is little value in the reports.   In the Bible, for instance, Methuselah was accredited with 960 years, but recent critical investigations into the source have reduced this figure to 74, as the original calculation was based on 28-day lunar years.

In other words, we are to read the *years* of Genesis as *months:* Methuselah really only lived 969 months, not 969 years!   This observation is a classic example of the nonsense that can emerge when otherwise intelligent individuals allow what is a proper caution in dealing with unverifiable data to degenerate into unwarranted scepticism entirely prompted by personal bias with respect to biblical statements.

They speak with complete confidence of "investigations into the source" of the information in Genesis, though there is *absolutely* no way of knowing what that source was!   Actually, it was probably 'common knowledge'.   But what incredible nonsense it is to speak about "the source" of something which must have been known to everyone in the community at the time.   And how utterly ridiculous to pronounce that lunar years were the unit of measurement, for if this principle is applied generally to the record in Genesis, we are left with the interesting conclusion that Adam begat a son when he was 10, Seth when he was 8½, Enos when he was just over 7, Cainan when he was 6, and Mahalaleel when he was only 5½ years of age!   The figures are patently absurd if we read the years as months.

Moreover, there is no evidence whatever that any other nation, or even the Hebrew people, at that time or subsequently used the word *years* when they intended *months* to be understood.[101]   Futhermore, it is obvious that by the time we get to the record of the Flood, the word *months* is being used as it has always been used.   At no point in the narrative of Genesis is there the slightest evidence of a change-over which would mark the transition in terminology where the record is no longer counting months as years but has adopted the normal reckoning found everywhere else in antiquity.   The observation is, in fact, puerile: and it serves only to show how, when people refuse to take

seriously the plain sense of the Word of God, their reasoning somehow
becomes inept.

The quotation is even, in some sense, dishonest since we are told
that "the investigations" are *recent*.   Just how recent this concept of
treating years as months really is may be judged by noting that when
John Peter Lange in 1864 wrote his *Commentary on Genesis,* the idea
had already been around long enough for him to be able to comment
on the observations of a number of scholars who had toyed with it.
This is over a hundred years ago!

Needless to say, those scholars who did favour the months-equals-
years concept did not have a very high opinion of the veracity of
Scripture.   The principle upon which they operated in making their
revised calculations involved them in some rather complicated adjust-
ments.   In view of the fact that from Adam to Noah (ten individuals)
the average age was 912 years, if we then read these years as months,
the average age is reduced to 76 years — which was felt to be more
"reasonable".   So it was proposed that the years were actually so
intended to be read.   But then from Shem to Abraham (the next ten
individuals) the average age is only 317 years.   It would not do to
take *these* years as months, for the average life span would then be far
too low (26 years).   But if we assume that the word *year* for this
period now means *three* months instead of only one, and if we convert
the average age accordingly, we again arrive at the very "reasonable"
life span of 79 years.   Thereafter we have to assume that the years
are normal years of twelve months each, or the figures once more
cease to make sense.   Thus having committed themselves to this
principle of adjustment, it becomes necessary to keep adjusting the
adjustment: a "year" is first of all one month, then three months, and
finally twelve months!   Yet this extraordinary manipulation of the
figures was seriously proposed by reputable scholars, such as Raske
(the one year = one month concept), and Hensler (the one year =
three months concept).[102]   On the whole it does not seem that
Acsadi and Nemeskeri have given very much thought to what they
were proposing.

Now, for many years it has been argued that the early chapters of
Genesis were concocted by the historians of the Jewish people on the
basis of information they borrowed from pagan traditions around
them.   They are admitted to have exercised more restraint with
respect to what their heroes were purported to have done, and with
respect to the length of time they lived.   But essentially the account
is mythical.   The figures which they incorporated into their history
were considerably more realistic, being in the hundreds of years rather
than the tens of thousands of years which the Babylonians and the

Assyrians attributed to their earliest ancestors; but the ages allotted were still felt to be ridiculously exaggerated and not to be taken seriously.

Fortunately, there are scholars today who view these early records with much greater respect than the Higher Critics were accustomed to do before Archaeology had begun to validate the Old Testament account in such an extraordinary way. At the present time, it hardly seems likely that we can hope for much in the way of validation of the pre-Flood portion of Genesis — in the sense that the later portions of Genesis have been confirmed — because the Flood probably obliterated most of the evidence. But it is possible by careful analysis of these early chapters to observe a sobriety and a reasonableness which is entirely lacking in the Cuneiform accounts covering the same events. And so pronounced is the difference between the two streams of tradition that it becomes most unlikely that the biblical account drew any of its inspiration whatever from the Cuneiform ones: on the contrary, the reverse is more likely to be the case.

There is, after all, no longer any reason to doubt that the keeping of records in some form was available even in pre-Flood times. Certainly the Genesis account of the Flood has all the earmarks of being a ship's log, a circumstance which surely suggests an adequate ability to keep a record. Such records may very well have been preserved and, as Wiseman has suggested, passed on through the line of individuals from Seth to Noah in the form of "heirlooms".[103] These heirlooms then were handed down from Shem to Abraham and finally to Moses who edited them,[104] perhaps reduced them to a uniform alphabetical script, and completed them by adding the rest of the Pentateuch. The extraordinary care with which the Hebrew scribes copied their ancient documents, even to the counting of the number of each letter in a line, must have preserved them almost perfectly.[105]

Perhaps the family of Shem allowed further copies of these ancient records to be prepared for other members of the family of man, for Hamites and Japhethites, though possibly they were made less carefully. The recurrence of the idea that there were ten generations from Adam to Noah in pre-Flood times is so common among the nations of antiquity, though often in a distorted form, that it can hardly be doubted they all represent a single tradition springing from a single source and arising from the same factual circumstance. As John Urquhart observed:[106]

> It is a significant fact that this very number *ten* re-appears with a most remarkable persistency in the ancient tradition of the various races. The Egyptians believed that ten deities reigned before man. The Sybelline Books speak of ten ages which elapsed between the Creation and the Deluge. The

Iranians looked back to their ten Peischaddin or monarchs, "the men of the ancient law"who drank of the pure *homa*, the drink of the immortals, and who watched over holiness. The Hindus speak of the nine Brahmidikas who with Brahma, their maker, are called the ten *Pitris,* or Fathers.

The Germans and the Scandinavians tell of the ten ancestors of Odin; the Chinese of the ten Emperors, who shared the divine nature and reigned before the dawn of historic times; the Arabs of the ten kings of the Adites, primitive inhabitants of the Arabian peninsula embraced between the Red Sea and the Persian Gulf. The Phoenician historian, Sanchuniathon, also gives ten generations of primitive Patriarchs.

It will be appropriate to examine the Cuneiform records which undoubtedly refer back to the same historical events, although — as will be seen — these pagan traditions *appear* to have been badly corrupted by transmission.

The first knowledge we have apart from Genesis, of a similar tradition came to us through Berossus, a priest of Bel in Babylon, who somewhere around 260 B.C. translated into Greek the standard Babylonian reference work on Astrology and Astronomy, and compiled in three books the history of his country based apparently on the archives in the Temple of Marduk, which archives were copies of ancient inscriptions. Unfortunately, most of his work has perished, but extracts have been preserved in Josephus and Eusebius. The latter may have got his extracts only indirectly through Alexander Polyhistor and Apollodorus. From Berossus we have a list of ten Kings who ruled the world in pre-Flood times. Against each name we are given the duration of their reigns in units of measurement called *Sari.* The value attached to a *Saros* by almost all scholars today has been 3600 years. Actually the *Saros* is not a measurement merely of *years:* it can mean 3600 of *anything.* The incredible thing about Berossus' list of pre-Flood Kings is that some of them lived as long as 18 *Sari,* which multiplied out gives them a reign of up to 64,800 years! And the whole period covered by these ten Kings comes to four hundred thousand years. When this is compared with the biblical time span from Adam to the Flood, a period of a mere 1656 years, it will be seen at once that the two accounts differ enormously in this respect.

However, there is a possibility, although it seems not to have been favoured at all by modern scholars either Christian or otherwise, that the Babylonian and Assyrian scribes had two systems of reckoning the length of a *Saros,* an alternative value of which was very much smaller indeed: the shorter or smaller value being only slightly over 18 years:

to be precise, 18 years and 11.2 days, though it does not appear that they had calculated it quite this accurately.[107]   Such an alternative unit of measurement, if applied to these otherwise incredible figures, reduces them to within reason in the light of what we suspect of the *potential* of human life, and the resulting tabulation accords remarkably well in its total with the biblical one.

TABLE III

KING LIST OF BEROSSUS

NAME	SARI	USUAL VALUE IN YEARS	SHORT VALUE IN YEARS
1. ALORUS	10	36,000	185
2. ALAPAROS	3	10,800	55½
3. AMELON	13	46,800	240½
4. AMMENON	12	43,200	222
5. AMEGALAROS	18	64,800	333
6. DAONOS	10	36,000	185
7. EDORANCHOS	18	64,800	333
8. AMEMPSINOS	10	36,000	185
9. OTIARTES	8	28,800	148
10. XISUTHROS	18	64,800	333
	120	432,000	2220

The circumstances surrounding this alternative value of the *Saros* and the details of the calculation based on the greatly reduced unit of multiplication will be found in Appendix II.   At this point the reader only needs to know the end result of this alternative reckoning.   In summary, the figures are as follows.

Berossus gives us a total period of 120 *Sari* for the ten antidiluvian reigns, which by the common mode of reckoning involves a period of 432,000 years.   If we allow the alternative value of the *Saros* as 18½ years instead of the longer value of 3600 years, this figure of 432,000 becomes 2220 years.   Bearing in mind that in the King List of Berossus we are concerned with *reigns,* not with total life spans as in Genesis, the figure still begins to approach a measure of concordance with the Genesis account.   Berossus allows 222 years for the average *reign,* Genesis allows an average *life span* of 912 years. Since many monarchs would presumably not succeed to the "kingship" till at least middle age, the two sets of figures are by no means incompatible.

There is little doubt that Berossus' first entry represents the biblical Adam, and he tells us himself that "in the time of Xisuthros the great deluge occurred", so that his last entry represents Noah. We thus observe from Berossus' figures that, on the basis of a short value for the *Saros,* this time interval (2220 years) was of the same order of magnitude as that given in the biblical account of 1656 years. One must allow for some divergence in the case of Berossus' figures since it is doubtful if the same care was taken in their transmission.

Since the shorter value of the *Saros* certainly brings greater harmony, it is a surprising fact that almost no biblical scholar of modern times has considered it a viable alternative in interpreting these ancient records.   Neither S. R. Driver nor George Barton nor F. Hommel nor any of the other Orientalists who have written at length on the subject make any mention of the alternative.[108]   Nor does A. H. Sayce who might have been expected to have done so in view of his strong Christian convictions.[109]   One of the few writers who has mentioned this alternative value was not an Orientalist at all and probably had very little sympathy for the Bible as a source of reference in such matters: I have in mind Professor George Sarton of Harvard, in his *History of Science.*[110]   On his observations the reader is referred to Appendix III.   Briefly, his argument is that the smaller value of the *Saros* must be a very recent discovery because the ancient Babylonian astronomers cannot possibly have been intelligent enough or observant enough in those earlier days to recognize the second and far shorter astronomical cycle.   Evolutionary habits of thought place extraordinary blinkers on the minds of scholars who are otherwise highly competent historians.

We have spoken of uncertainties about Berossus' figures.   We do have a number of what may very well have been copies of his original source — and among these there are certain variations.   A particularly relevant example is the case of the so-called "Weld-Blundell Prism", the details of which will be found in Appendix IV.

This Cuneiform 'document' is a King List currently dated about 2170 B.C.   It is known in several variant forms, a fact which suggests copyists' errors.   The basic errors are in the different spellings of the ten names listed.   At least one authority of note believes that all known versions go back, however, to a single original.   He does not suggest that the original was the biblical record.   All known versions clearly refer to pre-Flood times since each concludes with a reference to the Flood as terminal to the list.

One of the versions may possibly refer by implication to circumstances surrounding the premature 'departure' of Enoch (by translation) and Lamech (by violence).   The mention of Noah as "the eighth" (2 Peter 2:5) rather than "the tenth" from Adam, may thus be accounted for.

On two points all versions are agreed.   Men lived to very great ages *before* the Flood; and the number of generations from Adam to Noah was ten or less.   They occupied a period of years that accords well with the biblical record but not at all well with the evolutionary account.

In summary, therefore, we may repeat a statement already made. It is possible by careful analysis of these early chapters in Genesis to observe a sobriety and a reasonableness which is entirely lacking in the Cuneiform accounts.   And so pronounced is the difference that it becomes most unlikely that the biblical account drew any inspiration whatever from these Cuneiform ones.   On the contrary, the reverse is more likely to be the case.   In short, in the biblical account we may very well have the *original* record: and it is a record, I believe, that is truly historical.

Chapter 5

LONGEVITY IN GENESIS

All the days of Methuselah were
nine hundred and sixty nine years.
Genesis 5:27

The days of our years are
threescore and ten;
if by reason of strength they be
fourscore years,
yet is their strength labour and sorrow;
for it is soon cut off,
and we fly away.
Psalm 90:10

The biblical record has presented a problem for chronologists, which involves a paradox. The total period covered by the patriarchal list from Adam to Noah is far *too short* to satisfy the demands of current chronology which claims up to two million years for the time of the appearance of the first man; but the ages which are given are far *too long!*   In one respect, therefore, the record is much too circumscribed, and in another respect much too extended.   The usual method of dealing with this paradox is to say that the figures really have no meaning.   This is myth, not history.

In order to extend the total interval from the creation to the Flood without dispensing with the record, it is sometimes pointed out that the Septuagint versions give a longer period by approximately one third as shown in Table IV below, although this helps very little since it provides us with only an extra 600 years or so.   Two other chronologies for the period in question which might help are to be found in Josephus and in the Samaritan Pentateuch, also shown in Table IV. Unfortunately, Josephus essentially copies the Septuagint, while the Samaritan Pentateuch succeeds only in *reducing* the total by 350 years . . . .

In the Table which follows, figures are given for the ages of the fathers at the time of their firsborn according to the Hebrew text, the Alexandrian Septuagint, the Vatican Septuagint, Josephus, and the Samaritan Pentateuch.   By adding these ages together, along with the age of Noah at the time of the Flood, it is possible to calculate the total time which elapsed from the creation of Adam to that event.

TABLE IV

GIVING AGES OF FATHERS AT BIRTH OF FIRSTBORN

	Heb.	Alex. LXX	Vat. LXX	Josephus	Sam. P.
1. Adam	130	230	230	230	130
2. Seth	105	205	205	205	105
3. Enosh	90	190	190	190	90
4. Kenan	70	170	170	170	70
5. Mahalaleel	65	165	165	165	65
6. Jared	162	162	162	162	62
7. Enoch	65	165	165	165	65
8. Methuselah	187	187	167	187	67
9. Lamech	182	188	188	182	53
10. Noah	600	600	600	600	600
Totals:	1656	2262	2242	2256	1307

Now the question of which text is to be regarded as the original one was nicely summed up many years ago by Dr. James C. Murphy who showed that the internal evidence from the figures themselves is decidely in favour of the Hebrew text.*

> The numbers in the LXX evidently follow a plan to which they have been conformed.   This does not appear in the Hebrew, and it is greatly in favour of its being an authentic

---

* Murphy, James C., *Commentary on Genesis*, Belfast, n.d., p.196.

> genealogical record.   The numbers before the birth of a
> successor, which are chiefly important for the chronology, are
> enlarged in the LXX, by the addition of just one hundred
> years in each of six cases, making Adam 230 years old at the
> birth of Seth, Seth 205 years old at the birth of Enosh, and so
> on, while the sum total of each life remains the same as in the
> Hebrew, with a slight exception of 25 years in the case of
> Lamech.   The object here is evidently to extend the total
> life span of each individual.
>
> It is not easy to imagine what motive could have led in the
> other direction, i.e., to the shortening, if the original had been
> as given in the Septuagint; since all ancient nations have rather
> shown a disposition to lengthening their chronologies.   On
> physiological grounds, too, the Hebrew is to be preferred,
> since the length of the life does not at all require so late a
> manhood as those numbers would seem to intimate.

We shall have occasion to examine this evidence of internal pro-
portional consistency in a way that was not available to Murphy but
fully bears out his contention.

There is a further consideration also which we may touch upon
here in the analysis of the figures.   It is found that between the
period of childlessness and the total length of life *in the Hebrew text,*
there is a high correlation, but by an exactly comparable method of
statistical analysis the correlation in the Septuagint and in the text
given by Josephus is very low indeed.   The Samaritan Pentateuch
does a little better than the two latter.versions, but it has a peculiar
artificiality about it in that the numbers are arranged in a more or less
steadily declining order, which is cause for suspicion when it is realized that the total life spans of these same individuals show no such
steady decline.   In actual fact, Methuselah who lived longer than any
of the others, comes late in the list (eighth), while Jared (the sixth)
and Noah (the tenth) both lived longer than Adam.   This fact is
visually apparent in the graph shown in Fig. 1.

It is important to notice, therefore, that this decline in the period
of childlessness which makes the Samaritan figures look more "realistic" in one way, is badly upset when the figures for total life span are
correlated with them.   All in all, there is every reason to have far
more confidence in the Hebrew version than in any of the others: and
since the others do not really help to solve any chronological
problems, there are really no good reasons for preferring them.

Before proceeding to an analysis of the figures in the Hebrew text,
it may be useful to consider very briefly two suggestions which have
been made for the extension of the time interval of 1656 years between Adam and the Flood.   The first proposal is that we do not
have a complete and continuous genealogy from Adam to Noah, in

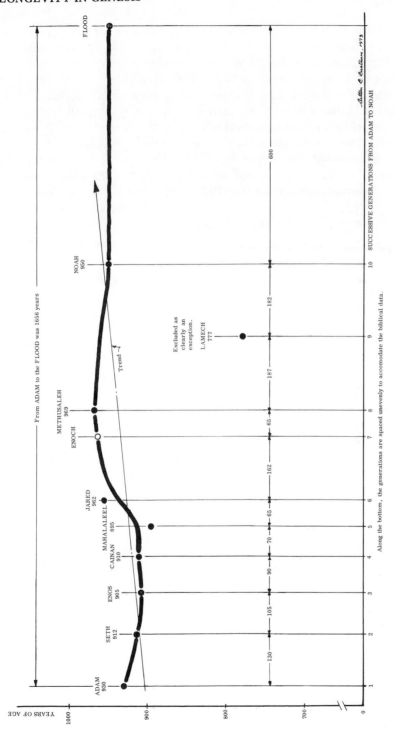

Fig. 1.   LONGEVITY FROM ADAM TO NOAH

spite of the fact that each successor is stated to have been the son of
his immediate predecessor.   The argument here is that the word *son*
in Hebrew can also mean grandson or great-grandson, to any degree of
distance one chooses, even as Christ is spoken of as a son of David, or
the woman who had an infirmity is spoken of as a daughter of
Abraham (Luke 13:16).   So there may well be gaps in the record for
all we know, according to the critics.

The second proposal is that the names of individuals in the genealogical list are not individuals at all, but dynasties.   This concept is a
little more complicated, as will be seen.   Let us consider these two
devices for the extending of the chronology.

I. The Supposed Gaps in the Record.

The proposal that there may be gaps in the record is reasonable
enough in certain contexts, for Scripture shows many such gaps, but
they are only discoverable by reference to parallel portions of Scripture where comparison of the details shows them up at once.   Did we
have but one account without any means of comparison with a parallel account, it would not be possible to discover that names were
omitted.   Sometimes a father is said to have borne a certain individual
as his son, whereas we learn from other parts of Scripture that the
individual was actually his great-great-grandson.   The fact is well
known to biblical chronologists.   Such "incomplete" genealogies are
not infrequent.   Two are illustrated below in Tables V and VI.   In
Table V will be seen, in parallel columns, the genealogy given in
1 Chronicles 6:6-10 and Ezra 7:3-4 for Zerahiah to Amariah, in which
it will be noted that in the second instance six names are omitted.

TABLE V

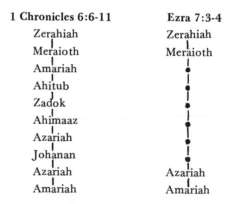

1 Chronicles 6:6-11	Ezra 7:3-4
Zerahiah	Zerahiah
Meraioth	Meraioth
Amariah	
Ahitub	
Zadok	
Ahimaaz	
Azariah	
Johanan	
Azariah	Azariah
Amariah	Amariah

Note: Ezra 7:3 lists the names in column 2 in reverse order.

Obviously in this passage the word *son* has a much broader meaning than it does in English when applied to the relationship between
Azariah and Meraioth who preceded him by seven generations. It will
be noted also, in this case, that the earlier Table is the complete one.

By contrast, in Table VI, we have two genealogies which are
parallel only in the sense that they cover the same period of time,
though not the same list of individuals.

TABLE VI

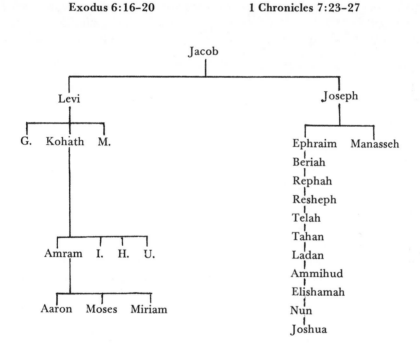

In this case, beginning with Jacob we have two contemporaries,
Levi and Joseph in the next generation, and then in Exodus 6:16-20
we have what appear to be only three generations till the introduction
of Aaron, Moses and Miriam.   Now Aaron, Moses and Miriam were
contemporaries of Nun the father of Joshua, but between Joseph and
Nun there intervened nine generations whereas between Levi and
Moses are shown only two generations.   This will be clear enough by
examining Table VI.   But if we did not have the right hand column
of this Table, then from Exodus 6:16-20 we might very well suppose
that Aaron and Moses were only the *third* generation from Levi.   If
we allow thirty years for a generation, this would represent a time

interval of about a hundred years.   But the parallel genealogy shows us that this would be a misrepresentation of the facts since there are nine generations in the interval which actually spanned approximately three hundred years.

A great deal has been made of such gaps in Scripture by those who would like to extend its chronology substantially.   I have dealt with these incomplete genealogies in some depth in another volume.* Here it is shown that it is not proper to assume, on the basis of these *known* gaps, that there may on that account be many *other* gaps which leave biblical chronology open-ended, since we have no proof of any such gaps.   The truth of the matter is that there is no evidence of any gaps in Scripture **except in so far as Scripture has itself directed our attention to them by supplying elsewhere the only evidence we have that the data in this instance has been abbreviated.**

If on an examination paper, for the sake of neatness in presentation, one were to work out a mathematical sum but omit some of the commonplace steps in the calculation, and then one were to append these omitted calculations on a final sheet of paper, it would be quite incorrect to argue that one had actually left gaps in the calculation — merely because the data was supplied elsewhere.   In the case of the biblical record, there has been even more confused reasoning because we would never have known of *any* of the gaps which are made so much of by Warfield† and others but for the fact that Scripture actually fills them in elsewhere.

In the absolute sense, we have no evidence whatever from Scripture that there really are missing names in any of the genealogies.   We only know that in certain cases they are omitted for specific reasons that are not always clear, but are then supplied elsewhere in order to make the record complete.   I think Philip Mauro was perfectly right when he said that God would surely not leave any missing links in the lineage leading from the first Adam to the last Adam, since it was essential that this relationship should be clearly demonstrable.‡

Because of the wide use made by those who appeal to these supposed gaps in order to bring the Word of God into line with current evolutionary doctrine, it is very important to observe that there is no evidence whatever of such gaps in Scripture unless one

---

* Custance, Arthur C., "Genealogies of the Bible" in *Hidden Things of God's Revelation,* Grand Rapids, Zondervan, Vol. VII, *Doorway Papers Series,* 1977, p.217-269.

† Warfield, Benjamin B., "On the Antiquity and the Unity of the Human Race", *Biblical and Theological Studies,* Phila., Presbyterian and Reformed Publishing Co., 1968, p.238 ff.

‡ Mauro, Philip, *The Chronology of the Bible,* Boston, Hamilton Bros., 1922, p.10.

adopts a policy of arguing from part of the record only.   The record as a whole does not leave any gaps.   The claim that such gaps exist is an argument based entirely on a selective reading of Scripture, while ignoring the rest of the evidence.

II. NAMES REFER TO DYNASTIES, NOT TO INDIVIDUALS.

We come, then, to the second alternative, namely, that we are really dealing with dynasties rather than individuals, a proposal which is believed to overcome two difficulties at once.   In the first place, the great periods attributed to each entry are not the life spans of individuals but periods during which a tribe or a dynasty founded by that individual, was in the ascendancy.   In the second place, it is proposed that the time periods ascribed to individuals who were con-temporaries for a large portion of their lives, are really consecutive and therefore may be added together as reigns are added together, thus considerably extending the time period from Adam to the Flood. In Appendix V will be found a Table showing how this scheme is applied to Genesis 5.   At this juncture it is only necessary to say that the total time span can be extended to a period of 7630 years from the birth of Seth to the Flood, by comparison with the biblical chron-ology of about 1656 years.   From the point of view of evolutionary anthropology, this is inconsequential.

I fancy this method of interpreting the genealogy originated with one who was acquainted with modern Arabian genealogies and family histories in which the whole clan may be treated as a single individual. It is sometimes pointed out that in Acts 7:16 the name *Abraham* refers to the clan or family of Abraham, the partriarch himself being dead at the time of the transaction referred to.

However, there is no doubt that some of the names at least are clearly intended to refer to individuals whose *personal* history is really the interest of the writer — Enoch, for example, whose 365 years of life clearly refer to the time he spent on earth before his translation and surely cannot be applied to the time period in which his clan was in the ascendance.   Noah who comes last in the list, is surely the same individual who, 600 years later, survived the Deluge with his immed-iate family, and the vignette of his life which follows the story of the Flood is obviously intended to be taken as *personal* history.   Alto-gether, it seems unlikely that anything is gained by re-interpreting the record as a list of dynasties.

The Genesis record contains the same kind of information *after* the Flood, giving us the age of the father at the birth of his son and in the end his total life span.   But in this instance no commentator has suggested that the figures should be interpreted as a succession of dynasties.

The post-Flood data show, moreover, that there is a steady decline in life span so that if a graph is constructed (see Fig. 3, p.70) the curve has the appearance of representing a genuine biological pheno- menon of declining viability until the age of man has fallen below 120 years.   It is as though the data were intended to show how the longevity of antiquity gradually decayed until man reached his present life span.   Thenceforth the subject was not worthy of further con- sideration in Scripture, and from this point on we are only once told what a man's age was when he died!   We shall have occasion later to examine the probable reason why this is so.

Altogether, I think it makes much more sense to take these lists of Genesis and treat them both statistically and graphically as though they are records of the lives of individuals.   The result of such an analysis is quite surprising for it is apparent that the figures display just that measure of variance, along with an over-all consistency, such as are normally observed in genuine vital statistics.   But this normalcy is observed only if we go by the figures in the Hebrew text and not by those in any of the other texts such as the Septuagint for example. In the latter, as we have seen, there is a certain artificiality, a kind of deliberate evening out of the figures, as though the editor was attempt- ing to give them a degree of uniformity which he felt was missing. But his emendations were not consistent nor were they effected right across the board, and the result is that statistical analysis of certain correlations clearly reveals that the data themselves have been in- expertly tampered with.

Now, in applying standard techniques of statistical analysis to the data provided in Genesis 5 on the ten pre-Flood patriarchs, it is nec- essary to exclude certain of the names as being too exceptional.   We must exclude Enoch since we do not have any figures which would have represented his natural life span, because he was removed pre- maturely.   Lamech also appears to be an exception.   This is clear from Fig. 1 where his name completely departs from the comparat- ively smooth curve drawn through the rest of the entries.   Evidently he died "young"; but also he appears to have matured slowly, for his period of childlessness was significantly greater than for any of the others.   Curiously enough, Lamech seems to have felt the burden of living more than the others, since he alone appears to have complained (Gen.5:29).   Perhaps he was frustrated by the fact that his old father, Methuselah, living on and on, delayed his own accession to a position of seniority in the family.   At any rate, if his name is included in the list for the purposes of statistical analysis, the effect is a total distort- ion of relationship between the period to the begetting of the first son and the total life span.   Finally, we must also exclude Noah, since he closed his life under different conditions in the world after the Flood and since there is some uncertainty as to the precise meaning of Genesis 5:32 where we are told that he was 500 years old when he bore all *three* of his famous sons — Shem, Ham, and Japheth.   Not only is this very late in life to beget a firstborn compared with the other patriarchs, but clearly there is some special circumstance involved unless these three sons were triplets.   Had they been so, we might expect to have been informed of the fact, as we are of Jacob and Esau. The use of the term *younger* when applied in Genesis 9:24 to Ham does not altogether rule this out because even if all three were born together, the first one to appear would be marked as the oldest and the last one as the youngest.

This seems a drastic reduction of the list, from ten names to seven. But it happens that, in statistics, seven is still accepted as a sufficient number of entries under certain circumstances.   Anything less renders the correlation formula which I propose to use unacceptable.

Using the Spearman Rank Order Formula, a very high correlation indeed is found between the figures given for the period of childlessness and the total life span of each individual as recorded in the Hebrew text, but when the figures given for the same individuals as found in the Alexandrine Septuagint and the Vatican Septuagint (Table IV, p.55) are treated in the same way, the result is entirely different.

The Spearman Rank Order Correlation Formula is:

$$r = 1 - \frac{6(\text{Sum of } D^2)}{n(n^2 - 1)}$$

The method of using this formula is straightforward.   The names are listed as they appear in Table VII in Column 1.   This is followed in Column 2 by the life spans.   Column 3 is the Rank Order, i.e., the largest life span is No.1, the smallest becomes No.7, and each life span is given a serial number representing its order in rank.   In Column 4 the period of childlessness is listed.   These figures are once more ranked as shown in Column 5.

Column 6, marked "Difference" (D), represented the difference between the figures in Column 3 and 5, i.e., the disparity between the relative rank orders.   The positive or negative sign is ignored because in Column 7, which is marked D^2, the process of squaring the figures cancels out the negative sign in any case.   The last column is then totalled to give the value as shown.   In the formula, *n* is simply the number of entries — in this case 7.

TABLE VII

Col.1	Col.2	Col.3	Col.4	Col.5	Col.6	Col.7
Name	Life Span	Rank Order	Childless Period	Rank Order	Diff'ce D	D^2
Adam	930	3	130	3	0	0
Seth	912	4	105	4	0	0
Enos	905	6	90	5	1	1
Cainan	910	5	70	6	1	1
Mahalaleel	895	7	65	7	0	0
Jared	962	2	162	2	0	0
Methuselah	969	1	187	1	0	0

Sum = 2

Applying the formula: $$r = 1 - \frac{6(\text{Sum of } D^2)}{n(n^2 - 1)}$$

We have: $$r = 1 - \frac{6(2)}{7(49 - 1)} = 1 - \frac{12}{336}$$

$$= 1 - \frac{1}{28} = 0.96$$

Now a word about the formula and the value of r (0.96). After years of analyzing data in a laboratory where the number of entries sometimes ran into three or four hundred and not merely seven as we have here, we took the trouble on a number of occasions to apply the Spearman Rank Order Formula as well as the usual far more complex formula which involves such high numbers that a calculator is necessary. We consistently found that the difference in the correlation values by the two methods was usually only in the second decimal point. Simple as it is, Spearman's Formula is, therefore, remarkably useful.

The value of r as found above has the following significance. Any group of figures such as these, because they are derived from vital statistics, are likely to fluctuate entirely due to chance in a way that

there will almost never be a perfect correlation.   There will always be
some individuals who mature more quickly than others for no evident
reason, and some individuals who die much younger or much later
than their peers — again, for no self-evident reason.   Where there are
evident reasons, one normally excludes their statistics from the calculations (as we have done with Lamech).   If the basic concept that
there is a firm relationship between the rate of maturing and the
length of life is sound, the longer a person has lived the more likely it
will be that he has matured more slowly.   Thus as the life span increases one expects, other things being equal, that the time to the
appearance of the first child will be correspongingly greater.   If this
always happened, we would have a perfect correlation and the value
in the Spearman Formula would then work out exactly at 1.00.   If
the figure works out to be very much less than 1.00 (say, 0.25), then
the correlation is poor.   It may even be reversed, the oldest persons
consistently bearing their children at the youngest period of their
lives, in which case the value of r is negative.

In the analysis of the Hebrew text it will be seen that the correlation is remarkably high (very nearly 1.00) and although such statistical
analysis is really only a measure of probability, it does imply that the
figures in Genesis 5 are genuine, undoctored by any scribe or editor:
OR they have been exceedingly carefully edited by someone thousands
of years ago who was aware of the kind of analysis they might be subjected to much later in history.   This alternative can be discounted.

The significance of the high correlation based on the figures given
in the text of Genesis becomes more apparent when we apply the
same technique of analysis to the figures in the Alexandrine Septuagint
which some authorities have preferred.   These values for r are shown
in Table VIII.

TABLE VIII

Hebrew Text	Alexandrine Septuagint	Vatican Septuagint
0.96	0.07	Minus 0.07

Assuming, then, that the figures in Genesis according to the
Hebrew text are the correct ones, we can construct a graph (Fig.1, see
page 57) showing that the viability of man from Adam to Noah has a
rather surprising trend upwards.   One could speculate that, immediately after the Fall, man's ability to compensate for his now lessened
vitality in extracting a living from the soil, was improved with time

and the ingenuity by those of later generations who developed a high technology with remarkable speed, as Genesis 4:17-22 indicates. Moreover, the smallness of the population at first would also contribute to the difficulties of achieving dominion over the earth.   But the very long lives of the earliest people would accelerate the accumulation of knowledge and experience so that civilization would all the sooner be advanced to the point where labour-saving devices and measures taken for the preservation of life and the curing of disease would gradually increase security and lead to a less exhausting way of life.   There may in that case have been a slight amelioration of the effects of the Fall on man's physical well-being which would be reflected by some gains in terms of life span, although the same advantages would undoubtedly tend to increase man's potential for wickedness, so that by the time of Noah technology was advanced enough not only to allow the building of a giant ship as large as the *Great Eastern* of comparatively modern times, but a spiritual condition so serious as to demand the almost total destruction of the human race.

Whether the Flood which was brought upon the world in judgment was *geographically* universal, or whether the world's population was still concentrated in a comparatively small area so that the Flood needed only to overwhelm that area, is a point of considerable argument.   In the present context, the really important point is that the race of mankind was literally reduced to eight sole survivors, Noah and his three sons and their four womenfolk.   The consequences of this in terms of the future life span of man were very great indeed — and for perfectly understandable reasons.

Post-Flood Decline in Longevity.

Immediately after the Flood the course of events in terms of human life span clearly changed very dramatically, as will be seen in Fig. 2. Something quite specific reduced man's life expectancy from nearly a thousand years to 120 years within a period of seventeen generations. When the data provided in Scripture are plotted in the form of a graph and these points are converted into a smooth curve, the end result is a graph which has such a normal appearance about it that no one who is accustomed to viewing scattergrams of biological data would doubt for one moment the validity of it — especially if they were not aware that it is based on biblical data.   It is a perfect example of what happens when some biological trend is explored and plotted routinely, provided that the original data have *not* been manipulated or gathered without sufficient precautions.   Speaking personally, having drawn hundreds of scattergrams of this nature from data derived from our own experiments using human subjects over a period of fifteen years

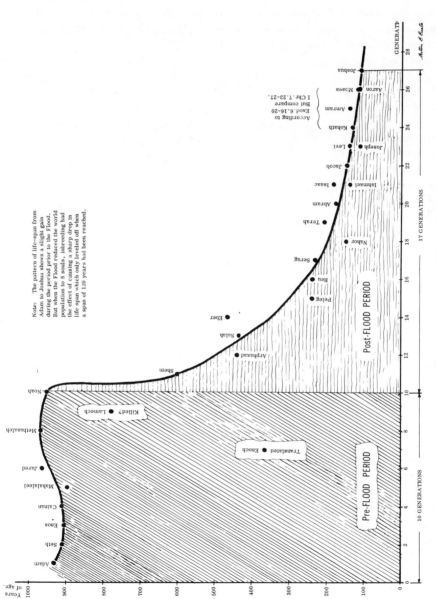

Note: The pattern of life-span from Adam to Joshua shows a slight gain during the period prior to the Flood. But when the Flood reduced the world population to 8 souls, inbreeding had the effect of causing a sharp drop in life span which only leveled off when a span of 120 years had been reached.

Fig. 2   DRAMATIC DECLINE IN LONGEVITY AFTER THE FLOOD

or so, there is not the slightest doubt in my mind that the relevant data provided for us in the Bible are genuine.   There is just that measure of inconsistency and variance between individual readings, combined with a certain over-all smoothness of trend which is so characteristic of experimental data where living things are concerned that we can have strong confidence in the genuineness of of the original figures.

But more than this: the decline continued for a long time, far beyond the period covered by Fig. 2, until a kind of equilibrium was achieved with a normal life span of about three score years and ten. What was the factor that caused the initial dramatic decline in life span from Noah's 950 years to Moses' and Aaron's 120 years, within sixteen generations?

It has been suggested — and it may very well be true — that a rather radical change took place in atmospheric conditions in connection with the Flood itself.   There are those who believe that prior to the Flood, man was shielded from harmful cosmic radiation and even possibly from direct sunlight, by some kind of canopy of water vapour which was more than merely an unusually heavy cloud cover. It is thus held that the collapse of this canopy contributed to the extraordinarily heavy rains which were partial cause of the Flood itself. The appearance of the rainbow as a special sign of assurance that such an event would not occur again on the same scale may be an indication that the conditions of ordinary rainfall as we now experience it, did not apply in pre-Flood times.   It is held that actual rain was not experienced before the Flood.   The earth was watered through the agency of a kind of water-saturated environment, rather like a hot-house situation.   It may be.   On the other hand, the sun and the moon (and the stars?) must surely have been visible, in view of the fact that they were given for signs. We are not told in Genesis 1:14-16 that the *stars* were given for signs, only that the sun and moon were.* But it seems to me to be implied that the stars were visible also; though it is difficult to see how even the existence of stars which would not actually be visible through such a canopy could be known to the earth's inhabitants.

It is certain that cosmic radiation and certain forms of solar radiation do have an effect upon life span.[111]   If there was a change from a wholly shielded environment in this respect to one in which, after the Flood, shielding was greatly reduced, then it might be

---

* The Hebrew *'oth* rendered *signs*, is generally considered to mean something more than markers, they would surely have to be rather clearly visible as distinct objects.   Would it fulfill the conditions of their appointment that they *only* distinguished night from day?

expected that the life-shortening consequences of exposure to such radiation would become immediately apparent. This could account for the sudden decline in life span shown so dramatically in Fig. 2.

However, there is another factor which I believe was a more potent one, that is only shown up by examining the nature of this curve more closely. Figure 3 displays the details of this period of human history on an enlarged scale to bring out two aspects of this sudden decline, one of which is related to the genetics of inbreeding.

When Adam and Eve were created, they were *perfect,* not only spiritually but physically also. None of their genes were defective by reason of mutation. What are known as mutations are errors of transcription in the basic coding of the DNA in the individual cell nuclei which appear to occur sometimes spontaneously when the cells multiply or which are caused by external agencies such as radiation and certain poisons, like mustard gas for example. Once such an error has occurred, the line of cells derived from the damaged original will all carry the same error or fault. Some of these faults appear to be comparatively harmless, although most authorities believe that *all* mutations are harmful. Certainly, all mutations can be harmful under certain conditions. These faults in replication, which are called mutations, are found to occur at specific locations on the chromosomes which determine the character of each cell. These locations are called genes. In man it is believed that there are possibly 40,000 such genes altogether in every cell. There is room, therefore, for a significant number of errors or mutations in any one cell: and it should be remembered that all the cells descended from a damaged cell will normally bear the same defect.

Now the only mutations that occur during the life time of an individual which can injure the next generation are those which have occurred in the ova or the spermatozoa, since these alone form part of the body of the next generation. Any agency which damages these reproductive cells has grave consequences for the future of the line thus affected. This is particularly so where close relatives marry. For they have not only shared the same environmental conditions and therefore been subject to the same damaging influences, but have also derived their reproductive cells from a common source. The result is that the damage in the cells of both partners is likely to have occurred at the same location in each cell, i.e., at the same gene on the same chromosome. When two such damaged genes are brought together by the mating of close relatives, the effect of the damage is tremendously reinforced and the offspring will suffer doubly from it. And technically, we say the effect is being expressed homozygously.

It is the discovery of this fact which has permitted biologists to explore the harmful effect of mutations by the simple process of

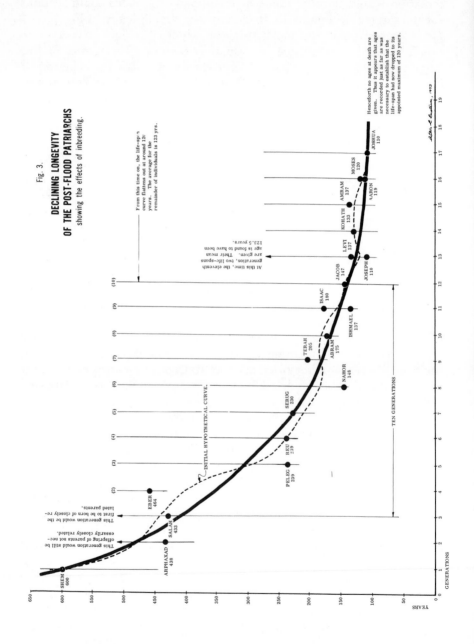

Fig. 3.

DECLINING LONGEVITY
OF THE POST-FLOOD PATRIARCHS
showing the effects of inbreeding.

exaggerating the effects of inbreeding.

Now what would happen when Adam's immediate sons and daughters married one another (Gen.5:4) is that chromosomes with the same gene content would be paired off homozygously, but the effects would not be very detrimental because at this stage in human history the number of damaged genes would be very small indeed. As time went on and more mutations began to occur with succeeding generations, partly perhaps because of the effect of the poison which Adam and Eve had introduced from the forbidden fruit and had passed on to their descendants, the danger of such mutations showing up harmfully in children would increase.   However, this increase would be compensated for by the fact that the population itself was expanding and the need for brother-sister marriages would become less and less.   More and more distant relations would be mated, and common lines of damaged genes would be conveyed in their less harmless or heterozygous form.   In view of the great ages to which people lived, it seems likely that the population would grow more rapidly than it does at the present time.   It is true that people were slower in maturing but there is no reason to suppose that this involved any lengthening of the *gestation* period.   It seems almost certain that families would be larger, and that the population growth rate would be substantially accelerated.

It seems likely that by the time of the Flood, the population could have been in the millions, even though man may not have spread very far from the original site of the Garden of Eden.   In modern times a single city may easily house a million people . . . . With such numbers and less than 2000 years of human history, the number of mutations that would be showing up homozygously in the population need not have been excessively large and up to that point probably had no significant effect on the average life span, although the mortogenic effect of the inherited poison itself brought every man to the grave in due time (with the exception of Enoch).

But then the situation changed fundamentally when the population was dramatically reduced to eight sole survivors, because close inbreeding was once again forced upon the community.   William Hollander, writing on the effects of lethal mutations in a population has this to say:[112]

> The quickest way to expose lethal traits is by intensive and continued inbreeding.   In man such matings are generally illegal or tabu; the experience of the race indicates bad results. But brother-sister matings in animals, and self-pollination in plants are a standard laboratory practice.   The outcome is generally detrimental unless it has become customary in the species.

> When inbreeding begins, the heredity seems to be breaking
> down, all sorts of defects and weaknesses appear.   The *average
> life span decreases* . . . .
> But if the family can weather the first few generations
> (five with plants, and *ten with animals*) a levelling off sets in.
> Members of the family may show defects and weaknesses but
> not new ones, and there is a striking uniformity.   The type
> has become fixed. (Emphasis mine).

This is essentially what I believe happened in the case of Noah's
family and their immediate descendants.   Moreover, we find that ten
generations were required to normalize the new expected life span.
The expected life span was not, however, the three score years and
ten of David's time (Psa. 90:10) but the 120 years *maximum* of
Genesis 6:3.   Figure 3 is designed to make these observations more
understandable.

The precise meaning of Genesis 6:3 has been a little difficult to
establish because the Hebrew is not absolutely clear.   It has been
proposed that the words, "My spirit shall not always strive with man
for that he also is flesh: yet his days shall be 120 years", meant only
that God would restrain his judgment for a period of 120 years for
man to mend his ways while Noah constructed the ark.   The problem
is to determine the exact meaning of the Hebrew verb which lies
behind the English words "shall not always *strive*".   I think the consensus of opinion today is that the intention of the original text is not
that judgment would be delayed for a period of 120 years, but rather
that God would normally call back to Himself the spirit of each individual before he reaches 120 years of age.   In short, this was to be
the maximum expected life span of man hereafter.   For example, the
Jerusalem Bible translates Genesis 6:3, "His life shall last no more
than 120 years".   By limiting his life span, God intended to limit his
potential for wickedness.

Since God used "natural" means to effect this limitation, the
decline follows a "normal" curve.   The curve of expected life span
fell very rapidly at first, beginning with Arphaxad who lived only 438
years and continuing through to Jacob who died when he was 147
years of age, *ten generations later.* By this time the curve is definitely
beginning to flatten out.   For the eleventh generation, we are given
two names, Levi and Joseph, who lived respectively 137 years and 110
years, with an average of 123.5 years.   Three generations later on the
chart, with Moses and Aaron, we have reached an average age of 119.5
years.   The final name on the chart is that of Joshua whose life span
had already fallen below 120, as will be seen.

The extraordinary thing is that from this time on, we are provided
in Scripture with almost no further data on actual life spans of individ-

uals — not even David.*   The figures given for Job come close, for we
are told that "after *this,* Job lived 140 years" (Job 42:16), but we are
not told what his age was *before this* and at the very end we are
merely informed that he died "being old and full of days".   Whether
I have failed to observe other exceptional cases where the age at death
is actually given, I do not know.   But certainly I have searched for
such cases without success thus far, and one concludes the silence
must be quite intentional.   We thus seem to have in this tabulation
clear evidence of a historic process of degeneration, most of which had
occurred by the tenth generation *of those who were born after the
Flood.*   Shem, of course, has to be excluded from this decade because although his life was shortened he was born before the Flood, a
fact which suggests that some environmental factors were indeed at
work contributing to the shortening of life.

There is one further point of interest: from Jacob (the tenth
generation) and onwards, the average life span of the remaining seven
individuals whose ages at death are given was actually 123 years . . . .
and it was still obviously declining, though much more slowly.   It is
therefore of interest to recall once again the observation made by
Acsadi and Nemeskeri that the probable maximum life span for man,
except under very unusual circumstances, is now set at 120 years.

Conclusion.

It is difficult to imagine how such data as these, the significance
of which could hardly have been recognized until modern times, could
have been fabricated by some author or authors who wished to add a
supposed dignity to the history of their own patriarchs by giving
them a fictitious longevity in keeping with the claims made by their
contemporaries.

There are ten generations from Adam to Noah but the phenomenon of reduction in longevity did not apparently take place.   The
reasons for this could hardly have been apparent to people writing
centuries later but who *were* aware of a drastic reduction in life span
in their own day.   They must therefore have been restrained from
trying to doctor the figures to show at least some decline which might
seem to them to make the figures more plausible.   That they did not
do so suggests the presence of a restraining Hand as they wrote. After
the Flood, the decline takes a form which has all the earmarks of truth

---

* A considerable search in Scripture reveals only one case, to my knowledge, namely, that of
Jehoiada, a priest (2 Chron.24:15), some fourteen centuries later.   One wonders why this
sole exception . . . .

about it.   The smooth curve of Fig. 3 is not arbitrarily drawn but has been imposed on the points by strictly mathematical arrangement. Towards the lower end of the curve several doubles of names appear at significant points.   The tenth generation mark is emphasized, as it were, by being preceded by the figures for Isaac and Ishmael (ninth generation) who nicely straddle the normalized curve, and is followed by the figures for Levi and Joseph (eleventh generation) who also straddle the normalized curve.

Even the *heroic* figures in Israel's history are not accorded the honour of having their ages at death recorded, the only near exception (as we have mentioned) being Job, a circumstance which may be intended to enable us to "place" him in history.   He seems likely to have been a contemporary of Abraham.

It is remarkable, therefore, that in those far-off days where one might expect to find the least specific information, there we find the most precise ages carefully recorded.   As soon as later historical times are under review where exact information would almost certainly be in official records, the precise statement of age seems to have been deliberately ignored — even in the case of the Lord Jesus Christ. Certainly God's ways are not man's ways.

We have now moved back further and further into the dim and distant past until we find ten patriarchal giants before the Flood covering with their individual lives a span of time exceeding that which has elapsed from William the Conqueror until the present.   It is hard to conceive what this really means in terms of the potential knowledge and experience that an individual might acquire in such a long lifetime.   And imagine the possibilities for firsthand communication!   Adam could have discussed his experiences with Methuselah over a period of 243 years, Methuselah could have discussed this information with Shem for 98 years.   And Shem was a contemporary of Abraham for 150 years.

But what would have happened to the world's population if natural death had never become part of human experience?   If death had *not* intruded, an endlessly growing population was a contingency which God had to take into account when He created Adam as a potentially immortal creature.   It is worth asking three questions: (a) what would have happened if man had not fallen and death had not entered, and if the population had thus simply gone on increasing century after century; (b) how did Adam lose that potential or, to put it slightly differently, how did death come to enter human experience; and (c) why was Adam created with such a potential in the first place if God knew that he would so soon lose it by his disobedience?   Was it not an exercise in futility to endow him thus to no purpose?

Chapter 6

THE ORIGINAL IMMORTALS

Made after the power of an endless life.
Hebrews 7:16

It has very commonly been held from the earliest times that Adam and Eve were originally immortal. Pagan writers of antiquity and the oral traditions of some contemporary primitive people reflect the same view: man at first was not subject to death. Moreover, we have seen that even after death had been introduced into human experience by sin, the longevity of the first few generations was held by all nations of antiquity to have still been very great, declining to the present limits only after two thousand years or so.

Early Jewish historians held that Adam and Eve need not have died, and they drew certain very logical conclusions from it. The Church Fathers of the first few centuries of the present era held the same opinion, basing it upon the same statements of Scripture which had guided the Jews. Church Councils later categorically asserted it and held it an important truth to be accepted by the faithful. And since that time many of the best informed commentators have explored the implications of it at some length.

Let us set forth the passages of Scripture in both the Old and the New Testaments which bear directly upon the circumstances surrounding man's creation and subsequent testing in the Garden of Eden.

Genesis 1:

26 And God said, Let us make man in our image, after our likeness; and let them have dominion over the fish of the sea, and over the fowl of the air, and over the cattle, and over all the earth, and over every creeping thing that creepeth upon the earth.

27 So God created man in his own image, in the image of God created he him; male and female created he them.

28 And God blessed them, and God said unto them, Be fruitful and multiply, and replenish the earth, and subdue it: and have dominion over the fish of the sea, and over the fowl of the air, and over every living thing that moveth upon the earth.

29 And God said, Behold, I have given you every herb bearing seed, which is upon the face of all the earth, and every tree, in the which is the fruit of a tree yielding seed; to you it shall be for meat.

30 And to every beast of the earth, and to every fowl of the air, and to every thing that creepeth upon the earth, wherein there is life, I have given every green herb for meat: and it was so.

Genesis 2:

7 And the Lord God formed man of the dust of the ground, and breathed into his nostrils the breath of life; and man became a living soul.

8 And the Lord God planted a garden eastward in Eden: and there he put the man whom he had formed.

9 And out of the ground made the Lord God to grow every tree that is pleasant to the sight, and good for food; the tree of life also in the midst of the garden, and the tree of knowledge of good and evil . . . .

15 And the Lord God took the man, and put him into the garden of Eden to dress it and to keep it.

16 And the Lord God commanded the man, saying, Of every tree of the garden thou mayest freely eat:

17 But of the tree of knowledge of good and evil, thou shalt not eat of it: for in the day that thou eatest thereof thou shalt surely die.

18 And the Lord God said, It is not good that the man should be alone; I will make a help meet for him.

19 And out of the ground the Lord God formed every beast of the field, and every fowl of the air; and brought them unto Adam to see what he would call them: and whatsoever Adam called every living creature, that was the name thereof.

20 And Adam gave names to all the cattle, and to the fowl of the air, and to every beast of the field; but for Adam there was not found an help meet for him.

21 And the Lord God caused a deep sleep to fall upon Adam and he slept: and he took one of his ribs, and closed up the flesh instead thereof;

22 And the rib, which the Lord God had taken from man, made he a woman, and brought her unto the man.

23 And Adam said, This is now bone of my bones, and flesh of my flesh: she shall be called Woman, because she was taken out of Man.

24 Therefore shall a man leave his father and his mother and shall cleave unto his wife: and they shall be one flesh.

25 And they were both naked, the man and his wife, and were not ashamed . . . .

Genesis 3:

22 And the Lord God said, Behold, the man is become as one of us, to know good and evil: and now, lest he put forth his hand, and take also of the tree of life, and eat, and live forever:

23 Therefore the Lord God sent him forth from the garden of Eden, to till the ground from whence he was taken.

24 So he drove out the man; and he placed at the east of the garden of Eden cherubims, and a flaming sword

which turned every way, to keep the way of the tree of life.

Romans 5:
12   Wherefore as by one man sin entered into the world, and death by sin; and so death passed upon all men, for that all have sinned:
13   (For until the law, sin was in the world: but sin is not imputed when there is no law.
14   Nevertheless death reigned from Adam to Moses, even over them that had not sinned after the similitude of Adam's transgression, who is the fig-

ure of him that was to come.

1 Corinthians 15:
21   For since by man came death, by man came also the resurrection of the dead.
22   For as in Adam all die, even so in Christ shall all be made alive.

1 Timothy 2:
13   For Adam was first formed, and then Eve.
14   And Adam was not deceived, but the woman being deceived was in the transgression.

Before proceeding to an analysis of the circumstances surrounding these events in Eden, it is important once again to underscore the fact that in the present context the term *immortal* is being used entirely in its biological sense.   It has reference here only to the physical life, not spiritual life (which is not the issue at the moment), and it means that the organism has the natural capacity to stay alive indefinitely.   It allows that death is possible from outside causes (predation, poisoning, etc.) but states that it is not an inherent principle of the life of the organism.

Man as *now* constituted, however, does not enjoy immortality, having forfeited it by eating the forbidden fruit.   It is most important to bear in mind, therefore, that the penalty of eating the forbidden fruit was not the mere *shortening* of a life which would have terminated later in any case, **but the introduction of death as an entirely new experience for man as a species.**

There are other forms of life which also appear to be subject to death, but not because they have *forfeited* something they once possessed.   It is rather that they seem to have a built-in or "programmed limitation" to length of life, designed to prevent over-population.   In unfallen man no such designed limitation was needed to prevent over-population because removal by translation would effectively have served this purpose.   The meaning of programmed limitation will be made explicit in Chapter 8.

The point of importance at this juncture is to recognize that for such creatures a mortal condition is not in any way the result of a judgment brought upon them as a species — except in so far as the Fall of man has made him destructive of all other forms of life.   It is part of the economy of Nature that no species shall be allowed to multiply at the expense of any other: it is in this sense *natural,* an essential factor in the total balance of Nature.   For man, by complete contrast,

death is *UN*-natural.   For him, it is forfeiture of a once enjoyed
potential.   Animals die: man, strictly speaking, is executed.   The
death of man is not the same thing at all as the death of an animal,
neither when considered in its theological aspects nor in its physiological aspects.   This means that the physical *life* of man is different
in some way also, and that Adam did not derive it from any animal
ancestor.*

In 1895 James Denny, inspired by James Orr, wrote a remarkable
forecast of the present position which was far in advance of the views
held by many of his theological contemporaries.   It is a long extract,
but seems worthy to be quoted in full.   He wrote:†

> There is one special question here to which Scripture
> teaching gives a peculiar importance − the question as to the
> connection of sin and death.   In the Old Testament and in
> the New alike the connection is maintained: man dies because
> of sin; or, as St. Paul puts it, the wages of sin is death . . . .
> All men must die.   Mortality is a consequence of sin.
>   But is this true?   Is it really because of sin that men die?
> The consenting voice of science seems to say no: death reigned
> in the world long before man and what theologians call sin,
> appeared.   Death is a law of nature; it is an essential lever in
> the great machine of the world.   Every living creature is born
> with the seeds of decay in it; it is like a clock, wound up to go
> for a certain number of hours, but liable, of course, to be
> stopped by a thousand accidents before it has run down of
> itself.   This line of argument, backed up by the actual univer-
> sality of death, has something imposing about it, and a good
> many theologians accept it without more ado.   Possibly they
> try to secure the truth of the Scripture idea by making death
> mean something else than death means in common language:
> they darken it by shadows of spiritual and eternal separation
> from God, as distinct from the purely natural experience
> ordinarily indicated by this name.
>   I do not think that these distinctions avail at all to secure
> the Scripture doctrine, and if it is to be maintained, as I think
> it ought to be, the line of defence must be drawn further back.
> The scientific assertion of the natural necessity of death, closely
> considered, really amounts to a begging of the question.   Man,
> it means, *must* die, must *always* have died, because he is a
> natural being, subject to the universal law of birth and decay;
> there is nothing but this for him.   But the whole ground on
> which the Bible doctrine is based is that man is *not* simply a
> natural being, with nothing but the destiny which awaits all

---

*   Hugh Miller was perceptive enough to see that the Theory of Evolution is fatal when
applied to man, on this account.   See reference # 113.

† Denny, James, *Studies in Theology*, Grand Rapids, Baker, 1967 reprint, p.97 ff.

nature awaiting him.   He is a being invested by his very constitution with a primacy over nature; he is related to God in a
way which makes him specifically distinct from every merely
natural being, in a way which those who understand it regard
as containing at least the promise and the possibility of immortality.   To say that he *must* die, because he is a natural
being, ignores all this: it amounts to a proof of man's mortality only in the sense that it is a disproof of his immortality.

But this disproof carries us too far: it would not be recognized as valid by most of those who have too hastily accepted
the inference which it includes, viz., that death is inevitable for
man, simply because of his incorporation in nature.   Once we
understand what man is, we see that death in him demands an
explanation which is not demanded in the case of creatures
whose whole life is bounded by nature; and that explanation
is supplied by Scripture when it makes death the punishment
of sin.   Death means, in this case, what we see when we stand
beside the dying, or rather what the dying experience as their
connection with the present order ceases.   It is a mistake to
minimise the significance of this by speaking of it as if it were
only natural, by speaking, as people sometimes do, even where
Christ is concerned, of "mere physical death".

There is nothing whatever, in human experience, which is
merely physical; death is not merely physical; it is human;
one, awful, indivisible experience, which cannot be analyzed,
and which is profaned when it is identified with anything that
could befall a lower than human nature.   We can be redeemed
from the fear and bitterness of it by Jesus Christ; but in itself
it has not a natural but a spiritual character: to the consciousness of man, in which it exists in its completeness, it is not the
debt of nature, but the wages of sin . . . .   The fact that man
is constituted for immortality, and has the promise of it in his
being from the first, forbids us to ascribe to death a natural
and inevitable place in his career.   It is an intrusion, and it is
to be finally abolished. [Emphasis his].

Now this once enjoyed potential may be termed "contingent
immortality".   And the term is entirely appropriate since man was
able by disobedience to nullify the conditions upon which his immortality hinged.   Although the immortality of the angels appears to be
*un*conditional, they are created beings as man is, and therefore their
existence is conditional upon the will of God and does not inhere in
their nature.   Immortality in the *absolutely* unconditional sense
belongs only to God (1 Tim.6:16).

Let us consider, then, what the biblical record implies by analyzing first of all the situation in the Garden of Eden *after* Adam and
Eve had eaten of the forbidden fruit.   The specific phrases which I
wish to elaborate upon are italicized in the following excerpt from
Genesis 3:22-24:

> And the Lord God said . . . . "and now, lest he put forth his hand,
> and take also of the tree of life and eat, *and live forever* . . . ."
> Therefore the Lord God sent him forth from the Garden of Eden,
> to till the ground from whence he was taken.
> So he *drove out the man;* and he placed at the east of the Garden
> of Eden cherubims, and a flaming sword which turned every way,
> *to keep the way of the tree of life.*

Genesis 3:22 is probably the only unfinished sentence in Scripture.   That it *is* an unfinished sentence has been recognized for a very
long time.   The *King James Version* has a colon after the words
for ever, and the sentence which follows is so structured as to show
that the translators did not consider it a direct continuance of verse 22.
They therefore adopted the colon as a device for showing that the
sentence was left hanging.   In place of a colon the *Revised Standard
Version* and the *American Standard Version* have both used a long
dash where I have used a series of dots.   The intention is clearly the
same.   Some other modern translations have re-phrased the sentence
and effectively concealed the potential danger implicit in the original
by its incompleteness.   They seem to have felt that something was
wrong with the sentence as it stood and corrected it accordingly.
Smith and Goodspeed have added the words "(suppose he were to)
reach out his hand, etc." and have concluded with an exclamation
mark.   The effect is somewhat the same, and so are the implications,
but it is not strictly true to the original.   The *Jerusalem Bible* has, to
my mind, spoiled the impact of the original by rendering it, "He must
not be allowed, etc.", which is more a statement of the precautionary
measures taken than of the reason for taking them.

Yet in all these diverse renderings, the implication is simply that
had Adam and Eve been permitted access to the Tree of Life, they
would have recovered the physical immortality which they had forfeited by disobedience.*

But why forbid *now* what had previously been clearly allowed and

---

* It is remarkable that in his *Institutes,* Calvin seems to have failed to see the biological implications of this passage. He makes only two references to Genesis 3:22 (Bk. IV, iv, § 12, 18).
In both cases he is concerned only or chiefly to stress the spiritual aspects of Adam's situation.
God excluded him from the Tree of Life lest he suppose that by resort to it, he should be
neutralizing the effects of his spiritual disobedience, thus circumventing the need for the operation of the grace of God in salvation through Jesus Christ.   Although Judaeus Philo (B. C.
20—39 A.D.), the wealthy Greek-educated Jewish philosopher of Alexandria, had many fanciful
interpretations of Genesis, he observed succinctly at this point, "It is unseemly to immortalize
evil, and it is unprofitable for him to whom it happens.   For the longer the evil and wicked
man lives, the more wicked he is and the more greatly harmful both to himself and to others".
[*Questions and Answers on Genesis,* tr. Ralph Marcus, Loeb Classical Library, Harvard, 1969,
p.34].

had not yet been abused?   Genesis 2:9 shows that the Tree of Life
had been there in the Garden from the beginning and, if we may argue
from the absence of any injunction to the contrary, it had been accessible to them, since Genesis 2:17 seems to indicate that only the Tree
of Knowledge had been forbidden.

All commentators who have engaged themselves with the story of
Eden have addressed this question.   The Rabbinic commentators
studied the record of man's fall and though their reasoning is sometimes a little strange to our way of thinking, they nevertheless reached
conclusions which have been shared by the Christian Church in all
ages.   First of all, they argued that angels are not propagated but are
immortal, whereas animals are propagated and are destined to die.
"Whereupon God said, 'I will create man to be the mirror of both of
them, so that when he sins, when he behaves like an animal, death
shall overtake him: but if he refrains from sin, he shall be immortal',
(i.e., like an angel)".*   There is another form of this view which states
more simply that "Every man could live forever if he should lead a
sinless life".**

Jacob Newman, in his edition of the commentary on Genesis by
Nahmanides written in the thirteenth century A.D., translates the
latter's comments on Genesis 2:17 as follows: "In the opinion of our
rabbis, if Adam had not sinned he would never have died, for the superior soul gives life for ever".†   But the Jews went further than this
and, reasonably enough, postulated that, so long as Adam and Eve remained sinless, their married life would have been pure and they
would have begotten immortal children.††

Ginsberg states the early Jewish understanding of man's original
condition: "Had it not been for the Fall, death would not have been
so terrible and painful, but a joyful incident in man's career".‡   He
gives several references where this view is clearly expressed in rabbinical commentaries.

Moreover, the Wisdom Literature of the Jewish people in pre-
Christian times reflects the same view.   In the apocryphal work *The
Wisdom of Solomon* at 1:13-15 it is written: "God made not death;

---

*Ginsberg, Louis, *Legends of the Jews,* Phila., Jewish Publ. Assoc. of Amer., 1955, Vol. I,
p.50, quoting from the Midrash, *Bereshith Rabba* on Genesis.

** Ginsberg, Louis, *ibid,* Vol. V, p.129.

† Newman, Jacob, *The Commentary of Nahmanides on Gen. 1—6:8,* London, Brill, 1960, p.71.

†† Ginsberg, Louis, *ibid,* Vol. V, p.134.

‡ Ginsberg, Louis, *ibid,* Vol. V, p.129.

neither delighteth He when the living perish. For He created all things
that they might have being and the generative powers of the world are
healthsome, and there is no poison of destruction in them . . . . For
righteousness is immortal". And in 2:23, "God created man for
incorruption". Both are from the *Revised Version* of 1884. It is
interesting that the word *poison* should have been employed here in
view of what is to be said later in this volume regarding the nature of
the forbidden fruit.

The early Church Fathers were certainly aware of this Jewish
traditional lore because, after all, the Christian Church was entirely
composed of Jews in its initial stages of development. For example,
Jerome (340–420 A.D.) in his Commentary entitled *Questions on
Genesis,* favoured the adoption of a translation for the latter part of
Genesis 2:17 which had been previously suggested by Symmachus (a
second century Ebionite who had translated the Hebrew Old Testament into Greek): "Thou shalt *become* mortal and liable to death".
Thus Symmachus had sought to indicate his belief that Adam had
potential immortality to begin with. Yet for some reason Jerome
himself did not adopt this rendering in the Vulgate, perhaps being
more strongly influenced by the Septuagint which does not agree with
Symmachus' version in this.*

Augustine (354–416 A.D.) thought much about the position of
Adam before he fell and, with characteristic insight, hit upon the exact
truth and expressed it with the simplicity of genius in words which we
have already noted. Before the Fall it was not impossible for Adam
to die but it was possible for him not to die. To use his actual words:
non imposse mori sed posse non mori.† The fact that Adam could
die, demonstrated to Augustine that the immortality he at first enjoyed was not the same kind of immortality that the angels enjoyed,
since the "death" of an angel would be annihilation. So Augustine
argued that Adam was "immortal by the benefit of his Creator". By
which he evidently intended that Adam could have lived on forever,
his body being so constituted that with the external aid of the Tree of
Life to preserve its balanced functioning he would have been continually renewed against any ageing of his cells. He was immortal, therefore, not because he had such power in himself to be so, but because
God had made such a thing possible, provided Adam maintained the

---

* Jerome: quoted by Harold Browne, *Commentary on Genesis,* N.Y., Scribner, Armstrong,
& Co., 1873, p.42.

† Augustine: *De Genesi ad Litteram,* Bk. I, 25, note 35 [in *Nicene and Post-Nicene Fathers,*
Buffalo, Christian Literature Co., 1886, Vol. I, p.73, fn.]

right conditions of life both spiritual and physical. Adam's immortality was contingent, not absolute.

Augustine continually reverted to the circumstances surrounding man's present mortal estate. In his treatise *Enchiridion* (chap.105), he said:

> (God) willed to show how good is a rational being who is able to refrain from sin, and *yet* how much better is one who *cannot* sin at all; just as that was immortality when it was possible for man to avoid death, yet there is reserved for the future a more perfect immortality when it shall be *impossible* for man to die.

Augustine spelled out with great clarity and precision the status of Adam and Eve as first created. In his *De Genesi ad Litteram* (Bk. VI, 25) he wrote: *"Aliud est non posse mori, sicut quasdam naturas immortales creavit Deus; aliud est autem posse non mori, secundum quem modum primus creatus est homo immortalis":* i.e., "It is one thing not to be able to die, as if what God created were immortal beings; however, it is another thing to be able not to die, after which pattern the first (Adam) was created an immortal human being".

Augustine felt there was a semantic problem here. What was one to call a creature that could die but need not, if one is to reserve the word "immortal" for a creature that *cannot* die? He tried to spell out this distinction in his treatise on *The Merits and Forgiveness of Sins* (Bk. 1. 5) where he titles one particular section thus: "The words MORTALE (*capable* of dying), MORTUUM (*dead*), and MORITURUS (*destined* to die)". Then he comments as follows:

> Now previous to the change into the incorruptible state which is promised in the resurrection of the saints, the body could be *mortal* (capable of dying), although not destined to die (MORITURUS)...
> In like manner was man's body then *mortal;* and this mortality was to have been superseded by an eternal incorruption, if man had persevered in righteousness, that is to say in obedience: but even what was mortal (MORTALE) was not made dead (MORTUUM) except on account of sin.
> For the change which is to come in at the resurrection is, in truth, not only not to have death incidental to it, which has happened through sin, but neither is it to have mortality (or the very *possibility* of death) which the natural body had before it sinned.

How Augustine would have delighted in finding out about the nature of the amoeba and the paramecia! They exactly fulfill the conditions of Adam as created: capable of being killed but not naturally subject to death. In his *City of God* (Bk. XII. 21) he wrote:

> Man whose nature was to be a mean between the angelic [which can never die, ACC] and the bestial [for whom death is programmed, ACC], was created in such sort that if he remained in subject-

ion to his Creator as his rightful Lord, and piously kept his com-
mandments, he should pass into the company of angels and obtain
without the intervention of death a blessed and endless immortality; but if he offended the Lord his God by a proud and disobedient use of his free will, he should become subject to death and live
as the beasts do — doomed to eternal punishment after death.

Moreover, in his treatise on *Merits and Forgiveness* (Bk. I. 2)
Augustine had written, "If Adam had not sinned, he would not have
been divested of his body, but would have been clothed upon with
immortality and incorruption . . . . passing from the natural body into
the spiritual body".

Perhaps the Tree of Life in the normal course of unfallen man's
life would have preserved the metabolic balance of his body in a state
of perfect equilibrium.   But it seems also to have the power to heal
even this mortal wound after he had fallen.   Thus it came about that
before the Fall only the Tree of Knowledge was forbidden to him: but
after the Fall only the Tree of Life was forbidden.   Each was equally
dangerous when taken out of place, and both of them were so in specific relation to the experience of physical death.

Here, then, we seem to have the basic truth which lies behind the
worldwide tradition of a period in history when man was immortal.
Such tradition virtually without exception places the Golden Age of
human experience in the past, not in the future as evolutionary optimism proposes.   Without revelation, mankind could not know that
this Golden Age will be *recovered* one day.   A Golden Age marks
both the beginning and the end of history — this is what revelation
tells us.

The implications of this tradition of immortality were explored by
many who took the biblical record as sober history.   Some of their
conclusions, as we know from the New Testament, were perfectly
sound: and, as we also know, were in anticipation of some of the
discoveries of modern biology.

Chapter 7

HUMAN DEATH: A PROCESS OF TRAGEDY

Dying, thou shalt die.
Genesis 2:17

Genesis 2:17 tells us that the effect of eating the forbidden fruit was to begin immediately: "in the day that thou eatest therof thou shalt surely die". Since Adam did not return to the dust until centuries later, it has sometimes been held that the whole import of this passage is spiritual not physical: that it was a spiritual death that occurred that very day, and that the Tree of Life was a tree for the healing of a spiritual disease rather than a physical one. But the implications are clear. It was a physical disease with fatal consequences that man had incurred from the forbidden fruit which the Tree of Life could have served to antidote. It is necessary, then, to read the words "in the day that . . . ." in some less literal sense. And here we have an interesting parallel in 1 Kings 2:36—46.

On this occasion Solomon had condemned Shimei to permanent confinement in Jerusalem for the rest of his life. Solomon's words in verse 37 are: "For it shall be, that on the day thou goest out (of the city) . . . . thou shalt know for certain that thou shalt surely die". We are told that Shimei stayed in Jerusalem according to the King's command for some three years, until certain of his servants ran away. Without stopping to think about the consequences, Shimei saddled his ass and went right out after him. After Shimei had returned to the city, Solomon learned what he had done and sent his official executioner to put him to death. The meaning of Solomon's warning was

probably quite clear to Shimei: he understood that the day he disobeyed, from that time he was a doomed man.   But after three
years, living freely within the confines of Jerusalem, he evidently
forgot all about the injunction of Solomon – and paid the penalty.

Now Augustine in his treatise on *Merits and Forgiveness* (Bk. I. 21)
illustrates how the threat of Genesis 2:17 can be viewed as certain
rather than immediate:

> By a certain disease which was conceived in men from a sudden-
> ly infected and pestilential corruption, it was brought about that
> they lost that stability of life in which they were created, and by
> reason of the changes which they experienced during the stages of
> life the disease issued at last in death.   However, many were the
> years they lived in their subsequent life, yet they began to die in
> the day when they received the law of death, because they kept
> verging towards old age.

Keil and Delitzsch, in their commentary on Genesis, consider
briefly not only the evil of death, the prospect of which was to plague
man throughout his life, but also the merciful aspect of its delayed
action.*

> This was the fulfilment of the threat "in the day thou eatest
> thereof thou shalt surely die", which began to take effect immed-
> iately after the breach of the divine command; for not only did
> man then become mortal, but he also actually came under the
> power of death, received into his nature (i.e., body) the germ of
> death [the mortogenic factor, ACC], the maturity of which pro-
> duced its eventual dissolution into dust.   The reason why the life
> of the man did not come to an end immediately after the eating of
> the fruit . . . . was that the long-suffering of God afforded space for
> repentance and so controlled and ordered the sin of men and the
> penalty of sin as to render them subservient to the accomplishment
> of his original purpose and the glorification of his name.

The poison must be slow acting or the whole of God's purposes
would have been rendered futile, since humanity would have perished
at once.   Thus Adam and his immediate descendants must be allowed
to survive for a sufficient length of time to allow the establishment of
the human race.   But once established, thereafter longevity could be
reduced for safety's sake lest the race once again destroy itself by its
very potential for wicked invention which this factor of long life made
so probable.

God therefore appointed that man should neither die at once, nor
enjoy undue longevity.   Death was designed as a *process,* not an event.

---

* Keil, C. F. and F. Delitzsch, *Biblical Commentary on the Old Testament,* Grand Rapids,
Eerdmans, reprint, n.d., Vol. I, *The Pentateuch,* p.105.

Moreover, if Adam and Eve had died *at once* before guaranteeing the continuance of the race, the whole creation would have been pointless. For the universe finds its meaning only in so far as the love of God has been effectively displayed in redemption.

Augustine had a tremendous influence by his writings on the subsequent development of Roman Catholic theology. The Roman Catholic view on this subject in the earlier centuries has been set forth by a Jesuit writer, Professor T. B. Chetwood, as follows:*

> The immortality of Adam is explicitly defined by the Church. The Sixteenth Council of Carthage (418 A.D.), the decrees of which were approved by Pope Zozimus, teaches: "If anyone shall say that Adam was created mortal so that he would have died in the body whether he had sinned or not, let him be anathema". And the same doctrine is confirmed by the decrees of Orange and Trent.
>
> The Scriptures, both the Old and the New Testament, have very many passages which speak of the "death" which came to us from Adam but there are none plainer than the Book of Genesis which gives the words of God to the pair in the garden: "But of the tree of knowledge of good and evil thou shalt not eat. For in what day soever thou shalt eat of it, thou shalt die the death".

Chetwood elaborated the argument first of all by pointing out that by his disobedience Adam did not die immediately but only after the passage of centuries. By which he concluded that God meant: "You will *at once* come under sentence of death, i.e., from that very day". And then, secondly, he observed that unless Adam really possessed immortality before he disobeyed, it would have been no punishment whatever to forfeit it afterwards. As Chetwood said, "He could not, clearly, be deprived for a punishment of something which he did not possess". Chetwood then remarks that the Fathers were unanimous in so understanding this passage and in their teaching of the original immortality of Adam and Eve.

Although Luther was diametrically opposed to Roman Catholic teaching on almost every point of importance, on this issue he found himself in agreement. In his *Lectures on Genesis,* he wrote:†

> If God had permitted Adam to eat of the tree of life, Adam would have overcome death by means of this food, since he had become subject to death after he had eaten of the tree of death....

---

* Chetwood, T. B., *God and Creation,* N.Y., Benzinger Bros., 1928, p.145 ff.

† See *Luther's Works: Lectures on Genesis Chapters 1—5,* ed. J. Pelikan, St. Louis, Concordia, 1958, Vol. 1, p.116. See also reference #114 for further excerpts from Luther.

I believe that if Adam had been permitted to go to the tree of
life, he would have been restored to the life he had lost, so that
thereafter he would not have died . . . .

In his commentary on Psalm 90 Luther deals at some length
with the tragedy of death which for man he calls "a genuine disaster".   It seems that in most evangelical circles today the fact has
been almost entirely overlooked.   The Theory of Evolution has made
its case so forcefully that many have abandoned their former position
and come to accept the animal origin of man's body, demanding only
that his soul be a special creation.

But this is to surrender an essential aspect of man's uniqueness,
namely, that he was created *immortal*.   If this is true, and the Word of
God most assuredly proclaims it in no uncertain terms, then man cannot have received his body by evolutionary descent because the
primate stock from which it is proposed to derive him consists of a
line of animals for whom old age and death seem clearly to be natural
and programmed.   For man death is *neither* natural *nor* is it programmed — save as a *penalty*.

Luther wrote in his commentary: *

This Psalm reveals in striking fashion that the death of man is in
countless ways a far greater calamity than the death of other living
beings.   Although horses, cows, and all animals die, they do not
die because God is angry at them.   On the contrary, for them
death is, as it were, a sort of temporal casualty, ordained indeed by
God but not regarded by Him as punishment.   Animals die because
for some other reason it seemed good to God that they should die.

But the death of human beings is a genuine disaster.   Man's
death is in itself truly an infinite and eternal wrath.   The reason is
that man is a being created for this purpose: to live forever in obedience to the Word of God and to be like God.   He was not created
for death.   In his case death was ordained as a punishment of sin;
for God said to Adam: "In the day that you eat of this tree, you
shall die" (Gen.2:17).

The death of human beings is, therefore, not like the death of
animals.   These die because of a law of nature.   Nor is man's death
an event which occurs accidentally or has merely an aspect of temporality.   On the contrary, man's death, if I may so speak, was
threatened by God and is caused by an incensed and estranged God.
If Adam had not eaten of the forbidden tree, he would have remained immortal.   But because he sinned through disobedience, he
succumbs to death like the animals which are subject to him.
Originally death was not part of his nature.   He dies because he
provokes God's wrath.   Death is, in his case, the inevitable and

---

* *Luther's Works: Selected Psalms II*, ed. J. Pelican, St. Louis, Concordia, 1965, Vol. 13,
p. 94, 95, 96.

deserved consequence of his sin and disobedience . . . .

Man's death is truly an event sadder and more serious than the slaughter of a cow.   This becomes most evident when one takes into account the propagation of evil.   Moses says: "Thou causest men to die".   "Men" refers to the entire human race.   Moses includes in this one word "men" all the offspring of our first parents. Therefore that which was created for life is now destined for death. This is the result of God's wrath.   So the entire human race plunged from immortality into eternal death.

Such is certainly the Scriptural view of human mortality: it is a penalty, and a tragedy.   In his *Biblical Theology* Geerhardus Vos nicely states the position of Adam before and after the Fall, as well as the position of man redeemed yet still destined to die, as follows:*

> *Immortality* is used in theological terminology for that state of man in which he has nothing in him which would cause death. It is quite possible that at the same time an abstract contingency of death may overhang man, i.e., the bare possibility may exist of death in some way, for some cause, invading him, but he has nothing of it within him. It is as if we should say of somebody that he is liable to the invasion of some disease, but we should not on that account declare him to have the disease.
>
> In this sense it can appropriately be said that man as created was "immortal", but not that after the fall he was so, for through the act of sinning the principle of death entered into him; whereas before he was only liable to die under certain circumstances, he now inevitably had to die.   His immortality in (the sense of his soul) had been lost.   Again *immortality* can designate, in eschatalogical language, that state of man in which he has been made immune to death, because immune to sin.   Man was not in virtue of creation, immortal in this highest sense: this is a result of redemption accompanied by eschatalogical treatment . . . .
>
> (Man) was (initially) *immortal* and *mortal* both, according to the definition employed: mortal as not yet lifted above the contingency of death, but non-mortal as not carrying death as a disease within himself.   Here, therefore, *immortality* and *mortality* co-existed.   In the next stage (fallen) he is in no sense anything else but mortal: he must die, death works in him.
>
> In the next stage the word *mortal* has only a qualified application to the regenerate man, namely, in so far as during his earthly state death still exists and works in his body, whilst from the centre of his renewed spirit it has been in principle excluded, and supplanted by an immortal life, which is bound in the end to overcome and extrude death.

The Tree of Knowledge might well have been called the "tree of death", for such it turned out to be.   But the Tree of Life seems

---

* Vos, Geerhardus, *Biblical Theology*, Grand Rapids, Eerdmans, 1975, p. 38, 39.

clearly to have been potentially a tree of health, this character being either in its leaves (Rev.22:2) or perhaps in its fruit. The circumstances surrounding the forceful exclusion of Adam and Eve from access to it (Gen.3:24) once death had been introduced into their bodies, reinforces the view that this Tree of Life was not for *spiritual* but for physical well-being. For it seems highly unlikely that if this tree had the power of spiritual healing, Adam and Eve would have been so rigidly excluded from further access to it, just when they most needed it .

The probability is rather that the Tree of Life supplied in their diet, while they were yet unfallen and immortal, that which would preserve them in perfect health indefinitely. But once they had disobeyed and destroyed by a single act of disobedience both their spiritual vitality as well as their physical immortality, the healing of the body could only have consigned them to an unending existence with a fallen nature. To continue for ever without the amendment of an evil spirit was a fate too awful to contemplate. Keil and Delitzsch put the matter thus:†

> Immortality in a state of sin is not the *zoe aionios* (eternal life) which God designed for man, but endless misery which the Scriptures call "the second death" (Rev.2:11; 20:6, 14; 21:8). The expulsion from paradise, therefore, was a punishment inflicted for man's good, intended, while exposing him to temporal death, to preserve him from eternal death.

Thus God thrust them out of the Garden and stationed at the entrance an angel with a sword that turned every way (i.e., was inescapable) specifically to keep the way to the Tree of Life. What had once been a guarantee of blessing had now become a potential hazard of immeasurable consequence.

The day that Adam and Eve disobeyed and ate of the fruit of the forbidden tree, they destroyed their unique constitution. They surrendered a potential physical immortality, and by a process of inheritance (to be considered later in this volume) they involved all their descendants (save One) in the same unnatural and unhappy state. As Paul says: "By one man sin entered into the world and death by sin; and thus death passed upon all men".* As A. H. Strong notes: "The

---

† Keil, C. F. and F. Delitzsch, *Biblical Commentary on the Old Testament,* Grand Rapids, Eerdmans, n.d., Vol. I, *The Pentateuch,* p.107. Erich Sauer rightly remarked: "The sinner's bodily deathlessness would be eternal death to his soul, and Paradise would have become a Hell". [*The Dawn of World Redemption,* Grand Rapids, Eerdmans, 1953, p.61]

* For an extended note on Romans 5:12, see reference #115.

death spoken of (in Rom.5:12) is, as the whole context shows, mainly though not exclusively physical.   It has passed upon all — even upon those who have as yet committed no conscious and personal transgression whereby to explain its infliction (i.e., infants)".* The fatal poisoning which had become the penalty of disobedience in the first pair was passed on and became the root cause of disobedience in all their descendants save One.   This has been stated succinctly: "In Adam a person made human nature sinful: in his posterity, nature made persons sinful".†

Luther spoke at some length on this matter.   He said:‡

> If Eve had not sinned, (man) would nevertheless have eaten, drunk, slept, etc., but all this without any sin and disorder.   Such a life would have continued as long as it pleased God, let us say for two or three thousand years.   Then we would have been changed in a moment without passing through death; and, completely sanctified, we would have entered into an eternal life free from trouble; such a life as, indeed, we are even now expecting.   But because sin has stolen into the world through the work of the devil and the consent of man, the judgment has been passed from the beginning and remains in force throughout this life: "In the day that thou eatest thereof thou shalt surely die".   This is the reason why we must die.

In another place Luther wrote:**

> Had man not fallen into sin, he would, of course, also have eaten and drunk.   The change of his food by the process of digestion would have taken place in his body, but it would not have been so foul as it is now.   This tree of life would have kept him in perpetual youth; nor would any man have ever felt the inconvenience of old age.   His brow would not have been furrowed; nor would his foot or his hand or any other part of his body have become increasingly weak and languid.   Through the beneficent effect of the fruit of this tree man's powers for procreation and all sorts of labour would have remained perfect until he would finally have been translated from this corporeal or natural life to the spiritual life.

Paul Althaus in discussing Luther's views on the entrance of

---

* Strong, Augustus H., *Systematic Theology*, Valley Forge, Pa., Judson Press, 1974 reprint, p. 622.

† Jones, J. C., *Primeval Revelation: Studies in Genesis I—VIII*, London, Hodder & Stoughton, 2nd ed., 1897, p. 256.

‡ *What Luther Says*, an anthology complied by E. M. Plass, St. Louis, Concordia, 1959, Vol. III, entry no. 4133.

** Luther: *ibid*, entry no. 4135.

physical death, observed that his theology of death is expressed particularly clearly in his powerful interpretation of Psalm 90.*

> Luther held that people usually understand death as a natural
> event, as a particular example of the transitoriness of all creatures;
> they therefore recommend that we should not take it too serious-
> ly . . . .   Holy Scripture, however, opens our eyes to what really
> happens when we die.   Dying is more than a biological phenomen-
> on.   It is a human reality; and this distinguishes it from the ending
> of plant and animal life.   Plants and animals do not come to an
> end because of God's wrath, but according to a "natural order"
> established by God.   As Luther says, "The death of a man is an
> infinite and eternal misery and wrath".   For man is a creature
> created in the image of God, to live eternally and immortally in
> relationship to God and not to die.   His death is not the result of a
> natural process created by God.   Rather death is "laid upon him
> and executed on him through God's wrath".   This is why men
> draw back in terror in the face of death and experience horror such
> as no other living being experiences.   We must understand our
> mortal fate theologically (i.e., not merely biologically) within the
> relationship between God and man; for this relationship is the
> decisive and all embracing destiny of man.

W. G. T. Shedd points out that physical death, as a mortal principle, befell Adam immediately, though he did not actually die on the
day he sinned.**

> When a man is smitten with a mortal disease he is a dead man,
> though he may live for months.   Adam's body became a mortal
> body . . . .
> The difference between the immortal body of holy Adam and
> the mortal body of fallen Adam is, that prior to the fall the human
> body was not liable to death from *internal* causes, but only from
> *external.*   It had no latent diseases, and no seeds of death in it . . . .
> It could however be put to death.   If it were deprived of food or
> air, it would die.

In speaking of the meaning of the phrase "in the day that thou
eatest thereof . . . .", Stephen Charnock (1628–1680), a Puritan
scholar and Presbyterian minister in London wrote: "It is to be
understood, not of an actual death of the body (that day) but the
deserving, and the necessity, of death".†

---

* Althaus, Paul, *The Theology of Martin Luther,* tr. R. C. Schultz, Phila., Fortress Press,
1975, p. 405 f.

** Shedd, W. G. T., *Dogmatic Theology,* Grand Rapids, Zondervan reprint, 1969, Vol. II,
p. 159.

† Charnock: quoted by W. G. T. Shedd, *ibid,* Vol. III, p. 336.

That death for man was something far more serious than death for any animal below him is certainly implied by much that is revealed in Scripture about the constitution of man as a spirit/body entity who was made in the image of God and for God's pleasure.   As James Denny put it: "Body and soul exist only in and for each other; the body is not *a* body, but the body of the soul; the soul is not *a* soul, but the soul of the body; in our consciousness of self the two are one . . . .   Man is a unity, not a tying together of separate parts or even separate faculties, and the Bible deals with him as such".*

In a similar vein, James Orr wrote:†

> Man is not a pure spirit like the angels, but an incorporated spirit.   Death therefore is not the same thing to him as it is to the lower animals unless, indeed, we deny to him, as we do to them, immortality.
>
> Neither, as I said, is the body to be regarded in his case, as the old philosophers thought of it, as a material prison house, from which he should be glad to escape in death.   It is *part of himself:* an integral part of his total personality, and body and soul in separation are neither of them complete man.
>
> It follows, if we deal firmly with this conception of man, that death is to him not a natural process but something altogether *un*-natural — the violent separation of two parts of his being which God never meant to be separated; a rupture, a rending asunder, a mutilation of his personality.

This is reflected in Paul's hope, a hope shared equally by every child of God, expressed so clearly in 2 Corinthians 5:1-5, in which he assures us of a new house, a new tabernacle, awaiting us for embodiment after resurrection.   We long for this, not because we long for death which must first intervene and might leave us "unclothed" (a kind of naked soul), but because we long to be "re-clothed" with an immortal body, one in which death is swallowed up by life.   And Paul says: "He that wrought us for this very thing is God".   It was never God's intention to turn us into anything else than a body/spirit reality.

This body is essential to our being.   And it is a body deliberately designed with enormous potentialities — especially to make the Incarnation of God in Christ possible.   This house, this body that is the house of man's spirit, is not just a complex electrochemical machine. It was designed from the very first for a special purpose.   It was so built that it would properly meet the requirements that God had in mind both for man *and for Himself* in the Person of the Lord Jesus

---

* Denny, James, *Studies in Theology*, Grand Rapids, Baker reprint, 1967, p. 76.

† Orr, James, *God's Image in Man*, Grand Rapids, Eerdmans reprint, 1948, p. 251, 252.

Christ.   In due course, it was to make it possible for God to objectify Himself, perfectly expressed in terms of human personality *as a Man.* And then, as a Man, to sacrifice his life vicariously for any man who would believe and appropriate that sacrifice as a full, perfect, and sufficient one.   In the face of the divinely appointed moral law, man must have this "satisfaction" against his own sinfulness, failure, and self-will.   God made man's body such that He Himself could assume it for a season as his own proper House without doing any violence to his own Person.   And then in the Person of his Son, Jesus Christ, He could die in it that we, who are dying in it even as we live, might be redeemed to live again and for ever in a new and even more glorious resurrected "house" throughout eternity.   Thus shall we exhibit the grace and love of our Saviour God as a matter of personal experience. No mere animal body could have sufficed for such a tremendous purpose.

Now this immortality, *surrendered* by the first man named Adam because of *disobedience* to the will of God, was in due time to be *sacrificed* by another man named Adam (Jesus Christ, 1 Cor.15:45) in *obedience* to God's will.   The conditions surrounding its forfeiture have already been examined in some detail: it remains now to examine some of the important circumstances under which the second Adam was able to sacrifice his immortality as an entirely free act of his own will without any other internal or external compulsion.   Both these two Adams are declared to have been immortals, the first implicitly by the wording of Genesis 2:17 and 3:22, and the last explicitly by the wording of Hebrews 7:16 which reads "made after the power of an endless life".   Of both, Augustine's words are true: it was not impossible for either of them to die, but it *was* possible for neither of them to have done so.

In the New Testament, there is presented to us a portrait of perfect manhood, such a perfection as any one of Adam's descendants might have achieved had the Fall not occurred.   Jesus Christ grew from birth to manhood, *flawlessly.*   Whereas the first Adam turned innocence into unrighteousness, the "last Adam",* the last truly human being to possess immortality, turned the innocence of childhood into moral perfection.   And when He had thus been "made perfect", that is to say, when He had reached full and perfect maturity by the things

---

* Anselm of Laon observed that Christ is the "Last Adam" because He is never to be succeeded by another as federal head of the human race. [*A Scolastic Miscellany*, ed. E. R. Fairweather, Phila., Westminster Press, 1956, Vol. X, p. 273]

which He experienced in the process of reaching manhood (Heb.5:8,9), He had arrived at the point which the first Adam and all his descendants might have come to had there been no Fall. Being thus ready, He might have been translated directly into a higher state of human existence *without passing through death.* *

I believe that in the case of the Lord Jesus, Peter and James and John actually witnessed on the Mount of Transfiguration the moment when just such an event might have transpired (Luke 9:27-36). At that time, the Last Adam was transformed and ready to be translated out of this world of time and space into that other world of which this world is merely a vestibule.

This, it would seem, was the prospect God had made possible for unfallen man: to turn innocence into virtue as a response to the daily challenges of having dominion over this world as God's appointee.†
When character had thus been perfected, then each individual would have arrived at the position that the Lord Jesus had arrived at when He was ready to be translated into heaven. That is to say, if there had been no Fall and no need for redemption, such an experience would have been the common lot of man — not as something to be dreaded and postponed at all costs, but as something to be striven for and longed for throughout the whole of life. As John Taylor put it:‡

> In the transfiguration of Jesus we see what could have happened, we see the ultimate perfection that God intends for man. No physical deterioration, no rending of the earthly body from the soul, but metamorphosis as smooth as sunrise into the full grown man.

I believe we have tended to miss the real significance of what happened on the Mount of Transfiguration. This is partly because of an unfortunate translation of one word in Hebrews 12:2. The Authorized Version, which I find still the most satisfying version of them all, has these words, "Looking unto Jesus, the author and finisher of our faith, who for the joy that was set before Him endured the cross, des-

---

* Two other men, Enoch and Elijah, seem to have experienced such a translation: but see on this some further discussion at reference #116.

† If man had not fallen, he need not have continued for centuries before translation. He might have matured much more quickly and therefore been translated within only a few centuries or even less. Indeed, the experience of Enoch may be intended to provide us with an illustration of this principle, for he achieved maturity in 365 years only: and this, be it remembered, in a world that had become increasingly wicked, so wicked in fact that within another three generations it was no longer salvageable and had to be destroyed by the Flood.

‡ Taylor, John, *Man in the Midst,* London, Highway Press, 1955, p. 51;

pising the shame . . . ." I imagine that most readers of this verse have assumed that in some way the agony, both spiritual and physical, of the events surrounding the crucifixion were anticipated by the Lord with a strange kind of "joy" because of what He knew that agony would in the end achieve for those He came to save. Perhaps this is true, though I honestly doubt whether it is the truth intended in this passage of Scripture.

Actually, the little word *for* in the phrase "for the joy that was set before Him" is not strictly correct as we now understand it. It really should have been rendered into modern English as "in place of" or "instead of the joy that was set before Him". Even today we use *for* in this sense as when we say "I will give you this for that", where our meaning is clearly *instead of*. Any good Greek lexicon will show at once that this is the meaning of the original,* even though only a few translations have actually observed it. The *Williams New Testament* has "who, *instead of* the joy that was set before Him, endured the cross". Smith and Goodspeed have "who, *in place of* the happiness that belonged to Him, submitted to a cross". There is really little doubt in my mind that these two versions have translated the original correctly.

So here we have "Adam" once again restored to view, perfectly fulfilling the role which man was intended to fulfil and passing into glory without seeing death. But then a deliberate choice was made by the last Adam in obedience to his Father's will, not to follow through with this immediate and wonderful prospect of joy to which He was now perfectly entitled, but to return to earth and sacrifice immortality, embracing death by a deliberate act of will: and not merely embracing death but embracing a shameful death — death on a cross. There were reasons why this particular form of death was ordained in this case which are profoundly important, but they must be left for consideration until later. Suffice it to say at the moment that no other form of capital punishment known then, or since invented, could have provided the necessary setting for the offering of this unique sacrifice.

I believe we are being told here, in Hebrews 12:2, that when the Lord came back down the Mount with the disciples, He had made a deliberate choice whereby, *instead of* the joy that might have been his from that moment on, He set his face to go up to Jerusalem, there to suffer a shameful death.

Until the time of this Mount of Transfiguration experience, we are

---

* For a more extended treatment of this passage in Hebrews 12:2, see reference # 117.

chiefly presented with a demonstration of the potential of human personality as revealed in the Lord Jesus Christ: but from this moment
on we see the cost to the last Adam of the first Adam's failure to
realize the potential he was originally endowed with.

If Adam and his descendants had realized that potential, I imagine
that we would not speak of the dead at all. There would only be those
who had "graduated" and those who were still "undergraduates".
And there is no need to suppose that there would be any separation
between them, any more than there was between the Lord and his disciples after the Resurrection.   John Taylor shows how idyllic such a
fellowship could be:*

> For six weeks of springtime nineteen centuries ago, perfected
> Man was seen and loved on this same earth upon which the unfall-
> en Adam, the germinal Man, had walked . . . . At will He showed
> Himself, at will He was unseen. He consorted with his friends, and
> went for walks, and shared a supper and picnicked by the lake.
> Nothing could have been homelier, nothing more natural. For it
> was *natural:* that is the point.

In such a world, then, man would have lived without dying. The
two worlds, the earthly and the heavenly, would not have been separated by a great gulf fixed. God would have dwelt with men and
walked and talked with them daily as He did in the Garden of Eden
and as He will yet do, according to Revelation 21:3. In such a world
there would have been no parting, and there would have been no last
enemy — death — to break the continuity of fellowship with those we
love.

In short, death is programmed for animals but is an *execution*
where man is concerned.   Death for animals is for the benefit of the
animal world.   Death for man is a catastrophe for both the world of
men and of animals.   Indeed, "the whole creation groaneth and travaileth in pain together until now . . . waiting for the adoption, to wit,
the redemption of our body" (Rom.8:22, 23).

---

* Taylor, John, *Man in the Midst,* London, Highway Press, 1955, p. 54.

Chapter 8

DEATH FOR ANIMALS: PROGRAMMED LIMITATION

Thou takest away their breath,
they die,
and return to the dust.
Psalm 104:29

Who knoweth the spirit of man
that goeth upward,
and the spirit of the beast
that goeth downward to the earth?
Ecclesiastes 3:21

It is sometimes held that when Paul wrote of death entering into the world as a consequence of man's sin (Rom.5:12), he was not speaking only of human death but of all death, the death of animals and man alike. It is argued that prior to the Fall animals did not die, and that, had Adam and Eve not sinned, death among animals would still be unknown. Presumably, plant death is accepted as inevitable since all the animals are seen by these writers as having been originally herbivorous, becoming carnivorous only after the Fall.

Those who hold this view see further confirmation of their view in Romans 8:20-22 which reads:

> For the creation [margin] was made subject to vanity, not willingly but by reason of him who hath subjected the same in hope. Because the creation itself also shall be delivered from the bondage

of corruption into the glorious liberty of the children of God. For
we know that the whole creation groaneth and travaileth in pain
together until now.

Now there are some problems in determining exactly what these
verses mean; among these, the question of the antecedent of *who* in
the phrase "who hath subjected the same in hope", as well as the significance of the words "in hope". For example, was it man or God
who subjected the creation in hope? But in the present context, the
critical phrase is "the whole creation" (verse 22), which is felt to be
clearly a reference to the whole *animate* creation (men and animals
alike). Yet is this the real intent of the passage?

The phrase "the whole creation" is perhaps an unfortunate rendering. The original Greek here *pāsa hē ktisis* (πᾶσα ἡ κτίσις) is found
only in three other places in the New Testament. These are:

Colossians 1:15
(Jesus) who is the image of the invisible God, the firstborn of
all creation *(pasēs ktiseos).*

Colossians 1:23
. . . . and be not moved away from the hope of the Gospel
which ye have heard, and which was preached to every creature *(en
pasē (ta) ktisei)* that is under heaven . . . .

Mark 16:15
And He said unto them, Go ye into all the world, and preach
the Gospel to every creature *(pasē tē ktisei).*

It seems clear enough that the Great Commission of Mark's Gospel
has reference to the human race alone. There is the familiar story of
St. Francis of Assisi preaching to the birds, but I doubt if it is really
the intent of the original that the Gospel is to be preached to animals
as well as to man, commanding them all alike to believe and be saved.
If it is, the command has certainly never been taken seriously by the
overwhelming majority of Christian people. So at least in Mark the
Greek phrase rendered "the whole creation" clearly refers only to
humanity, to human society.

This must surely be equally true of Colossians 1:15, for it would
be absurd to suppose that the Lord is to be called the firstborn of animals and plants. Nor can one suppose that Paul was including the
world of animals in Colossians 1:23.

So it seems clear that the same phrase occurring in Romans 8:22
must be taken to mean only that the whole of mankind has been subjected to dying *as a penalty,* and that the preaching of the Gospel
must accordingly be to all those under condemnation. Death as a
punishment does not seem to apply in the animal kingdom except

possibly in the case of an ox that gores a man (Exod.21:28) and even this is capable of a different interpretation.

It is perhaps pertinent to remind ourselves that death seems such a terrible thing to us largely because we have such a highly developed consciousness of our own existence *as individuals.* We not merely enjoy being alive, as animals most certainly seem to do, but we are very *self*-conscious about this aliveness. We reflect upon our enjoyment consciously: we plan for it deliberately, we seek to enhance it in a hundred different ways that animals never do, and so we develop culture. And normally we try to postpone its termination by every means at our disposal even when we are tired to death of it anyway! In the animal kingdom death is merely the annihilation of the animal: with man death is a violation of his very being, the tearing apart of body and spirit unnaturally. Since the animal does not live in the future, annihilation has no conscious reality for it. It is not anticipated as it is in man. Since man lives in the present *and* the future, the violation done to his person by death becomes a fearful thing. It is in this sense that man lives all his life in the fear of it (Heb.2:15).

Professor Carleton S. Coon rightly observes, "No animal knows that death is inevitable. The gazelle lives from day to day, now and then facing death but each time facing it as a separate event".[118]   It has been observed in Africa that when one animal in a herd is brought down by a lion, the general disturbance of the herd which accompanied the initial chase dies down instantly and the rest of the animals resume browsing with complete indifference to the fate of their poor brother. Even animal parents appear to be comparatively unmoved once they are certain, under natural conditions, that they cannot save their offspring.[119]   There is clearly no sense of individual anticipation whatever, at least not until the threat is immediate. Animals probably never reflect upon the death of others, or on anything else for that matter. Their memory is contingent memory, which is really more recognition than memory in any case. As far as we know, they must be in the presence of familiar things before their familiarity is observed or recognized, whereas we re-create mental images and so reconstitute situations from the past and project them into the future. We live in the future in a way animals probably never do, and the future that we anticipate includes our own decease and, hopefully, renewed existence hereafter. This is what makes us capable of dying many deaths where animals die but one. And they experience that one only when it is too late to reflect upon its consequences for their own individual existence.

Animals can hardly anticipate or fear death much in advance, and therefore it cannot be anything like the dread prospect it tends to be for man for a large part of his life.   It is not foreseen at all except when it is actually upon them.   Indeed, they probably have to experience it before it has any reality, and in experiencing it the reality of it ceases for them!   Moreoever, there is some doubt now, contrary to former opinion, whether the experience of death is accompanied by any suffering.[120] Prior to death they may suffer, but having no anticipation of the meaning of death at least frees them from unnecessary fear of it.   Even a trapped animal, suffering unnatural pain, probably does not foresee that its position is fatal to its life, that it is in *mortal* danger, though it is certainly aware of unnatural restraint upon its freedom.

Perhaps we have viewed the problem of death in creatures below man in an artificial way, anthropomorphically, with the use of too little and too much imagination: too little because we do not enter realistically into the animal's world of experience, and too much because we attribute to the animal mind our own prescience.

As we have already seen, the vast majority of living things suffer death by accident and not as an inevitable consequence of being alive. For such creatures death is unrelated to life per se, it is a hazard not inherent to life but "adherent" to it.   Death is more in the nature of a control external to the processes of life itself, serving in the economy of nature to place checks upon unlimited proliferation, just as the brakes we install on a car can stop the vehicle without really having anything to do with the operation of the engine itself.   The two are separate mechanisms.

Most Christians believe that there were geological ages before man while the earth was being divinely prepared for his creation.   "The testimony of the rocks", to use Hugh Miller's apt phrase, is that fossils of animals which were carnivorous, if we are to judge by their jaw and teeth structure, must have abounded.   The seas particularly seemed to have swarmed with large fishes which lived upon smaller ones, and smaller fishes which lived − in turn − on smaller ones still.   At the bottom of the food chain were, and are, the plankton which occur as both plants and animals and which must surely have experienced death by the million in order that life at higher levels might go on. [121] The whole chain of marine life is virtually inconceivable without the lower links being sacrificed for the higher ones.

Moreoever, fish eggs must surely be considered as being alive, yet in the present economy of nature only two or three codfish eggs, for example, survive to maturity at each spawning out of the millions laid by the parent fish.   Thus the accidental death rate is enormous.   It is sometimes said that the dying or destroyed eggs which do not survive contribute in some way chemically to the survival of the two or three which do reach maturity.   But this only seems to confirm that death is essential to life.   The survival rate of human spermatozoa is probably even lower since there is normally only one survivor (the one that fertilizes the ovum) out of several million forming the initial attacking host.[122]   Before Adam fell, or in an unfallen world, are we to suppose that codfish would only lay two eggs, both of which would survive?   And, indeed, the question might be asked whether the codfish could be allowed to lay any eggs at all after a little while, for the seas would soon become filled to bursting point.   What, otherwise, would prevent overflow?   And would only one spermatozoon be released to unite with the single ovum?   What has been said of codfish has to be said of all animals, including insects whose proliferation can be even more dramatic because of the short breeding cycle.

It therefore seems clearly necessary that death be programmed as a numerical balancing mechanism.   If millions are to be born, millions must die.   It is not at all certain whether death is a built-in limitation for any species, as Hayflick has proposed.[123]   It could be due to the very cricumstances in which the members of any species play their part in the web of life, some roles being more hazardous.   Or perhaps cell differentiation may carry with it some kind of programmed limitation *within* the individual, as the Gershons have recently proposed.[124] Possibly all three factors are at work governing the multiplication rate of any species and holding it in check as part of the natural balance to be seen everywhere, except where man interferes.

And there may be good reason for the need of death among animals apart from the danger of over-population.   The potential for variation of many species is important in relation to the part which that species will play in different areas of the world where foods, climatic conditions, altitude, temperature, etc., are different enough to require a modification of its form in order for it to meet the new exigencies of its habitat as it spreads or when the environment changes locally for geophysical reasons.   Every species seems to be able to respond to new environmental conditions when necessary with remarkable rapidity, and to adapt (within species specific limits) both its structural form and patterns of instinctive behaviour.   We see this in response to temperature, for example, where limbs are shortened to conserve heat, where body shapes are elongated to dissipate heat, where fur covering density is adjusted, where protective colouring is modified, and where even home building patterns are altered as the supply of raw material is changed.   But such adaptive responses occurring in any new generation have a much better chance of succeeding in future generations if the older generation dies off and thus clears the way for the new to take over entirely.   The older generation would otherwise constantly be tending to return the divergent form to the old and less viable one, or the better adapted behaviour pattern to the former and less effective one.

This can be illustrated very widely in nature:[125] the potential for variability which is resident in the genes does have definite limits but it enjoys sufficient flexibility that members of a single species can migrate and settle down in remarkably divergent habitats as variant forms of the original. Death thus becomes a benefit to the species. H. J. Muller, while certainly not sharing my views in relation to the purposes of God, underscores this fact when he observes:[126]

> .... death is an advantage to life. Its advantage lies chiefly in its giving ampler opportunity for the genes of the newer generation to have their merits tested out. That is, by clearing the way for fresh starts and new combinations, it prevents the clogging of genetic progress by the older individuals.

So, then, we have death programmed in the animal world for at least two good reasons: to prevent over-population and to open the way for adaptation to altered conditions.

Having said in the first chapter that functioning protoplasm is not subject to death, it may seem contradictory now to speak of built-in or programmed limitations. The point is that such limitations are not *inherent* in functioning protoplasm, even as brakes are not inherent in a car engine. If such limitations did not exist, living things would continue on indefinitely and multiply accordingly. Because numbers would soon be excessive and because the older generation would swamp any newer generations better equipped to fill some particular niche in the economy of nature (assuming both the economy and the animals have changed in some way), some means of limitation must be programmed for the system. This may be done in more than one way.

It may be done externally by the appointment of predators for the reduction of numbers. As we have seen previously, the life span of members of any particular species of animal may be externally limited by the circumstances of their existence. The members of most, if not all, animal species are constantly threatened and the longer they live, the greater are the probabilities of their being killed. If the individual lives "long enough" its death is "certain". The "how long" for any species is in some sense species specific, and this then effectively constitutes the average life span for the members of that species. Professor E. B. Edney and R. W. Gill of the University of California, in an article dealing with specific longevity, speak of this "hazard factor" which "thus sets a limit to longevity even in a population of potentially immortal individuals". They conclude: "If the hazard factor hypothesis is valid, differences in specific longevity in different species are seen primarily as phenomena with ecological aetiology . . . ."[127]

Alternatively, death may simply be the consequence of structural limitations. The insect, lacking a circulatory system, must obtain oxygen for its tissues by transpiration through its "skin". This severely limits the depth at which viable cells can exist below the surface and therefore the overall size of the animal. Any further enlargement starves these cells and the animal dies. No land animal can grow beyond a certain size, for the physical strength of bone and tendon limits the mass which can be successfully manoeuvred. So again, the animal reaches its limiting size and further growth increasingly endangers its existence.[128]

There is another kind of limitation which we have already noted in the case of salmon. The reproductive mechanism is so constituted that once it is set into operation, degenerative changes are initiated in the animal's life support system which bring about its collapse.

In the first case, the animal starves itself for oxygen; in the second, cripples itself by size; and in the third, commits suicide in its determination to reproduce. There are many such limitations placed upon life span in Nature, none of which are inherent in the principle of living tissue itself, only in the particular life style of the individual.

The scientific account of the phenomenon of death in the animal kingdom, to my mind, is not at all unreasonable. It serves to allow for the establishment of new lines of development, and it prevents over-population. Seen in this light, we find no conflict with the fundamental fact that living things are not doomed to death merely as a consequence of being in possession of life. Life and death are, of course, related in the sense that one must be alive in order to be able to die. But life and death are not *causally* related, for billions of living things never do die: they merely divide and go on living — leaving no corpses unless they are "executed".

God has, it seems, programmed the life processes of all creatures which, in the absence of adequate *external* checks, would otherwise proliferate uncontrollably. But this is in no sense a judgment upon them and is not connected, as I see it, with man's Fall. It is a *built-in* check, introduced to ensure that the web of life will be a harmony of inter-acting individuals, each of which makes its due contribution to the well-being of the whole,[129] except where man disrupts it. And here is the real problem for Science, because man, who is seen as the climax of a long progression of evolutionary improvements, seems almost from the very moment of his appearance to have been a disaster from nature's point of view,[130] *the* great disturber, 'the arch-destroyer' of the natural order, as Wood Jones called him.[131] He is the only creature in which something has evidently gone fundamentally wrong and for whom death appears indeed to be some kind of penalty. How *this* has come about, Science is not competent to say.

Chapter 9

THE TRIAL OF MAN: AND THE PRICE OF FAILURE

The Lord God caused a deep sleep to fall upon Adam,
and he slept:
And He took one of the ribs
and closed up the flesh instead thereof;
and the rib which the Lord God had taken from man
made He a woman,
and brought her to the man.
Genesis 2:21, 22

Adam was first formed,
then Eve.
And Adam was not deceived,
but the woman being deceived was in the transgresssion.
1 Timothy 2:13,14

We come now to an analysis of the events in Eden. Brief as the record is, these events had tremendous consequences for the subsequent history of man. The biblical record is deceiving in its simplicity. It could be said that the words are for children: but the thoughts are for men.

The first of these events is the physical separation of Eve out of Adam, signifying a profound difference between the origin of Adam and the origin of Eve. Anyone who tries to account for the origin of man in a naturalistic way while professing to have respect for the biblical record finds himself in difficulty at this point.

The unique formation of Eve played a part of crucial importance in making possible man's redemption.   It is difficult to deal with this first event without anticipating some of the data to be examined later. Nevertheless, it will be necessary to speak briefly about certain aspects of this data because the separation of Eve out of Adam brought about a radical change in the functioning of Adam's body.   And by reasoning backwards we soon discover that Adam's constitution at first must have been such that an evolutionary origin of his body is virtually out of the question.

It is often argued by those who have addressed the problem of the origin of man that one ought at least to allow the evolution of his *body*.   The uniqueness of our first parent would then lie in the possession of a soul or spirit which was created in the image of God.   There are a number of Roman Catholic theologians who take this position and apparently have the formal approval of their superiors.*   Not a few evangelical writers with a background in biology also adopt essentially the same position.

But this form of solution to the conflict between evolutionary claims and the biblical account is not really satisfactory because it does not explain how Adam could have been so structured physiologically that Eve could be taken out of him in the literal sense that Genesis 2:21 implies.   The King James Version reads: "(The Lord God) took one of his 'ribs' † and closed up the flesh instead thereof"; and the implication of a physical separation is reinforced by Adam's words in verse 23: "This is now bone of my bones and flesh of my flesh".

Eve's *body* was clearly derived from Adam's *body,* and in this surgical process the two genders were separated and sexual dimorphism *in man* was initiated. In the original, the two sexes must therefore have in some way been fused. That is to say, Adam was at first androgynous, male and female in form and function, and in temperament.

A compound of two chemical elements has properties that neither component has in itself.   So the compound of maleness and femaleness was expressed in Adam in a form which neither a male nor a female can ever exhibit individually.   Nor is it exhibited when maleness *and* femaleness (in some kind of aberrant form) occurs in a single individual. *It was something unlike anything we know today.*

---

* In the encyclical *Humani Generis*, [1950, paragraph 36], of Pope Pius XII, such an alternative to the direct creation of Adam's body was given official sanction.   The doctrine of evolution is left an open question provided that speculation is confined to the development only of Adam's *body*.

† The Hebrew word is not limited to the idea of a *rib*. See further on this, page 196.

It would therefore be a grave mistake to suppose that where, by accident of birth, both sexes find a measure of expression today in a particular individual that such an individual is approaching the original Adamic model.   Such congenital departures from the normal are, in a manner of speaking, in violation of what is implied in Genesis 2:21-24, a fact which bears witness to the long-range effects of the Fall.

Adam's body, as created, was made in the image of God in whom is neither maleness nor femaleness but something out of which maleness and femaleness could be separated in one of his creatures made in his image.   In this respect it is perfectly in keeping with his Being that God can therefore act and speak of Himself in the role of Father (1 Chron.29:10; Isa.9:6; 64:8) and Mother (Isa.49:15; 66:13; and by implication Matt.23:37) without confusion.   This "something", this *tertium quid,* of which we can have no accurate picture because it is entirely beyond our present experience, made deity entirely self-sufficient.   Such self-sufficiency is proper in God Himself, but in man such self-sufficiency appears to have been improper and was therefore not allowed to continue.   Genesis 2:18 may well have a more profound significance than merely of being alone.   I suggest that it is not a question of whether a man should *be* a bachelor or whether a woman should *be* a spinster but rather that neither a man nor a woman should be so self-sufficient as to feel no sense whatever of an incompleteness. We are in our relationships.

In short, it is difficult — if not impossible — to view the formation of Eve out of Adam without being driven to the conclusion that in Adam both principles (maleness and femaleness) were resident in something analogous to what we call androgynous form.   The biblical record has been so understood by both Jewish and Christian commentators alike, and classical tradition (as we shall see subsequently) reflected the same view though in sadly corrupted form.

We hope to be able to show that a literal reading of this account can lead to some surprisingly fruitful lines of enquiry — involving miracle, it is true, but miracle with an entirely intelligible objective.   The rationale can be taken apart piece by piece, as it were, and examined in depth.   And it will be found, if we take the text in complete seriousness, that a great deal of light is shed upon the constitution of Adam as created; on the purpose of the surgical operation involved in the formation of Eve; on the special significance of the "seed of the woman" as opposed to the seed of the man; on the differential effect of the poison from the forbidden fruit on Adam's body and on Eve's body; on the profound significance, in the course of time, of the Virgin Conception (the birth itself was surely natural enough) in relation to the vicarious death of the Lord Jesus Christ; and, in the present context, on the origin of death itself in human experience.

The sections of the biblical account with which we are here particularly concerned are as follows:

Genesis 2:18-25
And the Lord God said, "It is not good that the man should be alone; I will make him an help fit for him".

And out of the ground the Lord God formed every beast of the field, and every fowl of the air; and brought them unto Adam to see what he would call them: and whatsoever Adam called every living creature, that was the name thereof. And Adam gave names to all cattle, and to the fowl of the air, and to every beast of the field: but for Adam there was not found an help fit for him.

And the Lord God caused a deep sleep to fall upon Adam, and he slept: and he took one of his ribs, and closed up the flesh instead thereof; and the rib, which the Lord God had taken from man, made he a woman, and brought her unto the man.

And Adam said, "This is now bone of my bones, and flesh of my flesh; she shall be called Woman, because she was taken out of Man".

Therefore shall a man leave his father and his mother, and shall cleave unto his wife; and they shall be one flesh. And they were both naked, the man and his wife, and were not ashamed.

Romans 5:12-14
Wherefore, as by one man sin entered into the world, and death by sin, and so death passed upon all men, for all have sinned. (For until the law, sin was in the world; but sin is not imputed when there is no law. Nevertheless, death reigned from Adam to Moses, even over them that had not sinned after the similitude of Adam's transgression, who is a figure of him that was to come).

1 Corinthians 15:21-22
For since by man came death, by man came also the resurrection of the dead. For as in Adam all die, even so in Christ shall all be made alive.

Now it is widely acknowledged that in the animal world below man, creatures which multiply asexually, in which there is no true maleness or femaleness, enjoy a potential immortality on this account. It is held that when, in the course of evolution, sexual dimorphism appeared, this potential immortality had to be surrendered. Comte du Nouy expressed it this way:[132]

If several methods of asexual reproduction are known in plants and animals, it is evident that these processes reproduce indefinitely the same characters. The cell or organism separates into two individuals who live, grow, and in their turn, each separate into two others.

They never die except accidentally. They go on untiringly doubling their numbers according to their specific rhythm, so that if it were not checked by a more general or direct phenomenon [predation, ACC], they would soon smother the earth under their mass.

Asexual cells do not know death as individuals.   They are immortal.   All of a sudden, with sexual generation, we see the appearance of an entirely new and unforeseen phenomenon: the birth and death of the individual.

There is some doubt, however, about this because — as we have already noted — it is not at all certain that fishes, for example, though they reproduce sexually, are actually subject to natural death and have thereby surrendered their potential immortality. Although some, like salmon for instance, do die simply as part of the consequence of sexual reproduction.

However, we know from Genesis that Adam and Eve did not immediately surrender their immortality even though they were divided as to sex.   Death was still only a threat in the event of their being disobedient.   Thus Adam, as created, and then Adam and Eve as separated but unfallen, must have been differently constituted from other higher forms of life which shared their world.

Even yet, in spite of the long continued inheritance of the effects of the forbidden fruit on our bodies we still cannot detect precisely where the critical differences lie between the workings of the human body and the workings of the bodies of primates like man, but it would be a mistake to assume that such fundamental differences do not exist.   Adam and Eve as male and female were uniquely constituted by a surgical operation, which does not seem to have applied in the formation of any other species. It may well be that we simply do not have the appropriately designed tools of research to identify these differences, though differences *do* turn up in the laboratory where they were previously quite unexpected.[133]   Or it may be that we are not asking the right questions.

At any rate, there are excellent reasons for the creation of Adam with both seeds housed in his own body, and for the subsequent housing of the female seed and reproductive organs (including the ovaries) in a body that was distinct from his own both in form and function though *originally derived from it*. These reasons bear directly on the events immediately subsequent to the eating of the forbidden fruit, for the mortogenic poison which entered Adam's body and Eve's body had a similar effect on both of them in depriving them of their potential immortality.   But it appears to have had a significantly *different* effect upon their seed, upon what Auguste Weismann termed their *germ plasm*.   It is the latter circumstance which formed such an essential starting point in the chain of events by which man's redemption was put into effect.   For here we are dealing with the physiological background of the virgin conception of the Lord Jesus Christ.   It was only thus that He could be made after the power of "endless life" (Heb.7:16) by reason of which He could offer Himself vicariously in order that we might be reconciled to God (Col.1:22). And only thus by his bodily resurrection *without corruption* are we justified in God's sight (Acts 13:37-39).

We rightly think of the goal of redemption as being a spiritual one, but manifestly three of the prerequisites of the Plan — the virgin conception, vicarious death, and bodily resurrection without corruption — are all "hard facts" within the realm of physiology. The saving of man's soul is not completed without also the saving of his body: and the very fact of the Incarnation, when God was manifested *in the flesh,* underscores the important role which the body plays in the concept of the whole person.   Man is not a spirit only, but a body/spirit entity. Hence, as Redeemer, the Lord did not take upon Himself the nature of angels who are pure spirit, but was made for a little while lower than the angels for the suffering of death (Heb.2:9).

Luther was very clear on this point.   He says that the Saviour in order to suffer death, had to be incarnated, embodied, made man, for God (being pure spirit) cannot die, even as the angels cannot die — as we understand death.   Embodiment is a prerequisite to physical death and if we are to be saved by substitutional death, it must be substitutional *physical* death — and this required incarnation.   Luther's words as given in the *Formula of Concord* (Art. VIII, § 44) are: *Non enim in sua natura Deus mori potest.   Postquam autem Deus et homo unitus est in una persona, recte et vere dicitur: Deus mortuus est, quando videlicet ille homo moritur, qui cum Deo unum quiddam, seu una persona est.*   Translated literally this is: "For God is not able to die by his very nature.   However, after God and man were united in one person, rightly and truly is it said: God has died, when it is clear that he died a man, who so to speak is one with God, at least is one person [i.e., one with God] ".

The part which the Lord's *body* played in the redemption of man is sometimes lost sight of.   Consider the following verses:

Colossians 1:21, 22
".... reconciled in the *body* of his flesh through death".

Hebrews 10:10
".... sanctified through the offering of the *body* of Christ".

Hebrews 10:19
".... boldness to enter into the holiest by .... his *flesh*".

1 Peter 2:24
"He bore our sins in his own *body*".

Colossians 2:9
"In Him dwelleth all the fulness of the Godhead *bodily*".

The hope of bodily resurrection is not a sop to our materialism but an assurance of our real survival as persons.   The Lord Jesus sacrificed his whole Person for us, body and spirit; this is why the Incarnation, the embodiment of God, was absolutely essential for man's redemption.   The very first step towards this embodiment, the Incarnation, was the creation of Adam's body in such a form that Eve could be taken out of him as Genesis 2:21-23 reveals.

The second event of tremendous consequence in Eden was the temptation of Eve, followed by the very different temptation of Adam.   It was not Eve's failure but Adam's that resulted in the introduction of physical death into human experience. "By one man", not by one *woman*, nor even by one *pair,* death entered and passed by natural generation upon all men (Rom.5:12).   As we shall see, the reasons for this unexpected situation lie in the internal structural differences between the man's body and the woman's.   The language of both Romans 5:12 and 1 Corinthians 15:21-22 is precise and is surely to be taken to mean exactly what it says.

Consider, then, the circumstances surrounding this fatal test of Eve and of Adam in the Garden of Eden.   The actual record as we have it in several contributing passages of Scripture is as follows:

Genesis 3:1-13
Now the serpent had become more subtle than any beast of the field which the Lord God had made. And he said unto the woman: "Yea, hath God said, Ye shall not eat of every tree of the garden?" And the woman said unto the serpent: "We may eat of the fruit of the trees of the garden; but of the fruit of the tree which is in the midst of the garden, God hath said, Ye shall not eat of it, neither shall ye touch it, lest ye die".   And the serpent said unto the woman: "Ye shall not surely die. For God doth know that in the day ye eat thereof, then your eyes shall be opened, and ye shall be as gods, knowing good and evil".

And when the woman saw that the tree was good for food, and that it was pleasant to the eyes, and a tree to be desired to make one wise, she took of the fruit thereof, and did eat, and gave also unto her husband with her; and he did eat.
And the eyes of them both were opened, and they knew that they were naked; and sewed fig leaves together, and made themselves aprons.   And they heard the voice of the Lord God walking in the garden in the cool of the day: and Adam and his wife hid themselves from the presence of the Lord God among the trees of the garden.

And the Lord God called unto Adam, and said unto him: "Where art thou?"   And he said, "I heard thy voice in the garden, and I was afraid, because I was naked; and I hid myself".
And He said: "Who told thee that thou wast naked? Hast thou

eaten of the tree, whereof I commanded thee that thou shouldest
not eat?"   And the man said: "The woman whom thou gavest to
be with me, she gave me of the tree, and I did eat."
      And the Lord God said unto the woman: "What is this that
thou hast done?"   And the woman said: "The serpent beguiled
me and I did eat."

1 Timothy 2:13-14
      For Adam was first formed, then Eve.
      And Adam was not deceived, but the woman, being deceived,
was in the transgression.

I believe we should accept the fact that the forbidden fruit was a
real fruit, even as the Tree of Life was a real tree with leaves having
therapeutic value.   That both trees may also be used symbolically to
teach us spiritual truths is not in question.   But in this study it is the
actual trees in their physical character that we are examining.   By
gathering all the explicit and implicit information available from the
bibilical account we appear to have a situation in the temptation of
Eve and of Adam — in that order — which was far more complex than
the childish stealing of a forbidden fruit as traditionally presented.
      Consider the circumstances.   Scripture, it seems to me, has gone
out of its way to make it perfectly clear that Adam really was entirely
alone in the world.   First of all, it is apparent that although he was in
a real sense complete in himself, God evidently considered that this
kind of self-sufficiency was not a good thing.   Perhaps even in a state
of perfection Adam needed some fundamental human *inter-dependence* in order to develop his character.   As a potential companion,
God may have brought to him certain of the creatures which man has
since domesticated and whose company he has learned to enjoy as
pets.   In his fallen state, man can now often find solace in the 'companionship' of a dog or a horse — or even of a bird or a cat.   In his
unfallen state such creatures were inadequate companions. Certainly
God knew this of course: but perhaps He wanted Adam to discover it
for himself.   To none of these creatures which came to him by divine
impulse (Gen.2:19, 20) did Adam respond in such a way as to indicate
their sufficiency as true companions or mates.   His response was revealed by the names which he gave them.   He did not assign his own
name to any of them as a groom now assigns his name to his wife.
      So God performed an operation isolating part of Adam and con-
stituting that part into a new whole which, when brought to him, he
at once identified as the companion he had not found among the other
animals.   Accordingly, he named her "Woman", which is a translation
of the Hebrew word *Ishah* (אִשָּׁה).   And *Ishah* is the feminine form of
the word *Ish* (אִישׁ) which means *man*, the name by which he himself
was called.   Surely he must have loved her at once, for she was literal-

ly part of himself.

Without sin, radiant in health, and beautiful as only God could make her in the full perfection and maturity of womanhood, she must have returned his love. In the truest possible sense they were verily made for each other. Each completed for the other the cup of happiness in their idyllic garden home. Without doubt, her presence became as essential to his own fulfillment as his presence was to hers. And thus, in their earthly paradise, Adam and Eve passed cloudless days (because sinless) in fellowship and open communion with God,* with neither fear nor shame, and with complete freedom to do whatever they willed and to eat whatever they desired of the fruits of the garden, except one tree which was forbidden them.

And then Satan put Eve to the test. Whether Satan used a serpent as an agent by controlling its behaviour from without, or whether he indwelt a serpent (as the legion of demons indwelt the Gadarene swine, Luke 8:32, 33) or whether he assumed a serpent form, we cannot tell precisely from the record. Indeed, the word rendered *serpent* may not even mean a serpent at all.† But one could well imagine such a creature reaching up into the forbidden tree in Eve's presence and there eating its fruit with complete confidence and manifest enjoyment — and, to her amazement perhaps, with apparent impunity. Possibly the thought came to Eve that if other creatures could eat of the fruit with safety, why could not she? It is a common practice of country people in all ages to be guided in their choice of safe foods by observing what animals can safely eat. Why should the same thought not have occurred to Eve?

Yet the serpent may well have actually spoken to Eve in some language clear to her understanding, as Balaam was spoken to by his ass (Num.22:27-32). Or was it that Eve was really speaking to herself? Perhaps when doubts arose in her mind, the satan-inspired creature reassured her by deliberately returning to the tree sometime later and

---

* It has no historical value, but it is interesting that in an apocryphal book known only from an early Slavonic manuscript titled *The Secrets of Enoch* (Chapter XXXII, 3) the unknown author states that "Adam was five and a half hours in paradise"! The same view appears in several of the *Adam Books*. In the *Book of Jubilees* the life in Paradise is said to have lasted seven years: so also Syncellus taught. Josephus puts its duration as at least several days (cf. John Damasc., *De. orth. fide*, II. 10; Augustine, *De Civit.* XX. 26; Gregory (Great), *Dial.* IV. 1). These authorities are followed by Pererius and Ussher. R. Ammi (*Beresh. Rabba* II), Irenaeus, Ephrem, Epiphanius, and some scholastics fix upon one day as its limit. Eusebius (*Chron.* I. 16, 4, ed. Mai) said no one could tell anything about it! He was probably the most correct . . . .

† The Hebrew original *nachash*, which Driver suggests is onomatopoeic (= the word *hiss*) is of uncertain root but might possibly be related to the word for *bronze*, or even to a verbal root connected with divination.

taking the fruit a second or a third time, until in her own mind she came to doubt that there were any fatal consequences involved. And yet, her intuition persisted in warning her that she should neither eat the fruit *nor even touch it*. To touch was to take. In the end she was deceived as the New Testament tells us (1 Tim.2:14) and, having plucked the fruit from the tree, she tasted it and found it to be all she had anticipated, not only beautiful to look at but good to the taste and in some unexpected way enlightening to the mind . . . . as some modern drugs are.

But now a subtle change took place in her body, for she had unknowingly introduced a fatal poison. Even when she went back to Adam and invited him to share her experience, she still apparently had no real comprehension of what had happened to herself. And here we come to the crux of the story. For while Eve was, in one sense, as innocent as a child who has disobeyed but is not sure exactly in what way, Adam was not deceived at all. In a moment he realized that he was once again completely alone, but now it was an aloneness of a different kind, for he had lost his other self, his love, his sole human companion in the whole wide world. Part of him was missing.

We know that he was alone in this sense, for Eve *became* (Heb.) the mother of all living (Gen.3:20). There was no other woman who might have taken her place. She stood before him; yet she stood completely apart from him. They belonged to different kingdoms. Adam knew it at once, and in that moment he faced a trial surely more heart-rending than has ever been the lot of any man since who is called upon to surrender his dearest possession. For while many other men have made such a sacrifice for one reason or another (millions were forced to do so by the Nazis), Adam could never — for all he knew — expect to recover a helpmeet again. There *was* no other woman in the world . . . . Nor was there any other man who, placed in similar circumstances, might have shared the burden of loss with him. For a little while he had been alone before in his unidivided state as he came from the hand of his Creator but very probably without any awareness of loneliness as he now felt it in his divided self. He had to face the prospect of an aloneness made acute because of what he had experienced and what he had now lost. And for all he could see, this loss was for ever. Adam was still immortal: but for Eve a subtle change had already begun and she was, as God had said she would be, from that very day a dying creature. Here lay the gulf between them: a mortal creature could not be a proper companion to a still immortal one.

Thus God, who overrules all human history, had allowed the first man to be brought into a position of trial, the severity of which is far beyond our true comprehension. Adam was faced with a choice that was quite literally a matter of life and death for him. And it had all been brought about by the eating of the fruit of a forbidden tree.

In the Hebrew original, at verse 6. there is a small mark which in-dicates a pause after the words "and gave also unto her husband with her" and before the words "and he did eat". The little 'mark' in the Hebrew text at the word which is translated into English "with her", is called a *Tiphkha*. Every Hebrew sentence is given certain accents to guide the reader as to the appropriate emphasis, and some of these are called 'separation' marks. They are somewhat analogous to our comma, colon, and so forth. The strongest separation mark in a Heb-rew sentence is called a *Silluq*. It marks the end of a sentence, and usually in translation also marks the end of a verse. The strongest separation mark *within* the sentence, and therefore standing for a pause by way of emphasis, is called a *Tiphkha*. It is this little mark that tells us there is to be a pause after the words "with her".

It might be thought that this was hanging too much weight on so small a thread. But I think it is necessary to bear in mind that when a literary work is characterized by extreme simplicity and brevity, as Genesis is, and when the circumstances are of tremendous significance in human history, it is important to observe all the clues that the writer has given as to his intention.

Adam was about to make a choice which was to affect profoundly all subsequent generations. If he joined Eve, he was settling once for all the question of whether mankind would retain the potential im-mortality which God had provided for. When he followed his wife and ate the fatal fruit, *he*, not she (as we shall show), introduced death into human experience. Death entered by one man and passed upon all men so that every one of us now lives out his whole life under the shadow of a sentence of death. This was the consequence of Adam's decision.

There is no knowing what might have been the course of history had Eve been allowed to go out of the Garden alone, for ever separat-ed from Adam. We know from Genesis 4:1 that Eve was not pregnant at this time since Adam did not "know" her until sometime later. Such a separation would therefore seem to bring an end to the human race in terms of further multiplication, unless we suppose that God might have allowed Adam to go with her into exile even though he had not disobeyed. Their children would still have been immortal in such a case, for the seed of the man was still uncorrupted and the seed of the woman had been protected *against* corruption. Though she herself would die, since she had fatally poisoned her own body, yet Adam and her children would still have retained their potential im-mortality — for we know that the fatal poison is not transmitted through or in the woman's seed, and the seed of Adam still unfallen would in such a circumstance have retained its purity also.   But it seems most unlikely that God would have permitted Adam to leave the Garden, and the hypothesis has very little validity: but it is an interesting one to contemplate.

Adam cannot perhaps have anticipated all the profound consequences of his action, but we should not underestimate the perceptive powers of the human mind untouched by any poison and perfect as God created it.   As Rev. J. B. Heard rightly observed, even Aristotle was "but the rubbish of an Adam".*

I cannot imagine Adam simply agreeing to follow Eve's unhappy choice, blithely and without thought.   We know in fact that he was not deceived (1 Tim.2:14).   He must surely have known at least something of what the consequences would be.   When he decided to eat the fruit, he must have done so only after pondering the matter deeply. It must have been an agonizing decision to make.

He was faced with a choice, the choice of staying in the Garden and living for ever in complete and daily fellowship with God, in perfect health and sinless — *but without Eve.*   Or he could surrender his immortality and his innocence, and his sojourn in the Garden and his daily sense of the Lord's fellowship — but preserve the companionship of his love, the woman whom God Himself had "given to be with him". And who can tell but that his own awareness of the reality of the situation may have communicated itself to Eve.   Would she not appeal to him not to desert her?   How *could* he contemplate a separation on such terms as these which would leave *him* in the sunshine of Eden and God's presence, while exiling her to the unknown world outside the Garden.   I do not think we can really grasp the situation that Adam found himself in, because wherever we go we are likely to find people.   Adam and Eve were entirely alone in the world.

This, then, was the situation.   Can one imagine what must have been Adam's thoughts as he contemplated the sending forth of his beautiful help-meet out of the Garden into an entirely unknown and supposedly uninhabited world — while he remained within the Garden? And can we imagine what Adam's thoughts would be as he looked into the future and saw his beloved lying somewhere "out there" dying alone and unattended, in her aged condition?   There can be little doubt that he perceived at least something of what such a future could mean both for her and for himself.

It does not, of course, lessen his disobedience to realize at what a cost obedience would seem to have been demanded of him.   But it surely underscores the fact that those who thoughtlessly scoff at the

---

* Heard, J. B., *The Tripartite Nature of Man*, Edinburgh, T. & T. Clark, 1868, p. 163.

idea of a temptation story so childishly linked to a forbidden fruit have, by their refusal to take the record seriously, *entirely* failed to see how actuely was Adam being tried, and how by a completely reasonable series of circumstances his trial had been allowed to come about. Surely this is why we are told that Adam was not decieved and why it is indicated by the punctuation that he only ate the fruit after deliberation, and why, when faced with his disobedience, he (not altogether without an element of tragic truth) reminded God that He had "given" the woman to be with him as his companion (Gen.3:12).

Thus it came about that, like Socrates, he deliberately poisoned himself. He made his choice and surrendered his immortality because he preferred the company of Eve to that of the Lord.

I make no apology for the literalism which marks every aspect of my exegesis. I only regret that I have not the dramatic skill to paint a more accurate picture.   After some forty years of study and I am entirely convinced that the biblical account is a faithful record of what really happened.   In so far as Archaeology has confirmed the biblical account of history, it has always favoured a literalist interpretation over an allegorical one. Wherever archaeological confirmation is available, it consistently lends credence to the biblical record in its historical detail — not merely in its general tenor or broad implications, though it has done this too! We do not have archeological confirmation yet of the events in Eden in the sense that we do have confirmation of later events, but we seem to be getting another kind of confirmation now, namely, confirmation from studies in anatomy and physiology and, in less direct ways, from psychology also.

Let me re-state as succinctly as I can, even at the risk of being tiresome, what I think was really involved.   So much hinges upon what took place at the very beginning.   God, in his creative wisdom, set the stage for the working out of man's redemption, the redemption of his body as well as his spirit, by first creating an Adam who was potentially immortal and who encompassed within himself both seeds, male and female, containing within a single organism the mechanism for the production of both spermatozoa and ova.   We still have evidence in the human body to justify such an interpretation of the record, as will be amply demonstrated later.

The Lord then separated Eve out of Adam and entrusted to her one of the two seeds and the related reproductive mechanism, fashioning her body in a special way to preserve that seed uncorrupted even if she should poison herself with the forbidden fruit.   Her *body* was poisoned, like Adam's: but unlike Adam's seed, her *seed* (as we shall show) apparently remained untouched.   Thus although Genesis 3:6 affirms that Eve was in the transgression first, *her* ingestion of the forbidden fruit was not responsible for introducing death to the human race.   Adam's partaking of the forbidden fruit not only poisoned his own body but affected his seed also, and through his seed was transmitted to the human race our mortal condition.   It was *by one MAN* that death entered and passed upon all men.   It is when the seed of the woman is fertilized by the male seed that the fatal poison is transmitted to the next generation.   Via the man's seed came death (1 Cor. 15:21); via the seed of the woman was to come life.   It is literally true that *in Adam* all men die, as it is true that in Christ, who was both the Second Adam and the seed of the woman, all shall be made alive (1 Cor.15:22).

Abraham Kuyper stated this succinctly and in such a way as to demonstrate clearly that he took this biblical record as sober history. He wrote:*

> Death in connection with man's eating of the tree of knowledge can be understood in a twofold way: either as a punishment that was threatened, or as a result that would follow therefrom.   If death is fixed as the punishment of high treason this must be understood as a threat, for one does not die inevitably of high treason. But when I say, "Do not take of that Paris Green, for if you do you shall die", there is no question of punishment: all that is expressed is that this poison is fatal in its effect, and that one who takes the poison must die.
>
> In the last instance, I may, if one should, contrary to my warning take the poison nevertheless, make an attempt to counteract the deadly effect of the poison by the application of an antidote to make the patient vomit.   Then I certainly spake fully in accordance with truth: "When you take the poison, you shall die", and I do not at all come into conflict with myself when afterwards I make an attempt to save the reckless one that took the poison.   If this is clear, then it must also be admitted that the words: "If you eat of the tree of knowledge, you will surely die", are explained in their full implication when I understand them as implying nothing else than the declaration, the warning: "Know this, that when you permit yourself to be tempted to eat of that tree, you will see that death will be the result".

Here, then, is how physical death originated for man.   It was imposed upon him as a penalty for disobedience but it was a merciful imposition nevertheless.   Man had to be tested, and he had to be tested in a context which was meaningful for him.   The very simplicity of

---

* Kuyper, Abraham, *De Gemeene Gratie,* Vol. I, p. 209 ff; tr. by and quoted by Herman Hoeksema, *The Triple Knowledge,* Grand Rapids, Reformed Free Publ. Assoc., 1970, Vol. 1, p. 136.   It should be mentioned in fairness to Hoeksema that he expresses entire disagreement with Kuyper's interpretation of these events.

the test itself bears the stamp of truth and of the genius of God. His act of disobedience and the poison which he introduced into his body together ruined human nature and made it unsafe for man to continue alive indefinitely: and thus the same poison was made the agent for the termination of his life. It was an act of judgment that was also an act of mercy.

What kind of a poison could this have been?

Chapter 10

TOWARDS THE IDENTITY OF THE FORBIDDEN FRUIT:
(1) ACCORDING TO TRADITION

Hast thou eaten of the tree,
whereof I commanded thee that
thou shouldest not eat?
Genesis 3:11

In the sweat of thy face shalt thou eat bread,
till thou return unto the ground;
for out of it wast thou taken:
for dust thou art,
and unto dust shalt thou return.
Genesis 3:19

I do not really think that we shall ever be allowed to identify the poison with any certainty, for that would be to invite a search for an antidote. With our present sophisticated techniques of investigation, we might succeed! And my feeling is that the Lord would never allow such a thing to happen, because the consequences for man would be much the same as having allowed access to the Tree of Life which in the circumstances would have been worse than death.

Our minds being what they are, however, it is difficult not to find ourselves wondering whether a single poison really could be responsible for the sorry plight in which man now finds himself both physically and spiritually, and whether such a poison could be derived from the mere eating of some particular fruit that was: (1) good for food,

(2) pleasant in appearance, (3) in some way desirable to make one wise (possibly enhancing perception), as Genesis 3:6 tells us.

I think it is not altogether impossible that the royal physician to Henry II of France, Dr. Jean Fernel, was correct in his belief that if the plants and herbs of the world were examined with sufficient thoroughness, we would find a remedy "for each and every human illness that exists".[134] Whether he really meant that some single remedy would ultimately be found for all sicknesses alike is not clear, but I have the impression that this was in the back of his mind. A single cure implies a single cause at the first.

Nearly a century ago, J. Cynddylan Jones suggested that "in the leaves of the Tree of Life was medicine for all forms of sickness".* He said, "Today, healing virtues are distributed in hundreds of plants, specific plants being remedies for specific diseases; but in the Tree of Life were probably concentrated the medicinal virtues of all the vegetable creation, and special virtues of its own in addition, and thus it was a universal panacea against all the evils of sickness".

Even now we have some remedies (aspirin, for example) that have an extraordinarily wide application against all kinds of ills, which therefore certainly demonstrate that a single substance can be effective against a very broad range of common human ailments. Thus, it is not so entirely unreasonable to assume that at the very root of all human sickness there might lie some single basic defect in the body responsible for all other ills. If ever some plant extract should be found which could supply the single antidote, we should probably find, in effect, that we had discovered the identity of the Tree of Life.

It will be well to set forth the characteristics that the poison in this fruit must have had in order to cause the effects which Genesis seems to indicate it did. These are as follows:

> (a) It must be a protoplasmic poison, a poison that ultimately causes the death of cells, and therefore the death of the body.

> (b) It must have a more immediate short range effect, such that a perceptive individual would very quickly observe its effects in others or in himself. It might be expected that the effect would in some way heighten awareness of one's own body.

> (c) It must be obtainable from a fruit that is otherwise good for food and pleasant to look at.

> (d) It must produce an effect that is inheritable. If I am inter-

* Jones, J. C., *Primeval Revelation: Studies in Genesis I—VIII*, London, Hodder & Stoughton, 1897, p. 210.

preting the circumstances in Genesis correctly, the inheritable effect should be male sex-linked.

(e) It must have a detrimental effect not merely on the body but also on behaviour, contributing as a consequence to man's moral, not simply to his physical, deterioration.

(f) It must be potent in very small quantities, and ought to be capable of being neutralized in its physical effects but not in its moral effects, by some plant extract such as might have been derived from the Tree of Life.

There are two other considerations which it ought to satisfy. We should expect to find shadowy recollections of its characteristics reflected in the traditions of antiquity. And we should expect to find intimations of its identity in other parts of Scripture.

Having set forth these specifications, it may occur at once to a thoughtful reader that alcohol satisfies the requirements. It is very tempting to make this equation. Tradition, what we know of the aetiology of alcoholism, and the intimations in Scripture, all combine to reinforce this conclusion. Yet, personally, I doubt whether it was actually alcohol, at least not the common ethyl alcohol. Perhaps it was one of the higher alcohols which are far more potent. But I do believe that alcohol provides the most complete *paradigm* of the poison of which we currently have knowledge, and I believe that grapes as the source of the poison provide the best paradigm of the forbidden fruit.

It is important to underscore the fact that a paradigm is not to be taken as the thing itself but only as a useful parallel. I want to emphasize this, because I have some doubts whether grapes or their by-product (ethyl alcohol) *as we now know them*, are precisely to be equated with the forbidden fruit or with the poison it was capable of generating. My reasons for saying this are chiefly that I have not yet been able to satisfy myself completely about certain statements in Scripture which it seems to me could hardly have been made (approving the use of wine and of grapes) if the latter really were the original forbidden fruit which has caused all our ills.

The most serious of errors often arise by assuming as identical, things which merely correspond in obvious ways. The more nearly things are similar without being identical, the greater may be the danger of equating them. The more nearly a lie approaches the truth, the more dangerous it can be. So I should like to repeat that I do not yet believe that grapes, as we now have them, were the forbidden fruit or that alcohol was really the poison which introduced death to the human race — though I believe they may come remarkably close to it.

Thus we can usefully discuss the reality of that crucial event with some such fruit or by-product as a model, because it is close enough in

many remarkable ways to assist our imagination, and it assuredly demonstrates that such a situation could indeed have existed with precisely
the consequences to Adam and to Eve and to their descendants which
the Genesis record clearly indicates.

Having due regard, then, to the above cautionary observations,
consider first the following gleanings from the literature of antiquity
both pagan and Jewish; and then (in Chapter 11) some observations
regarding what is known about alcohol and the aetiology of alcoholism as a disease.   Following this (in Chapter 12), we will examine
certain intimations in Scripture which are interestingly illuminated if
we assume that the fatal poison shared many of the characteristics of
alcohol in its effect on both the body and the spirit of man.

Many of the nations of antiquity have traditions of the Fall of man
and relate the event in one way or another to the eating of a food or
the drinking of a fruit extract.   These traditions sometimes confuse
the circumstances by assuming that what the tempter said was actually
true; that the Tree of Knowledge was a tree whose fruit brought not
only benefit to the eater in the form of a superior kind of wisdom
(which in a sense it *did*) but also a higher kind of life (immortality
like that of the gods).[135]   Sometimes they state categorically that the
offending substance was the juice of a fruit or an extract like the sap
from a tree, and that it poisoned the body.   Some of them clearly indicate that the result was inebriation, but they attach to this a kind of
benefit in that the individual then transcends the ordinary limitations
of human experience and enters into special communion with the gods.
In some cases the plant or tree is identified by name, though the
precise nomenclature of the original is not always clear in modern
terminology.

The earliest of such non-biblical traditions are to be found among
the Cuneiform tablets of Sumeria and Babylonia.   Here are some extracts from such early records as reported in the literature at the time
when they were first found.   It is necessary to say this because *later*
collections of Cuneiform inscriptions do not always translate these
same tablets in precisely the same way, and in some cases the names of
the deities have been spelled differently.   In 1895 Dr. T. G. Pinches,
one of the earliest notable Cuneiform scholars in England, reported
the finding of a tablet which begins thus:*

> In Eridu grew a dark vine
> In a glorious place it was brought forth.

---

* Pinches, T. G., "On Certain Inscriptions and Records Referring to Babylonia and Elam",
Transactions Victoria Institute, London, Vol. 29, 1895, p. 44.

This is not very much to go on, but the tablet as a whole is clearly a reference to the beginnings of human history. The "glorious place" seems obviously to refer to the Garden of Eden. The problem here, however, is to decide whether this dark tree — perhaps the word *shady* might be equally appropriate — was the Tree of Knowledge which was forbidden *before* the Fall or the Tree of Life which was forbidden *after* the Fall. The tablet does not state whether the tree was forbidden — only that it was there; and therefore we really have no clue as to which of the two trees the writer had in mind: only that it was a *vine*.

The following year, W. St. Chad Boscawen published a translation of a fragment of a tablet which reads as follows: *

(1) The great gods, all of them determiners of Fate,

(2) Entered, and death-like the god Sar filled.

(3) In sin one with the other in compact joins.

(4) The command was established in the Garden of the god.

(5) The asnan fruit they ate, they broke in two:

(6) Its stalk they destroyed;

(7) The sweet juice which injures the body.

(8) Great is their sin. Themselves they exalted

(9) To Merodach, their redeemer, he appointed their fate.

As rendered by Boscawen, himself no mean Cuneiform scholar, the picture seems clearly to reflect the circumstances of the Fall and to connect it with an act of disobedience which was viewed as a great sin. I had considerable difficulty in tracking down the source of this excerpt from the Cuneiform literature, chiefly because — when I did finally find it — modern renderings are substantially different. This is actually a translation of the last nine lines of Tablet III of an Akkadian creation tablet. The same passage (l. 130-139) as translated by E. A. Speiser reads as follows: **

(1) All the great gods who decree the fates

(2) They entered before Anshar, filling (Ubshukinna)

(3) They kissed one another in the Assembly

(4) They held converse as they (sat down) to the banquet

(5) They ate festive bread, poured (the wine)

---

* Boscawen, W. St. Chad, *The Bible and the Monuments,* London, Eyre and Spottiswoode, 1896, p. 89.

** Speiser, E. A., "Akkadian Myths and Epics" in *Ancient Near Eastern Texts,* ed. James B. Pritchard, Princeton, 1969, p. 65, 66.

(6) They wetted their drinking-tubes with sweet intoxicant.

(7) As they drank the strong drink, (their) bodies swelled

(8) They became very languid as their spirits rose

(9) For Marduk, their avenger, they fixed the decrees.

It will be seen that there are marked differences between the two renderings. We have numbered the lines in order to assist the reader to see to what extent they match.

It seems important to examine this circumstance with care for several reasons. First of all, it should be understood that there are problems even yet in the reading of the Cuneiform text. The problems arise from the fact that each Cuneiform sign does not represent a letter of an alphabet which always has the same sound value, but may have as many as twenty different sound values. For example, the sign ⟨Ʈ may be read with the following sound values: UM, UMU, UD, TAM, PAR, HISH, and some other alternatives. There are certain guides to indicate to the reader which particular sound value the sign is carrying in any given circumstance. But these indications are not always clearly understood even by modern Cuneiform scholars, and different scholars sometimes adopt different readings for the same sign. Let me illustrate in completely modern terms what can be involved in translating a tablet. Let us suppose some particular sign could be read either as *CRI* or *HOC*, and this sign in a particular sentence could be followed by a second sign which is known to have two alternative values which are *KEY* and *KET*. I suspect that if it were known that the tablet was recording something to do with a game, an English Cuneiform scholar would almost certainly read it as *CRICKET,* whereas a Canadian Cuneiform scholar would almost certainly read it as *HOCKEY.*

Any such analogy can be misleading, but this is the nature of the problem, and when we compare the renderings of earlier scholars with those of later scholars we sometimes have an analogous bias, only the bias is not between English and Canadian sporting interests but between a not unnatural tendency among earlier scholars to look for reflections of the biblical story in contrast to the almost total indifference — indeed, even hostility — towards such a goal among modern scholars. Looking at the two renderings by Boscawen and Speiser, one has to admit that Speiser's knowledge of Cuneiform was far greater than that of his predecessors because he was standing on their shoulders. On the other hand, it must be admitted that Boscawen's rendering makes much better sense on the whole.

At any rate, even Speiser's translation, if we use Boscawen's as a background, does suggest that a beverage described as a sweet intoxicant with harmful effects both on body and spirit was involved. And admittedly, it is not easy to discern the figures of Adam and Eve since the chief characters in this little play are said to have been "all the great gods".

In a most useful little handbook on Archaeology and the Bible, S. L. Caiger gives a translation of a small fragment of a Cuneiform tablet, which also seems to have some bearing on the Fall, though it, too, is far from clear as to its meaning:*

> My King the cassia plant approached;
> He plucked, he ate,
> Then Ninharsag in the name of Enki
> Uttered a curse:
> "The face of life, until he dies, shall he not see".

This same extract is rendered slightly differently by S. N. Kramer, but the import of the words is essentially the same.† The identity of the fruit as coming from a cassia plant does not help us very much. But we do note that the effect was to exclude the eater from the presence of his god until he has paid the penalty of death.

We have to conclude, I think, that the only light at present available to us from the Cuneiform literature is very indistinct, a rather odd circumstance in view of the tremendous number of tablets that have been translated. It is to the pictorial representations of the Fall that we have to turn in order to find any unequivocal reflection of the Genesis story.

An ancient Babylonian seal, one of many seals that have been discovered by archaeologists, reproduced in Fig. 4 as a line drawing taken

Fig. 4: The Seal of Adam and Eve and the Serpent

The original   The woodcut from Smith

---

* Caiger, S. L., *Bible and Spade,* Oxford, 1936, p. 19.

† Kramer, S. N., *From the Tablets of Sumer,* Indian Hills, Colo., Falcon's Wing Press, 1956, p. 174.

from George Smith's *The Chaldean Account of Genesis* (published in 1880)*, clearly shows the temptation scene, with the tree in the centre, an erect serpent standing presumably behind Eve. The forbidden tree looks suspiciously like a trained vine with two clusters of grapes. Adam and Eve are each reaching out a hand towards the fruit. The shape of the tree itself which tempts one to assume it might be a vine, may not of course signify anything more than the artist's sense of symmetry.

In 1932 E. A. Speiser of the University Museum of Pennsylvania, discovered a seal near the bottom of the Tepe Gawra Mound twelve miles from Nineveh. He dated this seal at about 3500 B.C. It is the picture of a naked man and a naked woman walking as if utterly downcast and brokenhearted, followed by a serpent. The seal is about one inch in diameter, engraved on stone, and is now in the University Museum in Philadephia. Speiser considers it to be "strongly suggestive of the Adam and Eve story".† It is shown below in Fig. 5.

Fig. 5

---

* Smith, George, *The Chaldean Account of Genesis*, new ed., revised and corrected by A. H. Sayce, London, Sampson, Marston, Searle & Rivington, 1880, p. 88.

† Speiser, E. A., quoted by H. H. Halley, *Pocket Bible Handbook*, Chicago, published privately, 19th ed., 1951, p. 68.

Even in the matter of pictorial representations from the earliest periods we therefore admittedly have little enough to go on.   From later millenia (B.C.) we do seem to have more specific data.   Many years ago, Francois Lenormant reported the finding of a curiously painted vase of Phoenician manufacture, probably of the sixth or seventh century B.C.*   This had been discovered in an ancient sepulchre in Cyprus.   It exhibits a leafy tree "from the branches of which hang two large clusters of fruit" while a great serpent advances with an undulating motion towards it.

The *American Journal of Archaeology* some years ago carried an article by Nelson Glueck reporting on the general findings in Palestine and elsewhere during the years of excavation immediately prior to 1933.   He mentions that:†

> In one of the two tombs discovered southwest of the Jewish colony of Hadra, a lead coffin was found.   On one side it is decorated with an arch which rests upon two twisted columns.   Under the arch a naked body holds a serpent in his right hand and a bunch of grapes in his left.

A coffin seems a particularly appropriate setting for a picture of a man in his youth, naked, and holding in either hand the elements out of which physical death may have found its way into human experience.   The tradition of the forbidden fruit as being the product of a vine is widespread, though it is not always a *grape*vine that is in view. The Jewish people themselves, however, seem to have favoured the grape as the offending fruit, and this concept is clearly reflected in the *Book of Enoch.*   The *Book of Enoch* has always had a special interest for the Christian because it is the one book quoted from in the New Testament which is non-canonical and is not bound with the Bible even when the Apocrypha is included.   The allusions to it are not infrequent and it is generally held that the title, "the Son of Man", was taken from it.   In Chapter 32 the writer of the book tells how he went in search of the Garden of Eden and he says (verses 3 and 4):

> And I came to the garden of righteousness, and I saw the mingled diversity of those trees; many and large trees are planted there, of goodly fragrance, large, very beautiful and glorious, also the tree of wisdom; eating of it one learns great wisdom.
> It is like the carob-tree and its fruit is like the clusters of the vine, very good.

---

* Lenormant, F., in *Contemporary Review,* Sept., 1879, p. 155.

† Glueck, Nelson, "Palestinian and Syrian Archaeology", *Amer. J. Arch.*, Jan–Mar., 1933, p. 164.

The writer of the book then goes on to tell how he questioned his angelic guide about this particular tree (verses 5 and 6):

> And I said, "This tree is beautiful. How beautiful and pleasant to look at!"
> Then the holy angel Raphael who was with me, answered and said unto me, "This is the tree of wisdom from which thy old father and thy aged mother who were before thee, ate, and they learned wisdom, and their eyes were opened, and they learned that they were naked, and they were driven out of the garden".

Paul Isaac Hershon in his *Rabbinical Commentary on Genesis*, states that against Genesis 3:6 and the words "the Tree was good for food", there is this rabbinical comment:*

> Some of the sages say that it was a fig tree and that was why they plucked the leaves from the fig tree to cover their shame; for as soon as they had eaten of the tree of knowledge their eyes were opened, and they were ashamed to go about naked.
> But some sages say that the tree was a vine. Eve pressed the grapes and gave Adam red wine to drink, as red as blood.

The same author, in another work, in commenting on Genesis 1:27 quoted from the Talmudic *Tractate Sanhedrin* (folio 70, col. 1) as follows:†

> The Holy One, blessed be He! said to Noah, Thou shouldest have taken warning from Adam ("the man of the earth") and not have indulged in the use of wine as he did. Hence Noah is called (Gen.9:20) "the man of the earth". This accords with the Rabbi who maintains that the forbidden tree was a vine.

According to Louis Ginsberg in his *Legends of the Jews*, Origen in commenting on Genesis 9:20 maintained that Noah's vine was an offshoot of the Tree of Knowledge, and Ginsberg observes that the same view is reflected in the *Jerusalem Targum*.‡

So far, then, we see various traditional identifications of the tree.

---

* Hershon, Paul Isaac, *Commentary on Genesis*, London, Hodder and Stoughton, 1885, p. 27

† Hershon, Paul Isaac, *Genesis with a Talmudical Commentary*, London, Bagster and Sons, 1883, p. 67.

‡ Ginsberg, Louis, *The Legends of the Jews*, Phila., Jewish Publ. Assoc. of Amer., 1955, Vol. V, *From Creation to Exodus*, p. 190, note 59. Dr. Alfred Edersheim, himself a Hebrew Christian and author of that great classic, *The Life and Times of Jesus the Messiah* [London, Longmans, Green & Co., 1900], in a lesser known work of his, notes that a number of rabbis held this view [See his *The World Before the Flood*, London, Rel. Tract Soc., n.e., p. 55].

The Cuneiform records speak of it as a Cassia plant or an Asnan fruit. The *Book of Enoch* speaks of it as a Carob tree. The Talmud favours the grape vine. There is, of course, the famous apple which some scholars believe arose from a mis-translation. It happens that in Latin the word for *an evil thing* and the word for *apple* are the same, *malum*. The tree of good and of *evil* in any Latin rendering may possibly have been rendered by someone as a good *apple* tree.

There is another tradition to which Francois Lenormant refers:*

> The most ancient name of Babylon in the idiom of the first settlers in that region was "the Place of the Tree of Life", and even on the coffins of enamelled clay of a date later than Alexander the Great, found at Warka (the ancient Erech of the Bible and the Uruk of the inscriptions) this Tree appears as the emblem of immortality. Strange to say, one picture of it on an ancient Assyrian relic has been found drawn with sufficient accuracy to enable us to recognize it as the plant known as the Soma Tree by the Aryans of India, and the Homa of the ancient Persians, the crushed branches of which yield a draught offered as a libation to the gods as the water of immortality.

It might be argued that we have here better evidence to support a theory that it was the Tree of Life which was a vine rather than the Tree of Knowledge. But I think that Satan had something to do with this confusion in tradition, even as he had much to do with the confusion in Eve's mind. If we are dealing with a fruit capable of fermentation, it is not surprising that the *apparently* heightened prophetic insights which have often been claimed by priests under the influence of alcohol might soon transform something that was actually a poison into an ambrosia of the gods.

The soma or homa tree is generally considered to be the *Asclepias acida,* a tree associated in the Vedic hymns with the god *Soma,* just as the Asnan fruit may have been associated with the goddess *Ashnan.* It was important in Vedic ceremony, in the words of one encyclopedia, "because of its alcoholic character . . . ." In one hymn, those who have drunk the juice of the plant are said to have exclaimed together, "We have drunk the soma: we have become immortal: we have entered the light: we have known the gods!" Such a sequence reminds us of the assurances given by Satan when he tempted Eve to take the forbidden fruit.

Dr. Gordon R. Wasson, in an interesting paper on psycho-active drugs, speaks of the Indo-Aryans and the Soma as follows:[136]

---

* Lenormant, Francois, *The Beginnings of History*, N.Y., Scribners, 1891, p. 85, 86.

> An Indo-European people who call themselves Aryans conquer-
> ed the Valley of the Indus in the middle of the second millenium
> B.C. Their priests deified a plant which they called Soma, that has
> never been identified: scholars have almost despaired of finding it.
> The hymns that these priests composed have come down to us as
> the RigVeda, and many of them concern themselves with Soma . . .
> This plant, Soma, was an hallucinogen. The juice was extracted
> from it in the course of the liturgy and forthwith drunk by the
> priests who regarded it as a divine inebriant. It could not have
> been alcoholic for various reasons: for one thing, fermentation is a
> slow process which the Vedic priests could not hurry.

As we shall see, Wasson's last observation is not entirely justified, for there do exist fruit extracts which will ferment within a few hours in warm weather. One wonders whether such fruit juices were not originally drunk simply because they were sweet and pleasant to the taste, and that their intoxicating character after fermentation was an accidental discovery. The undesirable effects of intoxication may have come as a surprise in view of the original harmlessness and sweet- ness of the extract. It may be that this circumstance was responsible for the belief held by some people that this was really the work of the devil, turning sweetness into bitterness and corrupting man's taste. In some parts of the world it is specifically believed that it was evil spirits who persuaded man to take the first intoxicating liquor. Dr. S. H. Kellog gives a tradition from India which he believes owes nothing to borrowing from Christian missionaries. His account is as follows:*

> The Santals have a tradition . . . . that in the beginning they
> were not worshippers of demons as they are now. They say that,
> very long ago, their first parents were created by the Living God;
> and that they worshipped and served Him at first: and that they
> were seduced from their allegiance by an evil spirit Masang Buru,
> who persuaded them to drink an intoxicating liquor from the fruit
> of a certain tree.

On the whole, there is a certain concordance in this testimony both from pagan and Jewish sources. In the first place, man's down- fall was associated with the eating of a fruit. This action brought with it both a gain and a penalty. In some cases the gain is a superior kind of wisdom, prophetic wisdom, and in others it is "knowing the gods", whatever this signifies. On the other hand, most of the tradit- ions see it as an act of disobedience which of necessity also involved the penalty — death. The RigVeda, however, is an exception in this

---

*Kellog, S. H., *Genesis and the Growth of Religion,* London, Macmillan, 1892, p. 60, 61.

regard, for though the drink was intoxicating, it also was supposed to have guaranteed immortality.

In spite of this kind of contradiction, one has a feeling there is a link between all these accounts and that they bear witness to the fact that the human race is truly one and had one father Adam and one mother Eve, a knowledge of whose early history thus became the common property of all their descendants, i.e., mankind. The inconsistencies and contradictions of these traditions may actually strengthen our confidence in the original account in Genesis in the same way that a certain type of contradiction in the testimony of several witnesses to a crime may furnish the best proof that they have not borrowed their story from one another but are recollecting the original event without collusion among themselves.

Two facts seem to stand out: the fruit of some kind of tree was involved and the extract of the fruit was an intoxicant, a poison; whether it was some form of alcohol or not is a moot point, but it is a not unreasonable surmise.

Chapter 11

TOWARDS THE IDENTITY OF THE FORBIDDEN FRUIT:
(2) ALCOHOL AS A PARADIGM

At the last it biteth like a serpent
and stingeth like an adder.
Proverbs 23:22

Thou shalt be drunken
and shalt make thyself naked.
Lamentations 4:21

I was afraid,
because I was naked;
and I hid myself.
Genesis 3:10

As a paradigm of the original poison, alcohol serves in many re-markable ways. Reverting to the series of requirements listed on page 121 and 122, we find that the following characteristics of alcohol largely fulfill these requirements.

(a) It is a protoplasmic poison. To be in*toxi*cated is to be poison-ed. Its potent effect in small quantities has been known for many years. In 1908 Sir Victor Horsley quoted a Dr. Rauber, who experi-mented with the effects of alcohol on living cells, as follows:[137]

> Using principally a 10% solution (alcohol in water), Rauber found that alcohol acts as a definite protoplasmic poison upon all the forms of cell life with which he experimented. All these invest-igations proved clearly that animal and vegetable protoplasm is harmfully affected by even very small quantities of alcohol.

Rauber had found by experiment that blood containing only ¼ of 1% alcohol diminished within a single minute the work being done by the heart.   And blood containing ½ of 1% so seriously affected its working power that it was scarcely able to drive a sufficient amount of blood to supply its own nutrient arteries. Since that time a great deal of research has been carried out which serves to underscore the toxic effect of alcohol on cells in the animal body.

Subsequently however, the picture became rather less clear with continued research until opinion was somewhat divided as to whether alcohol was the bad character it had been made out to be.   No one who actually suffered from the effects of alcoholism personally within the family circle ever doubted its potential for disaster in human relations, but the pharmacologists became rather less certain as to its mode of operation and whether its cell-damaging effect was because it disturbed vital chain reactions or was acting directly as a protoplasmic poison in its own right.

Some object to any reference to alcohol as a poison at all, arguing that it is not a poison per se but only in the context of living tissue. This, of course, is quite true. Standing alone it is merely a chemical, as are a lot of other poisonous substances.   They are poisons in certain contexts only: and alcohol has been commonly accepted as a poison in the context of living tissue. Since, however, it cannot be poisonous in any *other* context than the living cell, it is proper enough to term it a poison with respect to the human organism. As Carlson and Johnson put it: "We may say that alcohol becomes a poison when an individual takes so much that body functions are impaired".[138] The problem, of course, is to determine just how much is required to constitute it as such. On this issue the best answer is "exceedingly little", for some people.   Much depends upon the damage already done by alcohol over a long period of time.   Records show that even the smell of brandy may have a profound effect in upsetting the normal functioning of the body of a person who, due to particular circumstances, has never had any experience of alcohol in any form whatever.

For some years it has been argued that alcohol is damaging to living tissue only because it causes a form of malnutrition. The steps by which this occurs are complex. There is evidence that malnutrition is effectively masked by indulgence in alcohol. But as George Watson puts it, this circumstance confuses the issue for the heavy drinker, who develops a kind of false sense of well-being:[139]

> One's tolerance to alcohol reflects the state of one's nutritional biochemical health.   The more one can drink without adverse effect, the worse off one (actually) is. It is just plain biochemical nonsense for people to pride themselves on being able to "hold" their liquor, for only those in very *bad* shape can do so.

And again, "Literally speaking, if you think you need a drink, you don't need a drink". Herein lies the deceptiveness of the situation. The organism reaches a stage at which alcohol seems to become essential to its survival. It is not unlike the experience of those who find that the more they yield to sin, the easier it seems to be to do so without ill effect, and the more necessary such harmful activity appears to be for mere survival. In both cases, of course, appearances are deceptive and the individual is headed for disaster at an ever increasing rate.

More recently, a better understanding of the mechanism which renders alcohol so damaging has begun to emerge. In 1975, the New York Academy of Sciences sponsored a conference on the medical consequences of alcoholism. In the Preface to the published report, Frank A. Seixas observed:[140]

> Medical science, having just awakened to the importance of vitamins, was prepared to go along and elaborately prove that cirrhosis (of the liver) was caused by malnutrition, not by a *poisonous* effect of alcohol . . . . This Conference marks a year in which a turning point has been achieved . . . . Alcohol has again become incriminated as *in itself* producing certain specific effects with pathological organ changes. (Emphasis mine).

Kenneth Williams, also a participant in the Conference, observed: "The red blood cell is pathologically affected at nearly every stage of its cycle in the body by the toxic effect of alcohol".[141]

Robert S. Hellman, who also took part in the Conference, subsequently said: "From clinical studies alcohol has now been implicated as a *toxin* at nearly every step of cell proliferation, maturation, delivery, and life span sequence".[142] And later, "Alcohol may affect the membrane or function of the cell in such a way as to shorten cell life or interfere with normal cell activities and distribution".[143]

Charles S. Lieber even more recently, in a paper dealing with the metabolism of alcohol, reinforces the above observation. Thus he writes:[144]

> For all the attention being directed toward heroin, cocaine, and marijuana, the favourite mood-altering drug in the United States, as it is in almost every human society, is alcohol. Its psychic effects, both pleasant and unpleasant, are well enough known. What is less well known is that alcohol, in different quantities for different people, is a *toxic* drug.

Later Lieber points out that as recently as 1949 the distinguished physiologist Charles H. Best and his colleagues wrote that alcohol's metabolic contribution was simply to supply calories and that "there is no more evidence of a specific *toxic* effect of pure ethyl alcohol upon liver cells than there is one due to sugar". Lieber comments on this, "Perhaps it was wishful thinking on the part of people in general and physicians in particular that installed as accepted fact the concept that alcohol lacked *intrinsic toxicity*" (emphasis mine).

This intrinsic toxicity has been confirmed specifically with respect to the germ plasm itself, a circumstance of particular significance in the present context.   Dimitrijevic, speaking of the pathogenesis neuroses in children, stated that among 678 neurotic children at the Children's Polyclinic at Sarajevo in Yugoslavia, 84 had alcoholic fathers.[145] The connection between alcohol and general irritability he attributed to the disruption of the nervous system **as a result of the toxic effects of alcohol in parents on the germ plasm in the first phase of conception.**

Starvation of the cells due to an induced inability to utilize the oxygen available to them is one of the consequences of the poisoning effect of alcohol in the body, even when the supply of oxygen is entirely normal.[146]   In the human body alcohol is a protoplasmic poison which in remarkably small quantities can be fatal to living tissue.

(b) We turn, now, to the second property that should apply to the Edenic poison, namely, its rapid action.

One of its short term effects in very small quantities is to cause peripheral vasodilatation, that is, it causes the minute blood vessels (capillaries) at the skin surface to open up and allow the blood to flood into them.   This has several consequences for the organism. For one thing, the increased vascular capacity for blood causes an immediate fall in blood pressure, and unless the subject is exercising and thereby increasing the pulse rate, the blood pressure may fall low enough to cause dizziness and unsteadiness on the feet with surprising rapidity.

A second consequence is that deep body heat is suddenly transferred to the skin surface where the heat receptors are, with the result that the individual experiences sudden heat flashes. The skin becomes flushed, especially in the face and neck areas.   There is a sensation of becoming heated up, but in fact one is only losing deep heat to the surface where it is suddenly felt in a new way; and from the surface the heat is radiated to the atmosphere whence it is lost to the body. The end result is that the body is not actually warmed by alcohol as commonly supposed, but *cooled*.   For this reason, Arctic expeditions prohibit the use of alcohol for any such "comforting" purposes.

People whose bodies have not become hardened to the use of alcohol or who are over-indulging, may feel so uncomfortably warm that they are tempted to remove their clothing.   Thus nakedness comes to be associated with drunkenness. The temptation to disrobe can be fatal of course in cold climates, but it may also be disastrous morally to those not in control of their emotions.

The reader will perhaps recognize that this discussion is relevant to the events in the Garden of Eden provided that the forbidden fruit was indeed of a kind capable of fermentation.

It could conceivably be that Adam observed the flush of Eve's body and even her unsteadiness; and that when they had both eaten the fermented fruit they both experienced the same sudden warming at the skin surface followed by a chill as body heat was lost by radiation. They may thus have become aware of their nakedness for the first time.   It could be also that the fact of the coolness of the evening (which is particularly noted in Genesis 3:8) accentuated this effect.

(c) Grapes are a particularly healthful food in themselves. So long as their skins remain intact and micro-organisms are prevented from reaching the sugar in the grape, no fermentation occurs and therefore no toxic substance is formed.   In 1958 a European periodical called *La Suisse* ("The Swiss Woman") had an article on grape juice by Dr. H. Mueller.   In this he referred to some forty companies manufacturing unfermented grape juice, each making a product with a recognizable taste that can be identified by an expert. Thus there are extensive uses for the juice of the grape which do not involve alcohol in any way, and these products clearly have quite recognizably different flavours.   Dr. Mueller extols the value of such juices.*

> The juice of the grape is an exceptional source of muscular energy.   Certain juices give 900 calories per litre (as over against milk with 670), coming from the grape sugar or glucose.   This is for muscle what gasoline is for a motor.   It is the drink for athletes as it is for labourers.
>
> But it is more.   It has been found that productive work after taking grape juice is distinctly higher than the calories in the grape juice would normally account for.   Certain substances in the juice, flavonols among them, which are related to vitamins, help the combustion of glucose by preventing the accumulation of intermediary products of oxidation, such as lactic acid.   Lactic acid causes muscular fatigue to the point of cramps and even runner's paralysis.   Nor is this all.   These same flavonols of the grape exercise a protective action on the walls of the blood vessels, diminishing their fragility.   This is so marked that it can be measured.
>
> White manufactured sugar, chemically pure, may be called the thief of vitamins and mineral substances, since the organism itself is obliged to furnish those needed for its digestion and combustion; grape sugar brings to the organism even more than are needed for the digestion and combustion of its own sugars.

---

* Mueller, H., quoted in *The Sunday School Times*, Phila., 7 June, 1958, p. 426, under the heading, "In praise of grape juice".

Certainly, then, grapes are good for food, and certainly they are pleasant to the eyes.   The micro-organisms which produce the right ferment to turn the grape sugar into alcohol, gather from the air and collect on the outside of the grape.   While there, they cannot attack the juices.   But as soon as the skin is broken, these micro-organisms begin to grow and increase very rapidly, at the same time producing their ferment which splits up the sugar in the grapes into alcohol and carbon dioxide gas.   It is only then that the fruit becomes harmful.

In the manufacture of grape juice the skins of course have to be broken; but fermentation takes time — a sufficient length of time, in fact, that the extracted juice with its sweetness can be preserved without fermentation by the proper treatment.   The sweet unfermented juice of the grape was termed *gleukos* (γλεῦκος) by the Greeks and *mustum* by the Romans — meaning essentially new or fresh wine. When it was desired to preserve it in a sweet state, according to Kitto* an amphora was coated with pitch inside and outside, and then filled with grape-trodden wine and stoppered so as to be perfectly air tight. It was immersed in a tank of cold fresh water or buried in wet sand and allowed to remain a month or two.   The result of this process was an unfermented grape juice which would remain sweet and unchanged for about a year.   Such new wine must be put into new wineskins for these alone would be entirely air tight; for old skins are sufficiently porous that fermentation may occur.   And under the pressure of gases formed, an old skin might well burst.   Kitto holds that this enduringly sweet wine was probably what was intended in the parable of the old and the new wineskins in Matthew 9:17.

According to Genesis, the fruit of this one tree was forbidden. There was nothing in its fruit per se that was harmful, had it been taken and eaten at once in faith.   It may have been doubt which caused hesitation; and hesitation after plucking it, perhaps allowed the fermentation of the otherwise highly beneficial fruit.   Such a reconstruction of events would remove from the Creator the stigma of having deliberately planted a fatally poisonous plant within an otherwise paradaisical Garden, a poisonous plant which would then be a strange thing to include in the comprehensive pronouncement that God saw *all* that He had created to be "very good" (Gen.1:31).

God had every right to single out any tree in the Garden and forbid it as food, as a test of obedience — even if its fruit was entirely harmless or even beneficial in its natural state.   The tempter could eat it unharmed, by which circumstance it would be demonstrated to Eve

---

* Kitto, John, *A Cyclopedia of Biblical Literature*, Edinburgh, Adam and Charles Black, 1845, Vol. II, p. 955.

that it was manifestly a food good to eat. Perhaps Eve also could have eaten it unharmed, had she but eaten it in faith and without hesitation.

The chief objection which might be raised to such a reconstruction of events, in the light of Gordon Wasson's remark about the slowness of fermentation, is circumvented if we assume that Eve plucked the grapes and kept them for some time before eating them, OR if the forbidden fruit was not actually grapes such as are familiar to us but more like a particular species of fruit known only in Africa from which natural juices may be extracted that require *only a few hours* for fermentation. David Livingstone came across one such plant extract. To quote his words: *

> The men of all classes of the Bango tribe (in Portuguese East Africa) trust to their wives for food and spend most of their time drinking a palm toddy. This toddy is the juice of a palm-oil-tree (*Eloeis guineensis*) which, when tapped, yields a sweet clear liquid, not at all intoxicating while fresh but, when allowed to stand till afternoon, causes inebriation and many crimes. This toddy, called *malova*, is the bane of the country.

As a matter of fact, the *Imperial Bible Dictionary*,† in dealing with two Hebrew words for wine, namely, *shechar* (שֵׁכָר) and *yayin* (יַיִן), points out that *yayin* simply denotes any of the liquid products of the grape, including of course unfermented juice. The word is probably related to the New Testament Greek word *oinos* (οἶνος) and consequently to the English word *wine*, showing how widespread was the knowledge of the substance itself whether fermented or unfermented.‡ Where water is scarce or apt to be contaminated, grape juice becomes the standard drink, especially in hot weather. It is not at all necessary to assume it signifies an alcoholic beverage.

By contrast, *shechar* is said to include all similar products of any fruit *except* the grape, which might therefore include pomegranate-wine, palm-wine, apple-wine, honey-wine, and perhaps even a beer as made by the Egyptians from barley. But if any single beverage is to be selected as most commonly intended by *shechar*, it is the palm-wine, procured easily and abundantly by tapping a tree.

When newly drawn off, this wine is a delicious, wholesome, and refreshing drink; and it is so inexpensive as to form an important part

---

* Livingstone, David, *Missionary Travels and Researches in South Africa*, N.Y., Harper, 1858, p. 445.

† *Imperial Bible Dictionary*, Vol. II, p. 1098, under *Wines*.

‡ The three forms, *yayin* (Hebrew), *wine* (English), and *oinos* (Greek) are closely related and probably originally belonged to the same root.

of the sustenance of ordinary people.   But in one day's heat it under-
goes a rapid fermentation, effervesces, and becomes possessed of about
the same intoxicating power as some of our light malt liquors.

Since some of the rabbis believed that the forbidden tree was the
palm, it is possible that their argument was based on this very fact,
namely, the rapidity with which an intoxicating liquor can be formed
out of a delicious and harmless fruit juice.   However, it seems unlikely
that Eve would have tapped a tree; and the serpent can hardly have
done so either!   It is because grapes would take rather too long to
ferment that I do not consider that grapes as we now know them can
have been the forbidden fruit, though they may have been very similar in many ways.

(d) There is still controversy about the inheritability of alcoholism.
The kind of evidence that can be presented in favour of inheritability
is of the following nature.   Wherever we find a family in which either
one or both parents are alcoholics, if alcoholism is inheritable, we
ought to find the incidence of alcoholism among their children to be
significantly higher than among children of non-alcoholic parents.   It
could be argued that such children become alcoholics because of the
example of their parents rather than because of an inherited predisposition.   It is necessary, therefore, to establish the fact that the children
of alcoholic parents have a significantly higher than average predisposition towards alcoholism *even when they have been brought up away
from all parental influences.*   This is what appears to be the case in a
substantial number of families investigated in many different parts of
the world.

Evidence that children of alcoholics may be born with genetic
damage predisposing towards alcoholism which satisfies this last requirement has recently been reported by Dr. George Winokur of the
University of Iowa School of Medicine.   He and his associates studied
the children of alcoholic parents who were raised in homes where one
or both parents were alcoholics and compared them with those who
had been removed from such an environment and raised in homes
where alcohol was not present.   In presenting his resume of this work,
Glenn Everett observed: [147]

> The psychiatrists discovered that 48% of the children of alcoh-
> olics raised in the alcoholic homes themselves became addicted to
> liquor upon reaching adulthood.   But they also found that 50% of
> the children of alcoholics raised in *non*-alcoholic homes (my em-
> phasis) also fell victim to the disease.
>
> Surprised by this finding, that home evironment did not seem to
> be as significant a factor as had been thought, they checked it by
> studying children of non-alcoholic parents who were raised in
> homes where alcoholism was present.   They found that only 14%

had become alcoholics as adults.   The rate for those raised in
non-alcoholic homes is said to be 8%.

In a manner of speaking, this could be interpreted to mean that
somewhere about 14% of the drive towards drinking results from example whereas 50% of the drive results from hereditary predisposition.

Moreover, it is not merely susceptibility to alcoholism that is found
much more frequently when parents are alcoholics.   There are much
higher frequencies of psychopathy and deviations in personality development in the families of alcoholic parents.

Furthermore, the risks of alcoholism among *brothers* in such a
family is far higher than among sisters (21% of the cases of sons of an
alcoholic father are likely to be alcoholics by contrast with less than
1% for daughters of an alcoholic father).   This compares with figures
for the general population which show that 3.4% of males are alcoholics as compared with 0.1% for females.   These figures came from a
study undertaken in Copenhagen in 1951.[148]   The figures reveal that
brothers showed a frequency of serious alcohol abuse three to eight
times greater than for the general population, but no difference was
found in any respect regarding sisters.   It is therefore concluded that
"in alcoholism there are certain groups in which hereditary factors
play a role.   The mode of inheritance is unknown.   The presence of
alcoholism in a parent is both a hereditary and an environmental fact-
or . . . . Criminality is at least four, and at most, eight times as high in
the present alcoholic subjects as among the general population".

In Stockholm, official registers of alcohol abusers in Sweden were
examined for men who had living twins of the same sex.[149] The 214
such men constituting the material for the investigation were members
of 174 pairs of twins in which 40 pairs showed both members as alcoholics.   Both twins were alcoholics in 54% of the 48 *monozygotic*
pairs but only 3.5% of the 126 *dizygotic* pairs.*   This meant that
where the twins shared identical genetic endowment, more than half
of them became alcoholics if either of the parents were alcoholics,
whereas if the twins did not share identical inheritance, only 3.5% of
them were alcoholics.   "These results are regarded as supporting the
assumption that drinking habits are influenced by genetic factors and
that such factors greatly determine the appearance of chronic alcoholism".

A study in Germany of the effect of alcohol intoxication on germ

---

* Monozygotic twins are identical twins who share identical heredity, being born from a
single ovum.   Dizygotic twins are born from two ova and are really nothing more than children of the same mother who happen to have been born at the same time.   Their hereditary
constitution will be no more similar (and no less) than any other children born of that mother.

cells and the reproductive mechanism concludes that damaging morph-
ological changes clearly occurred "even at low alcohol levels and are
not known to occur from other diseases or poisonings" (emphasis
mine).[150]   The motility of spermatozoa *in vitro* in alcohol solutions
from 0.1% to 20% was modified or completely undermined, in some
cases within seconds, and sperm death occurred within minutes.

A study was undertaken in the United States involving the family
histories of 500 alcoholic patients, 200 non-alcoholic psychiatric patients, and 200 controls with normal drinking habits.[151]   "A positive
history of alcoholism was shown in the family background of 62.4%
of the alcoholics, 28.5% of the psychiatric patients, and 16% of the
controls".   Of the 500 alcoholics 24% had alcoholic fathers but normal mothers, versus 13% who had alcoholic mothers with normal fathers.
The report concludes: "The usual explanation that alcoholism is
simply an expression of an underlying neurosis or inadequacy is insufficient . . . .   Rather, alcoholics seem to have an innate susceptibility to
alcohol which we believe is akin to an allergy to a food or an idio-
syncracy to a drug".   It is observed that the fact that alcoholism is
four times as frequent in the family history of alcoholics as in the
normal drinkers indicates that "there is a specific inheritance of the
disease in many cases".   Twelve cases were found in which the grandfather of the patient was an alcoholic but the father a total abstainer.
The authors note that "total abstinence (in such a case) may be an
equivalent to alcoholism, in that the patient realizes his susceptibility
to the drug and 'instinctively' avoids it".

As noted in some of these reports, the mechanism of inheritance is
still not clear, and even whether inheritance is a factor at all is not
certain either.   In the view of many investigators it is statistically
certain;   yet over this point there is still much debate.   Dr. Robert
Popham points out that the craving for alcohol of the compulsive
drinker may really constitute only a perverted appetite which arises as
a result of one or more dietary deficiencies.[152]   But then he admits
that these dietary deficiencies may themselves be traceable to some
genetic factor.   There is some experimental evidence that animals
maintained on a deficient diet may increase their consumption of
alcohol, if it is made available to them, merely as an alternative source
of calories.   However, such experimental animals, rats in this particular case, never become intoxicated but take only as much alcohol as
would supply them with the required energy.   Alcoholics, by contrast,
seek intoxication for its own sake and not for the energy it will provide.

It is reasonably certain that germ cell damage does occur, in which
case a hereditary factor would certainly be expected.   The literature
on this aspect of alcoholism is very extensive indeed.   The general consensus of opinion, as reflected in an article on drunkenness in the

current issue of the *Encylopedia Britannica* is mirrored in the statement that "some individuals have a specific susceptibility to alcohol due to heredity". And there is evidence of a substantial nature that the father's alcoholism plays a far greater hereditary role in the alcoholism of his children than the mother's.

We might sum up the situation, therefore, by saying that this particular type of poisoning does appear to reach the germ cells in a way that no other poison thus far investigated does, and that it reaches the male seed much more easily than the female seed in so far as the father's influence is several times more potent than the mother's. The poison of the forbidden fruit, as we have proposed, did not reach the seed of the woman *at all*, and therefore it is necessary once again to underscore the fact that alcohol serves only as a partial paradigm. Nevertheless, it indicates that such a protoplasmic poison with these specific effects is by no means to be ruled out as impossible or even unlikely.

(e) The effect of alcohol on the central nervous system, both the cerebrum and the cerebellum, is too well known to require much comment. Intoxication depresses the higher centres, removes inhibitions and lowers judgment and self-control, at the same time interfering with the normal functioning of all the senses. Sadly, it tends to be self-reinforcing in its detrimental effects because the distress following a period of drunkenness is most easily alleviated or entirely removed by repeating the *cause*.

In spite of the therapeutic effect of alcohol, medical men are increasingly unwilling to recommend its use, owing to the bad physical effects and the even more unfortunate moral degeneration consequent upon the use of alcohol which may become an addiction. The effect of alcohol on the central nervous system is particularly strikingly borne out by the fact that in post-mortem examinations traces of it may still be found in the cerebrospinal fluid, even when it has entirely disappeared from all other tissues.

(f) Alcohol is indeed a potent poison, exceedingly small quantities being quite sufficient to have a pronounced effect on those who have built up no immunity to it. It is evident that a very tiny quantity of the toxic substance had a tremendous effect upon Eve's body, as it did upon Adam's subsequently. Some people seem to be able to imbibe considerable alcohol without noticeable effect. Others are highly sensitive to very small quantities. Yet all of us are now born infected to a lesser or greater extent after centuries of forebears who were social drinkers. To any person whose body has never been subjected to alcohol in any form within their lifetime (they must still have had forebears who did, of course), the results of a small quantity are likely to be considerably magnified.

Singh and Zingg, in recording the story of the well known feral child, Caspar Hauser, remark upon the effect of alcohol on his body when he was given a small quantity for the first time in his life at the age of about seventeen years. Caspar Hauser had been kept in a tiny dungeon in almost total darkness since infancy, without any human attention except the occasional washing of his body and cutting of his hair by an attendant whom he never saw because he was always drugged before receiving this minimum of personal attention. There is some reason to suppose that he may have been confined because he was a contender for some hereditary position which was being occupied illegally by one of his captors. Singh and Zingg observed:[153]

> A certain person made the attempt to force some brandy upon him. Scarcely had the glass been brought to his lips when he turned pale, sank down, and would have fallen backwards against a glass door if he had not been instantly supported.
>
> A few drops of beer made from malted wheat, though much diluted with water, gave him a violent pain in his stomach accompanied with so great a (sense of) heat that he was all over dripping with perspiration; which was succeeded by ague attended with headache and violent eructations (i.e. passing of wind).

It is significant that such a minute quantity of alcohol could have such a profound effect on his totally unaccustomed body. The effect of fermented grape juice on Eve's perfect body could conceivably have been even more dramatic and quite evident to Adam. Eve had no forebears to pass on to her the slightest measure of immunity to its poisoning effects, whereas Caspar Hauser's body had at least *this* much preparation that he was born of a line of forebears with centuries of experience of alcoholic beverages, even though he himself may never have touched it.

In his commentary on Genesis, Lange rejected the idea that there could be any analogy between the experience of Adam and of Noah though both "discovered" their nakedness as a consequence of ingesting a damaging substance. He wrote: "(It) does not justify us in concluding that (in Adam's case) it was a wine, but some other fruit perhaps, whose effect for the first man was too strong, being of an intoxicating or disturbing nature".*

Lange then refers to Hartmann Beyer (1516–1577), a notable preacher in Frankfurt, Germany, who preached on this subject. Beyer

---

* Lange, John Peter, *Genesis: or The First Book of Moses,* tr. Tayler Lewis, Grand Rapids, Zondervan reprint, 1960, Vol. I, p. 245.

supposed that it was a "poison tree". But Lange adds "without any ground, for the human race is not poisoned corporeally, but distempered and disordered physically through an ethical consequence of its effects". Beyer may well have been closer to the truth, and it seems rather inconsistent of Lange to state that such a view is groundless while he himself admits almost the same thing in the same context. For Lange clearly saw the significance of the fact that the fruit may well have had an influence on Adam's body quite out of proportion to the influence that same fruit might now have on ours after long centuries of abuse.

Modern research may succeed in finding an antidote for the *appetite* of the alcoholic, but it is hardly to be supposed that the *basic biological effects* of the forbidden fruit as a form of protoplasmic poisoning will ever be eliminated from the human body. We shall not be rid of this poison which we inherit by natural generation until we sow our bodies in the dust to reap a harvest of resurrection in due course.

There are times when conversion has had the effect of instantly sobering a drunk man. And sometimes there is an equally complete deliverance from any further craving for alcohol. But this still does not confer immortality on the liberated individual. So the root defect remains, and clearly such miraculous cures of alcoholism do not really touch the mortogenic poison itself.

It is conceivable that pharmacology will one day find an effective "cure" in the form of some antidote, but it will not render the "cured" man any more physically immortal than conversion does. Mortality remains with us as an inherited penalty of the forbidden fruit, and dying as the only way to be finally rid of its effects. It is evident therefore that the Lord can deal with the effects of the paradigm we have been dealing with, in a moment, when He so pleases. But it will require physical death and bodily resurrection to undo the effects of the actual poison itself.

Were pharmacologists to find an antidote for this poison, it would be tantamount to allowing man access once again to the Tree of Life whenever he so desired. It is certain that the Lord will not allow such an eventuality.

I think it is remarkable how Scripture can enlighten the mind of the man who reads it believingly, even in matters about which he cannot possibly have previous knowledge by natural means. I have in mind a particularly striking insight of Luther's. He said: "Through the Fall of Adam, SIN entered into the world and all men in Adam have consequently sinned. For the *paternal sperm* (emphasis mine) convey the corruption from generation to generation".*

Similarly, Calvin wrote (*Institutes,* II, xiii, 4): "If Christ is free from all spot, and through the secret working of the Spirit was begotten of the seed of Mary, then woman's seed is not unclean *but only man's*" (emphasis mine).

Heinrich Heppe in his *Reformed Dogmatics*** demonstrates that such a concept as this — that the paternal sperm conveys the constitutional defect through each generation — was by no means a passing fancy quickly dismissed by subsequent theologians as too speculative. He singles out several "Reformed Dogmaticians" who kept the thought alive.

Peter Martyr (in his *Loci Communes*, London, 1576, p. 164) wrote: "If it be asked what is the seat of sin . . . . we answer that it has its place in the flesh as its root and principle . . . .   Therefore the seed (semen) is the instrument by which this sin is transmitted from parents to sons".†

Bartholomew Keckerman (in his *Systema Sacrosanctae Theologiae,* Geneva, 1611, p. 257, 258) expounds the view that not sin itself but its seed principle was procreated by the physical route.   The "disposition" to evil that is inherent in man is "propagated through semen".††

Amandus Polan (in his *Syntagma Theologiae Christianae,* Hanover, 1624,, Vol. VI, p.3) observed even more specifically: "Question: How was original sin sidetracked (i.e., passed on) to us and contracted by us?   Answer: Sin was transmitted by the paternal seed; propagated in the paternal semen, the corruption infected the soul".‡

John H. Hottinger (in his *Cursus Theologicus Methodo Altingiana,* Heidelberg, 1660, p. 165) wrote: "The manner of the derivation of original sin is a combination of the imputation of Adam's sin and *impure generation*" (emphasis mine).★

More recently, Professor Peter T. Geach of Oxford wrote: "Adam's continuing stream of germ plasm propagates itself: and his perverse

---

*   Quoted by J. L. Neve, *History of Christian Thought,* Phila., Muhlenberg Press, 1946, Vol. I, p. 230.   I think it is interesting that Karl Barth, in his *Credo,* claimed that "sin-inheritance came through the male parent only" [N.Y., Scribners, 1962, p. 71].

**   Heppe, Heinrich, *Reformed Dogmatics,* tr. G. T. Thomson, Grand Rapids, Baker reprint, 1978.

†   Martyr, Peter: Heppe, *ibid,* p.341.

††   Keckerman, Bartholomew: Heppe, *ibid,* p. 343, 344;

‡   Polan, Amandus: Heppe, *ibid,* p. 342.

★   Hottinger, John H: Heppe, *ibid,* p. 344.

will still lives on and reincarnates itself in a new human individual who by nature will want to be the sort of creature a fallen man is, not the sort of creature God made Adam at the first. For this situation, within the resources of human nature, there is no remedy".*   As we have already said, what became the *penalty* of disobedience in the first man, became the *cause* of disobedience in all his descendants.†

That a chemical poison could be the cause of moral degeneration should no longer surprise us in the light of what we know even now of the effects of alcohol.   That the poison itself is demoralizing in its effects does not lessen the moral responsibility associated with that effect, for man's guilt is not merely that he is a sinner, but that he is content — or even prefers — to remain a sinner when he might be a saint.

According to the Greek Fathers of the Church, original sin is a physical rather than a moral defect.   Adam's physical condition was deteriorated by his disobedience and that deteriorated natural constitution has been inherited by his descendants.   Since it has been customary to reject the idea that our ultimate moral failures stem from imitation of the evil ways of others but arise from some inherent defect in human nature which we call original sin, we are logically bound in the final analysis to look for a physiological (and therefore ultimately a *chemical*) cause.   Such a defect is not in itself the cause of guilt but certainly results in forms of human activity which are sinful.   The defect thus becomes the ground of our guilt before God by "poisoning" the spirit which as God's gift and creation must have been perfectly pure at its first infusion.

That the physical body can corrupt the soul was an idea commonly believed by medieval and scholastic theologians.   Anselm of Canterbury (1033 - 1109) wrote of the soul being "weakened from the corruption of the body" and "the corruptible body being a load to the soul".‡

Anselm of Laon (d. 1117) extended the idea and related it to the meaning of circumcision.   He wrote: "In the way in which the foreskin, after being removed by circumcision, remains in those who are begotten by the circumcised . . . . in this way sin which is cleansed by

---

* Geach, Peter T., *Evolution or Creation*, Birmingham, England, 1971, p. 7.

† Thomas Aquinas observed: "Had only Eve sinned, Adam's children would *not* have inherited the taint of original sin; had only Adam sinned, they would have" (quoted by Paul Jewett, *Man as Male and Female*, Grand Rapids, Eerdmans, 1975, p. 65).

‡ Anselm of Canterbury: *A Scholastic Miscellany*, ed. E. R. Fairweather, Phila., Westminster Press, Library of Christian Classics, Vol. X, 1956, p. 185.

(infant) baptism, remains in those whom the baptized beget".* Sin is deeply rooted in the body and the defect poisons each new generation equally.

Stephen Langton (d. 1228) put it this way:† "The flesh of Adam was corrupted by the eating of the apple, and this applies to all flesh which descends from him by way of concupiscence . . . . The soul is infused into a filthy and corrupt body . . . . From the corrupt and filthy vessel into which it is infused it contracts an inclination to sin, which is called *foment*".

I am convinced that human nature is as deeply rooted in the human body as it is in the human spirit, and in each of us it has been corrupted at its source by the poisoning of the body when Adam and Eve ate the forbidden fruit.

---

* Anselm of Laon: *A Scholastic Miscellany*, ed. E. R. Fairweather, Phila., Westminster Press, Library of Christian Classics, Vol. X, p. 262.

† Langton, Stephen: *ibid*, p. 352 f.

Chapter 12

TOWARDS THE IDENTITY OF THE FORBIDDEN FRUIT:
(3) SOME BIBLICAL INTIMATIONS.

He shall separate himself from wine and strong drink,
and shall drink no vinegar of wine,
or vinegar of strong drink,
neither shall he drink any liquor of grape,
nor eat moist grapes, or dried.
All the days of his separation shall he eat
nothing that is made of the vine tree
from the kernels even to the husks.
Numbers 6:3, 4

She may not eat of anything that cometh of the vine,
neither let her drink wine or strong drink . . . .
All that I have commanded let her observe.
Judges 13:14

There are intimations in Scripture regarding the nature of the poison. For some, these intimations carry considerable weight; to others they are merely far-fetched. It all depends on one's bias.

To the man who is convinced that evolution is true, the most implausible arguments and the most unlikely evidence in support of his conviction will suffice to confirm him in his faith. Our critical faculties are seldom applied with equal rigour in every direction. The convinced Christian is just as likely to find confirmation of his faith uncritically, as the evolutionist does. This is the way our minds

operate.   It is well to recognize the fact because each side is apt to
accuse the other of dishonesty, on precisely the same grounds.   It is
not possible for most people to take a middle course and see both
points of view with equal force, and I am not even sure that it is altogether desirable or healthy.   It is conviction that puts a cutting edge in
life, and it seems to me better to be completely convinced about certain things, even if they are unprovable, than to hold a totally open
mind.   A wholly open mind, unoccupied by any structured convictions, is apt to be vacuous, and a vacuum draws both foul and healthy
air into its void with equal vigour.   The difficulty is to find the balance
between having no convictions at all and therefore being equally re-
ceptive to all ideas good and bad alike (or *no* ideas), and having a mind
so made up that contrary evidence carries no weight whatever.   The
situation is complicated by the fact that whether evidence is contrary
or favourable does not always depend upon the nature of the evidence
itself but the direction of our own bias.   It is the set of the mind
which predetermines how we see and even what we see.   We see things
not so much as they are, but as *we* are.

Even if much of what I have said in the last two or three chapters
should turn out to be a mis-interpretation of the evidence, I hope I
should be able to recognize the fact.   But it would not in any way
shatter my faith, for **it all relates not so much to the fundamentals of
my faith but to the possible links which unify those fundamental elements into a single organic whole.**   I think this is a most important
point to keep firmly in mind at all times.   That Adam and Eve were
real people and poisoned themselves from a real fruit (which was forbidden to them) with terrible consequences for man and the world,
consequences that could only be effectively dealt with by God in
Christ, are clearly matters of revelation − as I understand Scripture.
I do not believe them because I can rationalize them in the light of
modern knowledge.   But I love to explore these things which I believe,
both with the light of Scripture and with the help of scientific research.   Such findings only enhance exploration: they can never
justify our faith.   Faith must always remain faith, this side of heaven.

Let us look, then, at some of the intimations in Scripture which
do seem to lend some support to the view that the poison of the forbidden fruit had about it something of the nature of such a poison as
alcohol is, always bearing in mind that if we should be shown in the
end to have been entirely mistaken about its identity, there is no likelihood of being mistaken about the reality of the forbidden fruit in
the first place, nor the fatal consequences to mankind of its ingestion
by Adam.

There is some evidence for a kind of unwritten law that the first mention of a particular object or the first use of an important word in Scripture often provides a special insight into its significance thereafter.   The first mention of the grapevine by name is in Genesis 9:20 where it is recorded that Noah planted a vineyard and later became drunk.   The immediate consequence was that he indecently exposed himself: a secondary effect was the pronouncing of a curse (Gen.9: 20-27).   It seems to me a remarkable circumstance that both Adam and Noah, who stood with respect to mankind in a somewhat analogous position (cf. Gen.1:28 with Gen.9:1, for example), should have become naked in a way that brought shame and a curse.   This might provide some justification for arguing that the same fruit, or at least a very similar fruit, was involved in both cases — though not a few commentators have flatly rejected the idea; as Lange did.

Throughout Scripture nakedness and the drinking of wine are linked together (cf. Lam.4:21; Hab.2:15, etc.).   We know how this association comes about from a physiological point of view.   There is, of course, another interpretation of Adam's and Eve's nakedness.   In this view it is held that they were clothed with some kind of radiance, a radiance which signified moral purity as well as absolute health.   On the Mount of Transfiguration the Lord Jesus Christ, having achieved perfect adult manhood, was clothed with light.   Moses, when he came down from communing with God, had a radiant face (Exod.34:29, 30) which may be a reflection of the same phenomenon.   It has even been suggested that if man was made in the image of God, he must have shared God's "clothing", a "garment of light", as Psalm 104:2 indicates.   And the familiar statement in Psalm 34:5, "they looked unto Him and their faces were lighted" could conceivably be a reference to the same association between purity and radiance.   In which case Eve's loss of this garment of light as she approached Adam with some of the forbidden fruit in her hand, may have been the first intimation that Adam had of the tragedy which had befallen her.

There is some evidence that living tissue in health can emit light. Certainly our bodies emit radiation which we detect only as heat but which some predatory animals, such as snakes, actually *see as colour*. There is a military device used for shooting at the enemy in the dark which has been appropriately called a "snooperscope".   This device converts heat radiation into light radiation, thus making people visible in the dark.

In England and on the Continent, a number of researches have established that the human body has an aura which can be used for purposes of diagnosis.   The physicist, Stomer von Reichenback, called it the *od*.   The German physicist, Otto Brueckner, measured it and believed it consisted of ultra-violet rays.   In America, an X-Ray specialist, Dr. Walter Kilner, uses the aura for diagnostic purposes.   It is believed that the aura is not a form of radioactivity since it would not then be extinguished by death, and it is doubtful if the human body contains sufficient radioactive elements to be responsible for it. Some years ago, three medical men in Italy, Drs. Sambo, Parenzan, and Contento, in collaboration with Professor Fabiovitali, investigated a certain Mrs. Anna Monaro whose body was so luminous at times (and for very short intervals) that "radiation" was clearly visible to the eye. In a report by an Italian physicist Dr. Giocondo Protti, it is concluded, "We have proved that we are dealing with a demonstrated fact of light", and he adds that observations under controlled conditions "enable us to conclude (against the most common assumption) that no element of electricity or radioactivity has any part in causing the phenomenon".[154]

There does not appear to have been any further research done in connection with this phenomenon, or at least it has not been reported in the literature with which I am acquainted, but the work undertaken in Italy and elsewhere at the time was well substantiated with documentary evidence in graph form and by cinephotography.   It is impossible to say whether this kind of phenomenon bears any relationship to the aura which has from time immemorial been associated with spiritual purity and health, and which lies behind the traditional use of the halo in sacred paintings.

So we have to be careful, when speaking of nakedness in connection with Adam and Eve, that we do not pre-empt entirely new possibilities as to the nature of the covering which they seem to have surrendered, for our bodies may yet have preserved some vestiges of a natural garment of which we have only slight and occasional evidence at the present time because we have not developed appropriate instruments to measure it.   But it is interesting that in the Bible the body is viewed as even yet possessing a natural "covering" of sorts.

This is illustrated, for example, in the covering which a woman's hair provides for her (1 Cor.11:15), and which in a special way a man's hair provided when he had taken the Nazirite vow.*   Anyone who took this vow was given the following instructions (Num.6:3-6):

> He shall separate himself from wine and strong drink, and shall drink no vinegar of wine, or vinegar of strong drink, neither shall he drink any liquor of grape, nor eat moist grapes, or dried.
> All the days of his separation shall he eat nothing that is made of the vine tree from the kernels [seeds] even to the husks [skins].
> All the days of the vow of his separation shall there no razor

---

* Incorrectly spelled *Nazarite* in the Authorized Version.   The word relates to a Hebrew verb meaning *to vow*, and has nothing to do with the village of Nazareth.

come upon his head: until the days be fulfilled, in which he separateth himself unto the Lord, he shall be holy and shall let the
locks of his hair of his head grow.
All the days that he separateth himself unto the Lord he shall
come at no dead body.

Here we have a list of requirements which must be fulfilled together; and they are explicit. Since we know from 1 Corinthians
11:15 that hair may have a significance of a natural covering, we have
here a linking together of three things: the "poison" from the vine, a
natural covering, and death. In the Garden of Eden Adam and Eve
took the fruit of a vine, somehow lost a natural covering, discovered
their nakedness for the first time, and became as good as dead.

In Judges 13 ff., we are given a story which seems to shed light on
the same theme. It is the story of Samson, a man placed under the
Nazirite vow (Jud.16:17). It was not possible for him to demonstrate
that he had been dedicated to the Lord by his parents in this special
way merely by testifying that he had never touched alcohol and that
he had never come near a dead body, for he could not prove this except to those who knew him well. What was needed was a continuing
and manifest testimony in some form that set him apart from his contemporaries, even before strangers. Such a public testimonial was his
long hair. The other two elements of his vow could be performed in
secret and constituted more of a private testimony.

Strictly speaking, no one 'took' a Nazirite vow: it was normally
imposed upon them from birth. In later rabbinical literature, it is the
father, and not the mother, who places his child under oath. Dedication of a child to the Lord normally occurred before the child was
born. It appears from Scripture that surprisingly few well-known
characters were dedicated to the Lord in this way *for life*. The only
such individuals that we know by name were Samson, Samuel, and
John the Baptist; though Jewish tradition adds Absalom by virtue of
his long hair. The vow was not limited to Israel. The Code of
Hammurabi (§ 110) contains several regulatory statements regarding
such people, including prohibition from even *entering* a wine shop,
much less the drinking of wine. It reminds one of Eve's cautionary
warning to herself, "neither shall ye touch it".

In New Testament times we appear to have reference to a temporary Nazirite vow taken by Paul (Acts 18:18) and shared by other
Christians in Jerusalem (Acts 21:23). Josephus (*Antiquities of the
Jews*, XIX, vi, 1) makes it clear that many Jews adopted the Nazirite
vow in his time, and there may be some connection here with the
community of the Essenes.

It has been argued that Samson cannot have conformed to the requirement of abstinence from the use of fermented wine since he is

clearly said to have given feasts to his friends (Jud.14:10). However, devout Moslems also give feasts to their friends. Yet no devout Moslem will touch fermented wine in any form. It is therefore quite possible to think of a *feast* in which alcoholic beverage plays no part in the festivities, though "wine" (i.e., the juice of the grape, unfermented) does indeed play a part. This is contrary to our cultural traditions, but it certainly suggests that the marriage feast in Cana of Galilee could have been a joyous occasion and entirely acceptable to the guests without any necessity of providing fermented wine.

Now, Samson undoubtedly knew well enough that his real strength in the Lord depended not so much on his long hair but on what that long hair represented, i.e., a witness to his dedication to the Lord. When he allowed himself to be stripped of his testimony, even unwittingly, he surrendered the joy of the Lord's known presence. As the Bible says, "He wist not that the Lord was departed from him" (Jud.16:20).

It is a familiar story. Samson was brought low by his subservience to a Philistine woman who succeeded by effectively destroying his public witness. The loss of his hair was symbolical: but the loss of his great physical strength at the same time was sadly real. Deeds which he might have done effortlessly before, he was now unable to perform. He found himself in bondage to the enemy and his vision gone: and he literally ate his bread by the sweat of his brow for he was put to work grinding flour in the prison house, while his feet were bound in chains. In all of these ways we see an analogy with Adam. This is not merely sober history but is remarkable allegory as well.

But this is by no means all we may learn from the story. For we find that the experience of his parents has relevance in the present context also. The promise of this 'heroic' son was given to his father, Manoah, and to his mother in Judges 13. What is significant here is the list of instructions given by the angel to Manoah's wife prior to the birth of her son. In verse 4 it is written: "Now, therefore, beware I pray thee, and drink not wine nor strong drink . . . ", a command which is three times reiterated in this one chapter (verses 4, 7, and 14). Today we have evidence of the reasonableness of this precaution, for there really is little doubt that some chemical substances which are harmful do cross the placental barrier and reach the unborn child. Thalidomide is a sufficiently tragic reminder of this possibility.[155] In order that the child might therefore be truly dedicated to the Lord, it was necessary to protect even the foetus from the contamination which the devotee himself was later called upon to avoid at all costs throughout his life.

There are some other intimations. Wine has from the most ancient times been a symbol for blood, and blood is very widely used as a symbol for death.   There was a time when men offered a sacrifice to the gods of the sea before launching a new vessel.   Today we simply break a bottle of wine over the bow instead.   The symbol of wine as death was used by our Lord (Luke 22:20), and this is perhaps the basic implication of the cup which He was given to drink by his Father (John 18:11).   There are passages in the Word of God in which the juice of the grape is actually spoken of as blood (cf. Gen.49:11; Deut. 32:14).

Blood is both a sign of life and a symbol of death; without it we cannot live and within it may be the very seeds of our dying.   As representative of blood, wine assumed both symbolic roles.   The presence of the blood in the dead body appears to accelerate its corruption.   Whatever the factor may be that thus accelerates corruption, removing the blood delays the process; and undertakers do this routinely.   The blood of the Lord Jesus was without this corruption by reason of his unique conception, and accordingly *his* body did not see corruption in the tomb (Acts 13:37).   Peter hangs an important "therefore" upon this very fact (verse 38).

In one passage of Scripture (Prov.23:31, 32) the action of fermented wine is linked with the action of the serpent.   "Look not thou upon the wine when it is red, when it sparkles in the cup, when it goeth down (too) easily.   In the end it biteth like a serpent and stingeth like an adder".   In this passage, the word *serpent*, in the original Hebrew, is the same word as is similarly translated in Genesis 3:1.

And this brings us to a further point.   Throughout Scripture leaven evidently stands for the same basic cause of corruption and death.   All types of Christ in the Old Testament as the *Bread of Life* of which man is to partake, involve unleavened bread.   Leaven was allowed in certain offerings (Lev.7:13 and elsewhere), but it was not for eating — even as fermented wine was permitted for certain drink offerings which were merely poured out before the Lord and not drunk (Exod.29:40).   The Lord's body which we are to eat and his blood which we are to drink as a memorial (John 6:54-56) are symbolized by bread without leaven and by wine without alcohol. Indeed, at the time of the Passover, leaven was not even to be found in the house on pain of death (Exod.12:15,19, 39; 23:18; Deut.16:3, 4). Although it is customary in certain of the older denominations to use fermented wine in the Communion Service, it does not seem to me likely that if the bread of that service was to be unleavened, the wine of that service should be fermented.   The very fact that at the time of the Passover such a rigid exclusion of leaven was commanded seems to me to require that we assume the same thing for the wine, for the ferment in both cases is comparable.

In the literature of the time of our Lord, leaven was always an evil thing. In the Talmud it is written:*

> Rabbi Alexander, when he had concluded his prayers, said, "Lord of the Universe, it is clearly manifest before Thee that it is our will to do Thy will. What hinders that we do not do Thy will? The leaven which is in the mass".

A glossary at this passage adds the explanation of the last sentence, "the evil which is in the heart". Thus leaven was associated with spiritual or moral evil. Plutarch says, "Leaven itself is born from corruption and corrupts the mass in which it is mixed".† The Latin word *fermentum* was synonymous with our word "corruption", and from it we derive the more familiar term, fermentation. Interestingly, it is largely the yeast which is introduced into bread that gives it its taste — especially when it is fresh — and the temptation of bakers to add more in order to increase sales by making their bread more tasty, led in time to the passing of a law specifying that the content of alcohol in fresh bread should not be in excess of 0.5%. I have seen it stated with some authority that fresh bread may actually have as much as 3% alcohol.

Chemically speaking, ferment and yeast are the same substance: but yeast or leaven is more correctly applied to solids, while ferment is applied to both liquids and solids. Fermentation is, in effect, a substance in a state of putrefaction. In the East the lees of wine are sometimes used as yeast, thus demonstrating that basically their action upon any body into which they have been introduced is the same. It is surprising that God should make it so very explicit that no leaven was to accompany any blood sacrifice (Exod.23:18; 34:25). It may also be worth mentioning that the Hebrew root of the word for *leaven* means "to be agitated". This is the very antithesis of the Hebrew concept of health which is synonymous with the word for *peace* (*shalom*). Priests were strictly forbidden in Leviticus 10:9 and 10 to drink wine or strong drink when they went into the service of God, as it says, "lest ye die".

Thus we seem to be led to the conclusion that whatever may have been the exact nature of the forbidden fruit, it was similar to a vine in so far as it contained the requisites for the production of something

---

* *Babylonian Beracoth*, 17.1.

† Plutarch, *Quaestiones Romanae*, CXIX, 6.

like alcohol.   In the present circumstances our bodies are already poisoned by generations of forebears who have made fermented wine and leavened bread.   Thus the addition of alcohol, in bread for example, is not likely to cause any further significant damage.   In Scripture we have a few occasions where it may even have been prescribed for its medicinal value, as in 1 Timothy 5:23 although it is not *certain* that fermented wine was involved here.   Recently, experiments conducted by Dr. Jack Konowalchuk and J. I. Speirs of the Bureau of Microbiological Hazards in Ottawa, Canada, have shed an interesting light on how Paul's instructions to Timothy may have been fully justified.

It has been found that wine can inactivate intestinal viruses.   It appears that soldiers in ancient Egypt always drank a wine and water mixture when fighting abroad and it was decided to investigate why this kept them free of many stomach ailments.   It was discovered that if the mixture was right, they were protected against a number of viruses, including polio virus.   And grape juice was more effective than wine! [156]

As we have already noted, the juice of the grape can be, and was, readily enough preserved without fermentation, and it seems to me highly probable that such would be the beverage at the marriage in Cana of Galilee (John 2:1 f.).   That the new wine which the Lord created was at once recognized by the master of ceremonies as of superior "vintage" by its taste need not at all require us to assume that it was fermented.   At least forty distinctly flavoured grape juices are bottled by different companies in Switzerland, each of which can be identified as to its source and quality by the connoisseur.   In view of the quite tremendous quantity of wine which would be involved in six stone vessels, each containing 18 to 27 gallons a piece, which the Lord commanded to be filled to the brim with water and which He then turned into wine, I think one must assume that this was non-alcoholic.   Otherwise we have to visualize the sudden production of between 100 and 175 gallons (or anywhere up to 700 quarts) of alcoholic beverage being produced by the Lord in circumstances which would certainly be conducive to widespread drunkenness.

In his *Archaeology and Bible History*, Professor Joseph P. Free has an excellent appendix on wine in the Bible, in which the various Hebrew and Greek words are analyzed.*   I do not think the manufacturers of alcoholic beverages will find much support from Scripture for their trade.   Above all, it seems to me exceedingly unlikely, if the main thrust of what we have said in these last three chapters is correct,

---

* Free, Joseph P., *Archaeology and Bible History*, Wheaton, Ill., Scripture Press, rev., 1962, Append. 2, p. 352.

that the Lord Himself would initiate a solemn feast in his own memory involving alcohol in any form, much less deliberately create a very substantial quantity of the poison in order to celebrate an occasion which marked the beginning of a new life for two of his young friends.

If a vine in Eden was the cause of all our shame and nakedness and of death for man, it is perhaps not so strange that the Lord should have spoken of Himself as the *true* vine (John 15:1).

There are undoubtedly problems which remain; and I do not consider that I have any more than opened up certain lines of inquiry. Moreover, I should like to reiterate the important fact that I have been talking about the rationale of the fundamentals of our faith and not about the fundamentals themselves. Whatever may be the fate of this rationale, it is quite certain that the fundamentals will remain. Let us then return to a matter of far greater theological importance.

Chapter 13

THE THEOLOGICAL IMPLICATIONS OF DEATH

Death is the wages of sin
Romans 6:23

All have sinned.
Romans 3:23

It is appointed unto men once to die.
Hebrews 9:27

As in Adam all die,
even so in Christ shall all be made alive.
1 Corinthians 15:22

We see Jesus . . . .
made a little lower than the angels
for the suffering of death . . . .
that He, by the grace of God,
should taste death for every man.
Hebrews 2:9

I lay down my life . . . .
No man taketh it from me,
but I lay it down of myself.
John 10:18

Hereby perceive we the love of God,
because He laid down his life for us.
1 John 3:16

To conclude Part I, let me try to put the death of the *last* Adam in the context of what has been said about the death of the *first*.

The death of the Lord Jesus Christ was an absolutely unique event in history.   There has never been another death like it, either as a punishment, as a suicide, as a martyrdom, or even as an act of self-sacrifice by any other human being on behalf of his fellows.   And yet it was for man and AS A MAN that He died.

In relation to the origin and nature of Adam as created, the circumstances surrounding the death of the Lord are of tremendous importance: and they are equally important in relation to the phenomenon of death itself in so far as it came to be part and parcel of human experience as a consequence of Adam's disobedience in eating the forbidden fruit.

We have, unfortunately, become so familiar with the concept of self-sacrifice and martyrdom that we have difficulty in discerning how entirely unique the Lord's death really was.   We readily acknowledge that He was master of his life and beyond the reach of his enemies until He chose to submit to them.   This we commonly take to be the meaning of his words, "no man taketh my life from Me. I lay it down of Myself" (John 10:18); or again, where we are told, "Then they sought to take Him: but no man laid hands upon Him for his hour was not yet come" (John 7:30).   In short, we assume that his choice was really a matter of *timing*: when the time was come, He would submit Himself to their designs and permit his own death by crucifixion.   This did, indeed, happen: but it is only part of what happened. Moreover, it is really the least part: for the cross itself was only the stage upon which a unique drama of death was acted out when the Lord Jesus Christ not only chose the TIME to die, *but chose to* die.

We have no choice in this matter.   We can sometimes choose the setting or the hour of our death by provoking martyrdom or by committing suicide, for example.   We can provoke others into effecting our own destruction, or we can voluntarily sacrifice our lives by some act of heroism in a time of crisis.   But how ever noble the act, we are after all only choosing the mode or the setting or the time for the fulfilling of an event which is inevitable in any case.   In the final analysis, we have no choice in the matter of whether we will die.   We *will*, in due course.   We know we will, for we are mortals.   Death is appointed for us as an inescapable terminus to life.*   It is merely a question of whether we die early or late, prematurely or protractedly.   Within certain limits we may hasten death or postpone it: but we cannot escape it and therefore we cannot pretend that we ever do any more than influence the *time* of our dying.   In the matter of being subject

---

* It is true that we shall not *all* die (1 Thess.4:17), but the circumstances here are quite exceptional.

to death as mortal creatures, we have no say. We shall die, willy nilly.

Yet we know now that it is quite possible to conceive of a situation in which this might not have been the case. As we have seen, death is by no means an inevitable consequence of being alive. Millions of creatures never do die, and even more millions never need to die, even though they do.[157]   And we still have no clear understanding of the cause of death for those creatures below man even when it does occur, unless it is the result of accident or disease — where of course the reason is clear enough. There is no certainty that death is ever "natural" in the commonly accepted sense for any creature. Functioning protoplasm in some organisms (especially plant life, but even in unicellular animals) is still potentially immortal.   Nor is it strictly "natural" for man either, but un-natural. **The penalty of eating the fruit was not the shortening of a life which had an appointed terminus in any case, but the introduction of an entirely new experience — PHYSICAL DEATH.**

We die because we are killed. Death is a penalty imposed upon us. Death is *passive* in the strictest sense, something that is done to us, something that we "suffer" — which is the meaning of the word *passive*. Strictly speaking, we are executed. We do not die *actively* in the sense that our wills decide at some particular moment that we shall now terminate our lives with no other compulsion to do so save that we will it. But Jesus did. He died by an act of will, a triumph of spirit over flesh rather than flesh over spirit as it is with us. Death came to Him only because He deliberately dismissed his life when, and only when, He had completely finished the work his Father had given Him to do. He died *on* the cross but not because of it. He may just possibly have died *with* a broken heart;* but a broken heart was not the real cause of his death. He was slain, that is true; but this was really only a slaying by intent, even as adultery may be committed by intent (Matt.5:27, 28). For it will be noted that He was slain *and* crucified (Acts 2:23). He had affirmed unequivocally that no man could take his life (John 10:18). He laid down his life of Himself.

We are subject to death, He *became* subject to death (Phil.2:8). We are humbled, He humbled *Himself* (Phil.2:8). We may, like Paul, be ready "to be offered" (2 Tim.4:6), which is *passive*; He offered Himself (Heb.7:27), which is *active*. He did not merely choose the *time* of dying: He had the choice of whether to die at all. We no longer have any such choice.

I do not wish to become too deeply involved at this point in this most wonderful of all truths. It is the more specific subject matter of

---

* See Appendix VII, *Heart Rupture: A Possible Cause of the Lord's Death?*

Part IV. But it is of fundamental importance to realize the uniqueness of this one death in history. Because He was made after the power of endless life (Heb.7:16), there was no time limit imposed on Him, no appointed life span. He could have sustained his life for ever, endlessly, effortlessly — not merely as God, but as MAN. Thus He was uniquely in a position to choose not simply the *time* at which He would permit Himself to be crucified (which even mortal men have the power to do under certain circumstances) but He could actually choose whether to die or not to die at all. This is such a simple truth: so easily missed. It is so seldom preached that the world is left even yet to assume that his death was merely a particularly noble martyrdom under circumstances which were unusually distressing because of its protractedness as a means of execution.

In the trial of the Lord Jesus Christ we have a very remarkable situation. He proved Himself to be totally un-judgeable! Not one person could be found to demonstrate any single fault by which to condemn Him to death. He was without blemish. Pilate, Pilate's wife, the centurion in charge of the execution detail, the thief on the cross, even Judas who betrayed Him — all gave the same unequivocal verdict, "Not guilty". Yet He was condemned as guilty and his guilt was established *on the basis of a statement which He made about Himself which was absolutely true!* (Mark 14:61-65). So He went to the cross in order that there might be laid on Him the sinfulness of others, having proved that He had none of his own. As we have noted, our *physical* death is *passive*: He died *actively*. Our *spiritual* death, by contrast, is *active*, for we deliberately choose to be and want to be the kind of people we are: his *spiritual* death, on the other hand, was *passive*; for God "laid upon Him the iniquity of us all" (Isa.53:6), and though He willingly accepted the burden, He nevertheless cried out in agony against it when the judgment fell (Matt.27:46); for it meant spiritual separation from his Father in heaven, and such a "darkness" that even the sun hid its face.

On the cross, the Lord thus died two deaths, even as we die two deaths: first a spiritual one and then a physical one. But whereas for us spiritual death is active and our physical death is passive, spiritual death *for Him* was passive whereas his physical death was active. The cross was a unique setting for this, as we shall have occasion to explore in depth in Part IV. Without any compulsion of any kind, least of all the compulsion of the poisonous stream which, through Adam, introduces death into our bodies and by which we are called upon in due time to surrender our lives, He *dismissed* his life (John 19:30) just as effectively as Pilate had dismissed Him from the court (John 19:16). The same word is used in the Greek (*paradidomi,* παραδίδωμι) in both cases, a fact which most translations obscure.

What the first Adam might potentially have been, the second Adam realized to the full both physically and spiritually. He died, it is true: but He died for us, for me, and not on his own account, being neither worthy of *spiritual* death nor subject to *physical* death.

Only if Adam had this same spiritual and physiological potential could the Lord Jesus Christ have stood as his counterpart as MAN and been in a position to perform these two vicarious functions. Only thus was He truly representative of fallen man. The Lord's death might still have been vicarious in the truest sense if He had been supernaturally born an immortal creature: but unless Adam was also such a creature, the Lord was not truly a second Adam and his death was not really legal tender *for man*.

But He had to be something far more than man. The legal principle requires an eye for an eye and a tooth for a tooth: and it requires accordingly two eyes for two eyes . . . . On the same principle, one man may sacrifice himself for one man but not for two, and certainly not for ten, or a hundred, or a thousand. This Man was more than man, for this Man was also God. Here, then, was an atonement sufficient, if need be, for the sins of the whole world (1 John 2:2). The "whosoever will" makes demands upon such a Redeemer that no mere man can possibly suffice for all who actually will. Yet the Redeemer must be truly *Man* and not superman if he is to stand as a substitute for any *one* of those who will. When we abandon any single part of the revelation of Scripture, we make shipwreck of the whole plan of redemption. From the record of Adam's creation in Genesis right through to the birth and life and death and bodily resurrection of the second Adam in the New Testament there is an unbroken thread of logical necessity. It is a single fabric of tightly woven historical exigencies.

Christian theology is not a system of beliefs loosely thrown together with no essential coherence between the component elements. It is an organic whole, a unified system, a closely connected framework of thought which is logically defensible if preserved in its entirety but irrational if merely presented selectively as a catalogue of traditional beliefs. There were physiological reasons for creating Adam first and then deriving Eve out of him as a second step, physiological reasons why Adam and Eve were expelled from the Garden of Eden, and physiological reasons why the virgin conception was necessary.

While the cause of the Lord's unexpected early death on the cross was not itself strictly a physiological one, all the steps that led up to it were. And so was his bodily resurrection without seeing corruption. The means by which our redemption has been secured are all firmly rooted in physiological processes.   It was a redemption achieved only because the Lord Jesus Christ was in a position to sacrifice his life in an entirely unique manner, a manner never before witnessed in history and never to be repeated again.

This does not mean that there were not *spiritual* reasons also, nor that these spiritual reasons were not equally or perhaps even more important.   It only means that we are in a better position today to gain some deeper insights into the physiological aspects of these events which were not available in former times.   Such new understandings will never generate faith, no matter how clear the evidence may come to be: but such understandings should surely be used to enable us to explore the faith we already have.   Whereas it is true that the actual APPLICATION of the redemptive process depends upon the nature of man's spirit, a nature which allows him to see his own need and to appropriate God's promises (which animals never could do), it is still a fact that the MANNER of man's redemption hinges upon the nature of man's body which permits the Son of God to be made flesh in order to achieve it.

It is customary to look upon man's body as a burden to him, as though only his spirit had eternal significance.   Yet Scripture is very clear in stating that the crucifixion by which his eternal redemption was secured was dependent upon One who also sacrificed his BODY. He was made *flesh* (John 1:14; 1 Tim.3:16) in order that He might bear our sins in his own *body* on the tree (1 Peter 2:24).   So that we are now reconciled to God in the *body of his flesh* through death (Col.1:21, 22), and perfected for ever by the offering of his *body* (Heb.10:5, 10, 20).   Man is not a spiritual creature who merely happens to have a body and who might, therefore, just as easily have been an angel.   The distinction between men and angels is very carefully drawn for this very reason, namely, that man's redeemability hinges upon his *physical* existence.   Man's body is as much a part of his total being as the Lord's glorious body became part of his total glory: and man's bodily resurrection is as essential to his completion as the Lord's bodily resurrection was to the completion of his sacrifice. Man is a body/spirit entity: not a body with a spirit or a spirit with a body but a reality resulting from the interdependence of both.   Though we have been already re-created in spirit if we have availed ourselves of the salvation which is in Christ Jesus, we still wait for the process to be completed by the adoption of − i.e., the redemption of − the *body* (Rom.8:23) which is yet to be fashioned like his glorious body (Phil. 3:21).   Though we do indeed groan in this body and desire to be freed from its limitations, we do not want to be bodiless but re-embodied, "reclothed" as Paul put it, that "mortality might be swallowed up of life" (2Cor.5:4).   As Thomas Boston put it so very beautifully:

> There is a vileness in the body (Phil.3:21) which as to the
> saints, will never be removed, until it be melted down in the
> grave, and cast into a new form at the resurrection, to come
> forth a spiritual body.*

It is the reality of man's bodily existence even after resurrection
that allows us to see something of the vital connection beween man
and the world he is a part of, and to find in man its ultimate significance.

It seems sheer presumption to suppose that such a stupendous
Universe should have been created merely as a setting for man.   Yet
the idea is not altogether irrational even from the scientific point of
view.   All the evidence tells us that this is truly a uni-verse, in which
every element plays some essential part.   Today there are those who
in all seriousness tell us that our world and its living inhabitants owe
their character to the structure of the rest of the Universe.

The nature of the Universe, by its total composition, determines
the nature of life itself.   In the past it was customary to say that life
was solely dependent upon the existence and character of the earth
itself.   This no longer appears to be entirely true: indeed, those who
are searching for the origin of life along purely naturalistic lines now
tend, generally speaking, to search elsewhere than on the earth. Russell
W. Maatman has this to say about the inter-dependence between the
phenomenon of life and the character of the Universe as a whole: [158]

> At the molecular level, there is only one element, *carbon*, which
> comprises the skeleton of the long chain molecules found in all liv-
> ing things.   Living things are similar to each other in this respect
> because no other element is capable of forming long chains: and
> this relation between the elements can in turn be shown (using the
> quantum mechanics) to exist because of the very nature of the
> universe.   Likewise, at the microscopic level, God made similar
> structures in living creatures because only these structures can
> carry out the functions intended for them.   Again, the basic reason
> a certain function can be carried out by only one structure lies in
> the very nature of the universe.

Harold Blum observed that "the stage upon which living systems
bowed their debut was set by all the preceding events in the history of
the earth, or for that matter of the universe . . . ."[159] D. W. S. Sciama
is now suggesting that even our ability to manipulate and handle the
objects of our environment, which is so enormously simplified for us
by the presence of gravity, may in fact be dependent upon the very

---

* Boston, Thomas, *Human Nature in its Fourfold State*, London, Religious Tract Soc., n.d.,
p. 99; originally published in 1720.

existence of distant galaxies elsewhere in the Universe.[160]

John A. Wheeler would pursue this line of thought beyond the realm of biology even into the realm of consciousness itself: [161]

> No one . . . . can fail to find thought-provoking a suggestion made by Dicke, half jokingly, half seriously. "What sense does it have", he asks, "to speak about a universe unless that universe contains intelligent beings?"
>
> But intelligence implies a brain. And a brain cannot come into being without life. As the foundation for life no biochemist sees any alternative but DNA. But DNA demands carbon for its construction. Carbon in turn comes into being by thermonuclear combustion in the stars. Thermonuclear combustion demands billions of years in time.
>
> But according to general relativity a universe cannot provide billions of years of time unless it also has billions of light years of extent. On this view it is not the universe that has dominion over man, but man who governs the size of the universe.

Julian Huxley saw man as unique above all other living creatures by reason of his power of conceptual thought.[162]   It is this faculty which makes man capable of entering into fellowship with God and of returning his love.   And this appears to be the fundamental reason why God created man.   If, as Sciama proposes, the Universe itself is essential for the existence of such an earth as ours, and such an earth as ours for the existence of such a creature as man, then God created the Universe in order that He might create man.   But a creature with the power of conceptual thought is a creature with a series of unique requirements.   For one does not have thought, where man is concerned, without a brain — and thought does not find expression without language.   And, tied together with these in a causal chain of necessity, is a whole series of further requirements which may be summed up in terms of freedoms and capacities which are uniquely true only of man. Julian Huxley seems to have been aware of these necessities, even though he attributes them to a process of blind evolution.   Thus he wrote: [163]

> There is only one group of animals which will fulfill these conditions — a terrestrial offshoot of the higher primates. Thus, not merely has conceptual thought been evolved only in man: it could not have evolved except in man . . . .
>
> Conceptual thought on this planet is inevitably associated with a particular type of Primate body and Primate brain.

It is sometimes said that there must be other intelligent beings not unlike man elsewhere in a universe of such fantastic dimensions as this Universe appears to be.   But those who make this assumption do not always take into account the extraordinary number of unique circumstances attendant upon the existence of such a creature as man is with all his potentiality, both for good and for evil. Without in any way surrendering his wholly agnostic position, no less an authority than Gaylord Simpson has expressed very grave doubts about such a possibility. In an essay entitled, "Some Cosmic Aspects of Evolution", he has this to say:[164]

> To what extent and in what way were the species of organisms that actually exist, and most particularly the species *Homo sapiens*, the inevitable or necessitated results of evolution? An attempt to answer that question is the central theme of this essay. The question is truly cosmic in at least two senses. First, its answer must depend on and at the same time shed light on the nature of the whole physical universe. Second, the probability that man-like organisms exist elsewhere in the universe can be estimated only if some answer to this question is first obtained . . .
>
> The chances that anything like man . . . . exist elsewhere in the universe are, I think, the same as the chances that any other planet had exactly the same history as the earth — and as its inhabitants (i.e., plant and animal) — in every essential detail . . . . In my opinion, these chances are effectively nil.

We are in fact, almost driven to the conclusion that man is indeed "possible" only because the Universe is what it is, and that the Universe was created to make this "possibility" a reality. Hugo St. Victor put it this way:*

> The world was created for man's body, man's body for his spirit, and man's spirit for God: the spirit that it might be in subjection unto God, the body unto the spirit, and the world unto the body.

A later writer, whose name is not known, said simply, "The cosmos was pregnant with man".** Later still, Hodge said, "Creation is in order to redemption".† Linnaeus said that the mineral Kingdom supports the vegetable Kingdom, and the vegetable Kingdom supports the animal Kingdom, and the animal Kingdom supports *Man*".‡ It is

---

* Hugo St. Victor: quoted by H. O. Taylor, *Medieval Mind in the Early Middle Ages,* London, Macmillan, Book II, 1938, p. 91.

** Ramm, Bernard, *The Christian View of Science and Scripture,* Grand Rapids, Eerdmans, 1954, p. 227.

† Hodge, Charles, *Systematic Theology,* Grand Rapids, Eerdmans reprint, 1973, Vol. II, p. 316.

‡ Linnaeus: quoted by John C. Greene, *The Death of Adam,* Iowa State Univ. Press, 1959, p. 132.

all of a piece, the setting was designed for the fulfillment of a special purpose by the Creator: namely, the exhibition of his love by an act of self-sacrifice on behalf of a creature whose *need* and whose *nature* specifically equipped him to be the recipient of its benefit. As Irenaeus put it, "Man had to be created from the first in the image of Him who was afterwards to be incarnate for man's redemption".*

One may ask, "How could man have borne a *physical* image of God who is pure spirit"? The question can only be answered by saying that it was looking forward to the time when God would objectify Himself by Incarnation in order to sacrifice Himself for man's redemption, a sacrifice which, as far as we know, could not have been made in any other form than through incarnation, because this sacrifice involved the tasting of death.

We have said that in order to redeem more than one man, the Redeemer had to be more than man. In Psalm 8:5 we are told that the angels partially fulfill the condition of being in some way more than man in the hierarchy of created beings, and therefore it is conceivable that the sacrifice of an angel *might* have sufficed for the redemption of more than one. But Scripture seems to make it reasonably clear that an angel is not capable of experiencing death and could not therefore become a sacrificial victim anyway. And, of course, God Himself, *as pure uncreated spirit,* cannot die either. As Luther stated it: "for God by his very nature is not able to die" (*non enim in sua natura Deus mori potest*). For this very reason, God in the Person of his Son the Lord Jesus Christ, had to become man and so be made for a season "a little lower than the angels for the suffering of death" (Heb.2:9), thus fulfilling the role of Saviour without surrendering his deity.

Man is not merely a spiritual creature who happens to have the kind of body he does and who might just as suitably have been equipped with any other kind of animal body. He is a creature whose uniqueness from the point of view of his humanness, both in terms of culture and spiritual aspiration, is as much dependent upon the structure of his body as upon the nature of his soul. It is quite wrong to imagine that the form of man's body is incidental and that he might have been structured like a giraffe or a dog or a mouse — or even an ape — and still have fulfilled the role for which he was created. This role required that he not merely be capable of redemption, but that he also be an appropriate proto-type of the One who was to be the Redeemer. Indeed, it would be more strictly true to say that the

---

* In *A Dictionary of the Bible,* James Hastings, N.Y., Scribners, 1906, Vol. II, p. 453.

Redeemer incarnate was the proto-type of man. In a sense, this is what man was *for*, and knowing this, we really have the answer to the more commonly asked question of what man IS. He must always have been such a creature that God in the Person of his Son could have become incarnated in the same form at any time in order to be his redeemer. And He must be able to do this without demeaning in any way his glory as the Son of the Father.

Perhaps we can illuminate this by the use of an analogy. If a man builds a house for his animals, he suits its construction to their nature and disposition, besides being guided by what he hopes to do with them. If he happened to be raising snakes in order to extract their venom for research purposes, it would be a house from which they could not escape but in which they would still thrive. For his cattle, he can build a house that is large enough to accomodate their greater bulk with facilities for keeping them fed and warm and clean, but they must be able to go in and out. Yet he would not need to take the same precautions against their escape as he would have to do with dangerous creatures like snakes, or destructive animals like pigs, or with vagrant ones like horses. For his dog, he would construct a house that in some small measure shared his own home comfort and style, for this is what his dog is likely to do.

Thus the nearer he gets to a house for a creature sharing his own likes and dislikes, the more like his own house it will be. For his hired man, he will probably build a house that he himself and his family would be willing to occupy — if he is a man of feeling and concern for those who work for him.

Ultimately, we come to his *own* house. How does he build it? He builds it not to suit his livestock, or his pets, or even his hired man. He builds it for himself. It takes on and reflects his own person in many subtle ways. It is likely, at least in so far as he has the resources and the design ability, to be uniquely suitable for HIM . . . . more suitable for him than for anyone else. When a man hands over such a house to someone else, either by sale or as a gift, it is almost certain to be modified by the next in-dweller: thus proving how special in certain respects it was for himself as a habitation.

Now what, then, will God do if *He* decides to build a house which is to be fit for Himself, which in due course will be *his* habitation, a house which is to serve Himself for thirty-three years, in which *He* will live and express his character, inhabiting it day and night, constantly, actively, fully, sleeping and waking, being born and dying? It will be a house capable of being so lived in, appropriately and worthily. It will be a house that can sustain the demands of habitability that *He will make* upon it.

It will be beautiful, for obviously God must rejoice in beauty that He should make so many beautiful things in the world, and it will be 'flexible' to allow the expression in the face, by the hands, by body movement, of the whole range of human mood from delight to mourning, from solitude to companionship in the way. It must have all the facilities (faculties in this context since it is a *body* that we speak of) which will permit movement, expression, communciation, gesture, comprehension, display of emotion, and even feelings of weariness, which are necessary for true sympathy of the human lot and to which others can minister upon special occasion. And above all, if the object from the very first was to be not merely the revelation of God but the redemption of man, it must be a house of such a nature that it can be deliberately sacrificed, not because it has worn out or is wearing out, but because He who is incarnate in it chooses to sacrifice it.

In order that this sacrifice could be truly and wholly an act of will and not something that had to be surrendered inevitably by the very wearing out of it, the house must be a house that would never wear out of itself, never collapse in the course of time as our houses do because it is their nature to do so, for otherwise it is merely being *prematurely* demolished. It *must* be capable of lasting indefinitely, even though it can be deliberately sacrificed. This house had to be of such a nature as to allow an event which was to signify something other than the mere premature breakdown of its structure: the house had to be of such a nature that its demolition could be purely an act of will unrelated to the condition of the house itself.

Moreover, precisely the same kind of house must be appointed as a habitation of both the first and the last Adam alike, in order that the conditions of physical life of *both* may have the same potential. It must be, for God's purposes, a house built with the capability of lasting for ever, even though that capability was twice sacrificed — the first time in Eden by an act of disobedience, and the second time on Calvary by an act of obedience. Remember Augustine's statement regarding Adam's constitution: "It was not impossible for him to die, but possible for him not to die". This *must* be true of both Adams, for unless it was, the death of Jesus Christ was not vicarious. **If Jesus was not immortal, his death was merely premature. If Jesus was immortal but Adam was not, then Jesus was not truly man and his death would not be substitutionary for MAN.**

This house, this body that is the home of man's spirit, is not just a complex electro-chemical machine. It was *designed* from the very first for a special purpose. It was so built that it would properly meet the requirements which God had in mind both for man *and for Himself* in the Person of the Lord Jesus Christ. In due course, it was to make it possible for God to express Himself perfectly in terms of human personality AS A MAN. And then, as a Man, to sacrifice his life vicariously for any man who would believe and appropriate that sacrifice as a full, perfect and sufficient satisfaction in the face of the divinely appointed moral law, against his own sinfulness and failure and self-will. God made man's body such that He Himself could assume it for a season as his own proper House so that in due time in the person of his Son Jesus Christ, He might die in it, that we who are dying from the day of our birth might be redeemed to live again and for ever in a new and more glorious resurrected 'house' throughout eternity. Thus was exhibited the grace and love of our God and Saviour in an entirely personal way. No mere animal body could have sufficed for such a tremendous purpose and we therefore see that Adam cannot have received his body by animal descent.

It is inconceivable that God could have expressed Himself as a Person in any other creature than man as we know him now. It is only in man's reprobate mind that the idea of God as a serpent or a crocodile or a bull or a wolf could have occurred with such force that he would bow down and worship such images, changing the truth of God into a lie and worshipping and serving such creatures rather than their Creator (Rom.1:23-25). No wonder idol worship is so strictly forbidden (Exod.20:4, 5).

Many devout people find it possible to make out some kind of case for the derivation of fallen man's body from some animal prototype. But in order to account for a body such as housed the spirit of the Lord Jesus Christ, which reflected in a unique way the unfallen Adam as created, one has to search outside the ordinary course of events entirely. For if Adam's body was derived from some prior animal form for which death was "programmed" and inevitable, then Adam's body must have shared this programmed character and for him too death would have been inevitable, not as a penalty but as a fact of life. So also, then, would the second Adam. For Him, death would have been likewise inevitable in the end. His death on the cross then becomes merely premature and not substitutionary at all.

As the second Adam, He voluntarily embraced death, a phenomenon foreign to his physiological constitution. When He died He did not merely surrender what remained to Him of his expected life, being then about thirty-three years old. He embraced death entirely as an act of will, being wholly free and able to make such a choice. Thus He undid what Adam had imposed upon the human race as a universal penalty, by "tasting death for every man" (Heb.2:9).

We have now to see how it came about that Scripture identified the Lord Jesus Christ as a second "Adam" (1 Cor.15:45).   In what sense was Jesus Christ both a "last" Adam and the "second" man? Were there then only two who could properly be called "men"? What of all the saints who came between Adam and Christ — the seven thousand, for instance, who had not bowed the knee to Baal (1 Kings 19:18)?   If we hold that by rebirth our true identity as "man" has been recovered, and if we hold that the Old Testament saints had a genuine experience of conversion, were there not therefore many who succeeded the first Adam as truly *men*?

How, then, does it come about that the Lord Jesus Christ is identified as only the *second* man?   Clearly He has title to this according to Scripture.   Yet upon what basis, within the framework of human history, does this title rest?   In Part II the grounds for this title are set forth.

PART II

**THE SEED
OF THE WOMAN**

The seed of the man and the seed of the woman are antithetical.

The seed of the man became the *carrier* of death; the seed of the woman the *viaduct* of life.

Chapter 14

SETTING THE STAGE FOR THE INCARNATION

When the fullness of time had come,
God sent forth his Son,
made of a woman,
made under the law,
to redeem them that were under the law,
that we might receive the adoption of sons.
Galatians 4:4, 5

And the Word was made flesh
and dwelt among us
and we beheld his glory.
John 1:14

We are now about to examine from the point of view of genetics, embryology, and developmental physiology, certain key events which finally prepared the way for the birth of the Lord Jesus Christ as the second Adam. It is desirable, therefore, in the interests of continuity to review briefly the nature of the problem and thus to clarify what are the requirements for a Redeemer who must personally represent sinners who are *dead or dying in two different ways.*

Man is dying as to his body, having lost the potential immortality with which he was originally endowed in Adam: and man is already dead as to his spirit, being cut off from fellowship with God and thereby severed from the fountain of all spiritual life. He thus stands before his God as a miserable sinner burdened with a defective and slowly disintegrating body, while his spirit is so corrupted that he cannot do the things he knows he should and constantly finds himself doing those things he knows he should not.

Even when his spirit aspires to better things he finds his best efforts thwarted by the weakness of the flesh. Man is in every respect a ruined creation. He is in need of both re-creation and redemption: he needs re-creation as to his spirit (John 3:7) and redemption as to his body (Rom.8:23). Two things must therefore be accomplished for him if he is to recover his manhood as God intended it to be.

In the story of Eden, after Adam had disobeyed and destroyed his original constitution both physically and spiritually, we are told that God cried out, "Adam, where art thou?" (Gen.3:9). I do not think that God was searching for *fallen* man (whose whereabouts He surely knew) but for unfallen Adam who had simply disappeared. It was Adam as created, physically immortal and spiritually alive, who had vanished.

In order to recover his true manhood, he must recover his physical immortality and he must recover his spiritual purity. He needs redemption and salvation; he needs a Redeemer and a Saviour. These two distinct needs cannot be over-emphasized, for if his need was only spiritual, the nature of the Lord's sacrifice could have been radically different — as we shall see.

This Redeemer and Saviour must himself be truly "human" with respect to both his body and his spirit. Only then can He be an acceptable substitute for such a creature as man is, in jeopardy of two kinds of death. To undo the damage introduced by the first Adam to himself and all his descendants, the second Adam must somehow reconstitute in Himself the perfection of the first Adam *before* he fell, thus to become Head of a new and truly human race.

The Redeemer must enjoy a physical immortality which He can then voluntarily sacrifice on behalf of others for the redemption of their *bodies* (Rom.8:23). And the Saviour must achieve a flawless perfection of character wholly without spot or blemish, which will permit Him to stand as a substitute for sinners whose character is totally unacceptable in the sight of God. Substitutionary sacrifice is at the root of this whole redemptive process. He who need never die must voluntarily embrace death (John 10:18), and He whose character has never in any way been corrupted by sin must be "made sin" (2 Cor. 5:21). Only so can the tragedy of Eden be undone. A new history must begin with a new Head of a new race.

Man is not, like the angels, a spiritual being only. Angels are purely spirit by divine appointment: man is *embodied* spirit by divine appointment. This body, indwelt by a God-given spirit, constitutes him a living soul (Gen.2:7). Because angels do not have bodies they are never termed "souls".

Man is a different order of being. While he shares something of the nature of the angels (having moral freedom and accountability, for example), yet he is an embodied creature (sharing something of the animal creation). He is thus entirely unique as a body/spirit entity whose soul has transcendant value in both this world and the next, belonging to both.

In the world to come, the resurrection of the body is therefore as essential to his wholeness as the continuance of his spirit is. Scripture is quite clear on this point. Some kind of ethereal, shadowy, ghostly existence throughout eternity is not in view for man, and accordingly there is not merely to be a new heavens but a new *earth* also (Rev.21:1). For his survival beyond death as man, he needs the recovery of embodiment: and although it will be a fundamentally re-constituted body it will remain as truly a human body as his spirit will remain a recognizably human spirit. The quality and nature of his human existence will thus be re-established in the presence of God throughout eternity, and therefore man will have potential that the angels can never have.

So the Saviour must be made flesh in order to become a substitute for the whole man. He must be incarnate, embodied, identified with the seed of Abraham (Heb.2:16) and therefore with the seed of Adam. Yet, on the principle of equivalence (an eye for an eye and a tooth for a tooth), He must be sufficient not merely for the redemption of *one* man but of *many*. How can He be truly man and yet be more than man that He may substitute for many men?

We have very specific clues as to how his body was to be "prepared" (Heb.10:5) for Him as He assumed the role of Redeemer: and Scripture tells us much on the subject of his worthiness to be the Saviour of *many*. It is revealed that before embodiment He was Himself God the Creator, the Jehovah of the Old Testament. It is written (John 1:1-3, 10, 14 and 1 Tim.3:16):

> In the beginning was the Word, and the Word was with God, and the Word was God. The same was in the beginning with God. All things were made by Him; and without Him was not any thing made that was made . . . .
>
> He was in the world, and the world was made by Him, and the world knew Him not . . . .
>
> And the Word was made flesh, and dwelt among us (and we beheld his glory, the glory as of the only begotten of the Father) full of grace and truth.
>
> Without controversy great is the mystery of godliness: God was manifest in the flesh . . .

So He did not become an angel, a *spiritual* being; but a man, a physical being.   And He did this with the express purpose of "tasting death" (Heb.2:9), of experiencing *physical* as well as *spiritual* death. Angels can experience spiritual death, for spiritual death is separation from God; and the angels which fell were excluded from his presence and therefore suffered this kind of dying.   In a purely spiritual way Jesus Christ as man might have suffered a like exclusion from God on man's behalf, and thus partially redeemed man in so far as he too is spiritually dead.   But man is not *only* a spirit being: such a substitut- ion could never suffice to redeem the whole man, the person, the individual body/spirit entity that he knows himself to be.   Such a salvation could conceivably have been achieved by the Saviour in those hours of darkness on the cross when He endured *our* due separ- ation from God.   But a half salvation is no salvation at all.   It is only our failure to perceive what an essential component of our humanness the body is, that makes such a "bloodless sacrifice" appealing.

No!   The Lord Jesus had two kinds of death to die in order to redeem us wholly.   In the present study we are laying particular em- phasis on what his *physical* death involved, though by no means overlooking its spiritual nature.   And the first step in preparation for this physical death was actually taken in Eden when Eve was not created as Adam was but was formed out of him in a separate operat- ion.   It may not seem that the two events could be so vitally connected but they are.   The formation of Eve bears directly on the redemption of man.

We therefore have to examine as fully as our present knowledge permits us to do so what was involved in such a process of "explant- ation", and in what way this gave special protection to the woman's seed and how this seed was thereafter preserved from generation to generation until it pleased God in due time to by-pass the male seed and by virgin conception initiate the preparation of that special body into which his Son was to enter (Heb.10:5) when the time was fully come (Gal.4:4).

Let us first set forth the biblical record of Eve's formation as re- corded in Genesis and then examine its implications in the light of what we know about the dimorphic constitution of man and of woman as we now observe them.   Here, then, are the words from Scripture:

Genesis 2:21-23
    And the Lord God caused a deep sleep to fall upon Adam, and he slept: and He took one of his ribs and closed up the flesh in- stead therof; and the rib, which the Lord had taken from man, made He a woman, and brought her to the man.
    And Adam said, This is now bone of my bones, and flesh of my flesh.   She shall be called woman, because she was taken out of man.

1 Corinthians 11:8 and 12
(Literally) For the man is not out of woman, but woman out of man . . . . For even as the woman (is) out of man, so also the man (is) through the woman.

1 Timothy 2:13
For Adam was first formed, then Eve.

We turn therefore to a subject which some readers may find hard going. As far as possible I have attempted to smooth out the difficult places. A few technicalities cannot be avoided. For the expert, most of the scientific background of the following chapters will be found spelled out with careful documentation at the end of this work in the Reference Section. The ordinary reader can safely ignore it.

The subject is indeed an involved one, and much of the data is new and has not yet percolated down in appropriate form for the general public. Nevertheless I am persuaded that this study will be well within the competence of any intelligent reader, especially one whose Christian convictions have predisposed his mind to receive what is said because Scripture is so wonderfully illuminated by it all.

I cannot do better than preface this section with one paragraph from a book review by Gordon Bermant of the University of Washington which appeared in the journal *Science* under the heading, "Human Sexual Development": [165]

> It is the fate of all serious interdisciplinary efforts to get hung on the horns of the communication dilemma: you either explain too much and bore some people or you move too fast and snow them. The more disciplines covered the more likely you are to accomplish both unfortunate ends at the same time with different groups of readers.

So we shall proceed with awareness of the dangers. We hope at least to provide some fresh insights into the actual moment of incarnation by laying emphasis upon the *physiology* of our redemption. My position throughout this volume is that God, in his creative wisdom, set the stage for man's redemption — the redemption of his body as well as his spirit — first by creating an Adam who was potentially immortal encompassing within himself both male and female seeds; and then by separating Eve out of him and entrusting to her one of the two seeds, fashioning for her a body specifically designed to preserve that seed through each successive generation uncorrupted because untouched by the fatal poison.

There is nothing arbitrary here, nothing purely miraculous as though God worked only by miracle, nor purely natural as though there was no need for divine intervention.

For God in his infinite wisdom had so designed the processes of conception and birth that He could use them without doing violence to his own created order as a means of entering into our world of space and time as the God-Man in the likeness of ourselves and for our redemption.

Chapter 15

MALE AND FEMALE CREATED HE THEM

And Adam said,
This is now bone of my bone and flesh of my flesh:
she shall be called Woman
because she was taken out of man . . . .
and they shall be one flesh.
Genesis 2:23, 24

For the man is not of the woman;
but the woman is of the man.
1 Corinthians 11:8

This chapter is really in two sections. The first, which comprises the text itself, is a general statement of what is currently known with reasonable certainty about the origin and development, in the maturing individual, of the differences in both form and function between the two sexes. It is important to be aware of these facts because, as will be seen in due course, they have a direct bearing on the taking of Eve out of Adam. The subject also has a direct bearing on the Virgin Birth and the Incarnation. The other section which might have appeared as supporting footnotes were it not as extensive as the text itself (!), will be found in the form of expanded notes which have been relegated to the Reference Section. These scientific excursions are primarily intended for those who by background and training will wish to have a more detailed treatment of the evidence. These notes can be safely disregarded without any harm being done to the thread of the argument by those who do not desire to become involved in technical detail.   The continuity of this study will not be seriously disturbed if they are simply ignored.   The body of the text itself, however, has a very direct bearing on the creation of Eve out of Adam and is therefore quite essential to what follows later.

When the female ovum is fertilized by the male, there is initiated an incredibly complex chain of events which culminate nine months later in the birth of a child.   During the very early stages of this gestation period the development of the embryo is predisposed in certain directions by the possession of the sex chromosomes which are composed of two elements, one contributed by the mother and the other by the father.   The mother can contribute only what is termed an X chromosome which predisposes towards the development of female structural, functional and temperamental characteristics, but the father can contribute either an X or a Y chromosome predisposing in the first instance to female, or in the second to male, structural and functional and temperamental characteristics.   In short, the sex of the child to be born is initially governed by the chromosomal contribution of the father.   All chromosomes are paired, and the Y is dominant over the X chromosome when combined with it.   A child conceived will therefore be subject during development thereafter to a predisposition towards femaleness if receiving an X chromosome from the mother and an X chromosome from the father (XX), or towards maleness if receiving an X chromosome from the mother but a Y chromosome from the father (XY).

In the earlier stages of embryological research it was believed that the contribution to the ovum of the X or the Y chromosome from the male parent *predetermined* the sex of the developing child.   It is now recognized however, that the word "predetermine" is too strong and should be replaced by the word *predispose*.   The truth of the matter is that in the very early stages of foetal development certain disturbing factors may neutralize this predisposition and despite the presence of the supposedly determinate sex chromosome contributed by the male, the individual may emerge oppositely sexed.   As Professor Dorothy Price put it: [166]

> Although its genetic sex has already been determined, depending on whether a Y-carrying or an X-carrying sperm fertilized the egg from which it has grown, the early foetus is structurally equipped to become *either* a male or a female (emphasis mine).

There are many factors which may disturb or confuse the relationship between the sex chromosome and the emergent femininity or masculinity of the individual, so that it has become useful now to make a distinction between sex and gender, between the physical appearance of the individual and his or her actual temperamental disposition which may belie the physical appearance. [167] It is apparent today that the chain of events during prenatal development may be influenced by factors other than the X or Y chromosome, though these other factors are by no means altogether independent of them.

If and when such disruption occurs the sex of the child as assigned by the attending physician at birth (or later) on the basis of the genitalia or external organs of sex, may either contradict the chromosomal sex or may be indeterminate, appearing in the form of a mixture of both male and female physical characteristics. [168] It then becomes a very serious, and often very difficult, matter for the physician to assign the correct sex so that the developing child may psychologically as well as functionally assume the appropriate role in society to suit the inner drives which he or she will be subjected to as the reproductive organs become mature and begin to produce those hormones that so strongly influence behaviour in adult life.   Any conflict between these stimulators of sexual behaviour and the organs of sex which are appropriate to their functional expression can be devastating in terms of the psychological well-being of the afflicted individual.

The truth of the matter is that a significant number of people are indeterminate to a more or less degree in this regard.[169] Indeed, comparatively few of us (some would say virtually *none* of us) are wholly male or wholly female.   We are all a mixture of both in adult life; and in the earliest stages of embryonic development we are actually *neither.* The body at first seems equally capable of developing into a male or a female, *in spite of* the predisposing presence of the XY or XX chromosomes which were formerly presumed to be the inescapable triggers of a purely uni-sexual development.

Among the factors which can disturb or neutralize this triggering device in prenatal life are the presence of a twin of the opposite sex and, in humans, inadvisable medication during pregnancy. Postnatally among the factors capable of upsetting or even reversing sexual characteristics are operational intervention and so-called parasitic castration in which some parasite destroys part of the function of the sex organ itself, the testes of certain animals.[170]

It is now well recognized that under such influences a genetic or chromosomal male may become a female, both structurally and functionally. The reverse, however, is apparently very rare indeed,[171] though there may be a tendency in this direction with ageing due to the failure of the female hormonal system and emergence of some residual male hormonal activity which has hitherto been kept in abeyance by the dominant activity of the female hormone.[172]   Thus an older woman may develop some male characteristics such as a deepening and coarsening of the voice, some incipient baldness on the head, beard growth, reduction of the breasts, and, psychologically, the development of a more aggressive disposition.   These changes may be enhanced by certain pathological conditions.

It has been found that "maleness" is for some reason not straightforwardly achieved by the developing male foetus, which does not therefore merely "drift" into the appropriate form simply by possession of the Y chromosome.   Maleness is, as it were, actively imposed on the growing organism against a tendency towards femaleness.   The tendency to femaleness is in part due to the fact that the whole embryonic development has to take place within the confines of a uterus which is bathed by maternal hormones.[173] The reverse does not appear to be true; a female foetus does not tend towards maleness.

This active imposition is, of course, dependent upon the presence of the Y chromosome which causes the medulla of the gonad* to develop at the expense of the cortex.   If this drive is weakened for some reason and the cortex begins to develop at the expense of the medulla, the hitherto neutral organism develops towards a female regardless of the presence of the Y chromosome.   The gonad itself is, up to this point, "indifferent", and can therefore develop into a testis or an ovary, although for some unknown reason the gonad more *easily* develops into an ovary than into a testis.   On this account the unborn male is said to have to "struggle" to maintain its integrity as a male. There is apparently no difficulty in the derivation of a female out of a male.

If the gonad develops into a testis, male hormones are produced which structure the developing organism as a male: if it develops into an ovary, the reverse takes place.   It is in this sense that the embryo begins as an entirely neutral organism from the point of view of its sexuality, the X and the Y chromosomes providing the necessary predisposition to decide which way the gonads shall develop, but not providing an infallible pre-determination.   In the *absence* of the Y chromosome the gonad has apparently no power to follow a course of development towards maleness, but even in the *presence* of the Y chromosome, the other influences acting upon the gonad may still override the influence of the Y chromosome.   To repeat, therefore, in the present state of our knowledge there are no barriers to the principle of deriving a female out of a male (an Eve out of an Adam),

---

* The gonad is the very first identifiable structure of the reproductive system to be formed in the developing foetus.   The medulla is the inner core of the gonad as opposed to its outer layers or cortex.

but there *are* evidently barriers to the derivation of male out of female.

At the present moment it appears that the best explanation of such sexual indeterminism is to assume that the sexes were at one time not differentiated at all, that the individual was bi-sexual. With respect to Adam as first created, this could very well mean that he was gynandromorphous in terms of his physical constitution, and androgynous as to his temperament, a man/woman creation, subsequently divided into two: and that the process of separation involved the removing of a female principle out of the male as "woman". The man thus retains both the X and the Y chromosomes whereas the woman carries only the X chromosome.

It must occur to the reader that such bisexuality as we are here attributing to Adam, converted into a monosexual being when Eve was subsequently separated from him, represents a situation that may well have applied equally to some of the other forms of animal life which also testify to a measure of residual bisexuality. I think this is quite likely. The surgical operation which separated Eve from Adam may not therefore have been the only occasion, or even the first occasion, upon which God acted in this way. This should not be a matter of any grave concern in that both man and animals alike also shared a similar experience of creation in the first place, similar at least in so far as both alike return to the dust (Eccl.3:20). It would surely not be so surprising that God should adopt a single procedure when introducing forms of life which share many things in common as to their over-all physiology.

Admittedly, it may seem to lessen the uniqueness of man's position a little but it cannot be denied and, as may be seen from the indexed references (chiefly #175, 176, and 177) animals also share a certain indecisiveness in the matter of sexual dimorphism which parallels that found in man though in a far more pervasive form. We are not really robbing man of his uniqueness; we are only saying, as we have already said in another connection*, that God prepared the natural order *before* Adam was created in such a way that it would serve (when it came time to create man) as a *natural* framework for the working out of his redemptive plan, a plan which required that Eve be first of all part of Adam and only later separated from him — for reasons which will become apparent subsequently. This is an arrangement which God did not merely use because it was already in operation, but put into operation because He intended to extend its use in a very special

---

* Custance, A. C., in the *Doorway Papers Series*, Grand Rapids, Zondervan: see particularly *The Virgin Birth and the Incarnation*, Vol. V, Part III, p. 115 ff., and Part IV, p. 171 ff; and *Evolution or Creation*, Vol. IV, Part I, p. 13 ff.

way.

The present tendency among biologists, where evolutionary thinking reigns almost unchallenged, is to assume in the light of what we
now know, that sexual reproduction is a somewhat latecomer in the
great chain of life.[174]   Before it appeared there were no such sexual
differences as we now observe widely among living things.   Either sexual reproduction was non-existent (i.e., multiplication took place by
simple division as in unicellular animals), or both sexes were combined
in each individual which was self-fertilized by its own seed.[175]   Such a
method of reproduction is common among plants and animals, including insects, birds and fish.[176]   In such animals it is not at all unusual
for their bodies to contain a testis (on one side) and an ovary (on the
other side), and not infrequently the individual has the power of self-
fertilization — though in some species there is normally cross fertilization with either sex.[177]   The problem of the origin of sexual
reproduction without which the concept of male and female has
virtually no meaning in biology, is one which has baffled evolutionists
because it is difficult to see what the intermediate stages could possibly be.   It is not without interest that the very word *Adam* has come
to be employed within scientific circles as a kind of code term to identify the whole question of the emergence of sexual dimorphism.[178]

It is clear today that man still shares some of the androgynous
character of certain species of animals and one must assume, I think,
that the constitution of these animals below man reflects a design
which the Creator adopted in anticipation of the creation of Adam
who was at first similarly constituted with a bisexual nature in order
that a certain further operation which is revealed in Genesis 2:21-23
might be performed to set the stage for man's redemption.   As we
shall see, the creation of Adam in this form and the subsequent taking
of Eve out of him was planned by God for profoundly important
physiological reasons in the light of man's foreseen history and fore-
known need for redemption.   The crucial connection between the
Plan of Redemption and the initial form in which Adam was created,
according to Scripture, will be explored subsequently.   What is
important at the present moment is to realize that this initiating surgical operation has left an indelible mark upon man, the evidence of
which can still be a subject of fascinating research and the antecedents
of which seem to have been witnessed in the prior existence of many
other forms of animal life in which the sexes have remained combined
in the individual.   Such an Adam would have been quite viable.[179]

In man as a consequence of the Fall, the effects of this separation
have been disturbed in various ways, to our distress.   Certain irregularities in the distribution of the X and Y chromosomes lead to anomalous
developments which nevertheless permit us to see something of the

specific influences of these specialized chromosomes by their exaggerated effects in such irregular forms.   Thus in Turner's Syndrome the Y sex chromosome has somehow been lost so that the normal XY appears as XO.   Only one X chromosome is found and this is presumably contributed by the female parent.   As might perhaps be expected the virtual disappearance of the male sex component is reflected in a corresponding diminishing of maleness in the female child which results.   Such an individual is considered to be a particularly "pure" female.[180]

Meanwhile, in human beings there are vestigial remains in both sexes of the organs of the opposite sex, the nipples in man being an obvious example.   However, there is some evidence that these particular organs in the male of the species are not entirely useless.   Several reports are now available of men who have suckled children in cases of extreme need.   David Livingstone notes a statement from the works of Humboldt who reported an instance of the male breast yielding milk.*   Livingstone remarks upon an occasion in Scotland, where a man whose wife had been put to death, in desperation put his child to his breast and found, to the astonishment of himself and his neighbours, that milk flowed.[181]   Farley Mowatt gives a translation of a portion of one of the old Viking Sagas setting forth a rather similar siutation:[182]

> All that night Thorgiol watched over his infant son and he could see that the boy would not survive unless something drastic was done.   He did not intend to let him die if he could help it.
> Then he shewed his mettle, for he took a knife and cut his own nipple.   It began to bleed, and he let the baby tug at it until blood mixed with fluid came out.   He did not stop until milk came out; and the boy nursed upon that.

Birds may be so completely convertible as to sex, in either direction, that there have been reports since the fifteenth century of roosters becoming hens and laying eggs, and hens becoming roosters with all their cocky characteristics.   *The Basler Chronick* of 1624 reported that in 1474 an egg-laying cockerel was executed! [183]   *The Edinburgh Evening Courant* in July, 1834, mentions a turkey cock in East Lothian which had hatched a brood of chickens.[184]

Among animals, therefore, such transformations of sex and such combinations of diverse sexual characters within a single individual are frequent enough;   and bisexualism or hermaphroditism is common in plants.

The word *hermaphrodite* is formed from the names of two pagan

---

* Livingstone, David, *Travels and Researches in South Africa*, N.Y., Harper, 1858, p. 141.

deities Hermes and Aphrodite, who are said to have loved so dearly that they begot a child combining both their natures in one. It is obvious that the ancients were well acquainted with sexual aberrations and sought to explain some of them in super-natural terms. Because hermaphroditism is by no means limited to man, I think one must assume that, like physical immortality, it was built into the Natural Order by the Creator in anticipation of the making of man whose history was to require a similar potential.

It therefore appears, in the light of present knowledge, that in living forms below man a clear distinction between male and female is not always to be observed. In plants, bisexuality is exceedingly common, in insects frequent, in birds it is not rare, and in higher animals the distinctions are often blurred.[185] Moreover, we know now that in animals conversion can be in either direction, maleness is easily converted into femaleness, and *vice versa*: whereas in man conversion from femaleness to maleness seldom occurs in spite of attempts by human intervention. We also know that a surprising number of people are almost equally male and female in some aspects of their constitution and character.

Let me try to sum up, therefore, for the non-specialist reader the substance of what we have been considering thus far. Not many of us, with the possible exception of those who "suffer" from the Turner Syndrome, are entirely male or entirely female: we are all a little of both and some are so much so that their sex and gender are contradictory and life may become a very confusing experience.

Present evidence shows that by so constituting Adam, woman could quite conceivably be derived out of man: but it is difficult to conceive how man could have been taken out of woman. To my mind, the creation of Eve was pure miracle: but the Christian who has once settled this fact in his own mind should surely not be surprised to find that research now provides him with a little better understanding of the background of what he has long since believed. There is no longer any excuse for *denying* the possibility that our first parents could very well have been united in one individual named Adam (Gen.5:2).

Neither can be wholly complete without the other and yet such have been the disruptive effects of sin through the centuries that *constitutionally* it is a rare thing when two are joined in marriage with entire success, for the true maleness or femaleness of both has been disordered. Consequently we are no longer two perfect halves which would make one complete whole even on a physiological plane: we are only two fragments and these fragments rarely match perfectly in more than a few areas of interaction.

Experience shows, moreover, that those whose sexuality is least clearly differentiated towards one pole or the other are often the most highly gifted but also the least fitted for marriage.[186]

I suspect that the original "wholeness" that was in Adam at first was not merely the sum of two halves, but a compound with qualities and characteristics of which we can have little knowledge.* As the compound of two chemicals is usually quite different in its nature to the elements themselves,† so the first Adam, as created, was such a creature as to be as full of mystery and glory as the last Adam was.

So it is not at all necessary for the child of God any longer to speak apologetically about his faith in the creation of Eve out of Adam. This is sober history, and if we do not believe it, it is not because we know too much but because we know too little. Eve was taken out of Adam by a surgical operation, divinely performed while Adam was in a deep coma. And this mode of creation for her was essential, as we shall see, for the later appearing of the virgin born Saviour who was truly to represent the original Adam as God created him. This is miracle — but miracle performed with a rational end in view and by a means that was essential to the service of that end. Every year sees further advances in our understanding of why and how this could be so, and leaves us with increasing wonderment at the ways of the Lord in creating man, and the extraordinary insight of the Genesis story.

We conclude, therefore, that the record of the formation of Eve out of Adam is not only entirely reasonable but may in fact give us a clue which we would not, except for revelation, have had regarding the origin of certain aspects of man's form and function *and temperament* as he is now constituted. And by extrapolation, we may judge something of his original constitution when God created him.

---

* According to Berdyaev, "man is really a bisexual being combining both the masculine and feminine principle in different proportions. A man in whom the female principle is completely absent would be an abstract being, and a woman in whom the masculine principle is completely absent would not be a personality. The masculine principle is essentially personal and anthropological, while the feminine principle is essentially communal and cosmic. It is only in the union of these two principles that we have complete humanity. This union is realized in every man and woman within their androgynous natures, but in the fallen world the two principles not only seek union but also wage war against each other . . . ." Man is a sick, wounded, disharmonious creature, in the thinking of Berdyaev, primarily because he is sexual, that is, a bisexual being who has lost his wholeness and original integrity. [Nicholas Berdyaev, *The Destiny of Man*, London, Geoffrey Bles, 1954, Chap.III, § 3, titled, "Sex: the Masculine and the Feminine".]

† As an example, salt is a compound of two elements that have very different characteristics. And even more remarkable is water with its incompressibility and other extraordinary qualities, composed as it is of two compressible gases.

Chapter 16

AND HE CALLED THEIR NAME ADAM

*Let us make man
in our image
and after our likeness.*
Genesis 1:26

*For (in Christ) there is neither male nor female:
for ye are all one in Christ Jesus.*
Galatians 3:28

*In the resurrection
they neither marry nor are given in marriage,
but are as the angels of God in heaven.*
Matthew 22:30

Traditions of the original bisexual nature of the first man and of his subsequent reduction to two sexes by the formation of the first woman out of him, are ancient and widespread. Probably the best known of these traditions are those of the Greeks whose ideas on the subject have been familiar to Classical scholars for centuries. Yet Jewish and Christian commentaries had very early reached the same conclusion on the basis of the Genesis account.

The Greeks seem to have derived much of their mythology from Egypt, and Egypt in turn had derived much of its mythology from Babylonia. In his *Legends of the Jews*, Louis Ginsberg notes that according to the German scholar, Jeremias (in a work available only in

German titled *Altes Testament im Lichte des Orients*), the view that Adam was originally andrognynous was familiar to the Babylonians.* So far I have not been able to find any unequivocal evidence of such a tradition in the currently available Cuneiform literature, though Ginsberg's reputation as a scholar should be sufficient authority. However, the Society of Biblical Archaeology pulished a three volume work in 1873 which contains a useful collection of Cuneiform texts relevant to Bible history translated into English under the title *Records of the Past,*† but there is no indication even in this collection of any such tradition.   Then in 1916, Barton published the first edition of his most useful work *Archaeology of the Bible,*‡ but again I found no evidence of any strictly parallel account of the formation of Eve out of Adam. Nor, to my knowledge, has one been added in later editions.

We now have Pritchard's authorative *Ancient Near Eastern Texts* § and a careful reading of the Sumerian 'Paradise Myth' reveals a brief incident towards the end of this poem which might possibly provide a link with Genesis 2:21 and Adam's so-called 'rib',# though it is certainly a tenuous one. We shall look into this more carefully subsequently.

Possibly the real source of Jeremias' reference is, however, the rather obvious parallel account that is to be found in the work of Berossus written about 260 B.C.   Francois Lenormant observed that this ancient historian, whose works are known to us now only from quotations by other authors of antiquity, has a statement to the effect that the first man was created "with two heads, one that of a man and the other that of a woman, united in the same body with both sexes combined".★

From India we have traditions preserved in the RigVeda which, however, have none of the sobriety of the biblical account though clearly pointing to a similar circumstance relating to the constitution of the first man.   According to the *Bundehesh*, (chap. xv — a work dedicated to the exposition of a complete cosmogony written in Pahlevi and known only from the period subsequent to the conquest of Persia by the Mussulmans), Ahuramazda completed his creative

---

* Ginsberg, Louis, *Legends of the Jews*, Phila., Jewish Publ. Assoc. of Amer., 1955, Vol. V, *From Creation to Exodus*, p. 88, note 42.

† *Records of the Past*, London, Soc. Biblical Arch., 1873, in 3 volumes.

‡ Barton, George, *Archaeology of the Bible*, Phila., Amer. Sunday School Union, 1916.

§ Pritchard, James B., *Ancient Near Eastern Texts,* Princeton, 1969.

Pritchard, James B., *ibid,* p. 40, 41, lines 263-266.

★ Lenormant, Francois, *The Beginnings of History*, N.Y., Scribners, 1891, p. 62.

work by producing a certain Gayomard, "the typical man". Unfortunately, Gayomard was later put to death by an enemy of Ahuramazda
but his seed germinated in the earth and there sprang up a plant rather
like a rhubarb.   In the centre of this plant was a stalk with a kind of
stamen in the form of a man and a woman joined together.   Ahuramazda divided them, endowed them with motion, and placed within
each of them an intelligent soul.   Thus were born the first pair from
whom all human beings are descended.

The same similar view is reflected in the Cosmogony of Zatapatha
Brahmana which is included in the RigVeda, though it is generally
considered to be very much later in origin — perhaps the fourteenth
century B.C. or even as late as the ninth century B.C.* It is apparently highly fanciful, yet it does bear witness to a very early tradition
about the original androgynous nature of man.

The same basic idea may also be found in early Chinese literature.
According to Lord Arundell of Wardour, quoting L'Abbé Gainet, the
Chinese cosmogony speaks of the creation of men in the following
way: "God took some yellow earth and he made men of *two sexes*",
which is generally interpreted to mean bisexual.†

Plato, of course, is unequivocal.   In his *Symposium* (chap XIV),
he wrote: "Our nature of old was not the same as now.   It was then
one man-woman, whose form and name were common both to the
male and to the female.   Then said Jupiter, 'I will divide them into
two parts'."   Subsequently Plato remarks, "When their nature had
been bisected, each half beheld with longing its other self".   Plato
elaborated his views in his work *The Banquet* by having one of his
characters, Aristophanes, say: "In the beginning there were three
sexes among men, not only the two which we still find at this time as
male and female, but also a third which partook of the nature of each
but which has now disappeared, leaving only the name *Androgyn* behind".   Aristophanes' speech confuses the issue somewhat by proposing that there were three sexes among men from the beginning, yet
the idea of androgynous man as the original type is clearly reflected in
Plato's reference to Jupiter's decision.   Lenormant believed that the
whole idea, common to the Ionian School of Greek philosophers, had
been borrowed from Asia in the first place.

Empedocles (c. 495-435 B.C.), a Greek philosopher of Agrigentum
in Sicily, set forth a reconstruction of the history of plant and animal

---

* Lenormant, Francois, *ibid*, p. 62.

† Lord Arundell of Wardour, *Tradition, Mythology, and Law of Nations*, London, Burns,
Oates, 1872, p. 134.

life which foreshadowed the theory of Evolution to some extent. It is highly fanciful, but a propos of the present subject it is of interest. *The Encyclopedia Britannica* article on his works states his position as follows:*

> His most interesting views dealt with the origin of plants and animals, and with the physiology of man. As the elements combined through the work of love, there appeared quaint results — heads without necks, arms without shoulders. Then as these structures met, there were heads and figures of double sexes. But most of these disappeared as suddenly as they arose; only in those rare cases where the several parts were adapted to each other did the complex structures last. Soon various influences reduced the creatures of double sex to a male and a female, and the world was replenished with organic life.

The Romans, of course, were much influenced by the Greeks, and like the Greeks they seem to have held that a bisexual individual was a superior one. In his book, *The Religion of Greece in Prehistoric Times*, Axel Persson underscores how very ancient this idea was.† The earliest deities were, like Cybele (the Mother of all other gods) hermaphroditic. According to their most ancient beliefs, Cybele generated the other deities by self-fertilization.

Greek thinking on this whole matter influenced the Hellenized Jews, as it had influenced educated Romans. Philo Judaeus (born about 20 B.C.) was one so influenced. He was aristocratic, eloquent, and a well informed Pharisee who seems to have been particularly familiar with the works of Plato. Indeed, he attempted to reconcile the Mosaic system with Platonic philosophy and is usually credited with having first made popular among the Jews the concept of the Logos as intermediary between God who is pure spirit and the physical world of matter. He became one of the more notable intellectual opponents of the Christian faith and his works were a source of constant concern to the early Church Fathers as they sought to elaborate and construct a Christian world view.

One of the much discussed issues in both Jewish and Christian circles was this question of the androgynous nature of Adam as first created. Philo, as shown in his *Quaestiones* (1:19), was well acquainted with rabbinic lore on this subject but he believed that the derivation of Eve out of Adam was not sober history but allegory. To this many of the Church Fathers took exception. In his *Contra Celsus* (4:38),

---

* *Encyclopedia Britannica*, 1958 ed., Vol. 8, p. 400.

† Persson, Axel, *The Religion of Greece in Prehistoric Times*, Univ. Cal. Press, 1942, p. 106.

Origen observed that Jews as well as many Christians considered the account of the creation of Eve out of Adam to be allegory. But Louis Ginsberg, when noting this fact, is careful to underscore that, "in the earlier rabbinic literature now extant, no such allegorical tendencies are known. Nor was Philo able to give firm sources for his own views from rabbinical literature".* Actually, according to Ginsberg, Philo is himself contradictory and it is thus difficult to know precisely what he believed. He seems to have thought that the best explanation was that Genesis 1:27 ("male and female created He them") implied a bi-sexuality and Genesis 2:7 ("formed man of the dust of the ground") no sex at all.†

Justin Martyr who lived from 100-165 A.D., in his *Hortatory*

---

* Ginsberg, Louis, *op. cit.*, 1955, Vol. V, p. 89.

† It is conceivable that Genesis 1:27, which seems to relate the maleness and femaleness of man as created with the image of God, is in fact telling us something about the nature of God Himself. Perhaps part of the 'image' of God in man is reflected in the compound of which we now observe only the two elements. As originally united in Adam, that compound of male/femaleness was an essential aspect of the divine image.

Karl Barth entertained such a view. He held that the simplest exegesis of Genesis 1:27 would equate a maleness and femaleness compound in Adam with the image of God. The subsequent division of man into two sexes was for man's own good by making him no longer self-sufficient and in some real sense potentially asocial. An important aspect of the image is the unity in fellowship between men and women under ideal conditions and Barth makes much of the uniqueness of this fellowship of love in purity [*Church Dogmatics*, III/1, tr. J. W. Edwards *et al.*, Edinburgh, T. & T. Clark, 1958, p. 214. See also Paul K. Jewett, *Man as Male and Female*, Grand Rapids, Eerdman's, 1975, p. 43 ff., and G. C. Berkouwer who says, "Barth is convinced that the text gives us a 'well-nigh definitive statement' of the content of the image", *Man the Image of God*, Grand Rapids, Eerdman's, 1975, p. 72, fn. 16].

There is another aspect of the male/female relationship in all higher forms of life. A. J. Thebaud suggested some years ago that one of the earliest concepts of the nature of God was hermaphroditic. "The principle of deity is always accompanied by a goddess, commonly called his wife but in reality his 'female energy' as we find in Hindustan, in the case of Siva in particular" [*Gentilism: Religion Previous to Christianity*, N.Y., D. & J. Sadlier & Co., 1876, p. 254].

The supposed 'wife-figure' is taken in this view to be a symbol of the deity's creative principle or energy. Some early Egyptian statues show 'God' as a giant figure signifying strength and majesty, while his generative energy is represented by a female figure, often relatively small in size, placed beside him.

Ideas of this kind tend to be discounted today. Our culture is fatally innoculated with the view that the new is better than the old, that novelty (even in ideas) is itself a virtue. Modern intelligence in such matters so far outstrips the intelligence of writers of only a century ago (let alone millenia ago) that such views can be quite safely ignored. Tradition was once held in very high regard, but it is now argued that this was due to lack of sophistication in former times.

But little by little we have come to accord greater respect to the thoughts of earlier times and have discovered how often archaeological findings have vindicated these ancient traditions — not just in a general way but almost always in a highly specific and detailed fashion. It could be that many of the traditions, and some of the symbols that were anciently shared by many nations about the original nature of man as a special creature of God and created in his image, reflect the truth of the matter in ways we did not suspect.

Address to the Greeks (chap. 30) follows Philo almost literally in his explanation of the double account in Genesis, but I do not think for one moment that he shared his cynicism.   Tertullian, who lived from 160 to 230 A.D., in his *Adversus Hermogenem* (chap. 26), and Hippolytus (d. c. 230 A.D.) both agree with the rabbinical view (*Baraita* 32 and *Middoth*, No. 12) which held that the Bible gives first a general account and then a detailed one.   That the rabbis truly believed Adam was originally hermaphroditic is clear enough from a number of sources, though they elaborated this simple truth along rather fanciful lines.   Louis Ginsberg gives a number of references,* and leaves one with the impression that these are merely some out of many.   *The Soncino Chumash*, edited by A. Cohen, has a note on Genesis 1:27 by the famous rabbinical scholar Rashi (b. 1040, d. 1105 in the Rhineland) who wrote a commentary on the Pentateuch and was credited with "an encyclopedic knowledge of rabbinic literature", in which the rabbi says, "The *Midrash* explains that man as first created consisted of two halves, male and female, which were afterwards separated".†

One of the most famous rabbis of Medieval times and one of the most philosophical expounders of Judaism was a man named Moses ben Maimon (1135-1202 A.D.), who is more popularly known as Maimonides.   He strongly supported the view that Adam was created as a man-and-woman being, having two faces turned in opposite directions, and that during a stupor the Creator separated his genuine feminine half (*Hawah*, Eve) from him in order to make of her a distinct and separate person.

A century later, Nahmanides (1220-1250) in his commentary on Genesis 1:1 - 6:8 which has been recently translated by Jacob Newman, has this to say on Genesis 1:27, "(Adam and Eve) were created with two faces".   Newman in a note (#144) interprets this to mean, "hermaphroditic".‡

Now *The Jerusalem Targum*, which may have been begun as early as the second century B.C., amplified the text of Genesis 2:21 and said that "Eve was formed out of the third rib on the right side"!   Whatever may be said of this kind of comment, it is surely quite clear that Hebrew scholars were interpreting the record very literally.   They

---

* Louis Ginsberg's references: *Midrash Bereshith Rabbah on Genesis*, chap. 8, para. 1, and chap. 17, para 6; *Berakoth*, chap. 61 a, a Talmudic Tractate on Prayers and Benedictions; *'Erubin*, chap. 18 a, a Talmudic Tractate on the Sabbath; *Midrash Weyikra Rabbah*, chap. 14; *Midrash Tanchuma hagidom Wahishon*, Bk. III, p. 32; *Midrash Tehillim*, chap. 139, p. 529; *Midrash Tanchuma Tazria*, 2.

† Cohen, A., *The Soncino Chumash*, London, Soncino Press, 1964, p. ix, 7.

‡ Newman, Jacob, *Commentary by Nahmanides*, Leiden, Brill, 1960, p. xx.

understood that a real cleavage by some kind of surgical operation divided Adam into complementary selves which, being thereafter "joined" in true marriage, were reconstituted as "one flesh". Modern Jewish scholars still either hold to this view or acknowledge it as by no means impossible; even those medically trained agree. Dr. Robert Greenblatt, in his little book *Search the Scriptures*, remarks in this connection:*

> Metaphorically we may assume that the original man, Adam, was hermaphroditic. Such an assumption is quite permissible, for it is twenty-one verses after reporting the creation of man that Genesis (2:18) tells us "and the Lord God said, It is not good that man should be alone: I will make a help meet for him".
>
> In this history of human events is thus recorded man's earliest conception of the establishment of the sexes. Some of the most distinguished Hebrew writers, according to Hans Selye, interpret the first chapters of Genesis as describing Adam as being of both sexes.

So now we may find it proper to trace back our ancestry until we arrive at a first father who carried in himself both seeds, and after the division had been effected, sinned and introduced into his body some disturbing agent which has upset the normal transmission of the chromosomal allottment assigned orginally by God to each sex once they had been separated. Any such disturbance, arising from chromosomal anomaly, surely suggests that the potential for both sexes is still resident in suppressed form in each individual. Such is the stuff of inheritance in all of us, a fact which seems to point to a past when the potential was effectively resident in a single person, and then to some occasion when the potential was modified — though not without leaving a vestige of itself to remind us that it is indeed a modification.

The quote from the *Jerusalem Targum* above brings us to a consideration of the meaning of the original Hebrew word (צֵלָע , tsela'), rendered RIB in virtually all our English translations. The Jewish version of this Targum by members of the famous Ibn Tibbon family (of the twelfth and thirteenth centuries, A.D.), and the version of Maimonides, both translate this word as *side* rather than *rib*.* This is not surprising since the Septuagint translators employed the Greek word *pleuran* ($\pi\lambda\epsilon\upsilon\rho\alpha\nu$) which, if we are to be guided at all by New Testa-

---

* Greenblatt, Robert, *Search the Scriptures*, Montreal, Lippincott, 1963, p. 50.

† Tibbon: see Robert Tuck, *Age of the Great Patriarchs*, London, Sunday School Union, n.d., p. 102.

ment usage has only the meaning of *side*.   It appears in John 19:34; 20:20, 25, 27; Acts 12:7.   It is important to notice that this is the meaning attached to it in the New Testament Greek.   Since the New Testament rests heavily for its usage of Greek words upon that already adopted by the Seventy-two who gave us the Septuagint, one should assume, I think, that the latter's use of *pleura* for *tsela'* indicates how they also understood the word: i.e., as *side* rather than *rib*.

Furthermore, the Hebrew word *tsela'* is only translated RIB in English versions in this one place.   Its renderings elsewhere, as in the King James Version for instance, are such as the following: *beam, chamber* (twice), *plank, corner* (twice), *sidechamber* (9 times), and *side* (19 times).   The rendering *side* appears mainly in connection with descriptive details of the tabernacle — in Exodus 25:12, 14; 26:27, 35; 27:7; 36:25, 31, 32; 37:3; 38:7; 2 Samuel 16:13; and Job 18:12.   These are all the occurrences in which the word appears.   In some of them it is so translated twice in a single verse.   In the Latin Vulgate it is rendered *side*; as it is also in the Syriac version.   It is therefore all the more surprising that so few modern English versions have adopted it in Genesis.

The question is, What really is the best word to use?   If we allow ourselves to be guided by the passages in which it is rendered *sidechamber*, we have possibly a closer approach to what may have been the intent of the original.   The word is so rendered nine times in the following places: Ezekiel 41:5, 6 (twice), 7, 8, 9 (twice), 11, and 26. Ellicott in his Commentary is surely correct in saying that "Adam could hardly have felt the loss of one rib out of 24 actual bones with which the body is provided — much less in view of the fact that the wound was completely healed after the operation".   Whether he would have been aware of the disappearance of some internal organ such as a gonad or a fully developed ovary is a moot point.   But he might very well have become aware of a new need, directed towards the woman.

It is worth noting in passing that, according to Moulton and Milligan, the general extra-biblical meaning of the Greek word used in the Septuagint is *side* of a human being or *lung* or *chest*.   But it is also noted that "an unusual use of the word is *vessel*, as found in one papyrus of the late third century A.D. in reference to some glass vessels". *

Liddell and Scott in their *Lexicon of Classical Greek* give the meaning of *pleuron* as *rib*, equating it with Herodotus' use of the word, but as they point out, "mostly in the plural like the Latin *costae*, i.e.,

---

* Moulton, James H. and George Milligan, *Vocabulary of the Greek Text Illustrations from the Papyri and Other Non-Literary Sources*, Grand Rapids, Eerdmans, 1972, p. 518.

'side' of a man". They give a secondary meaning as "the membrane that lines the chest". A third meaning is as the side of a rectangle, and a fourth meaning as a page of a book. It has also, they observe, the sense of *wife*. This is interesting in that among the Arabs a cognate word of the Hebrew *tsela'* is used to signify a bosom friend, a person who is "at one's side".* None of these comments are decisive, but I think in general they certainly allow the choice of the word *side* rather than *rib* as a meaningful translation of the Hebrew of Genesis 2:21.

Turning to the very oldest actual documents we have, i.e., cuneiform tablets, we find some curious indications that the Hebrew word *tsela'* had a more profound significance than merely the designation of one of Adam's ribs. One of the best authorities on Sumerian Cuneiform literature, Samuel Kramer, in his book *From the Tablets of Sumer* notes that the Sumerian word for *rib* is TI (pronounced TEE).† Now this sound value associated with the word TI forms part of several *names* under rather interesting circumstances. Some of the earliest tablets tell us that the name of one of the gods was EN-KI. This name seems to be compounded from two words meaning *Heaven* (and) *Earth*, a circumstance which may reflect something about the supposed nature of the being who bore the name. There is little doubt from a study of Sumerian mythology that EN-KI was really the counterpart of original man, exalted to the status of a deity. We are told that EN-KI became sick, and the sickness affected eight parts of his body — an observation which is probably intended to indicate only that the *whole* man was sick. The tablet which gives us the details of this event also spells out where the sickness afflicted him, although some of the words are not now decipherable. They do include his head, his arms and his chest. The ailment arose because of EN-KI's disobedience in eating a fruit which he had been expressly forbidden to eat and which is identified as a cassia plant, of which we have already spoken.

Being a highly favoured creature of the gods, steps were at once taken to heal him, and for this purpose a goddess was specially created. Her name was NIN-TI, which is a compound of two words meaning "the lady of the rib". Kramer tells us that NIN-TI came to be known later as "the lady who makes live". Thus the same compound name, NIN-TI, acquired by association two different meanings. The first compound (NIN) kept its sound value and meaning, but TI came to be

---

* Skinner, John, *Commentary on Genesis,* Edinburgh, T. & T. Clark, 1930, 2nd. ed., p. 68.

† Kramer, Samuel, *From the Tablets of Sumer,* Indian Hills, Colo., Falcon's Wing Press, 1956, p. 172 f.

associated with both "the rib" and "the one who gives life". The student of Scripture will see at once that we have here what looks like a confused reflection of the grand truth set forth in Genesis 2:21 and 3:20 which shows Eve as first formed from a *tsela'* (translated more correctly, I think, as *side*), later to become "the mother of all living". If EN-KI is equated with Adam, then clearly the female NIN-TI, created to heal the only ailment from which a perfect Adam could be suffering (i.e., a sense of aloneness) would logically be equated with Eve.

What Kramer did not note in either of the books in which he has made particular reference to this matter*, is the fact that the cuneiform sign or ideograph for TI sheds its own interesting light on the meaning of the word translated *rib*.   In Rene Labat's *Manuel d'Epigraphie Akkadienne,*† the cuneiform sign for TI is written as at (a) in Fig. 6, in late Assyrian.   But in the very earliest texts known this sign appeared as in (b), which is clearly the same pictograph in simplified form. However, it is known that these cuneiform signs were very early turned through 90° for some reason, so that they were originally written in the upright position.   The sign shown in (b) would therefore have been drawn at first as shown in (c); and there seems to be little doubt that it was once a simplified picture of a woman wearing a skirt.

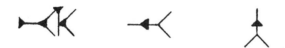

Fig. 6 Development of Sign for RIB

The *word* values which Labat attaches to the sign are various. They include *rib* or *side member* (of a vehicle or a boat); but the sign also forms part of the verb "to make alive".   We know from later texts employing this sign how it was to be pronounced.   The sign was not merely read as TI (as among the Sumerians) but by the Babylonians as TSILU, which is readily seen to be related to the Hebrew TSELU.

The Babylonians adopted the earlier Sumerian ideographs and used them to signify the same objects as the Sumerians had, but they applied to them their own sound values which were usually (though

---

* Kramer, Samuel, *From the Tablets of Sumer, op. cit.,* p. 172 f., or *The Sumerians,* Univ. of Chicago Press, 1963, p. 149 f.

† Labat, Rene, *Manuel d'Epigraphie Akkadienne,* Paris, Imprimerie Nationale de France, 1952, p. 68, 69.

not always) somewhat different.   This is a widespread practice.   The Japanese did precisely the same thing when they adopted the Chinese ideographs in order to put their own language into writing.   Looking at the sign ►◄〵◄ , the Sumerians would read it as TI but the Babylonians and Assyrians would read it as TSILU.   Each of them would immediately picture in their minds either a RIB (or a *side*, depending upon which is the correct interpretation) or LIFE-GIVING WOMAN, depending upon the context.   The word used in the Hebrew of Genesis 2:21 (*tsela'*) is certainly a cognate Semitic word with the Babylonian and Assyrian TSILU.

The reader may be misled here into supposing that I am supporting the view that the Sumerian language is earlier than Semitic languages such as Assyrian, Babylonian and Hebrew.   It is at present true that the earliest records (tablets) are in Sumerian.   But this is by no means absolute proof of any priority of the Sumerian language over Semitic.   For reasons which have been elaborated elsewhere,* I am persuaded that the language of Noah and his family was not Sumerian but Semitic in form — not necessarily Hebrew, though it might have been proto-Hebrew.   One of the strongest arguments in favour of this assumption is that the names of his immediate descendants as set forth in Genesis X are clearly Semitic words which, for the most part, have recognizable meanings even in Hebrew as we know it today.

It is clear that the names have not been translated or modified radically from their original form since they are still preserved with comparatively little change in their descendants who are now found to constitute the nations of the world.   Japheth, for example, is clearly recognizable in the *Japetos* of the Greeks whose ancestor he is, though the Greeks are certainly not Semitic people.   These names have been carefully traced by the author in another work.†   The importance of this fact is that people do not give their children names which are entirely foreign to their own language.   We do have a notable exception in the case of biblical names adopted in Christian families, but this is a special situation that did not apply on any wide scale in pre-Christian times.   A Chinaman who happened to be a metalworker would not call his son *Smithson*, because *Smith* is an English word, not a Chinese one.

People customarily give their children names that are meaningful in their own language, and the forms of such names provide a clue to

---

* Custance, A. C., "The Confusion of Languages" in *Time and Eternity*, Vol. VI of the *Doorway Papers Series*, Grand Rapids, Zondervan, 1977, p. 176 ff.

† Custance, A. C., "A Study of the Names in Genesis X" in *Noah's Three Sons*, Vol. I of the *Doorway Papers Series*, Grand Rapids, Zondervan, 1975, p. 52 ff.

to the language spoken by those who use them.   When Noah and his family gave names to their children they were clearly speaking Hebrew or something akin to it: and if Noah was doing so, it is a fair assumption to say that Adam also spoke the same form of language since the confusion of languages was much later.

From which I would conclude that the supposedly later form of the word *tsela'* is not *in fact* later at all, but the original.   The form TI is only assumed to be earlier because historical accident has placed in our hands Sumerian tablets in which the word TI appears and these happen to be earlier than any tablets in which the word TSILU occurs. We do not have any tablets, yet, which truly come from the pre-Flood world, but it seems virtually certain that a society which had metallurgy and could construct an ark larger than any vessel till quite modern times must have had some method of keeping adequate records.

It does not seem likely that we can filter from such indistinct leads very much in the way of concrete information of substantive value, but certainly there is a story here the details of which in the Scriptural account are clear enough.   The biblical record is free of the exaggerations and absurdities which mar all the pagan traditions.   It is sensible to view it as the original.

I do not think it altogether unreasonable to assume that when Adam exclaimed, "This is now bone of my bone *and flesh of my flesh*", he had an intuitive understanding of the fact (or was it revealed?) that Eve had been formed from something much more fundamental to himself and to his nature and constitution than merely one of his ribs. The supplementary statement made afterwards, "and they shall be one flesh", surely implies more than that Eve would in some mystical way merely make up for a missing rib — especially in view of the fact that man does not have, and is unlikely ever to have had, an odd rib on one side.

Adam was in no position to be able to understand in precisely what way he had been "divided" even if God had revealed to him the magnitude of the operation.   But it seems rather certain that if Eve had merely been formed from one of his *ribs* and the wound had then been completely repaired, he would hardly have discerned in Eve a creature so complementary to himself in such a profound way.   His sense of her complementarity was initially psychological not anatomical, though he felt it so concretely that he expressed it in anatomical language.   And surely, the two becoming one flesh when truly married reinforces the concept of an original "unity".

It is an interesting thing to note in the Sumerian account that the "Lady of the Rib" was formed in a way which was notable for the speed with which it all happened while not yet being actually instantaneous.   The normal nine months gestation period is reduced in the poem to a mere nine days: a day for a month.   Perhaps this was a way of saying that this "Lady who makes alive" was not formed by the ordinary processes familiar in human generation nor yet by a process totally independent of it, but by some quite exceptional means of which not the least remarkable factor was the short time it took to complete the operation.   But it *was* an operation; it did take time; it was not instantaneous creation but *formation**** (Gen.2:22).

And so we can perhaps add to the evidence from physiology the confirming voice of tradition, confused as it is, as well as the considered opinion of the more famous Jewish commentators who evidently found the Genesis account leading them to a similar conclusion: Eve was literally formed out of the man because Adam as first created was truly androgynous.   I believe he was androgynous not only physiologically speaking but in the very essence of his nature also: hormonally, he was truly male and female.

There are other important reasons why such a truly androgynous constitution should have characterized the first man, and these have to do with the method by which God was to redeem the race that sprang quite literally from *Adam's* loins, of one, i.e., a single individual, not "of one *blood*" (Acts 17:26) as the King James Version has it.†   And this is the subject of the next chapter.

---

* The Hebrew word used is *banah* (בָּנָה) meaning "to build".

† It is widely agreed by scholars of evangelical as well as liberal persuasion that the word *blood* should be omitted as it is in a number of MSS.   This is the procedure followed in the RV, RSV, Rotherham, Berkeley, and many others.

Chapter 17

GOD HATH MADE ALL OF ONE

Have we not all one father?
Hath not one God created us?
Malachi 2:10

(God) hath made of one
all nations of men
for to dwell on the face of the earth.
Acts 17:26

God is never devious. He acts simply and directly. When a certain leper came to the Lord Jesus and said, "Lord, if Thou wilt, Thou canst make me clean", Jesus simply put forth his hand and touched him saying, "I will: be thou clean". And immediately his leprosy was cleansed (Matt.8:2, 3). By contrast, the major surgery performed upon Adam's body for the formation of Eve may seem at first sight to be a devious way of producing the first parents of the human race. Why not simply create an Adam and an Eve instantaneously in the first place? Why this complex procedure?

I believe there are two very important reasons for the initial creation of Adam as androgynous and for his subsequent division into a male and a female to form the first father and mother of all mankind. Perhaps there are more than two reasons: but certainly there are two; and they are now made apparent in the light of what we know today from a study of human genetics. What has long been held by Christian commentators and theologians and proclaimed as a matter of faith —

that Adam was first formed and then Eve out of Adam — we are at long last in the privileged position of being able to understand with sufficient clarity to make it worthwhile to discuss the subject in physiological terms.   There is still much that is not fully understood, but we are beginning to perceive some of the reasons that necessitated the adoption of this less direct procedure which the Genesis account sets before us.

These two reasons of which we wish to speak can be examined from a *physiological,* or even more specificially, a genetic point of view: but their real significance remains essentially *theological.*   They both relate basically to the redemptive purposes of God.

The first reason relates to the method adopted by the Creator in the formation of Eve — a method made necessary for physiological reasons in order that all men might ultimately be derived from a single individual, Adam, and not from Adam *and Eve* as two separately created individuals.   The human race originates therefore from a single stem with one head, one source, one "original" — Adam.   The creation of two separate heads, a father of the race and a mother of the race, each formed by a distinct act of creation, would have physiological and genetic consequences respecting the true unity of the race which would present what seem to be insoluble problems in terms of provision of a single Redeemer truly representative of such a duophyletic line of human beings.

The importance of drawing Eve out of Adam and not making her a separate creation, and thus meeting the exact requirement of the statement in Acts 17:26 that God has made "of one" (not of one *blood*) all who dwell on the earth, is clearly brought out by the following consideration.

Every individual in the world who ever lived or is alive today is descended from a single person.   And this includes Eve herself.   It follows that Adam stood as a Federal Head, and in him we stand as one.   For this reason a single Redeemer tracing descent from Adam can truly represent any one (or every one) of Adam's descendants.

There are none to whom He is not related as a brother human being; whether male or female.   He was in Adam (as to his body) as we are in Adam, and therefore He is brother to all of Adam's seed. He can be the *Goel,* the Redeemer, of the whole family of man, none excepted.

We can grasp the significance of this more clearly by considering the difference between the angelic population of heaven and the human population of earth.   Each angel appears to have been a separate creation.   Angels are not brothers, or if one wishes to avoid all intimations of sex, they are not *siblings*. They have no familial relationships.

They are "angelic" only by virtue of having been all fashioned according to a single pattern, all "cast in the same mold", by their Creator. They do not form a race or a "species" in the sense that earth's creatures (including man) do.   By definition, a species is an interbreeding community and angels simply do not interbreed in order to multiply, and did not originate by breeding.*   They are not derived from a single ancestor.   But because of the formation of Eve out of Adam, man does derive from a *single* ancestor.

Thus having no federal head because they do not form a single "family", there could never be for the angels any single angelic redeemer since there is, strictly speaking, no angelic race but only an aggregation of angelic individuals of entirely independent origin. Thomas Aquinas was acute enough to see, in fact, that "each angel is itself a species".†   This statement demonstrated the genius of Thomas in getting at the nub of the issue — provided, of course, that he was aware of the truth he was annunciating so succinctly.   In a similar vein, Herman Bavinck observed:‡

> (Angels) do not constitute one race, are not blood relatives, and did not beget each other.   It is possible to speak of man*kind* but not of angel*kind* (emphasis mine).   When Christ assumed human nature He was immediately related to all men, related by blood, and He was their brother according "to the flesh".   But angels (merely) live next to each other, each one accountable for himself and not for the others, so that a portion of them could fall and a portion remain faithful to God.

In Adam are all men, and in Adam's Fall all are involved.   In the second Adam, therefore, all may again be represented, for He was by blood their *kins*man Redeemer.   Bavinck comments further that both animals and plants have, so to speak, multiple origins, "various ancestors" as he puts it.§   By contrast, all men are descended from a single parental pair.   The human race has only one ancestry and thus con-

---

* Some such idea seems to have been held by Gregory of Nyssa (330-c. 395). In his work *On the Making of Man* (chap. XVII) he notes that there are evidently billions of angels. But they cannot have multiplied by breeding, because they do not inter-marry. Since man is to become like the angels (Matt.22:30), and at the same time to regain his original constitution, he too was at first designed to multiply without conjugation. This means in effect that Adam was bisexual.

† Thomas Aquinas: quoted by H. O. Taylor, *The Medieval Mind*, London, Macmillan, 1911, Vol. II, p. 458.

‡ Bavinck, Herman, *Our Reasonable Faith*, tr. H. Zystra, Grand Rapids, Baker, 1956, p. 203.

§ Bavinck, Herman, *ibid*, p. 199.

stitues a single generation. To redeem the animal kingdom one would need as many saviours as there are species: a lamb could not redeem a lion and a mouse could not redeem an elephant. The same circumstance applies on an even wider scale in the plant kingdom, except that it is impossible to even conceive of redemption where there is no animation.

It therefore follows that if Eve also had been a separate creation, the human race would effectively have been composed of a line of descendants who were "pure Adam-ite" and owed nothing of their inherited constitution to Eve, and a line of descendants who were "pure Eve-ites" and owed nothing of their inherited constitution to Adam. In addition there would have been a mongrel line neither strictly Adam-ite nor Eve-ite. These three strains could never be *truly* represented by a single Redeemer.

The principle of the inevitable sorting out of the two strains (the Adam-ite and the Eve-ite) is clearly established by breeding experiments in nature. Ordinary conditions of misgenation of two separately created seeds would always result in a certain percentage of pure Adam-ites who owed none of their genes to Eve, and of pure Eve-ites who owed none of their genes to Adam, so that a single Redeemer-substitute in his individual person could only stand for one of these lines. The rest would be without the means of redemption. This would be the situation if Adam and Eve had been separate creations.

The situation is quite otherwise if Eve was not a separate creation but was derived out of Adam's loins. For in this case, all descendants are basically Adamic since all trace back to Adam, including Eve. A single Redeemer can thus stand in the stead of *all*, without exception.

It may seem absurd to suggest that in a race of men all descended from a first *pair*, Adam and Eve, there could still be a significant number of people whose hereditary constitution owed nothing to the first father, Adam, and an equally significant number whose hereditary constitution owed nothing to their first mother, Eve. Genetically speaking, Eve would not be the mother of all living — contrary to Genesis 3:20. Yet it is so. Remarkably enough, Augustine was aware of it! In his *City of God* (Bk. XII, 21) he states the matter thus: "And indeed He did not even create the woman that was to be given him as his wife, as he created the man; but created her out of man, that the whole human race might derive from one man". This was certainly an amazing insight from a man living 1500 years ago!

So we conclude that whether the word *blood* belongs in Paul's observation in Acts 17:26 or not, his statement was more profoundly true and important than appears at first sight. We are indeed the offspring of God through Adam (Acts 17:29) and because we are all truly Adamic in our constitution and share the same line of heredity and therefore stand undifferentiated in so far as human nature is rooted in a truly common clay,* it is perfectly appropriate that we should be saved by the same Redeemer and the world should be *judged* by the same standard (Acts 17:31) — since that Redeemer as the second Adam properly represents us all individually.

There is a second reason for forming Eve out of Adam.   It is related in a way to the first, and yet in some respects it stands as an entirely independent issue.   We have already touched upon it several times in Part I † but we must bring it forward again here because it forms the starting point for much that follows in the next two chapters.

One day, a Saviour was to be born in the line of Adam, made in the *likeness*‡ of sinful flesh (Rom.8:3) but escaping the entail of corruption which man can no longer escape in his flesh if he is begotten and born by the natural union of the male and female seed.

It now appears that the poison introduced into Adam's body also reached Adam's seed or *germ plasm*, as Weismann termed it (of which more anon).   By contrast, however, that same poison, though equally damaging to Eve's *body* as it was to Adam's, did not apparently reach her *seed*.   Adam *and* Eve were both literally poisoned to death, but the effect of the poison upon each seems to have been different in this important respect, that while the seed of the man was also infected by the poison, the seed of the woman evidently was not.   And in *this* respect the body of the man and the body of the woman were, and still are, constituted differently in a way that is crucial to the working out of the plan of Redemption.

I think we have to conclude from the subsequent course of events in Scripture which lead up to the Virgin Birth, that the body of Eve and the bodies of all female descendants of Eve from that day forward provided (and continue to provide) a housing which has uniquely protected her seed in a way that Adam's body did not protect his.   It thus becomes highly significant to refer, as Scripture does, to the promise of the coming Redeemer as being the "seed of the woman" as opposed to the seed of the man — while at the same time tracing the Saviour back, step by step, not to Eve but to Adam (Luke 3:38).   Clearly if Eve was indeed derived from Adam then the seed of the woman was

---

* Perhaps the "one blood" of Acts 17:26 is to be identified with the "same lump" of Romans 9:21.

† See page 109 ff.

‡ On the difference between *likeness* or similarity, and *identity*, see reference # 223.

originally the seed of Adam, and thus to call the Saviour the Son of Adam (i.e., the Son of "man") rather than the Son of Eve (in spite of the wording of Gen.3:15) is perfectly proper.

What if Eve had not been separated from Adam until *after* the Fall? When he ate the forbidden fruit, presumably the female seed within his body would be afforded no greater protection against the poison than the male seed. Consequently, her seed (now separated) would convey the same fatal poison in each generation just as Adam's seed. Thus there could never have arisen a Redeemer, even virgin born, who could escape the entail of sin — as we know the Lord Jesus Christ did. Eve must, therefore, be separated from Adam *before* the Fall in order to preserve that seed which was the sole guarantee and promise of such a Saviour.

For it was necessary that some step be taken to make possible the recovery of the first Adam in the form of a genuine descendant who was entirely uncorrupted by the stream of poison that runs without fail in all his other descendants. The seed of the woman which was once Adam's seed and therefore carried the Adamic line unbroken, had to be separated and set apart where it could be preserved uncorrupted to await the day when it would be germinated miraculously, the normal component which a male in Adam's line should have supplied being provided supernaturally by God Himself through the Holy Spirit (Luke 1:35).

In his wisdom God therefore set the stage for the coming of the Saviour who was to redeem man's body as well as his spirit, by first creating an Adam who was potentially immortal, encompassing within himself the reproductive mechanisms (both male and female) for the multiplication of his own kind, and then by separating Eve out of him and entrusting to her one of these mechanisms, fashioning for her a body specially designed to preserve that seed intact as it passed un-corrupted through each successive generation from daughter to daughter, regardless of the fate of her own body or of theirs. The record is set forth in Scripture without embellishment and it bears all the earmarks of simple truth. We are only now beginning to grasp the possibilities of such an operation as was involved in the formation of Eve, and its consequences in the light of developmental physiology.

That some such process of formation of Eve was involved has, it seems, been "in the air" for some years. Humphrey J. T. Johnson in his book *The Bible and Early Man,** notes that a Brazilian biologist,

---

* Johnson, Humphrey J. T., quoting Piza in a paper entitled "A Costela de Adao a luz da bio-logica" ["Adam's Rib in the Light of Biology"], *Revista de Agricultura,* Sept-Oct., 1946, p. 359 f., with English summary.

S. de Toledo Piza, in 1946 suggested that what God took from Adam's body for the purpose was not a rib but a chromosome, perhaps one of Adam's X chromosomes.   It should not be beneath the concern of any biologist with Christian convictions to contemplate what could be the meaning of this ancient record of what happened.   It is only our fear of being labelled "literalist" that puts the subject in the not-to-be-taken-seriously category by any biologist who has a weather eye on the safety of his or her professional reputation.

This seemingly roundabout way of providing a helpmeet for Adam proves to have been a necessary step in the provision which God foresaw was going to have to be made for the redemption of a creature who was to be allowed freedom of choice.   In the first place, it was necessary in order that a single Person could be the Redeemer of any member of that race, being kinsman to all men without exception. And in the second place, it was necessary because there was no other way in which One who was to be truly the Son of Man could be born of woman without the entail of sin.

There is nothing arbitrary here.   Nor is there anything *purely* miraculous as though God could only work by miracle, or *purely* natural as though there was no need for divine intervention.   God seems from the very beginning to have so designed the process of conception and birth throughout nature that He could use it, later on, without doing any violence to his own created order when the time finally came to *objectify* Himself by entering into this world of time and space in the likeness of ourselves as our Redeemer in the Person of Jesus Christ. He did violence neither to nature nor to Himself.

Just how this seed was preserved and carried in the female line from generation to generation (as it is still being carried even today) without surrendering its original immortality, is the subject of the next two chapters.   How wonderfully the Word of God is illuminated in so many familiar passages, once the meaning of these things has been understood, will be abundantly clear as we proceed towards the time of that most amazing of all events since the creation of the Universe, the moment when God became flesh and was dwelling among us.

Chapter 18

THE SEED OF THE WOMAN AND THE SEED OF THE MAN

I will put enmity between thee (Satan)
and the woman,
between thy seed
and her seed;
it shall bruise thy head.
Genesis 3:15

When Darwin formulated his theory of Natural Selection, it seemed obvious to him, and he easily persuaded many of his contemporaries, that any living thing which acquired a particular advantage over its competitors during its life time, would automatically pass that benefit on to its young by inheritance. Thus by a process akin to compound interest, the gains of each new generation were added to those of the last and linear progress in the development of higher and higher forms of life was guaranteed.

Any such supposed advantage accruing to an individual as the result of life experience is generally referred to as an Acquired Characteristic. For example, the man who becomes a blacksmith and develops tremendous arm and shoulder muscles would automatically endow his children with a superior physique, even though he himself may have been something of a weakling as a child. One of the strongest advocates of the inheritance of such acquired characteristics was the French naturalist Jean Baptiste Lamarck (1744 - 1829).

The fact seemed obvious and essential if any progress was to be made in improving the species of animals of particular value to man,

and superficially there seemed to be a great deal of evidence in support
of it.   Darwin was confident that he had the mechanism he needed to
make his hypothesis workable even when applied to human society.
But towards the end of the last century it was becoming increasingly
apparent that Lamarck was mistaken, that acquired characteristics are
either not inherited at all or so rarely that the assumed linear progress
of life through geological ages could not be attributed to the operation
of any such mechanism.

Moreover, it quickly became obvious that there were many examples in human history of "mutilations" persistently practiced by
men upon their fellows for centuries which nevertheless were not inherited.   Chinese girls, from time immemorial, had their feet tightly
bound because it was felt that small feet added to a woman's beauty,
yet Chinese babies were still born with normal feet.[187]

One of the most famous experiments of this nature in which an
attempt was made to demonstrate whether mutilation of the parents
could lead to defective offspring, was carried out by August Weismann
(1834 - 1914), Professor of Biology at the University of Freiburg and
Breisgau, whose chief interest was in Embryology.   Weismann cut off
the tails of hundreds of rats, generation after generation, but never
succeeded in getting any baby rats born without tails.   Some witty
individual with a literary background and inspired by Shakespeare
observed, "There is a divinity doth shape their ends, rough hew them
though we may"!

Weismann's conclusion, based almost entirely upon reflection
rather than on experiment, was that every body carried within itself in
some kind of concentrated form a deposit of hereditary substance
which he termed "the germ plasm".   This was the reservoir of specialized material out of which the elements of the *next* generation would
be derived.   He believed that unless external influences broke through
the defences surrounding this reservoir of germ plasm, there would be
no transmission of any characters acquired during the life time of the
parent.   Such characters affected only the body of the parent and not
his or her germ plasm.   If such characters acquired during life did
show up in the offspring, it must be presumed that somehow the influence of these characters had penetrated the defences and reached
the germ plasm.   He even went so far as to hypothesize that the germ
plasm was particulate in nature, the particles each in some way being
carriers of an inheritable factor.   He knew nothing about genes at the
time, a fact which makes his insight all the more remarkable.

Commenting on this apparent resistance to change which is built
into all living things, Sir Julian Huxley, in 1938, said:[189]

> Can the hereditary constitution be permanently changed by the
> environment?   It is clear that theoretically it should be possible to

induce such changes.   The hereditary constitution is seen to be
something material which only our lack of knowledge prevents us
from defining chemically; and as such it must be possible for us to
alter it.   The remarkable fact, however, is its stubbornness in resistance to alteration.

Sixty-nine generations of flies bred in the dark — and yet no alteration in their eyes or their instincts with regard to light.   Ninety
generations in an attempt to raise their resistance to heat by acclim-
atization and selection — without results.   Indefinite time spent by
dandelions in the lowlands not preventing their immediately react-
ing to mountain conditions by changing size and form and proportion — and vice versa on replanting from mountain to plain . . . .

In spite of all the work that has been done, we have only established the very definite certainty that to a great many apparently
outward influences the germ plasm is quite unresponsive.

Professor Raymond Pearl of Johns Hopkins University, after out-
lining experiments which involved the controlled breeding of over 300
generations of one species of fly, concluded: [190]

(This is) perhaps the longest bit of controlled breeding ever
carried out with the result in each successive generation carefully
observed and precisely recorded.   Allowing 30 years as a round figure for the average duration of a human generation, the time equivalent in human reproduction of this experiment would be of the
order of 9000 years . . . . considerably longer than the total span of
man's even dimly recorded history.

The objective of this experiment was, of course, to see whether it
would be possible in any way to influence the germ plasm by various
manipulations of the environment.   Raymond Pearl summed up the
situation by saying, "the demonstration of the inherent stability of
the genic mechanism of heredity that this experiment has given is extremely impressive".

Now the explanation for this negative conclusion is owing to a large
extent to the work of Weismann.   Quite early in his professional career
as an embryologist, he began to find that he could no longer continue
his research in developmental physiology due to failing eyesight which
seriously restricted his use of a microscope.   As a result, he turned to
the theoretical aspects of his subject — with remarkably beneficial
consequences in terms of our subsequent understanding of the earliest
stages in the development of the fertilized ovum.   His basic conclusions have since been "substantiated to a surprising degree by the work
in genetics in succeeding years", as Robert Briggs and Thomas King
have observed. [191]

The fertilization of the ovum by a spermatozoon initiates a process
of development in which the seed begins to multiply until a certain
number of cells are formed, all of which appear to share the constitut-

ion and totipotency* of the ovum itself. Then, for reasons which are only just now beginning to be understood, further division of some of these cells is accompanied by a change in their constitution which may be due to their reduced size or their orientation with respect to the rest of the cells, or to chemical alteration, or to internal re-organization related to the time lapsed since the process of cleavage began.[192] It has been proposed by Christian P. Raven that the cytoplasm has begun to develop a complicated spatial structure due to a re-orientation of its contents as it ages or due to some genuinely new structures arising as a result of chemical reactions taking place in the egg. At any rate, the various parts of the egg, which were all alike before, now begin to show differences in chemical composition.[193] Weismann rightly surmised that some such change signalled the beginning of the emergence of *body* cells, the rest of the original cells meanwhile preserving their character specifically as *germ* cells.   Thus the germ cells give rise to the germ cells or seed of the next generation: while the body cells give rise to the organs of reproduction which will house them and see to their ultimate fertilization, as well as to the body of which these organs form a part. The body cells merely serve as the arena in which this reproductive process is brought to maturity. Thus is carried forward the germ plasm from generation to generation in an unbroken chain. **The body cells are built out of, and by, the germ cells or germ plasm; the germ plasm is not built out of the body.** It was this basic hypothesis which was perhaps Weismann's most important contribution. It is commonly termed "the continuity of the germ plasm".

The following diagram (Fig. 7) may help to show what is really involved here, underscoring the rather humbling fact that the body is

Fig. 7   Seed gives rise to Seed.

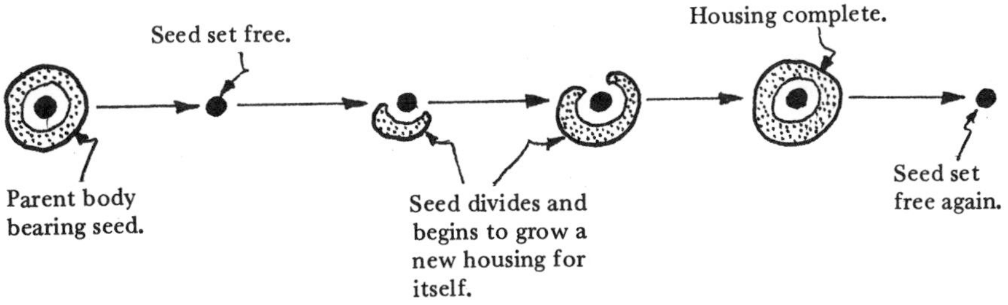

Seed set free.

Housing complete.

Parent body
bearing seed.

Seed divides and
begins to grow a
new housing for
itself.

Seed set
free again.

---

* Totipotency: the ability of a cell to multiply into a whole organism.

almost incidental, being merely the housing for the seed; whereas the seed is the only truly continuing element.

Generation after generation, bodies die and return to the dust, but the seed continues in an unbroken line reaching, in fact, uncorrupted in the woman from Adam to Mary — and of course it still continues to perpetuate itself.

The simplest way of explaining how physical death has passed upon all men through man is to assume that in natural generation the corruption which finally overwhelms the bodies of men and women alike is introduced to the ovum via the male seed but does not actually take effect **until the stage of embryonic development has been reached at which these differentiated body cells have begun to form.** The mortogenic factor has apparently had no influence upon the germ plasm of the woman but only upon the germ plasm of the man. By contrast, it does have its deadly influence upon the differentiating body cells of BOTH the male and female embryo once the body cells begin to form by diverging in their constitution from the germ plasm. In short, the germ plasm of the male, and the bodies of both males and females, are mortalized.   But the germ plasm of the female remains immortal.

That such a mechanism might be responsible for changes in cells subsequently derived from the germ plasm was suggested by Weismann. In 1881 he wrote:[194]

> It may be objected that cells of which the ancestors possessed the power of living forever could not become potentially mortal either suddenly or gradually, for such a change would contradict the supposition which attributes immortality to their ancestors and to the products of their division.   This argument is valid, *but it only applies so long as the descendants retain their original constitution.*   As soon as the two products of fission of a potentially immortal cell acquire different constitutions by unequal fission, another possibility arises.   It is conceivable that *one of the products of fission might preserve the physical constitution necessary for immortality, but not the other* (my emphasis).

Weismann certainly did not have in view the context presently under discussion, but his perceptive mind led him to a conclusion which is very relevant to the issue.   We have a situation in which two lines of cells, both with the potential of immortality, are housed in the bodies of two people (Adam and Eve) who subsequently surrender the immortality of their bodies.   The immediate cause of this loss of immortality is a poison which is fatal to all *body* cells.   The same poison also proves fatal to the male spermatozoa which will later be generated out of this germ plasm.   Unlike the oocytes in the female which are already formed at the time of birth, spermatozoa are manufactured

throughout the adult life of the male.   They are apparently susceptible to the influence of body cells, especially those of the tissues
which generate them.

When any attempt is made artificially to promote self-replication
and further development of a single spermatozoon, the results are
negative.   The sperm are not viable for more than a few days unless
fused with the ovum.   But when the female ovum is treated suitably
(at least in the animal world below man), it may develop into a mature
organism.   It is capable, therefore, of replicating itself indefinitely,
even in the absence of fusion with a spermatozoon.   When this is
observed in nature it is referred to as *parthenogenesis*, meaning essentially virgin conception leading to virgin birth.   The fact of parthenogenesis is clearly established for the female seed:[195] the same cannot
be said to have been observed for the male seed.

The ovum is, in fact, a unicellular organism.   And by virtue of its
ability to replicate itself indefinitely under appropriate conditions, it
must be assumed to have retained the same kind of physical immortality which other unicellular organisms (like amoeba or paramecia, for
example) still enjoy.   By contrast, although the individual spermatozoon has all the appearance of a highly active and extremely complex
unicellular organism, it does not have the power to replicate itself,
and therefore does not enjoy a like physical immortality.   It does *not*
behave like a unicellular organism.

Sometimes it is argued that the proportion of cytoplasm surrounding the nucleus of the male spermatozoon is too small to supply it
with the energy reservoir necessary to enable it to replicate itself.   As
a consequence, the nucleus cannot survive for more than 24 - 36 hours
or so, unless it is fused with the ovum: it simply runs out of energy.
The female seed has several thousand times[196] as much food available
to supply the energy for cleavage because it is so much larger, though
the *nucleus* itself is no larger than in the male seed.   To test whether
this is true, the male nucleus has been experimentally transferred by
microsurgery into an enucleated ovum in order to supply it with
adequate energy.[197]   The results, however, have been disappointing.
The spermatozoon nucleus still cannot perpetuate itself beyond a few
divisions.   It is thus apparent that there is a profound difference in
the constitution of these two seeds in respect to their potential
immortality.   Both will, or course, die if not housed appropriately
according to their nature, but whereas the mammalian ovum can with
surprising ease be made to divide and multiply[198] and grow into a
whole animal (though always a female[199]), the male spermatozoon
cannot.

Whatever the nature of the defect in the male seed brought about
by the entrance of the poison, it is almost certainly the channel by

which the mortogenic factor is introduced into the ovum at the time
of conception, even though the effect itself is not felt in the pre-
sumptive organism until the multiplying cells begin the process of
differentiation for the express purpose of forming *body* cells.[200]

Now Weismann set forth this theory of the "continuity of the
germ plasm" in the following way(Fig. 8):

Fig.8   Each seed gives rise to another seed
          and to the body which houses it.

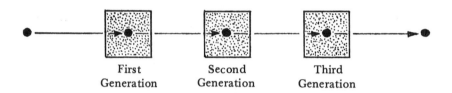

First   Second   Third
Generation   Generation   Generation

With remarkably few modifications, his conclusions have stood the
test of time.[201] His thinking triggered the somewhat facetious remark
which is often made to freshmen students when they are first introduced to these concepts: "The hen is merely the egg's way of laying
another egg". The thought is a depressing one if man himself is viewed merely as a plaything of Nature, a by-product of a process bent
upon a blind course of species-improvement without respect to the
worth of the individual. For the individual becomes simply one stage
in an entirely impersonal process. As Kenneth Walker put it rather
effectively:[202]

> All that the somatic cells, which form the main bulk of man's
> body are really called upon to do is to provide a refuge in which
> the immortal cells . . . . can find temporary lodging and sustenance.
> It is a little bit discouraging to our self esteem to be looked upon as
> merely useful wallets for conveying the valuable germ plasm down
> the ages.

It is, then, a simple fact that the body does not generate the ova
(in which case the ova would inevitably have become heir to the defect of the body) but the ovum generates the body. As Professor A.
S. Pearse put it, "through a series of divisions a germ cell gives rise to a
body or soma and to new germ cells. The latter, and not the body,
give rise to the next generation".[203] It appears that this mechanism is
by no means limited to human generation. It is a phenomenon of
very wide occurrence in sexually reproductive organisms below man.
Alfred Huettner describes this process as it occurs in the roundworm:[204]

In certain forms, as for example in *Ascaris*, the single primordial germ cell is set aside in the second cleavage of the ovum, and while this cell continues to divide it does so at a retarded rate. The other cells keep on cleaving at their usual rate and eventually form the body or soma of the animal, while the retarded germ cells become enclosed in the body to develop the gonads . . . . It is the function of these somatic cells to carry the germ plasm and nourish and protect it. The somatoplasm has to die some time and revert to the inorganic world. The germ plasm, however, is protected by and parasitic on the somatoplasm and is immortal so long as, during the life of the individual, one or a number of cells from the germ plasm (the gonad) with the total number of determinants is liberated and becomes activated by fertilization or by parthenogenesis and develops again into germ plasm (gonad) and somatoplasm (body) in the next generation and so *ad infinitum*.

Sir Charles Sherrington has a beautiful free-flowing passage describing this situation. Coming as it does from a man whose life was spent largely in medical research and whose reputation was international, his words so eloquently expressed are doubly worth pondering. Nor has recent research required their modification since they were penned. As applied to human beings his statement is still correct. He wrote:[205]

In its earliest stages the embryo's cells are not notably different one from another. Later . . . . they become so in spite of being by descent all members of one family . . . .

To this there seems at first sight one exception, one cell-type which, out of all the myriads, alone remains its original self and does not specialize. It retains the old original nature of the ancestral cell. Its sisters and their progeny pass on through chains of metamorphoses to form a world of different shapes and activities. But this one persists still unmodified and true to its own primitive forebear . . . .

All its sisters with their flights into far-fetched specializations, including the brain with its mysteries of mind, are powerless to produce again a germ such as they sprang from. From no one of them all, let them be ever so human, can any fertilization produce their like again in the shape of man or human child . . . .

From the old ancestral cell one narrow derivative line of descendants, nested in the rest of the immense collateral progeny, retains its original germinal and general nature: and this, even, has to ripen. Significantly enough, it then sets itself free from all the others. And so on from generation to generation.

It is therefore clear that these germ cells constitute a very slender thread in the continuity of immortality, for the initial cell (the fertilized ovum) retains its own identity for between two and five doublings (depending upon the species) before differentiated cells begin to appear which can no longer be considered as part of the original germ plasm. These few pure germ cells will continue to replicate themselves in isolation, though at a much slower rate, but for a short interval of time the stream of immortality is entrusted to a tiny handful of cells.

The expert in these matters will not need elaboration of this circumstance but the layman may find it helpful, in visualizing how the ovum provides for its own continuity, to have the following summary statement.

The sperm penetrates the ovum and shortly thereafter the ovum begins to divide into two cells, then each of these divide again and we have four cells. Shortly, there are eight and then sixteen, and so it grows into a ball of cells called a *morula*. A fluid-filled hollow develops and the whole growing mass assumes the form of a kind of thin-shelled ball like an orange peel without the orange inside. This is the blastocyst stage. The blastocyst then collapses on itself, looking rather like an air-filled ball with a small hole in it that has been stepped on and stays that way. In time, various parts of the structure begin to develop differently and the foundations for the reproductive system begin to emerge in what is called the genital ridge, which is approximately where the rubber ball indented and tended to close up the fold. Meanwhile, the germ cells have kept themselves apart in one place, multiplying slowly. Once the blood vessels and a kind of circulation system is in operation, these germ cells which have still retained their integrity migrate via the vascular system by a form of amoeboid motion towards the area of the genital ridge. When the gonads finally form in this area, they are invaded by the germ cells which then take up residence there. The gonads themselves now begin to develop as testes or ovaries, depending more or less on the chromosomal sex of the original germ cells.

It will be remembered that the presence of the X or Y chromosome determines whether the medulla or the cortex of the gonads will grow at the expense of the alternative and therefore whether testes or ovaries will form. These glands, once the decision is made as to which they shall become, begin to secrete hormones which act upon the maturing foetus to cause the appropriate internal reproductive organs to form, and later the appropriate external genitalia. By full term, the female foetus has its internal reproductive organs (ovaries, fallopian tubes, uterus, etc.) all essentially complete and supplied with a full quota of oocytes which, one by one, will later mature and be released as fully prepared ova throughout the whole fertile period of the woman's life.

If one wanted to think in purely biological terms, one might now convert a previous popular observation to read, "the woman is merely the ovum's way of creating another ovum". This is so because the seed of the woman perpetuates itself in a very special way — as we shall see in the next chapter.

Now various figures are given for the number of "pure" germ cells (from 16 to 32) after which further cleavage results in the appearance of the first somatic cells.[206]   Of *Ascaris megalocephala*, Alfred Kuhn says that the first somatic cells appear at the *fourth* cleavage when there are 16 cells present.   The experimental evidence is sometimes contradictory but it suggests a basic pattern: the differentiation of mortal cells from immortal cells is made very early in development.[207]

Thus the germ cells do not continue their uninterrupted development for very long.   They soon throw off differential cells which signal the development of body tissues.   But at the same time they preserve themselves as a reservoir of germ plasm throughout the life of the organism.

The subsequent history of the developing germ plasm in the female is, however, different from that of the male germ plasm.   As J. Money and A. A. Ehrhardt observe:[208]

> At birth the normal pair of ovaries is said to have between 300,000 and 400,000 ova, of which approximately 300 to 400 will eventually go through the process of ovulation.   The billions of sperm produced by the testes are not all present at birth as ova are believed to be, but are produced new throughout life.

Now this basic fact of the continuity of the germ plasm has been set forth diagrammatically in a number of ways by various authorities since Weismann's time.   In a paper entitled, "The Third Stage in Genetics", Donald Michie has the following figure showing in a simplified way two *opposing* views of the fate of the germ plasm from generation to generation.[209]   I have modified his drawing slightly in order to make its meaning more self-evident to those who find diagrams difficult.

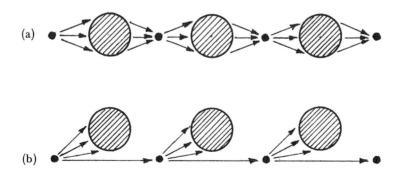

Fig. 9 Two opposing views of the fate of the seed
as it passes from generation to generation.

In Fig. 9 (a) the germ seed gives rise to a body which then gives rise to a germ seed. The latter then gives rise to a second generation body which in turn generates a second generation seed. And so the process goes on indefinitely. The important thing is that in *this* view the body really is giving rise to the seed. It is a view which was commonly held until the time of Weismann. In Fig. 9 (b) the situation is really quite different, for the initial germ seed gives rise to the next germ seed *and* to a body, the germ seed and the body thus generated being *almost* independent entities. This is not quite true and to this extent the diagram is unsatisfactory except in so far as it tends to point up the two different concepts very nicely. It is not quite true in so far as the seed *is* dependent upon the body to house it.

A more truly representative diagram is that which Sir Alister Hardy presents in his *This Living Stream*, re-drawn as Fig. 10.[210] In this view the initial germ seed gives rise both to the seed of the next generation and to the body. The seed is shown after migration into the body that is to house it.

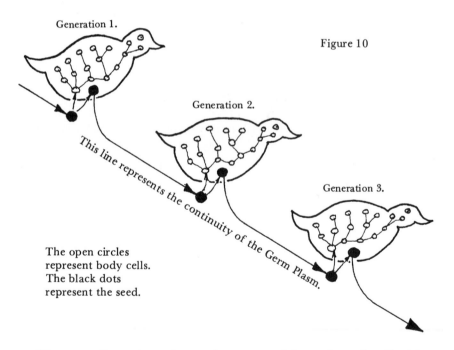

Generation 1.

Figure 10

Generation 2.

This line represents the continuity of the Germ Plasm.

Generation 3.

The open circles represent body cells. The black dots represent the seed.

The next figure is re-drawn from an article written by Fischberg and Blackler based strictly on experimental observation.[211] The initial germ plasm multiplies to the 8 cell stage by which time one or two cells have been partially isolated and are shown as solid dots. These cells, in the next stage, double and become effectively isolated. In due time these isolated cells become the gonad germ cells in the mature organism (in the Gall midge).

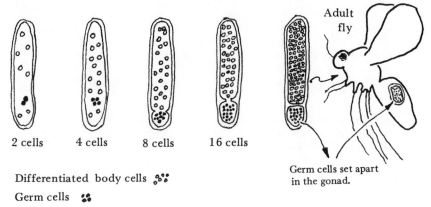

2 cells   4 cells   8 cells   16 cells

Differentiated body cells

Germ cells

Germ cells set apart
in the gonad.

Figure 11

It may help, finally, to bring this series of figures "home", as it were, by re-drawing an illustration from Fritz Kahn in his *Man in Structure and Function*, in which the same basic patter of continuity is transferred to the human context.[212]

Figure 12

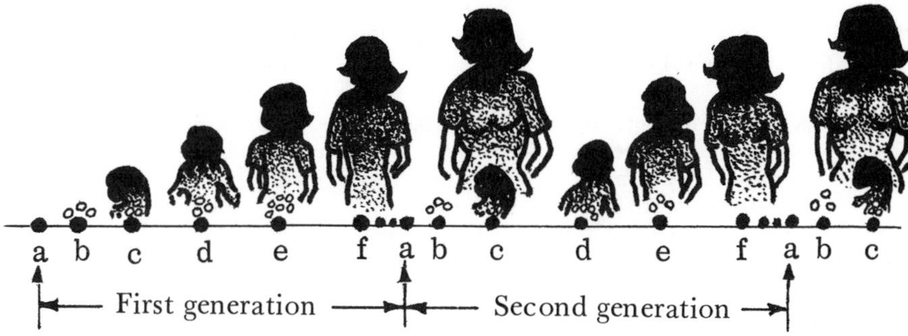

a   b   c   d   e   f   a   b   c   d   e   f   a   b   c

|← First generation →|← Second generation →|

Fritz Kahn published his book about 35 years ago and it might be thought that it would now be seriously out of date. In his discussion of this diagram, however, the facts remain essentially as he has described them. His work is still a very useful textbook, and the illustrations are both imaginative and effective for the communication of what is highly complex. He explains his diagram as follows:

The life of man begins at the moment when the paternal sperm cell unites with the maternal egg to form the egg-sperm cell that is the conceptus (a).   Through the union of the two chemically different cells an otherwise unknown vital energy is developed. The egg-sperm cell divides rapidly into 2, 4, 8, 16, 32 and finally into millions and billions of cells, thus giving rise to man.   Not all the cells participate in the development of the body, however.   Of the first four cells, one is retarded in its growth (b).   This quarter of the body which is laid aside during the first hours of human development forms the sex cells (c), and in its totality the sex gland (d).   Each of the four primordial cells possesses a certain supply of energy like a charged storage battery.   The three body cells use up this energy during youth: with this energy they build up and develop the body (e).   Their growth energy lasts for about twenty years.   Then growth ceases.   As long as the body cells grow, they inhibit the energy of the sex gland.   After this inhibitory influence has been removed, the sex gland begins to produce cells (f) . . . .   During youth the body cells multiply while the sex cells rest.   At the time of maturity the sex cells multiply and the body cells rest . . . .

Because of the division of the body into body and sex cells, man is not a unitary organism, but rather a kind of double creature, consisting of himself and his sex cells . . . .   The sex cells do not belong to us (as individuals) but rather to the entire species . . . . The sex cells are the truly immortal element in us, as Plato already sensed when he wrote, "The mortal creature harbours an immortal element" . . . .

It may be difficult to believe that any line of *mortal* creatures could convey from generation to generation a continuing stream of *immortal* cells without ultimately corrupting them.   But evidently this really is what takes place.   C. E. McClung tells us: [213]

A germ cell of one individual generation . . . . becomes detached and forms a complete organism of the next generation.   By *some insulating device* [emphasis mine] the germinal elements within the gonad do not participate in the somatic processes, but merely perpetuate themselves.   (But) on being freed from this inhibition (the insulating device) they are freed from the limited role of mere germ cells and may perform through their descendants all somatic activities.

But by nature, and if not experimentally interfered with, these germ cells are, as V. H. Mottram put it, "the only physically immortal things" in our bodies. [214]

Again, I would modify this statement slightly by noting that it is really the sex cells *in the female line* that are "the only physically immortal things".   The statement does, however, show how widely it is recognized that at the very root of our individual existence there is an immortal constituent, the seed of the woman.

Weismann, almost a century ago, in an essay published originally under the title *Uber die Ewigkeit des Lebens*, i.e., "Upon the Eternal Duration of Life", wrote (as we have already noted, p.14), "The immortality of the unicellular organism has passed over only to the ova or spermatozoa, the other (cells) must die, and since the body of the individual is chiefly composed of them, it must die also". Again, I would only modify Weismann's statement by excluding the spermatazoa.

So the seed of the woman dies with the woman because it is thus robbed of its home, even as seeds die month by month if not fertilized by the sperm, being rejected from the female body and to all intents and purposes killed in the process. In any case they do not die because it is their nature to do so or because they have limited energy. It is, as we have seen, remarkably easy in animals to trigger the seed into mitotic activity and thus to perpetuate itself indefinitely. Once so stimulated, the ovum will under appropriate conditions go on to full term in a viable form. There is considerable controversy, on the other hand, as to whether parthenogenesis in this sense has ever occurred in a woman, though there have been a number of claims made by unwed mothers with respect to the birth of supposedly fatherless daughters. [215]

Now all this has a direct bearing upon the present theme. Having been endowed with *immortality*, Adam and Eve acquired *mortality*. And, which is significant from a physiological point of view, their offspring inherited this acquired character. We have here therfore a clear case of something which actually happened that, until comparatively recent times, was ruled out as an impossibility. It has been the traditional wisdom among geneticists for about a hundred years that acquired characters are not inherited. Yet here was an acquired character that "passed upon all men" (Rom.5:12). It seems rather strange to me that no Christian biologist has given much thought to the matter. Indeed, it has taken a man actually opposed to the Christian view to note this unusual circumstance. Sir Gavin de Beer, an outstanding evolutionist in England, when reviewing the book *Mankind Evolving* by Theodosius Dobzhansky, makes this remark: [216]

> One wonders if Pauline theolgians realize that the doctrine of original sin involves the inheritance of an acquired character, for only genes can be inherited and, by the nature of the case, neither Adam nor Eve when they first appeared on the scene possessed the character they are alleged to have transmitted to all their descendants.

To all their descendants, *save ONE!* And here, if Sir Gavin had taken the thought seriously, is a further great truth which might have provoked him to think even more deeply upon the subject. For it is evident that the acquired character of Eden was indeed transmitted and *must* therefore have ultimately reached the germ plasm. The only mechanism which will satisfy all the conditions thus laid down in Scripture is one which assumes that the transmission was effected via the *male* seed only. Luther and Calvin (see page 145 f. above) and now Barth have all recognized this fact. De Beer's comment is therefore not entirely correct.

Now each spermatozoon is a single-celled organism of highly complex structure and form. It is not only the smallest cell in the body but quite possibly also the most complicated in its organization. In its head-piece, it has a nucleus containing the genes, suspended in a pool of surrounding cytoplasm containing a number of minute structures of various kinds called *organelles* (i.e., tiny organs), the whole being sheathed in a membrane like a soft shell, and provided with a quite complex tail portion by which a high degree of motility is achieved. Fig. 13 gives a good idea of its complexity.

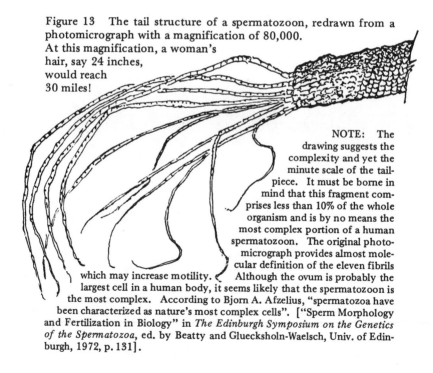

Figure 13 The tail structure of a spermatozoon, redrawn from a photomicrograph with a magnification of 80,000.
At this magnification, a woman's hair, say 24 inches, would reach 30 miles!

NOTE: The drawing suggests the complexity and yet the minute scale of the tail-piece. It must be borne in mind that this fragment comprises less than 10% of the whole organism and is by no means the most complex portion of a human spermatozoon. The original photomicrograph provides almost molecular definition of the eleven fibrils which may increase motility. Although the ovum is probably the largest cell in a human body, it seems likely that the spermatozoon is the most complex. According to Bjorn A. Afzelius, "spermatozoa have been characterized as nature's most complex cells". ["Sperm Morphology and Fertilization in Biology" in *The Edinburgh Symposium on the Genetics of the Spermatozoa*, ed. by Beatty and Gluecksholn-Waelsch, Univ. of Edinburgh, 1972, p. 131].

It is now believed that within the cytoplasm and among the minute particles which are suspended in it, there are certain carriers of hered-

itary material which have been termed *plasmagenes*.[217]   These cytoplasmic "genes" are distinct from the nuclear genes which hitherto
have been assumed the sole carriers of heredity, and they appear to be
(unlike the nuclear genes) susceptible to influences outside the cell.
Since there is constant interaction between the nucleus and the cytoplasm of each cell it is possible for environmental influences, by this
route, to reach the hereditary material and effect modifications in all
subsequent generations.   It is possible that the fact of the continuous
production of mature spermatozoa throughout the adult fertile life of
the male may expose them to such influences in a way that the ova
are not.

In the male the primordial germ cells are present from the very
beginning (as in the *female* embryo) but the complex free-living organism which is the mature spermatozoon (short-lived though it is) is
continuously being manfactured from puberty and throughout adult
life by extensive modification of the germ plasm cells.[218]   And these
mature spermatozoa are produced in the hundreds of millions.   This
fact may account for the greater accessibility of these cells to influences from the body which manufactures and houses them.   And
the fact that the spermatozoon actually penetrates into and becomes
absorbed in and fused with the ovum makes it a potential pathway
into the ova for male body cell influences.

Thus although the woman may have been the first to introduce
the fatal poison into her *body* cells, she did not by that act poison her
own seed, but the poison of death does enter through the male seed
into the seed of the woman by the fusion of the two.   By such a
mechanism the poison in Adam's body may have reached his seed, and
via the cytoplasm of the seed the poison is by fusion with the female
seed passed on to the embryo.

Now the substance of what we have been discussing in this chapter
may be stated as follows.   As we trace the history of biological theory
with respect to the mechanism of inheritance, we find Lamarck arguing
that any animal which responded to the challenges of the environment
by developing structures or instincts or chemical responses which gain
for it an advantage in the struggle to survive, was in a position to
further the chances of survival of its descendants by passing these
gains on by inheritance.   The key doctrine here was that acquired
characters were inherited.   It seemed self-evident and necessary that
this should be so in view of the apparent progress of life, and it very
reasonably accounted for the steady improvement in the breeding of
animals of particular interest to man.   It only remained therefore to
unravel the mechanism whereby acquired characters were transmitted.

It soon became apparent that this obvious "fact" was not true after all. Acquired characters did not seem to be *inherited*, or if they were, the mechanism was certainly not a simple one. Once this was acknowledged, all kinds of every day illustrations sprang to mind and made the older Lamarckian view seem patently absurd: mutilated parents do not bear mutilated offspring — daughters of Chinese mothers whose feet had been bound from childhood bore normal daughters, circumcised fathers did not beget circumcised sons, the blacksmith could have as many puny infants as anyone else. A new law was therefore announced: "Acquired characters are *not* inherited". And all biologists accepted this new law at its face value.

A few biologists with Christian convictions were disturbed by the new "law" because they could see that real problems were created in our understanding of the events which occurred in Eden. Mortality was *acquired* by man, yet it *was* inherited. To quote Romans 5:12 again, "Death entered . . . . and passed upon all men". This was an essential aspect of the Fall of man and his need for redemption. Was the Bible in error?

By the prodigious labours and elegant methods of research of a number of geneticists and microbiologists, the mechanism is now becoming clear. This research begins to show that there are certain conditions under which an acquired character can after all be inherited, not via the nuclear genes but by something analogous to them in the surrounding cytoplasm termed plasmagenes. The resistance to change in the germ plasm is due to the fact that it is not derived from the body cells — cells which are responsive to changes during life. It was this fact that made it so difficult to see how the germ cells could be influenced by what happens to the parents. It is the plasmagenes that respond to influences, not the germ plasm.

But it now appears that although the male germ cells, like the ova, are derived from the germ cells of the parent body and not from the body cells, these male germ cells are susceptible to the subsequent influence of the body cells in a way that the female germ cells are not. The end result is that by this roundabout way some acquired characters, whether hurtful or harmless, seem to be inheritable in mammals through the male seed. The pathway is from body cells to male germ cell *cytoplasm*, and from the male germ cell cytoplasm to the female seed by fusion at the time of fertilization. And thence these modifications appear in body cells of the resulting offspring both male and female. And these steps are repeated generation after generation so long as the seed of the woman is fertilized by the seed of the man.

But if the seed of the woman could be activated without fertilization by the seed of man, it must be supposed that the result would be the emergence of an individual escaping the mortogenic factor which Adam bequeathed via his seed to all subsequent generations. Such an offspring would recover in his person the original physical immortality with which Adam was endowed at his creation.

In short, to summarize a long and complex chapter, it may be said that the seed of the woman is the only remnant that has retained the original immortality possessed by our first parents. By contrast, the seed of man and the body cells of both the man and the woman have been mortalized. Furthermore, even the seed of the woman is fatally poisoned by fusion with the male seed.

However, this poison affects only that portion of the woman's seed which will develop into body cells: the remainder of her seed continues to form the immortal stream of germ plasm. Only if an ovum from this germ plasm reservoir can be fertilized by some means not natural to man can a body with the original endowment of potential immortality be recovered again.

Chapter 19

THE LIFE HISTORY OF THE SEED OF THE WOMAN

*A very brief consideration
of the concept
of the Continuity of the Germ Plasm
and its bearing
on the direct line relationship
between the First and the Last Adam.*

This chapter can quite safely be by-passed by anyone who is becoming impatient with technical details and prefers to move on to the more strictly biblical aspects of this subject. However, I do not think the intelligent reader will have any difficulty with it and it does show how wonderfully the Lord prepared the way, in his design and creation of the reproductive mechanism, for the recovery of Adam's original constitution in the midst of a dying world.

It may be helpful for those who are uninitiated in such matters to set forth in a generalized form which is admittedly very much over-simplified but nevertheless essentially correct, the life history of the ovum in one generation from the time of its fertilization until the time that it presents itself once again for fertilization to initiate the next generation.

This will help to show perhaps why it is possible to speak of a true *continuity* of the germ plasm and in what way it is quite correct to credit the seed with immortality in a situation where the vehicle or carrier (the female body in this case) has a very limited life span. Like the amoeba, the seed has the potential for unending self-replication without experiencing death in the sense that no corpse need be left behind to make a break in the continuity of the germ plasm unless the germ plasm is actually destroyed by some external agency or circumstance.

It is sometimes suggested that when the fertilized egg divides into two, it experiences a kind of death in that it is changed into something else. But I think Weismann's answer to this was effective. [219] He observed that the ovum no more dies in becoming two ova at a certain stage in development than the boy *dies* in becoming a man at a certain stage of development. The fact is that the ovum, considered as a living organism (which indeed it is), need never experience death provided that it is induced to divide and multiply by successive divisions. This may happen in nature without fertilization, but normally it is the result of fertilization by a sperm. With this one condition fulfilled, the single ovum becomes another ovum one generation later in history and no corpse is left behind as evidence of its death. The two "daughter" cells in turn divide, if fertilized, and so the line goes on unbroken and can continue endlessly so long as accident does not terminate it. Fertilization of the ovum is really only a means for preserving its integrity until one generation later it is again released and presented for fertilization. And so it is simply passed on and on, generation after generation, in an unbroken chain of continuous life. The living ovum is the ovum of yesterday perpetuating itself not as a mother perpetuates herself in her daughter and then dies while the daughter lives on, but as a girl perpetuates herself by growing up into a woman without experiencing death in the process. Such a process does not constitute death but fulfillment.

Now this can be set forth diagrammatically, granting much oversimplification, in such a way that these events can be visualized. First of all we allow a single black dot, (a) in Fig. 14, to signify the original

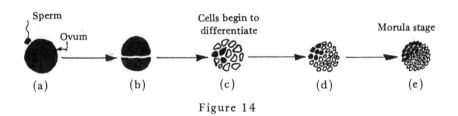

Figure 14

fertilized ovum. At (b), cleavage has taken place and the ovum has become two ova. The original ovum has not "died", it has merely converted itself into two viable duplicates half the size of the original. This process of multiplication continues, until a change takes place (c) and further multiplication leads to the emergence of cells which by now differ in their constitution from the original ovum.   These differentiated cells are shown from (c) to (e) as open circles.   The undifferentiated cells which have not changed their constitution but have retained the full potential of the original ovum, although they are now considerably smaller, are still shown as black dots.   From then on, the history of the two kinds of cells, the differentiated and the undifferentiated, follows a decidely different course.

In Fig. 15 the history of these cells is continued and the divergent end products of each group of cells is set forth diagrammatically by showing that the open circles become a separate entity, the *body*, while the black dots continue to replicate in a mass by themselves — *outside* the body of the embryo proper. This stage is therefore termed "extra-embryonic development".

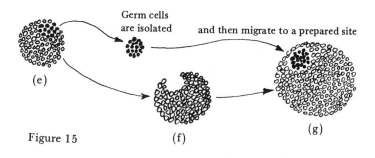

Figure 15   (f)

It should be understood that these germ cells really *are* multiplying outside the body of the developing embryo.   Later, this mass of multiplying germ plasm cells will migrate by amoeboid movement from its position beside the life-support system of the embryo into the embryo itself.   In the diagram the schematized growing embryo at (f) is shown with a kind of harbour facing towards the mass of germ plasm which is merely intended to indicate that there is an appropriate place being prepared to receive the germ plasm in due time as at (g).   From this "harbour" (the ovary), one ovum at a time is released for potential fusion with a spermatozoon, as shown in Fig. 16 below.

The mechanism governing the differentiation of the cells into germ cells and body cells appears to result not from any change in the nuclear content of the cells themselves but in some change in the surrounding cytoplasm in which the nucleus is immersed.   The initial process of replication by which the fertilized ovum multiplies itself until it forms a mass of germ and body cells is called a *morula*, (e) of Fig. 14, results in a gradual reduction in the *size* of each of the multiplying cells which, though their *number* is greatly increased, actually still occupy very nearly the same total space as the original ovum. This is called cell *cleavage*. It is not what will happen later when cells divide and multiply, because from then on the total *volume* of the cells begins to increase and not merely the *number* of cells. In this later process each body cell grows larger and larger until it has approximately twice the volume it originally had, at which critical point an internal change occurs in the cell and it divides into two, each the size of the original cell before it began to grow. This process is referred to as cell *division*. The multiplication of cells from the initial fertilized ovum to the morula stage is therefore quite different from cell division. The distinction is necessary because at this earlier period in cell life history the cells divide into two without first gaining in size. Each cleavage therefore reduces the *size* of the cell but the *number* of cells steadily increases. The ovum which begins as the largest cell in the body keeps dividing until its size is very substantially reduced. Then later in its life when the individual reaches adolescence, and just before one of the germ cells is presented for fertilization by a sperm cell, it increases in size and regains its status once more as the largest cell in the body. This will be observed in Fig. 16 below.

Now although the cell size decreases steadily from ovum to morula, the *nucleus* itself remains approximately the same size so that the ratio of cytoplasm to nuclear material steadily decreases. This means that a selection of the cytoplasm is being made with each subsequent cleavage, some of it being apportioned to one daughter cell and some to another. By this method the reduction in cell size can be achieved. Each successive cell during this process therefore receives not merely a different *amount* of cytoplasm but cytoplasm of a different *constitution* containing only a selection of the constituents in the parent cell as well as very probably a different internal organization. It is believed that this is what leads to progressive cell differentiation and therefore the growth, in due course, of specifically different tissues and the development of different organs within the body.[220]

Identical genetic material in the nucleus then finds itself surrounded by a series of different intra-cellular environments, and the interaction between nucleus and cytoplasm initiates the cell specialization which the developing organism demands. The subdividing of the substance of the egg qualitatively is believed to be a sufficient cause for the initial establishment of different lines of cells, most of which are body or somatic cells and each of which will develop along different lines — even though the nuclear material in every cell is thought to retain all the characteristics of the original ovum. Any cell nucleus transferred to an enucleated ovum is found to have the totipotency of the initial ovum. Cell character is therefore not merely the result of the nuclear material but the interaction of this nuclear material and its associated cytoplasm, and this cytoplasm is in a continuous state of change during foetal development.

In Fig. 16 we observe the final housing of the germ plasm. This in no way disturbs the integrity of the germ plasm itself which continues through certain stages of development that will prepare the individual germ cells for the time when they will be presented in the adult animal for subsequent fertilization. The important thing to bear in mind is that this reservoir of germ cells is given a safe haven within the foetus which, as far as is known at present, completely isolates the germ cells, thus preserving their integrity.

Figure 16

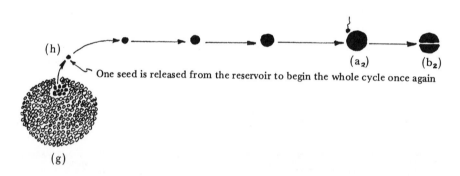

One seed is released from the reservoir to begin the whole cycle once again

In this Figure, one of the germ cells (h) is being ejected in enlarged form prior to being presented at the time of ovulation. At (a₂) the cell has become an ovum and is now fertilized by the sperm. At (b₂) the first cleavage has occurred and we are back at (b) of Fig. 14 and about to begin another cycle of development.

And so generation after generation, the seed of the woman re-iterates itself in its original form. Thus was preserved the continuity of the germ plasm from the first to the second Adam, from Eve to Mary. And just to keep the record straight, it has to be remembered that the process is still continuing. It did not *stop* with Mary.

PART III

WHEN THE WORD
BECAME FLESH

The Lord did not contravene the design of the natural order in bringing the Redeemer into the world.

He put nature to a higher service, a service for which it was designed in the first place.

Chapter 20

EMBODIMENT: ESSENTIAL TO HUMANNESS

And the Lord God formed man
of the dust of the ground,
and breathed into his nostrils the breath of life;
and man became a living soul.
Genesis 2:7

(When) the pitcher is broken at the source,
then shall the dust return to the earth as it was;
and the spirit shall return unto God who gave it.
Ecclesiastes 12:7

The body without the spirit is dead.
James 2:26

That men and animals share a similar life-support system is so obvious that an increasing number of people are willing to view man on this account as little more than an animal himself. In defence of the Christian view of man it is then customary to say that what distinguishes him from the animals is his possession of a *soul*. However, when it is pointed out that the word *soul* is applied to animal life before it is applied to human life*, refuge is then taken in the fact that

---

* Cf. Gen.1:20, 21, 24, 30; 2:19; 9:4, 10, 12, 15, 16. *Nephesh,* the normal Hebrew word for *soul* which is usually translated *pneuma* in the LXX and the New Testament, is in Genesis variously translated as *living creature, moving creature,* etc., as in these passages, and even as *life* itself in Proverbs 12:10.

man is also *spirit*, and it is his possession of a spirit that distinguishes him.   But again it has to be noted that the Bible also attributes the possession of a spirit to animals (Eccl.3:21).   So the question arises, What, then, *is* the difference between man and animals?

The answer appears to lie in the nature of the spirit that man has; and the distinctiveness of this nature is spelled out in the very passage which also attributes spirit to animals.   Ecclesiastes 3:21 states very specifically that "the spirit of the beast goeth downward to the earth" whereas "the spirit of the man goeth upward".   If the *destiny* of the two kinds of spirit involved is very different, then we are justified in assuming that the *nature* of the two kinds of spirit must be equally different.

But as we have already noted, there is also some funamental difference (as yet unidentified) between the animal and the human *body*, a difference which likewise has a profound bearing upon its destiny.   We have no indication from Scripture that when an animal dies it is in any sense a rending asunder of two constituents, a body and a spirit, which were designed to remain in union *forever*.   On the contrary, in human experience the tragedy of death is that the individual is overwhelmed by the horror of this anticipated rending asunder.   The Bible constantly supports him in this horror, and a very important part of the hope it offers to man is that the rending apart will be one day undone and he will be reclothed bodily.   Devoid of language, animals could never have such a hope revealed to them and one might therefore assume that it was never planned for them either.   For man the situation is quite otherwise.

Scripture places just as much emphasis upon his body as it does upon his spirit.   The uniqueness of man does not lie merely in the uniqueness of his spirit: it includes the uniqueness of his body.   We therefore learn that the uniqueness of the whole man lies not only in his possession of such a body *or* such a spirit as he has, but in the exceptional relationship between the two.   It is this relationship which constitutes his humanness.   He is not a human being except in the unity of his body and his spirit.   When death overtakes man it effectively dismembers the whole person contrary to every aspiration of his soul.   Then only the promise of the resurrection of the body fully reassures him.

James Orr observed that since death is not something natural to man at all, it is nothing less than a violent rupture of the parts of man's being that were never meant to be separated.*   Death is thus a mutilation of man's person; indeed it is more than mere mutilation, it is

---

* Orr, James, *God's Image in Man*, Grand Rapids, Eerdmans, reprint, 1948, p. 51, 52, 252.

experientally a temporary destruction of his person as a fully constituted human being.   This prospect devastates him: all his life he lives
in bondage to the fear of it (Heb.2:15), and not least because man is
deeply persuaded that death is not the end of his life.

Now the coming and going of the soul is a mystery.   We do not
even know what the precise difference is, if any, between the soul and
the spirit.   Nor is there any general agreement as to how the soul
originates, nor exactly when it is admitted to the body.   Is it created
or inherited?   Does it emerge by the act of conception, or in the drawing of the first breath, or does it arise at some critical point during
foetal development?

It seems rather unlikely at this late stage in the development of
theology that there will ever be a general agreement as to whether the
constitution of man is a dichotomy or a trichotomy, a duality of body
and spirit, or a trinity of body, soul, and spirit.   Does man have a
distinct spiritual component at all?

While the belief that man has a spirit which is distinct from his
body is virtually universal in the non-Western world, there is increasing unbelief among ourselves.   It is a recent phenomenon.   It is hard
to recall a single primitive society among the hundreds which have
been studied intensely that does not take it for granted.   Indeed
almost all primitive cultures place greater emphasis upon the spirit
than the body and have little or no doubt as to its continuance after
the body has been destroyed.   Western Man, meanwhile, seems bent
on reducing himself to a soul-less electrochemical machine.

Most higher non-Western cultures tend to favour a less materialistic
view of man's constitution.   It would be difficult to find an instance
where they have reduced man to a mere bodily existence.   Even the
Chinese with their truly remarkable knowledge of pharmacology from
the very earliest times,* never fell into the trap of making man's spirit
a mere chemical epiphenomenon of bodily existence.

Assumption of the existence of an independent soul or spirit has
always prompted speculation about its origin, and various alternatives
have been proposed.   For the most part these can be categorized

---

* The Chinese, from their earliest recorded history, were acquainted with thousands of cata-
logued medical formulations whose characteristics and uses were understood.   Their knowledge of pharmacology was literally encyclopedic.   Nevertheless, as Joseph Needham has
pointed out: "In accord with the character of all Chinese thought, the human organism was
an organism neither purely spiritual in nature nor purely material.   It was not a *machina* with
a single *deus* in it, which could go off and survive somewhere else; and for any recognizable
continuance of identity its parts were not separable". [*Science and Civilization in China*,
Cambridge, 1974, Vol. V, Pt. 2. p. 92].

under five headings.

(i) The Hindu concept of reincarnation makes soul as such part and parcel of the stuff of the universe. It is created only in the sense that the universe is a creation. It receives individuation because man's will has somehow detached it. By the suppression of his will he can return his private portion of soul-stuff to the universal pool and so find peace and rest in the surrender of his individual identity.

(ii) The Creationist view makes soul an individual entity uniquely created for the body which becomes its proper means of expression.

(iii) The Traducianist view holds that soul-stuff is derived from the parents, and through them therefore from Adam, in the same way that the body is derived from the parents and through them from Adam.

(iv) A fourth alternative, limited to a few primitive cultures but interesting nevertheless, is that the body is derived from the mother and the spirit from the father.

(v) And finally, the fifth view is the scientific one which holds that the soul is simply an electrochemical spin-off, an epiphenomenon of brain. This view reduces man to a strictly monistic entity in which the concept of an independent spiritual life is effectively annihilated. Such is pure materialism.

Each of these has a significant influence on the life style or World View of the individual who subscribes to it. Perhaps there is not much difference in the influence on life style between the Creationist and the Traducianist. But obviously the Hindu position greatly affects life style of the Eastern world even as the scientific view has had a profound influence in the Western world. The primitive view which attributes to the father the provision of a spirit for the foetus, has its own repercussions in social behaviour. It is improper in such a society, for example, to observe or remark upon any physical resemblance between the child and the father. On the other hand, a good character in a child is at once credited to the father, though he is also held accountable for the opposite.* The spirit of his child is his own spirit as the flesh of the child is the mother's.

In the present context we are only concerned with the Creationist and Traducianist views of the origin of the spirit or soul, since they are both strictly biblical; and fortunately they also provide a frame within which to examine the pros and cons of the dichotomic and trichotomic alternatives of the human constitution.

---

* Murdock, George P., *Our Primitive Contemporaries*, N.Y., Macmillan, 1951. p. 179: referring particularly to the Ainu of northern Japan.

It would seem a simple matter to resolve the dichotomy/trichotomy question by appealing directly to Scripture. For the trichotomist, the 'classical' proof text (1 Thess.5:23 — "I pray God your whole spirit and soul and body be preserved blameless . . . .") speaks of man as a trinity. The statement is so straightforward that it would seem to settle the issue — except for the fact that the weight of the balance of Scripture is strongly in favour of a dichotomy.

1 Thessalonians 5:23 does not stand alone in the arsenal of the trichotomists. They also appeal to Hebrews 4:12, "For the Word of God is quick (i.e., living) . . . . piercing even to the dividing asunder of soul and spirit, and of the joints and marrow . . . ." Yet if we take this statement quite literally we seem to have a quadrichotomy: of soul, spirit, joints, and marrow. Or if this is objected to as absurd, since the words "joints and marrow" may be intended to be taken together to represent the physical body, then we ought logically also to take soul and spirit together as representing the spiritual component. In which case we strictly end up with a dichotomy, though the trichotomists make this one of their "proof" passages. But we do have a quadrichotomy in the Lord's own statement recorded in Matthew 22:37 and Mark 12:30 in which He speaks of heart, soul, mind, and strength. Again, if it should be argued (very reasonably) that this is really an attempt to emphasize the totality of being, then the same argument can be applied to both Hebrews 4:12 and 1 Thessalonians 5:23.

How ever we may choose to interpret 1 Thessalonians 5:23, we have to recognize that for historical reasons, the Christian Church has adopted the dichotomic view of man throughout most of its history. We owe to Greek philosophy, chiefly to Plato, the trichotomic view of man, a view which was adopted by both the Eastern and Western branches of the Church at first. The reasons need not concern us except to remark that Plato was persuaded, on philosophical grounds alone, that the interaction between what is purely physical and what is purely spiritual must be mediated through some middle agency. Between matter and spirit (or mind) he placed the soul. The influence of mind on body and of body on mind was mediated through the *soul*.

As a result of the Apollinarian heresy, the Western or Latin branch of the Christian Church shied away from the Greek concept of a trichotomy and settled firmly for the concept of dichotomy. Unfortunately in doing so, they retained the words *soul* and *spirit* without discriminating their meaning precisely. They were considered interchangeable. The Eastern Church, meanwhile, retained the trichotomic view.

At the time of the Reformation, Luther adopted a position which was essentially that of the Greek philosophers. He said, in effect, that

if man is taken apart we find ourselves in possession of three components: body, soul, and spirit — the soul again being intermediary.* But
if man is viewed in terms of his *qualities*, then man is a dichotomy.
That is to say, there is a fleshly side to his nature and a spiritual side
to his nature, the outward man and the inward man.   The spiritual
side of his nature is composed of soul and spirit together, but they are
two distinguishable entities.   Nevertheless, each of the three parts
which form his constitution can be viewed as having either a spiritual
or a fleshly quality to it: even as Paul speaks of a fleshly *mind* (as in
Col.2:18).

Once the Latin Church had opted for a dichotomic view, many
attempts were then made to distinguish between the terms *soul* and
spirit as used in the Bible, and by far the simplest summary statement
found in the works of ancient and modern writers is expressed most
effectively in the observation that man *has* a body and *has* a spirit and
is a soul.   In effect, the soul is the person, the individual, the whole
man.   Unfortunately theologians have not always respected this useful
summation of relationships and have spoken (and continue to speak)
imprecisely, sometimes using the word *soul* where *spirit* would be
proper, and sometimes *spirit* where *soul* would be more correct.

In the last century and a half, the trichotomic view has been revived among non-Lutheran theologians by the writings of such men
as F. Delitzsch, C. J. Ellicott, H. Olshausen, and B. Jowett.   From
Delitzsch we have the fullest expression of the trichotomic view
spelled out in a classic work entitled *A system of Biblical Psychology*.
Yet it must be said that Delitzsch himself is not always unequivocal in
the meaning he attaches to the terms *soul* and *spirit*.   While he sees
both soul and spirit as having a reality in their own right, nevertheless
he says "according to the representation of Scripture man is a synthesis of two absolutely distinct elements".†   But he divides the
non-material side of man's nature into two separate and identifiable
realities, spirit and soul.   He bases part of his argument for the resulting trichotomy on 1 Thessalonians 5:23.   Thus at one place he seems
to be saying we have a dichotomy but in another a trichotomy.   This
equivocation is reflected in the heading he attaches to Section IV,
"The False and the True Trichotomy".

By far the most widely held view among systematic theologians

---

* Lutherans followed suit.   Martin Chemnitz is in this regard one of Luther's best known
protagonists [*The Two Natures of Christ*, reprinted in English, tr. by J. A. O. Preuss, St. Louis,
Concordia, 1971].

† Delitzsch, Franz, *A System of Biblical Psychology*, tr. Robert E. Wallis, Grand Rapids,
Baker, 1966, p. 205.

since the Reformation, exclusive of Lutherans, has been the dichotomic view.* And Roman Catholic theology has followed a similar course, revealing the strong influence of Thomas Aquinas. In fact, they have on the whole been more precise and consistent in dealing with the terms *soul* and *spirit* than we have.

The Church Fathers, as already noted, at first espoused a trichotomy, but largely because it had not yet become a matter of serious discussion, and thought on the subject was rather individual and random. The Apollinarian heresy resulted, among other things, in attempts to be more precise. Gregory of Nyssa (c. 335 - 395) abandoned the trichotomic view at this time. Augustine (354 - 430) held essentially to a dichotomy but viewed the soul as cognitive and mind as a faculty of the soul and the seat of awareness. Cyril of Alexandria (d. 444) was a dichotomist, body and soul constituting the whole man.

Medieval theologians followed in the dichotomic tradition, as Anselm of Laon (d. 1117) did, and Thomas Aquinas (1224 - 1274). Anselm of Laon spoke of "the creation of spirits which are then set in bodies". Aquinas developed his anthropology and its terms to a fine point of precision. He wrote: "Now we must look at the distinction between spiritual and bodily creatures; and first we take the purely spiritual creatures (angels), then purely bodily things (animals), and finally those composed of spirit and body, namely, man"[*Summa Theologica*, I a. 1, Prologue].† And again, "Man is not just a soul, but a compound of body and soul" [*Summa Theologica*, I a. lxxv. 4].

One of the most elaborate studies on the constitution of man in this respect was made recently by Robert H. Gundry. He traces the use of various terms relating to the constitution of man among Jewish writers during the Inter-testamental Period and demonstrates conclusively that the Jewish people came to interpret their Old Testament Scriptures as holding clearly to a dichotomic view of man.‡ He

---

* Among these will be found the following: Berkhof, Berkouwer, Calvin, Dabney, Gerstner, Gundry, A. A. Hodge, C. Hodge, Kuyper, Machen, Murray, Orr, Payne, Shedd, Strong, Thiessen, Turretin.

† This is an idea reflected in early Jewish literature: "Whereupon God said, 'I will create man to be the mirror of both (angel and animal) so that when he sins, when he behaves like an animal, death shall overtake him: but if he refrains from sin, he shall be immortal'." [Louis Ginsberg, *Legends of the Jews*, Phila., Jewish Publication Assoc. of Amer., 1955, Vol. I, p. 50]

‡ Gundry, Robert H., *Soma in Biblical Theology*, Cambridge U. P., 1976. His treatment is very full. Among Jewish works which reflect the dichotomy of man he lists the following references: *Judith* 10:13; *2 Macc.* 6:30; 7:37; 14:38; 15:30; *4 Macc.* 1:20, 26, 27, 32; 10:4; 13 (whole chapter); 14:6. Also the *Testament of Dan* 3:1-6; *Testament of Napthali* 2:2-4; and *1 Enoch* 71:11.

acknowledges that there are difficulties in such a study because the Jewish people did not feel the urge to crystallize their biblical anthropology, this crystallization being left to Paul to complete in his epistles.*   There is no question that if the dichotomic view of man is allowed, it is not only to be strongly supported in Paul's epistles but it is in no way contradicted by anything stated in the Old Testament provided that some small allowance is made for the fact that the Hebrew writers sometimes referred to the whole person under the term *soul (nephesh)*, even applying the word to Jehovah, and sometimes under the term *spirit* — essentially equating the two terms as synonymous.

Barton Payne in his study of the Old Testament view of man's constitution† adopts the position that the key to its understanding is to assume that man *has* a body and *has* a spirit and *is*, as a consequence, a soul.

From this position things fall remarkably into place and make very good sense of the data in both the Old Testament and the New.   At any rate, man is hereafter in this volume assumed to be a dichotomy of body and spirit.   The soul is what results from the infusion of the spirit into the body; it is a kind of summation as it were, of the two components essential for personal existence.

In reference to the spiritual side of man's being, it is important to observe how precisely Scripture (especially the New Testament) speaks of the regeneration of the *spirit*, of the departure of the *spirit* in death, of the return of the *spirit* in any case of resuscitation.   The state of the body is determined by the fate of the spirit, and what happens to the spirit in relation to the body determines what happens to the soul, to the person as a conscious individual.

In the following tabulation, the reader will notice — with some surprise perhaps — how the spirit, not the soul, is the subject of each passage.   This is not simply the result of an eclectic process of careful

---

* Gundry observes that "it is not fully appreciated how extensive and uniform is the anthropological duality in the Jewish beliefs which formed a major part of the milieu of Paul's own thought.   R. H. Charles does not overstate the case by writing that 'in all the remaining literature of this period there is only a dichotomy — either the spirit and body, or the soul and body'." [p. 107] He concludes: "What is most remarkable is the constancy with which man is portrayed as made up of body and soul/spirit.   Some affirm the resurrection. Others do not.   It is disagreed whether the body is a hindrance or a help.   But consistently body and soul/spirit form the constituent parts of man — throughout the period in question and regardless of the geographical provenance of the literature.   From the intertestamental literature to the later rabbinical statements, from Palestinian as well as extra-Palestinian sources, we hear the same opinion: man is body plus soul/spirit, united but divisible" [p. 109] .

† Payne, J. Barton, *The Theology of the Older Testament*, Grand Rapids, Zondervan, 1976, p. 224, 225.

screening for the purposes of writing this chapter. These passages in the great majority of cases are very specific, very basic, and quite unequivocal. In a number of instances the two constituents of man's nature are presented in such a way as to positively exclude any third component. The complete man is encompassed in the two terms, spirit and body. For example, if these are cleansed, the whole man is clean (2 Cor.7:1). To glorify God in body and spirit is to worship Him with all our being (1 Cor.6:20).

The *spirit* is given by God Eccl.12:7

In death man cannot retain this *spirit* Eccl.8:8

Ananias and Sapphira both surrendered their *spirits* . . . . Acts 5:5, 10

Stephen commended his *spirit*, not his soul, into God' keeping. Acts 7:59

The Lord Jesus Christ commended his *spirit* to his Father . . Luke 23:46;

Without the *spirit*, the body is a corpse . . . . James 2:26

In revival of the dead, it is the *spirit* which returns. Luke 8:55; Rev.11:11

It is the *spirit*, not the soul, which is born again. . . . . John 3:3-7

It is the *spirit* that is willing when the body is weak Matt.26:41

We are to glorify God in *spirit* and body 1 Cor.6:20

Both body and *spirit* need cleansing 2 Cor.7:1

There are two kinds of birth, one of body, one of *spirit* . . . . . .John 3:6

Mystically, the Church is one body and one *spirit* Eph.4:4

God is the Father of the *spirits* of the redeemed Heb.12:9

God is the God of all other *spirits*. Num.16:22

It is the *spirit* which is finally to be made perfect. Heb.12:23

It is the *spirit* that is to rejoin the resurrection body. Phil.3:21

Having said all this, it is important that we do not place an undue emphasis on the spirit to the neglect of the vessel that houses it. Man is not a spirit imprisoned in a body, though we may sometimes long to be free. This view inspired by Greek philosophy, was held by the Gnostics. As Paul discovered, it was a false view of the human constitution that in the Corinthian Church was proving very troublesome. He wrote to them, burdened by his own weariness, "In this (body) we groan, earnestly desiring to be clothed upon with an house which is from heaven . . . . for we that are (still) in this tabernacle do groan, being burdened: not that we would be unclothed but clothed upon that mortality might be swallowed up of life" (2 Cor.5:2, 4). We do not wish to be disembodied and *left* that way. We are whole only as embodied and this is something we sense with every fibre of our being.

The Gnostics were persuading many of the Christians in the early Church that the body was evil, that the resurrection was quite unnecessary and was, in fact, a fantasy. To the Greeks, the idea of bodily resurrection was absurd: Paul was a "babbler" even to talk about it!

(Acts 17:18). Yet verse 19 shows that the idea fascinated them never-theless. It was, to them, an entirely new idea and a challenging one.

The Gnostic view of the body as a prison to be shed when man achieves a truly spiritual life, invited not only the neglect of the body but even its abuse. "Prisoners" are more likely to abuse the cells that imprison them than they are to adorn them, and this is what the Cor-inthian believers were doing so long as they viewed the body as a mere prison.

Paul went out of his way to correct so entirely false a concept of the nature of man. Man is not a spirit: he is never called a spirit. He is frequently called a soul, for in Paul's thought a soul is a spirit/body entity. To keep the balance, Paul wrote to the Romans and said, "Brethren, I beseech you by the mercies of God that ye present your bodies . . . . and be not conformed to the world" (Rom.12:1). And to the Corinthians he wrote, "Your body is the temple of God"! (1 Cor.3:16). And again, "Glorify God in your body *and* in your spirit" (1 Cor.6:20); i.e., not merely in your spirit . . . .

Gnosticism came in like a great tidal wave into the early Church in the second century and corrupted its theology. It seems to have been a particular plague among the Corinthian Christians, especially at first. But John later also faced the same problem as is shown by his state-ments in 1 John 2:22 and 4:2 and 3, in which he twice warns against those who were denying that Jesus had really come in the flesh at all. It was being argued that if the body is an unwanted hindrance to spirituality, it was quite improper that He should be actually embod-ied. His incarnation was an appearance only, an accomodation, much as angels had accomodated themselves whenever they appeared to man. Their bodies were not real bodies, but only seemingly so.*

All this reflected the Gnostic distortion of the Christian world view. It saw the physical order not merely as unimportant but as a positive hindrance to the full realization of spiritual life. True spirit-uality was not merely to be achieved by "keeping the body under control" (1 Cor.9:27) or merely by denying its evil impulses, but by ignoring its existence altogether, by effectively denying it as an essential part of the human constitution. So Christ did not need embodiment to redeem man, since man is essentially a purely spiritual being. A "bloodless sacrifice" was quite sufficient. Gnosticism is still with us.

But Paul constantly rebuked this false view of man. And because there is to be a resurrection of the body, there is not merely to be a

---

* This entirely false argument led to the error called *Docetism*, from the Greek verb δοκεω (*dokeo*), "to seem".

new heaven, there is also to be a new *earth*.   It seems only proper to think of a new earth, for a new *body*.[221] What ever the nature of our new body will be, that will be the nature of the new earth also.

The promise of bodily resurrection is everywhere in Scripture. Job, perhaps one of the earliest books in the Bible, states it clearly.   "In my flesh I shall see God" (Job 19:26). Isaiah 26:19 gives us the same assurance with the words, "Thy dead shall live, together with my dead body shall they rise. Awake and sing, ye that dwell in the dust . . . the earth shall cast out her dead".   So also Daniel 12:2, "Many of them that sleep in the dust of the earth shall awake . . . ." And in the New Testament we have so many passages that we give only the most express and detailed of them: 1 Corinthians 15:14-18 and 35-53; Philippians 3:20-21; 1 Thessalonians 4:13-18.

While we are embodied, it is proper for us to be spoken of as *souls*: even in our dying (Gen.35:18) and in our resuscitation (1 Kings 17:22). The Hebrew writer, thinking in Hebrew, spoke ordinarily of the whole person as such, not of his composition.   They were not analytical as we are.   In the Epistle to the Hebrews and in James (both addressed to Hebrew Christians) the phrase "the saving of the soul" is found and is proper.   We do not find such a phrase in Paul whose thinking was analytical.   While the Lord Jesus during his earthly life addressed Himself almost wholly to the Jewish people, here too *soul* is used, where Paul would have used *spirit*.   All this is appropriate and in keeping with the particular audience addressed.

The precision which we find in the Pauline epistles is not to be found elsewhere in this regard.   In Paul's writings, by direct reference or by analogy or by implication, the basic constituents of man's being as a person are always (with the notable exception of 1 Thess.5:23) two only — a body humanly provided (which is of the earth earthy), and a spirit divinely appointed (which, when born again, is of heaven heavenly).

Of course, it is proper to speak of man as a soul whenever we view him in his wholeness as a unique individual person distinguishable from all other persons, the centre of a single self-consciousness. He is only by conscious effort aware of his dual nature, and this chiefly in times of conflict and spiritual stress.   The sense of singular identity remains, and it persists throughout life under normal circumstances, both as to man's view of himself and his friends' view of him.   Thus when the Lord says that a man may lose his soul (Matt.16:26) in a desperate attempt to preserve his body, we know what He means.

As we have already said, in the Old Testament we do not find reasoned theology but illuminated experience.   Any attempt to formulate an exact definition of man's constitution on the basis of

experience is bound to fail because we all interpret experience differently.   The thrust in the Old Testament is not doctrine as such but
behaviour, and quite properly much of that behaviour is described in
semi-poetic terms — as in the Psalms.   The reality which is given to
the word *soul* in the Old Testament is perfectly proper.   That the soul
should be a composite of body and spirit does not make it less real.

But that it *is* a resultant explains why the New Testament speaks
of the spirit being born again, and not the soul; of the spirit returning
to the body, and not the soul, in times of resuscitation; of the spirit
being perfected, and not the soul; of the spirit being committed to
God's care, and not the soul; it is the spirit, and not the soul, that is
willing in spite of the weakness of the flesh (though clearly this
weakness must reflect upon the soul); and it is the spirit, and not the
soul, that is saved.   Yet the *soul* will be saved when the perfected
spirit is clothed with the glorified body.   So in a sense we can understand why Paul should have broken out of his characteristic dichotomy
when he expressed the earnest desire: "And the very God of peace
sanctify you wholly; and I pray God your whole spirit *and* soul *and*
body be preserved blameless unto the coming of our Lord Jesus Christ"
(1 Thess.5:23).

An analogy of the relationship between body, spirit, and soul can
be found by the use of an overlay of two transparent sheets of plastic,
one blue and one yellow.   In this paradigm, the overlaying of the blue
(representing the spirit) and the yellow (representing the body) results
in the appearance of a colour that is neither blue nor yellow but *green*.
Two small coloured pieces of plastic will be found in a 'library pocket'
inside the back cover of this volume.   The effect of overlaying these
two sheets is immediately apparent.

In this analogy, the green is the *soul*, summing up the fusion of the
spirit and the body.   The green is the result of a fusion of blue and
yellow, as the soul is the result of the fusion of spirit and body. Green
is both blue and yellow, and yet we are aware only of green.   Soul is
both spirit and body, and the two components are so fused that we
have only one centre of consciousness.   Separate the two component
colours and the green ceases to be.   I suggest this is analogous to the
situation we are dealing with here.   The soul, in short, is both everything and yet nothing in itself.

The reality of the soul is as unquestionable as the reality of the
green, and yet it is the result of the existence of two entities which are
separable, and thus in itself it has no such *independent* existence.
So long as these two constituents overlap, soul has a real existence
with a destiny in the world to come by reason of the resurrection of
the body and the preservation of the spirit which is in God's keeping.

Soul, in short, is the person.   Soul is that with which other persons interact and which has consciousness of itself as a person.

As to the *time* of the introduction of spirit into body, there is again considerable disagreement.   Three possibilities exist: (1) at the time of conception, (2) some time during foetal development, and (3) at the time of birth.   All three positions present problems.

The first meets with difficulties in view of the fact that probably in at least 25% of conceptuses (and some authorities would place the figure much higher) spontaneous abortion occurs — often without the knowledge of the mother.   Such a high rate of rejection seems to cast doubt on the divine wisdom of creating a spirit to no purpose on so many occasions.   Furthermore, the circumstances surrounding the birth of monozygotic (single egg) twins 'seems to require the introduction of a second spirit some time after the initial fusion of the sperm and the ovum; for in such a case the ovum must divide and become two separate conceptuses subsequent to the initial fertilization.

The second creates problems because there seems to be no determinable structural stage of development which would mark the point of introduction of spirit and the resulting achievement of personhood.   If it is dependent upon the formation of a central nervous system at some fixed stage of organization sufficient to support mindedness of a sort, this stage has never been recognized accurately.   The status of the foetus cannot therefore be determined usefully in this respect.

The third presents problems to those who argue with considerable force that in the later stages of development there appear to be purposeful and responsive foetal movements that suggest a real awareness and therefore presumably a form of mindedness or actual consciousness.   The babe (John the Baptist) "leaping" in Elizabeth's womb is sometimes pointed to as an example.

The problems that surround (1) the origin of the soul or spirit, (2) the time of its admission to the body, and (3) the precise nature of the human constitution, seem therefore rather forbidding and unlikely to permit a single solution acceptable to the Christian community as a whole.   Each individual has to form a personal view on the basis of biblical data, scientifically established fact, and sound reasoning.

At the risk of being repetitious, I want to emphasize in every way possible that according to my view the *soul*, as such, has no independent existence.   It is not a creation per se.   It results from an overlap of spirit and body.   It is the spirit that is created and given to man (Eccl.12:7).   The key passage which seems to substantiate this view is Genesis 2:7 where soul is clearly an emergent.   Here it is written:

> And the Lord God formed man of the dust of the ground and breathed into his nostrils the breath of life;* and man *became* a living soul.

One thing is clear from this passage: man became a living soul when God added an appropriate spirit to a prepared body. Adam did not *acquire* a soul: he *became* one. The body was prepared for the spirit. The spirit was created only when the body was ready to receive it.†

Man did not begin as a soul for whom a body was then prepared. He became a soul when the prepared body received the animation of the spirit. The order always seems to be the same. The body first, then the provision of the spirit: and so the constituting of the soul, the "person". In the day of resurrection the body is to be raised and the spirit to enter it as the key to re-constitution of a truly human being. So the spirit of Jairus' daughter re-entered her body (Luke 8:55) and she became a living *person* again; and so with the two witnesses in Revelation 11:11. Likewise the Lord awaited the preparation of a body for Himself (Heb.10:5) that He might enter into it to assume a human nature when the time was fully come. To redeem man He had to be embodied, not assuming angelic nature, but taking up residence in a human body (Rom.1:3 and Heb.2:16) divinely equipped with a created spirit or soul‡ and thus truly constituted as to its human nature in the fullest sense.

There is no question that in order to be a whole person, man *must have a body and a spirit*. The origin of these two components is clear. The origin of his body is by human procreation: the origin of his spirit is by divine creation, as revealed in Scripture. From the interaction of these two, there emerges the soul or self, an individual whose identity persists, even through all forms of unconsciousness such as

---

* It is important to note that the Hebrew word (*neshamah*) rendered *breath* in this passage is the same word which is also employed to signify *spirit* in other places. Two passages in Job (27:3 and 34:14, 15) seem to indicate rather clearly that a man's breathing and his possession of a spirit from God are co-terminous. For the first reference reads, "All the while my breath is in me and the spirit of God is in my nostrils . . . ." and the second, "If God set his heart upon a man, he gathers unto himself his spirit and his breath", and so terminates his life — as verse 15 says, "man shall turn again unto dust". In Genesis 2:7 what was added to the body was *neshamah* (breath), something that came from God.

† Aquinas recognized this and observed that "it would be awkward for its creation to precede its union with the body" [*Summa Theologica*, I a. xc. 4].

‡ Augustine observed: "The Son of God created a soul for Himself as He creates souls for all other men". [Letter # 164; see *Nicene and Post Nicene Fathers*, Buffalo, Christian Literature Co., 1886, Vol. I. p. 521]

sleep and anaesthesia.

When conception takes place, a body begins its process of development. During almost the whole of its foetal development it displays "reactivity" to various external stimuli reaching it through the mother. But we simply do not know whether this reactivity is evidence of consciousness, since it may be observed before the cerebral cortex has had time to develop; and it is generally presumed that a functioning cortex is essential to consciousness. At some critical point, God sends a divinely created spirit. Although there may be some debate as to when that spirit is given, there is no question that when it is given it marks the beginning of the existence of the *person* as such. The analogy of the two colours (blue and yellow) superimposed to signify the joining of the spirit and body and the real coming into being of personhood as a resultant (the green) is to this extent perfectly valid. The giving by God of a spirit to each body when it is ready, certainly marks the appearance of a new individual person.

In just such a way, it would seem, when the time came for the Lord to dwell among us as Man, the announcement was made in heaven, "A body hast Thou prepared for Me" (Heb.10:5) and He who hitherto in his pre-incarnate existence was pure uncreated spirit, responded with the words, "Lo, I come" — and the Logos became flesh and dwelt among us from that moment in an entirely new way. He came, sent by the Father, to begin his assumption of human nature through the agency of a truly human body. So did He appear among us as a second Adam, born with the potential of unending life (Heb. 7:16), with the same physical immortality which originally belonged to Adam, that He might accomplish our redemption.

So there came into being — and it must be spoken with reverence — the Person of the Lord Jesus Christ *as Man*: He who dwelt in eternity now dwelt in time. We know whence his body came and we know from revelation whence He Himself had come, for in the volume of the Book it is written of Him (Heb.10:7). The conception of that "body prepared" was clearly supernatural, but it no longer seems necessary to introduce miracle into its foetal development.* It developed as a "holy thing" (Luke 1:35) but almost certainly at full term (Gal. 4:4?) it experienced a normal birth.

What we do know is that the Lord Jesus Christ assumed a truly

---

* A fact which Gregory of Nazianzen, in a Letter (#101) to Cledonius the Priest against Apollinarius, remarked upon as vitally important: "If anyone assert that He . . . . was not at one and the same time divinely and humanly formed in her (divinely, because without the intervention of man; humanly, because in accordance with the laws of generation), he is godless". [*Nicene and Post Nicene Fathers*, N.Y., Christian Literature Co., 1894, Vol. VII, p. 439] The issue was to establish not only his true deity but also his true humanity.

human nature by the act of taking up residence in that little body. And as to the time of his coming to dwell with men, I am persuaded that it would not be appropriate to Him who already had personal existence throughout all previous eternity, to have taken up residence in that body until it was fully prepared and fully formed and ready for independent existence outside the womb.* Whether this tells us anything about the vexing issue of the status of the human foetus in *natural* generation or not cannot be determined with certainty, for surely this was a very special case.

And so we turn now to the Scriptures which deal specifically with the actual provision of that little body, so uniquely prepared for Him by virgin conception.

⌒◯⌒

---

* According to Louis Berkhof, the foetus is not by definition a person: "The term *person* denotes a complete substance *endowed* with reason, and consequently a responsible subject of its own actions . . . . A person is a nature with something added, namely, independent subsistence . . . ." [*Systematic Theology*, Grand Rapids, Eerdman's, 1969, p. 321].

I may be reading more than I should into Warfield's words, but I think it significant that he should have written: "There is no reduction of the Godhead to the level of the human embryo" [*Biblical and Theological Studies*, Phila., Presbyterian and Reformed Publ. Co., 1968, p. 165]. Not until the body of Mary's firstborn was capable of housing the Lord Jesus appropriately did He take up residence in it, not until "the fullness of time was come" (Gal. 4:4) was He sent.

Long before this, Jonathan Edwards (1703-1758) had written: "As the embrio of Christ in the womb of the Virgin Mary tho it had no spirit or soul and no proper holiness of nature . . . yet it was from the spirit of God for it was a work wrought in the womb of the virgin . . . . for that was an holy thing that was born of her" [quoted by G. H. Gerstner and J. N. Gerstner, "Edwardsean Preparation for Salvation", *Westminster Theol. J.*, XLII, (1), Fall, 1979, p. 45].

Chapter 21

"A BODY HAST THOU PREPARED FOR ME"

> *When He cometh into the world He said,*
> *.... a body hast Thou prepared Me.*
> *Then said I,*
> *Lo, I come*
> *.... to do Thy will, O God.*
> Hebrews 10:5, 7

The Word of God is truly a wonderful book to study. Anselm, Archishop of Canterbury from 1093 - 1109, wrote what has become a classic study of the Atonement. This work, brief as it is, is full of profound insights. It is best known by its Latin title, *Cur Deus Homo*, "Why God Man?"

In dealing with the provision of the Lord's body, he said this – in the form of a conversation:*

> **Anselm:** Let us now examine the question, whether the human nature taken by God must be produced from a father and mother, as other men are, or from man alone, or from woman alone. For in whichever of these three modes it be, it will be produced from Adam and Eve; for from these two is every person of either sex descended. And of these three modes, no one mode is easier for God than another, that it should be selected on this account.
>
> **His friend:** So far it is well.

---

* *Cur Deus Homo*, LaSalle, Ill., Open Court Publ. Co., 1954, p. 248, 249.

> Anselm: It is no great toil to show that that man will be brought into existence in a nobler and purer manner if produced either from man *alone*, or woman *alone*, than if springing from the union of both, as do all other men.
>
> His friend: I agree with you.
>
> Anselm: Therefore must he be taken either from man *alone*, or woman *alone*.
>
> His friend: There is no other source.
>
> Anselm: In four ways can God create man, viz., either of man and woman, in the common way; or neither of man nor of woman, as he created Adam; or of man without woman, as he created Eve; or of woman without man, which thus far he has never done. Wherefore, in order to show that this last mode is also under his power, and was reserved for this very purpose, what more fitting than that he should take that man whose origin we are seeking [i.e., the God-man Redeemer] from a woman without a man? Now whether it be more worthy that he be born of a virgin or one not a virgin, we need not discuss, but must affirm beyond all doubt, that the God-man should be born of a virgin.
>
> His friend: Your words gratify my heart.

Perhaps in the end Anselm came to recognize another reason why the Lord had to be born of a *virgin*, though we do not have any record of it. For it will be realized that, had Mary given birth to other children before the Lord was born, these children could have contested the Lord's right to the throne of David and therefore his claim to be the Messiah. Mary certainly bore other children later, but when she conceived by the Holy Spirit and bear Jesus, she had known no man previously (Luke 1:34; and cf. Matt.1:18, "before they came together").

So we have four alternatives for the provision of the body by which the Lord was to become Man and dwell among us: (1) by creation ex nihilo, (2) by normal procreation, (3) by man without woman, and (4) by woman without man. The final alternative was the one chosen, and in fact was the only possible choice for the Saviour.

He must have a *real* body. It was not enough for Him to come as He had often come to men in the Old Testament in the form of a theophany with a mere appearance of humanness but not the reality. The emphasis which the epistles were to place upon the importance of the Lord's body in reference to his sacrifice on Calvary needs to be noted carefully. The following passages reflect this emphasis.

John 1:14
"The Word became *flesh* . . . ."

Romans 7:4
". . . . dead to the law, by the *body* of Christ . . . ."

1 Corinthians 11:24
"This is my *body* which is broken for you . . . ."

Colossians 1:21, 22
"You . . . . hath He reconciled in *the body of his flesh* through death . . . . "

1 Timothy 3:16
"Great was the mystery . . . . God was manifest in the *flesh* ".

Hebrews 2:9, 16
"We see Jesus who was made a little lower than the angels for the suffering of death . . . . that He by the grace of God should taste death for every man . . . .   For verily He took not on Him the nature of angels; but He took on Him *the seed of Abraham.* "

Hebrews 10:5
"A *body* hast Thou prepared for Me . . . ."

Hebrews 10:10
"By whose will we are sanctified through the offering of the *body* of Jesus Christ once for all."

Hebrews 10:20
"A new and living way . . . . through his *flesh* . . . . "

1 Peter 2:24
". . . . who his own self bore our sins *in his own body* on the tree".

It is important to underscore once again the fact that this sacrifice was not merely a spiritual one.   As man dies two kinds of death (a spiritual and a physical one), so man stands in need of two kinds of redemption.   But we have reached a point in modern preaching where the emphasis has been almost entirely concentrated upon the spirit of man to the virtual ignoring of his body, as if the spirit were the man. This easily tempts us to see the Cross as a spiritual sacrifice, the physical aspects of it contributing only as an exhibition of the love of God (which indeed it is: 1 John 4:10, 19), an exhibition which is then presented as an appeal to the individual to respond in like spirit.   All other aspects of the crucifixion are played down and the "moral influence" is emphasized instead.   The Lord's physical *suffering* has been the subject of eloquent appeal to the artist, but the significance of his physical *death*, the death of his body, has been largely overlooked.   And, not surprisingly, few preachers speak much about the fact of his bodily resurrection either — or our's, for that matter.   The whole drama is cast in a spiritual light to the exclusion of what happened to his body — a body so essential to his assumption of a truly human nature.

The creation of the body of Adam was nothing less than the first

step in the "preparation" of a body for the Lord Jesus.[222]   Such a
body had to be immortal, since the eternal Lord could not appropriately adopt as a vehicle for the expression of his Person a house that had
time limits placed upon it, and which would be progressively wearing
out while He dwelt in it.   Our bodies, as we have seen, are dying
slowly from the day of our birth.   Each day brings us nearer to the
inevitable total breakdown.   We dwell in a doomed house, a house in
a state of decay.   The body that was to house the spirit of the Lord
Jehovah had to be entirely free of such effects of sin.   It could only
be *like* our fallen bodies, not *identical* with them (Rom.8:3). [223]   It
must be identical with Adam's body in its *unfallen* state.   In us,
mortality is a consequence of sin (Rom.5:12) and sin is an inherent
defect, and such an inherently defective house is unthinkable for the
Son of God to occupy as Man.

This body, being prepared in Mary's womb, had to be both truly
of Adamic origin and adequate to allow the Lord (who through all
eternity had only a divine nature) now to express Himself also in truly
human nature.   While it therefore contributed nothing to the *reality*
of his existence as a person, it temporarily placed certain new conditions and limitations upon Him.   It caused Him to experience physical
fatigue to the point of falling asleep in a boat on a storm-tossed sea, to
be physically weary enough to rest at a well in the heat of the day, to
suffer the physical agony of thirst on the cross, and in a hundred other
ways to experience those "vulnerabilities" such as are common to man
(like weeping at the grave of a friend) and, in the end, tasting death
itself.   This vulnerability made his crucifixion possible (2 Cor.13:4).

Now each man's spirit is a unique creation.[224]   The created spirit
can be thought of as being given a form or a structure unique to itself.
The body which it is to indwell and through which it will find its
fulfillment must presumably also be providentally constituted to allow
the spirit to express itself in keeping with its specific nature.*   The
Lord of Glory was not a created spirit.   But even as all other created
human spirits perform the function of animating every newborn child,
so He created for Himself a human spirit (so Augustine, Letter # 164)
to complete his human nature.   And this extraordinary fact required
that the vessel which was thus prepared for Him should have an
appropriate form in order that He might be free to express both his

---

* Abraham Kuyper, using the word *soul* for *spirit*, reflects this view by saying, "The soul is
indeed directly and instantly created by God, but this does not happen arbitrarily, but rather
so that the soul is created in *this* man, at *this* time, in *this* country, in *this* family, with the
characteristics which are suitable" [quoted by G. C. Berkouwer, *Man: the Image of God*,
Grand Rapids, Eerdman's, 1975, p. 290].

divine and his human natures without the contamination of original sin.   For this reason I believe we must assume that a *perfect human body* was the only kind of body which could possibly fulfill such a tremendous role.*   Adam's body, as first formed, was structured by the creative providence of God as a first step towards the provision of *this* body.

Had it been God's intention, even Eve's firstborn could have been a perfectly appropriate body for the Person of the Lord Jesus Christ to enter as its animating principle.   The Word might indeed have been made flesh and dwelt among men at the very beginning.   Had Adam not fallen, no virgin† conception would have been necessary.   Then the purpose of the Incarnation would not have been to redeem man, but to reveal God.   In any case, a truly Adamic body would have been a fit abode for the Son of God at any time in history, provided it was supernaturally conceived.

Now the title of this chapter is a quotation from Hebrews 10:5 which reads:

> Wherefore when He [the Lord Jesus] came into the world, He said, Sacrifice and offering Thou wouldest not, but a body hast Thou prepared Me . . . .   Then, said I, Lo, I come (in the volume of the book it is written of Me) to do Thy will, O God.

The wording of this passage is somewhat cryptic but there is little doubt that it refers to the moment of the Lord's incarnation.   The words "Sacrifice and offering Thou wouldest not" refer of course to the Old Testament system of animal sacrifices and offerings, a

---

* The contamination of the soul by the natural born body was recognized by the Jews: "Only in the last centuries (B.C.) did the soul-body dualism and the concept that the soul was an independent substance joined to the body gain general credence; the soul originates in heaven and descends to earth joining a material body at the moment of conception or birth and *losing its original perfection*".   [*Standard Jewish Encyclopedia*, ed. Cecil Roth, N.Y., Doubleday, 1962, under *Soul*, p. 1743]   Hence the need of virgin birth.   This view was generally adopted by the Church and was widely held by theologians (Augustine, Hugo St. Victor, Anselm of Canterbury, Stephen Langton, Anselm of Laon, Ulrich Zwingli, Peter Martyr, Martin Chemnitz, Zacharius Ursinus, Andreae Hyperius, Benedictus Aretius, Bartholomew Kerkerman, Francois Turretin, Amandus Polandus, Johannes Wollebius, J. H. Hottinger, Samuel Endeman).   It is still widely accepted that the spirit is corrupted by the body.

† The seed of unfallen Adam, united with the seed of the woman, would have naturally produced a body as perfect as Adam's body when first created.   That body would have served as perfectly for the incarnation of the Lord as the body which was prepared in Mary's womb by supernatural conception.   The necessity of supernatural conception was occasioned by the fact that fallen Adam's seed would have communicated to it the defect of his own body.   It was not that a human body per se would have been an unsuitable habitation for the Person of Jesus Christ, but only that a defective human body would have been unsuitable.

system which had been only a temporary measure and was not intended to be the actual mode of man's redemption. These sacrifices were like a "stay of execution". It was now, at this moment in history, that the Lord in heaven announced his readiness to become Saviour and Redeemer, by incarnation as Man. The circumstance that made his announcement proper at that moment was the fact that a body was ready to receive Him. The time had finally come, in short, for the manifestation of God in human form.

The word *prepared* in the original Greek (*katartidzo: καταρτίζω*) has a special significance in this instance since it is a word which means something more than routine preparation. It means to "prepare *perfectly*".*

In view of our present knowledge of how the seed of the woman may be preserved untouched by accidents that happen to the body (even the ingestion of the forbidden fruit), and in view of the fact that the original seed of the woman was derived from Adam when Eve was first formed out of him in his unfallen state, and in view of the fact that in Adam this same originating germ plasm was exactly as created by God in the first place, we are in a position to see that in Mary was a seed which, energized by the Holy Spirit, would grow into an immortal body such as Adam had as he came from the hand of God. Thus was a body prepared for the Lord Jesus in which there was none of the inherited corruption that renders *us* mortal creatures and in its subsequent outworking turns us all into sinners. Consequently his body was a body without spot or blemish which, even while it lay in the grave, did not see corruption.

Thus Hebrews 10:5 was not merely an announcement that Mary's 'full-time' had come (Gal.4:4). It was an announcement that Adam's created body had been recovered as a house for the Lord's immediate possession, thus providing a new and second mode of expression of his

---

* It is a verb used in a number of contexts, all of which denote a special kind of making ready It can mean to reconstitute or to restore something as it should be. It is found in Matthew 4:21, for example, applied to the mending of broken nets. Barclay M. Newman gives such meanings as *to set right, to make perfect* [*Concise Greek-English Dictionary of the New Testament*, London, United Bible Societies, 1971]. J. H. Moulton and G. Milligan, on the basis of its use in Greek Papyri of New Testament times, give the meaning as *to prepare to perfection* [*Vocabulary of the Greek New Testament*, Grand Rapids, Eerdman's, 1972 reprint]. H. G. Liddell and R. Scott in their Greek Lexicon (of Classical and New Testament Greek) give the meaning as *to put in order again, to restore, to furnish completely*. G. Abbott-Smith gives the meaning *to render fit* or *complete, to mend, to repair, to perfect* [*A Manual Greek Lexicon of the New Testament*, Aberdeen, Clark, 1964, p. 238]. In the King James Version this Greek verb *katartidzo* is rendered "to make perfect" (Heb.13:21; 1 Pet.5:10), "to perfect" (Matt.21:16; Luke 6:40; 1 Thess.3:10), "to be perfectly joined together" (1 Cor.1:10), "to restore" (Gal.6:1) and "to frame" (Heb.11:3 — a passage of special significance for the biblical cosmologist in the light of this particular verb).

Person. God the Son was about to become true Man without jeopardizing his deity. And thereby, because He was now able to experience death, being embodied in a house that was *capable* of dying, He could become our Redeemer, in his own body bearing our sins on the cross, reconciling us to God in the body of his flesh through death; that we might be sanctified through the offering of his body once for all. It was (and still is) a great mystery — God manifested in the flesh: it provided a new and living way for us to recover our sonship with the Father and our place in glory with exceeding joy. And all this, because his Person was perfectly housed in a perfect body uniquely prepared. Supernaturally conceived, that little body developed in the womb without any *violation* of the laws of nature that God had originally designed and built into his created order for this very purpose.

The *Formula of Concord* clearly acknowledges this truth when quoting Luther who, as we have already noted, had said that the Saviour in order to suffer death must become man: "For God, by his very nature, cannot die. However, after God and man were united in one person, it is truly proper to say, 'God has died'." *

Only by becoming man could God become subject to death, and this is precisely what we are told He did — He was made in the likeness of man . . . . and He *became* obedient unto death (Phil.2:7, 8). It is in this sense that T R. Birks nearly one hundred years ago in his *Difficulties of Belief*, observed that man, unlike angels, may have been provided with a material body in order "to enable Christ to unite Himself to the race in order to save it".† In 1 Peter 3:18 we are told that "Christ suffered once for sins, the just for the unjust, that He might bring us to God, being delivered up to death‡ in the flesh but quickened by the Spirit". He thus died as to his humanity, but three days later was quickened again as a Man by the divine nature and energy that resided in his Person. In other words, there was no way in which He might bring us (as composites of body and spirit) back to God except through spiritual *and* physical death. And there was no way He could experience physical death except by embodiment, by incarnation, or as the Greek of Romans 1:3 has it, "being made according to

---

* *Formula of Concord,* Art. VIII, § 44. And see further, reference # 225.

† Birks, T. R., quoted by A. H. Strong, *Systematic Theology*, Phila., Judson Press, 1974, p. 488.

‡ The Greek here, $\theta\alpha\nu\alpha\tau\omega\theta\epsilon\grave{\iota}\varsigma$ $\mu\grave{\epsilon}\nu$ $\sigma\alpha\rho\kappa\grave{\iota}$ *(thanatōtheis men sarki)* often has the meaning of "condemning to death", or "delivering up to death". A good example is in Romans 8:36, and even more explicitly in Mark 14:55, in view of the fact that the Jews did not have this authority. "Delivering him up" was all they could legally do (Acts 3:13). He, as God, did *not* have his life destroyed by others, for He alone had the power to lay it down (John 10:18).

the flesh" (*kata sarka:* κάτα σάρχα).

Hitherto we have placed considerable emphasis upon the *scientific* account of the way in which preparation was made for the first coming of the Lord. We now turn, with some relief, to Scripture itself. What we have been dealing with *is* the scientific account extracted from the data of nature by human ingenuity, as God clearly foresaw it would be. And because He foresaw it would be, it was not necessary that such details should be *revealed*. But henceforth in this study we must depend more and more upon Revelation for the completion of those details which are inaccessible to us by any other means. And I must confess that it is with a sense of exhilaration because, in spite of all that we can attain for ourselves in the way of understanding by scientific means, we still only see through a glass darkly and need constant correction. The knowledge we gain by Revelation is so much more enduring.

One might ask, Do these scientific details really matter *at all?** They were hidden from our brethren in Christ who have gone before us, and clearly therefore they were not *necessary* to them. Why should they be necessary for us? Have they been omitted from Scripture for this very reason, simply because they are not important?

Not every one will *want* to know about such things, and certainly no one actually *needs* to be concerned with them. Those who have a simple faith usually find their faith serving them adequately and well, although analysis often shows that simple faith is, in reality, quite complex, the complexity being concealed by intuitive understanding, and therefore often unrecognized. But there are those who by circumstance and disposition are driven, or drive themselves, to enquire into the *how* of our redemption in greater depth. Such people have a thirst to know more, and find the quest an exciting one which sometimes amounts almost to an act of worship.

I think Benjamin Warfield has well stated the difference between the *desire* to know and the *need* to know. One is as real and undeniable as the other. But it is by no means essential for any man to know how he is saved in order to *be* saved, nor to know the intricacies of the circumstances by which God made this provision in order to have assurance of salvation. But if he does have the desire to explore the ways of God with man, then the means to do so are becoming increasingly accessible year by year.

---

* It is most important to keep constantly in mind that humanly discovered knowledge is always to *minister to*, not be *master of*, our understanding in the things of God. The role of reason and scientific knowledge must always be *ministerium*, not *magisterium*.

Throughout the centuries, many of the great theologians of the past struggled with the problem of the provision of a perfect body out of the sinful flesh that was Mary's (for she too needed a Saviour: Luke 1:47).   Roman Catholic theology evolved the dogma of Immaculate Conception.   But I believe such a dogma is not necessary and that many who sought to solve the problem by such means would have revelled in the kind of understanding which is now open to us and would have made the greatest possible use of it.   Such knowledge has been acquired almost entirely by those who are not at all concerned with the doctrines of the Christian faith.   Yet whether they know it or not, they are God's servants, even as Cyrus was a servant of God but knew it not (Isa.45:1, 5).   And I am convinced we should respect this service by making use of it, not merely to improve our lot in life but also to increase our understanding of the things we most surely believe.   We should not *depend upon* the findings of science to con-firm our Faith, though this may well happen; but it is certainly proper to use these findings to *explore* that Faith.

In his essay, "The Supernatural Birth of Jesus", Warfield points out that there are really two supernatural events involved in the virgin birth of Jesus Christ.   First, there is supernatural conception: and secondly, there is supernatural provision of the spirit to animate that little body.   These were the truly supernatural aspects of the Incarn-ation: the *actual birth* itself was almost certainly quite natural.* But while the creation of a human spirit to complete its humanness was indeed a supernatural event, do we need to suppose it was different in any way from the mode of provision of *our* spirits by which *we* achieve personhood?   In fact, only one miracle was really involved that was exceptional in nature, namely, the supernatural fertilization of the woman's seed.

The importance of the Virgin Conception in relation to the Christ-ian doctrine of Redemption was abundantly clear to Warfield.   He wrote:†

> It is only in its relation to the New Testament doctrine of re-demption that the necessity of the virgin birth of Jesus comes to its complete manifestation.   For in this (Christian faith of ours) the redemption that is provided is distinctly redemption from sin; and that he might redeem men from sin it certainly was imperative that the Redeemer himself should not be involved in sin . . . .

---

* This is implied by Galatians 4:4, "made of a woman, made under the law" — not merely birth but even pre-natal development was normal according to natural law.

† Warfield, Benjamin B., *Biblical and Theological Studies*, Phila., Presbyterian & Reformed Publ. Co., ed., Samuel G. Craig, 1968, p. 165.

> The sinlessness of Jesus, in the sense of freedom from subjective corruption as well as from overt acts of sin, seems to be involved in the incarnation itself, purely and simply; and in point of fact, those who imagine it was in principle sinful flesh which was assumed by the Son of God are prone to represent his flesh as actually being cleansed of its sinfulness, either by the act of incarnation itself or by the almighty operation of the Spirit of God as a condition precedent to incarnation.*

In other words, the body which the Redeemer was to assume had to be provided in some very special way if He was to fulfil the conditions of his office.   He must be born humanly, and yet He could not be born as we are born because He must then be as we are — defiled with the entail of sin.   But we know that He was not defiled as we are.   We know from Scripture that the Lord Jesus Christ was tempted as we are (Matt.4:1-11; Luke 22:28), but He was always tempted *apart from* sin (Heb.4:15).   For in Him was no inherited defect such as we are born with (contrast Psa.51:5 and Rom.7:8 with 1 John 3:5). When we are tempted, we are tempted from within (James 1:13-16), but when Satan came to tempt Jesus Christ he had to work entirely from outside, for he found nothing *in* the Lord that could possibly serve as a point of leverage (John 14:30).   The phrase "apart from sin" has in most translations, early and late, been rendered "without sin" or "without committing sin".   This is undoubtedly a truth, but I believe that the original supports an even more profound truth.   It is the root of sin, the inherited defect that gives Satan a headstart with us. Jesus was born without this defect in his body, and therefore although tempted with the kind of temptations that may come to us, it was always from without, never from within.   The basic inward root of sin was not there.   When we are told (in Heb.4:15) that He was tempted in all points *like as we are,* the Greek is careful to use the word which (as we have already noted, reference # 223) means only in a similar way, not in the identical way that we are tempted.   His temptations were real enough but not stemming from the same root cause as lies within us.

Now in Hebrews 4:15 the Greek word for "without" is χωρὶς *(choris);* and its basic meaning, according to Thayer, is "apart from".†

---

* Perhaps he had in mind the Roman Catholic doctrine of the immaculate conception. On this issue, see further reference #228.   Many other theologians of the past have shared the view that Christ's body had to be supernaturally protected somehow during gestation besides being virginly conceived.

† The *Definition of Chalcedon* (451 A.D.) clearly recognized this meaning: "Of one substance with the Father as regards his godhead, and at the same time of one substance with us as regards his manhood; like us in all respects, *apart from* sin".

This passage therefore tells us that when Jesus was tempted, his tempt-ation was not associated with inborn or original sin but apart from it, i.e., independently of it. It was, to use one of Thayer's alternative meanings, temptation "unconnected with" any internal defect in the one tempted. Unfortunately, Thayer then proceeds to suggest, with reference to Hebrews 4:15, that this means He was tempted "without *yielding* to sin". But surely the meaning is not this? The meaning is that his temptations arose entirely from a source external to Himself.

It is a pleasure to find that Rotherham in his *Emphasized Bible* and Robert Young in his *Literal Translation* have both adopted the render-ing "apart from sin": not merely indicating it in the margin as a possible alternative (as some other modern Bibles have done) but in-corporating it into their text.

Had the intent of the writer of the Epistle to the Hebrews been merely to express the idea of never actually committing sin (i.e., of being sinless in act), he would surely have not used the Greek prep-osition χώρις, but the normal word for this kind of sinlessness which is 'αναμάρτητος. This word is found in John 8:7, "Jesus said, He that is *without sin* among you, let him cast the first stone at her". The meaning here is quite clear; "he that has committed no sin". Thus Jesus was not tempted as we are tempted due to the entail of inward defect we acquire by natural generation. He escaped this entail by the very fact of virgin conception, a divine solution the purpose of which was not altogether clear to those who have struggled with this problem in the past.*

Thus Job foresaw the difficulty of redeeming man. He knew that a man must be redeemed by *a man*, and that animal sacrifices were only symbolic. But how is one to find a man, born of a woman, who is not under the same death penalty by the very fact of his human birth? Any man born of a woman will be brought into judgment on his own account: for, as Job put it, "Who can bring a *clean* thing out of an *unclean*? Not one" (Job 14:4).† Later on, Bildad faced the same

---

* For example, Calvin did not see that the virgin conception made possible the provision of a perfect body. He therefore proposed that the perfect body that the Lord must have was not *made* perfect merely by being "born of the seed of a woman unconnected with any man but because He was sanctified by the Spirit so that his generation was pure and holy, such as it would have been before the fall of Adam" [*Inst.* II. xiii. 4]. Calvin is really reiterating the argument put forward by Athanasius in his *De Incarnatione Verbi Dei* § 20. The child con-ceived in Mary's womb would still have been mortal like us, had it not been rendered immortal by the presence of the Logos within, a circumstance which "placed it beyond corruption".

† In the Hebrew original, "not one" is literally "not a man" (*lŏ adām*). This is a far more significant statement in the light of the virgin conception — which is God's answer to Job's question.

issue and stated the problem even more effectively in the form of a
two-sided question: "How then can man be justified with God? Or
how can he be clean that is born of a woman?" (Job 25:4). To be a
substitute, the Redeemer must be born of a woman, but somehow He
must escape our inherited corruption and be "clean".

The idea of a virgin conception was not revealed till much later in
history. We meet it first in Isaiah 7:14, where it is important to note
that Isaiah is speaking of a virgin *conception* (Hebrew *harah*) and not
merely of a virgin *birth* (Hebrew *yaladh*). I am well aware that the
Hebrew word used in Isaiah 7:14 can signify either a virgin or merely
an unmarried woman of marriageable age. The Septuagint took the
word to mean simply a virgin and so translated it, using the Greek
word *parthenos*. For myself, the New Testament use of the same
word (*parthenos*) when quoting Isaiah in Matthew 1:23, establishes
what was the intent of the Holy Spirit since the same Spirit inspired
both Isaiah 7:14 and Matthew 1:23.

Bildad's insight is perceptive. To have asked exactly the right
question in precisely the right form is a clear indication of his understanding of the problem. Today we can see how Mary might conceive
(by some freak accident) and bear a female child. But how she could
bear a *male* child* still remains a total mystery which only Revelation
can illuminate for us. It is significant, too, in the light of Job's question (in 14:4) as to how a "clean thing" could be born of a woman, that
the angel said to Mary (Luke 1:35) "that *holy* thing which shall be
born of thee shall be called the Son of God". This statement is so
explicit that it cannot but be in answer to both Job's and Bildad's
question.

Only by revelation do we know that the Holy Spirit supplied that
which a human father could not be allowed to supply in this single
instance.

It may seem that we are making too much of too little. We are
complicating the Gospel unjustifiably and destroying in the process
the simplicity of it which makes it so communicable to "all sorts and
conditions of men". Are we not then doing the truth a disservice? In
answer to this, I think an observation made by Warfield will be more
effective than anything I might say. Warfield wrote: "We are discussing not the *terms* of salvation, but the essential content of the Christian
system; not what we must do to be saved, but *what it behooved Jesus*

---

* Only via the male seed can a male child be conceived under normal conditions, for only the
male seed carries the Y chromosome required to bring this about. All virgin births (except
among birds) result in female offspring. See further on this, reference #198, final paragraph.

Christ to be and to do that He might save us"(emphasis mine).* That is to say, we are not talking about what a man must believe but what had to be done to make his salvation possible. On the other hand, Warfield rightly emphasizes that it is no virtue to be deliberately ignorant of these things if one has the opportunity of knowing them, on the ground that such knowledge is not essential to salvation. Thus he went on to say:

> The act of faith by which [Jesus Christ] is savingly apprehended involves these presuppositions, were its implicates to be soundly developed. But our logical capacity can scarcely be made the condition of our salvation. It will hardly do to represent ignorance or error as advantageous to salvation. It certainly is worthwhile to put our trust in Jesus as intelligently as it may be given us to do.

To which I can only add a fervent Amen! I am always amazed at the insights into truth of which the human mind is capable when relying upon the Word of God and enlightened by the Holy Spirit. In the Prayer Book of Edward VI, issued in 1548, there was read during the evening service a doctrinal statement of which I have extracted the following words, retaining their old spelling for interest's sake:†

> Perfecte God, and perfecte man: of a resonable [i.e., rational] soule, and humayne fleshe subsisting.
> Equall to the father as touchyng his Godhead: and inferior to the father as touchyng his manhoode.
> Who although he be God and man: yet he is not two, but one Christe.
> One, not by conuersion of the Godhead into fleshe: but by takyng of the manhoode unto God.
> One altogether, not by confusion of substaunce, but by unitie of person.

Let me give one further example of the elegant working of man's mind when called upon to grapple with the kind of unfathomable mystery here involved in the manifestation of God in human flesh, in what has aptly been called the "objectification of God". This is to be found in the *Tome of Leo*. Leo was Bishop of Rome from 440 - 461 A.D. and in his 28th epistle to Flavian, dated June 13, 449, he wrote:‡

> The Son of God therefore came down from his throne in heaven

---

* Warfield, Benjamin B., *Biblical and Theological Studies*, ed. Samuel Craig, Phila., Presbyterian and Reformed Publishing Co., 1968, p. 167, 168.

† *The First and Second Prayer Books of Edward VI*, Everyman's Library, London, Dent, 1957, p. 31.

‡ Bettenson, Henry, *Documents of the Christian Church*, Oxford, 1950, p. 72.

without withdrawing from his Father's glory, and entered this lower world, born after a new order, by a new mode of birth. After a
new order, in as much as he is invisible in his own nature and he became visible in ours; he is incomprehensible and he willed to be
comprehended; continuing to be before time he began to exist in
time.   By a new mode of birth, in as much as virginity inviolate
which knew not the desire of the flesh supplied the material of the
flesh.   From his mother the Lord took nature, not sin.   Jesus
Christ was born from a virgin's womb by a miraculous birth.   And
yet his nature is not on that account unlike ours, for he that is true
God is also true man.

It seems presumption to seek to amend a statement which has so
many wonderful turns of thought in it, but I think it is true to say
that we need not to speak of the birth itself as a miracle, only the
conception.   To this extent, our understanding has perhaps been
enlarged a little since Leo's time.   We now know more about the
Creator's reasons for designing the mode of human reproduction in its
initial stages in order to make his own incarnation possible.

It is clear that the Lord Jesus Christ could not become Man
without embodiment.   And because He was God, He could not be
embodied appropriately except in a housing that was altogether
without corruption or defect.   Such a body, to be human, must be
woman-born, but to be without corruption cannot be man-begotten.
All these conditions were perfectly fulfilled at the time of his incarnation, and yet the order of nature was not violated — only drafted to
serve an even higher purpose than before.   Such is the wisdom of God,
and such was his forethought in creating Adam and forming Eve as He
did.

On the following pages we have summarized in word and diagram
the substance of what has preceded in terms of the unfolding of the
plan for the redemption of man by the Incarnation of the Son of God,
though it seems almost presumption to attempt representation of any
kind of such a profound mystery.   Nevertheless the following may
help to show the continuity of events from the first to the last Adam.

Turning, then, to Figure 17 , we start at the top, level (1), with
the creation of Adam represented as containing within himself both
seeds, male and female, symbolized by open circles marked M and F.

We move down to level (2) and observe that Adam has now been
separated into two halves of himself, each of which contains one seed.

We drop down from these two representative figures to the next
stage (3) which signifies their fallen state.   Both figures are therefore
shaded.   But they are shaded differently and the difference is important.   In Adam's case the shading *includes* the circle which is the seed
of the man.   In the woman's case the circle is *not* shaded, signifying

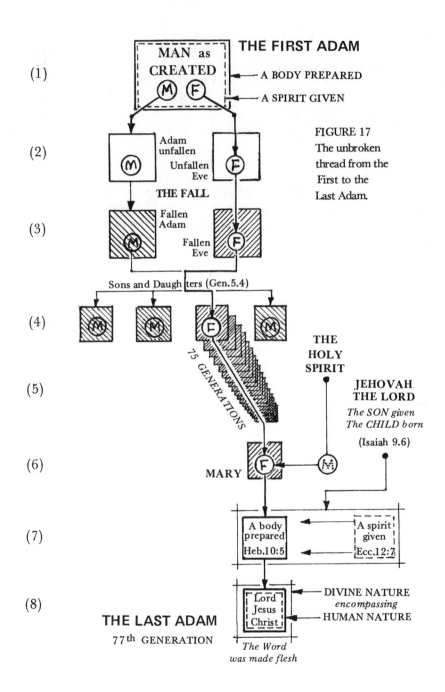

(1)

THE FIRST ADAM

MAN as CREATED
(M) (F)

A BODY PREPARED
A SPIRIT GIVEN

(2)

Adam unfallen
(M)

Unfallen Eve
(F)

THE FALL

FIGURE 17
The unbroken
thread from the
First to the
Last Adam.

(3)

Fallen Adam
(M)

Fallen Eve
(F)

Sons and Daughters (Gen.5.4)

(4)

(M) (M) (F) (M)

75 GENERATIONS

THE HOLY SPIRIT

JEHOVAH THE LORD

The SON given
The CHILD born

(Isaiah 9.6)

(5)

(6)

MARY (F)

(M)

(7)

A body prepared
Heb.10:5

A spirit given
Ecc.12:7

(8)

THE LAST ADAM
77th GENERATION

Lord Jesus Christ

DIVINE NATURE
encompassing
HUMAN NATURE

The Word was made flesh

that it was still untouched by the poison and has therefore all the potential of the female seed in Adam as first created.

At level (4) sons and daughters are born from the union of Adam and Eve.   It will be noticed that they are all shaded but that the shading in the male seed is total, whereas the female seed is still not shaded.   For the seed of the woman is preserved untouched.

From level (5) we have simply marked successive generations in the female line in which the seed of the woman continues untouched by the stream of the poison which nevertheless destroys the woman's body.   Throughout this line of successive generations the germ plasm retains the perfection that marked the female seed in Adam.   The continuity of the germ plasm is indicated.

At level (6) we arrive at Mary's generation.   The time has come for the appearing of the Lord: and from heaven the Holy Spirit over-shadows Mary, perhaps to provide the male component for her seed, a component therefore untouched by the poisoned stream that has been contributed in each generation by the male seed.   And out of this fusion, a body of a second Adam is in due time brought to birth. This is represented at level (7).

It is at this time that a human spirit is added to the body to complete it, while at the same moment the Logos declared, "Lo, I come", and took up residence in it, in order to assume a perfect human nature.   Thus He became what He was not before; while never ceasing to be what He had always been.   God had now become objectified in the only kind of body that was fitting, a body with the same potential of physical immortality originally enjoyed by the first Adam.   Accordingly He is called a last Adam.   At levels (7) and (8) the figure is thus no longer shaded.

Several significant passages of Scripture can be set forth sequent-ially in a way that may be helpful to show the parallelisms and yet the differences between our birth as mortal men and the birth of the Lord Jesus Christ as perfect man with the potential of endless life (Heb.7:16).

> In natural generation:
> 1. The father begets (Isa.45:10; Jer.16:3).
> 2. The woman brings forth (Isa.45:10).
> 3. God gives the spirit (Eccl.12:7).
> 4. And so emerges the person or soul (Gen.2:7).

> In the generation of the Lord Jesus Christ:
> 1. The Father, through the Holy Spirit, begets (Luke 1:30-35; John 3:16).
> 2. A virgin conceives (Isa.7:14) and a child is born (Isa.9:6).
> 3. The Logos creates a human spirit to complete a man-child nature; and then, sent by the Father (John 17:18; Rom. 8:3) the Son is given (Isa.9:6) to assume that nature and to become the seat of its self-consciousness.

4. And so the Word became flesh (John 1:14; 1 Tim.3:16), one
Person in two natures, human and divine.

The seed of the woman has fulfilled its highest appointed role. It is in this sense that the embodiment of Adam in the first place was nothing less than a first step in "the preparation" of a body for the Incarnation of Jesus Christ, the Lord.

We turn now to a question that must often have been asked in private but never seems to have been discussed in public — except by Roman Catholic theologians but from a perspective unacceptable to evangelicals as a whole. The question in its simplest form is, Why did God specifically choose Mary to be the woman whose seed should become a foundation of the Lord's humanity?

Chapter 22

WHY MARY?

And the angel came in unto her, and said,
Hail, thou art highly favoured,
the Lord is with thee:
blessed art thou among women . . . .
Fear not, Mary:
for thou hast found favour with God.
Luke 1:28, 30

I have implied by several statements made previously that, at any time in history, the Lord Jesus could have appeared as Man if God had chosen to prepare a body for Him from *any* woman's seed as He did Mary's seed. To this extent, physiologically considered, the Incarnation might have taken place any time at all: long before Mary or long after her, during the centuries that have intervened from Eve right down to the present moment. It may therefore be asked, "Why did the Lord appear just at that time?" and "Why was Mary chosen and not one of her contemporaries?" What particular circumstances converged to make that moment and that individual so propitious? In what sense, if any, was Mary herself unique so that she in particular should be chosen to become "the mother of the Lord", as Elizabeth called her (Luke 1:43)?

There are three main lines of enquiry which are worth pursuing in this matter. First of all, she may have had a unique kind of personality. After all, she was called upon to bring up as a child one who was her Creator! Secondly, she may have stood at a kind of 'genealogical crossroads', combining in her person (whether by marriage or by pedigree) both the Davidic titular rights to his throne and his actual blood line: on account of which two circumstances the Lord's claim to the throne of David was validated in a very special way. For it must be assumed that David had many other descendants by blood who nevertheless had no such title. Thirdly, she may have been the last in a line in which, for providential reasons, the genetic strain was particularly pure and free from the damage of mutant genes such as are assumed to be common to the rest of us, leaving us with damaged cells in every organ and tissue of our bodies. In the body of the Lord such damage, whether visible or invisible, is unthinkable.

Let us therefore examine these three lines of evidence. Such an examination will show at once that not one of these qualifying conditions is sufficient alone to account for the choice of Mary. But where we find all three of them converging in a single individual due to circumstances that cannot reasonably be taken as purely accidental, then we seem to have a clear demonstration of a unique situation entirely appropriate for such a unique event as the Incarnation of God in human form.

1. Mary as a special person.

Upon many occasions the Lord pointedly played down those family relationships which we count so important, expecially in times of stress. We find it disconcerting that He should never, according to Scripture, have referred to or directly addressed his mother by this term which seems to many of us one of the most beautiful words in any language.

But this same avoidance of directing attention to his mother, and his father also, is reflected in the Gospel accounts in other ways as well. It is customary in many societies, especially in the older ones that have changed little, to give credit always for a notable son to the *parents*, not to the child himself. When Saul desired to honour David after his valiant defeat of Goliath, he did not ask "What is his name?" He knew David well enough, for David had often soothed his frayed nerves with his harp. What he asked was, "Whose son is he?" For he wished, in accordance with an almost universal custom, to reward his father, not David himself. Such societies have always credited the goodness of a son to the worthiness of his father (1 Sam.17:55-58).

The reverse is also true, of course. A man must be held partially accountable for his bad son. Thus when Noah found what his son Ham had done to disgrace him, he could not curse his son — for that was to curse himself! So he cursed his son by cursing his grandson, Canaan (Gen.9:21-25).

In 1 Kings 11:11-13 we find that for his father David's sake, Solomon is not punished for his disobedience (verse 10) but his own son is punished. We are told this quite specifically: "Notwithstanding, in *thy* days I will not do it, for David's sake thy father: but I will tear [the kingdom] out of the hand of thy son". In 2 Samuel 3:27-29 we have a further illustration in which Joab is to be punished *in his descendants.*

By contrast, a woman who wished to compliment a man upon the greatness of his son could not with propriety address herself directly in such a fashion to the father and so she would praise the mother instead. Just such an occasion occurs in Luke 11:27 where a woman, recognizing the true greatness of the Lord, said, "Blessed are the breasts that have nursed thee". However, contrary to what was normal, the Lord rebuked the speaker for drawing attention to Mary in her role as his mother. For He said, "Yea, rather, blessed are they that hear the Word of God and keep it".

Now we run into this anomalous situation frequently in the Gospels. We begin with the Wise Men from the East who came with their gifts and these they presented not to Mary and Joseph (though doubtless Mary and Joseph took care of them afterwards) but to the Lord Himself, babe in arms though He was. And it is He, not Mary whom they worship (Matt.2:11). The text is most specific. "They fell down and worshipped *Him* . . . ." and "unto *Him*" did they present their gifts.

At the age of twelve we find Him staying behind at the Temple when his parents began the return journey to their home in Nazareth at the conclusion of the Passover festival (Luke 2:41-52). Naturally when his parents discovered his absence towards the end of the day, probably having assumed meanwhile that He was among the many other children from the village who would also be in the caravan, they anxiously returned in search of Him. They found Him in the Temple after visiting all the friends and relatives without success for three days. They were excusably amazed that He had not given them some warning as to his whereabouts. They were probably in fact not merely troubled but even possibly angered a little, but the joy of rediscovery dispelled their personal reaction.

Yet what must their surprise have been when He virtually repudiated any claim upon Him that they might have felt they had. It was his father's duty to teach Him a trade, by Jewish custom. Yet He said with surprising pointedness, "How is it that ye sought Me? Did you not realize that I must be about my Father's business?"

Joseph knew that he was not the Lord's true father, only a father by adoption. But his mother must surely have still felt a certain possessiveness: after all, He was only twelve years old. We are told, however, that though she (like Joseph) did not really understand what He meant, Jesus did obediently return with them — and Mary "kept all these sayings in her heart".

Then we come to the marriage in Cana of Galilee (John 2:1 ff.). At a crucial point in the celebrations, the host found himself suddenly in the embarrassing position of being out of wine. Perhaps Mary as a guest felt the embarrassment as keenly as her host, for her whole family was there. And in her concern she at once turned to her Son, expecting from Him some special action to relieve the situation simply because she *was* his mother. She said to Him, "They have no wine". That was all. Nothing more. No spoken request that He do something. Yet He knew it was actually a request. And He at once rebuked her for a kind of familiar presumption. Jesus said to her, quietly no doubt, "Woman, what have I to do with thee? Mine hour is not yet come".

Now *woman* is a term of respect. It does not in any way indicate a derogatory attitude. Nevertheless it seems strange that He so consistently avoided the use of the word *Mother* in direct address in public, though He must surely have used the word in private as He grew up. That there was no disrespect involved in the use of the term *woman* is clearly revealed at the end of his earthly ministry — in that last gracious act from the cross. Here He saw his mother, largely forsaken — the family was never wealthy it seems, and Joseph was dead; and his other brothers and sisters at this time appear to have repudiated Him. He thus, in spite of the agony of his position on the cross after several hours, turned to one of the few of his disciples who refused to desert Him and said to his mother, "Woman, behold thy son!" (John 19:26, 27). Then to the disciple, the beloved John, He said, "Behold thy mother!" And from that hour that disciple took her to his own home. Not one of her other children had come to her aid or offered her shelter. What a burden she had borne all through her life . . . . And now at the end she was as utterly forsaken as any mother has ever been. Yet even here, despite her loneliness in the last moments of her Son's life — so it must have seemed to her — He still did not call her by that most endearing of all names, *Mother*.

Again and again, Mary was thus challenged by a kind of repudiation that could only appear (to most women) like the worst kind of cruelty. Her whole life seems to have fulfilled the prophecy spoken to her in the Temple by Simeon, "Yea, and a sword shall pierce through thine own heart also" (Luke 2:35). In Mark 3:31-35 we have the story of his mother and his brethren coming to "rescue" Him whom they all felt was killing Himself with overwork. It seems they could not even get near Him! But he was soon notified of their concerned presence: "Behold", the people said, "thy mother and thy brethren outside seek for thee". What was his response? He asked, before the crowd, "*Who is my mother and my brethren?*" Then, to make his point clearer, He added, "Behold my mother and my brethren! Whosoever doeth the will of my Father which is in heaven, the same is my brother, my sister, my mother". No wonder his brothers and sisters were not there at the end, as far as we know . . . . But Mary was.

Throughout his whole ministry He exemplified personally what He had told his disciples in Luke 14:26, namely, that all such relationships must be held very lightly relative to our relationship to our Father in heaven as his children: so lightly, in fact, that it must seem we hate our parents relative to the love we have for God. It was, and is, a hard saying.

In all these things we see the Lord Jesus Christ restoring perspective regarding his true position as a member of the human family, not simply the son of Joseph and Mary. And we have proofs of Mary's extraordinary grace in that she kept these things and pondered them in her heart (Luke 2:19. 51) even though she could not understand them. She seems never to have raised her voice in protest, or sought in any way to assert her rights as his mother. She accepted humbly her calling as the "handmaid of the Lord" (Luke 1:38) and all that her unique position imposed upon her. No mother of such a great son was ever less possessive or less complaining.

Much has been made in a large part of Christendom of the angel's statement, "Hail, highly favoured: the Lord is with thee: blessed art thou among women" (Luke 1:28). Does this single Mary out *uniquely*?

In her song of praise when she was reassured by her visit with Elizabeth as to the reality of the visitation by the angel, she said, "All generations shall call me blessed". This would seem to justify her subsequent veneration under the title "The Blessed Virgin Mary". But actually the Greek verb (*makaridzo*) "call me blessed" means only "to *count as* blessed", exactly as it does in James 5:11 where the same word is used. The blessedness of Mary at this early time in her life was not due to herself but to the great fortune that had become hers by reason of her humble submission and her faith in the word of the Lord (Luke 1:45). As Elizabeth said to her, "Blessed (the same word again) is she that believed". Moreover, the angel had actually said to her, "Blessed art thou *among* women", not "Blessed art thou *above* women".

Other women besides Mary had been similarly declared "blessed" and indeed in the very same words. Jael, the wife of Heber the Kenite was one. "Blessed *above* women shall Jael the wife of Heber the Kenite be; blessed shall she be above women in the tent" (Jud.5:24). It is applied to Leah in Genesis 30:13 in reference to her pregnancy, and the Septuagint employs the same Greek word. Once again, using this same Greek word, Psalm 144:15 reads, "Blessed is the people whose God is the Lord".

Thus as the New Testament everywhere shows, nothing can be grounded in these declarations in behalf of Mary's character which may not be claimed for the partakers of grace generally. It is surely true that Mary was a gracious woman indeed and doubly blessed by reason of the part she was to play in the Incarnation. Yet the One of whom she was to be a virgin mother was also the One by whom she, like all others, was to be saved by grace. And she most gladly acknowledged the source of her salvation. "My spirit hath rejoiced", she exclaims, "in God my Saviour" (Luke 1:47). Mary was as much in need of a Saviour as any other sinner. She was not saved by being the mother of a Saviour-Son but by becoming a believer in her Son as her Saviour exactly as we do.

It is well to realize, perhaps, the circumstances of the events surrounding the annunciation and the nativity. She was a virgin, betrothed to Joseph, and by Jewish custom already legally his wife though not living with him until the wedding was actually celebrated. As she awaited this ceremony, the angel came to her and announced that she had been chosen of God to be the mother of the Messiah, the Son of God. This was wonderful enough in itself, but it may not have occurred to her then that she would become pregnant out of actual wedlock. Perhaps she understood something of the angel's words regarding the overshadowing of the Holy Spirit to mean she would become pregnant supernaturally (Luke 1:34, 35) *in due time*. But it seems unrealistic to assume that she supposed at that moment she would be called upon to endanger her marriage by appearing in the light of a faithless wife to her betrothed. Her spirit of submission, beautiful though it was (Luke 1:38), does not necessarily require us to believe that she had any immediate realization of what might be Joseph's natural reaction if she should become pregnant *before* they had come together.

But when she went to stay for a little while with her cousin Elizabeth in order to share with her the great promise made to herself that she was to be the mother of the Messiah (the hope of every Israelite woman, as we see from Dan.11:37) and when Elizabeth, under inspiration, declared her already to be indeed "the mother of her Lord", Mary must have suddenly realized what the angel meant. The open exultation of Elizabeth who, of course, knew that Mary was yet unwed by law, overwhelmed her spirit and reassured her: and by the end of her three month stay (Luke 1:56) Mary certainly knew she was indeed pregnant.

Yet she still had not "known" Joseph. Before leaving to visit Elizabeth, she may well have shared the angelic visitation with Joseph and perhaps both of them pondered its meaning without anticipating what the immediate consequences might be in terms of their betrothal. So as she returned to Nazareth, she may indeed have wondered what Joseph would say when he discovered she was already pregnant.

But the Lord had provided for this potential hazard. Joseph may already have suspected that Mary was pregnant, and at first have felt compelled to take steps to dissolve the betrothal. But he was now assured by an angel that he should receive his beloved not indeed *in spite of* her condition, but rather because of it. This pregnancy was a supernatural one.

Thus Joseph became her shield and provided for both mother and child a normal family relationship. And though Joseph was not the father of her child, he did perform the two duties required of any adopting father. First, he gave Him his name (a practice of very long standing — cf. Gen.48:16); and secondly, he taught him his trade. Edersheim tells us that it was deemed a religious duty, frequently and most earnestly insisted upon, to learn some trade — provided it did not minister to luxury or tend to lead away from personal observance of the law.* No father was truly a father who did not teach his son a trade — even when the family was well-to-do. Joseph could not better have demonstrated his adoption of Jesus as his son than by teaching Him his own trade. That he did perform both duties to ensure true adoption we know from Matthew 1:25 (he, not *she*, called his name Jesus) and by comparison of Matthew 13:55 with Mark 6:3 (where Jesus is called the carpenter's son and where Jesus is Himself called a carpenter!). One cannot doubt that Jesus was a good carpenter. Did He not Himself say — without fear of contradiction — that the yokes He makes are "easy" (Matt.11:30)? The Scriptures have hedged in the truth and built a firm fence about it.

There is no doubt that Mary was in an extraordinarily difficult position. She was indeed mother to her Son but had to learn that she could never "own" her Son in the sense that other mothers could (and do). On each occasion upon which she might naturally have felt proud of having borne such a Son, she was in one way or another rebuked. He rebuked her by refusing to allow that she bore any special relationship to Himself above any other of his disciples, whether men or women.

He never *once* (as we have said) referred to her as his "mother", not even from the cross in the one hour when her need of comfort must have seemed most pressing. He committed her to a beloved

---

* Edersheim, Alfred, *The Life and Times of Jesus the Messiah*, N.Y., Herrick, 1883, Vol. I, p. 252.

disciple John . . . . not even, be it noted, to his brothers or sisters* in the flesh (Matt.13:55, 56). A sword did indeed many times pierce her own heart. How could it be otherwise, her own motherly nature being what it was, and his identity being what it was. When Joseph died she must have felt alone in a very special way. Perhaps Luke was her physician and confiding in him was a particular comfort — which could account for the greater detail of the Lord's birth and earliest days which appear in Luke's Gospel.

Yet, for all this, it cannot be stated with certainty that there was no other "mother" in Israel who might not, with God's grace, have responded to the unique circumstances of Mary's life in an equally submissive and beautifully resigned way.

It does not seem, therefore, that Mary was chosen for spiritual or psychological reasons alone — and, humanly speaking, certainly not by reason of her social status, since her offering at the time of her ceremonial purification after giving birth to a firstborn male child was the offering appointed specifically for those who were to be numbered among the financially impoverished (Luke 2:22-24 and Lev.12:8). It is a striking irony that the injunction in Leviticus 12:8 reads, "If she be not able to bring a lamb, then she shall bring two turtle doves or two young pigeons". The irony is that she brought two birds *and* a lamb. For the Child she brought was indeed a sacrifical Lamb if she had but realized it at that time.

We look, then, for some other contributing reason for the choice of Mary and consider the possibility that she was chosen particularly because of her pedigree. And here we have two separate matters to examine: her title to the throne of David and her right by natural descent, by blood line. And it is in the latter we must ask also whether it is merely "continuity of seed" from David or whether there might not be some more profound "continuity" of a genetic nature that would in a special way provide in Mary an ovum of particular purity.

2. Mary's pedigree.

It has for centuries been noted with surprise by those not familiar with Jewish modes of reckoning pedigrees that Mary, through whom the Lord's body as to the flesh must be traced back to David's loins in order to validate his right to David's throne, does not actually appear

---

* This circumstance was clearly foretold in Psalm 69:8, "I am become a stranger unto my brethren, and an alien unto my mother's children". Although the Rabbis do not seem to have counted this Psalm as a messianic one, yet verse 9 shows clearly that the reference was to the Lord when it says, "The zeal of thine house hath eaten me up, etc.", words particularly applied to the Lord Himself in John 2:17.

in the only genealogies we have relevant to the issue. Why did neither Matthew nor Luke include her name when they traced the line from David to Jesus? Both pedigrees end with Joseph, not Mary.

It is perhaps not so surprising that Matthew did not include Mary. For there is some reason to believe that Matthew's account of the circumstances of Jesus' birth stemmed originally from the fact that Matthew was Joseph's confidant. Joseph probably sought advice from Matthew when he first heard rumours of Mary's condition. Matthew seems to have been a lawyer, or if not a practicing one, at least a man trained in the law, for he is elsewhere called Levi, i.e., *lawyer* (Mark 2:14). From Joseph he learned much that was very personal about Joseph's inward struggle — which he subsequently recorded in his Gospel. To present Joseph's relationship in the Davidic line seems to follow naturally from these circumstances.

By contrast we know that Luke was a physician (Col.4:14), and what more natural, therefore, than for Mary in her unusual condition to have sought him out as *her* confidant. Certainly the account of the circumstances surrounding the nativity in Luke's Gospel reflects Mary's point of view and her personal experience. For this reason we might surely have expected that Luke would have shown Mary's place in the Davidic line. Clearly he was not merely a physician but a historian with the mind of a scholar. He says (Luke 1:3) that he had been involved in the circumstances "from the very first", and if this is so he would surely have known Mary's father's name. But instead of tracing Mary back to Heli, Luke has stated that *Joseph* was the son of Heli (Luke 3:23) which not only seems to prevent Heli from being Mary's father but also contradicts Matthew 1:16 which makes Joseph to be the son of Jacob. If the blood line from David to Jesus must be established according to Jewish law, why was Mary's name omitted by both writers, for certainly the blood line could not be traced through Joseph since he was not the natural father of Jesus?

It is important to realize that in Israel a blood line was always traced officially through males only. No females are ever listed as actual links in the chain. If a man happened to have only daughters and no sons to continue his line line,[226] it was customary to set forth the daughter's husband as her representative in the pedigree and so to enter his name as a son — not as a son-in-law, as we would judge him to be.* Thus the line passes from the father to the son-in-law to the grandson: not from the father to the daughter to the grandson.

Occasionally both the son-in-law and the daughter (his wife) are

---

* According to Numbers 27:1-11 regulating birth rights in a "daughters only" family, the one stipulation was that a girl marry a man from her own tribe.

simply passed over so that a whole generation is omitted. The blood
line is then shown as passing directly from the father to the grandson.
These practices are exemplified in the two genealogies in question, as
will be seen in Appendix VI. This is the reason that Mary's name is
omitted in Luke's genealogy, while her husband's name stands in her
place. And this is the reason why her husband is shown not only as
Jacob's son (in Matthew) but as Heli's son (in Luke). Meanwhile,
there is no break in the blood line from Heli to Jesus, for although
Joseph had no connection, Mary is the physical link.

What we have here may be set forth as follows:

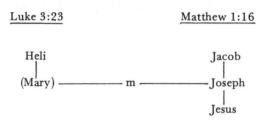

Jesus becomes by adoption the son of Joseph, and Joseph by
marriage to Mary becomes the son of Heli, even though he remains a
son of Jacob his natural father: and all contradiction is resolved.

But now the question arises, How do we know that Mary was the
daughter of Heli? We don't. It is a surmise on the basis of inference
from other Scriptures, and on the basis of certain traditions both
Jewish and Christian. These inferences, however, amount to virtual
proof, "proof from necessity". Let us examine them briefly.

According to rabbinical teaching, the wife of Joseph was listed in
the Jerusalem Talmud (*Hagigah* Book 77,4) as Beth-Heli, i.e., daughter
of Heli. This is an important piece of evidence, because the Jews who
made these records can hardly have been prejudiced by Christian
convictions. Added to this testimony is the account given of Mary's
parents in the so-called apocryphal 'Christian' work called *Protoevangelium of James*. This work is undoubtedly ancient and is quoted or
alluded to by a number of Church Fathers from the early fourth
century onwards. They speak as though it were a work long familiar
to their readers. It is attributed to James, the brother of the Lord.
It was apparently written either in Hebrew or Syriac (Aramaic?), and
a copy of it was brought from the Middle East by Guillaume Postel
(1503 - 1581) and translated into Latin. It was sent to Oporimus, a
printer in Basle, where a protestant divine named Bibliander, a professor of divinity at the University of Zurich saw it through to
publication in 1552. Postel asserts that it was publicly read as a

canonical work in the Eastern Church but rejected as such in the Western.*

Now the *Protoevangelium of James* tells us that Mary's parents were named Joachim and Anna of Bethlehem.† The importance of this piece of information is that Joachim is a shortened form of Eliakim (see, for example, 2 Chron.36:4). Subsequently the name Eliakim seems to have been shortened to Eli/Heli. The two lines of tradition therefore appear to converge in their testimony to the fact that Mary was indeed the daughter of Heli and thus continued in her body the seed line of David. The early Church was almost unanimous in making this assumption and the form in which Luke's genealogy appears is entirely concordant with what we know of Jewish practices in such matters.

But there are certain statements in Scripture not appearing in direct connection with the genealogies of Matthew or Luke, which virtually settle the matter. First of all, it is apparent from the angel's words to Mary in Luke 1:32 that she had a real title to David's throne. The angel said to her with respect to her son, "He shall be great and shall be called the son of the highest: and the Lord God shall give unto him the throne of his father David". Now it is true that this right might accrue to Him only by *title* through Joseph who was also clearly a lineal descendant of David according to Matthew. However, other Scriptures add somewhat to this simple statement. Romans 1:3 assures us that "He was made of the seed of David *according to the flesh*", and since Joseph contributed nothing to this *flesh* we have to assume that Mary was the link. The fact is re-affirmed in 2 Timothy 2:8 ("Jesus Christ of the seed of David"); and Acts 2:30 tells us that "of the fruit of his loins [i.e., David's] *according to the flesh* [God] would raise up Christ to sit on his throne". This was the fulfillment of Psalm 132:11 which reads, "Of the fruit *of thy body* will I set [one] upon the throne".

The root of this fulfillment was not through Joseph's loins, i.e., through Joseph's seed, but via Mary. We can therefore say with assurance that the evidence we have clearly reinforces the conclusion that Luke's genealogy is the line of Mary's seed and the blood line from David to Jesus the Messiah through her. This line, it may be said, passed through some very precarious but providentially preserved channels, both male and female, at the time of the Babylonian captivity. These are complex but they are so important that they are

---

* A translation of this work by Alexander Walker was published in the Scribner's edition of *The Ante-Nicene Fathers*, Vol. VIII, 1916, p. 361-367.

† See chap.I. v. i; chap. II. v. i; chap. V. v. 9.;

carefully explored in Appendix VI.

The evidence combined serves to show how God preserved both the seed and the title, and joined the two in Joseph and Mary in order to channel them and unite them in the Lord Jesus Christ. The *titular right* to the throne of David was channelled through Joseph according to Matthew, and the *blood line* of David's seed was channelled through Mary according to Luke. The circumstances which necessitated separating these two essential components of full title to David's throne are discussed in the above mentioned Appendix and they account for the need of two distinct genealogies and for the apparent conflicts between them. These same circumstances account, perhaps, for the divergence of tradition (Jewish and early Christian) regarding the actual name of Mary's father.

But Revelation 22:16 is also an important additional testimony to the reality of Mary's role according to Luke's genealogy. For Luke traces the line backward from Mary's father Heli, through David, Abraham, Noah, and so to Adam. But he does not stop here. He closes his genealogy with the words "which was the son of Adam which was a son of God" (Luke 3:38).

The last link in the chain is God Himself, the Creator of the world and the Creator of man. God therefore lies at the root of this long chain in the human family tree from Adam to Christ. But who was this Creator? It was none other than the same Christ Himself! By Him all things were created, man included (Col. 1:15 f.). Thus, through Mary's unbroken line, the Lord Jesus Christ is shown to have been not merely (by his bodily existence) the *offspring* of David, but also (by his pre-existence as the Creator in whose image Adam was made) the *root* of David as well. In Revelation 22:13 He said, "I am alpha and omega, the beginning and the end, the first and the last". And then in verse 16, "I am the *root* AND the *offspring* of David".* So He, the Lord Jesus Christ, now God made man, stands at the beginning and the end of this chain of seventy-seven generations stretching from Adam through Abraham, David, and Mary, to Mary's firstborn son who was indeed the "Word made flesh".

Thus while the majority of encyclopedias and dictionaries of the Bible take the position that there is no absolute proof that Mary was the daughter of Heli or that Luke's genealogy is really Mary's pedigree, and while this may be strictly true as to *absolute proof*, the total

---

* Nestorius wrote: "Learn how close a conjunction existed between the Godhead and the flesh of the Lord visible in the child. For the same (person) was both child and Lord of the child". [Quoted by Aloys Grillmeier, *Christ in Christian Tradition*, Atlanta, John Knox Press, 1975, p. 457] As the Son was "father" to Himself, so the child was "Lord" to Himself.

evidence is so strong that it cannot be seriously questioned. The blood line could not pass through Joseph because Joseph was the father of Jesus only in a legal sense, "as was supposed" (Luke 3:23), *hos anom-idzeto* (ὣς ἀνομίζετο). This Greek verb (*nomidzo*) has the meaning of "being by custom" when used in the passive voice as here.*

The number of hedges built around the stated relationships between Mary, Joseph, and Jesus to preserve the exact truth and avoid misstatement is truly amazing. For example, Matthew 1:15, 16 tells us that Mattan begat Jacob and Jacob begat Joseph — but it does not say "and Joseph begat Jesus". The truth is hedged by the words "and Jacob begat Joseph the husband of Mary of whom was born Jesus, who is called *Messiah*".

Again, in Luke 1:13 we find the words of the angel addressed to Elizabeth's husband with respect to the birth of John the Baptist, recorded thus: "Thy wife, Elizabeth, shall bear *thee* a son". But in Matthew 1:21 the words addressed to Joseph with respect to the birth of the Lord Jesus are thus recorded: "She shall bring forth a son". There is no "to thee" in this instance. It is a small omission but what a profound truth is preserved by it! Jesus was not a Son brought forth to Joseph but to the Father in heaven.

In the East it was normal for a father to rejoice publicly and to be congratulated by all on the birth of a son. But here we find Mary rejoicing publicly in the beautiful *Magnificat* (Luke 1:46-55). Of Joseph we hear nothing in this respect. By contrast, and in harmony with normal custom however, it is not Elizabeth but Zacharias who rejoices publicly over the birth of *John* (Luke 1:67-79).

In Matthew 1:16 Jesus is said to have been "of Mary" not "of Joseph". We find the words are: "Joseph the husband of Mary *of whom* was born Jesus who is called the Christ". It could be argued on the basis of the English translation that the words "of whom" revert back to Joseph. But the Greek is very clear on this matter, for the "of whom" is *ex hēs* (ἐξ ἧς) i.e., feminine, not masculine. The intent of the writer is effectively made quite clear.

We have noted that Jesus was by no means an only child: he had brothers and sisters (Matt.13:55, 56). We have also noted that this

---

* In the Papyri the word is so used regularly to signify "customary payments" in the form of dues. The basic root is *nomos*, law, and in the New Testament it has reference to social custom and to legal principle rather than to natural law. The present context clearly shows that Joseph was not the father of Jesus the Messiah. If he had been so, there could be no possible reason to say any more than simply that Jesus was the son of Joseph who was the son of Heli, etc., as it is in the rest of the pedigree. In the New Testament the word *nomidzo* appears fifteen times and always has the meaning of "supposing", of supposition rather than actuality (cf. Matt.5:17; 10:34; 20:10; Luke 2:44; 3:23; Acts 7:25; 8:20; 14:19; 16:13, 27; 17:29; 21:29; 1 Cor.7:26, 36; 1 Tim.6:5).

circumstance was anticipated in Psalm 69:8. It is striking to find that
the Word of God is careful even here: "I am become a stranger unto
my brethren, and an alien unto my mother's children". The passage
does not say "and an alien unto my parents' children". While He
shared their mother, He did not share their father.

Whereas the angel went first to Zacharias to announce the birth of
a forthcoming son before Elizabeth was informed (Luke 1:5-20), the
same angel (Gabriel) appeared first to *Mary* regarding the birth of hers
(Luke 1:26-38). For this was not Joseph's natural son in the sense
that John was the son of Zacharias. Hence in Luke 2:7 we are told
that Mary gave birth to *her* son, not to Joseph's son, or even to *their*
son jointly. Moreover, the angel had said to Zacharias "Your wife
Elizabeth shall bear *thee* a son" (Luke 1:13) and this was the normal
form of speech in such angelic annunciations. Thus had God spoken
to Abraham, "I will bless (Sarah) and give *thee* a son also of her" (Gen.
17:16). The son was brought forth by the woman, but it was always
the *man's* son. Nowhere else in Scripture, I believe, is a woman ever
said to have brought forth *her* firsborn son as Mary is said to have
done (Matt.1:25 and Luke 2:7).

In Luke 2:33 we find the words, "and Joseph and his mother marvelled at those things which were spoken of him". It does not say
"his father and his mother marvelled . . . ."

And so the truth is here always guarded and kept in every way
against the slightest contradiction or possibility of misunderstanding.
Thus was Mary's firsborn child, by supernatural generation and by
Joseph's adopting of Him, certified as the Messiah of Israel and the
Saviour of men.

As will be seen in Appendix VI, the pedigree of Joseph followed a
tortuous path but a firm one to its end in the Person of Jesus Christ to
whom now descended the *title* to the throne of David. By marriage
to Mary and by the act of adoption, Joseph became the "father" of
Jesus according to law and thereby passed to Him his titular rights,
while Mary fulfilled through herself the promise made to David that
of the fruit of his own loins should one sit upon his throne whose
kingdom would be everlasting. Each parent conveyed one aspect of
the two kinds of claims the Messiah must validate to possess rightfully
the throne of David.

Mary's pedigree was not traced through the first blood line from
David but through David's younger son Nathan — for reasons examined in Appendix VI. But she was nevertheless truly of David's loins
and bore David's "greater son" (Matt.12:42). What she could not
pass to her Son came to Him through Joseph's marriage to her and by
Joseph's official adoption of Him as his son.

While it is possible that another woman in Mary's day might have fulfilled the position that Mary did as the daughter of Heli and so of David, it seems that we do have in these circumstances a special situation that probably made her position unique.   And with the death and bodily resurrection of the Lord Jesus, the full title to the throne of David has passed forever beyond the reach of any other human claimant.

3. The existence of a 'pure' line from Adam to Mary.

We have considered at some length the psychological and spiritual qualifications of Mary, and the complete suitability of her pedigree from a legal point of view. We have now to give some thought to the suitability of her seed from the scientific point of view, genetically considered.   Some more cautious souls would say, Are you not trespassing into mystery?   Is this not unwarranted speculation?   Do not such secret things belong only unto the Lord?   The answer has to be, of course, It may indeed be so.

To one who has not given much thought to the matter, it may seem manifestly absurd to even think about it.   But if one *has* thought about it, it soon becomes apparent that there are some genetic problems that can hardly be dismissed — once they have been raised.   For there is no question that the Lord Jesus Christ was both the sacrificial Lamb of God and the High Priest who alone was worthy to present that sacrifice.   Both roles were undertaken by the one individual.   And both sacrificial victim and High Priest must be without spot or blemish, not to outward appearance only but inwardly as God sees.   This requirement would seem to mean a body (for both Lamb and Priest) free entirely of mutant genes.

A lamb offered according to the Mosaic Covenant might be approved for sacrifice by man's limited powers of observation and yet be far from perfect due to some hidden defect. The Lamb who was to fulfill all these prototype offerings in the Old Testament had to be not merely without blemish apparent to the superficial view of man but without blemish in the most absolute sense — in the sight of God. Such a body that was to be offered for man's redemption could not conceivably be one hiddenly marred in every cell by damaged genes.

Such damage *would be* in every body cell, for it seems virtually certain that there are very few individuals born today in whom, quite by chance, there are no mutant genes.   And it is equally safe to say that since all mutant genes are damaged genes and are in some measure detrimental, and since they will exist in every body cell, we are to that extent defective, every one of us, as to our tissues and organs — even though there may be no outward evidence of it.

The care which was to be exercised by the priests who approved the lamb of atonement was precisely set forth in Leviticus 22:17-23.

The very health of the whole nation depended upon minute examination of the victim.   Yet it was, after all, limited to what man could see.   The same must be said of the rigid examination accorded to all those who presented themselves as candidates for the priesthood. And this was even more true of anyone who was to be chosen as High Priest.   Such an appointee might be disqualified for any disfigurement whatsoever, no matter how small it was.   Basing their procedure on the instructions given in Leviticus 21:17-24, the Jewish authorities began with the enumeration of eleven characteristic blemishes that would exclude the holding of any priestly office involving the approach to any altar.   These blemishes included blindness, lameness, facial disfigurement, malformation of hand or foot, any extraneous growth, hunchback, short stature, defective eyes, scurvy, running sores, and damaged sex organs.   Any one of these defects disqualified the individual from officiating in the offering of sacrifices.

This Mosaic list of eleven disqualifying blemishes was extended in the Talmud to 142.   Later on the rabbis added two more, raising the total to 144 — perhaps for mnemonic purposes.   All of them were, of course, external and manifest.   They could not know of the hidden blemishes which were internal.

Any neophyte who desired to serve as a priest had to undergo an extremely rigid and probably sometimes embarrassing personal examination before admittance.   If he should subsequently be injured, he might be reduced to a wholly subservient role in the Temple services, such as preparing the wood for the fires for example.   Josephus notes that Antigonus cut off the ears of Hyracanus who had been High Priest in order to ensure that he would never be restored to this office again (*Antiquities of the Jews*, XIV. xiii. 10).

I think we must assume that so long as the nation of Israel had moral leadership, any candidate for the high priesthood would also be judged as to the suitability of his *character*.   But in terms of strict rules and regulations the emphasis was, of necessity, placed on physical suitability.   One Hebrew word above all others seems to have gathered under its head these qualifying traits — physical, moral, and spiritual. This was the word *tamim*.   It has, in a broad sense, the meaning of perfection.   The passover lamb was to be *tamim*, and so were all sacrifices offered to the Lord.   Of the 89 occurrences of the word, 54 refer to physical perfection and 35 to perfection of character.   The word is first used with reference to Noah, a just man and perfect (*tamim* — Gen.9:6).   The context of this reference may be particularly significant, for we are told that Noah was not only a just man but also *"perfect in his generations"*.

The Septugint translated the Hebrew *tamim* by the Greek word *amōmos* (ἄμωμος).   And the New Testament employed this word in

Hebrews 9:14 when speaking of the Lord Jesus who offered Himself *without spot* unto God, and in 1 Peter 1:19 in speaking of the Lamb *without blemish*.   But in other places in the New Testament *amomos* clearly has the sense of moral perfection or blamelessness.

The phrase "in his generations" is really the deciding factor.   In the Hebrew the word "generations" (*toledoth*) is a word consistently referring to the matter of pedigree in its 38 occurrences in the Old Testament. It is a word customarily written in a plural form, probably because any pedigree assumes a plurality of predecessors or descendants.   The Septuagint rendering of the Old Testament regularly translated *toledoth* by the Greek word *genea* (γενεα) which signifies *pedigree, line, descent, breeding, nation*: a word so used in this sense in Classical Greek to express the same idea. A concordance will show at once that *toledoth* is always associated in the Old Testament with pedigree, even as Matthew opens his Gospel (1:1) with the pedigree of the Lord Jesus and refers to it under the heading, "These are the generations of . . . ."

It could therefore be argued with good reason that at this critical point in human history the life-line from Adam was being preserved in one man (and his family) who qualified in his own person not only because he was a just man but because of the purity of his seed from a genetic point of view.   Through Shem he passed it on to Abraham and through Abraham to David.   Through David's son Nathan the line passed to Mary, and through Mary to the Lord Jesus Christ.

It was, of course, quite impossible for the authorities in those days to know of hidden defects in candidates under their scrutiny, whether youths for the priesthood or offerings for sacrifice.   But surely no such clemency could possibly be permitted by God Himself as He looked upon his own Lamb (John 1:29), and as He looked upon the High Priest who was to offer it.

The Lord Jesus Christ was both Lamb and High Priest: for "*He* offered *Himself* without spot to God" (Heb.9:14).   His perfection of body and spirit must have been absolute.   That He should have damaged genes in every cell is surely an unthinkable thing.   But how could He receive such a body through a woman, coming as it did after 6000 years and 76 generations of accumulated mutations?

Let us look briefly at what we do know from Scripture, which is the only data we have as to the requirements and the historical circumstances.   And then let us compare this with the known data of genetics which can be set forth with some measure of assurance because they are based for the most part on experimental verification.

First, then, the data of Scripture.

(1) We can be sure that since mutant genes are damaged genes, Adam had no mutant genes when God created him. His body was perfect and without spot or blemish.

(2) We can be sure that the Lord Jesus Christ had no mutant genes in his body either. As the Lamb of God, his body had to be perfect, without spot or blemish (1 Pet.1:19). It had to be as perfect as Adam's body.

(3) We know from Scripture that Mary's seed was supernaturally fertilized by the Holy Spirit, and therefore that no damaged genic material was *thereby* contributed to it. It was a "holy thing" (Luke 1:35).

(4) We know that Mary was only 76 generations from Adam, a fact of some importance in the light of the rate at which genetic damage accumulates from generation to generation.

This is our basic biblical data, though it has to be considered largely in the terms of implications rather than explicit statements.

Bringing to bear on this biblical data what we know from genetic research, we note the relevance of the following.

1. Mutant genes are damaged genes.

2. Mutant genes, contrary to popular opinion, are remarkably rare. G. G. Simpson has estimated that the chances of any one cell nucleus containing five mutant genes would be of the order of $1/10^{22}$ or one in ten thousand million million million!* To state it slightly differently, if there were available for analysis ten thousand million million million cells with a nucleus in each, only one of those cells would be found with five mutant genes in it. All the rest would have less than five mutant genes or none at all!

Since the ovum is a cell with a nucleus, the composition of which will be much like all other cell nuclei, this statistical estimate applied to it also. The ovum which Mary presented might therefore conceivably have five mutant genes (by this method of reckoning), but she might just as easily have fewer than five or even none whatever.

At any rate, the damage is of an extremely low order of magnitude relative to the number of genes in the cell which are estimated

---

The Major Features of Evolution, N.Y., Columbia Univ. Press, 1953, p. 96. Only where inbreeding enhances the probability of damaged genes being paired is the percentage likely to be higher. Bernard Rensch notes that H. J. Muller's genetic analysis of marriages among close relatives has demonstrated that every individual has an average of at least ten detrimental hereditary characteristics in his genetic make-up [*Homo Sapiens: From Man to Demi-God*, N.Y., Columbia Univ. Press, 1972, p. 11]. This is still a remarkably small number. Moreover, it is based on our generation, and it should be remembered that we today are not in the 76th generation as Mary was, but probably at least in the 150th generation from Adam. Mutant genes have had longer to accumulate and the mutagenic influences in our generation are probably much higher. Mary's generation was almost certainly less damaged than ours in this respect.

to be between 50,000 to 10,000: some would place the figure as high as 1,000,000!

And if there was a providential filtering out in the process of cell division at the time of fertilization, there might be none at all. Since one "parent" was the Holy Spirit, there would certainly be nothing surprising in the appearance of a body completely free of mutant genes. Even natural generation must result in individuals now and then being born in whom there are no inherited mutant genes in the cell nucleus, though their cytoplasm would of course still be carrying the mortogenic factor introduced by the male. It is this *cytoplasmic entail of sin* that virgin conception eliminated.

3. Furthermore, it is now known that a very large proportion of damaged genes revert to the original undamaged state by some built-in repair process which is only partially understood but clearly demonstrable.[227] Thus the figure of a possible five mutant genes would in any case probably be on the high side in most individuals.

4. Because of the nature of the chromosomes which carry the hereditary material in the nucleus of each cell, all genes are found in pairs called *alleles*. When a gene mutation occurs, only one gene of the pair is affected. The undamaged allele or pairing gene neutralizes the damaged gene. If, however, in the next generation the damaged gene by chance is paired with another damaged gene at the same position on the matching chromosome, the damage becomes manifest in the developing organism.* The chance of this happening is virtually nil unless the marrying partners are closely related by blood.

The Holy Spirit's contribution could not possibly introduce any mutant genes, so that there would be no *reinforcement* of any that Mary herself might have contributed. In point of fact they would be neutralized. But it seems clear that we have no right to suppose *any* damaged genes would be allowed through the sorting process† that precedes actual fusion of the nuclei of the two seeds in her case.

Moreover, it is by no means necessary to assume that such damaged genes were present at all. There is no evidence that we are all loaded with mutant genes. The evidence is quite to the contrary: mutant genes are rare to begin with. In natural procreation chance alone must allow their reduction by half in any case: and divine over-

---

* A determined effort has been made here to avoid the use of technical jargon — which would have made the description of these events easier but much less intelligible to the reader who does not "speak the language". To the geneticist, the shuffling processes involved here are very familiar.

† This sorting out process takes place at the time of the expulsion of the first and second polar bodies from the ovum after fertilization.

sight of this process of shuffling could very well assure that there were
in fact none in the woman's seed that was to be God's chosen vessel.

Furthermore, as we have already seen earlier, the cytoplasm of the
woman's seed would by its very nature be entirely free of any mortogenic factor.   The body of the Lord Jesus Christ could thus be not
only perfect in outward appearance but perfect in its inner constitution also.

In conclusion, I do not think it is necessary to introduce the
doctrine of immaculate conception in order to ensure that the Lord's
body would be free from the effects of original sin as it was being
prepared for Him.[228]

While Herman Olshausen can hardly have had Mary's genetic
constitution in mind when he wrote his *Commentary on the New
Testament*,* it is remarkable how apt his observation was when he
said: "We must look upon the incarnation of Christ as a fact for
which preparation was made by a vein of nobler life flowing through
the whole line of our Lord's ancestors". Mary's body came of a very
pure strain.

Taken together — her character, her titular standing with respect
to the throne of David, and her pedigree — all help to explain what
made Mary God's choice.   When Paul wrote to the Galatians (4:4) he
said, "When the fullness of time was come, God sent forth his son,
made of a woman, made under the law".   The immediate reference
may be only to the period of gestation, but it could also be to the
period of world history in which those events transpired, or it might
even relate back to the fulfillment of the predicted time interval of
Daniel's prophecy (Dan.9:25).   Mary certainly satisfied in her person
all the hedgings and fencings that were essential for the mother of the
Lord, in order that his title to the throne of David might be unchall-
engeable and that He might qualify as the Lamb of God without spot
or blemish.

Perhaps this is one of the few cases in Scripture where the reason
for the choice of a particular individual for a very special work of God
is not hidden in the secret councils of the Almighty but is revealed to
us and to our children (Deut.29:29).   All three of the reasons we have
considered in this chapter may together answer the question, Why
Mary?

---

* Olshausen, Herman, *Commentary on the New Testament*, tr. A. C. Kendrick, N.Y., Sheldon,
1861, Vol. I, p. 168.

We now turn to a consideration of the *moment* of incarnation and the change in relationship which took place between the Lord Jesus Christ and his heavenly Father as a consequence of his embodiment. In the history of the human race, indeed in the history of the Universe, it was for this moment that both the Universe and our race were created. The Incarnation was an event when time and eternity were scarcely distinguishable. And it was an event made possible by the very way in which God had designed man's body and the processes of human reproduction. The Incarnation was — and is — in fact, the key to the Universe. It is also the key to man's origin, to man's constitution, to man's history, to man's destiny.

There must have been a profound silence among the angels in heaven when that moment arrived: and not until Mary's firstborn had uttered his first cry did the angelic hosts burst forth with the praises heard by the shepherds (Luke 2:13)!

Chapter 23

WHEN HE BRINGETH THE FIRST BEGOTTEN INTO THE WORLD

Thou art my Son,
this day have I begotten Thee ....
I will be to Him a Father
and He shall be to Me a Son ....
Hebrews 1:5

When did the Lord Jesus Christ become a Son to the Father? In eternity? Or in *time*? Before the Incarnation or *after* it?

Was He not "the beginning of the creation of God" (Rev.3:14) and the very "firstborn of all creation" (Col.1:15) and yet did there not come a time when the Father said, "Thou art my Son, this day have I begotten Thee" (Heb.1:5)?

We ask, with the disciples, How can these things be? And throughout the centuries the people of God have wondered how a Son was begotten before all worlds and yet one day also begotten in time. Was He twice begotten of God or are there two Sons?

The answer is, No, there are not two Sons but One: not two Sons, but two *Sonships*. The Son was twice begotten — once in eternity, once in time, the Son of God and the Son of Man: the Son of God for the Father's sake and the Son of Man for our sake.

When did these things take place?

The time has come to examine closely what the Scriptures have to say on this matter, to sort out some of the truly amazing things revealed in the Word of God, and to attempt a synthesis of statements that

often seem contradictory.   Once ordered and arranged, their reconcil-
iation both increases our wonder at the condescension of God and
clarifies our understanding of the most extraordinary event in the
whole history of God's dealings with mankind.

The mystery remains: and yet enough becomes clear to enable us
to piece together the wonderful works of God so that we can say,
"Once I was blind, now I see" . . . . though it is but through a glass
darkly.

We have, in this Chapter, to turn our thoughts to two things that
have occupied men of God and exercised their minds to the limits of
human capacity: the meaning of the *Sonship* of Christ, and the
moment of Incarnation when the Word was made flesh and dwelt
among us — and we beheld his glory, the glory of the only-begotten
Son of the Father.

We have spoken of one Son, but of two Sonships.   This is what
Scripture reveals to us.   The Lord Jesus Christ was Son of God and
Son of Man.   Because the first relationship was established "before all
creation" (Col.1:15), it does not seem possible to reduce the nature of
such a begetting within the boundaries of human language.   All our
begettings are beginnings: His was not.

For centuries men have struggled to encompass a begetting that
was timeless within a framework of the boundaried comprehension of
events which always have a before and an after to them.   Eternity,
though set in the heart of man, is still entirely beyond our understanding.   The best we can do is to cast the mystery into an anomalous
phrase, the *Eternal Generation*, and pretend that it expresses the incomprehensible in a comprehensible way.   It doesn't, of course!   It
only appears to . . . .   And there we seem forced to leave it as an article
of faith not reconcilable with reason but to be accepted for what it
is: a mystery.

Arius, determining to apply reason, simply destroyed the truth he
sought to formulate.   He accepted the Scriptures which spoke of the
Son as begotten before all worlds and argued (logically enough) that
what is begotten is brought into being and that what is brought into
being must have been non-existent until then.   And so he made the
Son of God a creature, and said there was a time when He was not.   But
since we also know that the Son was always with the Father, eternally
present with Him, present before time began because present before
the world began, Arius had to deny what we now speak of as his
"eternal generation".   In fact, he denied his deity.

Arius took only part of the truth and, by extending it to its logical
conclusion, he ended up with a heresy that denied the very thing he
wished to prove.   The fact is that there is no way to reduce such a
truth to rational argument.   It is understood — in so far as a mystery

can ever be anything else — only by being believed.   By faith we understand.   What illumination our minds are capable of results from acceptance of the mystery and worship of the One who is its subject.

The Son of God was, then, always a Son.   The begetting was not like a human begetting which necessarily involves a beginning.   The terms used in Scripture (in Col.1:15 and Rev.3:14) are an accomodation to our limitations.   The limitation lies with us — not with God. We should never cease to wonder, nor presume to say we understand.

But what about the term, Son of Man?   Here we are on firmer ground.   We recognize that it is a title expressing a relationship far more intelligible to us, because the events which led up to its realization sufficiently partook of our experience of life and of what begetting a son means — humanly speaking.

What we have to accept is that any Mediator between God and man must be both God and Man in one Person. This one Person therefore stands not in some kind of middle relationship that is neither one or the other   — but is both.   The Son of God is, by Sonship, the express image of the Father (Heb.1:3).   But to be a mediator between God and man, He must also be in the express image of *man,* a second Adam, truly a Son of Man.   He must therefore be both Son of God and of Man.

One who is not "begotten of God" could not be a mediator merely by being "begotten of a woman" (Gal.4:4).   And thus the fact of the mystery of the *first* begetting is as vital a part of Christian Faith as the fact of the mystery of the *second* begetting.   The first begetting by its very nature must be in eternity: the second begetting must be in time. The only logic that is sufficient for these mysteries is the logic of necessity.

It does not seem likely that we can advance our understanding of the first begetting beyond what has already been stated in the great Confessions of Faith which deal with it.* But we do have considerable light from Scripture on the mystery of the *second* begetting.   Indeed even the events themselves which transpired at the very moment when that begetting became an amazing reality, are illuminated for us.

It is a remarkable thing that it is in the Old Testament we find most of the light we have on the manner in which the Lord Jesus Christ achieved his title "Son of Man": whereas it is in the New Testament that we find the most light we have on the manner in which He achiev-

---

* The *Belgic Confession* says simply and faithfully: "He is the Son of God not only from the time that He assumed our nature but from all eternity, as these testimonies, when compared together, teach us'"

ed his title "Son of God". It is a remarkable circumstance because it reverses what might be expected. While the Old Testament was being written, He was already Son of God, but his relationship as Son of Man was future. It is strange that the older revelation should be our chief source of light upon what was to be in the future, while the New should be almost our only source of what had happened in the past. But this is so often God's way — to surprise us.

Let us review what we have of light from the **New Testament** first on that relationship which is encompassed in the title "Son of God". We do not have very much to go on and it is not altogether clear what is meant. Essentially, only two verses are relevant. The first is Colossians 1:15 and 16 which speak of the Lord Jesus Christ as "the image of the invisible God, *the firstborn of every creature* . . . . by whom were all things created that are in heaven and that are in the earth". The second is Revelation 3:14 where we read, "These things saith the faithful and true witness, *the beginning of the creation of God*". From these two passages, it is revealed that the Lord Jesus was not only the firstborn of all creatures, but also the first creation of God. We can do little more than acknowledge that the concept of "eternal begetting" or "eternal generation" is about the only way to speak of what is here revealed, admitting that although it does little more than cover our ignorance, it does express our faith.

The begetting of which the **Old Testament** speaks was at that time still in the future. This prior begetting was already a *fait accomplis*, finished before the creation of anything else. It was, as Augustine rightly said, before the beginning of time itself. For time began with creation: creation was not *in* time but *with* time.* This was a begetting in eternity and therefore a begetting fundamentally different from our concept of begetting; and yet the relationship of the First Person of the Trinity to the Second Person of the Trinity cannot be expressed in any clearer way than by our term Sonship.†

---

* Augustine, *De Civitate Dei*, Bk. XI. 6.

† It has been observed that some form of heirarchy within the Trinity was necessary to the plan of redemption because it necessitated one member of the Trinity being incarnated as man and therefore made, for a season, a little lower than the other members. It was appropriate for the Son to assume an "inferiority" to the Father, but it would never have seemed appropriate for the Father to assume an inferior position to the Son. This principle, clearly implied in Matthew 22:41-45, forms the basis of the Lord's challenge to the Pharisees regarding his own identity.

The "inferiority" of the Son to the Father spoken of in John 14:28 ("My Father is greater than I") has always rightly been viewed as having reference only to Jesus Christ in his role as Son of Man, not as the Son of God. As the Athanasian Creed in one rendering states the matter: "(The Son is) equal to the Father as touching his Godhead: and inferior to the

There are passages which unequivocally state the fact of the pre-existence of the Son of God before He assumed human nature and became also the Son of Man. He Himself said that He was "before Abraham" (John 8:55) and that He shared his Father's glory before the world was (John 17:5). But these verses do not speak of a unique *Sonship*, except by implication. They do assure us of this, namely, that though the Lord Jesus was born in time, his goings forth had been from everlasting (Micah 5:2). W. G. T. Shedd observed that when the Son of God was begotten in eternity, there was no creation of a new essence, "but a modification of an existing one: and this modification is a kind of issue . . . ."* The issue was very God of very God, God of the very substance or essence (*ek tēs ousias*) of the Father, as the Athanasian Creed has it.

So we have One who was the only begotten Son of God, whose begetting is a mystery indeed, begotten in eternity, begotten before all worlds, God with God. This has been the Faith of the Church of God and is the first essential relationship for One who is to be a Mediator between God and man.

But there is, as we have said, a second necessary relationship for a Mediator between God and man — that He be also Son of Man.

The steps whereby this was to be accomplished are first intimated in the Old Testament. Here we find three prophetic utterances, all of which relate to the promise of the Messiah and each of which contains a recurrent phrase, "I will be to Him a Father and He shall be to Me a Son". It is never stated as a present fact, i.e., "I *am* his Father and He *is* my Son"; because what is in view is not the Son of God in that relationship which was already established, but the relationship as the Son of Man — which was yet to be realized in the Incarnation.

Father as touching his manhood". It coincided with the laying aside of his equality with his Father, for the more perfect expression of true manhood (Phil.2:6-8). But even in his now glorified state, it appears that his manhood remains a reality. It will never be relinquished and the relationship to the Father will remain one of subjection as Man throughout eternity (1 Cor.15:28).

Yet in his time of humiliation on earth, He by no means wholly laid aside his equality. For as Frank Weston rightly observed, such a laying aside even for an instant would still require the force of deity to sustain it [*The One Christ*, London, Longmans, Green, 1907). The Son of Man must have continued to exercise his powers as the Son of God to allow his manhood to be expressed. His powers of mind were limited by the circumstance of his humanity, and whenever they were, it was his divine power which prevented these limitations from being overwhelmed.

His glory was never diminished in any way by the assumption of human nature. It was enhanced by the acquisition of a new relationship with God and a new relationship with man. He became what He had not been without ceasing to be what He was.

* Shedd, W. G. T., *Dogmatic Theology*, Grand Rapids, Zondervan, reprint 1969, Vol. I, p. 294.

These three passages are the following:

2 Samuel 7:12-14, 16

And when thy days be fulfilled, and thou shalt sleep with thy fathers, I will set up thy seed after thee, which shall proceed out of thy loins, and I will establish his kingdom.

He shall build an house for my name, and I will establish the throne of his kingdom for ever.

I will be his father, and *he shall be my son* .... and thy house and thy kingdom shall be established for ever before thee: and thy throne shall be established for ever.

1 Chronicles 17:12-14, 16

Furthermore I tell thee that the Lord will build thee an house. And it shall come to pass, when thy days be expired that thou must go to be with thy fathers, that I will raise up for thy seed after thee, which shall be of thy sons; and I will establish his kingdom.

He shall build me an house and I will establish his throne for ever. *I will be his father,* and *he shall be my son* .... and his throne shall be established for evermore.

1 Chronicles 22:10

He shall build an house for my name. and *he shall be my son,* and *I will be his father*; and I will establish the throne of his kingdom over Israel for ever.

Now it may be asked why so much is being made of the fact that this relationship of Father to Son is spoken of as in the future. Since these are prophetic utterances and therefore looking to the future, how else could they have been written except by using the future tense throughout? The answer is that the italicized words could well have been written in the present tense without making the utterance any less a prophetic one. One merely re-reads the passages, changing the italicized words to "I am his Father, and He is my Son".

By this means there would have been no implication of a Sonship *yet to be established.* The use of the future tense in the italicized words must therefore be taken to refer to a relationship that was a future one, a Sonship relation clearly associated with Messiahship.*

There is no doubt that these prophetic statements had a measure of immediate historical fulfillment in the crowning of Solomon. Yet it is equally clear that a much more distant perspective was the real intent of the Lord's promise and that the Son whose kingdom was to have no end was not really Solomon but the Son of Man (Matt.12:40)

---

* The Hebrew scholar will know that these *future* tenses could just as well have been translated as *present* tenses. However, the New Testament in quoting the italicized words settles the issue for us, for here the future tense is used. The Septuagint of these passages is also set in the future tense, indicating how the Jews understood it.

who was a greater than Solomon (Matt.12:42).

Let me summarize the position being presented here. Jesus Christ had two titles — Son of God and Son of Man. These two titles represent in one Person two Sonships: one by reason of his deity and the other by reason of his humanity. The first is the result of an eternal generation and always existed — it is never spoken of as a future relationship. The latter was acquired by incarnation and is properly referred to as future until the Incarnation became a reality. The promise made by the Father in the Old Testament that the Messiah would be his Son in the future has therefore to do with the acquisition of a new kind of Sonship relation, which was to be additional to the eternal Sonship that already existed. When we enter the New Testament we see the fulfillment of this acquisition of a new relationship set forth in very explicit terms.

However, right at the outset we appear to meet with an apparent challenge to this position. In Luke 1:35 the angel announces to Mary that the Holy Spirit will overshadow her and she will conceive and bear a son, and "that holy thing which shall be born of thee *shall be called* the Son of God". Note that the title accorded is not Son of Man but Son of God. Now if the relationship of the Logos as the Son of God has always existed, how does it come about that the angel appears to be speaking of that relationship as yet to be established only by the bringing into the world of Mary's firstborn child? What is the significance of the angel's words "*shall be* called"?

Clearly it must mean only that when her Son is born, He will not simply become the Son of Man but He will be recognized as the Son of God also. In proof of which, many would acknowledge Him to be so by publicly *calling* Him so. It should be realized that the title Son of Man never was man's title for the Lord, but his own title for Himself. The angel did not say to Mary "shall be called 'Son of Man' '' for the simple reason that He never was so called by others — save on one occasion and that was only indirectly and seemingly in scorn (John 12:34). *Why* this was so is not clear but it is a fact — and the angel's predicition was therefore a simple statement of fact, which it would not otherwise have been.*

By contrast, He was time and again, by all classes of people, to be called the Son of God. Among the first to call Him Son of God was John the Baptist (John 1:34). In the wilderness, Satan acknowledged the fact (Luke 4:9). Unclean spirits added their testimony, unwanted

---

* The angel could not tell her that the Son of *God* would be begotten of her, nor that her child would be *called* the Son of *Man*. Both would be contrary to fact. The *Son of God* was begotten before all worlds: her child was never actually addressed as *Son of Man*.

as it was by the Lord Himself (Mark 3:11).   Nathaniel, perceptive of
the truth, recognized it at once (John 1:49).   The man born blind had
every reason to acknowledge it (John 9:35-38).   The centurion, overwhelmed by the events of the crucifixion, confessed it almost despite
himself (Matt.27:54).   And John wrote his Gospel to confirm it
(John 20:31).

Thus by the circumstances of his second begetting He became the
Son of Man, but it was very soon to become apparent that He had
never ceased to be what He had always been — the Son of God.

The question we now wish to answer is, At what precise moment
in time did the Son of God become also Son of Man?   When did an
event always spoken of in the future in the Old Testament become an
event that could be spoken of as now fulfilled?   Was it at the time of
conception, sometime during foetal development, or at the time of
Mary's full term when the child had been delivered?   Do we have any
information in Scripture with which to answer this question precisely?
In short, is there a passage of Scripture which changes the "shall be
my Son" to "now is my Son"?   I believe the answer is in the affirmative, and it provides us with a wonderful behind-the-scenes picture of
events which would be hidden from us but for the fact of revelation.

In Hebrews 10:4-7 and in Hebrews 1:5 and 6 we find the words we
seek.   They are as follows:

Hebrews 10:4-7
For it is not possible that the blood of bulls and goats should
take away sins. Wherefore when he [the Son of God] cometh into
the world, he saith, Sacrifice and offering thou wouldest not, but a
body hast thou prepared me: in burnt-offerings and sacrifices for
sin thou hast had no pleasure. Then said I, Lo, I come (in the volume of the book it is written of me), to do thy will, O God.

Hebrews 1:5 (NIV)
For to which of the angels did God ever say, You are my son,
today have I become your father? Or again, I will be his father
and he will be my son?

The first part of Hebrews 1:5 is a quotation from Psalm 2:7. The
Hebrew word in Psalm 2:7 rendered "begotten" (*yaladh*) has reference
normally to "bringing forth".   When it refers to the time of conception it is always used in a special tense form which gives it the meaning
of "*causing* to beget" rather than actually bringing forth. This is how
it is used throughout Genesis 5 in the long list of 'begats'. After all,
the man does not "bring forth" . . . . In Psalm 2:7 (and thus in Heb.
1:5) it is not used in a "causative" form and therefore refers not to
conception but to birth.   So here the meaning is "This day have I
brought thee forth", as the New International Version has correctly
rendered it.

In the Greek of Hebrews 1:5 where this Old Testament passage is quoted, the word *gennao* is used and it, too, has a double meaning — to conceive and to actually bring forth. In the Greek, only the context can determine which meaning is intended in any particular case.

We do have a further clue I believe in the next verse, as to which sense must be attached to *gennao*. Hebrews 1:6 reads as follows: "When He bringeth in the first begotten into the world, He saith, Let all the angels of God worship Him". And this was precisely fulfilled at the day of his *birth* (as shown in Luke 2:9-14), while there is no evidence whatever that the angels rejoiced at the time of conception. The conception was, as it were, a secret matter — perhaps guarded against because Satan might otherwise have sought to interrupt the divine program, even as he later sought to do so and brought about much weeping at Ramah.

This, then, would seem clearly to indicate that the Father only sent his Son when the vehicle through which He was to assume human nature was fully formed and ready to receive Him. That day, when Mary's firstborn drew the first breath of independent life, the Son of God said, "Lo, I come, a body hast Thou prepared* Me" — becoming at that moment also the Son of Man.

Carl Bernard Moll, who contributed the commentary on Hebrews in *Lange's Commentary on the Holy Scriptures,*† wrote in this connection:

> We are naturally led to look back to that prophecy (Psa.2:7) and to refer the "today" in its historical import to that day in which that "seed" was promised to David, who was to stand to God in the relation of Son and who on that day received .... his birth (*yaladh* rarely meaning "beget" but generally "to be born")...

Luther, it seems to me, was very clear on this matter, holding that Sonship was assumed at the time of *birth*. In the *Book of Concord* (page 608) his position is stated as follows: "In his Tract *Concerning the Last Words of David* which he wrote shortly before his death, Dr. Luther states: 'According to the second, temporal, human birth, the eternal power of God is also given to him — in a temporal way however, and not from eternity. For the humanity of Christ has not, like his deity, existed from eternity, but according to our calendar Jesus the Son of Mary is 1543 years old this year'."

We thus have a series of statements that can be placed together to

---

* On the word "prepared", see footnote on page 256.

† Grand Rapids, Zondervan reprint, Vol. II, p. 37.

provide us with a beautiful scenario that begins with the announcement in heaven that Mary has given birth to her firstborn, and ends with the assumption of that little body by the Son of God to become also the Son of Man, while the angelic hosts break forth into exultation. The "scenes" are as follows:

- A child is supernaturally conceived (Luke 1:35).
- Gestation being completed, the nativity is announced in heaven (Heb.10:5). The Son of God descends and, as a newborn child, becomes the Son of Man (Heb.10:7).
- The Father that day announces this new Sonship (Heb.1:5).
- The angels are commanded to worship Him (Heb.1:6) and the shepherds become witnesses to their exultation (Luke 2:9-14):

> And, lo, the angel of the Lord came upon them, and the glory of the Lord shone round about them; and they were sore afraid.
> And the angel said unto them, Fear not: for, behold, I bring you good tidings of great joy, which shall be to all people.
> For unto you is *born this day* in the city of David a Saviour, which is Christ the Lord.
> And this shall be a sign unto you; Ye shall find the babe wrapped in swaddling clothes, lying in a manger.
> And suddenly there was with the angel *a multitude of the heavenly host* praising God, and saying,
> Glory to God in the highest, and on earth peace, good will toward men.

All these Scriptures conspire to reinforce the view that the Son of God became Man not at the time of conception, nor sometime during foetal development, but only when Mary's firstborn had achieved independent existence. When the angel announced to the shepherds that unto them was *born that very day* a Saviour who is Christ the Lord, then the angelic hosts of heaven burst forth into praise. The nativity, not the conception, was the day of angelic exultation, for it was then that God became Man.

It is a remarkable fact that both in Matthew's account of the period of Mary's pregnancy and in Luke's, particular care seems to have been taken to ensure that the time of preparation was a time of preparation of a body and not the actual fulfillment of Sonship. In Matthew 1:20 the angel tells Joseph that "that which" (neuter) was conceived in Mary was of the Holy Spirit; and Luke 1:35 reinforces this restraint as the angel speaks to Mary of "that holy thing" (again neuter) which shall be born of her. Warfield said rightly,* I believe, "There is no re-

---

* *Biblical and Theological Studies,* Phila., Presby. & Ref. Pub. Co., 1968, p. 165.

duction of the Godhead to the level of a human embryo". And as far as Mary's part is concerned, I think W. G. T. Shedd was equally correct when he observed: "The substance of the virgin had no active, but only a passive disposition to this work; the matter of the body was earthly, the substance of the virgin".† As Augustine said, the Lord created for Himself a human soul to complete that body.‡ Then He entered it, in his own Person as the Son of God, to become the centre of consciousness of a complete human nature. Thus He acquired a new and added relationship to his Father as the Son of Man and to man as the Son of God.

All these wonderful events are set forth for us in such a way that their immediate connectedness can hardly be questioned. In every way a hedge is placed about the circumstances. Even when Mary visited Elizabeth, we find the latter saying (under inspiration), "Whence is this to me that the mother of my Lord should come to me?" (Luke 1:43). She did not say, "that my Lord should come to me", but only that his mother should come to her.

If it matters not what the precise words are, then clearly this method of studying Scripture is a waste of time. But surely we are right to adopt the Lord's own attitude towards the very minute details of the Word of God. He said that even the jot (its smallest letter) and the tittle (the smallest distinguishing mark) are worthy of scrutiny because they will not be lost until they have fulfilled their role as necessary to revelation. In that case, the words we have examined are not being excessively scrutinized. We are not worshipping the letter and neglecting the spirit. The tense *is* important; the gender *does* matter; the meaning *is* crucial. Attention to small cues in the Word of God *is* fundamental to understanding its message.

And what a wonderful insight this all provides into the moment of the Lord's acquisition of a second mode of Sonship to his Father, and of an entirely new relationship to us whom He is not ashamed to call his brethren! Here is the one Son, twice begotten of the Father: first by an eternal generation that was before all worlds, and now by a divine begetting entering into the world of time. Through channels clearly designed to work as they do in the natural order, the Word who created them becomes flesh and dwells among us: and his glory is not dimmed in the process.

---

† Shedd: *Dogmatic Theology*, Grand Rapids, Zondervan reprint, 1969, Vol. III, p. 385.

‡ Augustine: Letter #164, ch. VII. 19.

Chapter 24

IN THE VOLUME OF THE BOOK IT IS WRITTEN OF ME

Then said He unto them,
O fools, and slow of heart
to believe all that the prophets have spoken:
ought not Christ
to have suffered these things,
and to enter into his glory?
And beginning at Moses and all the prophets,
He expounded unto them in all the scriptures
the things concerning Himself.
Luke 24:25-27

I shall never forget the time when I first discovered that the Lord Jesus of the New Testament was the Lord of Hosts, the Jehovah, of the Old: that the God who in Genesis created the heavens and the earth was the Logos who in John's Gospel was made flesh and dwelt among us that we might behold his glory.

And I shall never forget the time when a young Hindu student at a conference where I was speaking of this amazing fact, suddenly broke into the discussion and said — with almost breathless comprehension, "You mean Jesus was the God who created the universe?"

I remember so well, too, sitting on a rug before an open fire with friends around an open Bible — and one of them said, "When people in the Old Testament talked with God face-to-face, was it really Jesus they were talking with?"

It is strange how this astounding truth suddenly strikes one. It is strange because the first chapter of John's Gospel is almost as familiar to most readers and as quotable from memory as John 3:16. We read here that "in the beginning was the Word, and the Word was with God, and the Word was God . . . . All things were made by Him; and without Him was not anything made that was made . . . . And the Word was made flesh and dwelt among us" (John 1:1, 2, 14). For all the familiarity of this passage, the meaning of it seems to escape us.

No wonder the Jews were staggered at his claim when He said, "Before Abraham was, I am" (John 8:58). To claim pre-existence was not so unbelievable to the Jews, for they had already considered reincarnation as a viable explanation not only of the origin of the soul but also of the reappearance in children and grandchildren of the mannerisms and characteristics of parents and grandparents. It was the basis of their questions about the relationship between Elijah and John the Baptist. And it may have been in the back of Nicodemus' mind when he asked, "Can a man enter a second time into his mother's womb and be born?" (John 3:4).

What they found utterly incredible was that the man who stood before them could actually be God, the very God whose name they dare not even mention and whom to see face-to-face was as good as receiving a death sentence (Gen.32:30; Exod.33:20; Jud.6:22, 23; 13:22). Here was a man whose mother and father they knew, whose brothers and sisters were just ordinary people and part of the community, a man who had little or no formal education and belonged to a family which was in no way remarkable and without social status. And this man was now claiming that He had been personally involved with his own Father in heaven as a coworker in the creation and running of the Universe (John 5:17). They understood what He meant — but it was worse than unbelievable: it was blasphemous.

They were appalled at his effrontery: and yet somehow his "presence" checked their resolve whenever they decided it was time to put an end to this nonsense.

In the light of their conviction that sickness was always the result of sinfulness, one can imagine their confusion when He said with absolute assurance to a total cripple, "Thy sins be forgiven thee". For who can forgive sins but God only? They must have thought that God would punish Him at once for his presumption. But God did not punish Him — for it was not presumption at all. The Lord Jesus then proceeded to prove this by saying, in effect, "You are right. But let me show you that my Father will not punish Me but will fully support Me in what I am about to do, for this man is a cripple because of sin and I can forgive sin". Then turning to the cripple, He said, "Arise, and take up thy bed and go thy way unto thy house". And immediately the man got up and took up his bed and went away before them all; and they were amazed and glorified God, saying, "We never saw it on this fashion" (Mark 2:1-12). It must have been clear to the Pharisees that He had indeed forgiven this man his sins and that was why he was healed. This was what made it such an exceptional healing. The Lord Jesus proved his point. Whether He said to the man, "Thy sins be forgiven thee" or "Take up thy bed and walk", made no difference. He had power to command both things, and his power was demonstrated by the result.

Some were overcome by the glory of his Person and simply fell at his feet and worshipped Him. And never once did He refuse their worship, nor rebuke it. Of the ten lepers healed on one occasion, one came back to say, "Thank You, Lord". The record is entirely artless in its simplicity. "One of them, when he saw he was healed, turned back, and with a loud voice glorified God, and fell down at his feet, giving Him thanks" (Luke 17:15, 16). He fell down at God's feet: giving Him thanks.

This, then, is He who, though born later than John by six months and to this extent came after him, was nevertheless *before* him (John 1:27) and whose very shoe latchet John felt himself unworthy to undo. This is He who said to the Pharisees, "and what if you shall see the Son of man ascending up where he was before?" (John 6:62). For this is He who shared the glory of the Father in his pre-incarnate existence (John 17:5).

No man can accept the worship of other men without doing damage to his own soul — unless he is God. The first commandment is that we should worship only God. We are not to bow down and worship any other. And we are so constituted that this commandment is for our own good. To disobey it is not merely morally wrong, it is spiritually damaging both to the worshipper and to the object of veneration. He who therefore accepts the worship of man as God and claims the right to do so is either indeed God or is the most wicked of men, for he is destroying both himself and them. For such a One as Jesus, whose whole life is universally recognized as epitomizing all that is noble in human nature and human relationships, to accept the worship of men as He did without damage either to them or Himself, can only signify that He was (and is) God. "Ye call Me Master and Lord, and ye say well, for so I am" (John 13:13).

In keeping with this claim about his true identity we may note that He knew, and openly proclaimed, the sinlessness of his own life (John 8:46). Never once did He apologize for his own behaviour or leave the slightest impression that He felt He might better have acted otherwise. Never once did He pray for Himself or ask forgiveness of either man or his Father in heaven. Never once did He feel the need to justify his claims of equality with God. He said without apology,

"I and the Father are one" (John 10:30); "Who hath seen Me hath seen the Father" (John 14:9).

But was it such a profoundly new thing — that Jehovah should become man?   Yes, and, No.   It was a new thing that Jehovah should become a man forever without surrendering deity.   But to become man for a particular occasion and for a season only was by no means a new thing.   Jehovah had already upon a number of occasions assumed human form so completely as to be able to walk and talk with man (with Adam and Eve in the Garden, for example), to be entertained at a man's table (by Abraham, for example), to wrestle with a man all night (with Jacob, for example), and to be seen and spoken to by many individuals, and on one occasion by a number of people together (by Moses and Manoah, for example; and by the elders of Israel on Mount Sinai).   Upon all these occasions, the Lord Jesus — the Jehovah of Hosts — must have assumed just that degree of real incarnation in human form as was necessary to make his direct contact or confrontation with man a real though unusual experience for them.

It was in this sense, speaking of his identity as the Jehovah of the Old Testament that He could say, "In the volume of the book it is written of Me" (Heb.10:7).   He need not have meant only that the prophets had everywhere predicted his coming, nor merely that throughout the Scriptures there were "types" of his Person and his work everywhere to be seen by the discerning.   He meant literally that He had walked with men throughout history — personally, concretely, even intimately at times.   He had, in fact, assumed a form of embodiment on numerous occasions in order to mediate between God and man, appearing in truly human aspect with such similitude that they scarcely showed surprise until, in retrospect, they suddenly realized that their encounter had been with no other than Jehovah Himself.

In Eden, Adam and Eve must surely have supposed themselves to be talking to one of their own kind.   After they had disobeyed, it does not appear that they had any reason to suppose hiding themselves was a waste of time.   Their action suggests that they genuinely believed they could somehow conceal what had happened from this One with whom they shared the Garden.   They heard his voice, and perhaps they heard his footsteps.   The Hebrew only tells us that they heard the *sound* of the Lord walking in the Garden.   Was this imagination?   Does a spiritual being make a noise like this?   In the Lord's post-resurrection appearances, his disciples are never said to have heard Him coming: He always appeared suddenly and silently in their midst.   Evidently in his dealings with Adam and Eve He approached them much as we would approach our friends — i.e., as a human being approaches another human being.

When the Lord approached Abraham, this is how He came — visibly from some little distance, giving Abraham warning as we are apt to give our friends warning. This is human behaviour. Abraham ran to meet Him (Gen.18:2). When he prepared food, did he believe that his visitor would only eat it in a token sense, transmuting it of necessity (mouthful by mouthful) into some ethereal substance commensurate with the ghostly nature of his guest? Or did he in fact arrange a place with cushions for his guest to be seated at his "table"? And did Jacob wrestle so vigorously with some purely spirit form as to put his hip out of joint?

Must we not assume that at least upon these occasions (if not all occasions) He whom all these people had to deal with was really there in very truth, accomodated somehow to their physical senses in a way that for the short interval of the experience left no doubt about the reality of Him? Must we not conclude that on these occasions the Lord Jehovah already partook of our nature in some sense: certainly as long as man himself has existed — and perhaps indeed before man was created in order that man might be created *in his image*?* And not a few of these divine interferences in human history must therefore have involved a kind of pre-incarnation "incarnation". It was no new thing or strange thing that He should one day say, "Lo, I come" when it was announced in heaven that a body was prepared for Him. Only, He was now to come among men in a new way, to remain permanently embodied.

We tend to overlook these pre-incarnation incarnations because we mistakenly suppose that whenever the record speaks of such appearances, it was God the Father who was seen. I believe it can be established from John 1:18 that every local manifestation of Jehovah recorded in the Old testament must have been a visitation of the Lord Jesus, anticipating the time when He would enter lastingly into just this kind of human association but by a more permanent form of incarnation in order that He might become Saviour and not merely Mediator.

Consider the wording in John 1:18. "No man hath seen God at any time; the only begotten Son who is in the bosom of the Father, He hath made Him known". I believe the sentence requires us to understand that *God* is to be identified as the *Father* in the first part of this sentence. So that we may legitimately rephrase this sentence: "No man hath seen God the Father at any time; the only begotten

---

* After all, we are to be conformed to his image (Rom.8:29) and even now, as his people, partake of something of the divine image (2 Pet.1:4).

Son who is in his bosom, hath made Him known". From which we must assume that those who saw the Lord, who spoke with Him, who had face-to-face encounters with Him in the Old Testament were not, in the personal sense, face-to-face with the Father *but face-to-face with the Son*. Unless we make this assumption, it is impossible to reconcile John 1:18 with the numerous theophanies of the Old Testament.

But can we demonstrate this proposition by a direct appeal to Scripture? I believe we can. And one way in which this can be done has not generally been noted by commentators in the past.

Let us take a few examples of such theophanies in which the identity of the One seen is established for us in the New Testament. Establishing identity presents no problems in such cases. For example, Isaiah tells us that he had a vision of the Lord (Isa. 6:1 ff.) and that he was given a commission to go and speak to the people of Israel even though they would refuse to hear him. In John 12:27 ff., this incident is referred to again. A close parallel is drawn between Isaiah's situation and the experience of the disciples who had also had a vision of their Lord and yet had discovered, to their surprise, that Israel still refused to hear what they had to say. John points out how similar the situation was, and makes the observation that it was really the same divine figure giving the same commission to his messengers with the same predictably unfruitful outcome — in both cases. So he says: "These things said Isaiah when he saw *his* glory and spake of *Him*". He whom Isaiah saw was the same Lord. The Jehovah of Isaiah and the Lord of the disciples was One and the same Person.

Throughout the Psalms, the work of creation is ascribed to Jehovah, and in John 1:1-3 and Colossians 1:15,16 the work of creation is ascribed to the Lord Jesus. In Hebrews 1:7-13 we find a number of such passages from the Psalms drawn together and identified clearly with the Lord Jesus, the divine Son of God, who had walked across the pages of history for thirty-three years. This Man, born of a virgin mother, was none other than Jehovah who had laid the foundation of the earth and fashioned the heavens!

Many passages in the Old Testament which we assume have reference to the Father are really references to the Son. Thus Exodus 17:2 and 7 records how the children of Israel tempted the Lord: and 1 Corinthians 10:9 tells us that this Lord was Jesus Christ. In Malachi 3:1 He who calls Himself the Lord of Hosts says, "I will send my messenger and he shall prepare the way before *Me*". In Matthew 3:3, Mark 1:3 and Luke 3:4 the identity of this messenger as John the Baptist is clearly established. The *ME* of Malachi 3:1 must accordingly have been the Lord Jesus, the Lord of Hosts of the Old Testament!

In Zechariah 12:10 we read: "And I will pour down upon the

house of David and upon the inhabitants of Jerusalem the spirit of grace and supplications: and they shall look upon ME whom they have pierced". It is important to note the wording here, since John 19:37 quotes this passage slightly differently by converting the word ME to HIM. But the ME in Zechariah 12:10 correctly represents the original Hebrew. Since the speaker is the Lord, Jehovah — according to Zechariah 12:4, 7 and 8 — the ME who is to be pierced must also be Jehovah.

Now there are a number of passages in the Old Testament in which the Trinity is not only intimated but the individual persons within the Trinity are identified for us by a simple device which, although it has seldom been commented upon, has nevertheless been faithfully adopted by many of the scholarly versions of the Old Testament, including the *King James Version.* The Old Testament speaks of God under various titles — Lord, God, Lord God, Lord of Hosts, the Almighty, and so forth. The title I wish to discuss here is the couplet *Lord God* which in many versions (*King James Version, Revised Standard Version, Revised Version, American Standard Version,* etc.) is printed using two different type styles. The remarks which follow apply equally to this couplet whether it is qualified by a personal pronoun or not. What I have to say therefore is true whether the text reads the Lord God, or the Lord thy God, or the Lord our God, and so forth. In short, the comments which follow relate to any combination of the two words *Lord* and *God*, but they *only* apply when these two words are presented together as a couplet. The rule I am about to explain cannot be applied where the word *Lord* or the word *God* appears by itself. This is an important observation to note carefully because many friends who have found this discovery a most exciting one have tried to apply it to the two words when they appear singly, only to find it cannot be so applied; and so the discovery has served to confuse rather than enlighten.

These two words, this couplet, will be found sometimes printed as (a) Lord GOD and in other instances as (b) LORD God. This may seem to be a small difference but it is an important one and it has been done to reflect faithfully a difference in the original Hebrew. In order to make sure that these distinctions are clearly understood, Fig. 18 (a) and (b) shows the difference between these two forms on an enlarged scale.

FIGURE 18 (a)

Lower case   Small capitals

Lord GOD

FIGURE 18 (b)

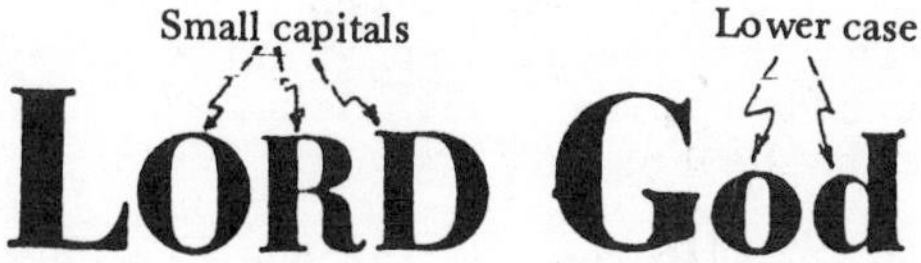

Small capitals   Lower case

LORD God

Now the first type style is used to represent an original in the Hebrew which may be transliterated as *Adonai Jehovah,* and the second as *Jehovah Elohim,* It is not important in the present context to explain why these forms of type were originally chosen by the scholars who produced the King James Version, but it is only necessary to note that the two combinations appear to have a different reference even though they share the name *Jehovah* (or Yahweh as it may originally have been) in common.   These two combinations are apparently intended by their difference to distinguish between two Persons in the Godhead. Thus, as an example, in the King James Version Isaiah 48:16 and 17 reads:

> Come ye near unto me, hear ye this.   I have not spoken in secret from the beginning; from the time that it [i.e., the beginning] was, there am I: and now the Lord GOD and his Spirit hath sent me.
> Thus saith the Lord, thy Redeemer, the Holy One of Israel, I am the LORD thy God who teacheth thee to profit, who leadest thee by the way thou shouldest go.

Looking closely at this, one sees that in verse 16 three Persons are clearly involved: two are responsible for the sending, and one is sent. One of the senders is the Holy Spirit, the other is identified as the Lord GOD.   The speaker ("me") is the Redeemer, the Holy One of Israel, whom we know without doubt to be the Lord Jesus.   Since we can now identify both the One who is sent and the Spirit who sends Him, we can automatically establish that the other sender, the Lord GOD , is God the Father.   We can also establish from verse 17 that the title, the LORD thy God , is the Jesus Christ of the Gospels.   We thus have this key:

> Lord GOD , in which the second word is entirely capitalized, is the *Father.*
> LORD God , in which the first word is entirely capitalized, is the *Son.*

As a simple mnemonic aid, we may note that when the word GOD is written entirely in capitals, God the Father is in view; and when the word LORD is set entirely in capitals, the Lord Jesus Christ is in view. With this key we may look profitably at some important passages rather similar to Isaiah 48:16 and 17.

rather similar to Isaiah 48:16 and 17. For example, in Isaiah 61:1 and 2 we have the following statement:

> The Spirit of the Lord GOD is upon me; because the Lord hath anointed me to preach good tidings unto the meek, He hath sent me to bind up the brokenhearted and to proclaim liberty to the captives, and the opening of the prison to them that are bound;
> To proclaim the acceptable year of the Lord . . . .

Everyone who is familiar with the New Testament will remember that this is the passage which Jesus Christ read in the synagogue (Luke 4:18, 19) to an audience spellbound by the graciousness of his words. When He had finished reading He closed the book, returned it to the minister, and sat down. And then He said (verse 21): "This day is this Scripture fulfilled in your ears". In short, He was saying that the reference here was to Himself, He was the *me* in this passage. Since there is no question as to the identity of the *me*, Lord GOD must clearly refer to the Father.

Now I do not want this to become too involved, but a note of caution is necessary at this point. When the words *Lord* and *God* stand alone and not joined together as a couplet such as we have been examining, either word may apply equally to the Father or to the Son or to the Holy Spirit, indiscriminately. Thus it is not possible merely by reference to the type style to know with assurance the identity of the speaker when either word stands *alone*. The key which we have been discussing above applies only when the two words appear as a couplet. Thus in the last two references considered above, the couplets 'the Lord thy GOD' and 'the LORD thy God' can both be assessed by this rule as to the identity of the Person intended, whether the Father or the Son. But the simple title *Lord*, as it occurs in Isaiah 61:1 for example (and in thousands of other passages), cannot be so identified except by some other means. This is the first important fact to bear in mind. The second important point to bear in mind is that this key is limited entirely to the Old Testament. It cannot be applied in the New Testament which is translated from the Greek, not from the Hebrew.*

There are, however, many illustrations of the common rule. Consider, for example, the import of Zechariah 14:4 and 5: "And

---

* The situation is complicated a little bit, as the reader will discover when seeking to apply these rules, by the fact that the Lord Jesus as the Second Adam and Federal Head of a new race is occasionally spoken of as *Father* (see, for example, Isa.9:6). And the Father appears occasionally in the role of Saviour (see, for example, Isa.63:8), a circumstance which is reflected in 1 Timothy 1:1. So that now and then the Lord Jesus appears in the Old Testament as Lord GOD, and the Father as LORD God . The context itself never leaves the issue in doubt.

his feet shall stand in that day upon the Mount of Olives, and the LORD thy God shall come with all his saints". This passage must be read in the light of two important facts revealed in the New Testament. First, that the Lord Jesus ascended into heaven *from the Mount of Olives*. Luke 24:50, 51 tells us that "He led them out as far as to Bethany [which is a village on the east slope of the Mount of Olives], and He lifted up his hands and blessed them. And it came to pass that while He blessed them, He was parted from them, and carried up into heaven". Secondly, that as He ascended from the Mount of Olives (according to Acts 1:10-12), "Two men stood by them in white apparel and said, Ye men of Galilee, why stand ye gazing up into heaven? This same Jesus who is taken up from you into heaven, shall so come in like manner as ye have seen Him go into heaven". Thus as He ascended *from* the Mount of Olives, so shall his feet "in that day" once again touch down upon the Mount of Olives. "This same Jesus" of Acts 1:11 is the LORD thy God who is to "come with all the saints with Him", according to Zechariah 14:5.

In Isaiah 50:4-7 there is another clear illustration of identification by the distinctive use of type style.

> The Lord GOD hath given Me the tongue of the learned, that I should know how to speak a word in season to him that is weary....
> The Lord GOD hath opened mine ear, and I was not rebellious, neither turned away back.
> I gave my back to the smiters, and my cheeks to them that plucked off the hair; I hid my face from shame and spitting.
> For the Lord GOD will help me: therefore shall I not be confounded; therefore have I set my face like a flint . . . .

The Lord GOD is here, without doubt, the Father; and it is the Lord Jesus who was both given the tongue of the learned to speak a word in season to him that is weary but also who set his face like a flint to go up to Jerusalem and gave his back to the smiters.

In Isaiah 56:8 we have one more such illustration: "The Lord GOD who gathered the outcasts of Israel said, 'Yet will I gather others unto *Him*, besides those that are (already) gathered unto Him'." Manifestly this reflects the "other sheep" of which the Lord Jesus speaks in John 10:16 and 29, and even more specifically in John 17:6 and 9. The *Him* of this passage is therefore clearly the Chief Shepherd Himself. And the Lord GOD must be the Father.

It seems appropriate that the Father should wipe away the tears from his children when the day of our true rest finally comes (Rev. 21:4) and accordingly the Old Testament pre-vision of this wonderful day in Isaiah 25:8 acknowledges this fact by the appropriate type style of the words, the Lord GOD:

> He (the Son) will swallow up death in victory; and the LORD GOD (the Father) will wipe away tears from all faces and the rebuke of his people shall He take away from off all the earth.

It is a wonderful thing to reflect upon the fact that the One whom Adam and Eve walked with in Eden was the LORD God , the Lord Jesus Christ.   The form of the title of deity and the type style used throughout the Eden story (Gen.2:7, 8, 9, 15, 16, 18, 19, 21, 22; and 3:1, 8, 9, 13, 14, 21, 22, 23) clearly demonstrates this.   Here we have consistently Lord GOD (with emphasis upon the word Lord) thus telling us it was Jehovah with whom Adam and Eve conversed so freely.

Now it is also worthy of note that the Jews understood there must be a Mediator of some kind not only between God and man but also between God and the world which He had created.   They believed that pure spirit either would not or could not act directly upon the physical order.   They came to view the One who stood as Mediator in this interaction as analogous to the part which is played by the spoken word as a bridge between thought and action.   Thus they held that the world was created by the spoken Word, and they referred to this Mediator by the name *Memra*, a Hebrew noun which signifies *Word*. Some of the Jewish paraphrases or *Targums* of the Old Testament substituted the word *Memra* wherever the original text speaks of Jehovah as acting directly upon his creation.   They had thus, in effect, recognized what we have spoken of previously as the pre-incarnation incarnation of Jehovah.   As an example of how they used the word, we may note that in the *Targum of Onkelos*, Genesis 3:10 is rendered: "And (Adam) said, I hid from the voice of the Memra and I was afraid because I was naked".   The *Targum* of Psalm 110:1 reads: "The Lord said unto his Word".

From all of which it is clear to the eye of faith the the Lord Jesus as Jehovah pre-existed his incarnation, and looms large indeed throughout the whole of the Old Testament, mediating between God (who is pure spirit) and the world and man which belong within the physical order.   The difference in this mediation in the two testaments is that in the Old He mediated with a kind of temporary incarnation whereas in the New He is mediating as embodied Man for ever.   And as such a Mediator, the Incarnation has not diminished but expanded his office, though He is still the same Lord and still one with his Father in heaven.

He who came down from his glory to take possession of that little body in order that He might truly experience our manhood, could indeed say, "In the volume of the Book it is written of Me"!   There are no "odd references" here.   The Son of God is everywhere to be found from Genesis to Malachi.

Joseph called his name *Jesus* as instructed by the angel. Why *Jesus*? *Jesus* is the Greek form of the Hebrew name *Joshua* (as Heb. 4:8 plainly shows*), which in turn is a shortened form of the original compounded name *Jehovah-Saviour*. His identity as both the Son of God and the Son of Man was therefore foreshadowed in his original name as Jehovah and Saviour, for it was because He would be a Saviour of his people that He received the name Jesus.

How wonderfully was this foretold in Isaiah 9:6, "For unto us a child is born, unto us a son is given". He was indeed, as the Son of Man, born as a child; He was indeed, as the Son of God, given for our salvation (John 3:16). Only the Child was born, not the Son. The Son of God was from all eternity.

---

* In the Septuagint, the Book of Joshua is "The Book of Jesus" and the name *Joshua* always appears in the form *Jesus*.

Chapter 25

WHAT IS MAN, AND THE SON OF MAN,
THAT THOU VISITEST HIM?

When I consider the heavens — the work of thy fingers,
the moon and the stars — which Thou hast ordained;
what is man
that Thou art mindful of him?
Thou hast made him
a little lower than the angels,
and has crowned him with glory and honour!
Psalm 8:3-5

My delights are with the sons of men.
Proverbs 8:31

A colleague of mine walked into my laboratories one day and said, "We've had this thing around the house ever since I was a kid. Any idea what it is?"

We both looked at it carefully. It was made of wood, obviously shaped by hand, about six inches long, and asymmetrical along its axis. It weighed only a few ounces and it had been nicely finished with a good lacquer. I have always felt I was quite sharp at this kind of guessing game . . . . but I could't identify it at all. Apparently nobody else had been able to either, not even the National Museum of Canada!

It was not simply a piece of wood that someone had doodled into shape as the fancy of the moment had suggested. It had without doubt been made for some purpose, and there were even unmistakeable wear marks on it in one place indicating that it had actually been made for something.   But what had it been made *for*?

And there's the point.   We could not say what it *was* because we could not imagine what it was *for*.   The fact that we could identify it as to its weight, colour, size, shape, or any of its other physical or chemical characteristics which are measureable, still did not tell us what it was because we did not know what it was for.   As far as I know, he never did find out.   One day, someone will say, "Oh, I know what that's for . . . ." and the problem of identity will be solved.

Nor can we say what *man* is — though we may know a great deal about him: his physical characteristics, his chemical constitution, his physiological functioning, and even his psychological make-up — unless we know what he is *for*.   We shall only really know what man is when we understand God's object in creating him.   As Aristotle was wise enough to observe, "The nature of man is not what he is born *as*, but what he is born *for*".[229]

We can see in a measure how each plant and animal fits into the web of life, even perhaps how each elemental substance in nature contributes to the whole; but man seems alien in some way to the scheme of things.   He is the great disturber of nature, the destroyer of order, the unbalancing factor in the web of life.   Among all creatures, man alone seems to be without the proper equipment for the survival of his species except by plundering the rest of the world in which he lives.   The pattern of his life as an individual and as a species is essentially destructive even in the midst of his most creative activities, and suicidal even when his objective is precisely the opposite. He is capable of a beastliness that is not of the beasts, and of aggressiveness that seems totally unrelated to the kind of aggressiveness animals display in their will to live.

He is, in fact, a fallen creature.   And yet he is so constituted that he can upon occasion do such noble things as to surprise even himself. He is capable of being a demon, but also of being a saint.   And his creative talents are, it seems, almost unlimited — whether in the composing of music, the building of a plane, designing a cathedral, or rocketing to the moon with a precision measured in mere seconds in terms of touch-down time and mere yards in terms of landing site.

For a host of reasons, such potential for good or for evil does not reside in the animal kingdom below him.   The form and functioning of his brain, his eyes, his ears, his face, his tongue and throat, his neck, his torso, his arms and his hands, his knee structure and his feet, all contribute in unique ways towards his being what he is.   His upright posture frees his hands, and his freed hands become an extension of his brain — even as his mobility of facial expression and his capacity for speech and the use of symbols become an extension of his mind. Above all else, he has a spirit with a different destiny from that of the animals (Eccl.3:21) and is a creature with a capacity for redemption that constitutes him a unique being, placing him in a "kingdom" by himself.   He is neither angel (without body) nor animal (without redeemable spirit).   He is man: made at first in the image of God, a child of eternity, and potentially capable of being a very habitation of God Himself.

Moreover, there are today some authorities who are prepared to say that in a sense man *is* the measure of all things, even of the very size and structure of the Universe itself! It seems clear now that man could not continue to exist, nor would he ever have come into being, unless the Universe had been constituted as it is.   This speck of dust which is our earth, floating in the immensity of space, would never have emerged as man's proper habitat except for the fact that the very constitution of the Universe itself has contributed to its being what it is — a home for living things of which man is both the objective and the justification.

Was the Universe really created for our earth, and our earth for man? Quite possibly. John A. Wheeler wrote in all seriousness that a very good case can be made for the view that it is not the Universe that determines the size of men but man who governs the size of the Universe! [230]

Even Sir Julian Huxley, as we have already seen, went so far as to admit that the kind of nature man has, including the power of conceptual thought and of making delayed decisions and moral judgments, can hardly be supposed to exist in any other type "of primate body and primate brain" than we observe in man. [231] And only such a Universe as we observe around us seems capable of accomodating this kind of primate body and primate brain.

The reader may recall Hugo St. Victor's words, written nearly nine hundred years ago:

> The world was made for the body,
> and the body was made for the spirit,
> and the spirit was made for God:
> the spirit that it might be brought into subjection unto God,
> the body that it might be brought into subjection unto the spirit,
> and the world that it might be brought into subjection unto the body.

It seems to us now that Hugo St. Victor was wrong only in this, that he should have prefaced his observation by adding also that "the Universe was made for the world". So he is suggesting — in answer to the question, "What was man made for?" — that man was made for God; and we would add that in the final analysis the Universe was made for man.

But in what way was man made for God?   And why was it necessary, if this is true, that he should be made the kind of creature he is?

Romans 8:20 tells us that this creature was made subject to failure *in hope*. In hope of what? And what does it mean to be "made subject to failure"? Well, I think it means that man had to be made free to choose, and this freedom of choice inevitably made him subject to failure. But God had a plan to cover the contingency of failure: and the fulfillment of this plan, the plan of redemption, necessitated that man be made just such a creature as he is — a redeemable creature. And by this I mean he has to be given just such a constitution — physical, chemical, moral, and in every other way — as he does indeed have. This constitution was given to man for one very important reason above all others, a reason which theologians have often tended to overlook. The reason relates to the circumstances surround the incarnation of God as Man.

In Part I (page 169 f.) I have used an analogy regarding the design of the human body. The analogy involved the building of a house for a particular purpose. A man builds a house to suit the occupant for which it is intended. Thus he designs a hive for bees, a sty for pigs, a stable for horses, a kennel for his dog. The design of each house is predetermined by the use to which it will be put. And man's body was designed as a habitation for a creature made in the image of God, and to this extent his house was to be a house of God. It might be more truthful to say a house *for* God. This is still true in spite of the Fall. Each individual who is born again is reconstituted individually, and not merely collectively, a Temple of God. As Paul says, "Your body is the temple of God" (1 Cor.3:16), and this is one reason why he lays such emphasis upon the sanctity of the body. "I beseech you therefore brethren, by the mercies of God, that ye present your *bodies* a living sacrifice, wholly, acceptable unto God, which is your reasonable service" (Rom.12:1). We are to return this house to the original Owner who designed it for his own purposes — which indeed is a reasonable thing to do. It is an awesome thought that God should take up residence in a human body, yet the New Testament is full of the idea. As Paul said in writing to the Galatians (2:20), "I live, yet not I, but Christ liveth in me". And in Romans 7:18 he defines what he means by "in me": he says, "that is, in my flesh".

The Incarnation of Jesus Christ as Man demonstrated once for all the fitness of the human body to be just this — a house of God. He did not take upon Him the nature of angels but of human seed (Heb. 2:16). The body in which He expressed Himself was a body like ours. It was not identical with ours (as we have already noted — see reference # 223), for ours is a body that is defiled by sin both inherited and actual. But his body was a human body in the most perfect sense, for it was the same as Adam's body when it was first created. The powerful persuasion that bodily existence is somehow evil is really pagan in origin and stems from the universal experience that while the spirit is willing the flesh is weak.   Sinfulness in action seems to be rooted somehow in a corruption of body.   But this is entirely due to the consequences of the Fall, not to the fact that God created man an embodied spirit.   The body is essential to man, a uniquely designed vehicle for the housing of his spirit: and it was entirely worthy of its design to carry the image of God — which no other animal body is.

When Solomon was preparing to build the Temple, God gave him very specific instructions. He did not simply say, "Build Me a temple", which He might well have done — for Solomon had plenty of temples of other gods all around him which might have served for prototypes. Indeed when he received instructions for this Temple, he may have felt that these other pagan temples were more impressive, larger, more richly equipped.   But God was not planning to build a house for Himself merely by elaborating upon the designs of other houses already in existence.   Perhaps this also reflects the fact that He did not build Adam's body by merely copying animal bodies which were prototypes. But as Solomon's Temple made use of materials and structures and architectural principles already in existence, so when God designed a body for Adam, He made use of materials and structures and architectural principles already existing in other animal bodies. However, in certain ways Adam's body was unique, and the chief aspect of its uniqueness stemmed from the purpose it was designed to serve. The body of Adam was to serve as a housing for creatures made in the *image* of God, and one day it was to serve for the incarnation of God *Himself.*

It was not therefore just another electrochemical machine. It was designed to make it possible for God to express Himself perfectly in terms of human personality: and there are millions of "electrochemical machines" that function successfully as living organisms which could never make a suitable housing for the purposes of divine incarnation. Man's body was created in such a form that the Creator Himself could assume it for a season as his own housing without in any way demeaning or violating his own divine nature.   Such a house, like Solomon's Temple, was not merely to be like any other pagan temple already in existence, any more than Adam's body was merely a copy of some other animal body already in existence.   It was to be exceptional, "exceedingly magnifical" (1 Chron.22:5) as the King James put it.

And so it was, originally.   It must have been glorious indeed. Imagine a human body which, despite all the defilement of sin to which it became subjected, still survived with its energies largely unimpaired for nearly a thousand years!   The body in which Jesus Christ took up residence for some thirty-three years was Adam's body recovered — and it, too, was "magnifical". The divine Architect had built it for Himself in the first place. "Every house is builded by some man; but He that built all things is God" (Heb.3:4), so we may be sure the Lord's body was not the tumble-down house in which we struggle through life. His body magnificently supported Him daily as He lived out his life among men: and it provided perfectly all the resources for the expression of the whole spectrum of his divine nature. His presence in the body was so magnificent that even the most callous of his enemies had to step back sometimes in awe, and they only had the courage to abuse Him because He deliberately veiled his glory. There is, even yet, an aura about this human body that is revealed now and then when a man draws very near to the Lord, even as it was with Moses when he came down from Mount Sinai (2 Cor.3:13).

There was, and is, nothing in the constitution of the human body (except in so far as it has been "defiled" by sin — Phil.3:21) that God is ashamed to take unto Himself and employ as a dwelling place. Undefiled by sin and indwelt by the Lord Himself, a superb human body appeared on the stage of human history and men worshipped without shame or hesitation the One who possessed it.

As we have seen, one of the fundamental differences between his body and ours was its potential for endless continuance (Heb.7:16), exactly as Adam's had been at first. Yet this did not mean it was a body incapable of fatigue or thirst or hunger — or physical injury. Adam unfallen was still given the night for rest, fruit trees for food, and a river from which to draw water. But it certainly was a body capable of expenditure of effort far beyond our own present resources even as his mind enormously exceeded ours in its intellectual reach. His energies nevertheless could be depleted, for He became aware of the depletion when a woman in the crowd touched Him and was healed (Mark 5:30).

Now such a body with its potential for unending continuance, and unfailing transmission of healing power to others, and housing what must be described literally as the mind of God, is not a mere animal body. In some way which it is not possible for us to grasp, it was different — fundamentally different. It is quite possible that with all the modern tools of research we now have at our disposal we might have identified some areas of physiological difference.[232] But the effects of the Fall upon *our* bodies have obliterated many of these differences and blurred others so that the human organism now looks like any other animal body. Indeed in some ways we are far less efficient organisms than they. But the human body unfallen made it a perfect vehicle for the Incarnation of the Creator Himself, who designed it. *This* body was what our body was intended to be and was designed to be and would have been but for the Fall.

The human body, then, is no mean organism. It is, in fact, still capable of serving as a worthy Temple for the majesty of God, a divine residence for the display of God's glory in the Person of Jesus Christ. It became such when conceived by the Holy Spirit and born of woman in perfection.

Thus, man is not a creature of spiritual significance who merely happens to have the kind of body he does and who might just as easily have been equipped with any other kind of body. He is a creature whose uniqueness from the point of view of his humanness is as much dependent upon the structure of his body as upon the nature of the spirit which animates it. It is quite wrong to imagine that the structure of man's body is incidental and that he might have been built like a giraffe or a dog or a mouse — or even an ape — and still have fulfilled the role for which he was created. The body that man inhabits was built with the capability of housing even God Himself. And the universe was designed to support that house, and probably when we know enough, we shall find everything in this universe contributes in some way to the sustaining of it.

In the final analysis, the creation of the body of Adam was really nothing less than the first step in the preparation of the body of Christ. And to this end the universe was made as it is. When seen in the perspective of history, man had to be created in the image of God in order that God might in due time appear in the image of man for his redemption. The nature of the first human body was thus predetermined entirely by God's intention to come as man's Redeemer. God incarnate, and man incorporate: each was the prototype of the other, depending upon perspective. Adam's body was designed for God because, as Irenaeus said, man's creation was for redemption. Here is where we shall one day find a complete answer to the often asked question, "What is the purpose of such a universe?"

So what is man? He is to be assessed by the purpose for which he was created. He was made for redemption and therefore made "redeemable": and this redeemableness hinged upon the incarnation and sacrifice of the Lord Jesus Christ who took upon Himself our human form. The means of man's redemption required that he should be a creature whose constitution, body and spirit alike, could be assumed by the Redeemer in order to effect our salvation, and this assumption must be possible without incongruity with his own divine nature.

Such, then, had to be the total constitution of man and such it has manifestly proved to be. In this we therefore have the answer not only to the question, "What is man?" but even a more basic question, "What is man *for*?" *Man is for God.*

PART IV

TRIUMPH
OVER DEATH

The Lord Jesus Christ did not merely choose the time of his dying: He was in a position to choose whether to die AT ALL.

Then He died *on* the cross but not *because* of it; and He died purely by an act of will.

Having disengaged spirit and body in death, three days later He personally re-engaged them in a bodily resurrection.

SUMMARY INTRODUCTION

So we come to the final act in the drama of the seed of the woman.
We have seen the provision of a perfect body, and we now observe
how the Lord Jesus Christ gave expression to his Person as Man,
through that body. We shall explore a few examples of how the
perfection of his character was displayed under conditions of appalling difficulty which increased until the moment of his death: and we
examine not merely the WHY of his dying but also the HOW of it in
the light of what has been learned thus far from this study. And from
it we are able to see how wonderfully the eternal sacrifice which was
made by the *last* Adam proved to be a full, perfect, and sufficient
satisfaction to redeem those who were lost through the disobedience
of the *first.*

Adam's sin had introduced, for man, two kinds of death: spiritual
death and physical death. These two kinds of death occur for us in
this order. Spiritual death occurs when the spirit is separated from
God by disobedience: physical death occurs when the spirit is separated from the body. We suffer the first death *actively* and by
conscious choice: the second we suffer *passively* — it happens to us.
Thus we die spiritually by an act of will: whereas we die physically by
a form of execution — willy-nilly. It appears that the first death is
probably an event whereas the second seems to be a process.

Jesus Christ suffered these two kinds of death on our behalf in
order to make our redemption complete. As with us, his spiritual
death took the form of separation from the Father: his physical
death resulted by the departure of his spirit from his body. Unlike us,
his spiritual death was passive, imposed upon Him for our sakes, and

contrary to his will but not to his resignation. His physical death was active: He was entirely responsible for it.

Both deaths occurred on the cross — the spiritual death preceding the physical death. The first was necessary in order that our SINS might be forgiven, the second that our SIN might be taken away (or put away). In Him our salvation is therefore complete, for both spirit and body are to be redeemed.

On the Day of Atonement, two goats — not one — were sacrificed. One was "sent away" into the wilderness, there to perish in isolation, the sins of God's people having been laid upon its head. This goat represented the break in fellowship between the Son and the Father during the three hours of darkness. The other goat was slain and its blood sprinkled on the altar in the Holy of Holies. The first sacrifice was an offering for SINS; the second was a SIN-offering.

These two requirements, an offering for SINS and an offering for SIN,* were both fulfilled by the Lord Jesus Christ on the day He made an atonement. Since these sacrificial animals which prefigured Him as Saviour and Redeemer had to be perfect, so He also had to be perfect both in spirit and in body.

In the Old Testament ritual on the Day of Atonement, the two goats were brought before the judges in the Temple. They were, first of all, declared satisfactory: and then both were "slain", one by banishment, the other by being slaughtered. Two goats were required because a single animal could not physically be both ritually slain *and* banished.

But the Lord Jesus Christ fulfilled both roles. His innocence having been established, He was then in a position to be appointed to both kinds of dying — under circumstances which were altogether exceptional. Moreover, the manner of his dying (by crucifixion) was not at all customary in Jewish law. Yet the mode of his execution was necessary in order to provide a stage which would allow both kinds of dying to be fulfilled.

But this is not the final act. The Lamb of God has been sacrificed. In this sacrifice He was both victim and High Priest. *He* offered *Himself*. It was then necessary that He, as High Priest, present the blood

---

* There is a vital distinction in the New Testament between the word SINS and the word SIN (when used generically). SINS are to be distinguished from SIN as the fruits of an evil are to be distinguished from their root, and as symptoms are to be distinguished from the disease. SINS are committed offences: SIN is the defect which we inherit from Adam by natural generation. SINS must be forgiven — for we are morally accountable for them. SIN, the disease, is not forgiven but covered (in the Old Testament), and cleansed, or taken away, or put away (in the New Testament). SINS are the cause of our spiritual death: SIN is the cause of our physical death.

of his own sacrifice before the very presence of God in the Holy of Holies which is in heaven.   For this, his bodily resurrection was essential.

He then returned in Person, bodily, to present Himself before his people, as the High Priest under the old Covenant presented himself again before his people — the signal that his atoning sacrifice had been accepted before God.   Any other form of resurrection than a bodily one would have placed in doubt the efficacy of his role as our sacrificial victim and his role as our great High Priest.

We may think of the Lord's work in salvation as a purely spiritual exercise.   Yet so much that He accomplished depended upon the possession of a *body*.   It was through his *body* that He lived out a perfect human life and thus qualified as our sacrificial victim.   It was through his *body* that He was able to die.   And it was in his resurrection *body*, a body which was not allowed to see corruption, that He returned to proclaim God's acceptance of the sacrifice He had made.

Man is neither a spirit who happens to have a body, nor a body that happens to be endowed with a spirit.   Man is a body/spirit *entity*.   The application of the redemptive process hinges not only upon his spiritual nature but also upon his physiology: indeed upon *His* and upon ours equally.   Unless these conditions of his life were fulfilled He *could* not die as a sacrificial victim, nor would his sacrifice have applied *for us*.

Chapter 26

LAMB OF GOD AND LION OF JUDAH

And Abraham said,
My son, God will provide Himself
a lamb for a burnt-offering.
Genesis 22:8

Behold!
the Lamb of God
who taketh away the sin of the world.
John 1:29

Weep not!
Behold, the Lion of the tribe of Juda,
the root of David
hath prevailed.
Revelation 5:5

The Lord Jesus Christ.   His full title!   Born to be a *Saviour* (Luke 2:11):   born to be a *King* (John 18:37):   *Lord*, the Alpha and Omega, the beginning and the ending;   who is, and was, and is to come;   the Almighty (Rev.1:8).

He is, first of all, LORD, the Jehovah of the Old Testament, the same whom Elizabeth acknowledged as Lord when Mary visited her in her home (Luke 1:43);   the same who said to the disciples, "Ye call Me master and Lord, and ye do well, for so I am" (John 13:13);   the same whose glory Isaiah saw (Isa.6:1 and John 12:41).

His second name, JESUS, identified Him in his role as Saviour: "Thou shalt call his name Jesus, for He shall save his people from their sins" (Matt.1:21). According to Jewish tradition regarding the meaning of Isaiah 52:7, Elijah* was to appear as a forerunner of Messiah, heralding his coming first of all with the words: "*Salvation* cometh to the world: *salvation* cometh to the world . . . .", and then after that, with the words: "Thy *King* cometh".† The wonderful thing is that the word *salvation* in the original Hebrew is JESHUAH, a word which underlies the Greek word so familiar to us as JESUS.

And thirdly, his title Messiah or CHRIST as the Greek has it, identifies Him as the one born to be King. He Himself said to Pilate, "To this end was I born, and for this cause came I into the world" (John 18:37).

Thus He is truly the Lord Jesus Christ, Jehovah-Saviour and Messiah the King. So here we have his full identity: Lord first, then Saviour, and finally King. And it is important to recognize that in the order of events He was first of all Lord, then Saviour, and only after that King. Herein lies a very important truth, a truth which was not altogether clear even to his disciples and much less so to the Jewish people as a whole. It is also a truth which has been blurred in our time, for we are often invited to accept the Saviour *as Lord* before we have accepted the King *as Saviour*. Even his contemporaries did not recognize the priority in time of his role as the Lamb of God. He had to become the Lamb before becoming the Lion .

Consider, then, the Lord Jesus in these two complementary roles; first as the Lamb of God and only then as the Promised Messiah They were two roles that were related and yet quite distinct, in which the fulfillment of the first was essential to the fulfillment of the second. These two roles are revealed clearly enough in the Old Testament when we look back in retrospect upon the events of his life, but they were not nearly so clear to those who witnessed them at the time. Even those who were spiritually perceptive in Israel had difficulty in

---

* In Ecclesiasticus 48:9 and 10 we find these words with reference to Elijah:

> Thou who wast taken up in a whirlwind of fire, and in a chariot of fiery horses,
> It is written that you are to come at the appointed time with warnings,
> To allay divine wrath before its final fury,
> And to turn the heart of the father unto the son . . . .

This mission of Elijah is clearly reflected in Luke 1:17, "And he (John the Baptist) shall go before Him in the spirit and power of Elijah to turn the hearts of the fathers to the children".

† Edersheim, Alfred, *The Life and Times of Jesus the Messiah*, N.Y., Herrick & Co., 1886, Vol. II, p. 708.

reconciling the statements of Scripture in this respect.   For on the
one hand they discerned that the sacrificial system of their Temple
worship looked forward to a day when God would provide Himself a
lamb, but they also shared with their less spiritual contemporaries the
hope that God would one day restore to them a glorious successor to
David.

They perceived, in part at least, that the "Suffering Servant", clearly portrayed in the passage which runs from Isaiah 52:13 through to
the end of chapter 53, was to be fulfilled by One who should bear the
sins of Israel as a nation.   This Suffering Servant was identified readily
enough with the Lamb of God foretold by Abraham in Genesis 22:8.
But it was very difficult to see how this Suffering Servant could also
be the Lion of Judah.   Thus while a spiritually perceptive minority in
Israel were expecting that one day it would be expedient for that One
to die for the nation, *everyone* in Israel looked forward to One who
would be the Messiah, or Anointed King, and who would elevate
Israel to the headship of the nations, making Jerusalem the capital of
the world.   The question was, How could one reconcile these two
roles — Lamb of God and Lion of Judah — in one individual?

So greatly in conflict were these two concepts that it came to be
quite generally believed they were not reconcilable in the coming of a
single Person.   And not unnaturally the glory to be revealed in the
latter, a glory to be shared by the nation as a whole, easily over-
shadowed the shame to be revealed in the former.

Even the prophetic writers themselves were puzzled by their own
inspired writings and kept turning over in their minds the strangeness
of some of the things they had been instructed to set down.   For it
was revealed to them that the suffering of the Messiah was to precede
"the glory that should follow" (1 Peter 1:11).   How could such a
dying One also reign for ever as King on the throne of David?

Thus it seemed simpler to hold the view that two separate individuals were involved;   and, human nature being what it is, the One who
was to be the Messiah attained far greater importance in the public
mind than the One who was coming to be the Saviour.   This became
increasingly so as the nation fretted under the oppressive heel of the
Romans.

The timetable set forth in Daniel (9:25) established the time when
Messiah should come.   But the rather less welcome cue regarding the
intermediate fate of the Messiah revealed in Daniel 9:26 (that He was
to be "cut off but not for Himself") probably contributed to an
almost total preoccupation with his coming as Messiah.   The Jewish
people were surely quite aware of the implications of Daniel 9:25, at
least within comparatively narrow limits, for the timetable there set
forth is very specific indeed.   Sir Robert Anderson worked out the

details of this timetable and established a terminal period falling somewhere around 32 A.D.*   We do not need to defend or challenge his
calculations for the present purpose but only note that by the time of
the appearance of John the Baptist, expectancy in Israel was high
(Luke 3:15).   Even if the exact year of Messiah's coming was not positively established, there is no doubt that everyone was conscious the
day was approaching.   They were longing to be freed, to be "delivered
out of the hand of their enemies" as Zacharias put it (Luke 1:74).   Yet
not everyone was fixing their attention upon national deliverance.
There were some seeking a personal Saviour, and Mary's psalm of
rejoicing establishes that she was one of them.   For she spoke of
rejoicing in God her *Saviour* (Luke 1:47).

John the Baptist himself seems to have shared the general messianic anticipation, for this is the initial burden of his message.   But he
was also attentive to the Spirit of God, for when Jesus finally appeared he did not identify Him as the Messiah at all — but as the Lamb of
God (John 1:29).

It appears that both the common people and the Jewish national
leaders failed to see the significance of John's actual introduction, and
they responded as though he had in fact said, "Behold the Messiah!"
For they submitted to baptism in order to fulfill at least the outward
requirements of public preparation for the coming of the King whose
Court they expected to be by obeying John's call for ceremonial
cleansing.   It has to be realized that after some four hundred years of
silence, John had appeared in the wilderness with all the hallmarks of
a prophet of old — the message, the dress, the food, and the aura.   He
was to them an object of intense speculation and many must have
taken it for granted that Elijah had returned at last to prepare the
people for their coming King.   Their hour of glory was fast approaching.

Edersheim provides us with a list of Old Testament Scriptures
which the Jewish doctors had interpreted as having reference to the
Messiah.†   They found such prophetic statements everywhere, bending

---

*Daniel 9:25 had foretold that Messiah would come 69 weeks of years (or 483 years) after the
decree to rebuild the temple had been issued by Artaxerxes (Neh.2:1-6).   Whether this was
the specific decree to which Nehemiah refers or not is a matter of debate (dealt with at some
length by Sir Robert Anderson, *The Coming Prince*, London, Hodder and Stoughton, 1895,
p. 51-129).   But certainly everyone was in a high state of expectation, and this expectation
was encouraged by the Lord when, at the time of his triumphal entry into Jerusalem, He had
said to the Pharisees that if the crowds had remained silent the very stones would have cried
out (Luke 19:40).

† Edersheim, Alfred, *The Life and Times of Jesus the Messiah*, N.Y., Herrick and Co., 1883,
Vol. II, Appendix IX, pp. 710-741.

words and stretching phrases to make them point to the Messiah, sometimes in a way which we find scarcely believable. In their eagerness they created a messianic image largely patterned after the order of the emperors of this world with whom they were all too familiar. It is no wonder they entirely failed to recognize the One who nevertheless did fulfill in his Person and in his ministry the hundreds of predictions made about Him by the prophets. With hindsight we find it hard to see how they could possibly have been so blind. But part of their blindness was due to the fact that all their attention was concentrated on the role which the Lord was to play as Conquering King, while they gave almost no attention whatever to the fact that He must first be the Suffering Servant.

It seems clear that some of them understood how the Suffering Servant was to give his life: but then how could He possibly be their Messiah at the same time? Daniel 9:26 might have forewarned them. The implication of being "cut off but not for Himself" ought to have prepared them. And Isaiah 53:10 could have given them a further cue that the cutting off would somehow be "undone", for He was to "prolong his days". How else than by resurrection from the dead? So they failed to see the resurrection as a solution to the problem. This was true of the disciples also. The truth is that the disciples did not anticipate his being cut off at all!

Whatever John the Baptist may personally have hoped, the essence of his message when he introduced the Lord was not that Jesus was the Messiah but that He was the Lamb of God. Previously in his preaching he had called upon the nation to prepare itself as a people for the coming of their *King*. This, he proclaimed, must be done inwardly and outwardly, by repentance and ritual cleansing. He had not preached a gospel of personal salvation.

I think we should assume that John shared to a large extent the current view that the Messiah and the Suffering Servant were two different persons. And it seems likely that for him, too, the messianic hope predominated.

When, *under inspiration* as a prophet in the Old Testament sense, he saw Jesus coming towards him, he did not see the Messiah at all but only the Lamb of God. He did not apparently see any anomaly in what he had been preaching about Messiah and what he actually declared about the identity of Jesus. This would not be surprising if he did indeed share the current concept of two persons rather than one.

And if he were perceptive, he may also have seen himself as a prophet with two roles: a voice preaching personal salvation, and a "forerunner" announcing the coming King. But he seems to have emphasized the latter role.

The fact is that John's actual role could have been either of these and in a sense was both. It all hinged ultimately upon the response of the nation as represented by their own appointed authorities to this One whom he identified as the Lamb of God. So long as the Lord was recognized only as the Suffering Servant, John's role was simply to be the Voice. Something more had to happen before he could assume also the role of a miracle-working Elijah, the forerunner of Messiah.

Whether he was merely a Voice proclaiming a Saviour or also Elijah proclaiming a King was dependent entirely upon the subsequent course of events. Had the nation responded to the Lord by accepting in his Person both Suffering Servant and Messiah, John the Baptist would have served likewise — both as a voice crying "Salvation!" and as Elijah crying, "Behold your King!"

John's role therefore hung in the balance until the Jewish authorities made their decision. Once they had made up their minds that the Lord was *not* the Messiah of their expectations, then John's role was limited to the introduction of the Saviour, not the King. It was almost certainly on the strength of this official rejection of the Lord's Messiahship that Herod felt safe in seizing John and putting him in prison. He had no fear of retaliation by the Jewish authorities. John was therefore never called upon to assume the second role: the role of Elijah, the forerunner of Messiah.

Consider the events which transpired in John's life while the authorities debated the issue of the Lord's identity. Had they accepted the Lord as the Messiah, John would then have assumed his second role as Elijah, Messiah's forerunner, his proclaimer to the nation at large. Unfortunately, the Jewish authorities were really only concerned with the coming of a Messiah of their own vain imagining. Their strong sense of self-righteousness did not dispose them to look for a Saviour in the personal sense at all. John's message had therefore had a comparatively brief impact upon their lives.

If he had assumed this second role, John the Baptist would not actually have become a different person: but his significance to the nation, his message, and very likely his fate, would have been different. And had the Jews themselves accepted the Lord as Saviour as well as Messiah, John's stature in the role of Elijah would have made Herod afraid even to imprison him, let alone putting him to death. And very probably with continued freedom, John's ministry would have paralleled Elijah's in terms of miraculous performance as predicted in the Old Testament.

That he did not fulfill this second role was not *his* fault but the fault of the Jewish authorities who had failed to recognize their own

Messiah.   Thus although as a consequence of this failure John actually
performed no miracles such as characterized the ministry of Elijah, the
Lord was careful to point out that this in no way diminished his stature as a prophet.   Indeed, the Lord said, "If ye *will* receive it, this IS
Elijah who was to come" (Matt.11:12-14), or to put this cryptic statement a little more explicitly, "If ye will receive the Kingdom with
Myself as King, this is Elijah who was to come".   It was for this reason
that the Lord was to say to the disciples later on, in a context of particular significance (Matt.17:12), that as they had killed John the
Baptist, so they would kill Him.   The two actions are inseparably
connected.   Because John could only fulfill half his mission, it would
transpire in time that the Lord also would only fulfill half his mission
before the Jewish people at that time.   But because He knew that in
the end He would indeed fulfill both roles, He could also tell them
with assurance that Elijah would indeed yet come (Matt.17:11).

Once John had completed his role as a Voice crying in the wilderness and had been the means of identifying the Lord as the Lamb of
God so successfully that men who had previously been *his* followers
now began to turn from John and become the disciples of Jesus, then
the Lord moved away from the area in which John baptized, being
sensitive to the effect that his presence was having on John's ministry
(John 4:1-3).   It was then that John's true greatness was manifested
as he openly declared his acceptance of his own lessening role: "He
must increase but I must decrease" (John 3:30).

Then, for reasons not directly connected with John's ministry in
preparing the way for Jesus, Herod imprisoned him.   The experience
must have come as something of a shock to John, for he may have expected he would receive special protection against such a contingency
from the Lord Himself.   As he languished in prison, it seems to have
troubled him even more that the Lord did not, as a proof of his true
identity, do something dramatic to secure his release.   John may have
thought to himself, "Could it be, after all, that Jesus is only the
Suffering Servant and therefore not really in a position to assert his
lordship?   Why does He not act on my behalf?   Because He cannot?"
So he sent word to Jesus asking Him, "Art Thou *He that should come*
[a common synonym for the Messiah] or do we look for another?"
(Matt.11:3).

I do not think for one moment that John ever had any doubts
about the Lord's identity as the Lamb of God.   But when he found
himself in prison it must have been very difficult for him, as he reflected on the events of the past months, to reconcile the Lord's apparent
acquiescence in his own imprisonment with his identity as Messiah.
Could it be that He was, after all, only the Suffering Servant of Isaiah

53 and no more?   Could it be that there was another who was yet to
come in the role of Messiah?   There seems to be little doubt that this
was the basis of his enquiry as recorded in Matthew 11:2 ff.

The Lord's reply to John was a gracious reminder of the fact that
He was indeed fulfilling the role of Messiah precisely as set forth in
Isaiah 35.   He was opening the eyes of the blind and the ears of the
deaf as verse 5 promised, the lame were wonderfully healed and the
dumb praised the Lord exactly as verse 6 predicted.   Since Jewish
commentators had always applied these verses to messianic times,*
John could only draw one conclusion: namely, that Jesus who was
indeed the Lamb was also the Messiah.

There is no doubt that the Lord must have longed to set John free,
for when He received the report of John's death by beheading, He was
deeply moved.   He had lost one who was personally important to Him
in a special way.   But the national die had also been cast, for Herod
had correctly read the common temper of his countrymen and had
confidence that there would not be any outcry at the execution of
Messiah's supposed forerunner.   The Lord, of course, knew what this
portended in its immediate context, although as we know from Mark
13:32, He was not yet certain as to the final outcome.   He Himself
was apparently kept at first from absolute certainty of his final
rejection, but John's death was certainly an ominous harbinger.

The confusion that clouded John's mind seems to have been
shared by the disciples also, although their confusion prior to the
crucifixion stemmed from a rather different cause.   Whereas John had
identified the Lord as the Lamb but evidently had doubts as to his
role as Messiah, the circumstances surrounding Peter's great confession
(Matt.16:13-16; Mark 8:27-33; Luke 9:18-21) show by contrast that
the disciples had identified the Lord as Messiah but had not understood his role as the Lamb of God.   In Mark 8:29 Peter made his great
confession, "Thou art the Messiah".   But in verse 31 the Lord "began
to show them that the Son of man must suffer many things, and be rejected of the elders and of the chief priests, and scribes, and be killed
and after three days rise again".   Moreover, we are told in verse 32 that
He "spake that saying openly" — that is to say, plainly, without equivocation, not as a remote possibility but rather as an absolute certainty.
And Peter at once took Him to task and began to rebuke Him.   Matthew
16:22 shows that Peter was very vehement.   "Be it far from thee, Lord;
this shall not be unto thee".   But the Lord turned and rebuked him in
no uncertain terms.   The fact is that Peter did not recognize the Lamb

---

* Edersheim, Alfred, *The Life and Times of Jesus the Messiah*, N.Y., Herrick and Co., 1883,
Vol. II, Appendix IX, especially p. 725.

even though it was as the Lamb of God that John had directed him to Jesus in the first place.* Moreover, it is doubtful if Peter paid any attention to the Lord's words, "and shall rise again the third day". He simply could not admit the Lord's death as a possibility. The Lord was the Messiah and Messiah was to reign for ever.

This may have been one reason why Peter's courage failed him when Jesus was brought to trial. He simply did not believe that the Lord, if He were truly the Messiah, would accept such indignities without any resistance whatever. And the doubt that wedged its way into his mind created an inner conflict in his heart that simply cancelled him out. He lost all his bearings, overcome with a crippling sense of indecision.

This same doubt had obviously been shared equally by those whom the Lord overtook on the way to Emmaus (Luke 24:13-31). This is a marvellous account, a masterpiece of inspired literature. The details will be familiar enough, but I want to draw particular attention to verses 21-27. Disappointment echoing in every word, the two travellers said, "We trusted that it had been He who should have redeemed Israel". I believe they thought only in terms of national redemption, of a Messiah who should set them free from Roman domination. They do not seem to have thought at all in terms of personal salvation. It was not a Saviour but a Messiah who had been their hope.

But now everything seemed to be in a shambles since obviously Jesus could not possibly have been the Messiah. He had been put to death and sealed in a tomb. He had *submitted* to the Romans, not *conquered* them. He had stood meekly in Pilate's court, flogged by Roman soldiers, crowned by Roman soldiers in mockery, abused by Roman soldiers in the most shameful way, and crucified by Roman soldiers. How could He possibly be the Messiah?

As He walked along beside these two disappointed travellers, Jesus gently rebuked them for their lack of understanding. So blinded were they that they did not even recognize Him. Perhaps it was already getting dark. But He said to them, "O fools, and slow of heart to believe all that the prophets have spoken: ought not Messiah to have suffered many things, and (only then) to have entered into his glory"? And beginning at Moses and *all* the prophets, He spoke unto them in *all* the Scriptures the things concerning Himself, for it is indeed "in the volume of the Book" that it is written of Him!

It is very important to keep these circumstances in mind, because this confusion between the two roles which the Lord had to play was shared by almost everyone, believers and unbelievers alike. That it

---

* Even then the disciples rejoiced in the appearance of *Messiah* (John 1:41, 49).

was a real factor in the rejection by the Jewish people of their Messiah and that it was *the* basic determinant in their insistence upon his crucifixion, can be shown very readily from Scripture itself. It can be said, in a manner of speaking, that it was this mistake on their part which really made possible the ultimate fulfillment of the Plan of Redemption in both its physiological and its spiritual aspects.

I believe it *was* a genuine mistake, yet it was a *mistake* for all that. They certainly hated the Lord (John 15:25): they hated Him partly because He revealed their hypocricy and thereby undermined their religious authority. But they hated Him also because they genuinely believed that the Messianic claims He made for Himself were invalid. Somehow they had to find a way to have Him discredited as a pretended Messiah, by placing Him in such a position that He would either be rescued by God from his predicament as a sign that they were mistaken in their judgment, or forsaken by God as a proof that they were correct. It seems to me important to separate two motivating forces underlying their behaviour towards the Lord. In the first place, they hated Him murderously because He had already disabused their pretended self-righteousness, openly and with tremendous force. But because they had imposed their own ambitious dreams upon their interpretation of the Old Testament prophecies, they seem genuinely to have believed He could not possibly be the Messiah since He was not fulfilling the kind of role they had created for Messiah.

In Matthew 9:2-8 we have a revealing incident in this connection. Although we have already had occasion to examine it, we must now view it once again in a new light. Here it is written:

> Behold, they brought to him one sick of the palsy, "Son, be of good cheer; thy sins be forgiven thee".
> And behold, certain of the scribes said within themselves, "This man blasphemeth".
> And Jesus, knowing their thoughts, said, "Wherefore think ye evil in your hearts? For which is easier to say, 'Thy sins be forgiven thee' or to say, 'Arise, and walk'? But that ye may know that the Son of man hath power on earth to forgive sins", — He then said to the sick of the palsy — "Arise, take up thine bed, and go unto thine house".
> And he arose, and departed to his house.
> But when the multitude saw it, they marvelled, and glorified God, which had given such power unto men.

Now, what was the Lord really doing here? In the context of Old Testament prophetic announcements about the coming Redeemer, forgiveness was to be the act of a Saviour, whereas healing was to be the act of a Messiah. The Lord Jesus was saying, "It makes no difference whether I act in the role of Saviour and say you are forgiven, or whether I act in the role of Messiah and heal his sickness. In either role, God is with Me and the man will be healed". And in order to demonstrate to them that God was not offended by the claim He had just made, He then said to the man, "Arise, take up your bed and go to your house". And the man did!

This must have genuinely puzzled the Jewish authorities. How could this be possible? How could this man make such claims with impunity? How could a man who appeared so unlike their envisioned Messiah, claim prerogatives belonging only to God without at once losing his power to do miracles? Some said, "He is a blasphemer"; others said, "Nay, but He has extraordinary powers to heal". So the Jews were divided among themselves.

As a consequence, because they discounted his messianic claims, they became increasingly determined to see Him disqualified by the only means they knew — by having Him crucified. Crucifixion was the surest way of demonstrating that the victim was not merely reject- ed of men but *cursed of God* (Deut.21:23; Gal.3:13). If God allowed Him to be crucified, that would surely settle the issue.

What, then, is the evidence that they really were mistaken in this respect and not merely hateful? Consider the following passages of Scripture. The stongest evidence must surely be the Lord's prayer from the cross: "Father, forgive them for they know not what they do" (Luke 23:34). Peter may have learned of this prayer later, for he was to say after the crucifixion, "And now, brethren, I know that ye acted in ignorance, just as your rulers did also" (NASB, Acts 3:17). Paul likewise supported Peter's contention when, in 1 Corinthians 2:8, he said that had the princes of this world known, "they would not have crucified the Lord of glory".

Certainly during the Lord's ministry there was much divided opin- ion among the authorities as to his true identity (John 7:43; 9:16; 10:19). There were many who did believe on Him even among the chief rulers (John 12:42), but they were afraid to confess Him lest they be turned out of the synagogues by the Pharisees. On the other hand, there were many who did not believe on Him at all.

It should be borne in mind that the Lord Himself warned them that after they had crucified Him they would realize their mistake: *afterwards*, but not before (John 8:28). And this came to pass. For it will be remembered that when He was buried, they were concerned that particular care should be taken to prevent his body from being stolen lest the claim should then be made that He had risen from the dead. In Matthew 27:64 they made the damaging admission that if it should be reported to the people that "He is risen from the dead . . . . *the last error shall be worse than the first*". At the time of his crucifixion, as Isaiah had foretold (Isa.53:4), they really did consider Him "smitten of God".

The final decision for an official rejection seems to have come after an event which above all ought to have produced precisely the opposite effect. This event was the Lord's ride into the city and the presentation of Himself under circumstances which, as we look back, were so obviously fulfilling the role of the Messiah that we can only wonder at their blindness. No doubt it was in precise keeping with the timetable set by Daniel that the Lord thus rode into Jerusalem just as Zechariah 9:9 had foretold He would: "Rejoice greatly, O daughter of Zion; shout, O daughter of Jerusalem: behold, thy King cometh unto thee: he is just, and having salvation; lowly, riding upon an ass, and upon a colt the foal of an ass". And this is exactly how He did ride into his city on this occasion (Matt.21:1-9).

Most of those in the crowd entered into the excitement, though perhaps hardly knowing why. But many of the disciples, believing they understood the portent of his action, welcomed Him in the appropriate words of certain messianic psalms. When the authorities advised the Lord that He ought to rebuke the enthusiasm of his disciples, He replied: "I tell you that if these should hold their peace, the very stones would immediately cry out" (Luke 19:40).

He proceeded then, as was proper, to the Temple — the seat of Jewish national authority. But there He found — as He must have known He would find — no signs of a genuine change of heart such as might have been expected at a time like this and in view of John's preaching and their public response to it. How sadly He must have left the Temple precincts and wended his way outside the city, weeping over its fate. "O, Jerusalem, Jerusalem . . . . your house is left unto you desolate; for I say unto you, you shall not see Me (as your Messiah) henceforth, till you, too, are ready to say (as these common people who welcomed Me this day have said) 'Blessed is He that cometh in the name of the Lord'." (Matt.23:37-39). And according to Luke 19:42 and 44 He said, "If thou hadst known, even thou, O Jerusalem, *at least in this thy day*, the things which belong unto thy peace! But now are they hid from thine eyes . . . . and they shall lay thee even with the ground, and thy children with thee; and they shall not leave in thee on stone upon another; *because thou knewest not the time of thy visitation.*"

Everything had combined to reveal his identity: yet they had missed it through prejudice and pride. Henceforth they could only be determined upon one thing, and that was to prove Him an imposter.

The national leaders were thereupon guilty of conducting a mockery of a trial designed to condemn Him to be worthy of death by crucifixion.   Yet this mock trial actually served a divine purpose, for it provided an opportunity for public disclosure not of his guilt as a false Messiah *but of his absolute innocence as the Lamb of God.*   It may have been entirely by inspiration or it may have been the result of some kind of awareness of this wonderful truth that the High Priest proclaimed at the end of the trial, "It was expedient one man should die for the people" (John 11:50).   At any rate, his utterance seems to have been the last prophetic statement ever made by a High Priest in Israel.

And so as an official body they performed the function of the priests in the Old Testament who had the solemn duty of examining the Passover Lamb.   Having first established that this Lamb of God was absolutely without blemish and without spot, they then declared it to be truly a worthy sacrificial victim.   This was not *their* intention and so it came about that "by wicked hands" (Acts 2:23) they effectively carried out the predeterminate council of God, a predeterminate council without which no man could otherwise ever be saved.

The rest of this volume is concerned with the events associated with that sacrificial death that had to be specifically upon a cross, and with the Lord's bodily resurrection, specifically after three days and without seeing corruption.   These two circumstances are crucial to our salvation for reasons that are apt to be overlooked and, as will be seen, their critical importance hinges upon the unique series of events surrounding the preparation of his body — for it was in his *body* that He bore our sins on the cross and it was by his *bodily* resurrection without seeing corruption that the validation of that death as a sacrifice on our behalf was finally secured in heaven.

Chapter 27

MANHOOD PERFECTED

Though He were a Son,
yet learned He (the meaning of) obedience
by the things which He experienced,
and being made perfect
He became the author of salvation
unto all that obey Him.
Hebrews 5:8, 9

The Incarnation brought to view man as God planned him to be. Adam was created for that kind of manhood. And this potential, which in the first Adam was lost, was fully realized in the last Adam. He not only made that manhood a reality, but by his sacrifice of it, made our recovery of true manhood possible. This is the "apprehension" Paul was striving to achieve (Phil.3:12). It is this "image of the Son" to which the Christian is to be conformed (Rom.8:29).

The perfection of the Lord Jesus *as Man* is the indispensible prerequisite for our redemption. Unless He is MAN, He cannot be *our* substitute: and only if He is perfect can He BE a substitute: otherwise He must bear his own guilt. The perfection pertains equally to his spirit as it does to his body. The perfection must be total. In Him we see the potential of man realized fully — physically, spiritually, morally, intellectually. The character of the Lord Jesus Christ as He walked across the stage of human history is entirely uninventivable. It is simply not possible to fashion such a figure out of human imagination. As someone has put it, "The creation of such an individual would be a greater miracle than the fact itself." And Renan, skeptic though he was, admitted frankly that it would take a Jesus to forge a Jesus.

The Gospels especially, but the whole of the New Testament also, are full of illustrations or allusions to the sinless perfection of the Lord Jesus Christ.   Peter, who was the activist among the disciples, could say with characteristic enthusiasm, "He *did* no sin" (1 Pet.2:22). Paul, who was the thinker, could say reflectively, "He *knew* no sin" (2 Cor.5:21).   John who seems above all to have loved the Lord so deeply (John 13:23 and 21:20) exclaimed with adoration, "*In Him* was no sin" (1 John 3:5).

He was without spot or blemish, a Man among men, blameless in everything He did.   In the presence of the elite intellectuals of the times, He was flawless in all his thinking.   In a day when society in the Roman world was falling as low in its moral standard as it had ever been, He displayed a purity in Himself that was almost terrifying in its luminescence.   Added to this extraordinary spiritual quality of his nature was his personal "presence".   Men were awed by it.   So powerful was it that He could in righteous anger drive out the entrenched and hardened moneymakers in the Temple precincts, overturning their tables and spilling their greedy wealth on the ground — and not one of them had the physical courage to oppose Him (John 2:13-16).

Yet his humanity was perfectly natural in its development.   There was nothing of unnatural progress in Him: He was first the child and then the man.   He learned by the experiences of life, and his understanding kept pace with his years.   Thus as a child we find Him being subject to his parents.   As a youth He learned his trade and knew the satisfaction that comes from a thing well done.   He knew that the yokes He made would not be burdensome in themselves.   Thus even as his bodily development was perfectly natural, so was his character entirely human in its expression according to his age.

When He reached manhood, his character was tested in two ways: He knew the pressures that come from the vulnerabilities of human flesh (weariness, hunger, thirst) and the temptations constantly requiring one to choose the right.   "In all points" He was tempted, though always from without, never from within.

At the very beginning of his public ministry, after a particularly wonderful event when the heavenly Father had audibly announced Him to be his beloved Son, came a severe trial.   For forty days He was tempted by Satan to use "worldly" methods to fulfill his mission.   We presume that as Man He did not know exactly what was involved in obedience to his Father's will.   His temptations were real.   We are told that He "*learned* obedience by the things He suffered" (Heb.5:8). Satan was vanquished in the wilderness but he only departed "for a season" (Luke 4:13).   Every situation presented a choice: and in every situation He demonstrated complete obedience.

It was as Man that He displayed perfect obedience.   In the first Adam the experiences of life had turned innocence into guilt and knowledge: in the last Adam the experiences of life had turned his innocence into virtue and wisdom.

What stands out in the Gospels particularly is the unfailing demonstration of his moral and intellectual perfection: in a word, his wisdom. For wisdom is by nature a combination of intelligence and purity (James 3:17).

We are constantly amazed at his extraordinary skill in dealing with the traps that were set by his enemies as they sought to undermine his authority and neutralize the exposure of their own miserable behaviour.   They sought again and again to place Him in what can only be described as "impossible situations".   And it must be admitted that they were very clever about it.   Yet He seemed always able with ease to turn the tables upon them and discomfit them utterly.   But, be it noted, never by evasion of the real issues at stake and never by the sacrifice of a moral principle.

Consider, for example, how He dealt with the question of whether tribute money should be paid to the Roman authorities or not (Matt. 22:17 f.).   "Is it lawful", they asked, "to pay tribute unto Caesar?" They reckoned that if He should say, "No", they would be able to accuse Him before the civil authority and thus have Him arrested and put out of action.   If however, He said, "Yes", they would turn at once to the crowds who were eagerly listening and say: "See!   He believes we must continue to be subservient to these taskmasters who oppress us!   Can such a man possibly be our promised King?"   He was, in short, on the horns of a dilemma.   This was not a matter of private decision to be wrestled with in secret and answered later, or solved perhaps by a subterfuge which might serve for the moment. The answer was demanded at once in the full hearing of bystanders who stood ready to publish it abroad.

And what did He say?   He turned to his detractors and asked *them* to show Him one of the coins they used as tribute money, a coin indeed of Roman mintage which was their accepted means of commerce. And when they produced one, unsuspectingly, He asked them a simple question: "Whose image and superscription hath it?"   They replied, still not realizing the trap they were getting themselves into, "Caesar's". "Then", said Jesus quietly, "render unto Caesar the things that are Caesar's and unto God the things that ar God's".   How wonderful! How simple his answer, but how complex its implications: and what a *perfect* rejoinder it was.

Consider another example.   As the end of his ministry drew near, He had entered the Temple and for a second time cleansed it of the commerce that continually blighted its spiritual mission.   The author-ities were infuriated but really helpless to intervene, for what He did was right — and they knew it!   So later on, they cornered Him and challenged Him, saying, "By what authority doest thou these things? And who gave thee this authority?" (Matt.21:23 f.).   And Jesus answered them, "I will also ask you one thing, which if you tell me, I will in like wise tell you by what authority I do these things . . . . The baptism of John, whence was it?   From heaven or of man?"   And they reasoned with themselves saying, "If we shall say 'from heaven', He will say unto us, 'Why then did ye not believe him?'   But if we say 'of men', we fear the people;   for all the people hold John as a prophet".   So they answered Jesus and said, "We cannot tell".   And He said unto them, "Neither tell I you by what authority I do these things".   A greater than Solomon was here.

Consider one further illustration which so impressed some of the bystanders that they never asked Him any more such questions.   In Luke 20:27-40 is an account of an incident in which the Sadducees (who did not believe in any resurrection) came to Jesus and said — and here I am abbreviating this rather long passage —   "A man is required to take upon himself the duty of husband to his brother's wife if he should die prematurely.   Suppose one brother after another dies, after each has taken over this duty for the same childless widow who has survived them all, whose wife will she be in heaven?"   Whose indeed!

Jesus said that there is no need of marriage in heaven — so the question is meaningless.   Then He added, "But touching the matter of resurrection, ye do err.   If there is no such thing as resurrection, how could God be the God of Abraham, Isaac and Jacob, which you your-selves admit He is?   He is not the God of the dead but of *the living* and therefore Abraham, Isaac and Jacob must be alive"!   It was then, we are told, that certain of the scribes observed, "Master, thou hast ans-wered well".   What a tribute this was from a group among whom were some of his bitterest enemies.   And we are told that after that "they dared not ask Him any questions at all".

Never once had He failed to put his detractors to flight — not by ridicule nor by evasion, but by what the Greeks would surely have called a "sweet reasonableness and an appropriate seriousness". . . . their definition of the ideal temperament in perfect man.   They had to admit that He had beaten them at their own game, effortlessly.

Perhaps the most crucial test of all was that of which we have the details in the disputed passage of John 8:1-11.   Admittedly, it is not against these verses.   But surely, if there is any place in Scripture where we ought to be guided by the spirit of a passage rather than its disputed history in deciding whether it belongs in the canon of inspired writings or not, it is here.   It seems to me that the whole atmosphere and feeling of this beautiful incident is so perfectly concordant with all that we know of the Lord's dealings with men that it should be included unless the reasons for its exclusion cannot possibly be gainsaid.   And in this matter, we do know that the reasons for its exclusion in some of the older manuscripts was because of the feeling that adultery was being condoned.   But surely this is not so.

The passage is luminous with the beauty of the Lord's Person, with the reflected graciousness of God's mercy.   And it provides us with such an unequalled example of the meeting of righteousness and peace (Psa.85:10) where circumstances otherwise seem to stand so completely against it, that it has the strongest possible claim upon our acceptance of it.

It is hardly necessary to set forth the details.   A woman, taken in the very act of adultery and therefore by Mosaic Law explicitly worthy to be stoned to death at once, is brought before the Lord. "Moses said that she must be stoned", they pointed out, "but what do you say?"

What could He say?   There seemed only one answer possible.   She was proven guilty; she was not denying it; she ought indeed to be stoned, there and then.   But can you imagine the Lord standing by while a woman, contrite enough neither to deny her guilt nor to ask for mercy, was mutilated to death (how else can one describe it?) by stoning, before the very eyes of Him who was everywhere recognized for the quality of his mercy?   Yet how could He possibly consent? To consent would be to deny mercy, even though unsought: to forbid was to undermine the Law of Moses, divinely given and everywhere honoured — even if only in the breach of it — as the standard of God's righteousness.

Jesus stooped down, we are told in verse 6, and with his finger began writing in the dust.   What did He write?   Perhaps the names of her accusers?   Jeremiah 17:13 may possibly tell us something about this, for there it is written: "O Lord, the hope of Israel, all that forsake thee shall be ashamed, and they that depart from me shall be written in the earth, because they have forsaken the Lord, the fountain of living waters".   And was He not already identifying Himself as that very fountain?

Consider the Lord's position here.   With men, forgiveness is the plainest of duties for we are all in the same position of needing forgiveness ourselves.   Not one of us is "without sin".   The righteousness of the law does not rest with us and is not therefore in danger when we,

who are unrighteous, overlook the unrighteousness of other men. But
with God forgiveness is the profoundest of problems. How *can* God
forgive the ungodly and still sustain the moral fabric of the Universe?
How can He be just and yet justify the deeds of the unjust (Romans
3:26)?   How can He wink at any one sin without in that instant
destroying the whole basis of morality in every other area? To forgive
once merely as an act of mercy and without in some way requiring the
payment of a penalty is to destroy righteousness, to abandon moral
truth, to justify the unjustifiable, and to remove all restraints against
wickedness. What, then, could Jesus do without betraying everything
for which He had come to give his very life?

Straightening Himself up He acknowledged their verdict, for He
said to them, "He that is without sin among you, let him cast the first
stone at her".   And then He again leaned down and continued to
write on the ground. It is important to recognize that his words had a
precise meaning to the woman's accusers, for it was required by law
that the *official* accuser be the one to cast the first stone. Not one
person could bring himself publicly to claim the sinlessness which the
Lord had now made the sole justification for casting this first stone.
And so, one by one, as He continued writing on the ground, they
unobtrusively left the threatening circle of men surrounding the
woman, from the oldest to the youngest, until not one of them remained.   She was left alone in the midst of the disciples and the
curious crowd.

Jesus again straightened up, and when He had looked around, He
said, "Woman, where are these thine accusers? Hath no man accused
thee?" She replied,"No man, Lord". And Jesus said unto her, "Neither
do I condemn thee: go and sin no more".

Surely here is a most beautiful example of the extraordinary presence of mind of the Lord Jesus Christ in a situation which must have
appeared to the disciples a moral impasse. In reflecting upon these
wonderful demonstrations of wisdom and moral courage, we have to
remember that they represent but a tiny fragment of what must have
been occurring every day of his active ministry. Whether it had to do
with polictical relations with Rome, the economics of the Temple
services, doctrinal matters among the religious parties, or with moral
issues in society, all were handled with complete propriety and superb
finesse.   And, be it noted once again, never by evasion of the real
issues nor the sacrifice of a moral principle. Was there ever such a
man as this in human history!   Was there ever a man so qualified to
be called upon in due time to judge the world?

We turn now to the matter of his personal relationships which demanded not merely intriguing or clever or intellectually satisfying

answers in the crucial moments of human encounter, but righeous answers as well.   And not merely righteous answers but righteous *responses*.   There must be no excess but no waste either, no indifference but nothing inappropriate to the occasion either: nor must there be any contradiction in the over-all pattern of response.   It must be all of a piece.   Our goodness is piecemeal, there is no consistency or wholeness to it.   It is always a patchwork.   As Isaiah 64:6 puts it so accurately, "All our righteousnesses (plural) are as filthy rags".   This is our way.   By contrast, the righteousness of God, which was perfectly expressed in the Lord Jesus Christ in terms of truly human behaviour, was a garment woven in one piece.   He is "the Lord our righteousness" (singular: Jer.23:6).   Look, then, at the moral glory of this Lord as witnessed in some facets of his daily circumstances by the beautiful balance and harmony of his judgments.

We see it in his relationship with his mother.   He knew when to acknowledge her claims upon Himself whenever they were appropriate (Luke 2:51), to resist them when they were sought inappropriately (Luke 8:21), and to recognize them unsought when it became Him to do so (John 19:27).

In every need He perfectly suited his response, rebuking any appeal that resulted from a lack of faith (Matt.8:25); but instantly meeting the need of a man whose faith encouraged him to say, "Lord, if thou wilt, thou canst make me clean", and He said at once, "I will .... be thou clean" (Matt.8:2,3).   He knew perfectly when waste was justified and when it was not.   With reference to Mary who expended a costly ointment to refresh his feet, He said, "She hath wrought a good work on me . . . ." (Matt.26:10), while rebuking those who suggested her devotion was wastefully misplaced.   But with reference to the thousands who had been miraculously fed, He said, "Gather up the crumbs that nothing be wasted" (John 6:12), where men would otherwise have taken no such steps.

He asked men to watch *with* Him, as though to underline the reality of his humanness (Matt.26:38): but never to pray *for* Him, as though He had need of an advocate with the Father.   Nor did He ever ask forgiveness of anyone.   But how could this be unless He never offended unrighteously?   The best of men are always those who are most conscious of their own unworthiness and their need of forgiveness.   We do not like people who do this too often, perhaps because it reminds us that we, too, ought to be asking forgiveness of one another.   So in a manner of speaking, confession of the need for forgiveness is evidence of an inherent goodness.   Never to ask for forgiveness could be a sign of total PERFECTION — *or* of total DEPRAVITY.   The verdict of history tells us that it was not total depravity but perfect goodness in the case of the Lord Jesus Christ.   He never at any time showed the slightest evidence of pangs of conscience or the least awareness of having done anything unworthy.   Either He was perfect or He was unbelievably evil.   But we know that in the end, although men did their very best to find whereof to accuse Him, they utterly failed in their purpose.

He never permitted anyone who was unworthy to bear Him witness (Luke 4:41).   This is a telling circumstance, for the very best of men suffer from a certain prideful awareness of their own public reputation and cannot resist accepting the compliments of the less worthy.   Were it not so, hypocrisy would disappear, for hypocrisy is only the compliment which vice pays to virtue and which the most virtuous among men, unfortunately, are not unwilling to accept.   The Lord Jesus *never* accepted it unless those who proffered it also acknowledged his true identity (Matt.19:17).

He never excused his actions, no matter how badly misunderstood, even by his friends.   When He slept in the boat and a great storm arose to threaten its other occupants, they cried out, "Master, carest thou not that we perish?" (Mark 4:38).   But He did not apologize to them for sleeping: He merely rebuked both them and the storm, to their utter amazement.   When the crowd pressed closely around Him and a woman with faith and a desperate need touched the hem of his garment, He asked, "Who touched me?"   His disciples asked Him how could He possibly raise such a question in the circumstances, but He did not answer them (Mark 5:30-32). When upon another occasion, they found Him talking to a woman of Samaria, a woman apparently of doubtful virtue, they did not dare to ask Him why He was talking to her alone — nor did He offer any explanation (John 4:27).

When Lazarus died while He delayed his coming, He made no attempt to explain his "failure" to come to their aid in time, though Mary's observation — "Lord, if thou hadst been here, my brother had not died" (John 11:32) — was certainly a pretext for just such an explanation.   One supposes that He might at least have satisfied her with some "excuse" if only to give her peace of mind.   We would have done so, no doubt, even if we had to tell a lie. He did not. He remained silent as to his reasons for delay.   Yet He shared Mary and Martha's grief very deeply (John 11:34, 35), even though He knew He would be undoing the tragedy within the next few minutes.

The picture which emerges from such silences is not, strangely, a disappointing one.   It leaves one only in amazement and wonder, and it reminds us so forcibly of our own eagerness to excuse our actions because they border so frequently upon the inexcusable, and we are insecure. This was not true of Him.

We cannot hope to exhaust the testimony of the inspired record which is like a treasure chest out of which God is constantly allowing his children to extract new gems, and we know for a simple fact that the record itself is only a tiny fragment of what might have been written had it been the intention of God to make the record complete. As John says at the very end of his Gospel, the earth itself could not have contained the volumes which might have been written (John 21:25): while Luke said of his Gospel account that it was, after all, only a beginning (Acts 1:1).

We have been talking here about the Lord Jesus Christ as *Man*. His wisdom, his power, his miracles, everything about Him as He walked among men, was the unfolding of the potential wrapped up in and acted out through truly human capacity.   I think it wonderfully opens up the record which we have of the Lord's doings in the Gospels to bear in mind that so much of what He did was done as *Man*.   He did not of course forgive sins in his human capacity, but as God.   But many of his miracles — indeed, perhaps all of them — were the work of a Person who was acting as a perfect man, and would have been possible for Adam (and his descendants) to have done equally, if sin had not entered.

We know this from many passages of Scripture.   Nothing would have been impossible to perfect man with a correspondingly perfect faith.   It is our faith that proves the barrier.   This is clear enough from such broad statements as Matthew 17:20; 21:21; Luke 10:19; John 14:12, and other parallel passages.   We could move mountains (literally) did we have perfect faith.   We simply do not know what a perfect man with a perfect faith might have achieved — we have only an inkling from what we witness of the activities of the Lord.   C. S. Lewis rightly says, "Whatever may have been the powers of unfallen man, it appears that those of redeemed man will be almost unlimited".*
It is true that man as he now is, even when he has been redeemed, has powers far beyond what he displays.   The trouble is that he has not the faith "beyond imagining" which is prerequisite to this greater display.

Does this sound absurd?   Well, consider Peter's experience of defying gravity!   In Matthew 14:22-34 we have the account of the great storm that overtook the disciples when the Lord had sent them on ahead across the Sea of Galilee to return to Gennesaret after the feeding of the five thousand on the opposite shore.   As they toiled to keep afloat, Jesus suddenly appeared through the blown spray and the roar of the waves, walking on the water.   They were naturally afraid, for in such a situation a figure calmly riding out the waves without

---

* Lewis, C. S., *Miracles*, N.Y., Macmillan, 1947, p. 140.

visible means of support must have seemed like a ghost. But the Lord called to them above the wind and reassured them while yet some feet from the boat.

Impetuous Peter, at once recognizing his Lord and seeing the "impossible" being done, said "Lord, if it be Thou, bid me come unto Thee on the water". And the Lord simply said, "Come"!

Now the wonderful thing about this is that Peter, in perfect faith, stepped over the side of the boat and walked on the water also! By faith he, too, defied gravity. But only so long as his faith was perfect. The moment he had doubts, gravity began to take over and, being (like so many other fisherman then and since) unable to swim, he cried out for help as he began to sink. The Lord Jesus immediately stretched forth his hand and caught him . . . . and rebuked him for his loss of faith. Once his faith had failed, even the Lord could not help him except *physically* by carrying his weight. He did not therefore say to Peter, "Float, man, float!" It had to be *Peter's* faith, and Peter's faith had collapsed.

Does this mean, then, that Peter and you and I could, in an emergency, walk on water? Yes, I believe it does, if we only had faith — just as we could move a mountain into the sea if we only had perfect faith. But, realistically, we do not have that kind of faith as normal to our daily walk, and we have therefore learned our limitations and, sadly, come to accept them and live with them. But had Adam never sinned . . . . what wonders might we do, yet without surprise!

Consider the significance of another somewhat similar event recorded in Matthew 14:15 f., just prior to Peter's experience of walking on the water. Here we have the story of the feeding of the five thousand. Notice how this miracle was prefaced. First, we have the situation of several thousand people far from any source of food and long after mealtime. The disciples, for some reason, were anxious to have them sent away before it was too late and the shops were closed. But Jesus said, "They need not depart; *GIVE YE THEM TO EAT*"!

What a challenge . . . . But they did not rise to it. The feeding of such a multitude was clearly beyond their resources which were composed of five loaves and two fishes. What they did *not* have were the resources of faith. But I think that if they had really understood the Lord's meaning and acted as Peter later acted in stepping out of the boat on to the water at the Lord's command, they would have performed the miracle which the Lord then performed for them in multiplying their physical resources. For there is surely no question that the Lord Jesus performed the miracle, not in his role as God, but in his role as perfect man exercising a perfect faith. Such faith is clearly creative.

Later on, in Acts, many such miracles of healing as the Lord had performed were indeed performed by the disciples, too. Although for reasons which may not merely reflect a diminishing faith, such signs and wonders gradually declined as the years went by. Whether this was due to a certain shift in the economy of God or merely a growing coldness among God's people, is a point hardly to be considered here. But certainly so long as the main thrust of the presentation of the Gospel was to the Jewish people such signs and wonders accompanied their preaching. Redeemed man obviously has residual powers of which we have little experience. What of *unfallen* man? To this potential of unfallen man we have the witness of the life and work of the Lord Jesus.

The Lord Jesus Christ was indeed Adam restored to view: not only as Adam, but even as his descendants might have been if he had not fallen. The humanity of the Lord Jesus had been tested in the crucible of daily experiences in all kinds of circumstances — but He had learned *perfect* obedience. He *could* say truly, "I do always those things which please my Father" (John 8:29).

Three times we are informed that God was pleased with his Son, the Man Christ Jesus. When He was twelve, at the time of the Passover He had stayed behind in Jerusalem, and for two days Mary and Joseph anxiously searched for Him. We read that, returning to Nazareth, He "was subject unto them" and that as He grew in wisdom and in stature, He also grew "in favour with God and man" (Luke 2:51, 52). Thus long after He had reached the age of accountability, He still had not displeased his heavenly Father.

When He was about thirty years old (Luke 3:23), He entered into his public ministry which was initiated by his baptism. Once more, God declared that He was well pleased with Him (Luke 3:22), attesting to the continuance of his perfection.

Almost three years later, when his public ministry had been tried to the full, Jesus one day took Peter, James, and John up to a mountain top where, before Moses and Elijah, the heavenly Father again affirmed that He was well pleased with his Son (Matt.17:6). He was now ready for "graduation" into glory without experiencing death.

In Him, then, was Manhood as planned, Man perfected to maturity, human nature finally and fully expressed as God intended it to be in the first place. What the first Adam might have become in an unfallen world, the last Adam did become in a fallen one. The innocence of the first Adam was destroyed and his manhood lost by his disobedience. The innocence of the last Adam was turned into virtue and his manhood was made perfect by his obedience. He was indeed a MAN altogether approved of God (Acts 2:22).

Chapter 28

THE SINLESS ONE BECOMES A SIN-OFFERING

For (God) hath made Him,
who knew no sin,
to be a sin-offering for us;
that we might be made
the righteousness of God in Him.
2 Corinthians 5:21

On the Mount of Transfiguration, God had declared that the Man Christ Jesus had matured faultlessly and, like Enoch, was ready for "graduation". He had earned the right to enter heaven. Before their very eyes, the three disciples had witnessed the glorification of Jesus, his face shining like the sun and his raiment white as light (Matt.17:2).

But then to their astonishment, instead of the joy that might have crowned the perfecting of his manhood, Jesus had come back down the mountain and had at once set out for Jerusalem — a course of action which could only end in his death. What astonished them was the commitment of Jesus to *death* rather than glory. In the succeeding days He explained what would happen at Jerusalem: "The Son of man shall be betrayed unto the chief priests and unto the scribes, and they shall condemn him to death, and shall deliver him to the Gentiles to mock, and to scourge, and to crucify him. And the third day he shall rise again" (Matt.20:18, 19). The disciples were amazed: they didn't understand. It was so contrary to all their hopes of a Messiah: for their hope was not in a Lamb. They looked for a kingdom, forgetting the prior need of personal salvation.

But Jesus knew what was involved in becoming the Lamb of God. The steps of the procedure He must go through were prefigured in the ceremony of the Day of Atonement. Like the victims for that Holy Day, He had to be examined according to certain specifications laid down by law and then officially and publicly declared to be without spot or blemish, an acceptable victim for sacrifice.

He must have been intensely aware of this deeper meaning when He shared the Passover Supper with the disciples, an awareness made more acute since the disciples were unable to comprehend despite his teaching.   To them this was the most important Holy Day of the year . . . . indeed a day of *rejoicing*! To Him . . . . an awful portent.

Earlier that afternoon Peter and John, representing the Lord's "household", had presented a pascal lamb before the priests in the Temple.   In a brief but carefully regulated ceremony, the lamb was slain.   A priest with a silver or gold vessel caught a small sample of the dying victim's blood, passed it to other priests near the altar who took this blood and cast it in one sweep at the base of the altar while at the same time supplying a fresh clean bowl to another priest for the next sacrificial victim.   The procedure was quick but reverent and orderly. At some convenient place nearby, the lamb was skinned and cleaned, parts were passed to other priests to be offered up as a burnt offering and the rest taken home for the Passover supper.   The whole procedure took but a few minutes, and hundreds of lambs were offered up in this way.

The Passover day began at 6 PM. An upper room — some believe it was in Mark's house (Matt.26:17-19) — had been prepared for Jesus to share this meal with his disciples.   While the lamb was roasting, the meal began with unleavened bread and wine (presumably unfermented, for why otherwise use unleavened bread?).   It was then that the Lord instituted the pattern of our communion service. The disciples seem to have been totally unaware of the deep significance of what was taking place at the table — the meaning of the Lord's words regarding the bread and wine, the whispered conversation between Judas and the Lord, his statement that He would not again eat this with them until He did so in an entirely new setting (Luke 22:16).

The passover lamb was now ready to be served and was brought to the table.   What can have been in the Lord's mind as He saw laid before Him this sacrificial victim, seeing the hour was so very near when He Himself would become the sacrificial victim of which this was but a symbol? He had said previously to his disciples, "Except ye eat of the flesh of the Son of man and drink his blood, ye have no life in you" (John 6:53), and now the time was almost come for its appalling fulfillment in his own Person. The meaning of his words at that time had been wholly lost to his hearers, except as an offensive idea grossly misunderstood by their carnal minds; and even now it is doubtful if any one of the disciples perceived the significance of the present circumstances.   Such total lack of understanding must have added to the burden of his spirit, especially as they were engaged in a heated argument as to who should have the highest position in the Kingdom to come (Luke 22:24).   What loneliness, humanly speaking, the Lord must have constantly suffered!   What patience He showed towards these blind followers!

After the meal was over, and Judas had already gone his way into the night to do his terrible work, they sang a psalm and together left the upper room heading in the bright moonlight (for Passover was at full moon) towards the Garden of Gethsemane.

From that moment events moved quickly.   Judas now knew where Jesus could be safely apprehended, and Caiaphas was allowed a small company of soldiers to conduct the arrest.   Since the soldiers might not identify Jesus quickly amid his disciples, all of whom would be rather similarly dressed, it was essential for them to have an unmistakeable sign.   Judas arranged to betray the Lord with a kiss, perhaps the touching of cheeks on each side as is done to this day in greeting. The events going on behind the scenes, though hidden from the disciples who therefore could profess an untested but fearfully frail courage beforehand, were of course fully known to the Lord Jesus Himself.   His agony in the Garden was not the response of a fearful soul who anticipated pain but of One who could foresee events which were to be filled with horror.   To be made a sin-offering!   That was the terrible prospect for the fulfillment of which He sought strength of body, mind, and spirit from his Father in heaven: and He was heard (Heb.5:8) in that He received angelic assistance (Luke 22:43).

In the semi-darkness, the approaching band of soldiers and some other people from Caiaphas' house including a servant named Malchus, with lanterns fastened to their spears or carried in their hands, must have been visible from some distance.   As they drew near, Judas ran forward and betrayed the Lord Jesus with an embrace and a greeting. For a moment there may have been some uncertainty and confusion, but the Lord offered no resistance to his arrest, as his disciples must surely have supposed He would do.   Indeed, He told Peter to put up his sword and at the same time undid the harm that Peter had done in using it by restoring Malchus' severed ear.

To the disciples such actions were totally unexpected and incomprehensible, and their courage being undermined by their puzzlement, they all deserted Him and fled.   The Lord Jesus remained alone, an unresisting prisoner of the soldiers.   The Messiah who was to destroy the enemies of Israel and rule over the world had meekly surrendered to the enemy, and now allowed Himself to be led away into the night apparently without protest!   No wonder the disciples had fled.   Thus was the Lord Jesus lead away unresisting to the High Priest.

Then began that extraordinary trial — perhaps the most infamous in history — which, while establishing the utter worthlessness of the court itself as a defender of human justice, served only to establish for all time the complete innocence of the Accused.

The *Jewish* authorities conducted a trial which contravened every single safeguard against injustice to the innocent that they had laboriously constructed over the previous centuries.   And so it was that by a travesty of illegalities the Lord Jesus Christ was publicly shown to be innocent — though this was not *their* intention — and thus identified as the Lamb of God, without spot or blemish, a worthy sacrificial victim to die for the sins of *others*.

Nor did the *Gentile* court prove to be any more just, though conducted by a nation whose law was universally recognized as fair and sound.   Nevertheless this trial also clearly demonstrated the innocence of the Accused, the court showed itself to be equally unable to fulfill its mandate in upholding justice.

Two trials were involved: a trial by Caiaphas officially representing Israel, and a trial by Pilate officially representing the Gentile world.   The Jewish court in a desperate effort to maintain their authority among their own people stooped to measures entirely illegal. The Gentile court did no better.   Coming to a right verdict of "Not guilty", Pilate then surrendered to expediency and perjured himself.

So the trial of Jesus Christ, whether religious or civil, was in fact and in every sense a miscarriage of justice.   Jew or Gentile, Herod or Pilate — it made no difference.   What was initiated by the envy and hatred of the religious authorities in the Court of Caiaphas was reinforced by the brutality and sadism of the soldiers under the authority of a Roman Governor in the Hall of Judgment.   It was a truth indeed that "against thy holy child Jesus, whom thou hast anointed, both Herod, and Pontius Pilate, with the Gentiles, and the people of Israel, were gathered *together* . . . ." (Acts 4:27).

Paradoxically, the religious and the civil trial proved both the innocence of the Accused and the guilt of the accusers!   In point of fact He was the Judge and they were on trial.   The Lord Jesus had foreseen this: his words, "Now is the judgment of this world" (John 12:31) had a double meaning.   Mankind was on trial. By their verdict they demonstrated their own unrighteousness and only underscored their need of a Saviour.

It was essential to the working out of the Plan of Redemption that He be condemned to death though innocent, and we shall see how it came about that the legally constituted authorities unwittingly performed their duty by "certifying" the Lamb of God, thus providing for mankind a full, perfect, and sufficient sacrifice and satisfaction once for all in the Person of Jesus Christ.

Let us consider these two trials separately, in the order in which they occurred: first the trial in the Jewish Court under Caiaphas, and then the trial in the Court of the Gentiles under Pilate.

One of England's most prominent magistrates, Frank J. Powell, made a study of the legal aspects of the Jewish trial of the Lord and was amazed at what he discovered regarding the procedures adopted by these authorities in the light of their normal practice in criminal cases as set forth in great detail in the *Mishnah*. The *Mishnah* was the more or less codified "Bill of Rights" protecting the individual in various life situations. Its instructions had been developed out of experience over the preceding centuries and had virtually the status of civil law. It was compiled in its final form by Rabbi Judah Ha-Nasi (c. 135 - 220 A.D.) but had already been in effect for a long time One important section dealt with criminal legislation under the heading *Nezikin* ("Damages"). Powell summed up his impressions of this code by observing:*

> It is sometimes said that the law of England is unduly favourable to the accused; but the safeguards in English law designed to reduce to a minimum the danger of an innocent person being convicted are as nothing compared with the "fences" put around an accused in a Jewish court. Indeed, with so many "fences" it is a wonder that anybody was ever convicted. But at the trial of Jesus these safeguards against a miscarriage of justice were thrown to the winds, and, judged by the Mishnah law standard, the proceedings ended in a riot of illegality with the Accused condemned exactly as the Presiding Judge and his colleagues had previously determined should be the case.

Virtually every single aspect of the trial of the Lord Jesus Christ contravened these safeguards and made the whole affair a mockery.

First of all, for humane reasons, the *Mishnah* ruled that a capital case could not be tried at night.† In contradiction of this injunction, the Lord Jesus was taken straight from the Garden of Gethsemane and tried at once.

Secondly, if the judgment went against the accused, sentence could not be passed on the same day as the trial. Since that night belonged to a day which did not end till 6.00 PM of the following

---

* Powell, Frank J., *The Trial of Jesus Christ*, London, Paternoster Press, 1949, p. 80.

† *Mishnah*: Sanh. IV. 1 "Judgments in souls are conducted by day and settled by day".

evening, the Lord should not in that twenty-four hour period have had sentence passed upon Him at all, let alone been executed.   The sentence "He is worthy of death", pronounced by the court within minutes of declaring his guilt was wholly illegal.*   Moreover, the same ruling laid down that no sentence of death could be passed on a Sabbath or a Holy Day.   Since it was now the day of Passover, a Holy Day, it was strictly forbidden to pass sentence: and since execution must be carried out within twenty-four hours of judgment, the trial itself could not even be legally held on that particular day!   The illegality of the proceedings was therefore doubly apparent — and Caiaphas and his court must have known this perfectly well.

According to E. M. Yamauchi, it was only legal to pronounce the actual death sentence in the so-called Hewn Chamber, in the innermost court of the Temple.† The purpose of this was to have such a sentence pronounced away from the excitement of the public court, in the seclusion of a restricted area.   But the death sentence was passed by this court in the palace of Caiaphas — and was therefore clearly out of order.

Again, an attempt must be made to find witnesses who would speak *for* the accused, since no *unanimous* verdict of guilty was allowable.‡   Here the purpose was to ensure that no one would be condemned without having at least one other person to support him in the ordeal.   No effort was made as far as we know to honour this requirement.   There is no record that any single person was appointed to oppose the verdict of guilty in order to provide at least one dissenting voice.

Then again, when witnesses proved false, they were to suffer the same penalty as the accused man would have suffered, if it turned out that they showed themselves to be false witnesses.★   No attention was paid to this "hedge" about the accused.   There is no evidence that the false witnesses were either punished or even rebuked by the court, though their witness was proved false by its inconsistency.

In the case of an accusation of blasphemy punishable by stoning, it was required that the accused should actually employ the sacred name

---

* *Mishnah*: Sanh. IV. 1 "Judgments in souls are finished on the same day for clearing and on the day after it for condemnation — wherefore there can be no judgments on Friday or on the eve of a festival".

† Yamauchi, Edwin M., "Historical Notes on the Trial and Crucifixion of Jesus Christ", *Christianity Today*, 9 April, 1971, p. 9.

‡ *Mishnah*, Sanh. IV. 1 "All must not express an opinion for condemnation".

★ *Mishnah*: Sanh. XI. 6 and *Makkoth* I. 6 "False witnesses are condemned to the same death which they had intended (for the accused)".   Compare Deuteronomy 19: 15-19.

of the Lord in the statement that was considered blasphemous.* The
Lord did not even use the word *God*, let alone the sacred name *Jehovah*.   It was Caiaphas who presented the question to the Lord Jesus, in
which the name of God was used.   The Lord merely answered in the
affirmative: "Thou hast said".   Indeed, the Lord's reply to Caiaphas'
question (Matt.26:64) seems to have been deliberately formulated
with the express purpose of giving no *legal* grounds for the immediate
accusation of 'Blasphemy'.   Technically, by their own definition, He
could never have been accused of blasphemy.   What had offended the
Court was the Lord's claim that He, the Son of Man, would descend
from heaven with the clouds.   For Daniel had seen a vision in which
"the Son of man came with the clouds of heaven" (Dan.7:13) and this
vision was applied by the Jews to the appearance of the Messiah.   But
although it may have seemed to them entirely heretical, this was not
actually blasphemy by their own legal definition.

And lastly, the crowning illegality: Jewish law expressly stated
that a man condemned to death may not be scourged before execution.†   Yet the Jewish authorities offered not the slightest protest
when Pilate scourged Jesus before He was crucified; nor did anyone
suggest for a moment that the act of scourging ought to have prompted a delay in the execution of the death sentence until his wounds had
healed — which was a further requirement of Jewish law.   It is just
possible that Pilate knew of this injunction and commanded the
scourging for this very reason in hopes that a delay in execution might
give him time to find another way out of his dilemma.

It is evident therefore that every illegality imaginable was practiced
at this trial.   It is an interesting fact that while these Jewish leaders
had not the least *moral* scruples about perjuring themselves before
Pilate, *religious* scruples prevented them from entering into his heathen
place of residence on a Holy Day.   Pilate "went forth" to tell them
his findings after each questioning of Jesus.   He did not require them
to come in before his judgment seat as he might otherwise have done.

It is also evident that these judges should have been disqualified
from presiding, for they were by no means unbiased.   They had no
liking for this Man.   In the last days of his public ministry, the Lord
had challenged the two chief ruling parties in the nation, the Pharisees
and the Sadducees, in a way that was almost fatal to them.

He had entered into the outer court of the Temple and ejected
those who exchanged money and sold sacrificial animals.   This

---

* Sanh. VII. 5.

† Edersheim, Alfred, *The Life and Times of Jesus the Messiah*, N.Y., Herrick, 1886, Vol. II,
p. 563.

business was under the care of the Pharisees and brought them no little financial gain. They were likely to lose this permanently if such interference was not stopped.

And then He had raised Lazarus from the dead, a fact which gave tremendous support to the popular belief in resurrection but which the Sadducees categorically denied. They believed that death was the end of existence and that life must be enjoyed to the full, here and now. But here was an undeniable case of a man truly and 'legally' dead (for he had been dead the minimum number of three days required to warrant a death certificate*), publicly resurrected by One who had assured everyone at the graveside that there would indeed be a resurrection at the last day — and furthermore that He Himself would raise the dead. To validate his statement, He had then calmly gone to the tomb and called Lazarus back to life. This was a severely discrediting blow to the Sadducees.

Both parties thus stood seriously in jeopardy, their reputations and their future clearly at stake. Something had to be done to put an end to this Man, not merely by having Him executed and possibly thereby turned into a hero, but by having Him crucified and thereby wholly discredited.

Their object in this instance was above all to invalidate the messianic claims of the Lord Jesus. This could only be accomplished by one means: having Him crucified and thereby rendering Him "accursed of God" according to Mosaic law (Deut.21:23). Such a one would never again be considered by the common people as a serious candidate for the messiahship. Thus their own position of privilege and authority, so severely challenged over the past three years, would be secure.

Furthermore, the soundness of their judgment of the imposter would be vindicated, for in their own way they genuinely believed that they were acting in everybody's interest. When, later, bystanders challenged the Lord Jesus to come down from the cross as a proof of his messiahship, they were acting on this principle (Matt.27:39-43). Unless God saved Him from the cross, or unless He saved Himself, He must indeed be an imposter in their view. When the authorities had said that if He were not stopped all men would come to believe his claims, and the Romans to protect themselves would come and take away their place and nation (John 11:48), they can only have been assured in their own minds that He was not really the promised Deliverer. Otherwise they would themselves have supported his claims in

---

* Ryle, J. C., *Expository Thoughts on the Gospels*, N.Y., Carter, 1881, Vol. II, p. 284. Here it is stated that the rule was based on the accepted fact that "after three days the countenance changes". See also Alfred Edersheim, *The Life and Times of Jesus the Messiah*, N.Y., Herrick & Co., 1886, Vol. II, p. 325.

hopes of getting rid of the Roman occupation.

They had already determined, even before the trial, what the verdict should be. "The chief priests and the elders and all the council sought for witness, for some charge against Jesus to put Him to death" (Mark 14:55). Their witnesses were obviously false; their testimonies did not agree and could not stand up in even this kind of a prejudiced court.

As a last resort, Caiaphas directly challenged the Lord Jesus with a question which, if answered in the affirmative, could at least be grounds for indictment on a charge of blasphemy (Matt.26:63-66). He said, "I adjure thee by the living God that thou tell us whether thou be the Messiah, the Son of God". As we have seen, Jesus entirely frustrated their design, but added, "Nevertheless, I say unto you, Hereafter ye shall see the Son of man sitting on the right hand of power, and coming in the clouds of heaven". Then the High Priest rent his clothes, saying, "He hath spoken blasphemy. What think ye?" And they all answered, "He is guilty of death".

The Lord Jesus was not guilty of blasphemy, by their own definition. But it mattered not: for such a charge brought a penalty of death — and this was what they sought.

However, the sentence of death for blasphemy was to be by stoning. While such a death would put an end to Jesus' career, it could not invalidate his claims to messiahship in the eyes of the common people. In fact, it might even make a martyr of Him. If only they could have Him crucified, then He would indeed be discredited, for everyone knew that a man hanged on a cross was not merely cursed by his own society but *cursed of God.*

There was a further complication. Under Roman rule, or at least under the Roman procurators of whom Pilate was one, the Jews were not actually permitted to execute a prisoner at all. They could condemn him to death in their courts, but the charges must be presented to and confirmed by the procurator who carried out the death sentence. Only in one circumstance were the Jews permitted to put a Gentile to death (even a Roman citizen) by immediate stoning, and this was for trespassing past the middle wall of Partition in the Temple which marked the boundary of the Court of the Gentiles.

In their own court they had "secured" a death sentence which must now be referred to the Procurator. They realized that they must bring an accusation against their Prisoner which could be referred to Pilate with assurance of a death sentence *by crucifixion.* Because this form of punishment was considered so awful and so degrading, the Romans limited it to the execution of slaves but no free man could be so put to death — *except for treason.* If they could establish an accusation of treason, there was hope . . . . But even in the Court of Caiaphas the witnesses, who would also appear before Pilate, could not agree in their testimony.   It was soon clear that such a charge could not really be substantiated, for He had *not* forbidden the payment of tribute to Caesar — indeed, He had actually *advised* the very opposite (Matt.22:21).

In the end the main thrust of their charge before Pilate was that Jesus had claimed to be a king — a charge which they hoped would be taken by Pilate as treasonable.   Even with such a shaky charge, their determination to secure a penalty of crucifixion forced them into the next step.   Only Pilate could execute Jesus in this way, so to Pilate they must go.

It is difficult to know from the records of history what kind of man Pilate really was, whether he simply did not care about justice or was caught up in events too large for him.   Certainly when faced with the Lord, he made a far better assessment of Him as a Man than the Jewish authorities had done.

Pilate was astute enough to recognize the charge that Jesus claimed to be a king was not really any challenge to Caesar.   In the presence of this regal figure he asked — without cynicism it seems to me — "Art thou then a king?"   Powell speaks of the Lord's defence action here as a case of "confession and avoidance".   For the Lord confessed that He was a king indeed, but not the sort of king alleged by the Jews, a king who might seem to be a rival to Caesar.   He explained that his Kingdom was "not of this world" — otherwise his followers would have fought against his seizure.   Pilate did not ridicule this affirmative answer;   rather he went out to the waiting accusers and, to their chagrin, said, "I find no fault in this man".

He had, perhaps, not reckoned with the hostility of either the religious authorities or of the crowds of people who had gathered outside — for it was now fully daylight.   All Jerusalem seemed to be demanding that He be crucified, be executed in the most terrible, most cruel, most degrading way known to the Roman world.   "Why? What evil hath he done?" asked a bewildered Pilate.

It may be, that, knowing crowd behaviour only too well, Pilate still supposed he could moderate their hostility to the prisoner by an appeal to *pity* for a broken man — at any rate he must have had some reason for what he did next.   For returning to Jesus, he handed him over to the brutal soldiery in the Common Hall to scourge Him and abuse Him as they wished.   Roman soldiers were hardened to physical suffering.   They were accustomed to seeing men torn asunder by wild beasts or slaughtering each other by the hundreds without mercy, for the entertainment of the degraded masses of the common people who daily thronged the Colosseum in Rome and screamed for blood.   It is a terrible thing when such men are given authority to abuse the bodies of victims who are helpless and unresisting, particularly of such a notable prisoner as this who had so recently been acclaimed by the common people as a man of tremendous power and authority. Sinful man takes pleasure in seeing the righteous brought low.

The Lord Jesus — the Creator and Sustainer of the Universe — could have demolished his oppressors with a single word, or turned upon them with such anger that they would have fled from his presence in terror. But He didn't. He meekly submitted, willingly, "turning his back to his smiters" (Isa.50:6), dumb as a lamb before its shearers (Isa.53:7). His very submission being mistaken for weakness, provoked the brutality of the soldiers to express itself so appallingly that when He finally emerged from their presence He had been so abused that Isaiah had to search for words to describe his appearance: he predicted that those who beheld Him *would be astonished*, his face and body so marred as to be scarcely recognizable as human (Isa.52:14).

The Lord Jesus had so absorbed in Himself the hatred and cruelty and corruption of unrestrained human wickedness, expressed both as spiritual venom by the Jews and as physical abuse by the Romans, that it is difficult to see how He remained conscious at all. That He could scarcely even support Himself, let alone the crossbar on the way to the crucifixion, is not surprising. Yet the crowds by and large seem to have been aroused to no pity, apparently genuinely believing that He had been a deceiver and was actually "stricken, smitten *of God*" (Isa. 53:4). And in a profound sense they were perfectly right. As Isaiah (53:10) had put it: "It pleased the *Lord* to bruise Him; *He* hath put Him to grief".

I believe that when Pilate presented this battered figure before the people, he was hoping to present Him as an object worthy of pity, now surely punished sufficiently for whatever crime they were accusing Him. Hence his words, "Behold the man!" As though he had said, "Just look at Him! Is this not enough?" And perhaps when he offered to release Him as an act of clemency (as his custom was at this time), he genuinely hoped they would accept his offer, their appetite for blood being finally appeased. But the appearance of the Lord whom they had once believed would overthrow their Roman oppressors, whom they now saw so utterly debased and apparently without the slightest resistance, drove them to even greater frenzy, for clearly He had proved Himself to be a deceiver indeed. "Crucify Him!" they screamed with one voice, "Crucify Him!"

I think this turnabout in the attitude of the common people was not really so surprising if it is borne in mind that they had hoped for only one thing from the Messiah. They were interested in his role as a conquering Deliverer of the nation, not as a dying Saviour whose

sacrifice of Himself would secure their personal forgiveness and recon-
ciliation with God.   Had they, as a people, recognized his identity as
the Lamb of God, as Saviour in this sense, they might at the same
time have seen that his death was essential.   But what then?   Would
they have undertaken to condemn Him to death on that account?   It
seems unlikely.   Even less likely does it seem that they would have
insisted so vehemently upon his death *by crucifixion*.   And yet
crucifixion was the only form of execution which, as we shall see later,
would have permitted the Lamb of God to offer Himself as a vicarious
sacrifice.   He could not in fact have made satisfaction for the sins of
his people in any other way.   Their blindness seems to have been
essential to the fulfillment of God's purposes.

That Pilate did really hope for some moderation of their hostility
seems clear from his insistence that the Lord Jesus should be released.
In Luke 23:15 and 16 we find him saying, "Nothing worthy of death
is done by Him.   I will therefore chastise Him *and release Him*".   And
when he re-affirmed this intention (verse 20), we are told that Pilate
really was *wishing to release Him*.   In verse 22 Pilate repeats this a
third time: "I will therefore chastise Him and *let Him go*'"

Pilate had every reason for this insistence.   He clearly had himself
become convinced of the Lord's innocence, and he said, "I find in
Him no fault at all" (John 18:38).   Again, later, he repeated, "I am
innocent of the blood of this just person" (Matt.27:24).   And once
more he declared, "Know ye that I find no fault in Him" (John 19:4).
What a testimony this was!

Meanwhile, his wife had sent him a disturbing note saying, "Have
nothing to do with that just man; for I have suffered many things this
day because of Him" (Matt.27:19).   Even Judas had realized his mistake but sought in vain to clear his conscience by returning the thirty
pieces of silver for which he had sold the Lord, saying, "I have sinned
in that I have betrayed innocent blood" (Matt.27:4).   And at the last,
one of those crucified with Him and watching Him in that final ordeal,
rebuked his other companion in crime with the words, "Dost thou not
fear God seeing thou art in the same condemnation?   And we indeed
justly; for we receive the due reward of our deeds: but this man hath
done nothing amiss" (Luke 23:40, 41).   What a triumph this was for
the Lord Jesus!   And though He was not alive to hear the tribute, He
would doubtless have been comforted by the testimony of the Roman
centurion in command of the detail of soldiers charged with the
execution of the condemned prisoners.   Witnessing the extraordinary
events which accompanied the Lord's expiration ("the earthquake
and those things that were done"), he was compelled to exclaim,
"Certainly this was a righteous man!   Truly this was the Son of God!"
(Luke 23:47; Matt.27:54).

But despite his inner convictions, Pilate was not prepared to sacrifice his career for this man whom the people were so determined to destroy. Yet he still seems to have made one last token effort. Knowing that they had no authority to crucify the accused, he challenged them — perhaps with a sneer — "*You* do it!" (John 19:6). He must have known full well that they would not have the stomach to do it themselves, even if they did have his permission, and he seems to have sought by this means to show his contempt.

But there is nothing so terrifying as the roar of an angry crowd united in an ugly mood and bent upon a destructive course of action. Faced with this situation and unable to make his voice heard, Pilate washed his hands of the whole affair publicly, making one final declaration that he was innocent of the blood of this just Person. And then he handed the Lord over to the soldiers for execution to satisfy the people.

It must have seemed to the Lord as He stood there that the cross itself, despite the agony that He knew it was to entail, would be almost a welcome relief from the open hatred of this violent people in their pitiless mood. We can know so little of his suffering that words fail us here and we can only repeat the Word of God and trust that the Holy Spirit will convey something of its sense to our hearts. "He was bruised for *our* iniquities: punishment was upon Him for *our* peace; by his stripes *we* are healed". It is as though the festered core of man's wickedness was poulticed and absorbed by Him — He who alone was utterly without infection, in order that our mortal wounds might be healed and we might live. We avenge ourselves upon one another but our avenging is never truly therapeutic because the one we try to hurt returns our vengeance in one way or another. The Lord Jesus did not. He accepted it entirely as though it was really his fault and not ours. He embraced the physical and spiritual torment of our sin, burying it in his own heart, praying that his tormentors might be forgiven on the grounds that they did not know what they were doing . . . .

It was essential to the working out of the Plan of Redemption that the Lord Jesus Christ be thus condemned to death though innocent. He was "delivered by the determinate council and foreknowledge of God" (Acts 2:23). It *had* to happen. Yet it was "by wicked hands" He was taken and crucified and slain. For *their* motive was not the desire to do God's will but to destroy a man whose whole life was a challenge to their shabby pretences. They could not abide the white light of his absolute sinlessness.

If the trial of Jesus Christ proved anything about human nature, it was that the heart is deceitful above all things and desperately wicked

(Jer.17:9).   In the presence of perfection, man is not filled with admiration but with hate.   Absolute holiness condemns us and we either seek to escape from its presence or to ignore it.   When we cannot do either, we seek to destroy it.   The trial proved man's need of a Saviour.

Thus did the Lamb of God stand before the bar of human judgment to be declared faultless as a human being by Jew and Gentile alike, only to be a sin-offering that we might be credited with his perfected righteousness in the sight of God.

The Altar for this sacrifice was a cross.   Only a cross could have sufficed.   For, as we shall see, no other form of capital punishment could accomodate the events which were necessary to make his death truly a sin-offering.

Chapter 29

WHY THE DEMAND FOR CRUCIFIXION?

Crucify Him!   Crucify Him!
John 19:6

Even so.
The Son of Man must be lifted up . . . .
And I, if I be lifted up,
will draw all men unto Me.
John 3:14 and 12:32

Looking unto Jesus
the author and finisher of our faith;
who, instead of the joy that was set before Him,
endured the cross,
despising the shame . . . .
Hebrews 12:2

It is now clear that the Jewish authorities really had in mind two rather distinct objectives in bringing the Lord Jesus to trial. The first was to have Him put to death because they hated Him, for they could abide neither the light of his life nor the truth of his words. The second was to demolish his messianic claims. They had so distorted the Old Testament prophetic previews as to the nature and work of the Messiah that they entirely failed to recognize the truth about his identity when He did appear before them.

To achieve the first objective they were dependent upon Pilate who alone could authorize his execution, unless they could secretly murder Him without attracting the attention of the Romans. This would have been extremely difficult without creating an uproar, and the more so as they delayed it, for his fame was spreading everywhere. Moreover, the one or two attempts they had made to stone Him had aborted because of their indecision or because of the sheer power of his 'presence'. To achieve the second objective was most easily effected by having Him arrested, publicly disgraced, and condemned to death. If possible, they would press charges of treason, for this would mean death by crucifixion, the ultimate disgrace. If it should happen that some sudden divine interference should effect his dramatic rescue, the Jews had probably persuaded themselves that they would at once accept his messianic claims. Some of those who agreed to this plan believed themselves to be moved by the best of motives, namely, the protection of the people from being imposed upon by a false Messiah. As we have already seen (page 333), there is a great deal of incidental evidence that in *this* they were genuinely mistaken, although the mistake was really due to their own spiritual blindness and religious prejudice.

Now, there were among the Jews only four methods for executing a man condemned for a capital crime. These were strangling, stoning, burning, and beheading. Crucifixion was *not* one of them. The first was the least severe by common opinion because it did not seriously mutilate the body. Burning may have been, like crucifixion, a way of desecrating the corpse: but only after death had been effected by stoning — although it seems to be listed in the Midrash as a *death* penalty.

If, in answer to Pilate's question, "What, then, shall I do with Jesus?", the Jews had demanded that Jesus be executed by burning, God's purposes for man's redemption would have been entirely thwarted. As we shall see, the same would have been the case had He been stoned or beheaded. Crucifixion alone could serve God's purposes in working out the Plan of Redemption, for only the cross could provide the altar upon which the Lord Jesus Christ could deliberately and under no compulsion but that of his own will, *offer Himself* as a sacrificial Lamb. In any other form of execution it would have required a miracle to keep Him alive long enough to make this voluntary sacrifice: whereas on the cross it was only by a miracle that He died when He did.

It is hard for us who have no first hand knowledge of crucifixion as a form of execution to realize how long a person could linger in agony in this awful predicament, and how the human body can endure such agony and continue alive and fully conscious under conditions

which would seem so inimical to life.   History shows that the powers
of the human body to survive physical injury are truly extraordinary.
Drs. G. M. Gould and W. L. Pyle in their study of anomalies and
curiosities of medicine, give many amazing examples.   One illustration
will suffice. [233]

> A most remarkable case of a soldier suffering numerous and
> almost incredible injuries and recovering and pursuing his vocation
> with undampened zeal is that of Jacques Roellinger, Comany B,
> 47th N.Y. Volunteers.   He appeared before a pension board in
> New York, June 29, 1865, with the following history (*Medical
> Record*, N.Y., 1875, p.685 f.).   In 1862 he suffered a sabre-cut
> across the quadriceps extensor of the left thigh, and a sabre-thrust
> between the bones of the forearm at the middle third.   Soon after-
> ward at Williamsburg, Va., he was shot in the thigh, the ball passing
> through the middle third external to the femur.   At Fort Wagner,
> 1863, he had a sword-cut, severing spinal muscles and overlying
> tissues for a distance of six inches.   Subsequently he was captured
> by guerillas in Missouri and tortured by burning splinters of wood,
> the cicatrices of which he exhibited; he escaped to Florida, where
> he was struck by a fragment of an exploding shell, which passed
> from without inward, behind the hamstring of the right leg, and re-
> mained embedded and could be plainly felt.   When struck, he fell
> and was fired on by the retiring enemy.   A ball entered between
> the 6th and 7th ribs just beneath the apex of the heart, traversed
> the lungs and isuued at the 9th rib.   He fired his revolver on recept-
> ion of this shot and was soon bayonnetted by his own comrades by
> mistake, this wound also passing through his body.   If the scars are
> at all indicative, the bayonet must have passed through the left
> lobe of the liver and the border of the diaphragm.   Finally, he was
> struck by a pistol-ball at the lower angle of the left lower jaw, this
> bullet issuing on the other side of the neck.
>
> As exemplary of the easy mannerism which he bore his many
> injuries, during a somewhat protracted convalescence, it may be
> added that he amused his comrades by blowing jets of water
> through the apertures on both sides of his neck . . . .
>
> Not satisfied with his experience of our war, he stated to the
> pension examiners that he was on his way to join Garibaldi's Army
> (in Italy).

Gould and Pyle then recapitulate these injuries under twelve sub-
headings, each with the potential for permanent injury, and comment
that the man can surely have had nothing but a charmed life!

They record the instance of another soldier (a Lt. Avery) who, in
the brutal capture of Fort Griswold, Connecticut, in 1781, had "an
eye shot out, his skull fractured, the brain-substance scattering on the
ground, was stabbed in the side and left for dead.   Yet he recovered
and lived to narrate the horrors of that day forty years later". [234]

One other case of facial mutilation is so extraordinary that one
can scarcely credit the account;   yet it is well authenticated in the

English medical journal *The Lancet*. [235] This man's whole face, including his two eyes, was literally blown away by the bursting of a Prussian shell. Yet he survived. A false face was made for him and a false nose, and he even recovered some sense of smell, learned to speak and play a flute! Such is the stamina of the human spirit and of the body.

It will therefore not seem quite so extraordinary to learn that men have survived crucifixion for days on end before succumbing to death by starvation, exposure, septic poisoning, or mutilation by predators (mammals, birds, and insects). A few have, for one reason or another, been taken down and have recovered from the experience.

Josephus had occasion to see untold numbers of his countrymen crucified by the Romans at the time of the fall of Jerusalem under Titus. He wrote of one instance: "I saw many captives crucified: and remembered three of them as my former acquaintance. I was very sorry at this in my mind, and went with tears in my eyes to Titus, and told him of them; so he immediately commanded them to be taken down, and to have the greatest care taken of them in order to aid their recovery; yet two of them died under the physician's hand while the third recovered" (*Antiquities of the Jews*, § 75, p. 21). At least one did recover: and with proper treatment perhaps all three would have done so, though we do not know how long they had hung on a cross.

How long can a man survive crucifixion? In 1617 Jacob Bosius published a work in Antwerp entitled *Crux Triumphans et Gloriosa* ("The Cross Triumphant and Glorious") in which he tells of the crucifixion of the Apostle Andrew who is said to have lived on the cross for two days.* He refers also to the crucifixion of Victor, Bishop of Amiterna, who although crucified with his head down — a circumstance most unfavourable to the continuation of life — survived in this manner for two days. Bosius notes that according to Origen this was the normal period of survival when death has not been hastened by other means. Death in the case of those being crucified in the head down position appears to have been hastened by starvation since it was impossible to take food or drink.

Bosius also repeats the well-known story of Timotheus and Maura, a married couple who suffered during the Diocletian persecution in the year 286 A.D. After being horribly tortured, these two godly souls were crucified together and, according to dependable witnesses, actually survived nine days while virtuously exhorting each other in

---

*Bosius, Jacobus, *Crux Triumphans et Gloriosa*, Antwerp, 1617, pp. 8, 43, 47, 94, 112-115. According to W. S. McBirnie, one record preserved in the Church of St. Andrew in Patras, Achaia, where he was martyred, says that he was crucified and survived for three days.[*The Search for the Twelve Apostles*, Wheaton, Tyndale Press, 1977, p. 85] .

the faith, expiring on the tenth day. It must be assumed, I think, that they had water either by rain or through the ministrations of some who were present. William Stroud, in his classic work, *The Physical Causes of the Death of Christ,** believed that this was possibly an exaggeration. But it need not be assumed so. Surviving for nine days without food is by no means exceptional provided that some fluid is available and weather conditions are comparatively mild.

In the year 297 A.D. by the order of Emperor Maximian, seven Christians at Samosata were subjected to various tortures and then crucified. According to Alban Butler,†

> Hipparchus (one of them), a venerable old man, died on the cross in a short time. James, Romanus, and Lollianus expired the next day, being stabbed by the soldiers while they hung on their crosses. Philotheus, Habibus, and Paragrus, were taken down from their crosses while they were still living. The emperor, being informed that they were yet alive, commanded huge nails to be driven into their heads — by which they were at length dispatched.

Much more recently, a Captain Clapperton reported on capital punishment in the Sudan in the year 1824.‡ He speaks of beheading as being reserved for Mohammedans, and impaling and crucifixion for "unbelievers". He says he was informed, just as a matter of interest, that these poor wretches who are crucified generally lingered for three days before death put an end to their sufferings. William Stroud referred to one case of a crucified man who, having no one to defend him, had his eyes pecked out by birds . . . .§ He also mentioned a report by a Bishop Wiseman written in 1828, in which a young man possessed of great physical strength was crucified, in 1247 A.D., under the walls of Damascus for murdering his master. The Bishop reported that though he was nailed to the cross in hands and arms and feet, he remained alive from midday on Friday to the same hour on Sunday, a period of 48 hours.☆

Kitto referred to two women who were crucified but for some

---

*Stroud, William, *The Physical Causes of the Death of Christ*, N.Y., Appleton, 1871, 422 pp. Arthur Koestler mentions a "curious tale about an obscure Christian saint, Eustratus. Around 1100 A.D., he was apparently a prisoner in Cherson in the Crimea, and was ill-treated . . . . Eustratus is said to have survived 15 days on the cross". [*The Thirteenth Tribe*, Popular Library, N.Y., 1976, p. 165].

† Butler, Alban, *Lives of the Fathers*, London, 1812-1815, Vol. VI, p. 251, 252.

‡ Clapperton, Captain: in Denham and Clapperton, *Travels and Discoveries in Northern and Central Africa*, London, 1826, p. 107.

§ Stroud, William, *op. cit.*, p. 60.

☆ Wiseman, Bishop, *Twelve Lectures on the Connection Between Science and Religion*, London, 1836, Vol. I, p. 265 f.

reason were taken down after a period of three hours on the cross.* They experienced most pain, apparently, from the extraction of the nails but otherwise seem to have suffered little injury and soon recovered.   He expressed the belief, on the basis of his perusal of a number of older classic works dealing with crucifixion in antiquity, that "thirty-six hours (is) the *earliest* period at which this form of punishment would occasion death in a healthy adult".

Now it is just possible that the Jews were really expecting Pilate would execute Jesus first and then hand his body over to them to do as they pleased with it.   I think the implications of their conversations with Pilate bear this out.   It would have served their purposes entirely, for Jesus would then be dead and they could, *by crucifying the dead body*, effectively demolish the force of his claims as the Messiah without running any risk of bringing the fury of the common people on their heads.   For by this one act, they believed they could secure general assent to the curse of God upon Him.   The fact that Pilate would have already undertaken his execution would shatter all the common people's hopes respecting the Lord's mission as Deliverer, and this would leave the way clear for the Jewish authorities to do as they would without any danger of an uproar by the people.

But when Pilate said, "Take ye Him and crucify Him" (John 19:6), the Jews responded with the rather curious statement, "We have a law and by our law He ought to die" (verse 7).   The statement is odd because it seems querulous.   One might have expected them to say, in effect, "Good!   Now you're talking.   Just hand Him over to us and we'll do the rest".   But their actual words were highly significant. What they implied was that granting them the right to crucify Him was not enough because, in the first place, they had no such practice of *executing* criminals by this means, and in the second place, they would have been forced by Mosaic law to take his body down by sunset and there was a very real possibility that He would not be dead by then.   In which case they would actually be forced to save his life! It is indeed possible that Pilate may have been aware of the injunction in Deuteronomy 21:22 and 23 which forbade leaving anyone on a cross *overnight*.   The injunction is very specific:

> And if a man have committed a sin worthy of death, and he be put to death, and thou hang him on a tree:
> His body shall not remain all night upon the tree, but thou shalt in any wise bury him that day: (for he that is hanged is accursed

* Kitto, John, *A cyclopedia of Biblical Literature*, Edinburgh, Black, 1845, Vol. I, under *Crucifixion*, p. 500.

of God) that thy land be not defiled, which the Lord thy God
giveth thee for an inheritance.

Since it was probably late morning and the new day began officially at 6 PM, there were only some twelve to fourteen hours that He
could possibly hang on the cross, and there was therefore a very real
likelihood that the Lord might survive the ordeal of crucifixion. Pilate
cannot have been unaware of the capacity of the human body to survive this kind of punishment. This contingency seems to have been
the reason why the Jews at once rejected Pilate's proposal that *they*
should crucify Jesus. Instead, they insisted that He must be put to
death, a statement which demonstrates clearly that they did not consider crucifixion a form of actual execution. They said, "We have a
law, and by our law He ought to *die,* because He made Himself the
Son of God" (John 19:7). And we are told that when Pilate heard
this, he was all the more concerned for the life of his prisoner, a fact
which surely demonstrates that he did not expect that handing Jesus
over to the Jews for crucifixion would actually result in his death.

So when Pilate wanted *them* (the Jews) to crucify Jesus, it was by
no means equivalent to their demand that *he* (Pilate) crucify Him. If
Pilate did it, the Jews knew Jesus would die. If they did it, there was
no such certainty in the matter. They thus recognized the implications of Pilate's suggestion that they crucify Him themselves. They
were being invited to crucify Him *but not actually to execute Him.*
For as we have now seen, it is quite possible to crucify a person
without executing him, unless the body is left on the cross for a very
considerable time. Indeed, one of the acts of mercy which was
occasionally permitted to a crucified man was to give him a *coup de
grace,* a merciful death blow to put him out of his misery. This was
done either by breaking the legs to hasten death (perhaps by a form of
suffocation resulting from the body weight being now chiefly suspended from the arms) or by shock. It is doubtful if the Jewish authorities
would have themselves undertaken to crucify the Lord and then have
deliberately applied this *coup de grace.* For all their hatred, they
were probably still not cold-blooded enough to murder the Lord
before all those who still stood around the cross.

Now most people do not see Pilate in this more favourable light.
Edersheim thinks that he was afraid simply because he was a super-
stitious man and stood in fear of the Lord as One who might do him
personal harm later by some magical means. But I believe the evidence supports a more favourable view of his real character.

Suppose, for a moment, that Pilate was not only convinced that
the Lord Jesus was not guilty of anything worthy of punishment by
death but that he was also genuinely impressed by the stature of the
Man before him. We do not have to assume that he understood the

Lord's identity or his mission.   He merely assessed Him as a man and was convinced that the Jews had delivered Him for envy — and for no other reason.   He must have been well acquainted with Jewish custom and law and with the Jewish national mood at that time.   The Romans were not fools but very capable administrators; and although they were ruthless in punishing offenders they seemed to have had a well developed sense of justice — except where slaves were concerned.   It is unlikely that they made Procurators of men who were total strangers to the customs and laws of the people they were sent to govern.   Pilate must certainly have known that crucifixion of the living was an agonizing slow death.   Indeed, according to Mark 15:44, he was amazed (ἐθαύμασεν, ethaumasen) that the Lord had died so soon, even in view of the tortures of the past hours.   It was most unusual for anyone crucified *alive* to die within a few hours.

Thus, leading Jesus out before the people after having Him appallingly scourged and abused, he presented this battered figure to the crowd and said in effect, "I have punished this man.   I do not believe him to be guilty of any treasonable offence worthy of anything more".   And he appealed to their pity.   But his appeal was wrongly aimed, for the very finding that Jesus was not guilty of any treasonable action against the Romans was precisely what the crowd did not want to hear.   Had Pilate said, "This man is guilty of treason: he was plotting to overthrow us", the sympathies of the crowd might well have shifted entirely in favour of the Lord Jesus as being indeed the messianic figure of their wishful thinking!   Pilate's hopeful appeal to the crowd for sympathy towards a broken Man may well have condemned Jesus because their aspirations were oriented in precisely the opposite direction.   It was a kind of ironic "kiss of death".

Perhaps, with some surprise at their increased hostility towards the prisoner, Pilate said, "Now what do you *want* of me?"   And they cried, "Crucify Him! Crucify Him!"   It was at this point that Pilate had said, "Alright, if it must be so for the sake of peace, do *you* take and crucify Him".   The response of the Jewish authorities we already know . . . .

So Pilate returned to the quietness of the Judgment Hall and again questioned Jesus: and I find it difficult to read the four accounts of these sad events without increasingly gaining the impression that Pilate was genuinely disturbed at what was happening.   Yet he could not make up his mind exactly what should be done.

Once more he took his regal prisoner before the crowd and said simply, "Behold your King!" (John 19:14).   And when they screamed back at him, "Away with Him! Away with Him!", he suddenly seemed to realize what they were really trying to get him to do.   "Are you really asking *me*", he said, "to crucify your King *for you*?" (John

19:15).   It must have been clear to Pilate now that while the Jews were determined to see Him executed, they did not have the stomach to undertake the crucifixion themselves unless He was already dead. Their reply, "We have no king but Caesar", now left Pilate with no alternative from a political point of view — and the political implications began to override what may have previously been humanitarian or even moral considerations.   So he surrendered Jesus to their will, delivering Him to the soldiers (the "them" of verse 16 is surely not the Jews who had no such authority) and they, the soldiers, took Jesus and led Him away to be crucified.

One thing stands out above all else in this whole frightful travesty of justice, involving both Jew and Gentile alike: the Jewish people had slain their King out of hate long before they crucified Him out of ignorance.   From the *historical* point of view, He was "crucified and slain" (Acts 2:23) by an act which was simply judicial murder.   From a *moral* point of view, He was "slain and crucified" (Acts 5:30 and 10:39).   *The words are now reversed.*

The changing of the word order in these passages is highly significant, but I do not recall seeing any commentary that has recognized its implications fully.   We often do not perceive a truth merely by the reading of it unless our minds have been brought into a state of preparedness.   Then the truth suddenly strikes us with great force and we find ourselves wondering why we did not see it sooner.   Unfortunately, in this particular case, some modern translators, having failed to recognize this wonderful truth, have now effectively denied the truth to their readers by concealing it through an alternative rendering, the implications of which are quite different.   The circumstance is worthy of a moment's further consideration, since it shows that translation is always dependent upon something more than scholarship, though scholarship is certainly an essential ingredient.

In the *King James Version*, both Acts 5:30 and 10:39 are rendered "whom ye slew and hanged on a tree".   In a number of modern versions the same words have been translated, "whom ye killed (or put to death) *by hanging on a tree*".   In the original, the Greek is ὃν ὑμεῖς διεχειρίσασθε κρεμάσαντε ἐπὶ ξύλου, literally, "whom ye killed, hanging on a tree".   This might quite fairly be taken to mean that the Jews did indeed kill the Lord Jesus by hanging Him on a tree.   Yet I think that the wording in the *King James Version* is perfectly justifiable in the light of the original, and is nearer to the truth.

In the first place, the Jews did not execute people by hanging them on a tree.   The Romans did: but even they had qualms about it. The Carthaginians appear to have been the first to make crucifixion a mode of execution.   Up to that time it had been only a method of shaming the condemned by desecrating his already dead body. The Jews had never adopted crucifixion as a means of *execution.** In the second place — and this is even more important — the Lord was not killed by being crucified. And in the third place, it is not at all necessary to render the original Greek as these modern versions have done so, the rest of Scripture being opposed to such a rendering. The translators of the *King James Version* allowed the rest of Scripture in fact to be their guide, and thereby preserved a great truth for us.

The Lord Himself had predicted to the Jews that in the years to come they would destroy other prophets sent to them as they had destroyed prophets in the past. "Some of them", He said, "you will kill and crucify" (note the order here — Matt.23:34). In this passage the original Greek is as follows: ἐξ αὐτῶν ἀποκτενεῖτε καὶ σταξρώσετε which is, literally, "(some) of them ye will kill and ye will crucify". The meaning here is unequivocal and the prediction is entirely concordant with Jewish procedure. Moreover, the Greek of this passage agrees in its structure with that of the Septuagint Version of Joshua 10:26 in which the English reads, "And Joshua slew them and hanged them on five trees". The original here reads as follows: καὶ ἀπέκτεινεν αὐτοὺς Ἰησοῦς καὶ ἐκρέμασεν αὐτοὺς ἐπὶ πέντε ξύλων. As in Matthew 23:34 the same verb ἀποκτείνω *(apokteino)* "to kill", is used, and as in Acts 5:30 the same verb κρεμάννυμι *(kremannumi)* "to hang", is used, thus nicely tying these three passages together.

The meaning seems to me to be clear enough, and the fact that the real murder preceded the crucifixion is reinforced. Were it not for our habit of thinking that the Lord Jesus was *put to death* by crucifixion, the more modern renderings of Acts 5:30 would perhaps have never been considered as appropriate. It is of great importance once again to underscore the fact that while Jesus died *on* the cross, He did not die *because* of it.

Now for years afterwards, people generally believed (particularly the Jewish people) that Jesus was indeed accursed of God because God had not "come to his rescue" nor had God either assisted or permitted Him to come down from the cross. When Paul wrote his letter to the Corinthians, people were still saying Jesus was accursed because He was crucified. But by inspiration, Paul warned that no man who called Jesus accursed could possibly be speaking by the Spirit of God (1 Cor.12:3). By his crucifixion He was made a curse *for us*

---

* Genesis 40:19, 22 show that even in Egypt a decapitated man could also be hanged, and thus hanging is shown to be a "punishment" applied *after* death — not as a means of execution. The order in verse 19 is clear.

(Gal.3:13), not because He was an imposter but because He was the Lamb of God as well as the Messiah. But the Jews found it impossible to believe that the Messiah, the *Anointed* One, could also be the Crucified, the *Accursed* One.

Later still, Trypho the Jew, in a dialogue with Justin Martyr, said, "Your Jesus, having fallen under the extreme curse of God, we cannot sufficiently wonder how you can expect any good from God, you who place your hopes upon a man who was crucified". Commenting on the fact that even Gentiles found this incredible, Justin observed, "They count us mad: that, next to the eternal God, the Father of all things, we give second place to a man that was crucified! ,Where is your understanding', say the Gentiles, 'that you worship as God One who is crucified!'"*

Trypho wrote further in explanation of his position as a Jew: "Moreover, resting your hopes on a man that was crucified, you yet expect to obtain some good thing from God". And in another place he wrote:

> Whether Christ should be so shamefully crucified, this we are in doubt about. For whosoever is crucified is said in the Law to be accursed, so that I am exceedingly incredulous on this point . . . . Bring us, then, by the Scriptures, that we may also be persuaded by you; for we know that he should suffer and be led as a sheep. But prove to us whether he must be crucified and die so disgracefully and so dishonourably by the death cursed in the Law. For we cannot bring ourselves to think this.

Paul was right indeed: "We preached Christ crucified (a *crucified* MESSIAH!), unto the Jews a stumbling block and unto the Greeks foolishness" (1 Cor.1:23). To the Greeks it was foolishness indeed, for they and the Romans alike reserved crucifixion essentially for slaves, i.e., for people who were in fact total non-entities, "nobodies". It was for them one way of stamping the condemned man as being utterly without significance at all. He did not even have the right to be buried. He was left to rot, a mere thing. Thus did the Jews hope to ensure the final repudiation of this self-proclaimed Messiah by having Him crucified.

Never has a mistake in establishing the identity of a single individual cost those who made it so dearly — for in repudiating their own Messiah the Jewish people committed national suicide. And when the time of their national eclipse arrived, they were themselves crucified in such numbers that the Roman soldiers could neither find trees suff-

---

* Justin Martyr, "Dialogue with Trypho the Jew" in *Ante-Nicene Fathers*, Scribner edition, 1913, Vol. I, p. 199 (chap. X), p. 244 (chap. LXXXIX), and p. 247.

icient to make the crosses nor space enough to plant them in the ground.   By crucifying Messiah they crucified themselves . . . .

Now Joshua 10:26 is by no means the only Old Testament instance of "hanging" the dead.*   Further examples will be found in 1 Samuel 31:10; 2 Samuel 4:12.   But it might be wondered whether hanging on a *tree* is really the same thing as hanging on a *cross*.

It should be noted that when we speak of hanging a man, we have in mind an entirely different form of punishment.   When the Jews hung a man on a tree, he was not fastened with a rope around his neck but with ropes around his arms and legs — a quite different concept, especially in view of the fact that they were dealing with a corpse, a carcase as Joshua 8:29 has it.   In so far as the word *cross* is an appropriate translation of the Greek words used in the New Testament in connection with crucifixion, namely, *stauros* and *xulon*, it is evident that the Jews themselves so understood it.   Undoubtedly, live trees were used at first for displaying the corpse in this fashion.   But trees became scarce in later times due to the practice by conquerors in those days of cutting down all trees in the countryside.   They even rendered the soil totally unproductive by sowing it with salt (commonly referred to as "laying waste the land").   So in due time some alternative to a live tree had to be devised.   And it appears from a study of the literature that the procedure was to erect a single upright pole or stake, firmly fixing it in the ground at some elevated spot used by the public and preferably at an intersection of two highways.

The object was to make an example by the display of the dead man's body slowly falling to pieces.   Throughout the Roman Empire *live* men were being crucified and left to rot on the cross.   For this reason it was customary to set the stake some little distance from the city because of the odour created.   Such stakes were a fixture around the countryside.   It is not certain whether the crossbar, which has traditionally been counted as part of the device, was also part of these earlier stakes or not.   There is some evidence that a standing tree-trunk with a single fork in it was used in some cases.

Certainly in early Christian times, the cruciform as we now know it, was not commonly used as a symbol among Christians.   In fact, during the first few centuries there is actually no evidence that it was used at all.   Dean Burgon questioned whether the Cross occurred as

---

* A cuneiform tablet from c. 2000 B.C. tells how the Queen of Heaven descended into Hades to rescue her beloved Dumuzi but was captured, slain, and then crucified.   A very ancient idea . . . . [J. B. Pritchard, *Ancient Near Eastern Texts Relating to the Old Testament*, Princeton, 1969, p. 52 f., at line 167, 168].

a Christian emblem during the whole of the first four centuries. Monseigneur di Rossi, speaking of the catacombs, observed that there is no authentic instance of the Cross, as we know it, prior to the fifth century.*   There are crosses but they are probably drawings made by visitors in later times.   As a matter of fact, so rare in the catacombs is *any* symbol of the Lord's death that it seems clear the early Christians were almost wholly absorbed in his resurrection rather than in his death.   As Sir Kenneth Clark, though speaking with a rather inadequate understanding of the elements of Christian faith, stated the case:†

> We have grown so used to the idea that the crucifixion is the supreme symbol of Christianity that it is a shock to realize how late in the history of Christian art its power was recognized.   In the first Art of Christianity it hardly appears; and the earliest example on the doors of Santa Sabina (425 A.D.) in Rome is stuck away in a corner almost out of sight . . . .   Early Christian art is concerned with miracles, healings, and with hopeful aspects of the faith like the Ascension and Resurrection.

The Anglican Church in 1563 even adopted a resolution to omit the making of the sign of the Cross in baptism, though the attempt does not appear to have been successful.   In 1689 a further attempt was made by an Anglican Committee consisting of bishops and ministers to exempt all who felt any uncertainty about the Cross from using it as a sign under any circumstance at all.   The Reformed Episcopal Church in England and in America and in Canada have officially omitted its use since 1789.‡

The English word *cross* is derived from the Greek *krauo* which means "to strike" or "fasten together", implying at least two components.   But the Latin word *crux* does not necessitate this interpretation and Livy used the word to mean simply a stake or a pole stuck in the ground.

Whatever may have been the formal arrangement of the structure itself, the actual penalty as the Romans employed it for executing

---

* Porcelli, Baron, *The Cross: Its History, Meaning and Use*, Protestant Truth Soc., n.d., p. 13.

† Clark, Sir Kenneth, *Civilization*, London, Brit. Broadcasting Corp. and John Murray, 1969, p. 29.   The matter has been frequently remarked upon.   Edward Hutton in an article on "The Wonder of the Roman Catacombs", observed: "(The early Christians) do not seem to have been pre-occupied with the crucifixion, the death of Christ; they thought only of the resurrection" [in *Wonders of the Past*, ed. J. A. Hammerton, London, Putnam's Sons, 1924, Vol. IV, p. 1015].   Indeed, Clifford M. Jones points out that it was not until the fifth century that Christian artists dared to portray Christ on the cross between two thieves [*The Cambridge Bible Commentary: New Testament Illustrations*, Cambridge U. P., 1966, p. 129.

‡ Porcelli, Baron, *op. cit.*, p. 3.

criminals was frightful.   It was frightful not only for the agony it
brought by the very fact of hanging in an attitude so full of stress, and
the shame it brought from personal exposure to the curious public,
and the prolonged nature of the suffering which could last for days, and
the total lack of defence against wild animals and birds (men sometimes had their eyes pecked out while still alive) — but from the sense
of total forsakenness which such a situation must have brought upon
the condemned individual in the long hours of darkness when there
was no one present with whom to share the agony of soul and when
the sense of desertion must have been utterly overwhelming. It is to
the everlasting credit of the Jews that up to this time they had not
condemned their own people to such an inhumane death.

If such a stake were left in place, then the condemned man must
have carried to the site something other than the upright. Presumably
it would be the crossbar.   We know from antiquity that the prisoner
was required to carry something which contributed to his own crucifixion, and we know from the Gospels that it was heavy.   The Lord
Jesus could not even carry this crossbar which is surely not surprising
in view of the terrible laceration of his body which must have resulted
from the Roman scourging as well as the probable absence of food for
many hours.   He certainly could never have carried a whole cross, in
spite of artistic representations to the contrary.

The Carthaginians, and the Romans who borrowed the idea of
crucifixion from them, appear to have used ropes to secure the body
to the cross.   But they also seem to have used nails through the hands
and probably through the feet as a double precaution against the possibility of the prisoner wriggling free from the ropes during the night or
being freed by the cutting of the ropes. If the hands were first nailed
and the arms tied to the crossbar, it could then be hoisted up and
fastened on the upright stake.   The feet were secured with ropes and
possibly with nails also, sometimes on a small platform for the feet.
Sometimes a peg, placed at the height of the crotch, was used instead
of the footrest.   It was driven into the upright.   This was called a
sedile (our "saddle").   It helped to carry the weight of the body and
relieved some of the tension on the arms and hands, but it also greatly
extended the suffering of the condemned man who would otherwise
have expired more quickly from a form of suffocation. Justin Martyr,
Irenaeus, Tertullian, and other early Church Fathers tell us that a
sedile was used in the crucifixion of the Lord Jesus.

It is my impression that in the absence of tying, a nail through the
palm of each hand would not suffice to carry the weight of a man's
body, especially with the writhing and twisting that must have accompanied the agony of the ordeal.   The nails served chiefly to prevent
the withdrawal of the arms from the binding ropes.   By themselves,

the nails would, I think, be insufficient to carry the weight alone since the structure of the bones of the hands would tend to allow the enlargement of the wound until the nails tore through the flesh.   It is for this reason that some writers have suggested the nails were driven not through the palms but through the wrists where muscle, tendon, bone, and other connective tissue would be sufficient to carry the strain. Whether this alternative can be harmonized with the action of the Lord in showing his pierced hands to the disciples as proof of his identity is a matter of debate.

Since the first such hangings made use of live trees, it is perhaps not unnatural that the later device, whatever its precise form, was still referred to as a tree.   The Greek word ξύλον *(xulon)* in the New Testament is used both for the instrument of crucifixion and for a living tree.   It is used for the Lord's cross in Acts 5:30; 10:39; 13:29; Galatians 3:13 and 1 Peter 2:24.   It is used for a living tree in Luke 23:31 and Revelation 2:7; 22:2 and 14.   *Xulon* is also used for what we would call lumber, i.e., wood in some prepared form.   Moulton and Milligan give an instance of a papyrus recording a request for shipment of "the remaining 200 beams *(xula)* as long and as thick as possible". The other New Testament Greek word used in the same connection, σταυρός *(stauros)*, is the preferred word for the cross itself, being used 28 times.

And so the soldiers nailed and probably also tied the Lord Jesus to the crossbar, hoisted it into place and secured it, and then tied and nailed his feet, and set over his head Pilate's superscription identifying Him as "Jesus of Nazareth the King of the Jews".   This inscription was probably written in Latin, Greek, and Aramaic.   His one-piece outer garment they also removed, and they cast lots for it rather than tearing it up and thus destroying its value.   Then they sat down to keep watch, not for the pleasure of seeing Him die — for this they can hardly have anticipated — but rather to see that no one assisted Him to escape.   Two others were condemned to a like fate.

For perhaps sixteen to eighteen hours He had been without food and possibly even without water: and during that interval He had endured indignities to his Person and brutal treatment from the common soldiers.   He had experienced the pain of a totally unjust trial in a hostile court as well as the appalling hatred of a crowd whose disappointment had given a cutting edge to their anger and who were wholly bent on his destruction and desecration.   Moreover, He had been entirely forsaken by all but a tiny handful of friends, especially by those who had assured Him of their most steadfast loyalty. But the end was by no means yet.

Even in the agony of crucifixion, those who passed by still taunted

Him, and their taunts must have reinforced the temptation to come down from the cross and thereby demonstrate the validity of his messianic claims and the wrongness of their judgment. "Come down from the cross", they challenged, *if thou be the Messiah!*" (Mark 15:32). And surely to any other man in such a position, if he had had any power to comply, the temptation to do so would have been overwhelming. To the passers by, it must have seemed a fair enough challenge. Surely He who could raise the dead, could have stepped down from the cross miraculously and saved Himself — if He really was what He claimed to be. And surely God would have supported Him in such a course of action. All He needed to do now, to prove that the Jewish authorities were mistaken and to validate his messianic claims, was to set Himself free! How else, indeed, could He become the triumphant Conqueror they were looking for?

Athanasius (c. 296 - 373), whose name has become for ever attached to one of the great Creeds of our Faith, wrote one of the most important early treatises on the Lord Jesus Christ. He titled it, "The Incarnation of the Word of God".

In Chapter 21, under the heading *Death brought to nought by the Death of Christ*, he asked: "Why did not Christ die privately or in a more honourable way?" And he answered that question by saying: "Well, it was not that He was subject to natural death, but that He *had* to die at the hands of others . . . . If, therefore, He had laid aside his body somewhere in private and upon a bed, after the manner of men, it would have been thought that He also did this agreeably to a natural vulnerability [i.e., to death] and because there was nothing in Him more than in other men".

Then in Chapter 22, he asked: "Why did He not withdraw his body from the Jews and so guard its immortality?" And he answered: "It became Him *not to inflict death upon Himself*, and yet not to shun it either. He came to receive death as the due of others . . . ."

Thus we see why, and know why, He could not act upon any such alternatives — not because He lacked the power but because He had another work yet to complete. And only when that work was done would He indeed do something that was tantamount to escaping the shame and the horror of death on the cross: He would escape from the tomb!* For this "other work" yet to be completed, a work that involved another kind of death, the cross alone of all forms of capital punishment was to be the stage on which the divine drama could be acted out.

〜〴〵〜

---

* The sequence of events from the arrest in Gethsemane to the Resurrection are shown in tabulated and graphic form in Figure 19 (pp. 378 and 379) and Figure 20 (p. 380).

Figure 19   The Order of Terminal Events

DAY	TIME	NO.	EVENTS
THURS.	About 10 PM	†(1)	● **ARREST** in Gethsemane. All night Trial begins . . . mocking . . . scourging . . . In early morning CONDEMNED to crucifixion.
FRIDAY	8 AM	(2)	● **WALK TO CALVARY** begins
	9 AM		● **CRUCIFIXION** "It was about the third hour" (Mark 15:25). Taunting: "Let Him come down if . . ." (Matt.27:41-44; Mark 15:31, 32). "Let Him save us if . . ." (Luke 23:39).
	12 Noon	(3)	●— **DARKNESS** of Divine Judgment. "About the sixth hour....until the ninth hour" (Matt.27.45; Mk.15.33; Lu.23.44).
	About 3 PM	(4)	●— **DARKNESS ENDS** Near the end of darkness, Jesus cries out in desolation (Matt.27.46). Jesus commends mother to John's care (John 19:25-27). All things now accomplished (John 19:28). "TETELESTAI" = "PAID IN FULL" (John 19:30). Commends Himself into his Father's hands (Luke 23:46).

ETERNITY

(continued on p. 379)

FRIDAY (cont'd)		
3.15 PM	(5)	● **JESUS DISMISSES HIS SPIRIT** (John 19:30); and so expires (Matt.27:50; Mark 15:37; Luke 23:46). Centurion deeply impressed (Matt.27:54; Mark 15:39; Luke 23:47). Bodies of many saints arise (Matt.27:52, 53). Veil of the Temple rent (Matt.27:51; Mark 15:38). Two thieves dispatched (John 19:31-33). Death of Jesus officially certified (John 19:34). Deposition from the Cross (John 19:40).
About 4.30 PM		
About 5.30 PM	(6)	● **BURIAL** and sealing of the tomb (Matt.27:60; Mark 15:46; Luke 23:53; John 19:41).
SATURDAY		
SUNDAY		
AFTER 6 PM BUT BEFORE DAWN	(7)	● **RESURRECTION**

† *Circled numbers correspond to the numbers on Fig. 20*

Figure 20

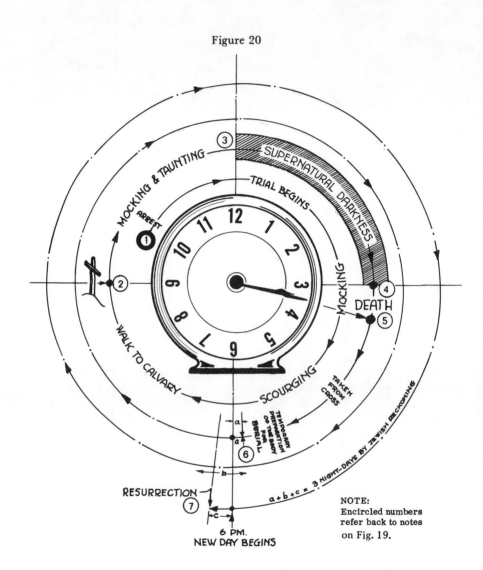

GRAPHIC ILLUSTRATION OF TERMINAL EVENTS.
(Read clockwise from ① on)

Chapter 30

THE GREAT DAY OF ATONEMENT

Never with these sacrifices
which they offered year by year
could the comers there unto be perfected . . . .
It is not possible
that the blood . . . . of goats
should take away sins.
Hebrews 10:1, 4

Ye know
He was manifested
to take away our sins.
1 John 3:5

And He is the propitiation
(lit., the atonement)
for our sins.
1 John 2:2

This He did once,
when He offered Himself.
Hebrews 7:27

Adam did not suffer one death *penalty*, but two. It is important to emphasize the word *penalty*. Adam received a double death sentence, and died twice.

The most obvious death sentence was physical: "Dust thou art and unto dust shalt thou return" (Gen.3:19). It was a conditional sentence.   It would never have been imposed had he not brought it upon himself as a consequence of disobedience.   Had physical death been *inevitable* for Adam, it could not have been presented as a threat, as a penalty, against disobedience.[236]   The result of his disobedience was not merely that he shortened his life so that he died sooner than he would have done otherwise.   What Adam actually did was to introduce an entirely new and foreign factor into human experience, the tragedy of physical death.   For man, it is indeed a tragedy, the rending asunder of spirit and body and the dissolution of human relationships. It is the "last enemy" that is to be dealt with in the plan of redemption (1 Cor.15:26).

Because Adam, like all other men, was a body/spirit entity, he was capable of experiencing both physical and spiritual death.   Although he need never have experienced either kind of death if he had remained obedient, he failed the test and by a single act of disobedience suffered two deaths.   His spirit died that very day, and his body died centuries later.   Disobedience was not forced upon him.   He was, as God first made him, free to choose, to sin or not to sin and therefore to die twice or never to die at all.

We know this to be the case because precisely the same thing was true of the Lord Jesus who stood where Adam had originally stood, as Federal Head of a race of truly human beings.   He, too, experienced two deaths — neither of which was inevitable.   The new human race which He is bringing into being as a result of his own two deaths, will never again die spiritually and will one day be placed beyond the power of physical death as well.   When that comes to pass, the redeemed of the Lord will not merely be able *not to die* and *not to sin* (as Adam had once been) but *not able to die* and *not able to sin* — which is a far more wonderful thing.   It will be constitutionally impossible for them to do either.   The very possibility of sinning and the very possibility of dying will be gone for ever.

The Lord as our substitute therefore had to suffer two deaths, the one spiritual and the other physical.   The spiritual death normally precedes the physical.   Death, in the most comprehensive sense, may be defined as "being cut off from the source of all *life*".   To be cut off from the source of spiritual life is spiritual death: to be cut off from the source of physical life is physical death.   With respect to the former, Ezekiel 18:4 tells us simply, "The soul that sinneth, it shall die"; meaning that the individual who commits actual SINS will be cut off from the source of all spiritual life which is in God.   This spiritual law is as much a part of the spiritual constitution of the Universe as the law of gravity is of the physical constitution of the Universe.   There are no exceptions.   If exceptions could be made in either case, the Universe would not be a Cosmos but a Chaos.

By contrast with spiritual death, physical death is not the result of actual SINS committed by the individual; since innocent babies die. Physical death entered into human experience as a defect in the organism.   It is inherited by natural generation which, in Romans 5:12, is spoken of as SIN (in the singular).*   This process begins with birth (if not sooner), and progressively ruptures the essential connection with the stream of physical life, which also resides in God.

The Bible everywhere bears witness to the fact that both kinds of death are real and that the only corrective for either is resurrection. The redeemed are resurrected with Christ *as to their spirits* when they are born again.   Ephesians 2:5 and 6 reads: "When we were dead in SINS (God) quickened us together with Christ . . . . and hath raised us up together (with Him)".   And the spiritually resurrected will never die again: "Whosoever liveth and believeth in Me shall never die" (John 11:26).   And in Christ we are yet to be made alive *as to our bodies* which will also be placed for ever beyond the power of death. Thus 2 Corinthians 5:1 reads: "For we know that if our earthly house of this tabernacle be dissolved, we have a building of God, an house not made with hands, *eternal* in the heavens . . . ." (my emphasis).   As is the order of the two deaths, so is the order of the two resurrections for the redeemed: first the spiritual and after that the physical.

As Adam died spiritually the very day he committed the first act of disobedience and only long after that laid his body in the grave, so we too die spiritually when we commit our first act of disobedience upon reaching the age of accountability: years later, like Adam, we are laid in the grave.†

This, then, sets the stage for what the Lord Jesus must experience upon the cross on our behalf.   He must die two kinds of death: first a spiritual one, separated ('cut off' − Dan.9:26) from the source of all spiritual life which is in God; and secondly a physical death.   The two experiences are clearly separated in time.   On the cross there was an interval between them, and each was experienced in its proper

---

* On the distinction between SIN and SINS, Calvin wrote: "Original sin, then, may be defined as a hereditary corruption . . . . which makes us obnoxious in the sight of God, and then produces in us works which in Scripture are termed 'the works of the flesh'. This corruption is repeatedly designated by Paul by the term SIN (Gal.5:19), while the works which proceed from it . . . . he terms the *fruits* of SIN . . . . also termed SINS" [*Institutes*, Bk. 2, chap. 1, § 5]. Similarly, Griffith Thomas wrote: "The Bible clearly distinguishes 'sin' and 'sins', the root and the fruit, the principle and the practice; and Article II (of the Thirty-Nine Articles of the Church of England) teaches that our Lord's Atonement covers both of these" [*The Principles of Theology*, Grand Rapids, Baker, reprint, 1979, p. 50].

† The case of death in childhood while in a state of innocence is of course an exception, since spiritual death does not precede physical death. But this is not the expected order of events.

order.   This is of crucial importance to an understanding of the circumstances surrounding the crucifixion: it has a direct bearing upon
the fact that *crucifixion* was part of God's intention as Acts 2:23
clearly implies.

Most systemic theologies recognize the fact implicitly but do not
spell it out explicitly.   The circumstances of the crucifixion are therefore not explored as they deserve to be and crucifixion per se tends to
be assumed as the death of God's appointment chiefly because of the
curse associated with it according to Deuteronomy 21:22 and 23. This
is a proper reason to emphasize, but I do not believe it is the most
important one.   After all, only the Jewish people saw crucifixion as a
mark of *God's* cursing.   The nations around do not seem to have regarded it in this way, but only as a mark of *society's* cursing. I believe
the cross was primarily appointed because it was required as a stage
upon which the Lord's *spiritual* death could be demonstrated during
the hours of darkness.   Only when this death had been accomplished,
could He then accomplish the second death, physical death by an act
of will.   It was the long interval between the beginning of execution
and the end of execution which made crucifixion unique.   It was for
this reason that we have the anomaly of a non-Jewish mode of execution appointed for their Messiah.

Now Peter is very explicit in his statement that the Lord Jesus "in
his own self bare our sins in his own body on the tree" (1 Peter 2:24).
"In his own self", i.e., He truly did Himself take the responsibility for
our personal SINS.   He did this "in his body on the tree", that is to
say, while *still alive* on the cross.   The circumstances of the Lord's
exectuion were such that opportunity was provided for an event
which any other kind of execution traditionally adopted by the Jewish people would not have permitted.   The factor in question was one
of time, of delay in dying.   Crucifixion was a terribly slow form of
execution.

We have already observed that the Jews employed several modes
of capital punishment: beheading, stoning, and strangling.   Burning
is also mentioned in Jewish law, but it seems rather to have been a
way of desecrating the corpse than actually carrying out the death
penalty.   It was like crucifixion in this respect, and yet unlike crucifixion in that it was still comparatively swift.   In none of the three
normal Jewish forms of execution was physical suffering unnecessarily
drawn out.   They were shocking — violent enough — but swift.   Pro-
tracting the actual dying of the condemned man was not part of Jewish
legal practice or philosophy.

Stoning normally required that the subject first be thrown to the
ground.   This was sometimes done by casting a large stone at the legs:

and sometimes by casting the accused down from a promontory of some kind. In either case stoning to death followed immediately and was done under controlled conditions. It was thus a reasonably swift death. Upon occasion the victim, by being pushed over a cliff, was killed in the process, and if death was believed to have already occurred, no further stoning was considered necessary. Paul escaped stoning on one occasion for this reason (Acts 14:19).

But such a swift death could not have been God's intention for the Lord Jesus, since part of the sacrifice He was to make on our behalf required a time interval that would not have been allowed for in beheading, stoning, or strangling. Several times the Jews had sought to stone Him, but He had protected Himself in each instance against their designs (John 8:59; 10:31; 11:8).

To set the stage for a better understanding of the part which this time interval played in the plan of redemption, we must examine briefly what happened to the two sacrificial goats on the Great Day of Atonement. And to do this meaningfully, it is necessary to review in a general way the arrangement of the Temple and especially the Holy of Holies, of which we must speak further later on in connection with the Lord's actions after his bodily resurrection. Having done this, we shall then be in a better position in the next two chapters, first to understand something of the meaning of the Lord's suffering during the hours of darkness, and secondly to understand the circumstances of his actual dying at the very end.

The Great Day of Atonement, sometimes referred to simply as *The Day,* was indeed the high point of the year in Israel's religious life. It marked the occasion for the re-establishment of a full covenant relationship between God and his people and guaranteed the continuance of sacrificial communion. It was the one day of the year in which the High Priest as a representative of his people, entered personally into the very presence of God within the Holy of Holies, the most sacred part of the temple complex, to make atonement. And atonement had to be made for both SINS and SIN, i.e., for spiritual as well as physical death. It covered all old debts and left the nation with a clean sheet for the coming year. It was a kind of "concealment" of guilt and corruption in the sight of God. It was therefore still only a temporary reprieve (Heb.10:1, 2, 11).

Now any plan of the Temple must be tentative, since the information we have to guide us from the Old Testament and from other sources such as Josephus is not precise enough for anything more than a general picture. As a consequence, a number of alternative reconstructions have been made, each claiming to be the intent of the original. The layout shown in Figure 21 must be considered as a

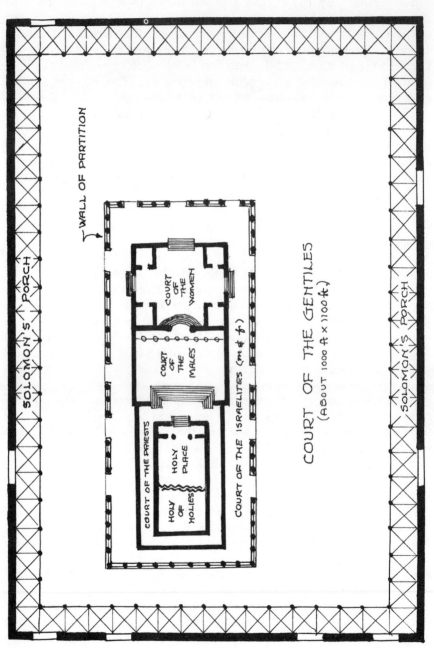

Figure 21 Basic Layout of the Temple Area.

compromise.   It is probably essentially correct in its general arrangement and any errors will not seriously detract from an understanding
of what took place on the Day of Atonement.

Basically the whole layout represents the Temple platform as
finally constructed under Solomon.   Around the perimeter was a
colonnaded shelter from the sun which became, later, the habitual
meeting place of the early Christians in Jerusalem.   Gentiles were
allowed in this peripheral area.   Approximately in the centre of the
platform and encompassing a much smaller area was a low wall about
four feet high which was probably colonnaded along the top.   This
was the Middle Wall of Partition beyond which no Gentile was allowed
to go, on pain of death.   Within this Wall of Partition was the Court
of the Israelites, male and female.   Occupying somewhat less space
within this wall were the structures of the Temple itself as shown in
the diagram, comprising at the eastern end the Women's Court which
then led up a number of steps into the Court of male Israelites. Moving towards the west and up another flight of steps one entered the
Court of Priests.

Within this area was the main structure, the Holy Place and the
Holy of Holies.   The Holy Place was entered via a kind of vestibule
as indicated, and in it were housed a number of important sacred
objects including the Table of Shewbread and an altar for the burning
of incense.   Apparently the width of this Holy Place was equal to that
of the Holy of Holies, which was thirty feet by thirty feet by thirty
feet high (1 Kings 6:20).   The Holy of Holies was separated from the
Holy Place by an enormous double* curtain or veil which must therefore have been thirty feet high and stretched from wall to wall.   It
was this double curtain which was rent from top to bottom at the
time of the Lord's death.

The Holy Place was a place of particular sanctity.   It could be
entered only by the priests, and only then upon appropriate occasions.
By contrast, the Holy of Holies was still more sacrosanct and could be
entered by the High Priest alone, and even then only once a year. This
supremely holy place was constructed without windows and, assuming
that the double curtain sealed it off completely, would accordingly be
in total darkness and very probably aboslute silence. It was an awe-ful
cavernous place of mystery.

The Holy of Holies originally contained only the Ark of the Covenant in which were placed the two Tables of Stone written with the

---

* See *Smith's Dictionary of the Bible*, Vol. IV, p. 3156, col. a: and for the possible reasons
for this dual structure, see C. R. Conder, *Handbook to the Bible*, London, Longmans, Green,
1880, p. 123.

finger of God (Exod.31:18 and 1 Kings 8:21). Later there was placed, either beside it or in it, the original text of Moses' *Book of the Law* (Deut.31:26). Subsequently some manna in a jar and Aaron's rod that had budded in vindication of Moses' authority (Num.17:1-13) were also placed in the Ark of the Covenant (Heb.9:4). However, when Solomon finally installed the Ark in its place in the Temple, only the two Tables of Stone were found within it (1 Kings 8:9). After the fall of Jerusalem in 586 B.C. and the destruction of Solomon's Temple, the Ark seems to have disappeared entirely, and we have no knowledge of what furnishings were put in their place in the Temple which was ultimately rebuilt by Zerubbabel and refurbished by Herod in our Lord's time.

It is a strange circumstance that of this one day above all others in the Jewish calendar we really have so little detailed information. In Hebrew, the Day of Atonement was referred to simply as "The Day", *Ha-Yom*. When Hebrew had been replaced by Aramaic in the time of our Lord, it was referred to as *Yoma* which means the same thing. It was also referred to commonly as *Yom Kippur*, which means "the day of covering". Our word *atonement* is a translation of the original Hebrew word which meant *covering*; thus the Day of Atonement was strictly a Day of Covering. This reflects the truth, which must have been understood by those who were spiritually discerning in Israel, that animal sacrifices could never really take away human sin but served merely as a temporary 'covering' until God Himself should provide the eternal sacrifice once for all.

It was the most solemn occasion of the year because if all went well during the ceremonies and no great judgment fell upon the officiating High Priest to signal God's displeasure, it was believed that their covenant was once more established with Jehovah for the coming year. Accordingly tremendous care was taken to ensure that everything required by law was precisely fulfilled.

The events which occurred on the Day of Atonement are described for us only in one place in Scripture and we have virtually no other information. We therefore are primarily dependent upon the descriptive details of Leviticus 16. It seems appropriate to set forth the injunctions as we find them here in order that we may more meaningfully draw attention to certain details that symbolize in a wonderful way the Lord's work on the cross. But in the interests of simplicity certain sections of Leviticus 16 will be abbreviated.

The first injunction is a warning. Aaron is to appear before the Lord in the Holy of Holies on one day in the year and on one day only. Disobedience in this matter would bring instant death. Leviticus 16:1 and 2 read:

> And the Lord spake unto Moses after the death of the two sons
> of Aaron, when they offered before the Lord and died . . . . Speak
> unto Aaron thy brother, that he come not at all times into the
> Holy of Holies within the vail before the mercy seat which is upon
> the ark; that he die not: for I will appear in the cloud upon the
> mercy seat.

Then there followed instructions for the High Priest, who was the
chief actor in this drama, that he himself might be forgiven and cleansed.   Great care was taken in this matter, and preparation for this Day
began some days before.   Every precaution was taken to ensure that
he would not be contaminated in any way by touching or being touched by anything that was dead or anyone who was unclean.   In case
such a thing should happen by accident during the preparatory period,
provision was made for him to step down from the office and a substitute to take his place.   Josephus tells us that only once in all the
centuries did it happen that the High Priest had to be replaced for the
ceremony.   On the final day, the Great Day of the ceremony, the
High Priest was bathed and clothed in several garments of linen, and
offered a sacrifice on his own behalf.   He then took up his position at
the entrance to the Holy Place for the presentation of two goats which
were to be sacrificed for the nation.

These two goats were to be male, and as alike as they could possibly be, preferably of the same mother, and of the same age.   They
were to be without blemish of any kind and great care was to be exercised in their examination to ensure their physical perfection.   They
were to be *kids* of goats, symbolizing the innocence of childhood.

Though two goats are involved, together they constituted a *single*
offering (Lev.16:5).   It is manifest that they are therefore to serve as
one offering but in two mutually exclusive roles.   It was for this reason
that they were to be, as far as possible, identical.   One of them was to
be presented *slain* before the Lord to serve as a true SIN-offering: the
other was to be presented *alive* before the Lord to serve as a living
sacrifice for SINS (Lev.16:10).   Instructions are given in the matter of
determining which of the two goats is to serve in each role.   It was
decided by lot in order to remove the choice entirely out of man's
hands, lest there should be a temptation to attach greater importance
to the one sacrifice over against the other and choose the more favourable kid on this basis.   Because the two kids really represented a single
sacrifice made by a single Person, such a mark of distinction and
preference had to be eliminated.

Leviticus 16:7-10 sets forth the following instructions:

> And he shall take the two goats and present them before the
> Lord at the door of the tabernacle of the congregation.   And
> Aaron shall cast lots upon the two goats, one lot for the Lord and

the other for the scapegoat.   And Aaron shall bring the goat upon
which the Lord's lot fell and offer him for a sin-offering.   But the
goat on which the lot fell to be a scapegoat, shall be presented alive
before the Lord, to make an atonement with him, and to let him
go for a scapegoat into the wilderness.

The High Priest approached the two goats carrying a gold vessel of
some sort containing two objects suitably distinguished, one of which
was marked "For the Lord" and the other "For the scapegoat".   He
put both hands into the vessel and took one of the two inscribed
objects in each hand.   The object in his right hand was to identify the
goat on the right as he stood facing them, and the object in his left
hand the goat on the left.   Thus one of the two goats was identified as
the appropriate victim to be slain before the Lord as a SIN-offering,
and the other to be presented alive as a scapegoat.   The scapegoat was
then marked by a piece of scarlet cloth tied to a horn.[237]

The meaning of the word rendered *scapegoat* (in Hebrew, *Azazel*)
has been discussed for years and remains uncertain.   Modern translations tend to transliterate the original into English as it stands.   The
simplest suggestion, and one of the oldest, is that it is a descriptive
adjective meaning "utterly banished".   The semitic root behind the
word, found in Arabic but not yet known in Hebrew, is *Azal* (עזל)
which according to Gesenius means to *forsake* or *banish*.   The form
Azazel (עֲזָאזֵל) may be a Pealpal form of the root verb *Azal* which in
Hebrew would be termed the *intensive form*.   Hebrew verbs are highly
flexible.   "To kill" could be changed to mean "to slaughter" by merely changing the vowels while retaining the root consonants.   To
convert the English verb "to break" into "to shatter", we employ a
different root: but Hebrew need not.   So here while *Azal* means to
banish, Azazel means to *banish utterly*.

The meaning of the words "for the scapegoat" might therefore be
literally rendered "for the one utterly banished", or possibly in prospect, "for the one to be utterly banished".   Although there are a
number of other explanations [238] of this word (which occurs nowhere
else in Scripture), a general consensus in modern times leans towards
that given above.

Now it will be remembered that the order of man's two dyings
is always the same: first a spiritual death, then the physical.   And so
also must be the Lord's sacrifice: first a spiritual sacrifice, then a
physical death.

It therefore follows that on the Day of Atonement these two
sacrificial victims, which symbolize the Lord's offering of Himself,
should be offered in the same order.   However, the scapegoat which
represents the spiritual sacrifice for SINS involves a somewhat pro-

tracted ceremony, as will be seen, just as the Lord's spiritual death occupied some hours. Consequently, the other goat would have to be kept captive right in the Temple precincts for two or more hours before being put to death. This would have presented certain administrative problems.   And it appears likely for this reason that the goat to be slain as a SIN-offering was dispatched before the sending away of the scapegoat.   Although the order of these two sacrifices was therefore reversed, it was almost certainly done as an accomodation to the fact that the two animals could hardly be handled in any other way.   The whole ceremony was orderly and reverent and dignified.   It was an expedient undoubtedly conducted in this reverse order by God's permission in view of these circumstances.

Thus the first sacrifice to be carried out, a sacrifice occupying perhaps half an hour at the most, preceded the ceremony of sending the scapegoat into the wilderness, a ritual that might well occupy a couple of hours as the circumstances clearly show.   This goat had to make a journey which may well have involved a distance of perhaps five miles or more which could scarcely have been made in less than two hours.

For this reason, then, the goat singled out as a blood sacrifice was slain first and its blood presented before the Lord in a ceremony that must have been awe-inspiring indeed.   Let us follow this ceremony as set forth in Leviticus 16:12 and 13:

> And he (the High Priest) shall take a censer full of burning coals of fire from off the altar before the Lord and his hands full of sweet incense, beaten small, and bring it within the vail: and he shall put the incense upon the fire before the Lord, that the cloud of the incense may cover the mercy seat that is upon the testimony [i.e., the two tables of stone within the Ark] , that he die not.

The dramatic effect of this preliminary ritual must have been heightened greatly by the fact that throughout the whole year the Holy of Holies had not been entered by anyone.   It had remained in darkness, the "thick darkness" in which God dwells.   As the priests officiated daily in the Holy Place, which was immediately outside it, they must often have looked at the curtain and wondered what was behind it.   They knew, of course, that the Ark of the Covenant was there, but in what form was the majesty of God in that place?   There seemed so little of substance between them and the very presence of God, a mere hanging curtain, double though it was and undoubtedly of very heavy material.   After all, it was thirty feet high and spanned the thirty feet from wall to wall.   Still, it was only a curtain.

When the time came for the High Priest to enter the Holy of Holies, according to tradition he entered at the south end where the outer of the two curtains met the southern wall, and then turned to-

wards the right and passed between the two curtains which were hung
with a passage of about eighteen inches between them. He followed
this passage towards the north wall and there passed around the end
of the other curtain directly into the Holy of Holies. Apparently the
object of the dual hanging was to prevent anyone from actually looking into the Holy of Holies during the admission of the High Priest.*

The High Priest carried with him some kind of container of live
glowing coals and probably another container to hold the powdered
incense.   The glowing coals might give him sufficient light to allow
him to approach the Ark of the Covenant; and on the lid of the Ark
he placed this container. He then took the powdered incense and cast
it on the coals. The immediate effect must have been startling indeed.
Billowing clouds of smoke would rise at once and fill the empty cavernous space illuminated by the live coals that would indeed seem a
most apt herald of the presence of God Himself who had said (Exod.
19:9) that He would come "in a thick cloud". The glow thus created
would probably light up the whole area, large as it was, while yet
concealing its boundaries — an effect that must have been tremendously enhanced by the gold sheeting covering floor and walls and ceiling.
The splendour must have bounced back and forth with a kind of gilded
irridescence, creating an atmosphere guaranteed to impress upon the
High Priest the sense of mystery in the sudden coming of Jehovah in
his glory.

The High Priest, walking backwards, then returned into the sanct-
uary, the Holy Place, from which all the priests who had previously
attended upon him had now withdrawn. Leviticus 16:15-17 continues:

> Then shall he kill the goat of the sin-offering that is for the
> people and bring his blood within the vail . . . . and sprinkle it upon
> the mercy seat and before the mercy seat: and he shall make an
> atonement . . . . and there shall be no man in the tabernacle of the
> congregation when he goeth in to make atonement in the Holy of
> Holies.

Having thus now presented the SIN-offering, the High Priest returned once again to the Holy Place, and taking up a position outside the
veil, he offered a prayer of thanksgiving which was kept short (according to tradition) so that the people who awaited his re-appearance
would be quickly apprised of his safety and therefore of the acceptance by God of the SIN-offering. Mosaic injunction ruled that if the
High Priest did not perform the ceremony acceptably, he would not
live.   Nor would Israel be "covered" for that year unless the High

---

* Conder, C. R., *Handbook to the Bible*, London, Longmans, Green, 1880, p. 123.

Priest survived the ceremony of presenting the blood and returned to the people.

So was fulfilled in anticipation the SIN-offering which symbolized the physical death and the shedding of blood which accompanied it, that marked the *second* death of the Lamb of God on the cross. We now revert to the fate of the scapegoat which anticipates his *first* death on the cross. The details are given in Leviticus 16:21-23 and 34:

> And Aaron shall lay both his hands upon the head of the live goat, and confess over him all the iniquities of the children of Israel and all their transgressions in all their sins, putting them upon the head of the goat, and shall send him away by the hand of a fit man into the wilderness.
> And Aaron shall come into the tabernacle of the congregation and shall put off the linen garments which he put on when he went into the Holy Place, and shall leave them there .... And this shall be a perpetual statute unto you, to make an atonement for the children of Israel for all their sins once a year.

Now clearly this goat is standing for a different kind of sacrifice. It does not suffer *physical* death but the death of absolute isolation. It is driven away as a creature fatally contaminated with man's SINS, utterly banished from all human association. It was sent into the wilderness only after the High Priest had publicly laid *both* his hands upon its head and thus transferred to it all the SINS of the people as a nation. The use of both hands is significant. The penitent who offered a personal sacrifice laid upon the animal's head only one hand as a gesture of *identity* (cf. Lev.1:2-4). Here the High Priest lays both hands upon its head as a symbol of *actual transfer*. An innocent creature becomes a guilty one.

Now it should be remembered that this injunction in Leviticus was given while the Tabernacle was still in the wilderness, so that only one man was needed to take the goat away and send it alone into isolation. The Temple presented new problems for the sending away of the scapegoat, problems which did not exist for the Tabernacle. The wilderness was in its immediate vicinity: the Temple was several miles from it. Since the Day of Atonement was a sabbath, a man could not be asked to lead the goat all the way from the Temple to the wilderness, for it far exceeded the distance any one individual was permitted to travel on a sabbath day. It therefore had to be arranged that this be done in stages or relays, each one a half a mile apart, and each relay being the responsibility of a separate individual. At each station a small shelter was constructed. The first man to take charge of the scapegoat took it the half mile to the first station and then returned, thus covering the allowed distance for a sabbath day's journey of one mile.   And so the goat passed from man to man until the last person took it out into the wilderness and there released it.   But on the way out, the people in the city and the surrounding countryside, considering the scapegoat as an object of desecration and horror, heaped upon it every conceivable form of verbal abuse and sought to hurry it on its way.   They genuinely believed that it was truly burdened with their sins and was now an object of shame and repulsion.

The goat had been identified by having a piece of scarlet cloth fastened to one horn.   There is no doubt that if it had attempted to come back again, it would have been driven away in horror.   But it seems more likely that God Himself would have seen to it that the goat remained separated for ever from the people whose sins it bore.   This assumes that the sacrifice was acceptable.   What if it had not been acceptable on some particular occasion?   According to tradition, this did happen once, and the goat returned from the wilderness.   Because of the horror with which the poor creature was viewed by the people, one can imagine their consternation.   That it should have returned did not, it seems, suggest to them that the sacrifice was not acceptable to God – only that the arrangement was not acceptable to the community!   The authorities determined that it should not happen again.   They therefore gave instructions thereafter that the last man should lead the scapegoat to the edge of a precipice and push it over backwards, with the reasonable certainty of breaking its legs, if not actually killing it.   This extraordinary precaution was necessary because, pushed over forwards, goats have been known to deliberately land not on their feet but on their head, in order to avoid breaking their legs, and they can apparently sustain a drop of fifty feet without injury in this position.   But the whole evolution of the ceremony involving such artificial precautions only demonstrates how far from a spiritual understanding of the truth the religious authorities had finally departed.

In the Temple, the people awaited news that the second ritual was completed.   When the last man let the goat go, he tore off a piece of the scarlet cloth and with it waved the signal back to his predecessor, who passed the news back to his predecessor in turn, and thus back to the Temple in a very short time.

The sins of Israel were removed *eastward*.   The distance was not great, only a few miles.   But when the Lord came to remove our sins in his own Person, He removed them to infinity.   As Psalm 103:12 states it, "As far as the *east* is from the west, so far hath He removed our transgressions from us".

Thus as soon as word was received from the Temple that the scapegoat was finally gone into the wilderness, there was general rejoicing throughout the land.   Their SINS had been utterly carried away, borne into the wilderness by an innocent victim.

So was offered in a compound ceremony a sacrifice for SIN and a sacrifice for SINS, a victim executed as a SIN-offering and a victim banished utterly as a bearer of the SINS of God's people.

In one Person these two sacrifices were made on the cross, when as a scapegoat the Lord Jesus took upon Himself the guilt of our SINS and was utterly banished from the Father's presence during the hours of darkness; and then as our SIN-offering (2 Cor.5:21*) took upon Himself the penalty of the deadly infection which has made us all mortals, and dismissed his life at the last.

We now turn in the next two chapters to examine these two separate deaths in the order of their occurrence at Calvary: first the spiritual, and then the physical.

---

* The use of the word SIN, in the phrase "made to be sin", is widely acknowledged to be an insufficient translation.   The Greek word is almost certainly to be rendered *sin-offering*, as it is frequently in the Septuagint.

Chapter 31

AN ETERNITY: IN THREE HOURS OF DARKNESS

It was about the sixth hour,
and there was darkness over all the earth
until the ninth hour.
And the sun was darkened.
Luke 24:44, 45

Jesus cried out with a loud voice, saying,
My God, My God, why hast Thou forsaken Me?
Matthew 27:46

The veil of the temple was rent in twain
from the top to the bottom.
Matthew 27:51

He said, "IT IS FINISHED!"*
And He bowed his head
and gave up the ghost.
John 19:30

I want to establish two points in this chapter and apply them to the circumstances in which Jesus Christ was placed during the three hours of darkness on the cross.

---

* Lit: TETELESTAI, meaning "PAID IN FULL". On this see page 409.

The first point I wish to establish is that the severity of any punishment has a profound influence upon the victim's sense of time, and that if it is severe enough, it becomes experientially *everlasting* — until it is "finished".

The second point I wish to establish is that there is a moral equivalence, universally recognized, between intensity of punishment and its extensity, between the severity of it and the duration of it. Punishment that is *brief but extreme* equals punishment that is *mild but prolonged*. There is a certain punitive correspondence between depth and time.

Both these principles have a terrible relevance to the Lord's experience during the three hours of darkness.

We are almost wholly time-bound. We have difficulty in understanding what the Lord could have meant when He said, "Before Abraham was, I am" (John 8:58). We feel it necessary to interpret this by changing the tenses. To say "Before Abraham was, I was" makes perfectly good sense. Yet this is not what the Lord said. On other occasions He introduced similar contradictions into his conversation — as when He said, for example, "The hour is coming and now is" (John 5:25). And as He seems to have transcended time (according to our idea of what is proper), so He transcended space. For example, He spoke of Himself as being both on earth and in heaven at the same moment (John 3:13).

It is noteworthy that statements of this kind are characteristic of John's Gospel, and there is no doubt that the emphasis in this Gospel is upon Jesus' trascendental nature. This transcendence is reflected in Luke 4:5 where we are told that Satan showed Him all the kingdoms of the earth "in a moment of time". It seems as though He did not experience the passage of time as some kind of continuous stream of cosmic reality by which the intervals between events are precisely measured. Nor was space for Him some kind of box, with the sides knocked out and no top or bottom, within which things are positioned in the correct relationships. During the violent storm described in John 6:21 we read that when Jesus entered the disciples' ship, then "immediately (ευθεως: *instantly*) they were at the land whither they went". Jesus' sense of both time and space was often different.

We have come to recognize since Einstein that time is a framework of a highly elastic nature, the amount of stretch being a very personal matter. We order and structure the conscious flow of events in a way that is subjective and private. The same event may be experienced by two individuals quite differently, by one as brief and by the other as prolonged. For both parties, the actual time interval as measured by the earth's movement in relation to the sun is experientially irrelevant.

Our *inner* clocks keep only a personal time.   Consciousness is the pacemaker of experienced time for each individual.   Each of us is his own point of reference both in space and in time.   The rate and even the order of events seem to share in this personal experience, and if this is true of us, we may be sure that God's time is just as uniquely *his*.

It is thus possible to say that the Lamb has been slain since the foundation of the world (Rev.13:8), but also somewhere around 33 A.D.   There is a contradiction here only because we try to fit the time-less consciousness of God into our own time-bound consciousness, and to view his time sense merely as an extension of ours rather than as something fundamentally different.   And if we do acknowledge the difference upon occasion, we do so only by assuming his time has in some way "temporarily" departed from the normality of things as we experience them.   We are time-bound because we are space-bound, for time is truly a dimension of space.   God is neither time-bound nor space-bound, for He existed *before* the Universe existed, before the creation of space or matter or time.   Einstein put the nature of the relationship between these three realities this way:[239]

> If you don't take my words too seriously, I would say this: if we assumed that all matter disappeared from the world, then *before relativity*, one believed that space and time would continue to exist in an empty world.   But, according to the Theory of Relativity, if matter and its motion disappeared, there would no longer be any space *or time* [emphasis mine].

Long before Einstein, Augustine had perceived the real equation of time with matter.   He saw that space and matter are co-existent, and he held that God created time when He created the Universe.*   Time began *with* the creation of matter.   Of God Himself, Augustine said this: "Thy years stand together at the same time . . . .   Thy years are one Day, and Thy day is not like our sequence of days but is today".†

It is extraordinary to realize that this was written over 1500 years ago.   All that has been thought on the matter since has been little more than embroidery or attempted demonstration.   Augustine had

---

* Augustine, *City of God*, Bk. XI, chap. 6: "beyond doubt, the World was not made *in* Time, but *with* Time".   As a matter of fact, the Jews themselves anticipated Augustine, though with somewhat less precision and sophistication. [See Louis Ginsberg, *Legends of the Jews*, Phila., Jewish Publ. Assoc. of Amer., 1955, Vol. V, p. 6, note 14, quoting from *Bereshith Rabbah* 3:7 and *Koheleth* 3:11].   It is also noted here that the Jewish philsopher, Philo, accepted the view held by his contemporaries.   He adopted the concept that time came into being when the universe was created [see Philo, *On Creation*, Vol. I, Loeb Classical Library, Harvard, 1971, p. 21].

† Augustine, *Confessions*, Bk. XI, chap. 13, § 16.

no problem with the statement that the Lord was, as a Lamb, slain since the foundation of the world. The present position is coming very close to this view of time. It is very effectively summed up by E. A. Milne when he said, [240]

> You can say *was* or *is* at your choice. There is no difference in the two propositions until a particular observer is mentioned . . . .
> The passage of time is a definite part of the experience of each individual, and from it may be constructed time measures . . . .
> (But) different individuals assign different spans of time . . . . to the same event.

When we speak of a *long* time, we are speaking relatively. When Malebranche first looked through a microscope, he is said to have exclaimed, "This is the end of size!" He was right . . . . It is evident that there is no absolute standard of bigness or smallness: nor is there of length of time.

To a creature that lives for only a few hours, these few hours must stretch out before it in its infancy as a life time — if it has any consciousness of time at all. Similarly, when it is dying, it may have some kind of "memory" of a long and happy past. If such a creature could contemplate the events of geology, they would appear to be virtually an infinity.

It is probable that animals have no conscious sense of the passage of time, that they are entirely *event*-oriented. Everything is experienced as a present reality or it is not given a thought. In flight from a predator, the gazelle flees with every appearance of fear but quite possibly with no actual sense of fear at all. Fear is related to a foreseeable evil in the future and in all probability the gazelle simply does not anticipate the future. Its flight is triggered by instinct, not fear. When the flight ends in escape, the gazelle may have had its instincts and reflexes sharpened and may therefore to this extent be more experienced, but in the human sense it has not been made more afraid. The sense of danger which appears to be the trigger for flight is dismissed from consciousness as soon as the situation returns to normal: the animal at once begins to forage again with a peculiar indifference to the danger just escaped. Its world, and probably the world of all living creatures in Nature, is almost entirely an untroubled one because it is lived in the present. It is only man who lives in fear because he lives in the past (with its unhappy memories) or in the future (with its disturbing anticipations). The short-lived insect crowds a life-time into a few hours: the long-lived tortoise likewise crowds a life-time into a century or two. Both almost certainly live moment by moment, even as a creature that lived for 20,000 years would do, if there were such a creature. Whether the allottment of years is many or few, the actual experience of time must be much the same for all such creatures: it is a thing of the moment.

Augustine pointed out that only the present really exists for any time-bound creature. As he put it, "The past is no longer and the future is not yet".* He then proceeds to ask, "If the past and the future do not exist, how *long* is the present?" He concludes that it has no length at all. What it does have is depth. And it appears that we mistake depth for length. This is a curious phenomenon, but quite common. One individual awaiting execution in a Spanish prison wrote:

> Time crawled through the desert of uneventful waiting as though lame on both feet. The greater the sum of blank days, the lighter their weight in the memory. The time that, when it is present, passes most slowly, passes swiftest of all in the memory. And the converse is also true. It is in flight that time leaves behind it the most visible traces. The only time that is unforgettable is that time during which one forgets that time exists.

I do not know the writer's name but it sounds very much like something Arthur Koestler would have written, looking back upon his prison experience in Spain as a man condemned to death. In any case, it is a sensitive observation, and it shows how flexible time-consciousness can be. We do not know whether animals experience this strange elasticity of time. It may, in fact, be a uniquely human capacity.

There is therefore for man a certain form of psychological temporality which is indeed relative and capable of expansion or contraction. If, for any reason, the mind or heart is disturbed, so is the time sense distorted. The more intense the disturbance, the greater is the distortion of time. If suffering is great enough, man's consciousness slips into a state of timelessness even though an observer's clock shows that it was really quite momentary. We recognize that there is a difference between suffering that is intense and suffering that is bearable, but it has always been difficult to find a definition for "intensity" in this context which would satisfy every observer. It may be that for the sufferer himself *intensity* is merely another way of measuring the degree to which the conscious passage of time is distorted.

To the extent that a man's time sense is eclipsed, to that extent is experience intense; and as it approaches the unbearable it approaches interminability. There are probably limitations to man's capacity for suffering and therefore his time sense may never be absolutely destroyed, except when he passes into a state of unconsciousness. Man still

---

* Augustine, *Confessions*, XI. xiv-xviii, *Nicene and Post-Nicene Fathers*, Buffalo, Christian Literature Co., 1886, Vol. I, p. 168, 169.

does not have sufficient *capacity* for suffering to turn his sense of time into an experience of eternity: *but God, made man, did have.*

He who shared his Father's glory in all eternity was Himself only subject to time in so far as He chose to limit Himself as Man to our experience of space.   To the extent that He became space-bound by incarnation, to that extent He became time-bound.   According to his divine nature, suffering as Man could be a timeless experience and therefore everlasting — even though our clocks deceptively measured only a few hours.   During these three hours the sun was eclipsed. Undoubtedly this was a historical event, yet it had far more significance than merely being an astronomical phenomenon. It was also symbolic, because the sun is our time-piece and, for the Lord on the cross, when the sun was eclipsed time was also eclipsed.   In the agony of his soul, He had no other reference point, no other clock.   Time slipped into eternity.

The factor which converts protracted suffering into endless suffering is the absence of any available time marker.   A time marker provides a yardstick, a gauge of "how much longer".   And such a gauge provides hope, even if it is far in the distance.   The prisoner who is sure of reprieve after a given number of years has hope, and hope is sufficient to make many kinds of suffering endurable.   When suffering is sufficiently intense however, the sense of future disappears and everything becomes present, NOW.   With the disappearance of the future goes also hope.

One of the things learned by survivors of concentration camps in World War II was that without hope of some kind a man dies.   In recounting his experience at Auschwitz, Viktor Frankl wrote in retrospect:* "What matters is not the meaning of life in general but rather *the specific meaning of a person's life at a given moment*" (emphasis mine).   In prospect and in retrospect we may think that hope would sustain us, but experience shows that if the agony is great enough so that life contracts to the moment, then hope simply disappears.   As Frankl put it, "It is a peculiarity of man that he can only live by looking to the future".   Thus when the suffering of the present shuts out all vision of the future end, that suffering becomes effectively endless, everlasting.   The man who can no longer see the end ceases to live for future release and dies in the very now-ness of despair.

All this must have been true of the Lord Jesus as He passed into the agony of being held responsible for all the sins of mankind — all the cruelty, hatred, viciousness, selfishness, violence, filthiness of mind

---

* Frankl, Viktor, *Man's Search for Meaning*, N.Y., Simon & Schuster, 1963, p. 112, 115, 171.

and wickedness of spirit that men have ever exhibited throughout history.   The tally is appalling.   We catch a glimpse of it occasionally when we read of some incident that makes us physically ill just to think about it.   All this was "laid upon Him" (Isa.53:6): for all this He assumed responsibility and blame.   And just as the more debased a man is the less is his spirit burdened by blame for his wickedness, so the purer a man is the greater is the burden upon his spirit of the wickedness of other men.   Jesus Christ was morally perfect, utterly without sin, entirely blameless as no other man has ever been.   Yet God made Him responsible for our sins and punished Him by the searing of his conscience and by turning away from Him as from an evil and contaminated thing of wickedness.   He was sent as a scapegoat, condemned, into utter banishment, into an outer darkness of such an appalling nature that hope ceased because time stood still.   The only clock which might have kept hope alive was blacked out.

What, then, is the significance of three hours?   Have *three* hours any meaning in such a situation?   If unredeemed man is to suffer eternal punishment, did Jesus Christ suffer eternal punishment in these three hours?   Should those hours have been much longer?   Could they have been far shorter and still satisfied the demands of justice?

This brings us to the second point posed in this chapter, namely, the actual amount of time required to fufill an eternity of penalty on our behalf.   And here, at the risk of seeming insensitive to the seriousness of the question, I want to use a simile that may appear to be frivolous.   But I believe it will help to establish this second point, which is that there is an equivalence between length and depth of penalty where depth of suffering can be such as to make length unimportant.

There are two schools of candy-eaters.   Both schools are composed mostly of children.   There is the youngster who plops a candy into his mouth and lets the sweet juices slowly dissolve, bathing the taste buds gently and for quite a long time.   Then there is the youngster who finds this gentle slow delivery system quite unsatisfactory.   He starts immediately breaking up the candy with his molars so that the flow of sweetness which results from the greatly increased surface area of the many smaller pieces proves much more exciting.   For a while the volume of taste is marvellous and it absorbs all his attention.   He stares into space wholly occupied with delight until suddenly he discovers the candy is all gone;   the last fragment has surreptitiously slipped down the throat with almost indecent haste.   All too soon there is nothing left: nothing that is, except the resolve to next time suck it much more slowly!   There are many in the first school — mostly girls I suspect;   but there are perhaps more in the second school —

mostly boys, I think. I always resolved to make the candy last, but always failed to keep the resolve — and still do, sixty years later.

Herein is a parable. Enjoyment may be prolonged but mild, or brief but intense: and so it is also with pain. Not infrequently we have a choice even in the matter of pain. We can stay away from 'the house' so that mother will not at once send us to that highly paid torturer, the dentist; and as a consequence suffer a gnawing ache until it becomes unbearable and cannot be concealed, or until it eases up and finally stops altogether — for a while. Alternatively we can go home like a martyr about to be thrown to the lions and in due course for a few agonizing moments allow some eager dentist to probe relentlessly, all the time asking, "Does that hurt?" when he can see that we are suffering agonies even from his mere looking at us.   .

So there we have the principle: long and mild, or short and awful. And it is a principle of very wide application. We can chop a man's head off (in France they still do) or imprison him for twenty years. [241] We assume, of course, that twenty years of imprisonment is to be preferred by the prisoner, but we do so because neither he nor we can truly anticipate what a long slow painful death these twenty years are likely to be. Being shot by a firing squad is quick, and perhaps hanging is not much more protracted, but given the choice men opt for the long and the mild rather than the short and sharp — except for a few brave or perhaps strangely misguided (?) individuals.

If such alternatives exist, if length of suffering can be replaced by depth, then clearly the capacity for experiencing this depth of suffering will determine whether a penalty that is to be endured will continue for a long time or a short time. Presumably if that capacity was infinite, the penalty could conceivably be applied with such intensity that it would not occupy *time* at all. But there is a principle in law very widely recognized which holds that justice must not only be done but that it must also *be seen to be done.* The question then arises, Could the time factor in the Lord's bearing of our sins have been eliminated entirely? I think the answer to this must be, No.

It is not possible for us, as mere human beings, to recognize the reality of suffering, no matter how intense it is, unless it also bears some relationship to duration. All our suffering involves time. We would have difficulty recognizing as an adequate penalty a kind of one dimensional suffering which does not occupy any time at all. Intensity would not therefore alone suffice to compensate for extension of suffering demanded by the offence, even if there was some way of demonstrating adequately afterwards that a real satisfaction had been effected.

For the God-Man who lived both inside and outside our time-frame (and who still so lives) there was undoubtedly no *need* for that three hours of darkness. It was in part an accomodation to our powers of comprehension, our sense of the oughtness of things. It is quite possible that in those three hours from twelve noon to three in the afternoon, time was converted from endless length (*everlasting* punishment) into unfathomable depth of nowness* (*eternal* punishment). Yet the time component could not be reduced to a single instant of infinite depth because the Lord Jesus suffered *as Man*, and therefore, as Man, had to experience some time component, even while his agony of soul must have plumbed the depths of eternity in a way which only his deity could make possible. Some compromise was necessary, some stretching of instantaneity to meet the limits of our comprehension, lest we should be misled into supposing that because his agony lacked the dimension of time it was not really a sufficient sacrifice at all.

We are not altogether without some helpful analogies in the face of this mystery. Viktor Frankl writes eloquently of the kind of torture that was the daily experience of men in the Nazi concentration camps whose position at the time seemed so utterly without hope. As he put it:†

> In Camp, a small time unit, a day for example, was filled with hourly tortures, and fatigue appeared endless. A larger time unit, perhaps a week, seemed to pass very quickly. My comrades agreed when I said that in Camp *a day lasted longer than a week* [emphasis mine].

In such a situation the sufferer and the observers (the guards) lived in entirely different worlds of time: the former in a time-frame distorted by expansion or contraction to the extent that suffering was painful or bearable; the latter went by a clock that was mechanical. For the sufferer, the more painful the experience the less did he measure time as the observer did. Within certain limits of suffering the future can still offer hope of an end, and some assessment of the passage of time is then possible. One can say to oneself, "I'm halfway through" or "It's nearly over, soon I shall reach the end". The existence of hope and the sense of the passage of time run together. As the suffering intensifies, the ability to escape into the future (or to retreat into the past) diminishes until extreme agony pins down all consciousness to the unbearable present, eclipsing both future and past and converting the momentary *now* into an eternity. Suffering takes on a conscious quality of endlessness and soon there is no time

---

* Luther defined eternity as the nowness of God's consciousness. He called eternity "total simultaneity" (*totum simul*).

† Frankl, Viktor, *Man's Search for Meaning*, N.Y., Simon & Schuster, 1963, p.112.

sense whatever.

We are told in Scripture that punishment will be *eternal*. Because we tend to think of the severity of punishment in terms of its duration, we assume this word is equivalent to *everlasting*.[242] But it is possible that the word *eternal* (*aionios* in the Greek) has to do with depth not length, with intensity not extensity.

In some unfathomable way the Lord Jesus Christ as our substitute must similarly have experienced eternal punishment and one has to ask then, How does this quality of eternity relate to the three hours of darkness on the cross?   Was this experienced by the Lord as three hours, or was this just the time period accounted for by the guards on duty and by the others present?   Is it possible that the supernatural darkness of those hours actually signified, among other things, that the one agency in God's economy by which our sense of time is regulated, namely the sun, had been "stopped"* for that interval?   Did time stop for the Lord?   Did He experience a present appalling reality in which there was no passage of time, no moments past with less moments yet to be endured?   Was his agony so intense that it was, in fact, eternal?

Was this, then, a form of eternal punishment, an experience of awful isolation and total separation from his Father, the only total loneliness He had ever known, now *experienced for ever*? His soul was made a scapegoat when there was laid upon Him the full responsibility for every evil, every wickedness, all the poison of human hatred, and the total horror of man's inhumanity to man since Adam fell.   In becoming responsible (and there is a sense in which there was justice in this, for did He not in the first place create man with such capabilities?) He could no longer pray, "Father forgive them": rather it might now have been time to pray, "Father, forgive ME".   But there was no ground of forgiveness for *Him*.   He became unforgiveably wicked: and even God turned from Him.   All He could cry was "My God! My God! Why hast Thou *forsaken* Me?"

Of course, He had known this had to be.   But anticipating that a fearful agony is to be borne even though, in prospect, we know that it must come to an end (for He told his disciples that He would rise again), is a different thing from experiencing that agony with such intensity that it becomes effectively endless.   In anticipation He knew what was to come: and while I do not believe He had a *fear* of it, He must have had a *horror* of what it would entail.   His prayer in Gethsemane bears this out.   But when the blow fell . . . .   Who can

---

* I don't suggest *literally* stopped: but effectively stopped because its movement could no longer be seen.   The Lord was, in experience, left on the cross without a clock.

possibly know what He endured in that eternity in order that our eternity of punishment might be commuted to total blamelessness because He had experienced it in our place.

John Taylor has eloquently expressed something of the way in which the Lord Jesus Christ identified Himself with man in his fallen condition:*

> The vicarious suffering of Christ was not, as it has sometimes been represented, a sort of legal fiction; "in all their affliction He was afflicted" was quite literally true through the imaginative sensitiveness of his perfect Manhood.   In a limitless compassion He Himself knew what was in man.   He groped in the darkness of blind Bartimaeus, and was filled with the self-loathing of the leper; his soul was sick with the Magdalene's sin, and was lost in the tortuous suspicions of Judas.

All this was part of the price that had to be paid.   But there was something more than mere identity with man's unhappy lot.   On the cross, as Albertus Pieters puts it, He took upon Himself as the eternal Son of God the *responsibility* for human sins.†   In human terms, when a man takes the responsibility for the misbehaviour of another, he says in effect, "I did it".   And the law punishes *him* as the actual offender.   Dare we suppose that the Lord Jesus Christ, whose moral purity shines forth with the brightness of the sun and whose flawlessness of character even his worst enemies have been forced to praise unstintingly, was actually counted as the perpetrator of all man's wickedness?   Was He really numbered among the transgressors (Isa. 53:12)?

Was He then accounted guilty of rape and murder, of the appalling cruelty of a Nero who lighted his gardens with Christians burnt on stakes like torches, of the utter ruthlessness of an oriental despot who piled up the severed heads of his victims into a pyramid outside the city walls — in short, of the veritable mountain of wickedness that has characterized the history of mankind from the murder of Abel to the atrocities of guerilla tactics in the troubled spots of the world or the vendettas of our cities?   Was He accounted to have been, in effect, the perpetrator of all *this* because He was responsible for the creation of man with all of his potential?   I do not see that we really have any alternative than to believe that in those three hours of darkness this is what came to pass.

Because He was *God*, his capacity for suffering was infinite. And we must suppose, I think, that it could have been over in no *time* at all.

---

* Taylor, John, *Man in the Midst*, London, Highway Press, 1955, p. 49.

† Pieters, Albertus, *Divine Lord and Saviour*, N.Y., Revell, 1949, p. 116.

But because He was *Man*, the time factor could not altogether be dispensed with, and even by our clocks that "moment of time" had to be stretched into hours.

But at last the sun burst forth once more, re-establishing the sense of time, thus signalling the end of an eternity of suffering, and restoring the fellowship once again between the Father and the Son. A full, perfect, and sufficient satisfaction against man's unrighteousness had been effected in the sight of God. It was not merely the suffering of sympathy: it was the agony of blame and assumed responsibility. That we might be truly saved, the Man Jesus Christ was actually *lost*. Here, surely, He descended into hell . . . . If we are permitted some freedom in paraphrase, Isaiah 53:10 and 11 sums up this transaction by saying:

> It pleased the Father to bruise the Son,
> The Father hath put Him to grief . . . .
> The Father shall see the travail of the soul of the Son
> and shall be satisfied.

The three hours of darkness which covered an eternity of suffering were an essential part of the price which must be paid. And this satisfaction for our sins would not have been possible in any other form of execution. Manifestly, all other forms of execution involve sudden death, or very nearly so. Beheading is instantaneous, stoning extends the time of reprieve by only a few minutes, and burning by very little more. Crucifixion alone of all forms of execution delays death not merely for minutes or hours but even for days. The cross thus provided a stage upon which this aspect of man's redemption could be wrought out so publicly that a historical record was made which satisfies the requirement that justice is seen to have been done. Crucifixion as the form of execution in this case was no historical accident: it was all part of the plan of redemption.

But the end is not even yet. The Lord Jesus had, as a scapegoat, suffered under the divine wrath of God for our SINS. One more penalty yet remained: He must take the sting out of death itself as a SIN-offering.

✦

Chapter 32

DEATH BY AN ACT OF WILL

No man taketh (my life) from Me,
I lay it down of myself.
John 10:18

He humbled Himself
and became obedient unto death.
Philippians 2:8

Because man is a body/spirit entity, we suffer two kinds of death and accordingly need two kinds of redemption. Redemption is therefore not merely of the soul, but also the redemption of the body which is every bit as necessary for the salvation of the whole man (Rom.8:23).

The Redeemer must assume man's place by experiencing both deaths. As the Redeemer must provide for the rebirth of the spirit that is dead in SINS, so must He guarantee the resurrection of the body mortalized by SIN. To die for our SINS only is but to half redeem us, and half a redemption is really no redemption at all. The penalty of SIN must also be paid.

We have now seen how He assumed our SINS. Now we must observe how He assumed our SIN: that basic defect we carry in our bodies which we inherit by natural generation from Adam, and which brings upon us a physical death that was never intended and is wholly unnatural for us. The two transactions are clearly separable, and the termination of each marked by a cry from the cross that was not a cry of despair but a cry of triumph!

When after an eternity of appalling darkness and isolation, the debt of SINS was finally paid, the sun burst through the blanket of cloud and the Father's face shone again upon his beloved Son.   Then the Lord Jesus Christ cried out in triumph "Tetelestai" — and the "My God! My God!" of despair became again the "Father" of restored fellowship.   This wonderful word, TETELESTAI, as Moulton and Milligan have shown from its use in Greek papyri of that day, was precisely equivalent to our PAID IN FULL stamped upon a cancelled debt!*   How is it that such a grand truth, widely known for half a century now, is so seldom mentioned from the pulpit?

It is true that this is a *Greek* word, and that the Lord almost certainly used *Aramaic* in ordinary conversation.   But such a Greek term could very well have been commonly adopted into Aramaic as a borrowed word, much as we have adopted many French words into English like *buffet, valet, café*, and scores of other words.   How better could He have conveyed the note of triumph?   The debt of our SINS has been marked in bold letters **PAID IN FULL**.   It is done.   It is finished . . . .   And so it was.

But there remains yet one more redemptive act to be performed. The body, too, must be redeemed.   This was his second great act of triumph and it involved a wholly unique dying, a dying of a kind never seen before in history and never to be witnessed again.   Let us turn all our attention now to the circumstances surrounding this second dying by which the Lord Jesus Christ completed his sacrifice and perfected our salvation.

We have already considered what physical immortality means. "Not impossible to die but possible not to die".   This was Augustine's description of the constitution of Adam as first created.   Adam could have lived for ever without tasting death.   If this had been said of any living organism a few years ago, it would have been considered as quite absurd: but today it is recognized among biologists as a simple reality for millions of living things below man.   Few if any non-Christian biologists would hold that this might have been true of the first *man*: but Augustine undoubedly had rightly interpreted the implications of the Genesis account of Adam's creation.

And such was the position also of the Lord Jesus Christ.   Virgin-born in order to escape the heredity of man's acquired mortal condition and therefore not made subject to the entail of Adam's disobedience and destined to die as we are,   He enjoyed a truly realizable prospect

---

* Moulton, J. H. and G. Milligan, *Vocabulary of the Greek Text: Illustrated from the Papyri and Other Non-Literary Sources*, Grand Rapids, Eerdmans, 1972, p. 630.

of living on for ever according to the potential of an endless life (Heb.7:16).   Like Adam, He too could die: for He, like Adam, *did* die.   But He, like Adam, need never have done so: and therefore his death could be a voluntary sacrifice of life made under no compulsion other than his own active will.

When Adam disobeyed and ate the forbidden fruit, he did not merely *shorten* his life: he introduced death into human experience as something entirely alien to it.   He deliberately rendered himself mortal and in due time paid the penalty of a body mortally wounded.

It was quite otherwise with the Lord Jesus.   For He never surrendered his immortality.   But in due course, at a time of his own choosing, He deliberately embraced death, dismissing his life by an act entirely free of any compulsion save that of his own willed intention.

Unlike ourselves, for whom life is contingent and must be surrendered in due time, the Lord Jesus Christ had life *in Himself* (John 5:26). The life which He enjoyed was not something borrowed for a limited period to be relinquished when the allotted term had become exhausted.   In this respect his body was fundamentally different from ours, not different from Adam's body as created but different from ours as we are now constituted as descendants of a disobedient Adam.   From the time we are born we are slowly dying from some kind of inherited poison; even probably from the time of conception.   The Lord Jesus Christ was conceived of the Holy Spirit, and was holy in Mary's womb (Luke 1:35).   It was not so much his birth that set Him apart in this respect as it was his conception.   And as the very beginning of his being as Man was supernatural, so was the termination of it on the cross.   Conceived supernaturally, He died super-naturally.

The death of Jesus Christ may be viewed in three different contexts.   It was a *historical* event, it was a *moral* event, and it was a *divine* event.

We have already explored the crucifixion from the strictly historical point of view — its ghastliness, its social function, its mode, its consequences for the individual, its religious significance in the light of Deuteronomy 21:23 and Galatians 3:13 in cursing the dead — and, in the case of the Lord Jesus, in providing a unique stage upon which the redemptive process could be carried out.

It is necessary to start here with its *historical* aspect because there are many passages in Scripture which seem to indicate that Jesus Christ was in fact *killed, executed,* in the process and as a direct result of human intervention in his life.   And this in spite of his assurance that no man would or could take his life from Him.

For example, Peter in his first sermon said, "Ye men of Israel, hear these words; Jesus of Nazareth, a man approved of God among you by miracles and wonders and signs, which God did by him in the midst of you, as ye yourselves also know; Him, being delivered by the determinate council and foreknowledge of God, ye have taken, and by wicked hands *have crucified and slain*" (Acts 2:22,23). And Peter repeated this in his first Epistle: "For Christ hath also once suffered for sins, the just for the unjust, that He might bring us to God, *being put to death* * in the flesh, but quickened by the Spirit" (1 Peter 3:18).

From which, along with the testimony of such other passages as Acts 5:30 and 10:39 (already examined), we gain the impression that He was indeed "slain". And we may wonder in what sense this could be true in the light of his own assurances to the contrary in John 10:18 which is most explicit.

So we are driven to the conclusion that there was a *moral* aspect to his death that was quite distinct from the purely historical aspect, in which actual responsibility for his death was incurred by both Jews and Gentiles alike. From this perspective they are indeed morally responsible and in this sense we can be said to have *slain* Him. He was executed by the Romans as an expedient and murdered by the Jews because they hated Him.

Yet from the *divine* point of view He was not slain at all! No man took *his* life from Him: He laid it down entirely of his own will. He did not merely choose the time when He would submit to man to destroy Him, a choice which even *we* might make. He actually chose to die — a choice that is never within our power.

He did not surrender to death as we are called upon to do when our allotted time is exhausted: He embraced death. Death conquers us: He conquered death. It conquers us because it is stronger than our will to live. He conquered it because He willed to die. He did not will to die as the man who is sick at heart may wish he were dead and prays for death to overtake him, or finds some artificial way in which to assist his own demise. Jesus simply dismissed life.

We are by birth subject to death: He *became* subject to death (Phil.2:8). We are humbled by death: He *humbled* Himself (Phil.2:8). We suffer death as a *passive* experience: He experienced death *actively*. Death *happens* to us, but it did *not* happen to Him. Death is always an accident in man but it was by no accident that Jesus died. There was nothing accidental about it. It was by an act of will that

---

* It should be noted that the Greek word θανατόω used here can just as properly be translated "being *condemned* to death", or "being delivered up to death". The act of slaying may not necessarily be attached to the phrase — only the fact of handing over for this purpose. For example, see Matthew 10:21, where the meaning cannot imply actual slaying. [See Rudolph Bultmann, *Theological Dictionary of the New Testament*, ed. G. Kittel, Grand Rapids, Eerdmans, Vol. III, p. 21. So also Bagster, *Analytical Greek Lexicon*, under θνῄσκω.

He Himself terminated his life just as soon as He had truly finished the work that his Father had given Him to do as the Lamb of God. Death did not happen to Him, He "happened" it.

Now we have, of course, four Gospels and each is different in its own unique way since only thus could all the dimensions of the Lord's Person and work be even remotely displayed. Three of these are termed synoptic because they seem to reflect a single point of view. There is a kind of down-to-earthness about them. The life of God made flesh is seen largely as man might have seen it. They are divinely inspired but human-point-of-view accounts, as it were. Events are set within a strictly human space-time framework. The fourth, by contrast, reflects another dimension, the timeless aspects of the Lord's Person and work. Accordingly, in dealing with the Lord's death on the cross, Matthew, Mark and Luke in referring to the fact of his actual death all use terms that are common to human experience — but John does not.

There are a number of words which may be used in Greek to describe the act of dying — just as in English one may speak of a man as expiring, as breathing out his last, as giving up the ghost, or euphemistically as merely "passing on". And so forth. In Greek we commonly find such words used as: ἀφίημι *(aphiemi)* as in Matthew 27:50 meaning "to give up"; or ἐκπνέω *(ekpneo)* meaning "to breathe out" as in Mark 15:37 or Luke 23:46. Both of these words are essentially equivalent to the English *expire*. In the new Scofield Bible at Matthew 27:50 there is this footnote:

> The Greek words used here and in John 19:30 are unique in the New Testament. In 15 other Bible verses, 'gave up the spirit' or 'yielded up the spirit', is used to translate a single Hebrew or Greek word meaning *breathe out* or *expire*. This is true of the description of the death of Jesus in Mark 15:37, 39 and Luke 23:46.
> But in Matthew 27:50 and John 19:30 alone these expressions translate a Greek phrase of two words meaning 'give over the spirit' or 'deliver up the spirit'. The death of Jesus was different from that of any other man. No man could take his life from Him except He was willing to permit it (John 10:18). Christ chose to die so that we might live.

I have no desire to be unnecessarily critical of a footnote which serves thus to draw particular attention to one of the most wonderful truths in Scripture. Yet this footnote does require to be qualified. First of all, it is true that there are 15 passages of Scripture in which a single Hebrew or Greek word is used which means "to breathe out" or "expire" and which is rendered by some such phrase as "gave up the ghost". Although the footnote does not list these passages, according to my search they are probably the following:

The Hebrew word גָוַע (gava') occurs in:

Gen.25:8	Gen.49:33	Job 13:19
25:17	Job 3:11	14:10
35:29	10:18	Lam.1:19

The Greek word ἐκψύχω (ekpsucho) occurs in:

Acts 5:5, 10 (2x)   Acts 12:23

The Greek word ἐκπνέω (ekpneo) occurs in:

Mark 15:37, 39 (2x)   Luke 23:46

So far, so good. The point at which the footnote could be misleading is in the statement that the Greek word used in Matthew 27:50 is unique in the New Testament. As it stands, the statement per se is correct: but the *implication* is not. The Greek word ἀφίημι (aphiemi) certainly does often mean in biblical Greek "to send away", "to bid depart", "to send forth", but it also means to "give up" or "surrender". Thayer has a full statement on this verb. I think the implication of the footnote is that in applying this particular verb to the sending away of the spirit, Scripture is singling out the Lord's death as being unique in the sense that He deliberately dismissed his spirit as an act of will.

I am absolutely certain that this is what the Lord did: but I do not think this truth can be established by reference to Matthew 27:50 because we have in extra-biblical Greek as well as in the Septuagint version occasions where the same phrase is used a propos *ordinary human death*. Thus in the Septuagint, Genesis 35:18 is rendered: ἐγένετο δὲ ἐν τῷ ἀφιέναι αὐτὴν τὴν ψυχὴν ἀπέθνησκε γὰρ — "and it came to pass that in the sending away of her soul, for she was dying . . . ." A similar phrase occurs in the Septuagint rendering of 1 Esdras 4:21, μετὰ τῆς γυναικὸς ἀφίησι τὴν ψυχὴν — i.e., "and with his wife he sendeth away his soul . . . ."

In classical Greek *aphiemi*, where followed by either the word for *soul* or *spirit*, is used the death of mortal men — as an example, by Aeschylus in his *Tragic Poems* written about 346 B.C., and earlier still by Euripides in his *Tragic Drama*, about 441 B.C.

Thus, in itself, the wording of Matthew 27:50 does not prove so exceptional, being on occasion employed for ordinary death in the Septuagint version of the Old Testament (written about 240 B.C.) and by classical Greek authors. These parallel passages do not by themselves signify that there was anything supernatural about the passing of those whose death is being recorded, and one could not therefore argue with absolute certainty that Matthew 27:50 necessarily implies something supernatural in the Lord's case, on this basis alone.

What has been said of Matthew 27:50 applies with equal force to Mark 15:37 and 39 and to Luke 23:46. In these three verses it will be remembered that the Greek word is ἐκπνέω *(ekpneo)*. This word is also used in Classical Greek with or without a noun corresponding to "breath" or "soul" or "life", for the death of ordinary human beings. For example, in his poem *Agamemnon* (line 1493) Aeschylus uses it; and Sophocles in his play *Ajax* (line 1026) uses it also.

However, when we come to John 19:30 where the Greek word παραδίδωμι *(paradidomi)* is found, the situation is very different. Neither in Classical Greek nor in the Greek Version of the Old Testament is there ever found any occasion upon which this verb is used in connection with the word "soul" or "spirit" for the act of dying. Moulton and Milligan, in their study of New Testament words in the light of the papyri and other non-literary sources such as inscriptions, etc., have provided numerous examples of the employment of this word with its basic meaning of *handing over* or *delivering*, but no instance is given whatever of the word being applied to the handing over of the spirit in dying.* The same is true of Kittel and Bromiley in their massive 9 volume theological dictionary of the New Testament in which it is normal to find extra-biblical references listed at some length wherever they are available or shed fresh light on New Testament usage.†

The verb itself has a very specific meaning, namely, "to deliver up", and although this kind of "delivering" is used in a wide range of contexts — such as "handing over (a torch)", "handing down (to posterity)", "handing over (to justice)", and so forth — the implication is always and without fail a free-will transfer and *not a surrender*. This is as true in the Septuagint occurrences as it is in Classical Greek usage. In every case someone deliberately hands over something or somebody to someone else, and the thought of surrender is *never* found in the context. In the Greek rendering of the Old Testament, *paradidomi* is used, for instance, wherever God delivers the Israelites into the hands their enemies.‡ There is no question of God's surrendering the people

---

* Moulton, J. H. and G. Milligan, *The Vocabulary of the Greek New Testament*, Grand Rapids Eerdmans, 1972, *loc. sit.*

† Kittel, Gerhard and Geoffrey W. Bromiley, *Theological Dictionary of the New Testament*, Grand Rapids, Eerdmans, 1973, Vol. II, p. 169.

‡ See, for example, Deut.1:8, 21, 27; 2:24, 30, 31, 33, 36; Num.21:2, 3, 34; Josh.10:8, 12, 19, 30, 32, 35; and so on almost indefinitely. In Liddell and Scott's *Classical Greek Lexicon*, no instance is to be found of the word being used in connection with giving up the spirit or the soul. I have been able to find but one single instance of this particular usage in Hatch and Redpath s *Concordance to the Septuagint*, which lists 197 passages exclusive of the Apocrypha. The Septuagint of Isaiah 53:6 reads in English: "All we like sheep have gone astray: everyone has gone astray in his own way: and the Lord *gave Himself up* for our sins" [*Bagster's*

against his will.

This same verb, *paradidomi*, occurs in John 19:30, and therefore signifies that the Lord's death was in no sense a surrender, as it is with us, but a unique form of dismissal.

It is clear that in this last Gospel a new aspect of the Lord's death is presented which cannot be positively demonstrated in the other three Gospels. It is customary in certain circles to say that Mark's Gospel is really the earliest of the Synoptics. But there is, I understand, evidence that the order in which the Gospels appear in our Bible is in fact the correct one, and that Matthew was inspired to write his record almost immediately in order to provide the Jews of the Diaspora with an account of what had occurred leading up to the events witnessed at Pentecost when many of them had assembled in Jerusalem. At any rate, it is quite clear that Matthew, Mark and Luke wrote their Gospels much earlier than John. All three of them recorded the Lord's death in terms which were commonly used. Perhaps they were not inspired to do otherwise partly because the full significance of the theological aspects of the Lord's death were not yet revealed at that time.

But perhaps, also, in view of the nature of the four Gospels which present distinctly different portraits of the Lord — in the first three of which He appears as an ideal representative of mankind in his role as a King, a Servant, and a Man respectively — it was not appropriate to attribute to Him a power in his death which neither kings, nor servants, nor men can have. The situation is quite different in John's account, for the Lord is here presented as the Son of God whose goings were from everlasting and who was the Lord of life. Writing later than the three synoptists, John had more time to reflect upon the events of that terrible day and to see how impossible it is that mere man should presume to put God Himself to death. If the Son of God died, He died "under his own hand" — not under the hand of man. On the Day of Atonement the goat of the SIN-offering died under the hand of the High Priest. On the day of his dying, Jesus Christ was Himself both victim *and* High Priest.

As Paul neared the end of his life, he spoke of himself as "ready *to*

Critical Edition]. In this translation from Hebrew into Greek, the italicized words represent the now familiar Greek word *paradidomi*.

Perhaps it is not without significance that on precisely the same grounds, in what must surely be one of the most revealing of all passages of Scripture, Paul wrote, "I am crucified with Christ: nevertheless I live; yet not I, but Christ liveth in me; and the life which I now live in the flesh I live by the faith of the Son of God, who loved me and delivered *Himself* up for me" (Gal.2:20). Once again, we meet with the verb *paradidomi*.

be offered" (2 Tim.4:6).   But of the Lord Jesus Christ we are told rather that *"He offered Himself"* (Heb.7:27).   Thus while Paul's death was indeed passive (he was probably martyred in Rome), the Lord's death was entirely *active*.

When we become sinners, we become sinners actively, wilfully, by choice.   It is an expression of our will.   On the other hand when we die, it is normally *against* our will.   In the healthy individual it is seldom that death is desired — even the aged cling to life.

By contrast, when the Lord became a sinner in our place, He became a sinner *unwillingly*: unwillingly in the sense that to do so He suppressed his own will in obedience to the Father's.   In Gethsemane He said, "Father, if thou be willing, remove this cup from me: nevertheless, not my will but thy will be done" (Luke 22:42).   This sin-bearing aspect of his sacrifice for SINS was imposed upon Him, and "we esteemed him stricken (passive), smitten (passive) of God, and afflicted (passive).   He was wounded (passive) for our transgressions, he was bruised (passive) for our iniquities . . . .   He was cut off [like the scapegoat] out of the land of the living: for the transgressions of my people was he stricken" (Isa.53:4, 5, 8).   All is passive.   In no way was his encounter with our sins something He sought except in the sense that He set Himself to do his Father's will.

It is in this sense that we may most properly speak of his assuming the place of the sinner against his will and not because He Himself had the slightest desire to become sinful.   Man, on the other hand, becomes sinful readily, almost with eagerness.   It is our *choice*: it was not his.   We become what we are because it is really what we want to be — until we are born again as a new person with a whole new set of motivations.   To sin is natural to us as we mature.   To Him it was never anything but abhorrent.

But in the matter of physical death the situation is exactly reversed. We die quite contrarily to our will, whereas He died precisely when He chose to do so.   Even this is not an adequate statement, for we are still likely to suppose it means only this: that while *we* submit unwillingly to death, *He* submitted willingly.*   The truth is far more profound. Death for us is a surrender, and it is in this sense that we *submit*, and submit against our will.   Jesus Christ *embraced death*.   *He did* not submit to it either willingly or unwillingly.   The use of the word *paradidomi* in John makes this abundantly clear.

This is borne out by John's use of the word in John 19:16 and 30. In the first instance we are told that Pilate "delivered up" Jesus to be

---

* Unfortunately, this is precisely what the note in the Scofield Bible at Matthew 27:50 suggests — but it is not the case, fortunately for us.

crucified, and in the last instance we are told that Jesus "delivered up" his spirit into the Father's hands. In a beautiful way, these two statements correspond to Isaiah 53:7, "He is brought as a lamb to the slaughter", and to Hebrews 7:27, "He offered Himself". The Lord became both Lamb and High Priest: Sacrifice and Sacrificer. As Tertullian put it, "Christ when crucified spontaneously dismissed his spirit with a word, thus preventing [i.e., anticipating and forestalling] the office of the executioner".* Origen observed that when life was no longer needed since He had now completed the work his Father had given Him to do, "the One who had the power of laying down his life, laid it down when He chose. This prodigy astonished the centurion who said, 'Truly this was the Son of God'."†

Origen was not alone in believing that the extraordinary circumstance of the Lord's actual dying was so manifestly exceptional that it convinced the centurion of its supernatural aspect. Jerome, in commenting on Matthew 27:50, likewise notes that when the centurion heard Him saying "Father, into thy hands I commend my spirit", and perceived that He immediately dismissed his spirit of his own accord, he was struck with the greatness of what he perceived to be something quite unique: a man commanding his own life to cease.‡

The act of dismissal must have been clearly a command rather than a submission. The centurion, standing by, recognized it for what is was. It is entirely appropriate that a Roman who could say to one under his authority, "Go!" – and he goes (Matt.8:9), should now perceive that the Lord was exercising the same prerogative of authority. Thus he exclaimed, "Truly this was the Son of God!" (Matt.27:54). For who else could give such a command in such a circumstance and see it instantly carried out?

Many others have struggled to find words to express the uniqueness of his death. John Murray wrote:*

> (The death of Jesus) was unique because of the way in which He died. No other died as He died. How can this be? All others die because forces other than their own wrest life from them and sever the bond uniting body and spirit. Not so Jesus on the accursed tree. He was indeed crucified by others; He did not crucify Him-

---

* Tertullian, Quintus, "Apology", *Ante-Nicene Fathers*, ed. A. Roberts and J. Donaldson, N.Y., Scribners, 1918, Vol. III, p. 35.

† Origen: See William Stroud, *The Physical Causes of the Death of Christ*, N.Y., Appleton, 1871, p. 64.

‡ Jerome: see William Stroud, *ibid*, p. 64.

★ Murray, John, "The Death of Christ" in *Collected Writings*, Edinburgh, Banner of Truth, Vol. I, 1976, p. 37.

self.   But when He died, He dismissed his spirit, He laid down his
life: He, in the exercise of his own agency and by the authority
given, severed the bond.

James Denny in 1895 wrote: *

> If death was precisely the same problem for Christ that it is for
> us, then the New Testament way of speaking about His death is
> simply incomprehensible.   If the first Christians had been of this
> mind, the phraseology we find in every page of Scripture could not
> have arisen.   But they were not of this mind.
> They believed that Christ was sinless, and therefore that death,
> although included in His vocation, had a unique significance, and
> presented a unique problem to Him.   His death is a solitary phen-
> omenon — the one thing of the kind in the universe — a sinless One
> submitting to the doom of sin.   It was *His* death, certainly, for He
> had come to die;   but it was *not* His, for He knew no sin;   it was
> *for us*, and *not for Himself*, that He made death His own.

Alfred Edersheim sought to express the same profound truth by
saying, "His death, His resurrection — let no one imagine that it came
from without!   It is His own act.   He has 'power' in regard to both,
and both are His own voluntary, Sovereign, and Divine acts". †
We shall probably never be able to find language sufficient for
this supreme event to which the whole of history before it and after it
was prologue or epilogue.

Once the great cry "Tetelestai" had rung out and the "O God!" of
the agony of separation had been replaced by the beautiful relationship
of the Son to the Father once more, there was no need for the Lord to
sustain his life on the cross any longer.   It is important to realize that
all which had occurred during the past six hours, and the climactic
event which was now to occur, was possible only because the setting
for it, the stage, was crucifixion and not some other form of capital
punishment.   Centuries before this, God had been moving in history
to set the pattern for a particular form of capital punishment which
would provide just such a stage.   The Chosen People were not called
upon to initiate this cruel form of punishment, for it was not their
invention as such.   But they were led to adopt it in a different context as a means of desecrating a *dead* person that he might be rendered

---

* Denney, James, *Studies in Theology*, Grand Rapids, Baker reprint, 1976, p. 136.

† Edersheim, Alfred, *The Life and Times of Jesus the Messiah*, N.Y., Herrick, Vol. II, p. 139.
He also wrote: "In the language of an early Christian hymn (by Scotus Sedulius, c. 855), 'It
was not Death which approached Christ, but Christ Death: He died without death..   He en-
countered Death, not as conquered but as Conqueror.   And this also was part of His work
for us" (p. 609).

accursed of God.   In due time the Jewish nation found themselves under the domination of a people who adopted crucifixion (not for Jewish reasons but for Gentile reasons) as the vilest form of capital punishment.

Thus it came about in the providence of God that, historically, the Lord Jesus was crucified and slain, while in Jewish eyes He was crucified and accursed of God — made a curse for us under circumstances which yet allowed Him to take upon Himself our sins and suffer in our stead the torments of eternity.

By any other mode of capital punishment, only a miracle could have preserved the Lord alive as an effective and voluntary sin-offering.   As it was, crucifixion became the stage that provided the setting for such a sacrifice.   And it was only *by a miracle* that He died when He did.   Even Pilate expressed surprise . . . .

And so, his work now completed, in one single gesture which demonstrated his dominion over life itself, He dismissed his spirit with the words, "Father into thy hands I commend my spirit" (Luke 23:46).

At the risk of being repetitious, let me see if I can draw together this amazing set of antitheses which set apart the action of the Lord in becoming first of all, an offering for SINS for our sakes (by contrast with the way in which *we* become sinners): and then an offering for SIN for our sakes (by contrast with the way in which death terminates *our* lives).

When we become sinners, our sinfulness proves to be an expression of our true nature.   As Dostoyevsky said, "Man commits sin simply to remind himself that he is free".*   When the Lord Jesus became a sinner, it was not according to his will, but by his Father's will.   Sinfulness was in no sense whatever an expression of his nature.   What we bring upon ourselves *actively*, He assumed entirely *passively*:   it was laid upon Him to his utter abhorrence.   For three hours (by our misguided clocks) He endured for us an eternity of punishment, utterly forsaken by both men *and God* in his experience, in order that we might recover the fellowship of God for which we were made.   He surrendered the Father's fellowship for an eternity that we might enjoy it for ever.

It may help to summarize in the form of a series of antithetical statements, the profound difference between the way the Lord Jesus died and the way we die.

---

* Dostoyevsky, F. M., *Letters from the Underworld*, quoted by D. R. Davies, *Down Peacock Feathers*, London, Bles, 1942, p. 10.

- We are humbled in death:
     He humbled **Himself.**

- We are subject to death:
     He **became** subject to death.

- We are offered in death:
     He offered **Himself.**

- We surrender to death:
     He **embraced** death.

- We relinquish our spirit:
     He **dismissed** his spirit.

- Our death is passive:
     His death was **active.**

- The very best we can do is choose *the time* of our dying:
     He **chose to die.**

- We can only *shorten* our lives:
     His life was potentially endless and could **never** be
          shortened.

- Our death is the final triumph of *flesh over spirit:*
     His death was the triumph of **spirit over flesh.**

- We are defeated by death:
     He **conquered** death.

     He died **on** the cross
               but not **because of** it.
     He may possibly have died **with** a broken heart*
               but not **because of** it.
     He **disengaged** spirit and body in his death
               and **re-engaged** them in his resurrection.
     His life by his own will was cut **off**
               not cut **short.**

---

* On this matter, see Appendix VII, "Heart Rupture: A Possible Cause of the Lord's Death?"

The cross itself was no more the *cause* of the death of the Lamb of God than was the altar the *cause* of the death of the sin-offering on the Day of Atonement. The cross was the occasion — but not the cause — of his dying.

When we die, even by some kind of self-sacrifice, we merely shorten our life. We only sacrifice what remains of our allottment. We cannot speak of his sacrificing what remained of his allottment of life — his life was potentially *endless* How can one define the sacrifice of what if left of what is potentially endless? He sacrificed life itself.

In reality, there is really no way in which we can compare his death and ours. We can only contrast them. All that we have surveyed in this study thus far serves only to show in some small measure how the setting for this transcendent event for which the whole order of Nature had been established could transpire as the climactic event of history. It tells us nothing of what really happened when God became Man and, as Man, died that men might live. Only spiritual perception can help us here, and the simplest of God's people may have as perfect an understanding as the profoundest Christian scholar.

The greater Day of Atonement of which the Mosaic institution was but a foreshadowing was now almost completed. The Lord Jesus Christ, in his own Person, had fulfilled the role of the two prototype animal victims. He had been sent into the wilderness of desolation "for ever" in those three dreadful hours of darkness: and then He had offered Himself as the sin-offering and shed his blood, a sign of his being truly dead (John 19:34).

Having completed the first work, He cried, "It is finished!" (John 19:30).* When He was ready to complete the second, He gave a great cry and, dismissing his spirit, committed it into his Father's keeping (Luke 23:46).

One more aspect of this ceremony, however, had still to be fulfilled. Our great High Priest must return to "the congregation" and, by presenting Himself *alive* before them, demonstrate once for all that the blood of his sacrifice had been placed before the true Ark of the Covenant in heaven and there accepted by God on our behalf. To this final act in the drama of the Plan of Redemption we now direct our thoughts in the two chapters which close this study.

---

* John H. Ruttan, in his *New and Complete Harmony of the Gospels* [Toronto, Briggs, 1906, p. 177], orders the terminal events as follows: John 19:30 a, "When Jesus therefore received the vinegar, He said, It is finished". Then, Luke 23:46 a, "And when Jesus had cried with a loud voice, He said, Father, into thy hands I commend my spirit". Then Matthew 27:50 b, Mark 15:37 b, Luke 23:46 b, and John 19:30 b — each of which close with the Lord's expiration.

Chapter 33

RESURRECTION WITHOUT CORRUPTION

*Thou wilt not suffer
thy holy one
to see corruption.*
Psalm 16:10

*For as much as ye know
that ye were not redeemed
with corruptible things
like gold and silver . . . .
but with the precious blood of Christ,
as of a lamb
without blemish and without spot.*
1 Peter 1:18, 19

"He whom God raised up saw no corruption" (Acts 13:37). Upon this fact hinges our salvation. For Scripture says, "Be it known unto you *therefore*, men and brethren, that through this man is preached unto you the forgiveness of sins and by Him all that believe are justified from all things from which you could not be justified by the law of Moses" (Acts 13:38, 39).

That there is an indispensible connection here is established by the use of the word *therefore*: and the things connected are (1) that his body did not see corruption, and (2) that we may accordingly be justified by faith alone without the works of the law. But in what way does our salvation hinge so specifically upon the physiological fact that the Lord's body did not see corruption?

Throughout our whole life there is a corrupting agent permeating every part of our body which is prevented from destroying us only by something in the force of life itself. But it is not held altogether in check, and it slowly subjects us to physical deterioration as the years roll by. When our allotted time has run out and life departs, this corrupting agent proves itself to be the victor. But it has still not finished its work. The restraining effect of life processes being no longer present to hold its baneful influence in check, the corrupting action suddenly accelerates and within a few hours changes take place which mark the beginning of the total breakdown of all organization of the body as such.

But it apparently marks something more than this. The breakdown of body tissues occurs in all animals which are subject to death or which, though not subject to death by nature (amoeba for instance), may have been killed by accident. The total breakdown of the organization of such bodies is clearly not due to sin; for although some of the higher animals might conceivably be accused of wickedness of a sort, this can hardly be said of unicellular creatures. Indeed, I do not think that Scripture supports the view that animals are morally accountable in the sense that man is, certainly not the very simplest of living forms anyway. Their death cannot therefore be attributed to the same cause that brings death to man. If this is so, one has to assume that the corruption which overtakes man's body in death (but which did not overtake the Lord's body while it was in the grave) results from some agency which is not at work in animals below man. Although the course of events after death is such that the bodies of both man and beast are returned to the dust, there is some fundamental difference involved in the process, a difference which has hitherto escaped our notice because we have not taken the trouble to look for it.

To make my point quite clear, consider the matter this way. No matter how much an ape or a monkey may look as though its body is essentially operating on the same bacis principles as man's, there must in fact be some fundamental difference. There are two reasons for saying this.

The first is that we know the first Adam need never have died and we know that the second Adam need never have died: yet both were truly human with respect to the constitution of their bodies. However, we know also that man has *become* a mortal creature due to an act of disobedience at the very beginning, a transformation in physiological terms which cannot be applied to the other primates. Man's death is now inevitable and results from a form of fatal disease which he inherits by natural generation.   Thus although both man and the other primates experience death, the *cause* of death is not the same in each case.

The second reason is that while man, as he now is, inhabits a body which after death appears to suffer the same fate as the bodies of other primates by returning to the dust, we know from the circumstances of the Lord's three days in the tomb that a truly human body *need* not disintegrate in this way.

We have probably been mistaken, therefore, in assuming that the real difference between man and the other higher animal forms rests entirely in his spiritual make-up.   I think we must reconsider this question and make allowance for the fact that a truly human body is not merely an animal body similar in constitution to other like creatures.   It must have been in some fundamental way *different* in its unfallen state (as witnessed in the body of the Lord Jesus).   And it must still be in some fundamental way different since its mortal condition has been imposed upon it in the form of a disease, a fact which surely cannot be applied to the animal body.

Now when the second Adam died, no protoplasmic poison existed in his body to initiate the process of corruption and decay.   This we know from Scripture — at least for the period during which it lay in the tomb.   There can be no doubt that the conditions favoured such decay.   The body of Lazarus had already begun putrefaction under very similar conditions, being in the tomb for approximately the same length of time and at the same season of the year.

If for some reason Adam had been killed in his unfallen state, one must then suppose his body would not have putrefied but *dehydrated,* or dried out — as many animal bodies do.   Under certain conditions man's body may still do this, due to some as yet unidentified quality in the local environment.   There is a city in Mexico in which the bodies of the dead having been allowed to dry first were then in a macabre fashion leaned against the wall of a long passageway where for some reason they have been preserved for centuries, immune from the normal processes of decay and from bacterial action.*   The subject is not a pleasant one, but there is every reason to believe that the natural course of events which now sees man's body putrefying

---

* This is the famous silver mining city in Mexico of Santa Fe of Guanajuato, capital of the Mexican State of the same name, founded by the Spaniards in 1554. Beneath the old public cemetry there are extensive catacombs and the mummified bodies of long departed Spaniards here stand leaning against the walls in a remarkable state of preservation. The faces are weirdly animated and I think it would be difficult to walk between the rows of figures without half expecting them to speak at any moment. [For photograph, see *The World's Greatest Wonders*, London, Odham's Press, (no author or date), p. 233].

before turning to dust may be suspended in certain circumstances, even for a body corrupted by sin.   The suspension is not total but it certainly is partial, and there is no reason to suppose that it might not be total if the human body was as God originally made it.*

In the case of the body of the Lord Jesus the situation is unique and we really have no parallels to guide us.   All that we know for certain is that in that beautiful human body there was none of the poison which brings us to the grave and returns our bodies to the dust by a process which usually involves putrefaction.   Scripture simply tells us, regarding the second Adam's body, that He died in a state of sinlessness and that *his* body did not see corruption at all.

It might be argued that even such a perfect body would have been consumed in time by the action of micro-organisms, but this is not what Scripture means by corruption when referring to the effect of the poison in the forbidden fruit.   It surely means the complete taking over of the body by a special kind of chemical upset which is inherited by all men naturally born and is only slowed up in its action by the force of vital processes which hold it in check for a season but have no power wholly to neutralize it.   Remove these vital processes with their restraining effects, and total decay follows which is shocking and distressing to behold.   It is not a natural process whereby an unwanted body is returned usefully to the good earth to enrich it as is the case with plants and animals. It is something that for man is un-natural because it was never intended to be. And being un-natural, it *is* distressing in a way we are not by nature equipped to accept.

Now this single physiological fact — that the Lord's body did not corrupt in the tomb — has tremendous significance because it is clear we are intended to learn from it that his death, unlike ours, was in no sense caused by anything inherent in his body.   He did not die as we die.   Dying, for us, is the inevitable terminus to our kind of life now corrupted by sin.   In Him was no sin and no corruption.   We are told specifically that we were redeemed by that which was not corrupt (1 Peter 1:18, 19).   The termination of his physical life as a Man was a unique event in human history and it left a unique body in the tomb and that uniqueness was witnessed to by the extraordinary fact that it did not see any corruption.   It was not that it did not *noticeably* corrupt.   It did not corrupt at all.

Scripture not merely affirms this fact as of the greatest importance to us, it goes further and supplies us with clues about certain subsequent events in order to tell us why that perfect body *had* to remain

---

* It is conceivable that some such special dispensation was granted to Moses' body, a circumstance which could lie behind the cryptic statement made in Jude 9.

so wholly uncorrupted.

Now the Lord foretold that his body would be three days and three nights in the grave (Matt.12:40). But why leave the body in the tomb at all? Indeed, why should resurrection not have occurred at once after his death on the cross? After all, his work on earth was done. "It is paid in full" was his last triumphant cry to the world before He commended Himself into his Father's care and dismissed his spirit. Once the certainty of his death had been officially established by the Roman centurion, could He not have been at once raised to life again and come down in triumph from the cross to the great comfort of his disciples and the utter confusion of his enemies?

There is an important reason for the delay. It was necessary that his body lie in the tomb for a certain length of time, and this length of time had to be spelled out as "three days and three nights". The fact is that it was essential for the Lord's death to be legally certified according to Jewish law, and no death was certified until the deceased had been 'dead' for a period of three days and three nights by their system of reckoning (see below, page 428). Until this interval of time had passed and putrefaction had begun (cf. John 11:39), they would not certify death or release a dead man's estate.

The Lord's mission was first of all to the Jewish people and these Jewish people had certain traditional beliefs regarding the dead which God was concerned to respect lest the reality of the Lord's death on the cross should later be challenged. Had any other course been adopted subsequent to his death, the Jews would, according to their understanding of the nature of life and the nature of death, have had every reason to doubt whether Jesus had ever actually died at all — in spite of all the circumstances so dramatically and so convincingly depicted by the four Evangelists. The Lord's death had to be unequivocally established, above all in the eyes of those who had been chosen to play so vital a role in the whole plan of redemption.

The fact is that death was not established, according to their understanding, merely by the apparent expiration of the individual. To demonstrate death without doubt, the body must be laid aside for a certain length of time, in order to ensure that there really was no evidence of life remaining. The Jewish authorities would not supply a death certificate until after the third day,* except in battle and

---

* Ryle, John C., *Commentary on John*, N.Y., Robert Carter, n.d., Vol. II, p. 284. The significance of Revelation 11:9 is at once apparent in this light. The two witnesses who are to prophesy for 42 months are to be slain and their bodies are to lie exposed ("not to be put in graves") for three days and a half. That is to say, their death is to be certified before the world. There are many who believe that these two witnesses will be Enoch and Elijah, the

in certain types of fatal accident.

There was some justification for taking these precautions since there is considerable evidence that many people have probably been buried alive as a result of faulty certification of death. It has happened upon occasion that, due to some circumstance necessitating the removal of a graveyard, bodies have been found in unnatural positions as though they had revived in the grave; and not a few individuals have revived just in time to save themselves from being buried alive by those who honestly believed them to be dead. Gould and Pyle have recorded some remarkable instances, particularly in cases of catalepsy or trance and during epidemics of malignant fevers or plagues in which there is an absolute necessity of hasty burial for the prevention of contagion. One such plague victim was burned alive, crying out only after it was too late to quench the fire.[243]

The view that a person should not be considered irretrievably dead until after the lapse of three days is very widespread. It is found among primitive and highly civilized people, ancient and modern. In his *History* (Bk. V, chap. 8), Herodotus reported that the Thracians laid out the bodies of their dead for three days and during this time offered many sacrifices while bewailing the departed, presumably in the hopes of inducing the spirit to re-enter the body. Failing this, at the end of the three days they either burned the body or buried it in the ground. In a certain initiation ceremony among the Egyptians, the candidate was laid in a stone coffin for three days, probably under the influence of some drug, during which time he experienced a state of transcendence.[244] At the end of the three days he was returned to a normal state of consciousness and told that he had died and been restored to a new life. The same period of three days is found reflected in the burial customs of one of the most primitive tribes in India, the Badaga, and among the Bhouyas of Bengal who appear to have been much more sophisticated.[245] Many of the Northwest Coast Indians of North America pay special respect to the third or fourth day after apparent death as marking the final break between the living and the dead.[246] Professor George P. Murdock observes that the Aztecs of Mexico believed the spirit of the dead remained near the body for four days before departing irrevocably for an underworld. On the

---

only two men who have been translated so that they have not "seen death". But it is appointed unto *all* men to die (Heb.9:27) and perhaps Enoch and Elijah are not to be excepted. For this reason their death is to be most clearly certified. There is one exceptional circumstance under which this appointment to death is to be laid aside, and that is when the Lord returns. For at that time those who are his children and remain alive will not die (1 Thess.4:17 and 1 Cor.15:51). But this is a mystery which was not revealed to the Old Testament saints, and is a unique situation in any case.

fourth day after death the body was placed on a funeral pile and burned with incense.[247]

But was Jesus Christ three days and three nights, a period of 72
hours, in the tomb?   The answer depends much on whether the
crucifixion took place on Friday, as traditionally held, or on some
previous day.   If tradition is right, then Jesus was buried late on Friday, lay in the tomb over Friday night and all day Saturday, and part
of Saturday night, rising so early that no one arrived on Sunday morning early enough to find his body still in the tomb.   I think that
Scripture has gone out of its way to emphasize this fact, as though
God were impatient and would not delay the raising of the Lord Jesus
one minute beyond the appropriate time that must be spent in the
grave to satisfy the Jewish law.   Matthew says that "Mary Magdalene
and the other Mary" were there *at dawn* (Matt.28:1) — and they were
too late (verse 6).   Mark, speaking of the same two women, tells us
that "It was *very early in the morning*" (Mark 16:2), and Luke uses
the same terminology (Luke 24:1).   John tells us that when they
arrived "it was *yet dark*" (John 20:1), just light enough for them to
see that the stone had been rolled away.
    Now this only tends to emphasize that the Jewish reckoning of
such a period as three days and three nights did not constitute the full
period of 72 hours which we with our more precise measurement of
time would demand.   When the Lord said He would be in the grave
three days and three nights (Matt.12:40), He was speaking within the
context of Jewish thinking.   Had He not done so, He would obviously
have had to elaborate what He meant.   But clearly He meant three
days and three nights as they reckoned them.   It is important again to
bear in mind that with them the day began at six o'clock in the evening.   Since the Lord was laid in the grave *before* 6 PM on Friday and
arose from the tomb *after* 6 PM on Saturday, He actually spent some
part of Friday, the whole of Saturday, and some part of Sunday in the
grave.
    For the Jews, as for many other peoples (including ourselves under
certain circumstances), any part of a day or any part of a year counted
as a whole day or a whole year.*   Thus a king who came to the throne
on the last day of one year, then ruled for the following year but survived only through part of the first day of the third year, was actually
credited with a three year reign!   In the *Babylonian Talmud*, the
Eighth Tractate of the *Mishnah* has this statement: "Our rabbis have
taught that if a king begins his reign on the 29th of Adar [our March,

---

* B. *Rosh Hasshanah*, p. 2 a and b.

and the last month of their calendar year], as soon as it is the first of
Nisan [our April], a year is reckoned to him . . . . and one day in a
year is counted as a year". This is repeated in the Third Tractate of
the *Mishnah* where it is written, "The portion of the day is as the
whole of it".*

In the *Jerusalem* or *Palestinian Talmud* and the First Tractate of
the *Mishnah*, there is a statement, "We have a teaching [from Rabbi
Eleazar ben Azaryah who flourished from 80 - 100 A.D. and was 10th
in descent from Ezra] which says, 'A day and a night are an *'onah* and
the portion of an *'onah* is as the whole of it'."

Edwin R. Thiele wrestled with what he called "the mysterious
numbers of the Hebrew Kings" and found that this principle resolved
all the apparent contradictions between the chronologies of the kings
of Israel and the kings of Judah and brought into complete harmony
all the cross references between the two accounts wherever they are
interconnected.† The harmony is literally complete so long as this
principle of allowing any part to stand for the whole is adhered to. It
usually happened, therefore, that the sum total of a succession of
reigns exceeded the available time span allowable only because, when
one king succeeded another, both kings were credited with having
reigned for that year in which the succession occurred. By *our*
reckoning, there are too many years to fit into the interval.

It is not altogether strange. We claim for ourselves a whole year's
tax credit when we are married or have a child even if these events
occur on the very last day of the year. And not a few routine "contracts" are considered fulfilled by the contractor if the slightest use
is made of the contracted service for only a few minutes of any one
day. Russian literature sees any portion of time, even a few minutes
before midnight, as a complete *sutkee*, i.e., a complete period of
twenty-four hours, and railway tickets which are made out for *sutkees*
are considered as used completely if they are employed for only a
minute on the specified day. It is a little analogous to our own
system which demands that we surrender a whole bus ticket whether
we travel one block which occupies two minutes or across the city
which occupies one hour. It was on this basis that the employer in
the Lord's parable of the labourers in the vineyard considered it perfectly just to have paid a day's wage of one penny equally to those
who had laboured all day and to those who only laboured for an hour
at the end of the day (Matt.20:1-15).

---

* *B. Pesachim*, p. 4 a.

† Thiele, Edwin R., *The Mysterious Numbers of the Hebrew Kings*, Univ. Chicago Press, 1951,
xxii & 298 pp.

Now the bearing of such beliefs upon the events of those dramatic days in Jerusalem is obvious. The Lord's body must be laid in a tomb for the specified three days in order to demonstrate that He had really died. As far as the officials were concerned, if the body was still there after three days, death was legally established. If, on the other hand, the body was not there at the end of those three days, they could argue that death had never actually taken place. The possibility of the Lord's bodily resurrection does not seem to have seriously concerned them. But as a precaution against his body being deliberately stolen, they had the tomb sealed and guarded. It was not surprising, therefore, that they were greatly disturbed when news began to leak out that in spite of the presence of the guards and the official sealing of the stone at the mouth of the tomb, the body had indeed disappeared. They must have had some terrible second thoughts. Their demand that the tomb be sealed lest the body should be removed and his disciples should then pretend that Jesus had been raised from the dead shows that the Jews were fearful of making any further mistakes in their treatment of Jesus (Matt.27:64).

It seems likely that the customary preparation of Jesus' body when He was hurriedly laid in the tomb had only been partially completed. Those who were concerned with his burial had had to move quickly, the day being nearly over (since it ended at 6 PM that same evening) and the next day was a special holy day. Presumably when the customary three nights and three days required by Jewish law to certify death were over, the final preparation of the body would have been completed and the tomb then closed by the family themselves. It is likely that it was the hope of seeing his body once again before the final closure of the tomb that took Mary Magdalene to the grave so early that first Lord's day morning.

It will be noted that the Jews had demanded only that the tomb be officially sealed under Pilate's orders till the third day (Matt.27:63, 64). Edersheim tells us that relatives and friends of the deceased were in the habit of going frequently to the grave until the third day so as to make sure that those laid there were really dead.* He also notes that the third day formed a kind of final day of special mourning because it was thought the soul hovered round the body until then, before finally departing from its earthly tabernacle. It is probable that the Jewish authorities were a little fearful lest the body should be removed by some of those who might well be expected to visit the tomb during those three days following this custom.

---

* Edersheim, Alfred, *The Life and Times of Jesus the Messiah*, N.Y., Herrick, 1886, Vol. II, 3rd ed., p. 631.

However, in spite of their precautions, their worst fears were realized — the body had indeed disappeared.   As Shakespeare has wisely observed, "Things bad begun make good themselves by ill", and the Jewish authorities now found it necessary to compound their error by bribing the guards to support them in their contention that the disciples had stolen the body in spite of these precautions (Matt.28:11-15).   It was at least a public confession that He was no longer in the tomb.

It is important to underscore the significance of the disappearance of the Lord's body after the lapse of the traditional three days.   Had his body disappeared earlier, the Jewish authorities would really have had no difficulty in persuading the nation that the Lord Jesus had simply revived.   His spirit had returned to his body because in point of fact it had never really left it permanently.   He had "died" on the cross but recovery of life was, in their view, still quite possible without involving anything particularly miraculous.   It was by no means exceptional for people to be to all intents and purposes dead, and yet revive again within the three days.   It was a kind of period of grace in which recovery was quite possible.   At the end of three days they believed that the features of the deceased were suddenly changed dramatically and that only then had the spirit truly forsaken its earthly home.

This circumstance is very significantly reflected by the Lord's actions in dealing with four individuals who were terminally ill.   There is evident design here.   The first instance is recorded in John 4:46-53 in which we are told that a nobleman's sick child was healed by the Lord, even though he was "at the point of death".   This event was wonderful enough, but did not apparently cause any particular stir.

The second instance is found in Mark 5:21-24 and 35-43.   In this case, the child actually died while the Lord was on his way.   Perhaps the child would not have died at all had it not been for the incident recorded between verses 24 and 35, where a woman was healed by touching the hem of his garment in faith.   When He reached the home of the sick child, He was in a manner of speaking too late.   Nevertheless, He exhibited his power over death and at once restored the child to her parents.   And although it was to the amazement of all, yet the incident still did not altogether convince the people since the child had, after all, so recently died.

The third incident must have created a greater stir among the people.   In Luke 7:11-17 we have the account of the raising of the widow of Nain's son.   This young man must have been dead for some hours, for he was being carried out to burial.   It is quite possible that under normal circumstances these preparations — washing the body, anointing the skin with oil, composing the figure, wrapping the body with linen and dusting with certain aromatic powders to preserve it against the attacks of insects — would occupy several hours. Indeed, such preparatory measures may very well have reflected the concern of the bereaved that if the deceased should recover, his body would be in a fit state to receive his spirit again. At any rate, this young man was certainly dead considerably longer than Jairus' daughter. When the Lord, stopping the funeral cortege, approached the bier and com-manded the young man to arise, those who witnessed his immediate revival were even more amazed than those who had witnessed the two previous recoveries. News of the event went quickly throughout all Judea and all the region round about (verse 17), and even the disciples of John ran to him to report the matter. The reaction was far more dramatic among the people than had been the case in the raising of Jairus' daughter.

Near the end of his ministry we have the case of the raising of Lazarus. And here, in the light of these three preceding events, we can see the significance of the Lord's seeming indifference when He first learned of the sickness of his friend Lazarus (John 11:6). In spite of the emergency, the Lord deliberately stayed "yet two more days in the same place where He was". His action could not have been more deliberate: and to many people it must have seemed only callous. The details of the story beyond this point hardly need re-telling. He arrived at the tomb only after the appointed period of three days was already passed and the stone had been rolled back to close the tomb because the body was already beginning to decay. This fact alone seems to me almost sufficient to demonstrate that the customary anointing for burial was not a process of embalming such as was common in Egypt but was merely a temporary measure intended to preserve the body through the three days during which revival might be hoped for. But Lazarus had clearly passed the point of no return, for Martha said to Him, "Lord, by this time he stinketh, for he hath been dead four days".

It is impossible to improve upon the simple account which follows. The stone was rolled away and the Lord of Life called to Himself one of his children who instantly obeyed, corrupted though his body was and starved and dehydrated. Lazarus walked from the tomb into the sunlight and, being loosed of his graveclothes, rejoined his two beloved sisters while the rest of the mourners stood in amazement. Never was there such a miracle as this performed in the history of man.

The really important thing is that Lazarus was unequivocally *dead*. 249   This was no mere revival by the return of a spirit which had not yet wandered away. The circumstance of decay was sufficient to prove that Lazarus' spirit had fled, and the return of Lazarus created an unprecedented stir in Israel. The news of this event spread from one end of the land to the other, and the Pharisees were forced to admit among themselves that they were impotent to do anything about it. "Perceive ye how ye prevail nothing? Behold, the world has gone after him!" (John 12:19). Here, then, was an absolute demonstration, pubicly performed under circumstances which allowed no possible deception whatever, of the bodily resurrection of one who had been legally and unequivocally dead.

It is as though the Lord had clearly foreseen the circumstances of his own resurrection and was determined that the Jewish authorities should, when that time came, be left without excuse. When the time did come, therefore, the Jews really had little alternative but to accept the fact either that the Lord was alive *again* or to announce that his body had been stolen.

It does not appear that they ever adopted a third alternative which is thus an entirely modern invention: namely, that Jesus merely revived in the tomb and was then nursed back to health. Some scholars now argue that the Lord did re-appear to his disciples — for how otherwise could the Church have ever been born — while yet denying that it involved a resurrection. They argue that the Lord was never really dead. He had merely swooned and been taken for dead by the centurion who, as a precautionary measure, did indeed wound the Lord severely enough with his spear but not fatally. Subsequently, in the cool of the tomb the Lord revived, they say, and somehow managed to get out and re-join his disciples who then nursed Him back to health and succeeded in completely fooling the public *and themselves* into believing that He had really triumphed over death. But consider what such a deception would involve.

It is difficult indeed to suppose, for example, that One who had suffered the appalling strains and stresses of the previous hours, both physical and emotional, could be nailed to the cross, receive a severe wound in the chest, be laid in a cold tomb, and there revive and find energy enough with such wounds in hands and feet and chest to brace Himself from inside the tomb against a stone which almost certainly could only be rolled back from the outside and which was far too heavy for the women themselves to move — and roll it right back out of the way so far clear of the opening that later on, while John stood looking in, Peter could run right on past him into the tomb (John 20: 4-6). And Jesus did this, apparently, without the soldiers on guard being awakened. Moreover, Pilate had given explicit instructions that the tomb was to be sealed against being broken open (Matt.27:62-66), a measure which would almost certainly make it impossible to open it from the inside, no matter how much strength the supposedly dead man might have.

Only a few hours later this figure, so mutilated that He was scarcely recognizable as human (Isa.52:14), now presented Himself before Mary who was overwhelmed with the joy of recognition when He made Himself known to her.   Shortly thereafter He walked for miles without manifest tiredness or evidence of mental anguish with two disciples whose attention would surely at least have been attracted to Him by the marks of utter exhaustion and physical injury but who apparently treated Him as simply a fellow traveller, inviting Him in at the end of the journey and only recognizing Him when He performed a simple familiar act, the breaking of bread (Luke 24:30 f.).   There is no evidence of any desperate need for rest or food or drink.   There is every evidence that when their clouded vision suddenly cleared they recognized Him because He had re-appeared to them in the same vital form they had known of Him *before* the events of those last terrible days, and not as He must have appeared when taken down from the cross.

There is nothing in the resurrection scenes to give the slightest hint that He was the one who needed ministering to, which must certainly have been the case were He a mutilated invalid verging on the border of total collapse.   As a matter of fact, precisely the opposite is the impression one has.   He was ministering rather to them, assuring them of his well-being and encouraging them in every way in the belief that what He had just passed through was not a near disaster but a mighty triumph.   That they were convinced of this is the only way of explaining how a loosely knit group of men with little or no courage and, at the moment of crisis even less cohesion as a group, were suddenly turned into a band of courageous men who were fearless of death or imprisonment or ridicule or the threatenings of the authorities, and ended up by turning the Roman world upside down.   Such a transformation requires a sufficient cause.   Those who, like Sir Robert Anderson, have set themselves *with an open mind* to examine the evidence from the Gospels and Acts have been thoroughly convinced that the bodily resurrection of Jesus was cause enough.   Years ago, C. A. Row wrote:*

> A Messiah who crept out of his grave, took refuge in retirement, and afterwards died from exhaustion, was not one who could satisfy the requirements of a community which had been crushed by his crucifixion.   His followers had fully expected that He was going speedily to reign . . . .
> Yet it is the most certain of historical facts, that the Christian

---

* Row, C. A., "The Historical Evidence of the Resurrection of Jesus Christ from the Dead", *Present Day Tracts*, Rel. Tract Soc., London, 1883, Vol. I, Tract II, p. 31.

community commenced a new life immediately after its basic conviction that Jesus was the Messiah of popular Jewish expectation, had been totally destroyed by his crucifixion.   Nothing but a resurrection could have served the purpose.

As one reads the record in Acts one is amazed at the transformation which has taken place in the disciples, especially Peter, as a result of the resurrection of the Lord Jesus.   The same Peter who trembled before a little girl whose question may very well have been prompted only by idle curiosity (Luke 22:56, 57) now stood before the Sanhedrin (that most august body of Jewish authorities) and boldly rebuked their unbelief.   And the other disciples stood with him, equally unafraid.   It is necessary to find an adequate cause for such a transformation and it will surely not be found in some self-deception regarding the fate of the One whom they now claimed to be the Messiah.

Their confidence was manifest to everyone.   In Acts 4:13 we are told, "Now when they saw the boldness of Peter and John and perceived that they were unlearned and ignorant men, they marvelled . . . ." Later on, the same religious authorities, exasperated by what can only be described as the remarkable results of their courageous testimony, rebuked them saying, "Did we not straitly command you that ye should not teach in this name? And behold, ye have filled Jerusalem with your doctine!" (Acts 5:28).

What we read in the Gospel accounts of the resurrection is so simple, so artless, and so unlikely, as to be impossible of invention. Consider just a few of the scenes which Luke portrays, for example. In Luke 24 we have that wonderful story of the two, perhaps Cleopas and his wife Mary (not sister to Jesus' mother: John 19:25), who made a memorable journey to Emmaus.   As they walked on their way and talked in a subdued voice of all their shattered hopes because of the crucifixion, Jesus Himself drew near and went with them. But they didn't recognize Him — their vision perhaps clouded by loss of hope. He asked them why they were so sad and why they were talking so earnestly with one another.   Cleopas asked the Lord if He was a stranger in Jerusalem that He should be so unaware of what everyone was talking about; and he recounted to Jesus the events of the past few days.   Then he explained the most surprising element of all, namely, that certain women of their company had visited the tomb and there had been told by angels that Jesus was alive!

The Lord proceeded to explain to them that nothing had happened which had not already been foretold or implied in all that the prophets had said: that the great problem which the Jews had had in the past of reconciling the fact that the Messiah was to be both Suffering

Servant and King, found its resolution in the fact that the Suffering Servant had been raised again from the dead in order to assume his position as anointed King.

We are not told in any great detail what He said to them as they walked along, only that beginning at Moses and all the prophets He expounded to them in all the Scriptures the things concerning Himself. What extraordinary restraint on the part of the disciples that they did not leave a record of what He said!   As Wright put it:*

> With what singular indifference to apparent effect did these men throw away the brush the moment His form was sufficiently outlined for those in distant ages to see!   The utmost effect seems to have been produced with the smallest amount of material.

How extraordinary is the effect achieved!   In the passage we are reading in Luke, we are told that by the time He had finished his expounding, they were nearing home.   And the text continues (verses 28-31):

> He made as though He would have gone further.   But they constrained Him, saying, "Abide with us: for it is towards evening and the day is far spent".
> And He went in to tarry with them.   And it came to pass as He sat at meat with them, He took bread and blessed it, and brake, and gave to them.   And their eyes were opened, and they recognized Him!
> And He vanished out of their sight . . . .

Almost immediately, even though it must have been dark by now, they went back to Jerusalem where they found the eleven disciples and others who were with them, and they told them of their wonderful experience and how He had revealed Himself to them in the breaking of bread.

In spite of the fact that their testimony fully corroborated what others had been telling the disciples (verse 34), and the fact that the Lord had appeared also to Simon, they were all very frightened indeed when, after Cleopas and his wife (?) had just told of their experience, the Lord Himself suddenly stood in their midst (verse 37).   Knowing that many of them would suppose He had not really risen from the dead but was only a ghost of his former self, He quietly invited them to examine Him, to see the wounds in his hands and feet, to *handle* Him and discover for themselves that He had a real corporeal existence (verse 39).   Apparently they were so amazed and overcome, half with joy yet mingled with doubt, that He sought to give to them the final

---

* Wright, G. Frederick, *The Logic of Christian Evidences*, Draper, Andover, 1890, p. 281.

proof of the reality of his presence by eating food. He said, "Have you any food?" And when they gave Him a piece of broiled fish and a honeycomb, He took it and ate it then and there before their very eyes.

Thus in this one chapter, in some thirty short verses, we are given a series of kaleidoscopic cameos of the drama of those hours which surely could not be improved upon. And together these provide absolute proof that it was the Lord Himself, identified by the wounds on his body, by his overall "presence", by his voice when calling Mary Magdalene by name, and by his behaviour at the table. What possible additional means would contribute to such a demonstration? At the same time, unequivocal evidence is provided that He possessed a real body and yet a new kind of a body, a body perfectly capable of transcending time and space and matter. These accounts have none of the qualities of visions or hallucinations. The resurrection appearances do indeed break every known law of visions.

Even if we did not have the testimony of the other Gospels, in this one chapter of Luke alone we have long conversations, protracted appearances over what must have been a considerable period of time — an appearing to two people on the journey to Emmaus, then unexpectedly to perhaps twenty people (the disciples and others), along with a clear demonstration of materialization in a familiar form which invited not only handling but also observing the eating of real food before them all. In 1 Corinthians 15:6 it is recorded that the Lord appeared before over 500 people at one time; and it should constantly be borne in mind that these people were for the most part unprepared and still unconvinced at the time. Even 'Doubting' Thomas was only completely convinced when he was invited to examine the proofs of the reality of the Lord's body for himself (John 20:27, 28). And Matthew 28:9 tells us that they actually *held* Him by the feet. Nothing like this ever happens in visions.

The fact is that we do not have the slightest change in the personal identity of this same Lord who has already walked through the Gospels during his earthly ministry. Any changes associated with his power to materialize at will, do not in any way mask his identity as the same real living Person that they had known before. The identity is total, resurrection has only increased his potential in certain directions. Ghosts created by literary artists of later generations were very unsubstantial and unimpressive creatures. They are failures really — ghosts of ghosts only, as William Alexander put it.

But such was the effect of those forty days upon the disciples that when the time came to say "goodbye" in terms of visual contact, there were no tears, no expressions of disappointment, no lingering at the point of departure, but rather an immediate return to Jerusalem "with

great joy" (Luke 24:52).   What an extraordinary thing this is!   Only
once in the long history of separations which are expected to be permanent (at least visually), has there resulted such an effect as Luke here
describes.   Something very wonderful and very unusual had been
transpiring during those forty days of constantly recurring, yet
quite unpredictable, personal appearances in their company.

It seems to me that there is a beautiful propriety in the Lord's
successive appearances to his disciples during these forty days.   The
first thing He accomplished was to make absolutely sure that not the
slightest doubt remained in the minds of his disciples that He had risen
from the dead.   Yet while easily convincing them that it was truly
Himself and not merely a ghost, He undertook to show them also that
He was now living within a world that transcends our own.   He therefore came and went without regard to any physical barriers, and
appeared and disappeared without leaving any visible trace of his
presence.   The consequence of this very unexpectedness was that it
soon ceased to be frightening and came to be accepted by the disciples
as normal behaviour for the Lord.   Perhaps as the days went by He
continued to appear unexpectedly but with less and less frequency.

Yet because the disciples had absolutely no way of anticipating
when He would re-appear in their midst, they would inevitably come
to suppose that He was in fact always present with them, but just out
of sight.   By the time this truth had become firmly implanted in their
minds, He could now clearly afford to show them that while He would
indeed be with them always, his presence would not be a visual one
but one mediated to their consciousness through the Holy Spirit. This
truth was demonstrated by his visible ascension into heaven from the
Mount of Olives.

His ascension was accompanied by the assurance (given by angels)
that this same Lord, unchanged and as beloved to them as ever, would
in due time return to earth in visible form.   In the meantime they had
his promise that wherever they might be, even unto the ends of the
world, He would actually be present with them always.   It was very
important for the disciples to recognize that the environs of Jerusalem
were not to remain for ever the only scene of his presence.   But it
would have been confusing if, throughout history, the Lord had been
suddenly appearing in this very concrete way in Egypt, in Rome, in
England, in China, in North America.   How many shrines would then
have been erected!   And how strong would have been the tendency to
single out those places of his appearing.   So He ascended — never to
be seen as hitherto until He would return to remain visibly with men
once for all.   Propriety marks every stage.   It is a beautiful display of
gentle instruction graciously imparted and learned almost unawares by
those who had known Him in the flesh.   A bodily *ascension* was as

important as a bodily resurrection.

Such a period of gradual conditioning seems essential to account for their "joyful parting", and seems clearly to have been one of the purposes of the forty days spent with them before a cloud received Him out of their sight (Acts 1:9).

Thus by the time of the Ascension they seem to have come to realize that the days of surprise engagement were over, that the Lord's presence would continue to be with them but not visually as before. Yet this knowledge brought no sadness with it! Was there ever such a parting from One who was so dear!

Meanwhile, if we were to ask, What would be the best way of refuting the accusation of forgery or fraud?, we might set forth such requirements as follows:

(a) The Lord's death must be public.

(b) It must be witnessed by people who were used to seeing that kind of death.

(c) It must be certified by experts that death had really occurred.

(d) Some specific steps must be taken by someone in authority to make death doubly sure.

(e) The responsibility for securing the body must be left, ultimately, with enemies — not with friends.

(f) The tomb should be sealed after burial and guards placed near it who were in no way involved.

(g) If resurrection has occurred in spite of all these precautions, it must be testified by many witnesses, and they must be witnesses who honestly did not believe such a thing would occur.

(h) These witnesses must give clear evidence by their *actions* that they had no such expectations.

(i) Some of the witnesses to his resurrection must be intimate friends who could never have mistaken somebody else for Him, and would only have been convinced of his identity by rather subtle and characteristic personal forms of behaviour.

(j) The proofs which He Himself would supply must be such as to completely convince the most sceptic amongst his followers.

All these requirements were met by what appear to be almost incidental observations made by the writers. There is nowhere the

slightest indication that they had formulated such a list of requirements and then deliberately undertook to satisfy them.

   In considering these requirements rather briefy, nothing need be
said of (a) — except that even Roman records support the reality of
the event. 250   In connection with (b), it need only be said that crucifixion was well known to the Romans, and even Pilate was quite
familiar with the fact that it was a slow death: hence his surprise that
Jesus was so soon dead (Mark 15:44).   The fulfillment of (c) and (d)
is certified by the action of the centurion (John 19:34) and the eye
witness account of what happened (John 19:35).   In connection with
(e) and (f), we note only that the Jewish people themselves received
permission to have the grave secured and guards placed nearby.   In
regard to (g), we are told that there were many witnesses to his resurrection and the great majority of them were surprised.   It seems that
not a single soul among the disciples really anticipated it, not even
Mary Magdalene who thought somebody had taken the Lord's body
away (John 20:2), nor Cleopas and his wife(?) who "had hoped . . . .
but . . . ." (Luke 24:21).   All his disciples, especially his inner circle,
had to be convinced.

   With respect to (h), we note that the leader of the small band of
disciples said, "I'm going fishing", clearly declaring his intention to try
to forget all his disappointments.   And his decision was shared by
those who said, "We go, too" (John 21:3).   In connection with (i), we
find that Mary Magdalene was the first to be absolutely persuaded,
and she of all those who were not actually relatives was perhaps the
one who was most completely devoted to the Lord's Person as witnessed by her willingness to anoint his feet with oil at such a cost to
herself (Luke 7:37).   She undoubtedly recognized Him first by the
way in which He pronounced her name.   How subtle this is: but how
completely convincing!   Cleopas and his wife had their eyes opened
by his simple act of breaking bread. So run all the accounts — without
artifice.   Here, then, is no studied attempt to win by force of argument.

   Finally, as though in the providence of God, the intimate circle of
disciples included among its number one who was inherently sceptical
about anything which he did not have adequate firsthand experience.
And so the Lord was provided with an occasion for satisfying this
requirement also that a man, still quite unconvinced, should be
converted to an unhesitating faith not only in the identity of the
 resurrected One as the same Lord whom he had known previously,
but to the claims which the Lord made for Himself as God (John
20:27).

   What more could be asked of a written record: by what better
standard of evidence could one assess whether these events are romance

or history?

He was, then, physiologically dead and bodily resurrected. With what kind of body? There is evidence that it was at first the same body which had been laid in the tomb, but that this was subsequently changed in some way. And the timing of the change is significant, as we shall see in the final chapter. Moreover, it is clear from the accounts of the resurrection scenes that the change re-constituted Him in a way which was quite remarkable. For He passed through closed doors or vanished at will — which suggests some kind of *spiritual* rather than *physical* bodily existence. And yet He clearly ate the food of his friends which certainly had physical reality (Luke 24:41-43), and He invited them to handle Him and see that He was not simply a spiritual being. He enjoyed a real corporeality. And one cannot help but wonder of course, what became of the food which He had eaten before them all, when a few minutes later He vanished from their sight! Here indeed is a whole new order of being. Nevertheless, his body was still recognizably *his*. This was truly the same Lord whose company the disciples had shared continuously for the three previous event-filled years. We can say unhesitatingly I believe, that He suffered under Pontius Pilate, was cruficied, died, and was buried: and that He rose again the third day.

He did indeed rise on the third day: *and without seeing corruption*, for He had yet one duty to perform in order to consummate the sacrifice which He had made of Himself. And this duty was the presentation of his blood before that altar in heaven (Rev.9:13) which the "altar" in Jerusalem symbolized, thus fulfilling the office of the High Priest on the great Day of Atonement.

At what point did He enter into the most Holy Place not made with hands (Heb.9:11), there to present the final proof of his sacrifice once offered for sins (Heb.10:12)?

We must bear in mind that the High Priest in the Tabernacle (and later in the Temple) showed himself alive to the people as proof of the divine acceptance of the sacrifice he had offered on their behalf. If our High Priest entered into the Holy of Holies in heaven to present his blood, when did He do so? Before He showed Himself alive to Mary Magdalene? Or immediately afterwards? Or only after He had ascended into heaven from the Mount of Olives? We have not, I think, been left altogether in the dark on this matter.

We turn therefore to an examination of the post-resurrection scenes in order to establish, if possible, what really happened in those first few hours after He left the tomb.

Chapter 34

THE PRESENTATION OF THE BLOOD

Without shedding of blood
is no remission (of sins).
Hebrews 9:22

It was necessary therefore that
the (representations) of things in the heavens
should be purified by these (means);
but the heavenly things themselves
with better sacrifices than these.
For Christ is not entered into the holy places
made with hands (which are the figures of the true);
but into heaven itself,
now to appear in the very presence of God
on our behalf.
Hebrews 9:23, 24

For many years I wondered why it was so important that the Lord should have been raised *bodily* from the dead. It did not seem sufficient that the real reason was to fulfill his prediction that He would raise up his body again ("this temple", John 2:19). No prophecy is made merely to provide a justification for fulfilling it.

What great importance attached to his body that He could not have manifested Himself to his disciples in a spiritual body and left his physical body in the grave, sealed and never to be seen again? So long as He appeared in a truly recognizable form to those who needed the assurance of his being alive from the dead — that seemed to me to be quite sufficient.   It surely was not meant as a sign to the unbelieving Jews, because He never did actually appear to any of them.

I have come to the conclusion that He had yet one more task to fulfill *in his physical body* before the plan of redemption was completed.   As He had given his physical life in the role of a sin-offering, so like the High Priest under the Mosaic covenant, He also must present the *evidence* of his sacrifice in person.   And I believe that "in Person" means in Person *as a Man*; and to fulfill that role He must still have a truly human *body*, a body of which blood is an essential component.

But this implies a real correspondence of some kind between the Holy of Holies of the Mosaic covenant and a Holy of Holies in heaven; otherwise where would He go to present his blood?   Is there thus some counterpart in that other world that does correspond to the Holy of Holies in the Tabernacle (and later in the Temple)?   Which is the real and which is the shadow: the earthly or the heavenly?

I want to suggest a simple means of testing the answer we give to this question.   The earthly seems so real, so tangible, so objective: the heavenly seems so invisible, so intangible, so subjective.   What criterion would serve to enable us to evaluate reality apart from the bias of our own immediate sensory experience?   The answer to this, I believe, lies in the concept of *permanence*.   What is truly real is permanent. Whatever has about it a certain temporality, passingness, impermanence, is not real in the same absolute sense.   What is lasting, is real.

But how *long* must a thing last to be real?   The question is an interesting one, and one that bears directly upon certain phenomena in modern physics.   There are subatomic particles, for example, that have a life of only a few seconds.   Can they be said to be *real* objects? While they last, Yes!   What if they last only a fraction of a second? How big a fraction?   Would a billionth of a second be long enough to establish real existence?   At what point does something have an existence so fleeting as to surrender any right to being called real at all?

We begin to run into philosophical problems when we reach this level of temporality, and the problems are actual enough because we now "know" of one subatomic particle that does indeed have such a fleeting existence!   It is called a *antiomega-minus baryon* particle and it has a life of 15 billionths of a second . . . .

We thus have to adjust our thinking somewhat about the nature of reality.   Let us go to the other extreme.   Would we not say that an object was "more real" that had a life of billions of years — the earth itself, for example — when compared with the *antiomega-minus baryon* particle which has such a fleeting existence that it can only be demonstrated at all by the most refined scientific equipment imaginable and even then only by inference?   Our thinking tends to look upon perm-

anence as a mark of reality.   What lasts a long time is more real than
what is short-lived.   What then of something that is *eternal in the
heavens*?   If it lasts for ever, even though we cannot yet actually see it,
is it not by this principle more real than the earth itself — which will
pass away (Matt.24:35) even though we *can* see it?   A thing does not
have to be seen to be real.

I believe we have to look again at certain passages of Scripture in
the light of this kind of assessment of reality: the reality of the permanent though yet unseen, against the unreality of the transient though
visible while it lasts.   Long after this world has passed away, that
other world will remain (Heb.12:26, 27).   Which, then, is the real and
which is the shadow only?   I think we must conclude that our world
is the shadow of the eternal reality which is in heaven.

We thus have to divest our minds of the idea that the spiritual
world is a kind of mental creation which uses the imagery of the
material world that alone has real existence.   For the truth is that all
we see and touch and handle is a mere extension of the spiritual world.
It is a momentary crystallization of spiritual reality, a reification that
exists only for what we call "the present". It will no longer be needed when the everlasting reality supercedes the temporal one.   In short,
the spiritual is the real, not the physical.

The divinely appointed festivals and rituals and ordinances of the
Mosaic Law which marked the seasons throughout the year in the Old
Testament were no more than temporary transcriptions of a basic
reality in the spiritual world.   They were "a mere shadow of things to
come but the substance (the reality) belongs to Christ" (Col.2:17,
ASV).

Thus the Tabernacle was not the materialization of something that
was an idea only.   It was patterned after an original reality that was
already in existence in heaven.   It was not the *original* of its counterpart in heaven but a *copy* of it, a "figure" of it (Heb.9:24), a kind of
temporary representation, an "antitype" as the Greek actually has it
($\dot{\alpha}\nu\tau\acute{\iota}$-$\tau\upsilon\pi\alpha$, *anti-tupa*).   The same word is applied to baptism (1 Peter
3:21) as a symbol of a higher reality already in existence.   When we
die, we are not deserting a solid world of reality for an ethereal world
of unreality: quite the reverse.   We are forsaking the ephemeral for
the eternal, the shadow for the substance, the copy for the original,
the antitype for the prototype.

The blood which symbolized the sin-offering of the goat sacrificed
under Mosaic Law on the Day of Atonement had to be carried into
the presence of God.   When the time came for this antitype sacrifice
to be superceded by the prototype sacrifice of the Lamb of God, the
blood of *this* sin-offering had also to be carried into the presence of
God.   But this time the presentation was not in a temporary tabernacle

made with hands, or by a Priest who served only for a little while, but in heaven itself and by a High Priest who abideth for ever (Heb.7:23, 24).

When the blood sacrifices were offered in the Tabernacle, and later in the Temple, an innocent creature had indeed to be put to death; but in itself the mere slaughter of an animal was not enough. In the first place, an *animal* sacrifice will not suffice to redeem a *man* under sentence of death. The balancing of justice requires that a *man's* life blood, and not merely an animal's, must atone for a *man's* capital offence. It is not possible for the blood of goats or bulls or any other creature below man, how ever innocent it may be, to atone for human sins (Heb.10:4). In the second place, the *proof* of death in the form of shed blood, had to be brought and presented before God in acknowledgement of the commonly accepted principle of jurisprudence that justice must not merely be done but must also *be seen to be done*. The visual evidence of substitutionary death had to be brought before the bar of justice in testimony of the penalty paid.

The proof of a full, perfect, and sufficient sacrifice for man's sins in the form of a *man's* shed blood (not merely in the form of the shed blood of an animal) must finally be presented before God in order that justice may be both actually done and actually seen to have been done. This is the basis of all satisfaction in legal matters; to establish the fact of an adequate penalty paid, proof of which is witnessed in an appropriate manner.

We have already observed that the Lord Jesus was not merely the Lamb of God, but stood also in the place of the High Priest who sacrificed the Lamb. *He* offered up *Himself* (Heb.9:14). He was, in fact, *our* High Priest (Heb.4:14, 15); and the blood which He presented as proof of his having sacrificed Himself as MAN was the presentation of his own shed *human* blood. With this, He entered into the true Holy of Holies in the presence of God and there offered, once for all, proof that the penalty of our sins had been paid: justice had been done and our eternal redemption therefore secured. Here was the ground for our forgiveness, a forgiveness which in every way satisfied the demands of the moral law because it was upon an acceptable principle of balance, accompanied by a visible proof of satisfaction.

Consider, then, in this light, the following series of passages of Scripture which bear upon it. And although these passages are familiar, they should be read, bearing in mind what has been said above about what is real and what is only a shadow of reality.

Leviticus 17:11
The life of the flesh is in the blood: and I have given it to you upon the altar to make an atonement for your souls: for it is the blood which maketh an atonement for the soul.

Hebrews 9:22
> Without shedding of blood is no remission.

1 Peter 1:18, 19
> For as much as ye know that ye were not redeemed with corruptible things as silver and gold . . . . but with the precious blood of Christ, as of a Lamb without blemish and without spot.

Hebrews 9:11-15
> Christ being come an high priest of good things to come, through a greater and more perfect tabernacle not made with hands, that is to say, not of this order of creation; neither through the blood of goats and calves, but *through his own blood, He entered in once into the Holy Place having obtained eternal redemption for us.*
>
> For if the blood of bulls and goats . . . . sanctifieth to the purifying of the flesh, how much more shall the blood of Christ, who through the eternal Spirit offered *Himself* without spot unto God, purge your conscience from dead works to serve the living God?
>
> And for this reason He is the mediator of the new covenant, that by means of death for the redemption of the transgressions that were under the first covenant, they which are called might receive the promise of eternal inheritance.

Note that when He thus entered the Holy Place, He had already obtained our redemption.   His entering *followed* the accomplishment of our redemption and was not therefore to *achieve* it but rather to testify to the fact of its having already been accomplished.

Hebrews 9:24
> For Christ is not entered into the holy places [i.e., the Holy Place and the Holy of Holies] made with hands, which are figures of the true; but into heaven itself, now to appear in the presence of God for us.

Hebrews 10:19-22
> Having therefore, brethren, boldness to enter into the holiest [i.e., the Holy of Holies, the very presence of God] by the blood of Jesus, by a new and living way which He hath consecrated for us *through his flesh* . . . . let us draw near with a true heart in full assurance of faith.

Now there is little doubt that we have here a revelation of something which the Lord accomplished as part of his saving work: and it was done *after* He had obtained our redemption: that is to say, having *already* obtained eternal redemption for us (Heb.9:12).   Clearly, He presented his blood as proof of his sacrifice, exactly as the High Priest under the old covenant had presented the blood of the sacrificial victim as proof of that sacrifice.

The question arises, therefore, When did the Lord Jesus perform this part of his office?   I suggest that a careful reading of the events immediately following the resurrection will give us adequate clues, while at the same time shedding a wonderful light upon certain special circumstances surrounding these events.

Putting together the accounts in the four Gospels, we are presented with an empty tomb very early before the dawning of the third day after the crucifixion, a day which by Jewish reckoning would actually begin *at 6 PM on Saturday evening.* Two Marys — Mary Magdalene and Mary the mother of Joses — and one other woman named Salome (Mark 16:1), were at the tomb while it was yet dark (John 20:1) before the dawn of Sunday morning. The tomb was empty. Mary Magdalene ran to tell Peter and the other disciples (John 20:2), and Peter and John ran at once to see for themselves. John, being the younger, reached the tomb first but also being more restrained, did not go in. Peter came puffing up behind and, with characteristic impetuosity, brushed past John standing at the opening and went right on in. He found the linen clothes lying there disposed in such a way as though the Lord had risen and carefully divested Himself of them, laying the head cloth neatly folded in a place by itself. But there was no sign of the Lord Himself; and presumably with many questions in their minds, Peter and John returned to the city.

Meanwhile, Mary Magdalene returned to the empty tomb and stood weeping, deeply grieved that He was no longer there. As she did so, someone whom she failed to recognize through her tears, asked her why she was weeping and whom she was seeking. Supposing Him to be the gardener, she asked at once where her Lord's body had been taken. The very simplicity of this record is surely the most substantial proof of its veracity. It is an uninventable scene. We all have those among our closest friends whose way of calling us by name at once identifies them, and this is clearly what happened here. Recognition was immediate. Mary fell at once to her knees before Him and would have held Him by the feet . . . . *but He forbad her to touch Him.*

And here we have the first clue to the sequence of events which trasnpired between heaven and earth before the Lord returned and again showed Himself openly to the other disciples. He said to her: "Touch Me not, for I am not yet ascended to my Father; but go to My brethren [how wonderful!] and say unto them, I ascend unto My Father and your Father; *and to My God and your God*" (John 20:17).

What did this mean? It is significant that on three occasions the Lord either addressed or spoke of his Father as GOD. When He first entered upon his mission by becoming Man we are told that He said, "Lo, I come to do thy will, O God" (Heb.10:7). When that mission was being accomplished in its most crucial aspect, He cried out, "My God, My God, why hast Thou forsaken Me?" (Matt.27:46). And now,

here, when it seems He was about to ascend and present the proof of
that mission fulfilled, He again refers to his Father as his GOD.   In
each case it seems clear that He was addressing his Father not in the
old familiar relationship but rather as Judge of all men, before Whom
we stand guilty and He, as Man, stood as our mediator.

Since He was now about to present his blood before the divine
judgment seat as a visible symbol of his sacrifice, *any touching of his
body by sinful man could only have fatally defiled Him* and rendered
Him unfit to fulfill his office as officiating High Priest.   That this
must be the reason for his warning to Mary is borne out by the fact
that subsequently He not only permitted the disciples to hold Him by
the feet (Matt.28:9) but actually *invited* them to handle Him and see
that it really was Himself who stood before them (Luke 24:39).   Moreover, the ascension that He spoke of to Mary can hardly have been a
reference to that *final* ascension which marked the end of his visual
presence with the disciples during the forty succeeding days, because
He assures her that He will yet *return* to be with the disciples once He
has ascended to his God and his Father and completed the last stage
of his mission as Saviour.

It was necessary, or perhaps one should say rather an act of
graciousness, that this encounter should be allowed in order to provide
a natural occasion for revealing to us the wonderful fact that He was
indeed about to present his blood in the true Holy of Holies in heaven.
But for this incident we could not have known the circumstances which
lie behind the statement made in Hebrews 9:11-15 which we have
already quoted.   The wonderful thing is that we know this "presentation" of his blood did actually occur, for the body with which He
returned to his brethren to spend the next forty event-filled days with
them was a *different* body.

To begin with, Mark's account of his first appearance to two
witnesses — and two witnesses were required by Jewish law to establish
the truth of anything — states that He appeared to them "in another
form" (Mark 16:12).   The Greek here is very specific: $\dot{\epsilon}\nu$ $\dot{\epsilon}\tau\dot{\epsilon}\rho\alpha$ $\mu o\rho\phi\widehat{\eta}$
(en hetera morphe).   The implication of these words is that although
the form in which He appeared to them was still recognizably Himself,
yet it was a *changed body*.   It was no longer the identical body in
which He had appeared to Mary Magdalene, even though both appearances were *after* the resurrection. A change of some sort had therefore
taken place within the interval between the two appearances.   The
shape was the same but the vital force which animated it was different.

The vital force in our earthly bodies is in the blood, which is the
life of the soul: but a new vital force had now replaced the original
vital force in the blood.   Blood was no longer the conductor of the
energies of that changed body.

In Luke 24:39 the Lord's words seem to indicate just such a change.   This change did not involve the *spiritualization* of his body, for He assured his disciples that a spirit did not have flesh and bones as they could see for themselves his body had.   This was a real body, even though He could pass with it through solid substances, through closed doors for instance: and He could eat meat before them all and yet so transform the food thus ingested that it disappeared instantly when He Himself disappeared from their view.   And He invited them to make real contact with his body, to handle Him and see for themselves.   This is incomprehensible to us as we are now constituted.   How could a body be handled and yet pass silently through a solid object like a closed door?

To these disciples He said, "Behold, my hands and my feet, that it is I Myself: and handle Me and see; for a spirit hath not flesh and *bones* as ye see Me have" (Luke 24:39).*   Such an expression, "flesh and bones", is unique as a description of his body in the New Testament, even of his mystical Body which is the Church (Eph.5:30).   We are members of that Body, "of his flesh and of his bones".   The phrase *flesh and bones* is common enough in the Old Testament (Gen.2:23; 29:14; 2 Sam.5:1; 19:12,13; for example), but in the New Testament this is not the case: the normal Greek phrase being flesh and *blood* (for example, Matt.16:17; 1 Cor.15:50; Gal.1:16; Eph.6:12; and in a slightly modified form in John 1:13, "not of blood, nor of the will of the flesh").   In some real way, the Lord Jesus Christ had for our sakes "*shed* his blood", and in making this sacrifice not only secured our redemption but also achieved a higher form of bodily existence in which blood no longer played a vital role.

In summary, it may be that we can now place in chronological sequence the seemingly incidental notices of events relating to the first few hours after the resurrection and find ourselves in possession of a remarkable scenario somewhat as follows.

The Lord's terribly mutilated body had been taken down from the cross, given a very hurried treatment with temporary wrappings and anointing to preserve it against insect attack while it remained in the tomb for the official three days and nights to qualify for a death certificate.   The Jews, knowing that the body was still legally "in the possession of" his disciples, persuaded Pilate to see that the tomb was sealed and guarded so that it could not be "stolen" and the pretence then made that Jesus had risen from the dead.   After three days and nights, they felt assured that such an event was wholly unlikely.

---

* With this, contrast 1 Corinthians 15:50.

The sealing of the tomb is the first "fact" we have in our scenario, for it means that if Jesus was to come forth from the tomb, either (a) the stone must be rolled away, or (b) Jesus Himself must come *through* the stone — as He was later to pass freely in and out of locked doors (John 20:19, 26).

In the case of (a) one has to ask, "Why did Jesus not roll away the stone Himself?"   After the resurrection He surely could do anything He wished to do . . . .   In the case of (b) it would seem that by merely passing through the stone without disturbing it or breaking the seal He would have once for all shattered any possibility of such a rumour as Matthew says was later to be "officially" sponsored, to the effect that the disciples had stolen the body while the guards slept (Matt.28: 13-15).   The unbroken seal would have been the disciples' best proof of the reality of his emergence in some unique way from the tomb.

Was there, therefore, some good reason why an angel was called to roll away the stone (Matt.28:2)?   I believe there was and the reason is indeed significant.   It seems that the body which was first raised that Sunday morning was exactly the same mutilated body that had been laid in the tomb on Friday evening.   It was not metamorphosed until some time later (Mark 16:12).   The body which Jesus re-engaged was a body of flesh *and blood* — in short, the same battered and bruised and wounded body which had been taken down from the cross.   It was, in fact, that same "temple" which He had said He would indeed raise up again (John 2:19):   and the Jews had obviously so understood his words if we are to be guided by the fears they expressed afterwards in Matthew 27:64.   Since throughout his earthly ministry He had deliberately limited Himself to the normal capacities of that body, so now — even as He rose again in the sealed tomb — He continued to limit Himself.   For this reason an angel had to come and roll away the stone.

Shortly afterwards Mary Magdalene found Him, still in the garden and still, I suggest, in that same flesh and blood body.   And here we meet with a second fact in the record.   When Mary recognized her beloved Lord she fell at his feet and would have immediately touched Him, but He instantly forbad her to do so (John 20:17).   It has often been suggested that the reason for this injunction was in order to discourage an attachment to Jesus on the part of Mary which was no longer appropriate.   It is possible.   But I suggest that there was another reason, a reason that relates to the High Priestly role of the Saviour, who could not be touched *by anyone* until his priestly duty was completed.   Did He not Himself suggest the reason when He said He had yet to ascend to his God and hers?

The fact is that He seems to have been at that moment on his way with his own blood to leave it in the heavenly Holy of Holies as the symbol of his death for all eternity. He delayed long enough to put on record this one encounter which was to provide the occasion to fill out the scenario of his still uncompleted mission. Without the details of this particular meeting we could not have known that the body with which He entered the Holy of Holies of God with his blood was a flesh *and blood* body.

The next incident recorded is his first meeting with his disciples since his death. This time He by no means avoided the kind of contact which in the former situation would have disqualified his High Priestly mission, but actually *invited* contact as a proof of the reality of his Person (John 20:27). But why should this have been necessary? If Mary had recognized Him unquestionably once He had spoken her name, what possible reason was there for the disciples not to be able to? The answer must surely be that Mary had seen Him in his old familiar body, wounds and all: whereas the disciples were seeing Him in an entirely new form, clothed in a metamorphosed body (*en hetero morphe* — Mark 16:12). Obviously the form is different, for He had come to them silently through a locked door (John 20:19. 26): whereas the body which Mary saw had been *imprisoned* by the locked "door" of the tomb.

What He had now assumed was not the old body of flesh and blood but a new, changed, and glorified body, a body of flesh and bone and therefore real as no ghostly "body" could ever be, yet different in its vital principle in the absence of blood as the sustaining medium of its life.

So we have, revealed to the eye of faith and to the energetic mind, certain details which wonderfully assure our hearts that the Lord was raised without corruption in order that, transported in his uncorrupted body, his uncorrupted blood might be presented before heaven and placed for all eternity as a witness to the one full, perfect, and sufficient sacrifice and satisfaction which He offered for our redemption — an event for which the orderly development of the Universe had been but a preparation. Natural law in the development of life had been so ordered that, in the setting of the stage for man, the way had been opened for the objectification of God as Man by incarnation in the Person of Jesus Christ, who might thus become our Redeemer. Physical life had been designed with this event in view: and the Universe as the ampitheatre of this physical life thus finds its meaning. It is all of a piece.

And the signal of God's acceptance of the sacrifice which the Lord Jesus had made of Himself was that He raised Him from the dead, a circumstance which in the Old Testament is reflected in the return alive of the High Priest from the Holy of Holies after he had placed

the blood upon the Ark of the Covenant containing the emblems of
God's moral law.   Thus was the sacrifice validated in both situations.
But whereas the veil of the Temple had continued to separate God
from direct access by his people, this veil had now been ripped apart
from top to bottom, indicating symbolically the possibility of immediate access to God (Matt.27:51).

   The factual proof of a life given, the shedding of blood, had been
transplanted into a world of non-physical but greater reality, and
presumably there transformed in some way to make it agreeable in its
permanence to that other-worldly reality.   Perhaps its new form was
the result of a transformation similar to that which seems clearly to
have taken place in the Lord's glorified body which thus placed it
beyond the spoiling powers of this present world — even as we have
the promise that our bodies will likewise be fashioned in due time
(Phil.3:21).

   These things are not spelled out in a simple narrative of connected
events in such a way as to make them self-evident.   The method of
presentation adopted is such that they are likely to be concealed from
the casual reader.   But the serious student will rejoice as one who
finds great spoil.   Such is always the reward for searching the Scriptures.   This is the delight of all who love the Word of the Lord — and
the puzzlement of all who treat it with insufficient respect.   These
fragments of truth have been dispersed throughout the Scriptures to
give a special form of comfort and delight to those who are willing to
dig for them and thus to secure their spiritual bread as they do their
daily bread, "by the sweat of their brow".

SUMMING UP

It is not that we have new light on the Articles of Faith themselves: they are still the grand fundamentals we have always believed.

It is rather that we have new light on the connecting links between them. This new light underscores the organic unity of our Faith, and shows how each Article contributes an essential element to the whole structure.

SUMMING UP

> *Now unto the King*
> *eternal, immortal, invisible,*
> *the only wise God,*
> *be honour and glory*
> *for ever and ever.*
> 1 Timothy 1:17

If John Owen had not pre-empted the phrase "The Death of Death" as part of the title of one of his best known theological works, it might have made an excellent title for this volume. For this is largely what it is all about. Alternatively, it might have been titled *The Unique Relationship Between the First and the Last Adam*, since this too would have been appropriate. Yet its theme has a broader compass than either title.

For a long time we were in the habit of referring to the volume as *The Physiology of Redemption* since it lays emphasis on those factors in the great scheme of redemption which have to do with matters physiological. Yet we were persuaded in the end that the title did not adequately declare the theme of the book which is the salvation of the *whole* man. So we ended up with the present title, *The Seed of the Woman* — that Seed being the Lord Jesus Christ, our Saviour. It is a fresh examination of how the Lord Jesus Christ, the Jehovah of the Old Testament and the Creator of the Universe, when He designed the order of nature, prepared the way for Himself to become Man in order to die as Man that we who had lost true manhood might live.

We have indeed been dealing with the nature of death as a consequence of disobedience and with the promise of its final elimination. But we have been dealing with an even more profound problem: how can such a tragedy in human experience as death has proved to be, be reconciled with the claim that God who declares Himself to be altogether gracious in all his intentions towards man is also sovereign? How can such an evil have been allowed to bring so great an avalanche of tears to a race conceived in love by a Creator who desires only the good of his creatures? Was the Fall and its penalty unforeseen? Was it an accident? Was it merely allowed? Or was it *planned*?

The conclusion seems to me to be somewhere between allowing and planning, for it was both allowed and *allowed for* and therefore part of the plan. It was planned in hope, not after the event had happened but from the very beginning of creation — indeed, before creation was actually begun. The whole process of creation, whether it took millions of years to set the stage or only a few days, was directly related to and designed with the plan of redemption in mind.

Natural laws, including those governing all living processes, were engineered as a direct preparation for the creation of man as a free agent with the power of making a choice between right and wrong, and with the capacity for redemption if the choice was wrongly made. The process of redemption itself was ultimately bound to the nature of the penalty that disobedience would bring, namely, the experience of dying. And the origin and nature of man's dying as distinct from the origin and nature of plant and animal death provides the key to an understanding of the physical basis of this plan of redemption: in short, the *physiology* of redemption. *Human* death makes redemption possible.

Only revelation can help us here. All the sophisticated research in the world cannot tell us what kind of physical life Adam enjoyed at first that made it possible for him not to die unless he disobeyed. We see something of the meaning of a form of physical immortality in certain lower orders of life, but we cannot know by experiment whether the form of Adam's immortality was the same. And we still do not know even in animals what actually happens when a creature begins to die. If we should get closer to understanding this strange phenomenon for *them*, we still have no materials for experiment with man as God created him because man is no longer *man*. Adam ceased to be himself when he disobeyed and became something essentially different, for he no longer had the power to continue his life unendingly. If we experiment with man today, we are not experimenting with man as God created him in Adam.

All we know is that the original kind of life system was not entirely lost to the human race when Adam fell. By the unique formation of Eve out of Adam, provision was made in the woman's seed for its continuance and recovery in the Person of Jesus Christ. The Universe seems to have been designed for this: and the earth was prepared specifically as the stage within the theatre of the Universe upon which the drama of redemption was to be worked out.   The nature of the Universe predetermined the nature of man's corporeality, and it was only possible for man to be redeemed by a Redeemer who assumed man's corporeal constitution. The Redeemer was God Himself, taking upon Him the nature of man as a permanent part of his own personal existence without in any way surrendering his deity.   And the constitution of man as a hyphenate body/spirit entity made this 'assumption' possible.

His death *for man*, by incarnation *as Man*, meant that his manhood could suffer death when his human body died and could be recovered again when his human body was resurrected.   He died as Man even though He continued to live as God; and it was in his capacity as God that He raised Himself again as Man from the dead.   What He raised up again was his human body and what He thereby reconstituted was his manhood.   He was perfectly correct when He said that *He* would raise his body up again in three days (John 2:19).   But Peter was equally correct when he said that it was *God* who raised Him up (Acts 2:24).   For He was God.   It was the Lord **Jehovah** who raised up his own human body and reappeared to the disciples as the Lord **Jesus** whom they had known before.   As such, even Thomas acknowledged Him when he exclaimed, "My Lord and my God" (John 20:28).

The death of God as Man incarnate is only comprehensible to the extent that we grasp the fact that it was by the destruction of the human body which He had assumed, that He died as Man.   And the re-constitution of God *as Man* is only comprehensible to the extent that we recognize He was able to raise that body and assume it once again in a glorified form.

Man was created with the possibility of dying but not the necessity of doing so, and thus accordingly a Redeemer could be made with the same potential and be truly human.   Since redemption involved the Redeemer's death but without internal necessity, this is precisely how true man had to be constituted at first.   No angel could die for man since angels do not experience physical death, and no animal can suffice by its dying either.   Only God could suffice as Redeemer of men; and therefore God became neither angel nor animal, but Man.   And He became Man specifically that He might taste death not for some solitary individual, as a man may do today in giving his life for a friend, but that He might taste death for every man (Heb.2:9).   That was why He had to be both man and more than man: God-Man.

As we have seen, while death must be possible for man even in his unfallen state since otherwise an unfallen redeemer could not himself have experienced death on man's behalf, it had to be possible for him not to die since otherwise the redeemer could not embrace death *voluntarily*.   Unless these two alternatives were present in Adam, there could have been no Redeemer and no redemption.   It is necessary to underscore these two potentials because so much hinges upon them.   Unless it is possible for man to die, no *man* can possibly die as a substitutionary sacrifice.   Unless it is possible for man not to die, such a redeemer if truly man would be subject to death by nature and could not therefore offer himself in man's place.   We know that both these conditions were met in the creation of the first Adam, and we know now that the processes of conception and birth and hereditary transmission were so designed that out of Adam's loins there might still arise a second Adam who could be just such a Redeemer.

So the plan is of a piece in every element.   To surrender any link in the chain is to make the plan unworkable.   For man to be redeemable, the race must have begun with an Adam whose physiology was precisely that which Scripture reveals it was in Adam.   Such a creature was not evolved but was a special creation.

And in order for the Redeemer to escape the necessity of death while remaining truly man, what is revealed in Genesis to have happened is precisely what had to happen to make the plan of redemption work.   The creation of Eve out of Adam in order to separate the two seeds, the housing of the woman's seed in a unique way for its preservation, and the virgin conception and birth of a sinless and immortal Redeemer — these form a single theme.   Bodily resurrection without corruption was proof of its success.

In following this sequence of events, we have seen how research has shed more and more light upon the matter until continued unbelief is well-nigh inexcusable.   We see now that the great fundamentals of the Faith need not be abandoned because of the advance of knowledge, but ought to be even more securely embraced than ever before. Only those ignorant of the facts can today justify their departure from the Faith.

But it may be argued that the approach taken in this volume is inherently dangerous.   In the past, apparent confirmations of faith have been hailed with enthusiasm only to prove in the course of time to be misinterpretations of the evidence which, properly understood, offered no confirmation at all.   In a few instances the evidence has in fact been the invention of an over-eager mind, although with the best of intentions.   Such claims can only do harm.   The argument is, therefore, that we should never bolster Faith by such means.

With this I agree.   Faith based on humanly acquired knowledge is precarious, since all such knowledge is subject to correction.   Yet it is undoubtedly a mistake to go to the other extreme and refuse to explore the implications of such new knowledge in the light of the strong convictions we do have. The worst of all fears is fear that the discovery of the truth will be damaging to our Faith. Yet a fact established is as sacred as a truth revealed.

Moreover, almost all the evidence here presented is experimentally verifiable or can be documented historically. Much of it is repeatable evidence, observable, and in essentials hardly deniable. It is not likely that we shall suddenly discover it is all a mistake. Theories come and go, but experimentally established data remain. And I believe it is time that the implications of these findings should be explored by the Lord's people. The supposed conflict between science and faith lies not in the facts themselves but in the way they are interpreted. We are challenged to interpret them in the light of the Word of God.

Just when our theological colleges and seminaries are tending to lead the ministers and pastors of to-morrow away from the old Faith on the grounds that modern science has made that old Faith untenable, modern research is in many ways tending in exactly the opposite direction.

That Adam could have been 'divided' for the formation of Eve, and that two such creatures could have had a potential physical immortality is no longer a concept foreign to current biological findings — though few biologists would risk their reputations yet by openly declaring such a position as I have taken. But human genetics and developmental physiology do combine to show that the unique formation of Eve out of Adam could very well serve the purpose of providing a means whereby the potential immortality they both enjoyed at first could be preserved via the woman's seed, even after it had been surrendered by both of them personally. However, what the evidence really tells us is not so much that this could be done, for we know by the implications of Scripture that this is what *must* have been done. What this new knowledge does is to enable us to gain a deeper insight into the means whereby God brought it all about. And it shows that the natural order had been designed with this in view.

We should not therefore turn our backs upon this new light, but rejoice in it and explore our Faith along new lines. The result of such exploration is to provide new understandings of Scripture itself and new insights into passages, the meaning of which has lain dormant hitherto. Such passages are suddenly unlocked, and many old familiar passages are illuminated in new and surprising ways. In short, this new knowledge is not to engender faith but to enable us to gain a deeper understanding of *the things we already believe.*

But there is an important distinction that needs to be made between what are strictly the fundamentals of our Faith when viewed as a series of propositions to which we assent wholeheartedly, and the rationale with which they are organized into a coherent and defensible system of theology. The existence and nature of God, the creation of man in God's image, the formation of Eve, the fact and nature of the Fall, the entrance of death (both spiritual and physical), the promise of a Redeemer, the Incarnation whereby God became Man for man's redemption through the miracle of a virgin conception, the sinless life and vicarious death of that Redeemer, his bodily resurrection without corruption, and his promised return — all these are the elements of our Faith, the basis of our hope as Christians, and the subject headings of our systematic theologies. How one element follows from the preceding one and relates to it and to all the rest is something which God has left us to work out by thinking about the matter, though He has provided pointers throughout Scripture.

Such pointers illuminate the whole fabric of our Faith and make it beautifully satisfying to the sort of minds we have, if we do but accept these fundamental elements to begin with. But because our minds are at different stages of development, so we each take from Scripture that which is most suitable for us personally. Scripture encourages this selectivity by its constant use of parable and symbol and metaphor, since such devices lend themselves to different purposes according to the mind of the reader. By which I mean that one may have in a single household a child reading a Bible story and being stirred in imagination to make noble resolves, while at the same time in another room grandfather is sitting at a desk poring over the same passage and drinking in the deep things of God, which the child would never discover nor needs to know at that stage of development. The words are for children, but the thoughts are for men. Each draws from the same Word food convenient for himself. Yet the truth is not thereby compromised.

However, what I think we have to avoid at all costs is the temptation to confuse the rationale (the theology which we construct for ourselves in relation to our Faith) *with saving faith itself.* Such systematic theologies are built up partly on the basis of explicit statements of Scripture, and partly upon its implicit statements and upon knowledge gained from other sources. We must not equate faith with reason in such a way that it becomes dependent upon reason. Faith that is dependent upon reason is not a biblical faith. Saving faith is something granted to our darkened minds by the Holy Spirit. We reach it by a leap not a ladder, by a jump not a climb. It is something that suddenly grips the mind, as though a light were switched on unexpectedly. Afterwards we may back-track and construct a rationale but we do not arrive at our faith this way to begin with. Christian evidences may serve the purpose of removing some of our objections so that our blindness is not quite so strongly 'willed': but this is not how saving faith itself is acquired.

We do not simply decide to believe, having been convinced by factual evidence. We first grasp the truth, being enabled by the Holy Spirit, and then the external evidence for the truth suddenly takes on a new significance. Thus we 'understand' by faith rather than believe because we have first understood. Anselm said, "I believe in order that I may understand". It was years later that Abelard set the modern trend by saying instead, "I seek understanding in order that I may believe". Abelard led us astray.

The reason I believe the fundamentals of my Faith is not because I can rationalize them. For some years I believed them with all my heart without being able to systematize them in my own mind. Systematization, and rationalization, came long after faith. But today I find it exciting indeed to explore the implications of these things not only in the light of Scripture but with the help of scientific research also. Such findings do not certify faith but they can indeed broaden understanding: and they help to show the organic unity of that Faith.

It is important to note that the fundamentals of Faith are sometimes abandoned because their interrelateness as a system of belief has not been made explicit. For example, it is easy to abandon the concept of the direct creation of Adam and to substitute some form of evolution at least of his body, if the true significance of the body in man's constituted being is not recognized. If Adam's body is animal in origin, regardless of where his 'soul' arises, then man is half animal and the Lord Jesus when He became Man became half animal also. If we once accept the erroneous view that man is only truly man by reason of his 'soul', and that his body has little significance except in so far as it is an adept housing for his soul from a physiological point of view, then we are really losing sight of what man is. The human body forms as much a part of man's humanity as his spirit does. Neither is more important than the other, or less important.

If Adam had his physical life by virtue of animal ancestry, then his death was not a penalty but was programmed as it was for animals. He becomes a unique spirit in an animal body, all the physical elements of which are shared by other primates. But Scripture does not seem to take this view at all. The death of a man is quite different from the death of an animal because it is a rending apart of a bond originally designed to last throughout eternity. So important is the body of a man that he must have his *own* body resurrected in order to be reconstituted as truly himself. When we bow to the implacable offensive of science in such an issue as this, as the Roman Catholic Church has done officially, we are left with a totally indefensible theology of salvation, and a biblical psychology that is no longer truly biblical.   It is only a matter of time before the logical relations of this betrayal of sound doctrine will become evident.   Professor Gresham J. Machen said many years ago:*

> The true way in which to examine a spiritual movement is in its logical relations: logic is the great dynamic and the logical implications of any way of thinking are sooner or later certain to be worked out.

Few people realize when they begin to take a supposedly broader view of human origins that they are initiating a process of reasoning which will work itself out in their minds, willy-nilly, until they find they are shifting their position even with respect to some elements of their Faith which they never had any intention of abandoning.   And very soon the whole Faith, the whole *system* of Faith, begins to collapse.   It is quite hopeless to defend the fact of the Virgin Birth and the Incarnation if we abandon the record of the formation of Eve as given in Genesis.   The Virgin Birth apart from the background of original sin and the communication of mortality through natural generation becomes meaningless.   Indeed such a scholar as William Barclay, who accepted the evolution of man, has stated quite candidly that he cannot see the significance of either the virgin birth or the bodily resurrection of the Lord.   If one can see no reason for these great truths, can they remain great convictions?   The fatal step from a little doubt to no faith is sometimes delayed for a long time, but it is almost always taken in the end.   And we have seen how unnecessary it is for us to surrender our Faith in any of its fundamentals so far as factual evidence goes.

Whatever else in Karl Barth's theology we may feel uneasy about, he was unquestionably right in insisting that the creation of man in such a form that the Fall of man took place as it did, was an essential step in the revelation of God's redeeming love; and the story of Eden must be viewed as preparatory to Calvary.   In this sense creation was conceived after the plan of redemption had been formulated, because that plan predetermined the form that creation must take.   As Barth put it:†

> To proceed from creation to original sin, from original sin to actual sin, and from actual sin to grace, is a wrong method in dogmatics.   The true method of a believing theology is in reverse.

---

* Machen, Gresham J., quoted by J. I. Packer, *Fundamentalism and the Word of God*, London, IVF, 1958, p. 26, 27.

† Barth, Karl, quoted by N. H. Ridderbos, *Is There a Conflict Between Genesis and Natural Science?*, Grand Rapids, Eerdmans, 1957, p. 14.

That is to say, in the mind of God the exhibition of his love at Calvary was the prime cause of his decision to create man at all: the creation of man in the form in which it is revealed to have taken place was a necessary but dependent consideration. Calvary preceded Eden and the plan of redemption preceded the Fall. This means that the crucifixion was not an emergency measure planned later to offset an unfortunate incident in Eden. What happened to the first Adam had everything to do with what was achieved by the last Adam. By distorting the former we completely confuse the significance of the latter.

We should be exploring the new evidence that science is uncovering in the fields of genetics, embryology, and developmental physiology with a view to enlarging our sense of wonder that God in his wisdom should so design the processes of conception and birth that He could use them, without doing violence to his own created order, as a means of entering into our world of space and time in the likeness of ourselves for our redemption. He did not need to supercede these laws. He put them to a higher service, a service for which they were designed in the first place.

It is not that we have discovered unexpectedly that the natural laws governing these things at last permit us to present a scientific argument for our Faith. It is rather that we can now see how these laws were from the very first intended to serve the purpose of God. Our Faith perceives them to have been essential if that purpose was to be fulfilled. God was not limited by natural law which by some adjustment permitted Him to do what He wished: He designed those laws in the first place to serve his own purpose. He first made his plans and then designed the natural order accordingly.

It is time to return to the old Faith, for the old Faith as traditionally understood is far nearer to the truth than the newer versions of it. The revised versions are often the result of ignorance rather than the understanding of modern research. We have abandoned our Faith too easily. We were fearful of being 'out of date' where in point of fact we might even have inspired some new fields of biological research which just now are beginning to excite the scientific world (the basis of longevity, for example). If only we had had the courage to explore without apology the consequences of those things which the Lord's people have most surely believed from the beginning, we might have led the way to exciting new understandings of both the world we live in and of the Faith we profess.

I cannot do better than close with a beautiful succinct summation of the whys and wherefores of much that has been discussed in this volume than by quoting some words of W. Ian Thomas in his quite remarkable little book, *The Mystery of Godliness.* *

- He had to come as He did
  to be what He was.
- He had to be what He was
  to do what He did.
- He had to do what He did
  that you might have what He is.
- You must have what He is
  to be what He was.

In short, the Lord Jesus had to come by virgin conception to be a *truly* human being.   He had to be a truly human being to redeem fallen man.   He had to redeem fallen man in order that you and I might have his kind of eternal life.   You and I must have his kind of eternal life in order to be a truly human being.   Amen!

We have for too long thought of the salvation of the soul as a salvation of the spirit only.   But man is not a spirit only.   Angels are spirits, but man is man: and he is man by reason of the duality of his constitution as a body/spirit entity.

Whereas it is true that the *application* of the redemptive process depends upon man's spiritual nature which permits him to see his own need and appropriate God's promises, it is nevertheless true that the *manner* of man's redemption hinges upon the nature of his physiology which was so designed that the Son of God might be made flesh in order to achieve that redemption for him without doing violence either to his own nature or to the natural order of things.

The salvation of his soul is not possible except his body be redeemed as well.   Nor is the body incidental: it is as fundamental a part of man's being as his spirit.

Furthermore, the emphasis upon man's spiritual being to the exclusion of his bodily existence has led us to overlook the physiology of his redemption.   Redemption is not simply a matter of the Lord's spiritual sacrifice of Himself.   In spite of the great emphasis in Scripture upon the *blood* of his sacrifice, we tend to find repugnant the thought that the shedding of his blood is the ground of our salvation.   Yet this shedding of blood is what made his embodiment, his Incarnation, a prerequisite.   It involved not merely taking upon Himself for our sakes the *appearance* of man, as angels already have done throughout biblical history.   It involved being human as to his body

---

*Thomas, W. Ian, *The Mystery of Godliness*, Grand Rapids, Zondervan, 1972, p. 121.

including his brain: i.e., *physiologically*. So we rediscover the importance of Adam's body as created, not evolved: of Eve as formed miraculously, not by natural process: of the Fall as a physical Fall as well as a spiritual Fall: of the virgin conception as an essential step in the redemption of man: of a death that need never have happened for internal reasons but was truly substitutionary both spiritually and physically: and of a resurrection of that body that allowed the symbol and proof of divine satisfaction to be placed on record in heaven to protect for ever those whose souls have been redeemed at such a price.

The whole man is body and spirit, a hyphenated entity in which neither constituent is whole in itself, nor is either superior or inferior to the other in importance. As Robert H. Gundry argues, the biblical touchstone for truly human life is not a spirit that has consciousness nor the mere existence of a physical object such as a body.* Man is only himself in the unity of his body and his spirit, wherein the body is animated and the spirit can express itself actively in obedience to God. Once redeemed, both parts of the human constitution share equally in the dignity of the divine image, a dignity which lies in man's service as God's representative caretaker over the material world. For such a task man needs just as much the physical instrument for action, his body, as he does the incorporeal source of conscious willing to action, his spirit. Thus we come full circle and find ourselves reiterating the words of Hugo St. Victor, that the world was made for the body, the body for the spirit, and the spirit for God. And we may remind ourselves that the Universe was made for the world.

Man in his *whole* constitution becomes the reason for the *whole* creation, which now waits for his redemption, the redemption of his body (Rom.8:23), because upon it the proper ordering of the world hinges and without it, its proper master is missing.

It becomes us to recognize once again the fundamental importance of the long chain of events which has been the subject of this study of the physiological aspects of man's redemption. All too often we have tended to ignore these aspects of salvation and consequently to lose sight of the vital importance of the events which necessitated such a kind of redemption and also made such a kind of redemption possible.

The human body is as essential to the existence of a truly human being as is the human spirit. In spite of the effect of the Fall upon man's body, his body is still essential to his spirit because it supplies the spirit with its *means* of expression and action, just as the spirit provides the body with its animation and capacity for purposeful

---

* Gundry, Robert H., *Sōma in Biblical Theology*, Cambridge Univ. Press, 1976, p. 160.

activity.   By their separation body and spirit both die; and so dies the whole man.   Thus by the redemption of the body and by bodily resurrection wherein the physiology of redemption is made complete, the whole man is reconstituted personally, and the original creation of man is finally fulfilled and justified.   Thereby is also fulfilled and justified the creation of the whole Universe.

The whole creation awaits the redemption of man, a redemption made possible because both the cosmos and man himself were prepared for this contingency — perhaps even designed for it. Certainly the design encompassed the necessary mechanisms for the appearance in due time of one unique Seed of woman in the person of the Lord Jesus Christ, who by special means escaped the entail of sin and death transmitted through the seed of man.

By his sacrifice of Himself, He who was the Creator of the Universe effected our salvation by temporarily laying aside the glory He had shared with his Father and being made one with us within the framework of space and time, becoming subject to two kinds of death in our place. So that, by rebirth of our spirit and by resurrection of our body we are thus wholly redeemed.

As there is to be a race of new men in Christ — new in spirit and new in body — so there is to be a new *heaven* and a new *earth* accordingly.   Nothing has been in vain, nothing was unforeseen. He who promised He would make a new people out of us who are really no longer people at all (1 Peter 2:9), promised also that He would make all other things new as well (Rev.21:5).   And indeed He will!

Even so, come Lord Jesus . . .   Amen.

APPENDIXES

APPENDIX I

(Page 39-41)

TABULATION OF SUPERCENTENARIANS.

EXPLANATORY NOTES:

(1) The data are not listed alphabetically but serially with increasing age.

(2) The data come from a great number of different sources, many of which are only newspapaer reports. Such data are not always reliable and a certain amount of scepticism is proper in assessing them.

(3) The original sources often contained considerable information of general interest and some of this has been included where it seemed of importance.

(4) It will be noted that certain areas of the world appear to favour longevity to an exceptional degree — notably Abkhazia (an eastern border of the Black Sea in the Georgian Soviet Socialist Republic), Hunza (in the Karakoram Range of Kashmir, Pakistan), and in Vilcabamba (southern Ecuador, South America).

(5) It may seem that most of these supercentenarians are of non-white origin, but this is not the case. The people of Vilcabamba are almost certainly old Spanish stock.

(6) It should be borne in mind that the absence of written records such as birth certificates, marriage certificates, etc., is not necessarily a reason for doubting the general validity of the data. Where a people do not have such records they are apt to be habitually more adept at *remembering* such things. It is essential for any culture to know the relationships of its members to one another since these relationships determine rights and privileges and responsibilities, and form the basis for many small but highly significant forms of social interaction and courtesies. Patterns of behaviour in all non-literate societies are almost wholly built up on age relationships, in ways that are sometimes exceedingly precise. Australian aborigines recognize 70 to 80 different degrees of relationship and have specific terms for them which are entirely foreign to Indo-Europeans. This network of remembered past fact and acknowledged present relationship serves as an excellent frame of reference in which to check out ages: and where this has been done, considerable confidence in the general correctness of the ages claimed has resulted.

(7) Whatever may be a critical reader's reaction to *some* of the entries, the data *as a whole* surely demonstrate that there must have been in the past and still are today many people who attain ages which to the purely sceptical mind are quite beyond reason; yet they cannot *all* be seriously questioned. We ought not to assume, as we read how easily the scientific community can be misled by forged data from within its own camp (Haeckel's forged diagrams, Dawson's Piltdown Man, Kammerer's frogs, and so forth), that Western man has a monopoly

on accurate reporting or recollection of past events.

We need only a few authenticated cases to show that, even today, man can indeed live well past the century mark without becoming a mere vegetable. We really have no hard evidence that men might not formerly have lived far longer. Why should we suppose that the Chinese, whose technology was *far* advanced above ours in Europe when we in England were dressed in sacking and they were dressing in silk, were more credulous than we are today?

(8) Finally, we have not included "mere" centenarians, for they are even now far too numerous to allow space for them. According to Elinor Langer, there were in the United States alone, in 1963 over 10,000 of them ["Growing Old in America", *Science:* 140: 1963, p. 471].

The tabulation which follows is drawn from many sources of varying value. In a number of cases documentation is very incomplete. In column five, in the interest of saving space, data derived from *books* is documented only by author, date, and page. The bibliography below gives the rest of the documentation as far as it has been possible to gather it. The volumes are listed by author, alphabetically.

Acsadi, Gy. and J. Nemeskeri, *History of Human Life-Span and Mortality*, Budapest, Akademiai Kiado, 1970.

Airola, Paavo, *Are You Confused?*, Arizona, Health Plus, 1971.
      Rejuvenation Secrets Around the World, Arizona, Health Plus, 1974.

Baily, T., *Records of Longevity*, London, 1857.

Dublin L. I., *Length of Life: A Study of the Life Table*, rev. ed., N.Y., Ronald Press, 1949.

Gould, George M. and Walter L. Pyle, *Anomalies and Curiosities of Medicine*, N.Y., Julian Press, 6th printing, 1966.

Gris, Henry and Milton Merlin, *"May You Live to be 200"! A Study of the Centenarians of Russian Georgia*, London, Barnes & Co., 1978.

Halsell, Grace, *Los Viejos*, Emmaus, Pa., Rodale Press, 1976.

Hufeland, C. W., *The Art of Prolonging Life*, ed. E. Wilson, Phila., 1870.

Humboldt, Baron von F. H. A., *Political Essay on New Spain*, 1807, Vol. I.

Marston, Sir Charles, *The Bible Comes Alive*, London, Eyre & Spottiswoode, 1937.

Prichard, James C., *Researches into the Physical History of Mankind*, London, Houlston and Stoneman, 1836, 5 vols.

NAME	AGE	COUNTRY	BIOGRAPHY	SOURCE
Maude Tull	103 in 1975	Los Angeles USA	Learned to drive after husband's death in 1965, given licence again this year. Works full time at a home mortgage company.	San Francisco Chronicle, 3 May, 1975, p. 8.
Leonor Cartujana	103 in 1976	Vilcabamba	Knows much about medicinal herbs. Attributes good geyesight to plants.	G. Halsell, p. 158.
Anna Schwab	104 in 1972	Ohio, USA	Reads Bible daily, knits and sews, hearing not so good, but mind keen.	Good News Broadcaster, (USA), July-Aug., 1972.
John Walker	104 in 1969	Port Arthur Ont., Can.	Acknowledged his birthday greetings with typed letters "unable to have usual open house on account of daughter's illness"! Photograph shows a young looking man.	The Bulletin (Can.), May, 1969.
Micaela Quezada	104 in 1976	Vilcabamba	Never married.	G. Halsell, p. 9.
Frances Johnson	107, d. Sept. 8, 1832	Jamaica	A Samboo slave, "retaining all her faculties to the last".	Gent's Mag, Supplement, Eng, Dec., 1832.
Robert Thomas	107, d. 1821	Fairfax Co., USA		Morning Herald, Eng., 2 June, 1823.
Emma E. Mills	108 in 1973	Toronto, Can.	Has never been ill and never missed a meal in her life.	Toronto Star, 25 Jan, 1973.
Mary Holoboff	108, d. 1942	British Columbia Canada	A Doukhobor, emigrated from Russia in 1842. She has 103 descendants.	Toronto Evening Telegram, 26 April, 1942.
Thomas Robinson	110, d. Jan. 6, 1970	Windsor, Ont. Can.	Died the day before his birthday.	Toronto Evening Telegram, 6 Jan, 1970.
Elizabeth Lambe	110, d. Sept. 1830	St. Helena West Indies	In 1731 was housekeeper for General Pike. Married 8 times. "She died in full persuasion that the Millenium will happen in 1836, and that the charter will be renewed to the East India Company".	The Times, London, 8 Sept., 1831.

NAME	AGE	COUNTRY	BIOGRAPHY	SOURCE
Astana Shlarba	110 in 1966	Georgia USSR	Picture shows him in riding garb with gunpowder cartridges on chest.	*Life*, 16 Sept, 1966, p. 123.
Jim Ho	111 in 1976	Prince Edward Island, Can.	Born in Canton, China, in 1865. Came to Canada at the turn of the century. Laundryman and chef for CPR. Attributes long life to Chinese food, likes cigarettes and liquor.	*Recorder & Times*, Brockville (Can), 13 Nov., 1976, p. 1.
Spencer Church	111 in 1961	Ontario Can.	Chopped wood when 110.	Item on CBC News, 17 Feb., 1961.
Ada Roe	111, d. Jan. 11, 1970	England	British birth certificate verified.	*New Scientist*, 1 Feb., 1973, p. 237.
John Turner	111, d. Mar. 22, 1968	England	British birth certificate verified.	*New Scientist*, 1 Feb., 1973, p. 237.
Luceja	112	Rome	An early Roman actress who performed for a whole century and even made a public appearance when 112.	Gould & Pyle, p. 377.
Mittelstedt	112, d. 1792	Prussia	In 68 years of army service, participated in 17 engagements, braved numerous dangers, was wounded many times, and a prisoner of the Russians. After a turbulent life, he married a third wife at 110. Until shortly before his death, he walked 2 miles every month to the pension office.	Baily, 1857.
Cesar Paul	112 in 1975	Ontario Can.	A Cree Indian. Married twice with 6 children. In good health, smokes a pipe, a hockey fan.	*Recorder & Times*, Brockville, 15 April, 1975, p.16.
Gabriel Sanchez	113 in 1976	Vilcabamba	Goes up the mountain at dawn every day and works all day in his plot.	Halsell, p. 45, 71-76.
Francis Hongo	113, d. 1702	Venice	Father of 49 children, married 5 times.	*Toronto Evening Telegram*, 26 April, 1942.

Name	Age	Place	Notes	Reference
Arma Darendonian	113, d. 1972	France	Emigrated from Armenia in 1924. Attributed long life to the nuts and honey she ate as a young woman.	*Toronto Globe & Mail*, 5 Dec, 1972.
Annie Firlotte	113 on July 15, 1954	New Brunswick Can.	Until that winter, she walked several hundred yards every day to the grocery store. Has never been to a dentist, has her teeth. Memory is crystal clear, speaks both French and English, does not read or write, listens to the radio.	*Toronto Evening Telegram*, 17 April, 1954.
Amina Orujeva	114 in Mar., 1967	Azerbaijan, USSR	Celebrating their 101st wedding anniversary!	*Toronto Evening Telegram*, 15 Mar, 1967.
Zibeida Sheidayeva	114 in 1974	Azerbaijan, USSR	After 100 years as a worker in a rug factory, was awarded the Red Banner of Labour. She ties 7000 knots a day, makes a rug in 20 to 25 days.	*Toronto Evening Telegram*, October, 1974.
Teb Sharmat	115 in 1966	Abkhasia USSR	A singer-raconteur, member of a 50 voice choir of centenarians.	*Life*, 16 Sept, 1966, p. 126.
Murtee Johnny	115, d. 1976	Australia	An aboriginal rancher.	*Recorder & Times*, Brockville, 18 Sept., 1976, p. 10.
Walter Williams	117, d. Dec. 19, 1959	Houston Texas, USA	Last survivor of the Civil War.	*Ill. Lon. News*, 2 Jan., 1960, p. 27.
Mary Mills	118, d. 1805	West Indies	"Passed away peacefully". 295 descendants attended the funeral.	*Toronto Evening Telegram*, 26 April, 1942.
Mr. C. Cotterel	120, d. 1760?	Philadelphia USA	His wife was aged 115 at her death. They were married 98 years.	*Benjamin Martin's Miscell. Corresp. in Prose & Verse*, Jan., 1761.
Jane Morgan	120, d. 1830	Jamaica	A negro woman belonging to George Crawford Ricketts, Esq., Attorney-general of the Island.	*Gent's Mag.*, England, March, 1831.
Mary Goodsall	120, d. 1820	Jamaica	Black lady.	*Blackwood's Mag.*, England, 18 Jan., 1822.

NAME	AGE	COUNTRY	BIOGRAPHY	SOURCE
Mrs. Gray	121, d. 1770	Kent, England	A deaf mute, noted for her cheerful disposition and manifest enjoyment of life.	Gould & Pyle, p. 377.
Charles Layne	121, d. 1821	Virginia, USA	Left a widower aged 110 years. A numerous and reputable family to the fourth generation.	London Mag., Aug., 1821.
Sabir Kurbonadadov	122 in 1973	Tajik Republic USSR	Oldest dweller in the Andarob village.	Health Mag., Spring, 1973, p. 16.
Rev. Toby Crosby	122, d. 1976	Florida, USA	Born of slave parents. In 1932 built a church. Sight and hearing impaired; preached and travelled two weeks prior to his death.	Christianity Today, 18 June, 1976, p. 31.
John Gilley	123, d. 1813	Maine, USA	Born in Ireland, came to Maine at age of 60. Remained single till 75 when he married a girl of 18 and they had 8 children. She survived him, stating he was virile till 120.	Boston Medical Journal, 1869, p. 432.
Noah Raby	123, d. 1895	New Jersey USA	Discharged from the "Brandywine", USN, 83 years ago (in 1812).	New York Herald, 21 April, 1895.
Demetrius Liondos	123 in 1970	Greece	Walked erectly and easily. Until a few years ago had walked over a long difficult road for his monthly cheque. He was thin, bony hands, sallow skin and his long beard grey, his hearing poor but eyesight quite good.	Christianity Today, 5 June, 1970.
Thomas Wishart	124, d. 1760	Dumfries Scotland	He had chewed tobacco 117 years! When a child, his father gave him tobacco to allay hunger while shepherding in the mountains.	Gould & Pyle, p. 377.
Francisco Rubio	124, d. 1943	Mexico	A few days before his death played pool. Survived by 23 children, all born of his second marriage.	Toronto Evening Telegram, 1943.
Attila	124, d. 453?	Germany	King of the Huns, and nicknamed "Scourge of God". Ruled over the Vandals and Ostrogoths.	Prichard, p. 121.

Name	Age	Place	Description	Source
Anton Pilia	124 in 1966	Azerbiajan USSR	Tends his orchard regularly.	*Recorder & Times*, Brockville, 15 July, 1966, p. 1.
Sylvester Magee	126 in May 1967	Missouri USA	A former slave. His eyes bright and alert, his face marvellously expressive; until four years ago still worked in the cotton fields.	*Time*, 14 July, 1967, p. 50; *Toronto Globe & Mail*, 30 May, 1967, p. 8.
Mary, wife of Joseph Yates	127, d. 1776	England	At 92 married a third husband; at 110 had walked into London (from Lizard Commons); and at 120 was strong and hearty.	Gould & Pyle, p. 377.
Miguel Carpio	127 in 1976	Vilcabama	Still has nearly all his black hair, is over 6 feet tall; hoes in his garden. Says his long and full life is due to "destiny".	*New Scientist*, 1 Feb., 1973, p.237. Halsell, p. 32.
Eglebert Hoff	128, d.1764	New York USA	Was a lad driving a team in Norway when Charles I was beheaded. Never used glasses, read fluently, retained his memory and his senses till his death which was due to an accident.	Gould & Pyle, p. 377.
Margaret Darby	130, d. April 6, 1821	Jamaica	A free black woman: died with all her faculties to the last.	*Blackwood's Mag.*, England, July, 1821.
Francis Peat	130, d.Nov. 1830	Jamaica	Black slave, leaving many descendants to the fourth generation.	*Gent's Mag.*, England, April, 1831.
Ramonotowane Seran	130. d.1945	Bechuanaland Africa		*The Times*, London, 31 Aug. & 5 Sept., 1945.
Balakishi Orujeva	130 on Mar., 1967	Azerbiajan USSR	Married at 30, celebrating 101 years of married life. In good health.	*Toronto Evening Telegram*, 15 Mar., 1967.
Ephriam Zithundu Zulu	130, d. 1975	South Africa	Member of the Zulu royal family.	*San Francisco Chronicle*, 6 Feb, 1975, p. 19.
Peter Garden	131, d.1775	Edinburgh	Lived during 8 reigns. Was of gigantic stature and retained his health and faculties to the last hour. He	*Toronto Evening Telegram*, 26 April, 1942; and

NAME	AGE	COUNTRY	BIOGRAPHY	SOURCE
Mathayo Achungo	132, d. 1976	Kenya, Africa	was 26 years old when Henry Jenkins (died at 169) related to him the Battle of Flodden in 1513 where he was present. Incredible that he could thus say he had heard an eye witness report of an event occurring 260 years ago!	*San Francisco Chronicle*, 4 Dec, 1976, p. 9.
Gabriel Erazo	132 in 1976	Vilcabamba	A romantic poet who laughs easily.	Halsell, p. 19.
Charlie Smith	133 in 1976	Florida, USA	Born in Africa, brought to States as a slave at 12. Worked steadily picking fruit until 113. In 1976 he received an honorary diploma from Polk County School System, though had little formal schooling.	*Time*, 14 July, 1967; *Toronto Star*, 19 Sept. & 2 Oct., 1972; and 13 May, 1976.
Henry Francisco	134, d. 1820	New York, USA	Present at Queen Anne's coronation (1702).	Baldwin's *London Mag.*, Jan., 1821.
Beim Mekraliyeva	134 in 1966	Azerbaijan USSR	Chief baby sitter for her village.	*Recorder & Times*, Brockville, 15 July, 1966.
Anton Pilya	135, d. 1965	Georgia USSR	Member of the village council till his death. At 135 married a woman of 27; died of a stroke 5 months later.	*Sunday Times*, (London), 3 April, 1966.
Nicholas Petours	137, d. 1775?	Germany	Canon of Cathedral of Constance, always healthy and vigorous, celebrated mass 5 days before his death.	Gould & Pyle, p. 378.
Juan Moroygota	138 in 1828	Columbia S.A.	At this advanced age enjoying perfect health and working every day as an agricultural labourer.	*Gazeta de Columbia*, S.A., 28 Nov., 1828.
Gentleman	140 in 1838	South America	Was a witness in a trial held in 1838 — recorded as born the night of an earthquake destroying Ambato, in 1698.	Gould & Pyle, p. 376.

Name	Age	Place	Description	Reference
William Hotchkiss M.D.	140, d. 1895	St. Louis USA	Known as the "colour doctor" because of his black patients.	*Nat. Pop. Review*, Aug., 1895.
Khfaf Lazuria	140, d. 1975	Azerbaijan USSR	In 1965 picked a ton of tea leaves; when over 100 held the record as the fastest tea leaf picker. Retired in 1970. Had smoked for over 100 years and still rolled her cigarettes herself. Preferred vodka to tea. Still had her own upper teeth. Only 4 feet 2 inches tall, with a marvellous smile, known as "coquette of the Caucasus".	*Life*, 16 Sept, 1966, p. 124; *Reader's Digest*, May, 1973, p. 55; *Toronto Star*, 8 Nov. 1974. Gris and Merlin, p. 167-183.
Medzhig Agagev	140 in 1976	Azerbaijan USSR	Still hale and hearty, active in the local council.	*San Francisco Chronicle*, 21 Jan., 1976, p. 13.
Jose David	142 in 1973	Vilcabamba	He is neither feeble nor bedridden but cultivates his patch of soil daily.	*New Scientist* 1 Feb., 1973, *Toronto Star*, 28 Feb., 1973.
Hilario Pari	143, d. circa 1807	Lima, Peru S.A.	This old Peruvian went, at the age of 130, from 3 to 4 miles daily on foot.	Humboldt. 1807.
The Countess of Desmond	145, d. 1619	England	Mentioned by Raleigh and Bacon. She appeared in court in 1614, being 140, in full possession of her powers, physical and mental. Several portraits of her at this advanced age were then known.	Gould & Pyle, p. 375.
Joseph Bam	146, d. 1821	Jamaica	Black man, belonging to the estate of Morice Hall.	*Gent's Mag*, Eng, Dec., 1831.
Bridget Devine	147, d. 1845	England	A well-known inhabitant of Oleon St., Manchester.	Baily, 1857.
Catherine Hiatt	150, d. 1831	Jamaica	Creole woman beloning to Hon. Capt. John Hiatt. Retained all her faculties to the last moment, did coarse needlework shortly before her death.	*Gent's Mag*, Eng., Dec., 1831.
Unnamed Lady	150, d. 1894	France	Died peacefully in the hamlet of Haute Garonne, subsisting during the closing decade of her life on goat's milk and cheese. She preserved all her mental faculties to the last but her body became attenuated to an extraordinary degree; her skin was like parchment.	*London Telegraph*, Oct., 1894.

NAME	AGE	COUNTRY	BIOGRAPHY	SOURCE
Christen Jacobsen Drakenberg	150, d. 1772	Denmark	A sailor for 91 years, fought in the war against the Swedes, then became a merchant seaman. In 1694 taken prisoner by Algerian pirates but set free after 15 years of slavery, and resumed his life as a seaman. In 1737, at the age of 110, he married a widow of 60 years. Known as 'the old man of the north'.	Acsadi & Nemeskeri, p. 17; Dublin, 1949.
Mahmoud Nivazov	150 in 1959	Azerbaijan	"Living among his 173 descendants".	Acsadi & Nemeskeri, p. 17.
Judith Crawford	151, d. 1829	Jamaica	Retained her bodily strength and faculties until within a few days of her death.	Gent's Mag., England, April, 1830.
G. Stanley	151, d. 1719	Wiltshire England	Black marble monument to him in the chancel of Honington Church.	Gould & Pyle, p. 375.
Thomas Parr	152, d. 1635	England	At the age of 130 was an active farmer, did not marry till 80, then again at 120. Presented to King Charles I in 1635. The excitement of the journey to London brought on his death — its immediate cause was over-eating. He was autopsied by Harvey who found the "internal organs in a perfect state; his cartilages were not even ossified".	Toronto Evening Telegram, 9 Sept., 1939; 26 April, 1942. Acsadi & Nemeskeri, p. 17. Gould & Pyle, p. 373.
Thomas Newman	153, d. 1542	England	Data confirmed by his Yorkshire monument.	Gould & Pyle, p. 375.
Asmar Salakhova	154 in 1966	Soviet Armenia	Spins wool yet.	Recorder & Times, Brockville, 15 July, 1966.
Iwan Yorath	156, d. 1621	Wales		Marston, p. 54.
Sampson Skakoragaro	158 in 1969	Tanzania Africa	In that year, had a successful cataract operation and "was in high spirits and talkative". He had fathered his youngest son at 136. Married in 1934 at age 123 with sons born in 1935, 1941, and 1945 — the two eldest are teachers and the youngest a tailor. He has	San Francisco Chronicle, 21 Jan, 1969, p. 15.

Name	Age	Country	Notes	Source
Robert Lynch	160, d. 1830	Jamaica	had three wives and 16 children. He himself was the eldest of 58 sons. His father lived to 123 years, had 39 wives, and 45 daughters.	Gent's Mag., England, June, 1831, supplement.
Joseph Surrington	died at 160	Norway	"Property" of Sir Edward Hyde East, "a slave in comfortable circumstances".	Hufeland, 1870.
Zaro Aga	164, d. 1932	USA	He had, living at the same time, a son of 103 and a son of 9 years. A Turk who worked as a porter in Constantinople where his strength (at age 160) so impressed an American that he arranged for him to tour the States. Aga did so for two years but then died from eating meat.	News Review, 22 Dec., 1938, under Medicine; probably from Edmond Szekely's book, Medicine Tomorrow, tr. P. Weaver, Daniel, Lon., 1938 (?).
Sarah Desson Rovin	164, d. 1741	England	Wife of John Rovin, 172 years old.	Prichard, p. 121; Acsadi & Nemeskeri, p. 16.
Jonas Warren	167, d. 1787	Balydole Ireland?	Called the "father of fishermen" for he followed his trade for 95 years.	Gould & Pyle, p. 374.
Shirali Mislimov	168, d. 1973	Azerbaijan USSR	On his birthday (1971) he rose at dawn to do his daily chores in the garden and orchard. Among his well-wishers were doctors who gave him his annual physical and judged his health perfect. He has never been ill, though forced to give up riding horseback recently. At 160 he journeyed to the capital city (his first visit). There a doctor recorded his pulse at 72 and blood pressure at 120/75 — but then this was after a three storey climb! He neither smoked or drank. Survived by his third wife, 107 years old, 219 other family members, including a grandchild aged 100 years.	Toronto Evening Telegram, 20 May, 1971; Ottawa Citizen, 13 Feb., 1967, p. 18. Life, 16 Sept., 1966, p. 121; Gris & Merlin, p. 88-115. Time, 17 Sept., 1973.
Ali Ashraf Husseini	168 in 1976	Iran	Today married his thirteenth wife, a fifteen year old.	San Francisco Chronicle, 23 Dec., 1976, p. 9.

NAME	AGE	COUNTRY	BIOGRAPHY	SOURCE
Javier Pereira	169, d. 1958	Columbia S.A.	Only 4'4" tall, weighed 75 pounds. Taken to New York Hospital - Cornell Medical Centre in 1956. At that time he had all his hair without any gray, teeth were all gone, skin like old brown wrinkled leather, eyes cloudy but still serviceable, hands arthritic but a powerful handshake firm and surprisingly youthful. Arteries showed no signs at all of deterioration. His endurance and feats were remarkable — like standing on one leg and pirouetting without losing his balance, walking three blocks and climbing two flights of stairs without losing his breath. He had no immediate relatives (though married 5 times), his last grandchild had died 15 years ago at age 85 years. He was known by oldsters in his own village when they were in *their* teens as the "old Indian who liked to dance".	*Toronto Star Weekly Mag.*, 15 Dec., 1956, p. 2 ff. Death notice appeared in *Time*, 14 April, 1958, p. 88.
Henry Jenkins	169, d. 1670	England	Present at the Battle of Flodden (1513) at age of 12. When over 100 he was still an excellent swimmer.	Gould & Pyle, p. 373.
John Rovin	172, d. 1741	England	He and his wife Sarah were married 147 years.	Prichard, p. 121; Acsadi & Nemeskeri, p. 16.
John Gower	died at 172	England	His wife, Susan, lived to 164 and, at the time of this report, their eldest son was 115.	Lejoucourt, "Galerie des Centenaires".
Jean Korin	died at 172	Hungary	His wife died at 164 had lived together 148 years. At the time of their death a son was 116.	Gould & Pyle, p. 373.
A Negress	174 in 1775	South America	This was reported by a witness who attested to the veracity of her age by events she recounted.	Reported in *Journal de Madrid*, 1775.
Baba Harainsingh	176 in 1952	India	He had grown a complete set of teeth, the previous ones having fallen out when he was about 100 in the 1870s, his gray hair was also turning black again.	*Toronto Daily Star*, 15 Dec. 1952.
Elizabeth Yorath	177, d. 1668	England	According to parish records.	Marston, p. 54.

Name	Age	Place	Notes	Source
Kentigren	185, d. 5 Jan. 600 A.D.	Scotland	Founder of Glasgow Abbey.	Acsadi & Nemeskeri, p. 16
Peter Torton	185, d.1724	England		Prichard, p.121.
Petratsh Zartan (Setrasch Czartan)	187, d.1724	Hungary	A few days before his death he walked a mile. Shortly before his death a Count Wallis had his portrait painted. When he died he was more than 10 years older than Abraham and 35 years older than "old Thomas Parr".	Acsadi & Nemeskeri, p. 16 Baily, 1857.
Gentleman	died at 192	Vera Cruz Mexico	In a town of Teluca where registers are "carefully and efficiently kept".	*Practical Medicine*, New York, 1895.
Gentleman	died at 207	England	More than one such case is reported in *Sammlung von Natur-geschichte und Medizin-geschichte*, Breslau, 1724, p.636.	Gould & Pyle, p. 375.
Li Chang Yun	256, d. May 1933	Szechun Pov. China	At the age of 100 he was awarded by the Chinese Government a special Honor Citation for extraordinary services to his country. This document is available in existing archives. It is reported that he gave a series of 28 lectures at the University of Sinkiang when he was over 200 yrs. old. He attributed his longevity to his life-long vegetarian diet and regular use of rejuvenating herbs plus "inward calm". A renowned herbalist, he used Fo-ti-tieng and ginseng daily in the form of tea. He enjoyed excellent health, outlived 23 wives, and kept his own natural teeth and hair. Those who saw him at age of 200 testified that he did not appear much older than a man in his fifties.	*Toronto Evening Telegram*, 26 April, 1942. Airola, 1971, p. 203. Airola, 1974, p. 79, 80.

THE TWO VALUES OF THE SAROS.

The Babylonian system of counting involved a process of multiplying by an alternate number instead of multiplying by the same number. We use the number *ten*. We start with *one* and multiply it by 10 to give us TEN, then again by 10 to give us a HUNDRED, and again by 10 to give us a THOUSAND, and so on. In the Babylonian system, they began with *one* and multiplied by 10 as we do. But then they multiplied this by 6. The next step they multiplied by 10 again, and then once more by 6. They did not, of course, use the word TEN or HUNDRED or THOUSAND which are English words: they used the words SOSSOS, NAROS and SAROS. Thus:

A SOSSOS was 10 x 6, or 60.

A NAROS was 60 x 10, or 600, i.e., 10 SOSSI.

A SAROS was 600 x 6, or 3600, i.e., 6 NARI.

They had a further term which signified a SAROS multiplied by 10, i.e., 36,000: and the next number in the series was 36,000 multiplied by 6, or 216,000. This was referred to as *Shar-ges*.

Now according to the above system, the usual value of a *Saros* for ordinary purposes of mathematical calculation was 3600 and this is the value which has been given to it by scholars in interpreting the Table of Berossus in which the reigns of the Kings were listed as so many *Sari*. This Table was set forth as follows:

TABLE IX

TABLE OF BEROSSUS

NAME	SARI	USUAL VALUE IN YEARS
1. ALORUS	10	36,000
2. ALAPAROS	3	10,800
3. AMELON	13	46,800
4. AMMENON	12	43,200
5. AMEGALAROS	18	64,800
6. DAONOS	10	36,000
7. EDORANCHOS	18	64,800
8. AMEMPSINOS	10	36,000
9. OTIARTES	8	28,800
10. XISUTHROS	18	64,800
	120	432,000

But, as we have noted, there was the alternative value to the *Saros*.   This shorter value was first reported by Suidas, a Greek lexicographer of whom little or nothing is known except that he must have lived before Eustathius (12th — 13th century A.D.) who frequently quoted him.   Under the heading ADAM, Suidas in his lexicon gives a brief chronolgy of the world ending with the death of the Emperor John Zimisces (975 A.D.).   This would indicate that Suidas lived in the latter part of the tenth century.   His lexicon is in the nature of a dictionary and encyclopedia combined, and it includes numerous quotations from ancient writers such as Aristophanes, Homer, Sophocles, and Thucydides.   A prefatory note gives a list of earlier dictionaries, and although the work is somewhat uncritical it contains much information on ancient history and life.   It also gives the length of reigns of the antediluvian Kings in *Sari*.   But at this point Suidas informs us that this unit of measurement had a double value among the Babylonians.   His words are:[251]

> *Sari* are, with the Chaldeans, both a measure and a number . . . . According to the calculations of the Chaldeans, the *saros* contains 222 lunar months which is equivalent to 18 years and 6 months.

The mathematics of Suidas can be bothersome unless one realizes that he is using a year of 360 days and a month of 30 days.   With these equivalents his figures of 222 months does work out at 18 years and 6 months.   But the modern *Saros* which is given the value of 18 years, 11 days, and 8 hours does not satisfy his calculation.   The point is not important unless one is a mathematical purist. From the point of view of Suidas, we simply have an alternative value of the *Saros* attributed to the Babylonians which makes an enormous difference to the figures in the tabulation of Berossus as will be seen from the following:

TABLE X

MODIFIED TABLE OF BEROSSUS

NAME	SARI	SHORTER VALUE IN YEARS
1. Alorus	10	185
2. ALAPAROS	3	55½
3. AMELON	13	240½
4. AMMENON	12	222
5. AMEGALAROS	18	333
6. DAONOS	10	185
7. EDPRANCHOS	18	333
8. AMEMPSINOS	10	185
9. OTIARTES	8	148
10. XISUTHROS	18	333
	120	2220

It should be borne in mind that the figures given by Berossus are not life spans as in Genesis but lengths of reigns.   The average length of reign from the above Table will be seen to be 222 years, which is far more reasonable than the figure of 4320 years which is the average length of reign according to Berossus' list when calculated on the basis of the higher value of the *Saros*.   If we assume that each King ascended to the "throne" upon the death of his predecessor, we can add together the ten successive reigns and take this to be the total period from Adam to the Flood.

CRITICISMS OF THE SHORTER VALUE OF THE SAROS

The Greeks adopted the Babylonian asterisms and appropriated their knowledge of the planets and their courses, and they learned to predict eclipses by means of the *Saros*.   This cycle of 18.03 years is the time in which the moon returns very nearly to her original position with respect to both the sun and to her nodes and perigee.   A, M. Clerke notes that there is no getting back to the actual beginnings of such knowledge of the heavens, but records dating from the reign of Sargon of Akkad (2350 B.C.) imply that the varying aspects of the sky had even then been long under expert observation.[252]   There is reason to suppose that the star groupings with which we are now familiar had even then begun to be formulated.[253]   Clerke observes that clay tablets preserved in the British Museum have supplied detailed knowledge of the methods practiced in Mesopotamia in the second century B.C. and that these show no trace of Greek influence.   The Babylonian observers were not only aware that Venus returns in almost exactly eight years to a given starting point in the sky, but they had established similar periodic relations of 46, 59, 79, and 83 years for Mercury, Saturn, Mars, and Jupiter.

They were accordingly able to fix in advance the approximate positions of these objects with reference to ecliptical stars which served as fiducial points for their determination.   The dates and circumstances of solar and lunar eclipses were predicted.   Clerke notes that F. X. Kugler made the discovery that the various periods underlying their lunar predictions were identical with those hitherto believed to have been reached independently by Hipparchus, who accordingly must be held to have borrowed from Chaldea the lengths of the synodic, siderial, anomalistic and draconitic months.   Evidently a steady flow of knowledge began from East to West in the seventh century B.C.   A Babylonian sage founded a school about 640 B.C. in the Isle of Cos, and possibly may have counted Thales of Myletus (c. 639-548 B.C.) among his pupils.   Clerke believes that the famous "eclipse of Thales" in 585 B.C. has not yet been authenticated by research, yet the story as told by Herodotus appears to intimate that a knowledge of the *Saros*, such as would have allowed such a prediction to be made, was indeed possessed by Thales.   The question is, Where did he get it from?   If Thales obtained it from the Babylonians either by studying their records or by having been taught it at school, then obviously the shorter value of the *Saros*, upon which such knowledge depends, must have long antedated the Greeks and there would be no fundamental reason why the antediluvian patriarchal ages might not actually have been recorded by the early Babylonians in *Sari* having this shorter value.

This is a point at issue in Sarton's view.   He argues that the Babylonians could not have been acute enough to extract this eighteen year cyclical period from their observations of the heavens, and he supports this conclusion from a work by a Dr. Antone Pannekoek, a Dutch astronomer, who wrote a paper entitled, "The Origin of the Saros" which appeared in the *Proceedings of the Royal*

Academy of Amsterdam in 1918.[254] According to Sarton, "neither the Babylonians nor the Greeks had any idea before the fifth or fourth century B.C." of the shorter value of the *Saros*.[255]   He argues that such a period would have been exceedingly difficult to discover if for no other reason that that it does not embrace a whole number of days.   It involves a certain number of days, *plus eight hours*. In his view the discovery of the *Saros* was therefore "not simply difficult but impossible".[256]

Any writer who holds categorically that something is impossible is asking for trouble.   There *are* impossible things, of course.   But in a case like this, the word *impossible* means that no document can ever be allowed to be discovered which contradicts it.   And this, of course, is an impossible prohibition!

Now Pannekoek, in his original paper, makes the following observation.[257]

> The forecast of eclipses, which to the uneducated is such a convincing proof of the power and accuracy of astronomical science, is not the fruit of highly developed modern theory, but belongs to the oldest products of human science.   Greek writers tell us that the Babylonians were already able to predict the eclipses by means of a period of eighteen years, which they called a *saros*, and which rested on the fact that 223 synodic lunar periods and 242 draconic revolutions are practically equal (both 6585.3 days), that after the period therefore, full and new moon return to the same position relative to the nodes . . . .
>
> According to the theory of Hugo Winckler's school, Babylonian astronomy had reached its highest perfection as early as 2000 to 3000 B.C., and therefore the origin of the *saros* lay in such a far off time that there is no possibility of following the road to its discovery.

Pannekoek proceeds to show that the Babylonians could not possibly have had the insight to observe this astonomical measure on the grounds that it would require someone to make a continuous compilation of events and then to notice from his own compilation the almost exact recurrence of events over a cycle of eighteen years.   The argument, in effect, is that their minds were not keen enough to observe the recurrence of events over a comparatively short period, although as we now know they did observe cycles of considerably longer lengths, which would require even greater powers of observation!   As a matter of fact, Pannekoek himself refers to a list of lunar eclipses arranged according to *Saros* periods which is now in the British Museum (Sp.11.71) of which Strassmaeir had given a transcription in 1894.   Pannekoek stresses that it could only be after such lists of eclipses had accumulated "in the course of centuries" that their periodical recurrences could be noted.   He did not have a very high opinion, obviously, of the competence of these people whose mathematics is now known to have been highly advanced, as Professor T. J. Meek has shown.[258]

So he concludes, "This shows that the familiar story according to which the Greek philosopher Thales predicted a total eclipse in 585 B.C. by means of a knowledge of the *saros* borrowed from the Babylonians can only be regarded as a fiction.   At that time the *saros* was still unknown . . . ."   But then, of course, Pannekoek (and Sarton) may be quite mistaken!

APPENDIX IV

(Page 52)

WELD-BLUNDELL PRISM.

The Weld-Blundell Prism is believed to have been written by a certain NUR-NINSUBUR and has been dated about 2170 B.C. This Sumerian King List is known in several variant forms, the variance being chiefly in slight differences in the spelling of the names and in the appearance of only eight names rather than ten in some editions. In Table XI we give the ten-name variant after Halley but corrected to more exact figures.[259] Halley seems to have rounded his figures to the nearest thousand years.

TABLE XI

ACCORDING TO HALLEY

NAME	SARI	LONG VALUE	SHORT VALUE
1. ALULIM	8	28,800	148
2. ALALMAR	10	36,000	185
3. ENMENLUANNA	12	43,200	222
4. KICHUNNA	12	43,200	222
5. ENMENGALANNA	8	28,800	148
6. DUMUZI	10	36,000	185
7. SIBZIANNA	8	28,800	148
8. EMENDUEANNA	6	21,600	111
9. UBURRATUM	5	18,000	93
10. ZINSUDDU	18	64,800	333
		349,200	1795

Average reign = 180 yrs.

In Table XII we give two eight-name variants, of which the first column of names is the form in which they are presented in Barton's translation based on Professor Stephen Langdon's text, [260] and the second column of names is the form in which Pritchard presents them on the basis of Thorkild Jacobsen's Sumerian King List.[261] Jacobsen attempted to reconcile all the available variant readings and to produce a kind of *textus receptus* or "standard version". He believed that all currently known texts went back to a single original written at the time of UTU-HEGAL, King of Uruk, around 2100 B.C. I have shown two numbers, (4) and (10), as blanks in the list merely to preserve the pattern of ten names which more or less correspond with the lists in Tables X and XI (p. 483 and above).

TABLE XII

ACCORDING TO JACOBSEN

ACCORDING TO BARTON	SARI	LENGTH OF REIGN IN YRS.	ACCORDING TO PRITCHARD
1. ALULIM	8	28,800	ALULIM
2. ALALMAR	10	36,000	ALALGAR
3. ENMENLUANA	12	43,200	ENMENLUANNA
4. ——	——	——	——
5. ENMENGALANNA	8	28,800	ENMENGALANNA
6. DUMUZI	10	36,000	DUMUZI
7. SIBZIANNA	8	28,800	ENSIPAZIANNA
8. ENMENDURANNA	6	21,000*	ENMENDURANNA
9. UBERRATUM	5	18,600*	UBARTUTU
10.——		–	——
	Total	241,000	for 8 kings.

Average length of reign:

Long reckoning   30,150 years

Short reckoning   155 years

* The two final figures appear to be somehow in error (presumably in the original) if whole *Sari* are the units, since 21,000 would be 5.83 *Sari* and 18,600 would be 5.16 *Sari*.   Probably these figures should be 21,600 (i.e., 6 whole *Sari*) and 18,000 (i.e. 5 whole *Sari*).   The 600 has somehow been transposed from the 21,000 entry to the 18,000 entry.

In order to reconcile Berossus' version with Jacobsen's (i.e., Table X with Table XII), we have to deal with three points of disagreement: the first is in the number of names (10 as opposed to 8), the second is in the spelling of the names, and the third is in the lengths of the reigns.   The common factor which is assumed to equate these lists in point of fact, is the concluding comment by the originator in each case to the effect that what followed next was the Deluge.   In the Berossus version after number 10 we are told, "in the time of Xisuthros the great deluge occurred".   In the standard version of Jacobsen, following his entry of UBARTUTU are the words, "then the flood swept over the earth".   These all, therefore, refer to pre-Flood times.

With respect to the divergence in numbers, nothing can be said at the present time.   With respect to the difference in names, it could be argued that Berossus' List gives the names in a form which had become familiar to the Greeks. Although none of the proposed reconciliations in this respect are very satisfactory, there are some rationalizations.   For example, in view of the fact that L and R are commonly interchanged, ALOR- (in Table X) could conceivably be a corruption of ALUL- (in Table XII) for entry No. 1.   In No.2 ALAPAR- (in Table X) could be ALAMAR- (in Table XII), in view of the fact that P and M are interchangeable.   In this case, a hypothetical ALAMAR- would be a broken down form of the ALALMAR- (Table XII).   S. R. Driver suggested that OTIARTES (Table X) is a corruption for a hypothetical OPARTES, which in turn might be a broken down form of UBAR-TUTU (Table XII), which means "father of UT-

NAPISHTIM" who was the "Noah" of one of the Cuneiform Flood stories. OPARTES would then be equated with No.9 of Table XII.

However, it is very generally agreed that this kind of bridge building has a somewhat doubtful value, and at the present moment we have to accept the fact that Berossus' King List does not match very well in this respect with the Weld-Blundell Prism which it is nevertheless probably "descended from".

The question of the difference in the number of entries possibly finds its explanation in a more exciting way.   First of all, it is necessary to bear in mind that these Cuneiform Lists provide us with lengths of *reigns* only.   They are strictly "King Lists".   It might be supposed, therefore, that individuals who did *not* become *kings* in the line would be omitted.   By contrast, the biblical list is a straightforward genealogical table, giving us merely the names and ages of the firstborn sons from Adam to Noah.   The wonderful thing about the latter list is that it also informs us, indirectly, that two of the ten died before their fathers, namely, Enoch and Lamech.   Assuming that the head of the house of the leading family was "king" until his decease, then there could only have been eight such kings: though there were actually ten generations.   Enoch was removed by translation 435 years before his father Jared died; and Lamech, being a man of violence, seems to have come to an end earlier than expected at the age of 777 years, just five years before his father Methuselah died.   He must have been a very frustrated prince!

Thus the figures in the Bible are sufficient to provide us with a possible key to the difference between the Weld-Blundell Prism of 2100 B.C. or thereabouts which was a list of "chiefs", while the Berossus' account perhaps is a list of the names (as then remembered) of the full ten generations.   If they are in the correct order, Enoch would be represented by EDORANCHOS in Berossus' List, a name which might be composed of two elements: EDOR and ANCHOS.   Conceivably ANCHOS is a corruption of Enoch.   Lamech would be represented by the name OTIARTES, which is not easy to account for.

Although I do not think much weight can be attached to the argument, it is just possible that in 2 Peter 2:5 where Noah is spoken of as "the eighth", and not "the tenth" as might have been expected, the reference could be to his position as eighth chief or "king" from Adam.   In Jude 14 where Enoch is spoken of as the seventh from Adam, the reference would presumably be to his position merely in the line of descent.   At any rate, it is an intriguing thought that we may have in the Genesis account an explanation for the apparent divergence between Berossus and his original source.

Perhaps even these pagan accounts from the Cuneiform and elsewhere, in spite of their gross exaggeration of the figures (due possibly to a mis-reading of the units of measurement somewhere along the line) are genuine reflections of an actual phenomenon in the early history of the human race.   Such a tradition, as we have seen, is remarkably widespread among the nations of antiquity, and virt-ually all such traditions agree among themselves at two important points: man lived for centuries before the Flood, and there were ten generations only from the creation of the first man to that event.   It is true that the number *ten* might con-ceivably be artificial, chosen as a mnenonic aid on the basis of the number of fingers on both hands.   By the same token, it would surely *not* be reasonable to account for the *eight* names of what is believed to be the Sumerian King List on the ground that we only have eight fingers — the two thumbs being excluded!

GENESIS 5: NAMES VIEWED AS DYNASTIES

The family of Seth originated when Adam was 130 years old (v.3)	130 years
Adam and his direct line were at the head of affairs for 930 years (v.5) when they were superceded by —	930 years
The family of Seth. In Seth, 105 years after it attained leadership, the family of Enosh took its rise (v.6).	
After being at the head of affairs for 912 years (v.8) Seth was succeeded by —	
The family of Enosh.	1842 years
Ninety years after Enosh attained to the headship, there sprang from it the family of Kenan (v.9).	1932 years
After Enosh had held the leadership for another 815 years (v.10), Enosh gave place to —	
The family of Kenan.	2747 years
Seventy years after Kenan had founded his dynasty, the family of Mahalaleel began its rise to power.	2817 years
Meanwhile Kenan's dynasty survived another 840 years and was then replaced by the family of Mahalaleel.	3657 years.
Sixty-five years after the rise of the dynasty of Mahahaleel, the family of Jared began to be prominent.	3722 years
The dynasty of Mahalaleel meanwhile continued for another 830 years, but was then overthrown by the dynasty of Jared.	4552 years
One hundred and sixty-two years after the rise of Jared's family, the family of Enoch began to become powerful.	4714 years

But Jared's family retained power for another
   800 years and then died out, to be succeeded
   by the dynasty established by Enoch.   5514 years

Sixty-five years after the rise of the family of Enoch,
   however, the family of Methuselah began to be
   prominent.   5579 years

The dynasty of Enoch survived for 300 years
   to be replaced by Methuselah's dynasty.   5879 years

One hundred and eighty-seven years after the
   rise of the family of Methuselah, Lamech's
   family became prominent.   6066 years

However, the supremacy of Methuselah's dynasty
   continued for another 782 years, to be replaced by the family of Lamech.   6848 years

One hundred and eighty-two years after Lamech's
   family had begun its rise to power, the family
   of Noah came into existence.   7030 years

And six hundred years later, the Flood came and
   brought to an end all these dynasties. This
   makes a grand total, from Adam to the Flood, of   7630 years

THE COMBINED GENEALOGIES OF MATTHEW AND LUKE

The study of an ancient genealogy can be quite fascinating but it takes a little getting into and demands more than ordinary dedication.

The two genealogies of our Lord which together establish his absolute right to the throne of David, both by blood relationship through Mary and by title through Mary's husband, bear close examination. For they show how the two lines were preserved at one particularly critical period when almost all family relationships in Israel were being disrupted. This was at the time of the Captivity in Babylon. It is shown in the genealogy (inserted at the end of this volume), as a kind of "wasp-waist" joining the head and the body of the genealogy above and below Zerubbabel.

The details of this gate are the subject of this Appendix. It seemed important to say something about the circumstances here because it is at this point in the line that the blood relationship between the Lord and David comes nearest to being destroyed.

The numbers which appear against the names in the Tabulation represent the two different systems of accounting adopted by Matthew, on the left side, and Luke, on the right. In Matthew, David appears as the 14th name from Abraham: in Luke David is the 34th name from Adam. The *red* line represents the blood line connection: the *yellow* line represents the carrying of title to the throne of David.

David had two sons who figure as heads of the two branches of the family as indicated in Matthew and Luke, namely, Solomon and Nathan. In Matthew's genealogy Solomon becomes No. 1 in the second group of 14 names: and in Luke's genealogy Nathan becomes No. 35 on the other branch line.

From Solomon we move down to Joram, No. 6. Joram married Athaliah, the wicked daughter of a wicked father and mother (Ahab and Jezebel). As a consequence of this evil man and his wife, his seed was cursed for four generations in accordance with the reference made in Exodus 20:5. Thus Matthew, who probably follows the Temple records faithfully in his list, omits the next three names (Ahaziah, Joash, and Amaziah) from his genealogy. There is little doubt that these Temple records had, by divine providence, removed these three generations from the register, so that Ozias (No. 7) appears as though he were the son of Joram, No. 6, in the accounting of Matthew 1:8. We know from 1 Chronicles 3:11 and 12 that in the original court records, these three missing names were written down. In this court record, Ozias (No. 7) is given an alternative name Azariah (1 Chron.3:12), and elsewhere he is also called Uzziah (Isa.6:1). These are merely variants of the same name.

We pass on to No. 14, Jehoiakim. It is important to note that his name ends with an *M*, not an *N*, and he is not to be confused with his son whose name was Jehoiakin (or alternatively Jeconiah, Jechonias, Coniah, and Conias). This multivariant form of a name applied to a single individual is common in many of the older cultures. It seems to be particularly prevalent in Russia, even today.

Now, with Jehoiakim (No. 14) we begin to see the hand of God at work in a very special way separating the thread of continuity of blood relationship and titular right to the throne in David's family. Jehoiakim was the last king of Israel to come to the throne as a free man. Unfortunately he was both an evil man and a foolish one. He began his reign just when the Fertile Crescent was in a state of political turmoil, Nebuchadnezzar in particular having very ambitious designs for empire building which were challenged by Egypt. In this see-saw contest for power that habitually characterized the relationship between Egypt and Babylon, Palestine stood at the pivot point. But Jerusalem itself need not really have become involved, for the city actually stood off the main route between the two warring parties. Any king of Judah who kept out of the fray and conciliated the antagonists as they marched their armies back and forth to attack each other, could expect to be left more or less alone except for paying token tribute.

Jehoiakim was not humble enough or wise enough to realize this, and provoked Nebuchadnezzar to attack Jerusalem. This was the Lord's way of punishing a wicked man who had unwisely aligned himself with the king of Egypt. His immediate punishment was to have his city beseiged and overrun, and to be carried captive to Babylon (2 Chron.36:5, 6). But for some reason Nebuchadnezzar decided to return him to Jerusalem as a puppet king while he completed his unfinished business in Egypt. His long range punishment was foretold by Jeremiah (36:30) that none of his seed should ever sit upon the throne of David. This was a severe blow to him because he was in the direct line, as Matthew's genealogy shows, and probably had every expectation of seeing this greatest of all honours accorded to his seed in due time.

Meanwhile Nebuchadnezzar, having completed his Egyptian campaign, soon discovered that Jehoiakim was a teacherous man who could not be trusted by friend or foe. Indeed, so treacherous was he that even the people of his own city, Jerusalem, turned against him, murdered him, threw his body over the walls and left him unburied outside the city — exactly as predicted by Jeremiah (22:18, 19). Nebuchadnezzar must surely have known what had happened, but he did not interfere when Jehoiakin (i.e., Jechonias, No. 55) succeeded his father.

But this young prince who was only eighteen years old when thus honoured (2 Kings 24:8) proved to have no more good sense than his evil father. He provoked Nebuchadnezzar (after only three months and ten days on the throne) to invest the city once more and depose him (2 Chron.36:9). Jechonias and all his court were taken captive to Babylon while his uncle, Zedekiah, was left as regent. Unfortunately, Zedekiah behaved as the rest of his family had done and eleven years later, Nebuchadnezzar seized Zedekiah, put all his sons to death before his eyes, and then deliberately blinded him. Zedekiah was taken to Babylon and died there. Jerusalem meanwhile was utterly destroyed (2 Kings 24:17—25:16).

Now Jechonias, after being taken to Babylon, was put in prison where he remained for some thirty-seven years. It appears that either before he was taken captive or possibly during his captivity he was married to a woman of appropriate status who appears to have been a daughter of Neri (No. 54 in Nathan's branch of the family) and therefore of David's line. In order to account for the subsequent relationships shown in the two converging genealogies, we have to assume that this woman was a widow whose husband had probably been killed in one of the many seiges which Jerusalem had suffered. It seems as though the prophet Zechariah had this circumstance in mind (12:12). This widow already had a son by her deceased husband when Jechonias took her as a wife. This son's name was Pedaiah. His name is not numbered in the genealogy shown in the foldout at the end of the volume. It appears only in 1 Chronicles 3:18 where he is shown as a son of Jehoiakin (i.e., Jechonias). If his widowed mother was married to Jechonias, he would by Jewish custom become the son of Jechonias automatically.

But Jechonias appears to have had a son of his own by this widow of the royal line. This son's name was Salathiel (No. 2 and No. 56 in the two pedigree lines). By this marriage of a widow to Jechonias, these two boys — sons of the same mother — would become brothers by Jewish custom.

However, Salathiel appears to have died childless, though not until he had reached manhood and married a wife. Jehoiakim's *blood* line thus came to an end in his grandson Salathiel — indicated by termination of the red line. But as it happens the actual *title* to the throne remained active. The curse of Jeremiah 36:30 was to be fulfilled not by the removal of the title itself from Jehoiakim's line but by the denial of that title to anyone who happened to be a blood relative in the line. With the death of Salathiel this blood line terminated.

But now, according to Jewish custom as set forth in the principle of the Levirate (Deut.25:5, 6), it became encumbent upon Pedaiah, the deceased Salathiel's (step-)brother, to take his widow and raise up seed through her who would not therefore be of Salathiel's blood line but would be constituted legally as Salathiel's son through whom the title would pass to his descendants. The son of this levirate union was Zerubbabel. In Matthew 1:12 and Luke 3:27 Zerubbabel is listed legally as Salathiel's son: but in 1 Chronicles 3:19 he is listed as the son of Pedaiah by actual blood relationship.

In the terms of biblical reckoning these two statements are in no sense contradictory. We might wish to be more precise by substituting such extended terms of relationship as son-in-law, stepson, and so forth. But Scripture is not required to adopt our particular terminology. It is required only to be consistent with itself, and the facts of the case as recorded of those who were the actors in the drama are precisely as stated.

We thus have a remarkable chain of events. Jehoiakim has a son, Jechonias, who has a son, Salathiel, who by levirate custom has a son named Zerubbabel. This son, Zerubbabel, has no blood line connection whatever with Jechonias, for he has no blood relationship with Salathiel. The blood relationship of Zerubbabel is with Pedaiah, and through Pedaiah with Pedaiah's mother, and through this mother with Neri. Thus Neri begat a grandson, Salathiel, through his daughter; and Salathiel "begets" a son, Zerubbabel, through Pedaiah.

The blood line thus passes through Zerubbabel: but so does the title also. The former passes via Pedaiah's mother, the latter passes through Salathiel's father. And though this mother and this father were also man and wife, the blood line stopped with Salathiel who literally died childless. It is necessary to emphasize this word *literally*, for it appears that it was *literally* true. Jeremiah 22:30 had predicted that Jechonias would also die "childless" — but we are reasonably sure that this was not *literally* the case, for he had a son Salathiel whom we cannot otherwise account for. But Jechonias' subsequent history tells us the sense in which childlessness was to be applied to him.

Jechonias seems to have matured and softened during his thirty-seven years of imprisonment in Babylon, and Nebuchadnezzar's son, Evil-Merodach, evidently took a liking to him and set him free, giving him a pension for the rest of his life (2 Kings 25:27-30; Jer.52:31-34). He would by now be nearing sixty and probably be counted a harmless old man.

Reading these two records of Scripture concerning this surprising act of clemancy accorded to the last genuine king of Israel (until Messiah shall be crowned), one has a strange sense of the mercy of God and the potential for gracious action that even pagan kings could display in those days.   It is a touching swan-song to the old kingdom of David's line which will yet be renewed in glory.   At any rate, when Jechonias died, he seems to have died alone without male descendants, "childless" in his old age, as Jeremiah had predicted he would.

As to Zerubbabel, he became a very prominent and worthy man in the re-building of Israel's fortunes after the Captivity, under the benevolent authority of Cyrus.   He stands as No. 3 and No. 57 in the dual pedigree.   He appears to have had several sons and one daughter (1 Chron.3:19).   We do not know why his sons were disqualified: we only know that their sister, Shelomith, inherited the title and carried the blood line.   Both of these she passed on to her eldest son, Abiud, and so to Joseph.   But with Joseph, as with Salathiel, the blood line terminated once again in so far as the Lord Jesus received nothing from him by natural procreation.   However, Mary drew her line, the blood line, through Heli from Joanna (No. 59), the second son of Shelomith.

And thus the Lord Jesus received the two guarantees of right to the throne of David: the blood line through his mother directly, and the title through his adopting father, Joseph.   With his death and resurrection these two rights became locked for ever in his Person and cannot be passed on to, or henceforth claimed by, any other man.

HEART RUPTURE: A POSSIBLE CAUSE OF THE LORD'S DEATH?

Did the Lord Jesus die from a broken heart?

Not a few commentators of recent years have suggested that He did, and the evidence adduced in such a work as that by Dr. William Stroud carries considerable weight.   Yet I believe it is important to distinguish between dying *with* a broken heart and dying *from*, or as a result of, a broken heart.   In the Lord's case the former, I am persuaded, may be a sad truth but the latter is a profound error. I believe that the circumstantial evidence from the Gospels lends some support to the view that the Lord's heart was broken, ruptured in the most literal sense, when He died.   But I am also persuaded that this was not the cause of his dying, nor even a contributing factor in it.   But this, in turn, means it must be possible for a man with a ruptured heart to continue an active life.   It means that heart rupture is not necessarily immediately fatal.   *Is* this the case?   Can a man survive for any length of time after the heart has ruptured, and what would be the symtoms during that survival time?   And what are the known causes of heart rupture in the first place?

Poets speak of a broken heart without meaning that the organ itself is physiologically ruptured: and we commonly speak of men and women (and upon occasion of pets, too) as having died of a broken heart in consequence of breavement or very great disappointment.   History also shows that great and unexpected joy can be fatal in a strikingly similar manner.   Commonly, we suppose that such an experience is so emotionally overwhelming that the rhythm of the pulse is severely disturbed causing a fatal malfunction of the vagus nerve which regulates the beat.   We do not necessarily mean the actual rupture of the walls of the heart's chambers.   It is as though the engine were "stalled", rather as a car engine may be stalled by feeding it too strong a mixture of fuel.

But actual heart rupture is well known in medical histories and if autopsies were performed as frequently and as routinely today as they were during the last century, we might well find as frequent reference in current medical literature to it as there was a century ago, especially in Europe.   However, there are still many accounts of death by heart rupture, verified by post mortem examination.   And in a surprising number of instances rupture was not immediately fatal.   From some quite extensive accounts it is clear that a man may live for some hours and, though in great discomfort, may continue the daily round of activities until, suddenly, there comes a dramatic end — sometimes in great pain, but sometimes quietly during sleep.

Is this, then, the cause of the death of the Lord Jesus?   Personally, I do not think so: but let us look at some of the evidence which has led not a few commentators to assume that heart rupture was indeed the immediate cause of the

Lord's death.   It is a view which has a certain sentimental appeal and should therefore be examined all the more carefully.

Before embarking on a brief historical summary of the evidence regarding heart rupture, it will be proper to note a fact which helps to account for the comparative paucity of medical reports on the subject in the enormous literature of the present day.   One is hard put, in fact, to find many references in current medical literature guides such as *Index Medicus*, and one may note also that the world famous authority on human stress, Dr. Hans Selye of Montreal, scarcely even mentions the subject in his very extended bibliographies.   Is this because heart rupture is now so rare and therefore seldom considered a likely cause of premature death, and is therefore unrecognized because not expected?   One contributing factor may be that post mortems, so common formerly at least in Europe, are now somewhat rarer because it is necessary today to obtain permission either beforehand from the patient or afterwards from the nearest of kin, whereas previously this was not a requirement.   As a consequence such post mortems are less often carried out, especially since the rather general term 'heart failure' seems to be accepted as a sufficient description of the cause of death.

The literature of antiquity and the medical literature of the last century or two abounds in detailed accounts which we have no reason to suppose are not authentic and quite correctly diagnosed.

In a recent study of this aspect of medical diagnosis, Dr. George L. Engel of Strong Memorial Hospital, New York, published the results of a survey of 275 newspaper reports of sudden death attributed to heart failure due to traumatic shock.[264]   He commences by saying, "Few folklore notions have enjoyed as widespread and persistent popularity as those that ascribe sudden death to emotional shock.   As far back as written records exist, people are described as dying suddenly while in the throes of fear, rage, grief, humiliation, or joy".   He notes that physicians writing before 1900 often ascribe sudden deaths to intense emotion, but with the coming of the germ theory of disease in the late nineteenth century which cast doubts on much folklore about medical matters, such notions fell into disfavour.   "In the eighteenth and nineteenth centuries medical writings abounded in such accounts . . . .   Since then consideration of the relationship between emotion and sudden death has virtually disappeared from the medical literature."   Yet he adds: "Many physicians in private conversations are quite ready to recount from their own practices examples of patients who apparently died suddenly under precisely such circumstances".

Engel gives a breakdown of his findings, stating that of the 275 reports studied, clearly the most common (135 deaths) cause was an exceptional traumatic disruption of a close human relationship, whether actual or anticipated, or confrontation with events of great emotional consequence impossible to escape. He observes that in experiments with animals this was most likely to occur with already damaged hearts, but it was not a hard and fast rule.   Animals with undamaged hearts also suffered heart rupture under certain conditions of stress. And as to humans, an 88 year old man without known heart disease was reported to have developed acute pulmonary edema after receiving tragic news, dying just as the doctor reached the house.   A similar report of an otherwise healthy 27 year old army captain is also noted.

As to the cause: it frequently appears to be the result of severe derangement of the cardiac rhythm — particularly in the case of humans.   Certain hormonal substances are secreted in excess during stress which predispose the heart to lethal arrhythmias.

Engel comments: "We can only speculate about the mechanism of death in such cases.   Most would agree that effective cardiac arrest, whether caused by ventricular asystole or by ventricular tachyarrhythmias, is probably responsible for the death of those who die within a few minutes . . . .   But such are not present in all cases . . . .   Some of the lethal influences may involve rapid shifts between sympathetic and parasympathetic cardiosvascular effects".

Such shifts back and forth can be invoked experimentally in animals and the usual consequence is sudden death for no other accountable reason.   This has been demonstrated in squirrel monkeys.   Engel therefore concludes: "Certainly, the use of 'folklore' or 'old wives' tales' as pejorative labels, as some sceptics are wont to do, is hardly compatible with the scientific attitude requisite for the study of natural phenomena involving life and death".

It is curious that there seem to be as many reports from antiquity of death from heart rupture caused by sudden *joy* as there are by sudden grief!   Later reports tend in the opposite direction.

Valerius Maximus (c. 30 A.D.) tells us that Sophocles, the writer of Greek tragedies, had died in 405 B.C. in consequence of a decision being pronounced in his favour in a contest concerning his honour.[265]   The Roman historian Livy, writing about the same time, mentions the case of an aged mother, who while she was in the depths of distress due to tidings of her son having been slain in battle, died in his arms from excess of joy on his safe return.[266]   Pliny, writing somewhere around 100 A.D., informs us that the Lacedemonian, Chilo, died upon hearing that his son had won a prize in the Olympic Games. [267] The Greek physician, Galen (about 175 A.D.), mentions death from joy, commenting that the emotion of joy is more dangerous to the heart than anger.[268] Aulus Gellius (second century A.D.) mentions the remarkable example of such in the case of the Greek poet Diagoras of Melos whose three sons were crowned the same day as victors in the Olympic Games, one as a pugilist, the second as a wrestler, and the third in both roles.[269]

Among the fragmentary remains of a kind of official Journal of contemporary events authorized by the Roman Emperors and known under the title *Ephemerides*, there are instances of death from sudden joy.   Similar reports are also known from Marcellus Donatus (1586) and other writers.[270]   In recent times Gould and Pyle, speaking of this fact, observed that heart rupture is known to have occurred from sudden joy by post mortem examination; in one particular case the pericardium   (the sac around the heart) being filled with blood as a consequence.[271] The general assumption made by these writers is that rupture resulted from the sudden and excessive increase in cardiac output.[272]   Such medical histories seem to bear out not only that excessive joy is as damaging to the heart as excessive grief but that the damage is likely to be more immediately fatal.   Perhaps this is a reflection of the fact that we are less accustomed to joy than to grief and therefore build up a greater capacity to sustain the shocks of the latter.   At any rate, it seems as though the individual may survive heart rupture caused by an excessive disappointment for several hours, or even for *days*.   Nor is heart rupture from external injury always immediately fatal either.

If not all, at least the great majority, of instances of heart rupture are probably because the heart tissue has already been weakened by fatty degeneration or some other damage such as infarct, for example, due to strain, although a surprising number of post mortems of the last century were unable to demonstrate any such predisposing condition, the walls of the organ being firm and healthy at the time of actual rupture.

As we have already noted, one of the most complete studies vis-a-vis the death of the Lord Jesus is that undertaken by William Stroud.   Stroud quotes from many sources, especially during the nineteenth century when such interest in the subject of heart rupture was evidenced by the numerous reports in the medical literature.   Thereafter, interest seems to have declined, partly as a result of the greater restrictions imposed upon post mortem examination. Today, however, there is renewed concern.   *MD of Canada* recently had the following note under the title, "Subacute Heart Rupture". [273]

> Rupture of the heart has now become the second major cause of death in the coronary care unit, second only to myocardial failure. Investigation by Dr. Michael O'Rourke of Sydney, Australia, [274] shows that in some instances heart rupture is not sudden and dramatic but subacute. If recognized early, this rupture can be repaired surgically.

Perhaps two factors have contributed to this resurgence of interest: life is more hectic and heart failure of one kind or another has become more common. At the same time, the tremendous advances in heart surgery technique, and perhaps the temptation of surgeons to prove their own skills, has improved chances of survival by corrective measures.

In the meantime, it is now rather well established that rupture can be sustained for a remarkable length of time without fatal consequences though not without severe pain.   It is not at all impossible, therefore, that Jesus may have indeed suffered some form of subacute heart rupture in Gethsemane and yet have sustained the subsequent abuse at the hands of the soldiers and the final torture of crucifixion some hours later, without succumbing to the effects of the rupture itself.   We have some well authenticated instances of survival for several days after severe heart rupture which were later fully confirmed by a post mortem examination.   But it must still be borne in mind that such examination generally suggested previous tissue degeneration, a circumstance which it is difficult to admit in Jesus' case.

A German physician, Dr. Daniel Fischer, whose chief interest was heart pathology, in the December, 1817, issue of the *Journal der Practischen Heilkunde,* reported such a case in some detail. [275]   A summary statement of the case is given herewith.

A gentleman, aged 68 (his initials only are given as V.K.), in apparently robust health, was forced by an unfortunate circumstance to retire from a prominent position in the German court.   The experience proved excessively burdensome to his sensitive nature.   On the 16th of October, 1817, he was suddenly seized with a violent pain while walking, which he supposed to be a stomach cramp.   He reached home half a mile distant only with great difficulty, but after some medication (Hoffman's Anodyne) he quickly recovered and did not complain further that day.

On the 17th, after a good night, he felt so fully recovered that he visited a neighbour travelling by carriage, there held a conference, and returned home again later on foot accompanied by his coachman.   During the return trip, however, he sustained another attack of pain so violent that he had to be entirely supported by his servant.   Arriving home he rested, soon recovered, had supper, and slept as usual.

On the morning of the 18th, he sent a note to his physician, Dr. Fischer, and gave him an account of his health, requesting his advice.   His appetite and digestion, he said, were quite unimpaired.   Dr. Fischer prescribed a diaphoretic mixture to relieve what appeared to be gas, and the rest of the day and the succeeding night were spent comfortably.

On the 19th, he went to church and exerted himself in singing with the congregation.   He then returned home, and almost at once experienced a dreadful pain in the region of his stomach.   Dr. Fischer was called and arrived within one hour to find the paroxysm had almost completely subsided, but he noted that

circulation was poor as evidenced by coldness of the extremities. In the afternoon the patient seemed improved, and by evening he felt so much better that he
wanted to get up and join his family for dinner.

Early on the 20th, Dr. Fischer learned that his patient had passed a fairly
good night, and that body functions seemed to have responded to the medication
prescribed for his stomach. The patient, however, after sending off the messenger
with this report, got out of bed, smoked a pipe, and began to walk about. The
pain instantly returned accompanied by a paroxysm "with the rapidity of light-
ning". The doctor was at once called, arriving about ten o'clock. The patient's
suffering subsided slowly and the doctor left at 11:30 — but he was at once
re-summoned to find his patient in an awful agony "roaring for relief or death".
After several heroic attempts to relieve his suffering, some of which were partially
successful, the doctor again left. But the next morning, the 21st, he received the
unexpected news that his patient had died very suddenly during the night.

Eighteen hours after death a post mortem examination was carried out. The
sternum being removed, and the pericardium punctured, it having the appearance
of being distended by a substance of dark blue colour, a quantity of reddish fluid
escaped followed by bright red blood to the amount of two or three pounds. The
pericardium was then opened up completely and the heart itself was found to be
surrounded by a coagulum of more than three pounds in weight. When this was
cleared away, a rupture was disclosed in the aortic ventricle. The heart was then
removed entirely and the rupture was found to extend upwards about an inch and
a half on the external surface while the internal rupture was about half an inch in
length. This indicated that rupture was caused by excess pressure from the inside.
According to the methods of tissue analysis then available, the heart tissue iteslf
was otherwise found to be firm and healthy.

Whether this conclusion would be accepted in the light of present diagnostic
technique is difficult to say. However, the subsequent discussion which followed
the publication of Fischer's report showed that other similar cases of heart rupture
were known where the heart tissue was in no way pathological.[276] A Dr. Portal
is quoted as stating in two medical reports dated 1784 and 1794 that the aortic
ventricle "commonly bursts without any previous weakening of the substance of
the heart". And in the second of these reports, Portal quotes a certain Dr. Whytt
as "having seen the heart burst from protracted grief" and therefore "not regarding the term *broken heart* in the light of a mere metaphor".[277]

Dr. Portal also notes some authorities who do not believe that heart rupture
can occur unless the heart has been subject to insidious inflammation or over-
burdened with excess adipose tissue. Heart rupture would then be the fatal
termination of a previously existing morbid state. But as Dr. Fischer observed,
such was clearly not the case in the instance of his report. Possibly rupture is not
therefore fatal at once in a healthy heart but only in a diseased one. Fischer
reported in this case "no morbid state of heart capable of diminishing its cohesive
properties".

Survival for some hours or even some days would thus seem to be quite possible, though undoubtedly accompanied by considerable pain. Moreover, the
protracted survival of Fischer's patient must be viewed in the light of his mature
age (68 years), and we must assume therefore that in the case of the Lord Jesus
who was still in the prime of life, emotional stress and not a diseased condition
could have caused rupture — if indeed rupture did occur. Fischer believed on the
basis of all the evidence that rupture had "occurred gradually" over the previous
few days. The first pains felt on the 16th he believed to have been due to the
violent extension or aneurism rather than actual rupture. Actual rupture probably occurred at the first devastating attack of pain while the subject was out

walking on the 17th. That would mean that this particular individual survived heart rupture with a surprising amount of activity in the interval for about three days.

A number of other cases established by post mortem examination are cited in the follow-up of Dr. Fischer's article, in one of which the left ventricle was found to have ruptured in three places. Heart rupture was also reported as having occurred during sleep, although severe pain in the area had been experienced for some time previously.

From current literature one gathers that most authorities would now attach greater importance to pathological conditions than to sudden emotional stress, and in view of Stroud's fascinating conclusions regarding the case of Jesus, I think this fact has to be kept in mind. Krumbhaar and Crowell attribute rupture to coronary disease which has produced infarction and partial or complete aneurism. Death is then said to be due to *haemopericardium*, i.e., infusion of blood into the pericardial sac.[278] Karsner observes that in *haemopericardium* from rupture of the heart wall, the intraventricular pressure is communicated directly to the pericardial sac.[279] This compresses intrapericardial pulmonary veins and also inhibits cardiac diastole. The result is usually rapidly fatal. It is referred to as cardiac tamponade. History is replete with cases of men who have died from this form of heart failure in their prime upon hearing shocking news. J. G. Zimmerman noted that Philip V of Spain died suddenly on learning of a major defeat of his army: and autopsy showed that his heart *had* ruptured in this way.[280] It seems highly likely that there are other examples if we had an adequate medical history of every individual whose death has been attributed to some form of heart failure.

Charles K. Friedberg, in his *Diseases of the Heart*, observes that rupture of the heart is "one of the commoner causes of sudden death" but only in the first two weeks after acute myocardial infarction.[281] Nearly 5% of one thousand consecutive cases of acute myocardial infarction confirmed at autopsy indicated death due to rupture. Much higher percentages (up to 19%) were reported by other investigators in 1960. In all such cases, rupture occurs at the point of infarction and usually while the infarcted area is still soft and freshly damaged. After some weeks it hardens somewhat and the patient is then likely to survive for some time. In mental institutions where hypertension is frequent, the incidence of rupture in acute myocardial infarction has been recorded as high as 73%, but this high relationship between hypertension and rupture has not been observed in a normal population. In all cases it is a general rule that rupture occurs only when previous degeneration of the heart tissue has occurred.

A suffusion of blood is commonly found in the pericardium in various amounts depending upon time of death, severity of rupture, and level of activity. It may exceed one litre (2.2 lbs.) but averages 250 c.c. (about ½ lb.). Death may occur within a few minutes, but occasionally there is a survival period of a half hour to several hours. However, mention is made of survival in one instance for more than five years due to the formation over the rupture of fibrous pericardial adhesions.

While older reports seem to indicate cases of rupture in healthy hearts, the general consensus of opinion at the present time is that rupture only occurs where previous degeneration of heart tissue exists. The issue is crucial, if this is really the case, for it implies either that the Lord's heart had in this sense already "degenerated" and the Lamb was not therefore without blemish, or that the phenomenon of bloody sweat and the escape of "water and blood" from the wound on the cross must be explained in some other way. That the rule is *not* hard and fast, however, is suggested by Friedberg's remarks under a general heading *Traumatic Heart Disease*.[282] He observes: "There are instances of so-called spontaneous rupture, perforation or tear of a cardiac structure, in which physical strain may be a significant contributory factor". Yet if applied in the Lord's case, this would still not be the *cause* of death but merely an accompaniment. In other words, the Lord died *with* a broken heart perhaps but, in my view, not *from* it. To my mind the distinction is a real one and one of great importance.

The actual course of events in the case of rupture, considered from the purely physiological point of view, was many years ago very ably described by a Dr. Allan Burns who shows what happens to the blood escaping from the rupture into the enveloping pericardium. New knowledge has not essentially required any change of this descriptive paragraph.[283]

> The immediate cause is a sudden and violent contraction of one of the ventricles, usually the left, on the column of blood thrown into it by a similar contraction of the corresponding auricle. Prevented from returning backward by the intervening valve, and not finding a sufficient outlet forward in the connecting artery, the blood reacts against the ventricle itself which is consequently torn open at the point of greatest distention, or least resistance.
>
> A quantity of blood is thereby discharged into the pericardium, and having no means of escape from that capsule, stops the circulation by compressing the heart from without and induces almost instantaneous death.
>
> In young and vigorous subjects, the blood thus collected in the pericardium soon divides into its constituents parts, namely, a pale watery liquid called serum, and a soft clotted substance of a deep red colour termed crassamentum.

Now we are told in Luke 22:44 that in Gethsemane the agony of spirit which anticipation of the horror of the pending ordeal brought upon the Lord was so severe that, as it were, great drops of blood burst like sweat from his forehead and poured down his face. Luke, the physician, was the one who obtained this piece of information from some eye witness to the event. The disciples may not have been asleep at the beginning of Jesus' spiritual struggle but had fallen asleep by the time He returned to them after it was over. Luke may have received his information from one of them, for he certainly records it as though it was an eye witness account. He makes no effort to explain the phenomenon.

In Hebrews 5:7 we seem almost certainly to have a further reference to this event. We are told here that in the days of his flesh, the Lord offered up prayers and supplications evidently under the stress of pending death and was heard and preserved at that time. This clearly cannot refer to his death a few hours later on the cross, since He could not possibly be spared from this if man was to be redeemed. What prospect of immediate death was He then preserved from if not death by heart rupture?

Certainly the Greek verb *sodzo* appearing here in the phrase "able to *save* him", often means "to preserve". Probable instances of this meaning in other places where the same word occurs will be found as follows: 1 Timothy 2:15, the preservation of the woman in childbearing; 1 Timothy 4:10, the Lord who preserves all men but takes particular care of the redeemed; 2 Timothy 4:18, Paul is preserved against every evil device brought against him. One might argue, therefore, that in Gethsemane the Lord's heart suffered a subacute rupture, and that the Lord Himself was fully aware of what had happened within his body. Certainly the form and functions of the human body were of his design in the first place and He was Himself the master Physician. There is no reason at all why He may not have correctly recognized the symptoms in his own case. It could be, therefore, that the trauma of anticipation of what was to be truly an awful spiritual and physical agony, was sufficient to rupture his otherwise perfectly sound heart, with fatal consequences to Himself and to his mission if death ensued prematurely as a result. He would have recognized this only too well.

The question then arises as to whether, if weakened by this serious internal wound, his frame would be able to sustain the ordeal that it was about to undergo. We have to remember that although He was made with the potential of unending life, that life could still be destroyed. If such an internal wound should prove fatal now, the whole plan of salvation — for which the Universe was created as a setting and to which all history had moved up to this moment — would have aborted.

Many commentators have habitually associated Hebrews 5:7 with the events of Gethsemane, as Barnes does for example, though he does not indicate any awareness of the possibility of heart rupture.[284] In response to the Lord's cry for help, an angel came to strengthen Him (Luke 22:43), a circumstance which suggests that the prayer was indeed for *physical* support, since it is most unlikely that He would appeal for *spiritual* help from an angel. Almost immediately after this appeal, the bloody sweat broke out on his forehead as though in confirmation of the internal injury which may have prompted his cry for help.

The significance of "sweating" blood as a physiological phenomenon is not clear, although a great deal is known about the sweating mechanism itself. It is referred to technically as *haematridrosis*. It has, however, been observed to be always associated with deep emotional stress. It was reported frequently enough in antiquity, during the Middle Ages, and even in modern times.

When a man's body overheats, several automatic corrective measures are at once initiated. These include an increased flow of blood through the vascular bed just below the skin surface, causing a sudden reddening or flushing, and resulting in a much greater transport of deep body heat via the blood fluid to the skin surface where it is radiated away if conditions permit. If this proves insufficient and body temperature continues to rise, then the sweat glands are triggered into activity. A very pure water, filtered from the blood vessels, is expressed via about two million sweat glands onto the skin surface where it evaporates and in so doing removes a quite remarkable store of heat very efficiently, provided that the surrounding air has the requisite capacity to absorb the water vapour. In conditions of high humidity it is therefore characteristically difficult to keep cool.

This filtrated water is one of the purest fluids in the body, since it contains a total of less than 1% of other substances such as uric acid, lactic acid, etc. Under normal circumstances this exudate contains no other blood components than water. However, under very great emotional stress, perhaps in part due to a rise in pulse rate and blood pressure, red blood cells may find their way into individual sweat glands, chiefly those which are under the control of the sympathetic nervous system — which the majority of sweat glands are not. The areas particularly involved here are the forehead, the axillary vaults (the arm pits), and some areas of the hands. The forehead region is especially involved, being for some reason highly supplied with sweat glands that are particularly active.

According to Shelley and Hurley, such coloured sweat does not relate normally to a rise in body temperature but only to emotional stress.[285] The coloured droplets are turbid and they suggest a possible connection with hysterical stigmata in the hands. Rothman, in his classic work on the biochemistry and physiology of the skin, believes that this form of sweating (which may also be found in the palm of the hand) probably accounts for the phenomenon associated with the well-known Theresa of Konnersreuth.[286] Bloody sweat has been reported also among primitive people, especially shamans from Siberia when seeking a state of ecstasy, as reported by Bogoras.[287] William Stroud refers to a number of works from the sixteenth to the nineteenth centuries in which are to be found case histories of men who, being condemned to death under unexpected circumstances, have broken out into a bloody sweat. [288]   One young boy is mentioned who, having taken part in a crime for which two of his older brothers were hanged, was exhibited to public view under the gallows at the time and was thereupon observed to sweat blood from the exposed parts of his body (presumably his hands and his face).   In a *Commentary on the Four Gospels* published in 1639 in Paris, Joannes Maldonatus refers to a robust and healthy man who had, on hearing a sentence of death passed upon him, been bathed in a bloody sweat. [289] In 1743 J. Schenck, in a work entitled *Medical Observations*, referred to the case of a nun who, falling into the hands of soldiers threatening her with instant death, was so terrified that "she discharged blood from every part of her body and died of haemorrhage". [290]   In 1800 S. A. D. Tissot, in a work on the nervous system, referred to a sailor who was so alarmed by a storm that he collapsed, sweating blood from his face continuously throughout the whole episode.   He mentions that the bloody sweat renewed itself like ordinary sweat as fast as it was wiped away. [291]

One of the best known and most famous examples is that of Charles IX of France, a monarch of great cruelty but also of great energy both in mind and body, who died of a similar cause in his 25th year.   According to Voltaire, he suffered a fatal haemorrhage, the blood flowing from the pores of his skin.   He expressed the opinion that it is usually the result either of excessive fear or of great passion. [292]   In his *Histoire d'France*, the historian de Mezeray, refers to the same circumstance noting that it was on the 8th of May, 1574. [293] He says that in his last illness near the end, Charles was found on one occasion *bathed* in bloody sweat.   There is an interesting discussion of this subject, from a purely medical point of view, in the work by Gould and Pyle to which reference has already been made. [294]

I would conclude, then, that while heart rupture may not have been the *cause* of the bloody sweat on the Lord's brow, extraordinary emotional stress might have been the common cause which lay behind both phenomena.   The agony of Gethsemane was the agony of anticipation of the events which were about to transpire, and the effect of that agony upon the Lord's body may have been sufficient to cause both subacute heart rupture and bloody sweat.   But I would go further and say also that heart rupture was, nevertheless, *not* the cause of the Lord's death on the cross.   In Gethsemane his cry for help was heard and this injury was not permitted in the interval between Gethsemane and his death to anticipate the sacrifice of his life which He was to make voluntarily and in his own time.

Adding enormously as it must have done to the ordeal of all that He endured from the evening of his arrest to the moment when He dismissed his spirit by an act of will, and no doubt contributing largely to the sheer physical impossibility of carrying the crossbar of his own instrument of death to the place of execution, the Lord Jesus still did not *succumb* to death — did not die — *because of* heart rupture.   He died perhaps with, but not because of, a broken heart, for the circumstance of the outflow of "blood and water" (John 19:34) seems to indicate that the pericardium had indeed been pierced by the soldier's spear.   Extravasated blood, which had escaped through what was perhaps a very small rupture, had accumulated and separated out into coagulum and serum.   This could possibly account for a phenomenon which Scripture has seen fit to include in the record as a circumstance of significance.   But his death was entirely of his own doing, not forced upon Him because of the failure of his heart.   Sentiment might favour such a supposition, but I believe that theology demands recognition of something of greater consequence.

His death was in no sense a final collapse of the life support system of his body, but a glorious triumph of will, of spirit *over* body.   On this super-natural fact Scripture has spoken unequivocally and with beautiful precision, as we have seen in Part IV, Chapter 32.   These signs of possible rupture may serve perhaps to give us *some* idea of the awful prospect the Lord faced and the unimaginable burden it placed upon his nervous system and therefore also upon his heart.   It could have been a literal fulfillment of Psalm 69:20, "Reproach hath broken my heart: and I am full of heaviness: and I looked for some to take pity but there was none: and for comforters, but I found none".   "Could ye not watch with Me *one* hour?" (Matt.26:40).

DOCUMENTATION:
REFERENCES
AND NOTES

NOTE:
With the following key (pp. 505 and 506) it is a simple matter to be able to locate in any particular case where an extended note in this section belongs within the body of the text itself. For every call number the table gives the page where it applies in the text.

KEY TO LOCATION OF CALL NUMBERS

Continued over

INDEX OF REFERENCES

1. Tennyson, Sir Charles, *The Listener*, 8 July, 1971, p. 39, in an interview.

2. Acsadi, Gy. and J. Nemeskeri, *History of Human Life Span and Mortality*, Akademiai Kiado, Budapest, 1970, p. 15.

3. Acsadi, Gy. and J. Nemeskeri, *ibid*, p. 16.

4. Ludwig Aschoff: in the editorial, "Old Age in Mind and Body", *Lancet*, 9 July, 1938, p. 87.

5. Selye, Hans: quoted by Stephen E. Slocum, "Length of Life", *J. Amer. Scient. Affil.*, **13**, *1*, 1961, p.19.

6. Casarett, George W., "Radiation Slows Down Aging in Dogs", *Science News Letter*, 30 Aug., 1957, p. 136.

7. West, Irma, G. L. Nielson, Allen E. Gilmour and J.R. Ryan, "Natural Death at the Wheel", *J. Amer. Med. Assoc.*, 205, 1968, p. 226-271.

8. Simms, H. S: quoted in *Brit. Med. J.*, 5 July, 1947, p. 14 from *J. Gerontology*, 1, 1946, p. 24.

9. Simms, H. S: quoted by Ernst LaFrance and Sid Ross, "Can We Live to be 120?", *Mag. Digest*, Nov., 1950, p. 46.

10. Selye, Hans, "Is Death Inevitable?", *MacLean's Mag.*, 15 Aug., 1959, p. 13.

11. On this, see Hayflick's findings discussed in reference #123.

12. Korenchevsky, V., "Conditions Desirable for the Rapid Progress of Gerontological Research", *Brit. Med. J.*, 28 Sept., 1946, p. 468.

13. Haldane, J. B. S: reported in *Genetics, Paleontology and Evolution*, Princeton Univ. Bicentennial Conference (series 2, Conf. 3), 1946, p. 26.

14. Woodruff, L. L: noted by Florence Moog, "The Biology of Old Age", *Sci. Amer.*, June, 1948, p. 41.

15. Dorsey, George A., *Why We Behave Like Human Beings*, N.Y., Blue Ribbon Books, 1925, p. 105.

16. Pearl, Raymond, *The Biology of Death: Monographs on Experimental Biology*, Phila., Lippincott, 1923, 275 pp., reviewed in *Brit. Med. J.*, 3 Mar., 1923, p. 382.

17. Muller, H. J., "Life", *Science*, **121**, *1955, p. 5.*

18. Dobzhansky, Theodosius, "Man Consorting with Things Eternal" in *Science Ponders Religion*, ed. H. Shapley, N.Y., Appleton-Century-Crofts, 1960, p. 118.

19. Zahl, Paul A., "Need There Be Death?", a contribution in a report published by the New York Joint Legislative Committee on "Problems of the Aging", 1950, p. 134.

20. Zahl, Paul A., *ibid*, p. 135.

21. Sturgeon: Ontario Government Service Bulletin, 1 May, 1954.

22. Huxley, Sir Julian, "The Meaning of Death" in *Essays on Popular Science*, London, Penguin Books, 1938, p. 105.

23. Huxley, Sir Julian, *ibid*, p. 105.

24. Lancaster, Sir Edwin Ray: quoted by Alex Comfort in "The Biology of Old Age" in *New Biology*, 18, 1955, p. 19 [publ'd by Penguin Books].

25. Medawar, Sir Peter B., *The Uniqueness of the Individual*, N.Y., Basic Books, 1957, p. 57.

26. Bidder, G. P: reported under "Senescence" in *Brit. Med. J.*, 2, 1932, p. 583.

27. Barnett, Lincoln, *The World We Live In*, N.Y., Time Inc., 1955, p. 150.

28. Huxley, Sir Julian, *op. cit.*, (ref. # 22), p. 104.   Plants that die bearing one crop of seeds can, if kept under conditions that prevent flowering, be made to continue indefinitely in their vegetative form.   Their life is extended probably without limit provided that the ageing effect of seed and flower production is prevented.

29. The factor of size is dealt with subsequently, see ref. # 128.

30. Went, F. W., "The Size of Man", *Amer. Scientist*, 56, 4, 1968, p. 400-413.

31. Comfort, Alex, "The Biology of Old Age" in *New Biology*, 18, 1955, p. 18 (published by Penguin Books).

32. Walker, Kenneth, *Meaning and Purpose*, London, Penguin, 1950, p. 63.

33. Weismann, August, *Essays Upon Heredity and Kindred Biological Problems*, tr. E. B. Poulton, S. Schonland and A. E. Shipley, Oxford, 1889, 1892, in 2 vols., Vol. I, p. 25, 159.

34. Weismann, *ibid*, Vol. I, p. 111.

35. Weismann, *ibid*, Vol. I, p. 158.

36. Special Communication, J. *Amer. Med. Assoc.*, 205, 1968, p. 337.

37. Camps, F., *The New Scientist*, 27 Feb., 1964, p. 558 f.

38. Doskaoh, E., *Worldwide Abstracts of General Medicine*, 5, 2, 1962.

39. Negovsky, V. A. and V. I. Soboleva, "Delaying the Process of Death", *Discovery*, Dec., 1964, p. 20.

40. Dr. Leo Davidovich Landau: *The Man They Wouldn't Let Die*, Alexander Dorozynski, N.Y., Macmillan, 1965.

41. "Death Needs Better Definition", *Science J.*, Feb., 1969, p. 11, 13, over the signature of Hadassah Gillon.

42. The problem of determining when death has occurred is particularly acute when the dying individual is a potential donor of some organ such as a kidney, to a living individual who may be seriously in need, because such

tissue deteriorates very quickly in the dead and must be removed at the earliest possible moment for transplant. Early in March, 1974, it was reported that a sixty-five year old man who had been injured in a road accident, and whom two doctors had presumed dead, began breathing again in a Birmingham hospital when an attempt was made to remove his kidneys in just such an emergency [Robert Jones, "Organ Grafting Dilemmas", *New Scientist*, 7 March, 1974, p. 595].

43. "Human Heart Beats After Extraction", *New Scientist*, 28 Oct., 1965, p. 248.

44. Hillman, Harold, "When is Death?", *New Scientist*, 19 Mar., 1970, p. 552.

45. Parkes, A. S: quoted by R. C. W. Ettinger, *The Prospect of Immortality*, N.Y., Macfadden-Bartell, 1966, p. 16.

46. G. M. Gould and W. L. Pyle in their book *Anomalies and Curiosities of Medicine* [N.Y., Julian Press, 1966] observe concerning this phenomenon: "The hair and beard may grow after death, and even change colour. Bartholinus recalls a case of a man who had short black hair and beard at the time of interment but who, some time after death, was found to possess long and yellowish hair. Aristotle discusses post mortem growth of the hair, and Garmanus cites an instance in which the beard and hair was cut several times from the cadaver. We occasionally see evidences of this in the dissecting rooms. Caldwell mentions a body buried four years, the hair from which protruded at the points where the joints of the coffin had given way. The hair of the head measured eighteen inches, that of the beard eight inches, and that on the breast from four to six inches. Rosse of Washington mentions an instance in which after burial the hair turned from dark brown to red, and also cites a case in a Washington cemetry of a girl, twelve or thirteen years old, who when exhumed was found to have a new growth of hair all over her body. Nails sometimes grow several inches after death, and there is on record the account of an idiot who had an idiosyncrasy for long nails, and after death the nails were found to have grown to such an extent that they curled up under the palms and soles" (p. 523).

47. Ettinger, R. C. W: in his introduction to R. F. Nelson's *We Froze the First Man*, N.Y., Dell, 1968, p. 8.

48. Morison, R. S., "Death: Process or Event?", and L. R. Kass, "Death as an Event: A Commentary on Robert Morison", *Science*, 173, 1971, p. 694-702.

49. Morison, R. S., *ibid*, p. 695.

50. Decerebrate cats: Sir Charles Sherrington, *Man on His Nature*, Cambridge, 1963, p. 149 f.

51. Decerebrate birds: A. J. Carlson and V. Johnson, *The Machinery of the Body*, Univ. Chicago Press, 1941, p. 422; see also Walter B. Cannon, *The Way of an Investigator*, N.Y., Hafner, 1968 reprint, p. 121.

52. Decerebrate dogs: G. H. Bell, J. N. Davidson and H. Scarborough, *Textbook of Physiology and Biochemistry*, London, Livingstone, 1954, p. 860.

53. Decerebrate cats: H. C. Bazett and E. G. Penfield, "A Study of the Sherrington Decerebrate Animal in the Chronic as Well as the Acute Condition", *Brain*, XLV, 1922, p. 218, 261.

54. Wakerlin, George E., "The Biology of Aging", editorial, *J. Amer. Med. Assoc.*, 16 Mar., 1957, p. 950.

55. Kass, Leon, *op. cit.*, (ref. #48), p. 698.

56. Medawar, Sir Peter B., *op. cit.*, (ref. #25), p. 117.

57. Sauer, Erich, *The Dawn of World Redemption*, Grand Rapids, Eerdmans, 1953, p. 56.

58. Scheer, Bradley T., *General Physiology*, N.Y., Wiley, 1953, p. 428.

59. Total life span versus birth-to-maturity ratio = six to one: see Paul A. Zahl, *op. cit.*, (ref. #19), p. 134; and Fritz Kahn, *Man in Structure and Function*, N.Y., Knopf, 1960, Vol. I, p. 57.   Maturity is marked by birth of first-born.

60. Progeria: see Willian Reichel, Rafael Garcia-Bunuel, and Joseph Dilallo, "Progeria and Werner's Syndrome as Models for the Study of Normal Human Aging", *J. Amer. Geriatrics Soc.*, 19, 5, 1971, p. 369 - 375.   See also A. L. Rosenbloom and Franklin L. DeBusk, "Progeria of Hutchinson-Gilford: A Caricature of Aging", *Amer. Heart J.*, 82, 3, 1971, p. 287 - 289; and B. Schaman Danes, "Progeria: a Cell Culture Study on Aging", *J. Clin. Invest.*, 50, 1971, p. 2000 - 2003.   For a popular account, see S. Katz, "Old Age at Eleven", *MacLean's Mag.*, 11 Aug., 1962, p. 12 f., photograph p. 40.

61. Progeria: reported in *Toronto Evening Telegram*, 9 Mar., 1967, p. 9, under the heading, "MDs probe death of boy 'aged 95'."

62. Reported in *San Francisco Chronicle*, 17 June, 1970, p. 4.

63. de Beer, Sir Gavin: in a book review, *Sci. Amer.*, Sept., 1962, p. 268.

64. On this see J. B. S. Haldane, "On Being the Right Size" in *The World of Mathematics*, ed. J. R. Newman, N.Y., Simon & Schuster, 1956, Vol. 2, p. 952 f.

65. As reported in *New Scientist*, 25 Mar., 1976, p. 2: the species is *Cryptomeria japonica*.

66. A tiny organism believed to be two billion years old *and still alive*, has recently been reported in *MD Canada*, Feb., 1971, p. 144.

67. *Think*, Sept., 1939, p. 19.

68. Bonner, J. T., *Size and Cycle: An Essay on the Structure of Biology*, Princeton, 1965, p. 66.

69. Godwin, H., "Evidence for Longevity of Seeds", *Nature*, 120, 1968, p. 708 f.

70. *Juglands australis: Science J.*, Jan., 1969, under News, p. 16.

71. Black, Michael, "Arctic Lupines Bloom After 10,000 Years", *New Scientist*, 19 Oct., 1967, p. 148, 149.

72. Bacteria have been recovered from the deepest strata of salt mines, first in Europe and then in America, completely insulated by rock salt.   These bacteria on being removed proved to be still viable.   They are dated from the strata in which they were found as half a billion years old.   See H. J. Dombrowski, *Lebende Bakterien aus dem Palaozoicum* (1963) for an excellent account of their discovery and characteristics.   Theodosius Dobzhansky observed: "Life carries the potentiality of endless self-replication, but the realization of this potentiality is restricted by the resistance of the environment" [in *Science Ponders Religion*, ed. by H. Shapley, N.Y., Appleton-Century-Crofts, 1960, p. 118].

73. Josephus, *Antiquities of the Jews*, Bk. I, chap. 3, § 9.   According to Stanley M. Burstein who has published a complete transcript of all the known works and fragments of Berossus, "Berossus was probably the ultimate source of Josephus for the underlying theory concerning the extraordinary ages of the patriarchs" [*The 'Babyloniaca' of Berossus*, Malibu, Cal., Undena Publ., 1978, p. 29].   What Josephus has said is virtually an exact quote from Berossus whom Burstein had already noted as a very careful reporter of the materials he had at hand.

74. Lenormant, Francois, *The Beginnings of History*, N.Y., Scribners, 1891, p. 293.

75. Lenormant, Francois, *ibid*, p. 294.

76. Rawlinson, George, *Historical Illustrations*, p. 14, quoted by Marcus Dods, *The Book of Genesis*, Edinburgh, Clark, n.d., p. 29, fn. 2.

77. Needham, Joseph, *Science and Civilization in China*, Cambridge, 1954 to the present.   Eight substantial volumes have been published so far.   See especially, Vol. V, Pt. 3, pp. 1 - 167, "The Golden Age of Alchemy".

78. Needham, J. and Lu Gwei-Djen, "Sex Hormones in the Middle Ages", *Endeavour*, XXVII, 1968, p. 131.

79. Polo, Marco, *The Travels of Marco Polo*, N.Y., Library Publications, n.d., p. 276.

80. *Roy. Anthrop. Inst. News*, Sept./Oct., 1975, p. 13.

81. Leaf, Alexander, "Every Day is a Gift When You are Over 100", *Nat. Geog. Mag.*, Jan., 1973, p. 99.

82. Warthin, A. S., *Old Age*, N.Y., 1929, p. 166, 167.   Dr. Clive Wood of Oxford pointed out that between 1789 and 1963 the expectancy for white American men who had reached the age of 60 remained almost stationary at fifteen years, for "The old men of the Revolution were as old as the old men of today.   There were just fewer of them" ["Longevity, Catalyst of Social Revolution", *New Scientist*, 24 May, 1973, p. 469].

83. Pearl, Raymond, *Man the Animal*, Bloomington, Ind., Principia Press, 1946, p. 52.

84. Acsadi, Gy. and J. Nemeskeri, *op. cit.*, (ref. #2), p. 69, 251, 255.

85. Soviet Census: news item, *New Scientist*, 22 May, 1969, p. 412.

86. Acsadi, Gy. and J. Nemeskeri, *op. cit.*, (ref. #2), p. 22.

87. Gould, G. M. and W. L. Pyle, *op. cit.*, (ref. #46), p. 370.

88. Prichard, James C., *Researches into the Physical History of Mankind*, London, Houlston and Stoneman, 1936, Vol. I, p. 127.

89. Pearl, Raymond, *op. cit.*, (ref. #83), p. 47.

90. Davies, David, "A Shangri-la in Ecuador", *New Scientist*, 1 Feb., 1973, p. 237

91. Gould, G. M. and W. L. Pyle, *op. cit.*, (ref. #46), p. 378.

92. Gould, G. M. and W. L. Pyle, *op. cit.*, (ref. #46), p. 373.

93. "Inheritance of Longevity", *Brit. Med. J.*, 4 Oct., 1952, p. 767.

94. Gould, G. M. and W. L. Pyle, *op. cit.*, (ref. #46), p. 379.

95. Acsadi, Gy. and J. Nemeskeri, *op. cit.*, (ref. #2), p. 251 and elsewhere.

96. Gould, G. M. and W. L. Pyle, *op. cit.*, (ref. #46), p. 379.

97. Sebastian Kresge: feature article, "Adding Life to Years", *Time*, 20 Oct., 1958, p. 52 f.

98. Kahn, Fritz, *op. cit.*, (ref. #59), p. 57.

99. For Simms, see ref. #8; Selye, ref. #10; and Huxley, ref. #22.

100. Acsadi, Gy. and J. Nemeskeri, *op. cit.*, (ref. #2), p. 16.

101. Note: Tayler Lewis, in *Lange's Commentary on Genesis*, has a most interesting editorial comment of some length showing that such a confusion of terms is exceedingly *unlikely(* [Zondervan reprint, p. 271].

102. Raske and Hensler: referred to in *Commentary on the Holy Scriptures: Genesis*, John Peter Lange, Grand Rapids, Zondervan reprint, p. 271.

103. Wiseman, P. J., *New Discoveries in Babylonia About Genesis*, London, Marshall, Morgan and Scott, 1936, p. 47 ff. especially.

104. Such editing is apparent in the following:
    Gen. 14:2, 8 — "Bela *(which is Zoar)* . . . ."
    14:3 — "Vale of Siddim *(which is the Salt Sea)* . . . ."
    14:7 — "En-mishpat *(which is Kadesh)* . . . ."
    14:15 — "Hobah *(which is on the left hand of Damascus)* . . . "
    14:17 — "Valley of Shaveh *(which is the King's Dale)* . . . ."
    The italics in parenthesis are clearly editorial comment to identify a place name no longer likely to be familiar to the reader.

105. Accuracy in copying: not only did the Jewish scribes adopt exceedingly high standards in copying but pagan nations did also. J. Černy gives a good example from an Egyptian funerary papyrus of about 1400 B.C. which bears the following colophon: "The book is completed from its beginning to its end, having been copied, revised, compared, and certified sign by sign" [*Paper and Books in Ancient Egypt*, 1952, p. 25, quoted by K. A. Kitchen, *Ancient Orient and New Testament*, London, Tyndale Press, 1966, p. 140].

106. Urquhart, John, *The Bible and Modern Discovery* London, Marshall Bros., 1898, p. 158.

107. Moore, Patrick, *Atlas of the Universe*, N.Y., Rand McNally, 1970, p. 146.

108. Driver, S. R., *Commentary on Genesis*, London, Methuen, 3rd ed., 1904; George Barton, *Archaeology and the Bible*, Phila., Amer. Sunday School Union, 1916; Fritz Hommel, *The Ancient Hebrew Traditions As Illustrated by the Monuments*, London, SPCK, 1879.

109. Sayce, A. H., *Higher Criticism and the Monuments*, London, SPCK, 1895.

110. Sarton, George, *The History of Science*, Harvard, 1952, p. 120.

111. Casarett, George W., "Acceleration of Aging by Ionizing Radiation", Univ. Rochester Atomic Energy Project, U.R. # 492, N.Y., 1957; Howard J. Curtis, "Biological Mechanisms Underlying the Aging Process", *Science*, 141, 1963, p. 689 - 691; and "Effects of Radiation on Human Heredity", *WHO*, Geneva, 1959.

112. Hollander, Willard, "Lethal Heredity", *Sci. Amer.*, July, 1952, p. 60.

113. Here are Hugh Miller's words: "If, during a period so vast as to be scarce expressible by figures, the creatures now human have been rising, by almost infinitesimals, from compound microscopic cells . . . . until they have at length become the men and women whom we see around us, we must hold either the monstrous belief, that all the vitalities, whether those of monads or of mites, of fishes or of reptiles, of birds or of beasts, are individually and inherently immortal and undying, or that human souls are not so. The difference between the dying and the undying, — between the spirit of the brute that goeth downward, and the spirit of the man that goeth upward, — is not a difference infinitesimally, or even atomically small. It possesses all the breath of eternity to come, and is an infinitely great distance . . . . Nor will it do to attempt to escape from the difficulty by alleging that God at some certain link in the chain might have converted a mortal creature into an immortal existence, by breathing into it a "living soul"; seeing that a renunciation of any such direct interference on the part of the Deity in the work of creation forms the prominent and characteristic part of the scheme, — nay, that it constitutes the very nucleus around which the scheme has originated . . . . If man be a dying creature, restricted in his existence to the present scene of things, what does it really matter to him, for moral purpose, whether there be a God or no?' [*Footprints of the Creator*, Boston, 1850, p. 38, 39].

114. In his *Commentary on Genesis 1—5*, Luther explores the implications of Adam and Eve's potential immortality in interesting ways. On Genesis 2:17 he wrote: "Adam was created in a state of innocence . . . . Therefore if Adam had obeyed this command, he would never have died. for death came through sin. Thus the remaining trees of Paradise were all created for the purpose of helping man and maintaining his physical life sound and unimpaired.

"For us today it is amazing that there could be a physical life without death . . . . If (Adam) had remained as he was he would have done the other things physical life demands until at last he would have been translated to the spiritual and eternal life.

"This, too, we have lost through sin, because now the present life is separated from the future life by that awful intermediate event, death. In the state of innocence that intermediate event would have been a delightful one; by it Adam would have been translated to the spiritual life or, as Christ calls it in the Gospel, to the angelic life (Matt.22:30)".

Subsequently on the same verse he wrote: "It is as if God were saying: 'You can indeed remain in the life for which I have created you. And yet you will not be immortal in the same way as the angels. Your life is, as it were, placed in the middle: you can remain in it and afterwards be carried to an immortality that cannot be lost; contrariwise, if you do not obey, you will become a victim of death and lose your immortality'."

In other words, Luther is saying — as Augustine had said — that there were two kinds of immortality. There was the immortality which means that the individual *need* not die, and the immortality which signifies that the individual *cannot* die. The first is contingent, contingent upon obedience: the second is absolute. The first is potential but not certain unless the requisite conditions are fulfilled: the second cannot be lost under any conditions whatever. As Luther puts it, "This (first kind of) immortality had not been made so sure for him that it was impossible for him to fall into mortality".

In commenting on Genesis 3:23, 24 Luther notes that "Adam was not created to remain forever in this physical life, but from this physical life and from the physical eating he was to pass over into spiritual life . . . . no death intervenes on that occasion . . . . Adam, without any intervening death would have exchanged his mortal life for an immortal one". That is to say, he would have exchanged his contingent immortality for an absolute immortality.

115. Note on Romans 5:12.

> Wherefore, as by one man sin entered into the world, and death by sin; and so death passed upon all men, for that all have sinned.

> Διὰ τοῦτο ὥσπερ δι' ἑνὸς ἀνθρώπου ἡ ἁμαρτία εἰς τὸν κόσμον εἰσῆλθεν καὶ διὰ τῆς ἁμαρτίας ὁ θάνατος καὶ οὕτως εἰς πάντες ἀνθρώπους ὁ θάνατος διῆλθεν ἐφ' ᾧ πάντες ἥμαρτον –

"As by one man, sin entered into the world, and death by sin": by one man, single and singular. I think this is a profoundly important phrase: not "by two people" as might have been supposed since Adam and Eve were both in collaboration. It is apparent that the seed of the man is the viaduct that carries the corruption Adam introduced into the body to all succeeding generations.

It may be remarked that non-canonical literature on the subject of man's fall is just as likely to attach the entrance of death to Eve as to Adam. Thus Sirach 25:24 reads: "From a woman sin had its beginning and because of her we all die". So also a Latin work from a group of Jewish writers on Adam, edited by Meyer (1878) and titled Vitae Adae et Evae ("Lives of Adam and Eve": see G. Kittel, Theological Dictionary of the New Testament, Grand Rapids, Eerdmans, 1964, Vol. II, p.856, fn.191), and Strabo, Bk. I, p. 137 f., and Bk. III, p. 646. In a sense this is true; but there is an element of only half-truth about it, and therefore of half-falsehood, which Scripture studiously avoids by never attributing the entrance of death to Eve. The seed of the man and the seed of the woman play antithetical roles in the redemptive history of man. Thus physical death was introduced, it "entered", it was a novelty for human kind, and it entered by man not by woman, and it is passed on from generation to generation via the male seed. The seed of the woman is not the viaduct of death, but of life.

Paul continues, "and so death passed upon all men, for that all have sinned". The last part of this sentence has occasioned a great deal of controversy. Lange's Commentary [Grand Rapids, Zondervan reprint, 1960, Vol. X at Rom.5:12, p. 177 - 180] gives a most useful summary of this debate. The assumption is commonly made that the word sin here means a sinful act. In Adam's case this is, of course true; his disobedience. But is this true thereafter? Do we die physically because we become active sinners, or are we active sinners because we are physically dying creatures? Or to put the matter slightly differently, do we finally return to the dust because we, individually, commit sins that have the effect of making us mortals, or do we commit sins because of the weakness of the flesh (Rom.8: 3) which "weakness of the flesh" is demonstrated by the final death of our body?

The usual view, if I read the commentaries correctly, is that the former is the truth of the matter and the intent of Paul's words. Physical death overcomes each one of us in due course because we inherit some spiritual malaise that turns us into active sinners, the penalty of which is physical death.   But not a few commentators have seen the situation in reverse.   We become sinners because we inherit from Adam by natural generation a defective body that becomes a source of infection of our spirit as we mature. The initial corruption of the spirit (or soul) by its union with the body has been a view very widely held from the earliest times.   It was explicitly maintained by the following who are representative.

New Testament: Paul (Rom.7:17,18).

Patristic: Augustine (354 - 430).

Medieval: Anselm of Canterbury (c. 1033 - 1109), Anselm of Laon (d. 1117), Hugo St. Victor (c. 1096 - 1141), Peter Lombard (c. 1095 - 1161), Stephen Langton (d. 1228.

Reformed: Ulrich Zwingli (1484 - 1531), Zacharius Ursinus (1534 - 1583), Andreae Hyperius (1568), Benedictus Aretius (1589), Bartholomaeus Keckerman (1611), J. H. Hottinger (1620 - 1667), Amandus Polanus (1624), Francois Turretin (1632 - 1687), Johannes Wollebius (1626), Samuel Endemann (1777).

Jewish: Standard Jewish Encyclopedia (1962) under *Soul.*

The question of how soon this occurs, at what young age, is not at issue here.   It is assumed to be in *youth*, for so Scripture states it (Gen.8:21; Jer.22:21; 32:30 and cf. 2 Kings 24:8,9) but obviously this could be interpreted rather broadly depending upon how quickly a particular culture encourages the maturing processes.   But certainly there is an age of innocence before the malaise has time to express itself.   Babies die, though innocent.   The possibility of dying has therefore also become the lot of those who have not yet reached the age of accountability.   Meyer was one of the earlier commentators of modern times who acknowledged the force of this argument.

It might be argued that when an infant dies, it is really "killed", by disease in one form or another.   But we know now that our bodies appear to be dying anyway, from the day of our birth — if not even prenatally.

So mortality replaced immortality by the action of one man and this physiological defect was then transmitted by natural procreation to all his descendants.   This defect now appears to be at the root of our spiritual death which seems in the end as inevitable as physical death.   Augustine said: *Persona corrupit natura, natura corrumpit personam*:   "A person (i.e., Adam) corrupted (human) nature, (human) nature corrupts the individual".   This is why the law fails to produce moral behaviour. The pure spirit with which each new body is endowed by a creative act of God is soon infected by the corruption in the body.

When God gives this spirit, what was previously only a body is constituted a *person*.   Conscious life thereafter turns this person into a personality: but sadly, time also turns innocence into guilt, and this process is somehow initiated by a defective body.   It is a form of somato-psychic influence, of which medicine is becoming increasingly aware in cases of chronic forms of poisoning due to industrial pollution of our environment, for example.

Paul longed to be rid of this "body of sin" (Rom.7:24) and confidently asserted that physical death alone could guarantee the final perfecting of the spirit.   When the perfected spirit is re-introduced into a perfected resurrection body, the whole man is at last made perfect.

Now the universality of this experience by which we all become active sinners is a clear demonstration of the universality of the root cause. That which has rendered every naturally procreated body a dying organism is shared by us all. This is the universal cause of a universally observed effect. Born mortals, we become inevitable sinners if we live long enough. If we die prematurely, we remain innocent of moral guilt but, alas, we die physiologically nevertheless.

And so the phrase "for that all have sinned" can be translated (as many claim) "on account of the fact that all have sinned". Active sinfulness then becomes the *proof* of the common root cause, the cause being that physical death passes upon all men by inheritance.

F. W. Farrar, in his *Life and Work of St. Paul* [London, Cassell, Pelter, Galpin, 1879, Vol. II, p. 215, fn. 2) wrote: "There can be no doubt that ἐφ'ῷ ("for that") means 'in as much as'. Since the argument of Paul seems simply to be that sin was universal and that the universality of death *was a proof of this* [emphasis his], it certainly seems advisable to understand ἐφ'ᾦ in the sense of 'in accordance with the fact that'." With this agree the majority of grammars which refer to this passage, such as Dana and Mantey (*Manual Grammar of the Greek New Testament*, Toronto, Macmillan, 1957, p. 106], other aids to study such as Vincent [*Word Studies in the New Testament*, N.Y., Scribner's, 1890, Vol. III. p. 62] and Abbott-Smith (*Manual Greek Lexicon of the New Testament*, Edinburgh, Clark, 1964, p. 166], Kittel's *Theological Dictionary of the New Testament* (under various word headings, especially Vol. I, p. 427, fn. 14), and *Expositors Greek Testament* [ed. W. R. Nicoll, Grand Rapids, Eerdmans reprint, 1976, Vol. II, p. 627 f.].

In summary, it seems that we are justified in understanding Paul's words to mean that Adam, endowed with immortality by the Creator, forfeited that immortality by his sin and entailed to all his descendants the poisoned constitution which he had acquired, the proof of this entailment being the universality of human wickedness.

We can interpret these words in Romans 5:12 to mean either that all are mortal and dying, and as a consequence became sinners; or that all have an inherently sinful nature by spiritual entailment from Adam and that this condemns the body of every individual to physical death. The grammar of the sentence does not speak unequivocally and we have to decide which is cause and which is effect. About the only telling factor, in helping us to make the decision, is the knowledge that an innocent baby may die as easily as a guilty old man or woman. Physical death can overtake those who have as yet committed no sins, which seems to demonstrate that it is at work before any display of a disobedient spirit.

116. It is appointed unto men once to die (Heb. 9:27). This being so, we must assume that both Enoch and Elijah have yet to keep this appointment. There are some commentators who believe that the two witnesses referred to in Revelation 11:3 f. are none other than Enoch and Elijah who, after giving their testimony for an unspecified length of time, will be overcome and slain. Their dead bodies will lie in the street for three and a half days (vv. 8 and 9), a figure which has particular significance in that there is a widespread belief that the lapse of three days is required to certify that the deceased really is dead. The two witnesses are then raised from the dead and both ascend into heaven (vv. 11 and 12). If this surmise as to their identity is correct, then man's appointment with death has been truly universal, even with respect to the Lord Jesus Christ.

117. With reference to Hebrews 12:2, in his *Greek-English Lexicon of the New*

Testament [Edinburgh, T. &. T. Clark, 4th ed.], J. H. Thayer under the Greek ἀντὶ *(anti)* gives the following meanings: (1) it properly seems to have signified *over, against, opposite to, before,* in a local sense.   Hence (2) indicating exchange, succession, *for, instead of* (something).   Dana and Mantey [*op. cit.,* p. 100] say in this connection: "There is conclusive proof now that the dominant meaning for ἀντὶ in the first century was *instead of.* Professor Whitesall (Chicago) made a study of αντι in the Septuagint and found thirty-eight passages where it is rightly translated *instead of* in the *Revised Version.*   Since ἀντὶ is used in two atonement passages in the New Testament, such a translation needs careful consideration.   Notice the following: Genesis 22:13, "and offered him up for a burnt offering *instead of* (ἀντὶ) his son"; Genesis 44:33, "Let thy servant, I pray thee, abide *instead of* (ἀντὶ) the lad a bondman to my lord"; Numbers 3:12, "I have the Levites from among the children of Israel *instead of* (ἀντὶ) all the firstborn".   These three sentences unmistakeably deal with substitution.   This translation applies especially to the following: Matthew 2:22;   Luke 11:11;   I Corinthians 11:15;   and Hebrews 12:2, "Jesus . . . . who *instead of* (ἀντὶ) the joy that was set before him endured the cross".   The *New Testament: An Expanded Translation* by Kenneth S. Wuest has also adopted this rendering [Grand Rapids, Eerdmans, 1959].

An excellent illustration of the use of the Greek word ἀντὶ with the meaning of "instead of" but translated by the English word *for* will be found in the King James Version at Isaiah 61:3 which reads, "To appoint unto them that mourn in Zion, to give unto them beauty *for* ashes . . . . the garment of praise *for* the spirit of heaviness".   The Septuagint Greek version has here:

δόξαν ἀντὶ σποδοῦ. . . . στολὴν δόξης ἀντὶ πνεύματος ἀκηδίας

Translated literally this is: "Glory instead of ashes . . . . the garment of glory instead of a spirit of heaviness".   Bagster's edition of the Septuagint so translates the first phrase but then adopts the English word *for* in the second, presumably for the sake of avoiding reiteration.

In the Hebrew of Isaiah 61:3 the words "glory *for* ashes" are represented by the Hebrew word *tachath,* תַּחַת .   It is a pity that in *The New Testament in Hebrew and English,* published by the Trinitarian Bible Society and chiefly the work of Louis Ginsberg I believe, the translator was influenced and misled, I regret to say, by the English versions.   Instead of being guided by the Septuagint usage where the Hebrew *tachath* meaning "instead of" is replaced in Greek by *anti,* Ginsberg replaced the Greek *anti* in Hebrews 12:2 by a Hebrew word *ba'abor,* בַּעֲבוּר , which means "because of" or "on account of".

Actually, in the Hebrew original of Isaiah 61:3 *tachath* occurs three times. In each case Rotherham has rendered it "instead of", as is proper.

The Greek word *anti* is frequently used in the Septuagint with this meaning.   See for example, Genesis 2:21; 4:25; 9:6: 22:13; 29:27; 30:2; 36:33, 34, 35, 36, 37, 38, 39; 44:33; 47:17; etc.   This is not to say that the Hebrew word and its Greek equivalent *anti* never have the sense of "because of", but only that the meaning "instead of" where ever it is found in the Hebrew regularly requires the form *tachath,* which the Septuagint has then replaced by *anti.*   A particularly good illustration of how the English word *for* could be misinterpreted, is to be seen in Genesis 47:17 where the King James Version made the meaning explicit by inserting the words "in exchange for" in its first occurrence.   The verse therefore reads as follows: "And they brought their cattle unto Joseph: and Joseph gave them bread in exchange for their horses, and for the flocks and for the cattle of the herds and for the asses: and he fed them with bread for all their cattle for that year".

If the King James Version had not inserted the words "in exchange for", the transaction could have been interpreted to mean that Joseph supplied feed for the animals. This is not the intention of the exchange: it was the owners, not the animals, who were supplied with food. They traded their cattle for bread. Verse 18 makes this clear, for although they managed to save their lives, they lost all their possessions in so doing. All they had left to barter for bread was their land and themselves as slaves (v. 19). And in the end, these too became Pharaoh's possessions (v. 23).

It therefore seems entirely appropriate to translate *anti* in Hebrews 12:2 by the words "instead of". To render it any other way requires an unnatural and unlikely exegesis. Can one really suppose that the Lord faced the eternity of that ordeal of separation from the Father in a spirit of joyful anticipation because of the prospect at the end of it, when such a prospect was just as certain whether He subjected Himself to such a frightful ordeal or not? Would He not have been joyfully received into glory even if He had not suffered the penalty on the cross?

118. Coon, Carleton, S., *The Story of Man*, N.Y., Knopf, 1962, p. 67.

119. Skutch, Alexander, "The Parental Devotion of Birds", *Sci. Mon.,*, April, 1946, p. 369.

120. Hirst, J. Crowther, *Is Nature Cruel?*, London, James Clark & Co., 1899. This work is a most valuable assessment of the amount of pain actually inflicted on their victims by predators. It is based on studies of some 60 individuals mauled severely by wild animals. Almost without exception they experienced no pain at the time. Interestingly, the same has now been reported for those attacked by sharks. A good summary of Hirst's findings (which may be more accessible to most readers than his book) will be found in the British *Spectator*, 3 June, 1899, p. 782, 783.

121. Plankton: Fred Bodsworth, *The Natural History of Canada: the Pacific Coast*, Toronto, McClelland, 1970, p. 97.

122. There is some evidence now that the sperm which do not actually fertilize the ovum nevertheless contribute by their disintegration to the total environment in which the fertilized ovum will survive and develop in its earliest stages by forming some essential part of its nourishment [B. Baccetti and B. A. Afzelius, *The Biology of the Sperm Cell*, Monographs in Developmental Biology, #10, Basel, Karger, 1976, p. 78].

123. In recent years the concept of the inherent immortality of excised tissue in vitro has been challenged by the findings of Leonard Hayflick who reported that cells derived from human foetal lung tissue cultured under rigidly controlled conditions would survive only 50 ± 10 doublings [*Exper. Cell Res.*, 25, 1961, p. 585]. These findings were reported in great detail and were confirmed by others later. (See also L. Hayflick, "The Limited in Vitro Lifetime of Human Diploid Cell Strains", *Exper. Cell Res.*, 37, 1965, p. 614 - 636.

In 1974 Hayflick contributed a paper under the title "Cytogerontology" in *Theoretical Aspects of Aging* in which he again summed up his findings to that date. In this same volume S. Gelfant and G. L. Grove wrote, with reference to Hayflick's findings: "These studies originally reported by Hayflick

and Moorehead in 1961 showed that normal animal cells cannot be maintained in vitro indefinitely, but rather have a limited life span. The life span
is expressed in the proliferative capacity of the cells in culture and it is also
directly related to the age of the donor from which the cultured cells were
taken.   The maximum life span of human diploid cells in vitro is about ten
months.   This life span represents approximately 50 cell population doublings, and it applies to cells taken from the youngest possible tissue, that is,
from foetal tissue. By comparison, shorter life spans and progressively fewer cell population doublings are observed in cultures originating from adult
and old human tissue" [*Theoretical Aspects of Aging*, ed. M. Rockstein,
N.Y., Academic Press. 1974, p. 107, 108].

David E. Harrison, on the basis of Hayflick's reported results, confidently
asserted that "his work refuted the fifty-year-old dogma that normal cells
could be immortal in tissue culture" [Letter to the Editor, *Science*, 192,
1976, p. 614 under a heading "Hayflick's Achievements"]. Harrison clearly had in mind such experiments as those conducted by Alexis Carrel [*J.
Exp. Med.*, 15, 1912, p. 516] and A. H. Ebeling [*ibid*, 17, 1913, p. 273] in
which chicken tissue cells were maintained for years until the experiment
was terminated by failure of the equipment.

It is important to note that Hayflick's experiments involved normal
diploid cells.   Under certain conditions of cell culture abnormal (hetero-
ploid) cells may suddenly appear for some reason, and these cells are capable of maintaining their viability indefinitely.

Hayflick is careful to note in his paper "Cytogerontology" that "the in
vitro end point measured by us as loss of capacity for division is simply a
very convenient and reproducible system, but may have little to do with the
actual cause of in vivo aging" [in *Theoretical Aspects of Aging*, p. 94].

It should also be noted that Hayflick himself, in 1968. had reported:
"Restudy of the experiments in culturing mouse cells has brought to light a
highly interesting fact.   It has been found that when normal cells from a
laboratory mouse are cultured in a glass vessel, they frequently undergo a
spontaneous transformation that enables them to divide and multiply indefinitely.   This type of transformation takes place regularly in cultures of the
fibroblasts (i.e. cells of connective tissue) of man and other animals. These
transformed cell populations have several abnormal properties but they are
truly immortal: many of the mouse derived cultures have survived for
decades" ["Human Cells and Aging", *Sci. Amer.*, Mar., 1968, p. 32].

There are therefore at least two possible explanations for Alexis Carrel's
findings and for the findings of a number of others since: the culture medium may have contributed something to the extended survival of the cells
which was lacking in Hayflick's experiments, or the cells themselves may
have spontaneously transformed to an abnormal condition.   It was for this
reason that Hayflick later underscored that his cells were *normal*.   He specifically states that they are not the same as the HeLa cells from cervical
tissue which George O. Gey of the Johns Hopkins University School of Medicine had started with in 1952 and which were still growing and multiplying
in glass cultures in 1968, and may even yet be flourishing.   These exceptional cells did not have the usual 46 chromosomes of a normal human cell but
anywhere from 50 to 350 per cell.   They were cells that sometimes behaved
like cancer cells and would form tumours when implanted in live animal
tissue.

Rona Cherry and Lawrence Cherry, under the heading "Uncovering the
Secrets of a Longer Life", noted that while cells from foetuses died around

the fiftieth division, cells from young adults divided about fifty times before dying, and those from mature adults only about twenty times [*The New York Times Magazine*, 12 May, 1974]. This circumstance seems a clear validation of Hayflick's findings that cells so cultured in vitro do have a limited life span.

Accordingly, Hayflick considers that normal animal cells are programmed with a limited life. This may be true of animals by divine design, to prevent over-population. It may be true of human beings *now* because of the penalty imposed on man for his sin. It need not have been true of Adam as created.

Paul T. Libassi notes that if Hayflick's experiments reflect aging in the whole organism, "man's biological clock is wound for about 110 - 115 years" [*The Sciences*, New York Academy of Sciences, 14, (9), 1974, p. 7]. This seems remarkably close to a statement made in Genesis 6:3 that after the Flood man's life span should not be allowed to exceed 120 years. To take the words to mean that God would grant the old world only 120 years of grace before the Flood would destroy it, is — in Kalisch's view — "utterly at variance with the context". Kalisch has a long note on this passage that pretty well covers (and invites rejection of) all the then current alternative interpretations [*Historical and Critical Commentary on the Old Testament: Genesis*, M. M. Kalisch, London, Longmans, 1858, p. 175 ff.].

August Weismann, with extraordinary foresight, addressed the same question of whether there is really a limit placed upon cell multiplication many years ago when he wrote: "The hypothesis upon the origin and necessity of death leads me to believe that the organism did not finally cease to renew the worn-out cell-material because the nature of the cells did not permit them to multiply indefinitely, but because the power of multiplying indefinitely was lost when it ceased to be of use" [*op. cit*, ref. #33, Vol. I, p. 25]. Unicellular forms seem to have no such limitations imposed upon them, so that the *base* of the food chain is virtually guaranteed so long as conditions that will support life are maintained.

One criticism of Hayflick's experiment may have to do with the nature of the culture medium. In a special report under the title "Cellular Theories of Senescence" [*Science*, 186, 1975, p. 1105, 1106], Jean L. Marx noted that "Lester Packer of the University of California, Berkeley, and James R. Smith of the Veterans Administration Hospital in Martinez, California, added vitamin E to cultured WI-38 cells. These cells which they obtained from Hayflick are the same human embryonic cells that normally have an in vitro life span encompassing only about 50 divisions. But in the presence of vitamin E, an antioxidant that can interfere with reactions mediated by free radicals, the cells continued to divide and to have youthful characters for about 120 population doublings: after that they, too, became senescent and died out. Packer and Smith estimate that the concentration of the vitamin in the enriched culture medium is approximately the same as that in serum in vivo. Packer said that these results do not necessarily conflict with Hayflick's hypothesis that the cells have a built-in "biological clock" that determines the number of population doublings. He thinks that they may have such a programmed potential but that it is not always attained. Addition of antioxidants to the (cell) environment may allow the cells to reach their full potential for dividing and thus achieving an apparently lengthened life span".

Here, then, we have the same cells treated with a culture medium that more nearly approaches the medium in which cells would be bathed in a healthy body with a proper diet, living not for 50 doublings but for 120.   If modern man has a life potential of, say 70 years, the new potential for cell population doublings should ideally give him a theoretical life span of approximately 170 years — which comes close to the Vilcabamba, Azerbaijan, etc. people.   Moreover, it should be remembered that these cells are taken from human tissue of man as he *now* is, not as he once was in pre-Flood time — and certainly not as he was before he fell.

Indeed, it now appears that the so-called "Hayflick limit" may, in a sense, be an artefact, that is to say, "the inevitable consequence of normal culturing procedures".   It should in fact be quite possible to produce "an immortal steady state culture".   Such a population "might be propagated indefinitely".   [See R. Holliday, *et al.*, "Testing the Commitment Theory of Cellular Aging", *Science*, 198, 1977, p. 366 f.].

Even more recently, E. Bell and co-workers have questioned whether the Hayflick phenomenon is a sign of aging or whether it is not rather evidence of cell differentiation.   They observe: "The notion that diploid cells age in vitro is based on the observation that they undergo only a limited number of population doublings . . .   In this article we examine these assumptions and provide evidence for an alternative interpretation — namely, that cessation of proliferation of diploid cells . . . . represents a step of differentiation and not one of senescence".

Hayflick's technique of subculturing is seen to be an "upsetting" factor in cell culture which "forces" the cells to "exchange immortality for specialization".   They conclude that "cells of organisms need not be programmed intrinsically to die".   ["Loss of Division Potential in Vitro: Aging or Differentiation?", *Science*, 202, 1979, p. 1158 - 1163].

124. Gershon, Drs. Harriet and David, Technion-Israel Inst. of Technology, Dept. Biol., Haifa: "Inactive Enzyme Molecules in Aging Mice: Liver Aldolase", *Proc. of Nat. Acad. Sci.*, 70, 1973, p. 909.   Dr. Clive Wood of Oxford has suggested that the appearance of "errors" in cell reproduction is under direct genetic control.   "The cell carries its own ageing programme which ultimately results in programmed death" ["Longevity — Catalyst of Social Revolution", *New Scientist*, 24 May, 1973, p. 470].   The word "error" must, therefore, be used in a rather special sense.

125. Many years ago Sir William Dawson remarked upon this both for plants and animals.   From a study of post-Pleiocene molluscs and other fossils he concluded that "new species tend rapidly to vary to the utmost extent of their possible limits and then to remain stationary for an indefinite time".   [*The Story of the Earth and Man*, London, Hodder and Stoughton, 1903, p. 360].   It has been found true for birds, according to Ernst Mayr [*Mathematical Challenges to the Neo-Darwinian Interpretation of Evolution*, Phila., Wistar Inst. Symposium Monograph, No. 5, 1967, p. 47].   Charles Brues reports the same for insects   ["Contributions of Entomology to Theoretical Biology", *Sci. Mon.*, Feb., 1947, p. 130].   Adolph Schultz has confirmed it for primate populations [*The Origin and Evolution of Man*, Cold Springs Harbor Symposium on Quantitative Biology, 15, 1950, p. 50].   And it has been remarked upon for man by Ralph Linton [*The Study of Man*, N.Y., Appleton-Century, 1936, p. 26 ff.]; LeGros Clark ["Bone of Contention", Huxley Memorial Lecture, *J. Anthrop. Inst.*, 88, 2, 1958, p. 136 138]; and Ralph Goldschmidt ["Evolution as Viewed by One Geneticist", *Amer. Scientist*, 40, 1952, p. 97].   This built-in variability is an advantage to man, for it allows him to breed lines of domestic animals select-

ively to suit his own special needs.

126. Muller, H. J., "Life", *Science*, 121, 1955, p. 5.

127. Edney, E. B. and R. W. Gill, "Evolution of Senescence and Specific Long-evity", *Nature*, 220, 1968, p. 282.

128. Size: see an excellent discussion of this point by J. B. S. Haldane, "On Being the Right Size" in *The World of Mathematics*, ed. J. R. Newman, N.Y., Simon and Schuster, 1956, Vol. II, p. 952 ff. In this connection with man, see a valuable paper by F. W. Went, "The Size of Man", *Amer. Scientist*, 56, 4, 1968, p. 400 - 413. See also T. McMahon, "Size and Shape in Biology", *Science*, 179, 1973, p. 1201 ff. I have a copy of a diary kept by a Parson for forty years in the latter half of the eighteenth century. He tells how he went to see, in Norwich (England), a giant pig which was nine feet long and four feet high! He observes as a by-the-bye that it had to be supported on its legs and when it fell over was unable to raise itself [Woodforde, James, *Diary of a Country Parson*, ed. John Beresford, Oxford, 1926, in 5 vols., Vol. I, p. 245].

129. Good, Ronald, in a review of a book by Lee R. Dice, *Natural Communities*, [Ann Arbor, 1952], in *Nature*, 11 July, 1953, p. 46. A very refreshing volume.

130. In 1967 *The National Academy of Sciences* sponsored a special congress to deal with the problem of the cause of the extinction of a great number of species in Pleistocene times. Some sixty-two pages of animals that were ex-tincted are listed, some of these pages covering as many as forty different species, and the total involving at least two hundred genera. The conclusion of the Congress as a whole was that "this global extinction pattern" was the result of over-kill by early man. Other possible causes, such as climatic change, are not considered to be of primary importance. It was concluded, however, that man's over-kill of many species of interest to himself had the effect of depriving other species of their natural source of food so that they, too, suffered extinction indirectly. It appears that man has always been the great disturber indeed — and still is. As late as 1627 he killed probably the last of the European aurochs. During the last 2000 years about 200 species of mammals and birds have become extinct, 70 of them within the last 50 years — and the rate is increasing. About 350 species of vertebrates, nearly a third of them mammals, are currently endangered [*The Living World of Animals* London, Reader's Digest Assoc., 1970, p. 370; *Pleistocene Extinct-ions: The Search For a Cause*, ed. Paul S. Martin and H. E. Wright, New Haven, Yale Univ. Press, Vol. VI of the Proc. of the VII Congress of the Internationsl Assoc. for Quarternary Research, 433 pp; also Lynn White Jr., "The Historical Roots of Our Ecological Crisis", *Science*, 155, 1967, p. 1203 - 1207].

131. Jones, F. Wood, *Trends of Life*, London, Arnold, 1953, p. 18.

132. du Nouy, Comte, *Human Destiny*, N.Y., Longmans Green, 1947, p. 61.

133. An illustration is the peripheral circulation which performs some very im-portant functions in the regulation of man's body temperature and thus his viability. This peripheral circulation is found to be strkingly different in some of the most commonly used experimental animals, including those believed to be nearest to man in their biological make-up [R. H. Fox and O. G. Edholm, "Peripheral Circulation in Man", *Brit. Med. Bull.*, 19, 1963,

.p. 112]. J. D. Hardy remarks particularly upon the differences between man and some species of monkey in the matter of body temperature regulation. In fact he concludes one of his reports by saying: "In summary, although the monkey was selected originally for this type of experimentation because it was hoped that its physiology in respect to temperature regulation might be nearer to man than that of the domestic cat or dog, it would seem that the monkey does not simulate man in its method of regulating body temperature" ["Control of Heat Loss and Heat Production in Physiological Temperature Regulation", Harvey Lecture Series, XLIX, N.Y., Academic Press, 1953-4, p. 242-270]. See also the author's "Is Man An Animal?" in *Evolution or Creation?*, Vol. IV, Doorway Papers Series, Grand Rapids, Zondervan, 1976, p. 208-320, which deals at some length with these questions.

134. Sherrington, Sir Charles, *Man on His Nature*, Cambridge, 1963, p. 33, 34.

135. The nations of antiquity often have traditions that seem to be reflections of the two Trees in the Garden of Eden, though the role of the two trees is sometimes reversed. There was in the old world in classical times a very widespread association in certain festivals between the drinking of an alcoholic beverage (which might be seen as a recollection of the forbidden fruit) and the acquisition of immortality (which would seem to be related rather to the Tree of Life). The ancient gods of Greece and Rome drank fermented wine (nectar) or ate a food associated with such wine (ambrosia) to preserve their immortality.

Ambrosia was commonly described as the "food of the gods", and nectar as the "drink of the gods". There is no question that both were related and sometimes the terms were used interchangeably, or reversed in meaning. The ancient Greek Poetess, Sappho (seventh century B.C.) and Anaxandridas (d. 520 B.C.) both say that ambrosia was a drink. Homer refers to it however as like an ointment or an oil for anointing the bodies of the dead to preserve them from corruption, whereas he describes nectar as resembling red wine and states that its continued use brings immortality [*Iliad*, XIV, 170; and XIX, 38].

The word *ambrosia* is held by some authorities to be of Greek origin, composed of α (not) and βροτος (mortal), i.e., *not mortal, immortal*. Liddell and Scott suggest an etymological connection with the Latin root MORT-.

Homer also refers to ambrosia as being an unguent for the treating of wounds, an observation again reflected in the widespread use of fermented wine in the same connection. This practice is observed in Luke 10:34, where the good Samaritan treated the severely wounded man that he found beside the road on his way to Jerich by "pouring oil and wine" into his wounds.

Ambrosia was a central element in several Festivals observed in Greece (and elsewhere) in connection with Dionysus, "the god of peasants". It was a time of celebration for the grape harvest and, according to Johannes Tzetzes (c. 1120-1183) a Greek author who wrote commentaries on Homer and Hesiod, it was held when the must of the newly harvested grapes had fermented. Other non-Hellenic peoples adopted these festivals but turned them into orgies which the more sober Greeks felt were "scandalous".

Hindu mythology has a drink termed *Amrita*, believed to be derived from Sanscrit *a-* (not) and a root word related to the Latin *mort-*, and the Greek *brot-*. The gods of the Scandinavian pantheon preserved their perpetual youth by eating apples guarded by one named Idun. It is tempting to see this guardian figure as a corruption of the word *Eden*!

Clearly, there has been preserved among the nations a certain connection between alcohol and immortality, a reversal of the biblical connection obviously, and perhaps an illustration of just the kind of reversal that mythology experienced when it made the serpent the symbol of health.

136. Wasson, Gordon R., "Fly Agaric (*Amenita muscaria*) and Man", in *Ethnopharmacological Search for Psycho-Active Drugs*, ed. Daniel H. Efron, published U.S. Dept. of Health, Education and Welfare, Public Health Services Publ., No. 1465, 1967, p. 413.

137. Horsley, Sir Victor, *Alcohol and the Human Body*, London, Macmillan, 1908, p. 54.

138. Carlson, H. J. and V. Johnson, *op. cit.*, (ref. #51), p. 341.

139. Watson, George, *Nutrition and Your Mind*, N.Y., Harper and Row, 1972, p. 104.

140. Seixas, Frank A., "Medical Consequences of Alcoholism", *Annals of New York Academy of Sciences*, 252, 1975, p. 5.

141. Williams, Kenneth, "Medical Consequences of Alcoholism", *Annals of New York Academy of Sciences*, 252, 1975, p. 296.

142. Hellman, Robert S., "Medical Consequences of Alcoholism", *Annals of New York Academy of Sciences*, 252, 1975, p. 297.

143. Hellman, Robert S., *ibid*, p. 304.

144. Lieber, Charles S., "The Metabolism of Alcohol", *Sci. Amer.*, Mar., 1976, p. 25.

145. Dimitrijevic, D. T., "Alcoholism of The Parents in the Pathogenesis of Neuroses in Children", *Med. Arch.*, Sarajevo, 12, *1*, 1958, p. 81-85.

146. Ruch, T. C. and J. F. Fulton, *Medical Physiology and Biophysics*, Phila., Saunders, 1960, p. 809.

147. Everett, Glenn, "Alcoholism: A Matter of Genetics?", a brief note in *Christianity Today*, 16 Feb., 1973, p. 53.

148. Aamark, C., "A Study in Alcoholism: Clinical, Social-Psychiatric and Genetic Investigation", *J. Acta Psychiat.*, Supplem. 70, Copenhagen, 1951, 283 pp.

149. Kaij, L., *Alcoholism in Twins: Studies on the Aetiology and Sequels of Abuse of Alcohol*, Stockholm, Imqirst and Wiksell, 1960, 144 pp.

150. Doepfmer, R. and H. J. Hinckers, "On the Question of Germ Cell Damage in Acute Alcohol Intoxication", Z. Haut-U., *Geschlechstkr*, 39, 1965, p. 94 - 107.

151. Lemere, F., *et al.*, "Heredity as an Etiologic Factor in Chronic Alcoholism", *Northwest Med.*, Seattle, Wash., 42, 1943, p. 110, 111.

152. Popham, Robert E., "A Critique of the Genetotrophic Theory of the Etiology of Alcoholism", *Quart. J. of Studies on Alcohol*, 14, 1953, p. 228-237.

153. Singh, J. A. L. and R. M. Zingg, *Wolf Children and Feral Man*, N.Y., Archon Books, Harper and Row, 1966, p. 294.

154. Protti, Giocondo, "The Luminous Woman: The Mystery of Anna Monaro", *Ill. Lon. News*, 19 May, 1934, p. 780.

155. It has been found that vitamins (especially A, C and thiamine), antibodies, products of metabolism, the sulfonamide compounds and other drugs cross the placental membranes. It has also been found that penicillin and streptomycin administered to the mother appear rapidly in human foetal blood. It has been reported that hormones, narcotics and chemotherapeutic agents are transmitted across the placental barrier.

In a brief note in the *New Scientist* (8 Dec., 1977, p. 632) it was recently reported: "The US Food and Drug Administration wants to have alcoholic drinks labelled to warn pregnant women that excessive alcohol consumption could harm their babies. According to one US federal organization, The National Institute of Alcohol Abuse and Alcoholism, something like 1500 babies born in the US each year may be mentally or physically damaged because their mothers drank too much alcohol when they were pregnant. Dr. Donald Kennedy, the FDA Commissioner, says that two glasses of wine or one and a half (imperial) pints of beer a day is an excessive alcohol intake.

Another recent report in *New Scientist* (11 Jan., 1979, p. 76) indicates that the strictly poisonous nature of alcohol in human tissue is being increasingly recognized. Under the somewhat undignified heading "Mother's ruin is baby's downfall", it is noted that evidence has now clearly indicated the often severely detrimental effect on the unborn and newly born of the mother's alcohol intake. The number of pregnant mothers studied is very substantial and the evidence confirms experiments with animals that there is a marked foetal effect of alcohol poisoning via the mother. The effect of alcohol poisoning appears to be direct and not indirect.

At least 20 different patterns of drinking can lead to some form of congenital damage. But it is not yet clear precisely how alcohol disrupts embryonic development, nor whether it is a poison in its own right or disrupts the flow of nutrient to the embryo. Whether by direct or indirect action, its effects on the embryo are "strikingly toxic".

156. Konowalchuk, J. and J. I. Speirs reported their findings in the *Journal of Applied and Environmental Microbiology*, 32, 1977, p. 757. Polio, herpes simplex, echo, and coxsackie viruses were all suppressed or inhibited. Polio virus infectivity was reduced by a factor of 1000 when incubated at 4°C at pH7 for 24 hours with grape juice. Wines were less effective.

The authors believe that the amount of inhibition exercised by the juices is related to the concentration of tannin-like phenolic compounds present. Inhibitory activity is confined to the extract from the skin of the grape rather than the pulp. The mechanism of inhibition probably depends on the phenolics' ability to bind especially to virus protein, upon which the ability to infect depends.

157. Richard J. Harrison and William Montagna in their book *Man* remarked upon the necessity of death and the potential hazard it would be to life as a whole if the majority of creatures were not "programmed" to die [N.Y., Appleton-Century-Crofts, 1969, p. 354 f.].

"One can conceive that under ideal circumstances tissues could remain unchanged and animals live forever. This 'foreverness' seems to be man's goal in studying the aging processes. Had this goal been achieved in the past, the numbers of each species would, eons ago, have exceeded the limits of their natural ecological niches. The total inhabitable surface of the earth and the oceans, lakes, and streams would have long ago been overpopulated, and the competition for survival would have been magnified to such an extent that the destruction of life might have resulted . . . .

"It is singularly true of animals with a circumscribed reproductive function that when this function ceases the individual dies, as if nature had
ordained that organisms that are no longer useful in genetic succession are
ipso facto useless and must be eliminated. Some justification can be found
for such belief when one analyzes the situation in all vertebrates *except man*
[emphasis mine]. The perpetuation of each species, after all, can only be
assured by reproductively vigorous animals. Hence the elimination of those
no longer able to reproduce seems to establish a natural order of things".

All this is true provided that the only purpose in the system is that each
species shall survive. The question of what a species is to survive *for* is un-
asked. If individual worth has some significance, then the mere serving of a
reproductive function in the life of the species is not enough to determine
how long an *individual* organism is to survive. To die off as soon as reproductive capacity is ended, does indeed suggest that life was allocated only for
this purpose. But man may live long after he is no longer reproductive. His
life therefore must serve some further objective.

Animals would, if given unlimited longevity, soon swamp every available
nook and cranny of the globe. But man was never originally planned to
come to an end by dying but by being "graduated" to another sphere of
living without passing through death. In such an order of life, the earth
would never have been "knee deep in human bodies". This signifies that he
is something more than just a reproductive machine. But translation of
animals below man does not seem to have been part of the plan, and death
for them must therefore have been programmed. Yet there is still no hard
evidence that life per se has to be terminated in death as a natural process of
wearing out by the exhaustion of its vital resources. It is simply that the
longer an animal lives the greater are its chances of being killed. All life had
to be constituted with the *possibility* either of dying or of being translated,
otherwise there is no safety valve against over-population.

158. Maatman, Russell W. (Dept. Chemistry, Dordt College, Sioux Centre, Iowa),
"Inerrancy, Inspiration and Evolution: the Position of Russell W. Maatman",
J. Amer. Sci. Affil., 24, 2, 1972, p. 88.

159. Blum, Harold, *Time's Arrow and Evolution*, N.J., Princeton, 1951, p. 76.

160. Sciama, D. W. S., quoted by R. E. D. Clark from Sciama's *The Unity of the
Universe* (1959) in *The Christian Stake in Science*, Exeter, Paternoster Press,
1967, p. 113.

161. Wheeler, John A., "Our Universe: the Known and the Unknown", *Amer.
Scientist*, Spring, 1968, p. 18.

162. Huxley, Sir Julian, quoted by E. L. Mascall, *The Importance of Being
Human*, N.Y., Columbia Univ. Press, 1958, p. 6.

163. Huxley, Sir Julian, *ibid*, p. 7.

164. Simpson, G. G., "Some Cosmic Aspects of Evolution" in *Evolution and
Hominization*, ed. Gottfried Kurth, Stuttgart, Fischer, 2nd ed., 1968,
p. 2.

165. Bermant, Gordon, "Human Sexual Development", *Science*, 180, 1973,
p. 588.

166. Price, Dorothy, quoted by Graham Chedd, "Struggling into Manhood", *New
Scientist*, 5 June, 1969, p. 524. As Chedd notes, it is now believed that
maleness is dependent not merely upon the presence of the Y chromosome

but, at two critical points, upon two masculinizing substances, one as yet unidentified and the other testosterone or something very like it.   It is virtually certain that these two substances appear only in the presence of the Y chromosome but apparently they may not be manufactured by the developing organism at the appropriate time and when this happens the foetus becomes feminized instead.

Ursula Mittwoch, an outstanding authority in this area in Great Britain, observed: "It is now accepted that the embryonic testis plays a major role in mammalian sexual development.   If testes are present in the young embryo, a male phenotype will develop, whereas if the embryonic testes are removed the phenotype will resemble that of a female *whatever the chromosomal sex of the embyro*" [emphasis mine: "Do Genes Determine Sex?", *Nature*, 1 Feb., 1969, p. 446].   From which we conclude that not only does the human embryo have the capability of developing into either a male or a female regardless of the presence of the X or Y sex chromosomes but the genetic male may rather easily emerge as a female if certain irregularities in sequential development occur.

The same author in another paper on the subject underscores the now apparent indeterminacy of the X and Y chromosome by saying, "Indeed, the assumption of sex-determining genes is beset with difficulties . . . . Furthermore, the facts of embryology suggest an inherent bisexuality" ["Sex Differentiation in Mammals", *Nature*, 6 May, 1967, p. 554].   Mittwoch quotes Korens in Berlin as having stated that there can be no question of the segregation of genes for sex differences during gamete formation, but that on the contrary the gametes trasmit the hermaphrodite condition on which the characteristics of one or the other sex are imprinted during subsequent development.   It is because the potentialities for both sexes are present in both male and female determining germ cells, that Korens postulated the existence of some additional sex determinants ["Do Genes Determine Sex?", *Nature*, 1 Feb., 1969, p. 446].

This is a point which has been emphasized also by A. D. Jost who says: "The concept has been progressively developed that in the absence of any sex gland the body is fundamentally neutral sex, and that maleness or femaleness is imposed by male and female hormones produced by the sex glands . . . . As early as 1913, E. Steinach was convinced that the early embryo was neither unisexual nor bisexual but asexual or indifferent until sex is imposed by the sex glands".   And later he adds, "I have come to the conclusion that the simplest explanation of gonadal differentiation would accept that some mechanism — perhaps the production of a special local hormone, correlated with the presence of the Y chromosome in the male [which Jost elsewhere terms an 'inducer' substance] — triggers an early and rapid development of the testis in the rudimentary sex organ which otherwise would follow the slow pattern of development characteristic of the ovary" ["Development of Sexual Characteristics", *Sci. J.*, June, 1970, p. 67, 70].

In a similar vein, R. G. Edwards wrote: "The essential unanswered question about primary sexual differentiation is the mechanism which causes switching of the gland into male or female development.   Various theories have been expounded involving the more rapid synthesis of DNA and cell division due to the smallness of the Y chromosome, the heterochromatic regions of the X and Y chromosome, and balance between the medullary and cortical regions of the gonad.   Early in differentiation, an inducer-like substance evidently determines whether development will be ovarian or testicular.   Once determined, the gonad will evidently not support the growth of germ cells of the other sex" ["Sex and the Developing Embryo", *Sci. J.*, Sept., 1969, p. 89].

167. Ideally, it appears that the X or Y chromosome initiates the programmed development of the appropriate sex glands internally (ovaries or testes) and the external genitalia as well as the accessory organs of the whole reproductive mechanism.   While the gonads are developing into paired ovaries or testes, the germ cells are migrating to these glandular structures in which they will be housed and further prepared for later presentation as ova or spermatozoa.   Migration of the germ cells is believed to take place at first through the vasculature by amoeboid movement [R. G. Edwards, "Sex and the Developing Embryo", *Sci. J.*, Sept., 1969, p. 89].

According to C. R. Austin, primordial cells "are seen first in tissue that originates from the fertilized egg but lies *outside* the true body of the embryo and are thus said to have an extra-embryonic origin.   Shortly, in the course of embryonic development, the cells migrate from this site into the body of the embryo and move towards the genital ridges, regions in which the future gonads, the ovaries or testes, are to develop" ["The Egg and Fertilization", *Sci. J.*, June, 1970, p. 37].

So we have first, genetic or chromosomal sex determination.   This is followed by a gonadal determination whereby either testes or ovaries are formed.   These gonads produce hormones which stimulate development of the appropriate reproductive organs of either sex.   Finally, by visual inspection of the external organs, the sex of the neonate is assigned by the attending physicians or by the parents and the child is thus cast in a special role by society which hopefully will reinforce, and be in harmony with, the physiological constitution.

168. Fritz Kahn observed: "In all mammals including man, the sex gland is very often accompanied by more or less well defined elements belonging to a gland of the opposite sex . . . .   On the one hand, it is not uncommon to find children whose external genitalia exhibit such a combination of male and female structures at birth that it is often difficult, if not impossible, to decide whether the infant is a boy or a girl.   A child is born with a closed genital cleft like a boy but the ostensible penis is small like a clitoris, and the sex glands (testes) cannot be found because they have remained in the abdominal cavity.   Or, on the other hand, two glands have become prominent like a boy's testicles but the genital cleft has remained open like a vagina and one faces the question as to whether the child is a girl with descended ovaries or a boy whose scotum has remained open" [*Man in Structure and Function*, N.Y., Knopf, 1960, Vol. II, p. 734].   This helps to point up the difficulties which may face an attending physician who, for various social reasons, must make a quick decision.

D. R. Keller of Basel, writing on hermaphroditism, remarked, "From our discussion, it is clear that while sex when *fully* differentiated is easy enough to recognize, it is rather difficult to define biologically.   Indeed, according to Lillie, there is no such thing as sex but rather several dimorphous states with contrasting characters.   It is evident that this applies to all living creatures" [*Ciba Symposium*, 2, 3, 1940, p. 485].

The number of individuals who experience a conflict between their inner drives and their assigned sex and role in society seems to be on the increase. Peter Scott, in an article entitled "Identifying Gender", and speaking of the newborn whose sex is not easy to determine, observes: "Most of these babies are normal females (that is, their sex chromosomes are those of a female) who have been to some extent masculinized by male hormones which have either arisen within the baby's body or within the mother's body or have been administered to her during pregnancy". He lists at least six criteria that under ideal conditions might be used, but in real life are not all of them useful either because they are applied too late in life or because they delay assignment of sex too long. These are: (1) internal organs (there is not usually time for this kind of examination); (2) external genital organs (fully formed breasts would be identified too late to correct an error in assignment of sex at birth); (3) type of sex chromosome; (4) characteristic hormones; (5) assigned sex by the physicians or parents; and (6) gender role in society [*New Scientist*, 24 July, 1969, p. 182].

169. According to Hamilton, Boyd and Mossman: "True hermaphroditism is very rare, and among humans there are only twenty proven cases" [W. J. Hamilton, J. D. Boyd, H. W. Mossman, *Human Embryology*, Baltimore, Willams & Wilkins, 1945, p. 220]. This was given on the authority of H. H. Young, *Genital Abnormalities: Hermaphroditism and Related Adrenal Diseases*, written in 1937. In 1946 Charles W. Hooker noted five new cases reported during that single year and states that this brought the total known to him up to 35 or 36 at the time ["Reproduction" in *Annual Review of Physiology*, 8, p. 470]. In 1957 John L. Morris describes a number of cases of confused sex in some of which both male and female gonads were present in the same individual, and some clearly structurally opposing their chromosomal pattern. He notes that there were by then at least 50 histological cases reported. Some of the subjects underwent surgery to correct the malfunction of both internal and external organs and were able to bear normal children thereafter ["Intersexuality", *J. Amer. Med. Assoc.*, 163, 7, 1957, p. 538-542].

M. Bobrow and M. H. Gough of the Medical Research Council in England reported in *Lancet* a number of cases of otherwise completely normal young men with no testes whatever, the *vas deferens* ending "blind" behind the bladder. It has been estimated that as high as two or three in every thousand are biologically neither straightforward males nor females. Rarely are such individuals able to have children ["Bilateral Absence of Testes', *Lancet*, 14 Feb., 1970, p. 366]. And now we learn from John Money and Anke A. Ehrhardt that over the last twenty years more than 900 cases of hermaphroditism and related reproductive and psychosexual disorders have been seen in the psychohormonal research unit at Johns Hopkins Hospital in Baltimore [*Science*, 180, 1973, p. 586]. And this is only *one* reporting agency.

As a matter of fact, Morris' opening statement is: "While the differences between the sexes are the subject of considerable emphasis, male and female are not mutually exclusive, and both have certain anatomic and endocrinal characteristics of the opposite sex. The six-week old embryo is ambisexual, with gonads which may develop into either ovaries or testes, and two systems of tubules, the Wolffian and the Mullerian ducts, which develop into the male or female reproductive organs respectively. Sexual differentiation commences about the seventh week, but many rudimentary structures of the opposite sex persist after birth" ["Intersexuality", *J. Amer. Med. Assoc.*, 163, 7, 1957, p. 538]. According to Money and Ehrhardt who probably have more experience in this area than any other researchers, true hermaphroditism by definition is that condition of incomplete external sexual differentiation at birth in which both testicular and ovarian structures are represented internally in the gonads. There may be one ovary and one testis, or even a pair of each: although most frequently both gonads are of mixed structure. That is, they are ovotestes.

An ovotestis is a gonad which has developed both its cortex and its medulla components, where normally *either* the cortex *or* the medulla would have developed at the expense of the other. The rule is that when the medulla develops, the cortex gradually disappears until only a trace remains, and the structure becomes a testis: when the cortex develops, the medulla gradually disappears leaving only a trace, and the structure becomes an ovary. When both medulla and cortex develop equally, an ovotestis results, in which the medulla produces spermatocytes (later to become spermatozoa) while the cortex simultaneously produces oocytes (later to become ova). [John Money and Anke A. Ehrhardt, *Man and Woman, Boy and Girl*, Baltimore, Johns Hopkins Univ. Press, 1972, p. 38, 39].

It is thus apparent either that the incidence of confused sexuality is actually increasing (possibly due to the widening use of denatured foods and/or inappropriate medication during pregnancy [See Isobel W. Jennings, *Vitamins in Endocrine Metabolism*, London, Heinemann, 1970, 148 pp.], or existing cases are receiving greater publicity. The news media in recent years have reported a number of instances of surgical intervention which has successfully corrected previous sexual indeterminacy, suggesting a changing attitude on the part of the public towards this unfortunate condition.

In the New Testament the word *eunuch* is used to signify a male castrated according to the practices of the nations at the time: but it is also used in the spiritual sense to signify an individual, man or woman, who has deliberately sacrificed all that is involved in sex life in order to dedicate himself or herself entirely to the Lord's service. When the Lord refers to this circumstance in Matthew 19:12, He also notes that in the physical sense there are some who are actually born eunuchs, i.e., born without sex organs. Such abnormalities are not solely a modern phenomenon.

170. Whether there is a positive effect of such twin prenatal influence in humans or not, is perhaps an open question. The case is quite otherwise with animals, where such effects are well-known. D. R. Keller in an article entitled "Hermaphroditism in the Animal Kingdom", mentions pigs and cows as among the more familiar examples. He observes: "Especially in the pig have a relatively large and varied number of cases of hermaphroditism been observed and studied for a long time". Of cows he says, "A particular form of abnormal hermaphroditism designated at present as hormonal intersexuality, occurs when cows bring forth twins of different sex. The female animal may then exhibit marked male characteristics. Such 'Freemartins' have been known to farmers and animal breeders from time immemorial. The origin is ascribed to hormonal action arising from the male embryo, stimulating the female foetus to develop in a masculine direction. Embryologists have demonstrated that the production of testicular hormone can begin earlier than that of ovarian hormone, because the testis in mammals begins to differentiate in an earlier developmental stage than the ovary. Consequently the testicular hormone can exert an inhibitory effect on the development of the genital apparatus in the female twin. Such Freemartins may exhibit varying degrees of intersexuality owing to the circumstance that the two placentas can fuse at various times during embryonic life" [*Ciba Symposium*, June, 1940, p. 478].

P. K. Basrur *et al* have reported similar abnormalities in a horse which was registered as a male at birth but exhibited several intersexual aberrations of internal and external genitalia. This was attributed to an interchange of blood cell precursors and primordial germ cells between heterosexual twins through vascular anastomoses in the foetal membranes during pregnancy ["Further Studies on the Cell populations of an Intersex Horse", *Can. J. of Comparat. Med.*, Oct., 1970, p. 294-296].

Such disturbing hormonal influences may reach the foetus from the mother where hormones are administered in treatment of threatened abortion. Money and Ehrhardt refer to data on genetic females whose mothers were given large pregnancy-saving doses of progestin. All these infant girls suffered from progestin induced hermaphroditism (androgenization) of the external genitalia which was surgically corrected. The authorities state that these girls nevertheless retained in some aspects the masculinization which the operation was intended to correct against [*Man and Woman, Boy and Girl*, Baltimore, Johns Hopkins Univ. Press, 1972, p. 95 ff., especially p. 99 on Tomboyism in girls].

Operational intervention is not usually thought of as *upsetting* the normal sexual development, but rather correcting for it. However, there are cases where normal development has been upset by accident. One such example is that of a child, raised as a girl, though actually a boy "whose penis was completely lost due to clumsy circumcision at seven months" [Money and Ehrhardt, *ibid*, p. 118].

To my knowledge, the term "parasitic castration" has not yet been applied to man, but it has been found in animals. G. E. and N. MacGinitie state: "Barnacles of the genus *Sacculina* are among the most unusual parasites in the animal kingdom. At one stage of its development the barnacle larva attaches itself to a 'hair' on a crab's body and penetrates the covering of the hair and travels down its hollow tube to the interior of the crab. It develops inside the crab, but the only external manifestation of the parasite is a formless reproductive sac that grows in the region of the crab's abdomen. The creeping spreading growth destroys the testes of the host, whereupon organs of the other sex begin to develop and to produce female reproductive hormones. These hormones will initiate the growth of secondary sexual characteristics, such as a wider abdomen and female genital pores. Thus, as a result of parasitism, an almost complete sex reversal occurs. Biologists sometimes call this 'parasitic castration'." [*A Natural History of Marine Animals*, N.Y., McGraw, 1968, p. 261-263].

V. H. Mottram. in his *Physical Basis of Personality* and speaking of a hen which after a year of normal "henny" characteristics had become dominating and cocky in her relations with the rest of her sisters, notes that she grew feathers, comb and spurs appropriate to a rooster and begat a number of chickens "before her sacrifice on the altar of genetics". Then it was discovered that avian tuberculosis had destroyed her ovaries and that from undifferentiated germinal tissue she had grown testes. Since birds (unlike other animals) are heterosexual, the possession of a Y chromosome leads to a *female* sex and it may therefore be that the female can more easily convert to a male in the way that among other animals species it is the *male* which can convert to female [London, Penguin Books, 1949, p. 11].

171. Transexualists are people who wish to become members of the opposite sex not merely in behaviour and dress but by operational intervention if possible. Transvestites wish only to dress in the clothing of the opposite sex. According to an editorial in the *British Medical Journal* [1, 1966, p. 872] under the title "Transexuality", "Transexuality is more frequently reported

in man than in woman, the excess varying anywhere from 50:1 to 3:1, according to different estimates". There is a very large difference between these estimates, but the editorial quotes J. H. Schultz as asserting categorically that true transexuality occurs *only* in man, *never* in woman [in *Intersexuality*, ed. Claus Overzeir, London,1963]. According to R. G. Edwards, development is always female unless a testis is present, when male patterns of differentiation are then imposed on the foetus almost irrespective of the genotype of the foetus, and he refers to the condition known as testicular feminization. In such cases of hermaphroditism the subjects are generally XY and are often found to possess testes (as would be expected) "but the internal and external genitalia are predominately female and the patient behaves as a woman" ["Sex and the Developing Embryo", *Sci. J.*, Sept., 1969, p. 89].

Isobel Jennings observed: "In the presence of functioning pituitary the gonad in the genetic male begins to secrete androgen . . . . Loss of this activity by castration or by chemical means or by parasitism inhibits this process and feminization occurs" [*Vitamins and Endocrine Metabolism*, London, Heineman, 1970, p. 140]. By contrast, at least in mammals, the gonadectomized female has no such tendency towards the development of male sexual characteristics. I do not recall any report via the news media of an assigned female being operationally transformed into a male, but there are numerous reports of the reverse, and such reports demonstrate clearly that if the social and environmental conditions are favourable, the transformation can be carried through with success. Moreover, such transformations have occurred in men who had already fully matured and had even fathered children successfully. *The Toronto Telegram* of 6 March, 1954, carried the story in some detail of an ex-Royal Air Force hero who was the father of two children, aged 10 and 12, who is now to all intents and purposes an entirely different individual — different in name (Robert became Roberta), different in sex, different in habits of life, and different in temperament. The medical report states categorically that in spite of having fathered two children and raised them to adolescence, "she is undoubtedly a woman". They also say that they had known of no previous case where the change had occurred so late in life (at 35 years of age). As we have already noted (see ref. # 169), J. L. Morris reported some instances of hermaphroditic subjects with testicular feminization who underwent surgery and later delivered a normal child, provided only that the ovaries were still present and the vagina not blind ["Intersexuality", *J. Amer. Med. Assoc.*, 163, 7, 1957, p. 540]. Here, then, we have what amounts to a full cycle conversion, male into female and father into mother. Eve who was formed out of Adam became the mother of all living (Gen.3:29).

172. On this subject, Fritz Kahn has observed: "The male and female sex glands, as well as the male and female hormone, are antagonistic in their actions. If a female sex gland is implanted in a man, it is rapidly destroyed, and the same thing happens to a testicle implanted in the body of a sexually immature woman. Nevertheless, throughout its entire life, every organism retains some genital tissue belonging to the opposite sex . . . . When the sex gland becomes weak in the course of the ageing process, it sometimes happens that the tissue of the other sex begins to predominate. This explains the well-known fact that after the menopause women become masculinized to some degree by developing facial hirsutism and acquiring coarser masculine features, a deeper voice, and a gruff manner" [*Man in Structure and in*

Function, N.Y., Knopf, 1960, Vol. II, p. 737, 738]. Kahn has a photograph of a woman who had experienced what he terms "a crass case of masculinization". He says of this woman that until a few years previously she had been completely feminine. One day, however, a tumour had developed due to a proliferation of cells which belonged to the opposite sex and which then flooded her body with male hormone.

173. Short, R. V., "Germ Cell Sex" in *The Genetics of the Spermatozoon*, ed. R. A. Beatty and S. Gleuchksohn-Waelsch, Edinburgh, International Symposium at Edinburgh University, 1972, p. 325.

174. In this connection, Ursula Mittwoch observes: "It is evident that both the evolutionary and the embryological evidence demonstrate that the origin of separate sexes is in hermaphroditism .... We may thus picture the evolution of sex chromosomes as having occurred in three stages. During the first stage individuals were hermaphroditic. This was followed by the second stage in which separation of the sexes was achieved by environmental factors such as temperature .... Lastly, a pair of unequal chromosomes was set aside under whose influence males and females would develop in equal numbers ["Sex Growth and Chromosomes", *New Scientist*, 15 July, 1971, p. 127]. This *could* be viewed as a reflection of what happened at an accelerated rate in the case of Adam and Eve. At first the two sexes were combined in one individual: their separation was effected: and each separated half was then reconstituted as a whole organism in its own right — all this taking place perhaps in a matter of minutes?

175. E. A. Lapham and H. Morowitz, speaking of the *Dicyemida*, point out that these simple creatures develop a structure that may be thought of as a kind of hermaphroditic gonad. This is in a sense the only organ that the Mesozoa possess, and it produces both eggs and sperm. The eggs produced are fertilized by sperm frequently from the same organ ["The Mesozoa", *Sci. Amer.*, Dec., 1972, p. 95]. It is evident that how ever sexual dimorphism has come about in man, among lower animals the division was sometimes highly uneven. According to V. Geodakyan, in the mountains of Armenia on the shores of Lake Sevan, colonies of lizards exist which are entirely female, laying only unfertilized eggs and hatching them, thus breeding strictly by parthenogenesis ["Why Two Sexes?", *Meditsinskyia Gazeta* (Medical Gazeteer), Moscow, 23 Mar., 1966 — trans. Joint Publication Research Service, US Dept. Commerce, Washington, and issued as JPRS No. 35321]. There is a small fish known under the name *Labroides dimidiatus* which is specifically sexed as either male or female but the females have the power of becoming males if the male happens to desert the harem. The most dominant of the ten or so females in the harem begins to change its sex within a few hours of the departure of the male [Ross Robertson, "Sex Changes Under the Waves", *New Scientist*, 31 May, 1973, p. 538].

176. John Burton observes that parthenogenesis takes place in insects, fishes, reptiles and even birds. He notes that it has been clearly established that the eggs are not being fertilized by any males ... though the eggs *can* be! ["Virgin Birth in Vertebrates", *New Scientist*, 9 Aug., 1973, p. 334].
Under the heading *Hermaphrodite*, the *Encylcopedia Britannica* [Vol. 11, 1953, p. 503] makes reference to what is called "functional hermaphroditism in animals, a condition in which both male and female gametes are produced by one and the same individual ... occasionally fish and birds have both sex organs, one on each side. Gynandromorphism leads to two

half-animals (male and female) united in one . . . . (chiefly in insects)".

More recently the National Institute for Agronomical Research in France reported the breeding of bisexual trout which produce both eggs and sperm. "The breeding process is fairly simple and requires feeding young normal trout with small doses of substances which act on the biological sex differentiation. About 30% of those treated become bisexual within two to three years. Each bisexual trout can produce about 1000 normal trout and experiments are just starting to find out exactly how the process can benefit fish farms by giving rise to trout of superior quality" [*New Scientist*, 12 Jan., 1978, p. 93].

177. The common earthworm night crawler *Lumbricus terrestres* is both a complete male and a complete female. It cannot, however, fertilize its own eggs: there is reciprocal cross fertilization in this species. This may be contrasted, therefore, with the behaviour of the Mesozoon *Dicyemida* which can fertilize itself [H. Armstrong, *Creation Res. Soc. Quart.*, Sept., 1972, p. 132]. This is known as *autogamy*.

178. Ulam, Stanislaw M., "How to Formulate Mathematically Problems of Rate of Evolution", *Mathematical Challenges to the Neo-Darwinian Interpretation of Evolution*, Wistar Symposium, Phila., Wistar Institute Press, No. 5, 1967, p. 23.

179. A work was published in 1974 dealing with the clinical, morphologic and cytogenetic aspects of hermaphroditism. The author is Professor W. van Niekerk, Dept. of Obstetrics and Gynaecology in the Tygerberg Hospital, Parow, Cape Province, South Africa. This is perhaps the most complete study of the subject to be published in recent years. Among the case histories in this volume is that of an individual who developed to maturity with a truly hermaphroditic constitution including an active testis and an active ovary. Normal sperm were found in the testis on the left side, and an ovary with numerous follicles and some ova were observed on the right side [*True Hermaphroditism*, Willem A. van Niekerk, N.Y., Harper and Row, 1974, 200 pp., especially p. 112].

180. Money and Erhardt point out that girls with Turner's Syndrome are "more extremely feminine" than normal XX females. They conclude from this that masculinity and femininity are not really discrete entities but lie along a unidimensional continuum which would see pure masculinity at one extreme and pure femininity at the other extreme and a continuous graduated series of mixtures in between. Turner's Syndrome, as they interpret the evidence, places the individual further to the feminine pole than the normal female, thus leading to a "purer" sexual type [Review in *Science*, 180, 1973, p. 587; and *Man and Woman, Boy and Girl*, Baltimore, Johns Hopkins Univ. Press, 1972, p. 107 ff.].

181. Gynecomastia or gynecomazia, a condition where the male mammary glands are well developed and may secrete milk, is a recognized phenomenon, being reported by early writers including Aristotle and referred to by the French as *la couvade*. More recently, the famous physiologist, John Hunter, records the instance of a sailor who, having lost his wife, took his son to his own breast to quiet him and after three or four days was able to nourish him. He also mentions the case of a man of 50 who shared equally with his wife the suckling of their children. In Franklin's *Voyage to the Polar Seas*, he quotes the case of an old Chippewa who, on losing his wife in childbirth, had put

the infant to his breast and earnestly prayed that milk might flow; he was fortunate enough to eventually produce sufficient milk to rear the child [See further on this G. M. Gould and W. L. Pyle, *Anomalies and Curiosities of Medicine*, N.Y., Julian Press, 6th printing, 1966, p. 395-397].

Under the heading "Milk Hormone Produced at the Slightest Touch", the following observation is made: "Prolactin is one of the galaxy of peptide hormones secreted by the anterior pituitary gland and its main function has to do with the production of milk in lactating females. Biologists in Washington University School of Medicine have been looking at the way prolactin secretion is initiated in non-lactating individuals — *both males and females* [my emphasis]. Occasionally milk is produced in individuals following mechanical stimulation of the breasts . . . . Simple stroking of the breast and nipple in the female subjects for five minutes induced a dramatic increase (at least ten times) in the prolactin output of the pituitary. Curiously, when wives manipulated their husband's nipples prolactin output rose". Reference is made in a Note, in *Nature*, 238, 1972, p. 284; quoted in *New Scientist*, 10 Aug., 1972, p. 277].

In a *Bulletin of the New York Academy of Medicine*, there occurred the following observation: "It is not a very uncommon circumstance to find both among human kind and animals, males whose breasts contain milk. Among the lower orders of people in Russia milk in the breasts of men is much more frequent than among the more southern nations . . . ." It may be of interest to note with respect to the last observation that the Scyths who migrated into Russia, according to Hippocrates showed a high incidence of hermaphroditism as though it were almost a racial character, and some sceptics of reports of male breast feeding have suggested that only a hermaphrodite could possibly perform this function. Perhaps Hippocrates' observation sheds some light on this matter. This information was published by the *Medical Librarian*, Evansville, Indiana, in a local paper dated 2 Aug., 1972.

The *San Francisco Chronicle* [6 Nov., 1976] reported a billy goat which was observed by two scientists at Garhwal University in the State of Delhi, India, to be producing milk from normal mammary glands, yet all its other sex organs were clearly male.

As Dr. Wilder Smith points out, both sexes synthesize both male and female hormones. Males synthesize female hormones and females synthesize male hormones. In fact after certain operations it is often necessary to treat the female to prevent the undue expression of the male hormones as a result of the depletion of the female hormone and in old age with the decline of the female glands which produce these hormones, the female body may occasionally assume a number of quite marked male characteristics. Wilder Smith observes wisely that if human ancestry from an evolutionary standpoint is ultimately to be traced through reptiles which do not nurse their young and therefore have no nipples, it is difficult to account for the possession of nipples by the male unless we assume that they served a purpose at some time in the past [*Man's Origin, Man's Destiny*, Wheaton, Shaw, 1960, p. 105]. For this is how the evolutionists must account for nipples in the *female* of the species. He therefore concludes that we have to assume that they were at one time functional, or at least potentially so. If Adam were originally bisexual, his nipples would undoubtedly have been routinely functional and only ceased to be so because Eve was taken out of him.

It has more recently been discovered that males also produce *relaxin*, a substance which softens the pubic bone in the female, allowing the fetus a little more freedom of passage.   In the male it is produced by Leydig cells which also produce the male sex hormone, testosterone.   This was reported by M. P. Dubois, of the National Institute of Agricultural Research, and Jean-Louis Dacheux of the Laboratory of Comparative Physiology in Tours, France [*Cell and Tissue Research*, 187, 1978, p. 201].

It should be said that when, for pathological reasons, the genetic male does not respond to the androgen produced by the testes (a condition known as androgen insensitivity) the body develops with essentially female external genitalia and with female sensitivities, and will almost certainly be assigned a feminine sex role.   This condition is also termed testicular feminization, for obvious reasons.   The male testes therefore produce sufficient estrogen to impress female characters on what should have been a male body.

Thus, a male can give rise to a male or to a female, but a female cannot give rise to a male — or only so rarely that many authorities deny the possibility, and reports of such are probably misrepresentations of the actual facts.   Eve can easily be conceived as having been derived out of Adam, but not Adam out of Eve.   In 1866, Franz Delitzsch, in his *System of Biblical Psychology*, made a remarkable observation regarding the forming of Eve. He said: "Eve is certainly not Adam's child, but Adam himself in a different sex" [See p. 133 of the Baker reprint, 1966].

Even in the matter of the external genitalia, it has so far proved impossible to convert a female to a male by surgical intervention or by the administration of hormones, but the reverse operation is now quite successful when it is considered proper.   An actual case of the conversion of a true male into a female, an event necessitated only as a result of an unfortunate accident, is given by Money and Ehrhardt [*Man and Woman, Boy and Girl*, Baltimore, Johns Hopkins Univ. Press, 1972, p. 95-116 and 118 f., esp. p. 113].

182. Mowatt, Farley, *West Viking*, Toronto, Little, Brown, 1965, p. 147.

183. *Ciba Symposium*, June, 1940, p. 495.

184. Turner, Sharon, *The Sacred History of the World*, London, Longman, 1837, Vol. II, p. 191, footnote.

185. R. V. Short has a very good summary statement at this point: "In this review I would like to consider the essential differences between sexual and somatic tissues in mammals, and the way in which these two cell lines may be subject to separate genetical control mechanisms.

"Natural sex reversal occurs commonly in a number of lower vertebrates (Chan, 1970), and complete, functional sex reversal can be achieved in fish and amphibia by adding steroidal sex hormones to the water in which they are swimming (Ohno, 1967).   There are occasional reports of spontaneous functional sex reversal in birds (Crew, 1923), and if the single ovary of a hen is removed surgically, the contralateral gonadal remnant will develop into a testis and may produce spermatozoa (Miller, 1938).   Partial gonadal reversal occurs when male chick embryos are treated with oestrogen (Erickson and Pincus, 1966), or when embryos of opposite sex develop within the same egg and acquire extensive vascular interconnections (Lutz and Lutz-Ostertag 1959).   In the Virginia opossum, a marsupial, partial gonadal sex reversal can be produced by treating the pouch young with steroids (Burns, 1961). But in mammals, complete functional sex reversal never occurs naturally, and even partial gonadal sex reversal cannot be induced experimentally with steroids (Burns, 1961). It is therefore tempting to conclude that the plasticity of gonadal development in fish, amphibians and birds had to be forsaken in mammals, where the whole embryonic development has to take place within the confines of a uterus which is bathed by maternal hormones. Such a situation demands a much more immutable genetic control if the foetus is to develop its sexuality independently of its mother"["Germ Cell Sex" in *The Genetics of the Spermatozoon*, Proceedings of International Symposium at Edinburgh, August, 1971, ed. R. A. Beatty and S. Gluecksohn-Waelsch, Edinburgh, 1972, p. 325 f.]. His references are:

Chan, S. T. H., "Natural Sex Reversals in Vertebrates", *Phil. Trans. Roy. Soc.*, London, B. 259, 1970, p. 59-71.

Ohno, S., *Sex Chromosomes and Sex-linked Genes*, Berlin, Springer-Verlag, 1967.

Crew, F. A. E., Studies in Intersexuality. II: "Sex-reversal in the Fowl", *Proc. Roy. Soc.*, London, B. 95, 1923, p. 256-278.

Miller, R. A., "Spermatogenesis in a Sex-reversed Female and in Normal Males of the Domestic Fowl, *Gallus domesticus*", *Anat. Rec.*, 70, 1938, p. 155-189.

Erickson, A. E. and G. Pincus, "Modification of embryonic development of reproductive and lymphoid organs in the chick", *J. Embryol. exp. Morph.*, 16, 1966, p. 211-229.

Lutz H. and Y. Lutz-Ostertag, "Free-martinisme spontané chez les Oiseau", *Develop. Biol.*, 1, 1959, p. 364-376.

Burns, R. K., "Role of hormones in the differentiation of sex" in *Sex and Internal Secretions*, 3rd ed., Vol. I, Baltimore, Wilkins, Williams, 1961, p. 76-158.

186. The world famous Vienna psychiatrist, Carl Gustav Jung, was convinced that if personalities could be arranged in some kind of order from superior to inferior, at the very top of the list one would have to place those who somehow seem to combine within themselves in almost equal measure male and female personality traits and characteristics. Jung believed that such people under favourable conditions are likely to achieve "the highest human perspective and creative expression. But this gynandromorphic admixture appears to introduce a peculiar delicacy and a hair-trigger emotional intensity into the human machinery" [quoted by W. H. Sheldon, *The Varieties of Human Physique*, N.Y., Harper Bros., 1946, p. 257]. More recently Getzels and Csikszentmihalyi reported the results of some interesting psychological experiments involving particularly creative people, and came to the following conclusions: "The creative person is not stereotypic in temperament. The male exhibits some of the feminine sensibilities: the female some of the masculine sensibilities. In our own work with artists, the males were more feminine on a sensitivity scale than other males, and the females more masculine on a tough-minded scale than other females" [J. W. Getzels and M. Csikszentmihalyi, "Scientific Creativity", *Sci. J.*, 3, 9, 1967, p. 80, 84].

I think this reflects the same situation. There are differences in temperament and in other significant psychological ways between the sexes which are mutually contributory to the total well-being of both. Where they can be combined in one individual, or where two individuals (man and wife hopefully) can pool their best resources, there we ought to find human potential at its highest levels of creative expression. Presumably, in Adam as first created all these potentials were maximized in a single individual. What is at issue here is not physiological function but temperament.

The best explanation of the facts as presently understood seems to me, in the light of Scripture, to be that the earliest forms of life which multiply by propagation rather than by simple division were almost certainly bisexual, each individual combining the organs of both sexes within his own body: in the higher forms each containing both a functional testis and ovary. Perhaps when God planned the organic world, of which man was to be a working member, He introduced this mode of multiplication in anticipation of the time when man should be likewise created bisexual for reasons already intimated.

187. Many of the examples of acquired characters that seem to have become inheritable which are now being discussed by such men as Waddington, seem to me of dubious value because they could be viewed equally well as pre-adaptations.   This is true of the thickening of the soles of the feet in the human foetus.   It was noted by Darwin and elaborated upon subsequently by R. Semon [*Arch. mikr. Anat.*, 82, 1913, p. 164 ff.], and it has since been discussed by C. H. Waddington in an article entitled "The Evolution of Adaptations" [*Endeavour*, 12 July, 1953, p. 136].   Among evolutionists, it is customary to point to this phenomenon as having resulted from the bipedal locomotion of man which has had the effect of toughening the soles of his feet, an advantageous acquired character which is then inherited after millenia of use.   The human foetus now therefore is born already prepared for walking, in this respect, according to this view.

Waddington refers to a similar situation in connection with the ostrich. This bird has two conveniently located callosities on its breast which bear the brunt of friction and pressure when the bird squats on the ground. According to Waddington, these callosities have become inherited and they are therefore found to be already formed during foetal development ["Experiments in Acquired Characteristics", *Sci. Amer.*, Dec., 1953, p. 92 f.]. However, this particular case is not as straightforward as Waddington makes it appear, for as Sir Gavin de Beer has pointed out, the ostrich is born with other similar callosities which it cannot make use of at all [*Embryos and Ancestors*, Oxford, 1951, p. 87].   It could therefore be argued that we have here a case of the accidental development of callosities due possibly to some gene mutation, two only of which callosities happen to be of some use to the animal.

A somewhat analogous situation has been observed in man in the form of so-called squatting facets of the Indians of Punjab.   These Indians easily assume a restful squatting position which the European finds difficult, because of a modification of the bone structure of the tibia.   No such modification is ever found among chair-users, according to Wood Jones [quoted by Kenneth Walker, *Meaning and Purpose*, London, Penguin, 1951, p. 154], but the Punjabis are born with them.   Is this, then, an acquired character that has become inheritable or is it merely that they have made use of a chance modification once they discovered its advantages?

Such proposed examples of inherited acquired characters have, it seems to me, doubtful validity.   On the other hand, there is much experimental evidence on the genuine inheritance of acquired characters in many forms of life from the simplest to the more complex which seem most easily to be accounted for by assuming that they are inherited cytoplasmicly rather than via the nuclear genes.   Some further observations on this point will be found in a later reference, #217.

One of the most eloquent supporters in recent times of what may be called Neo-Lamarckism was the English naturalist, Professor F. Wood Jones. In his *Trends of Life*, he has a whole chapter titled, "The Inheritance of Adaptations", which is well worth examining [London, Arnold, 1953]. And in the same year, Dr. Carlos Monge reported an impressive example of what seems clearly to be a case of an acquired character being inherited in man. Monge found that Andean highlanders had developed considerably larger chests, presumably a compensation for the rarified atmosphere in which they live.   The interesting thing is that many of their descendants who came down and have now lived along the sea-coast for many generations, still have the same large deep chests and broad shoulders of the highlanders. If this were simply a superficial response of the highlanders to the need for an increased lung capacity, one would expect it to disappear quickly in their lowland descendants.   That it has not done so, seems to indicate that the character became inheritable ["Biological Basis of Human Behaviour" in *Anthropology Today*, ed. A. L. Kroeber, Chicago Univ. Press, 1953, p. 127 ff.].   Why this lung enlargement should become heritable but not the black-smith's muscular build, is hard to say.   The mechanism is obviously not a simple one.

188. Weismann, August, *op. cit.*, (ref. #33), Vol. I, p. 419 ff.

189. Huxley, Sir Julian, "Inheritance of Acquired Characteristics" in *Essays in Popular Science*, Penguin, 1938, p. 36, 37.

190. Pearl, Raymond, "Biology and Human Trends", *Smithsonian Institute Report*, Washington, 1935, p. 331.

191. Briggs, Robert and Thomas King, "Nucleoplasmic Interactions in Eggs and Embryos" in *The Cell: Biochemistry, Physiology, and Morphology*, ed. J. Brachet and A. E. Mirsky, N.Y., Academic Press, Vol. I, 1959, p. 539.
      There is some evidence that some of the body cells retain the full potential of the germ cells. Writing in *Science* under the heading "Some Characteristics of a Continuously Propagating Cell Derived from Monkey Heart Tissue", J. E. Salk and Elsie N. Wood report that it has been possible by the right techniques to isolate heart tissue cells and induce them to go on multplying indefinitely [126, 1967, p. 1338].   The phenonmenon suggests that some of the potential for immortality which is characteristic of germ cells may have been retained even by the body cells which have differentiated some distance from the originating germ plasm.
      Recently *MD of Canada* reported that Dr. John Gurdon and his co-workers at Oxford had grown fully mature and fertile frogs from single body cells extracted from the intestinal lining of other frogs.   With his present technique more than 30% of the intestinal cells could be made to grow at least to the tadpole stage [10, *3*, 1969, p. 53].   Neither lines of proliferating cells were human.   It must surely be assumed that the fall of man has made his body cells unlike all other animal cells.

192. In a manner of speaking, Weismann was both right and wrong in assuming that differentiating cells lose the totipotency of the initiating ovum to the extent that such cells are no longer individually capable of giving rise to a whole animal but only to specific organs and tissues.   In plants, of course, the cells in a slip taken from almost any part of the plant are capable of reproducing the whole organism, roots and all.   But experiments have now shown that complex animal forms may also be reproduced by highly refined techniques from cells which have long since differentiated into specific tissues and have lost their identity as germ plasm.

The technique involves extracting the nuclei from tissue cells and transferring them to enucleated cells of germ plasm origin. Such reconstructed cells are evidently capable of initiating the process of cell cleavage and division and proceeding normally through embryological and foetal development to maturity. It no longer seems likely, therefore, that cell differentiation is due to the loss of gene material *in the nucleus* during earlier stages of cell division but rather to changes in the cytoplasm; although Briggs and King were able to demonstrate that nuclei of cells taken from tissue which has formed later in foetal development less frequently retain their totipotency than do nuclei of cells derived from tissue formed earlier in the developing embryo. It therefore seems likely that even the nucleus may change slightly with time, although it is fairly certain now that the major change occurring within the cell relates to the chemistry or organization or structure of the cytoplasm as successive cell divisions occur. The differentiated cytoplasm interacts with the nucleus and this in turn leads to the emergence of new directions for cell development along specific lines towards the growth of tissues and organs which form the body or housing for the original germ plasm.

Professor Bernard D. Davis, Harvard Medical School, stated: "We now know that all the differentiated somatic cells of an animal (those of muscle, skin, and the like) contain in their nuclei the same complete set of genes. Every somatic cell contains all the genetic information required for copying the whole organism. In different cells, different sub-sets of genes are acting while the remainder are inactive. Accordingly, if it should become possible to reverse the *regulatory mechanism* responsible for this differentiation, any cell could be used to start the embryo. Though differentiation is completely reversible in the cells of plants (as in the transfer of cuttings), it is ordinarily quite irreversible in the cells of the higher animals. The stability, however, depends on the interaction of the nucleus with the surrounding cytoplasm . . . ." ["Prospects for Genetic Intervention in Man", *Science,* 170, 1970, p. 1280, 1281].

Cell differentiation is therefore mainly the result of modifications of the cytoplasm rather than the nucleus. A. C. Enders and S. J. Schlafke, in a Ciba Foundation Symposium, observe that the cytoplasm of cells, even by the time the blastocyst has formed, is clearly different from the cytoplasm of the ovum. "During the late cleavage stages and the blastocyst stage, the structure of the cytoplasm alters a great deal in most species. Characteristically, there is a diminution and re-organization of the cytoplasmic inclusions . . . ." ["The Fine Structure of the Blastocyst: Some Comparative Studies" in *Preimplantation Stages of Pregnancy*, ed. G. E. W. Wolstenholme and M. O'Connor, London, Churchill, 1965, p. 45, 47]. Alfred Kuhn puts the matter this way: "It is certain that the nuclei of some tissues need not forfeit some of their talents to reach a certain stage: rather they can replace the egg nucleus, and their derivatives can satisfy all the demands of the developmental steps which the various cells must pass through" [*Lectures in Developmental Physiology*, tr. Roger Milkman, N.Y., Springer-Verlag, 1971, p. 488]. It seems, therefore, that the cell *nuclei* retain their totipotency to a far greater extent than the cytoplasm. In the natural order of things, cells do fairly quickly become differentiated and lose their totipotency — except perhaps in plants. While *most* of the cells to which the totipotent ovum gives rise soon become differentiated cytoplasmicly for the development of body cells, not all of them do. A few remain for the perpetuation of the germ cell line. It is these few that form the thread of continuity from generation to generation.

The following readily accessible articles dealing with this subject are useful: J. B. Gurdon, "Transplanted Nuclei and Cell Differentiation", *Sci. Amer.*, Dec., 1968, pp. 24-35; C. H. Waddington, "How Do Cells Differentiate?", *Sci. Amer.*, Sept., 1953, pp. 108-114; Michail Fischberg and A. W. Blackler, "How Cells Specialize", *Sci. Amer.*, Sept., 1961, pp. 124-140; Robert Briggs and Thomas J. King, "Changes in the Nuclei of Differentiating Endoderm Cells as Revealed by Nuclear Transplantation", *J. Morphology*, 100, 2, 1957, pp. 269-311; Lewis Wolpert, "Developing Cells Know Their Place", *New Scientist*, 14 May, 1970, p. 322 f.

193. Raven, Christian P., *An Outline of Developmental Physiology*, tr. L. de Ruiter, N.Y., McGraw Hill, 1954, p. 62.

194. Weismann, August, "Upon the Eternal Duration of Life", *op. cit.*, (ref. # 33), Vol. I, p. 139.

195. Parthenogenesis is so well established for so many species that it scarcely needs the reinforcement of this note. However, for those who may not be aware of how widely it has been demonstrated below man, the following brief comment may be useful. Few proven cases of *mammalian* parthenogenesis *in nature* have ever been clearly established, though as we have already seen (ref. # 175) it has been observed for lizards and is common enough among insects and some fish. To the list of insects in which parthenogenesis occurs naturally, B. I. Balinsky adds aphids, phyllopods, and rotifers at certain times of the year, and of course bees in which the fertilized egg produces a female and the unfertilized egg develops into a male [*An Introduction to Embryology*, Toronto, Saunders, 1970, 3rd ed., p. 126].

The situation is very different in the laboratory where experiment has shown that a very wide range of animal forms can be induced to propagate parthenogenetically. According to Albert Tyler, "Extensive investigations . . . . have shown that in practically all the main groups of animals, normal development can be obtained by artificial activation of eggs" ["Artificial Parthenogenesis", *Biol. Reviews*, Cambridge Univ., 16, 1941, p. 292 f.]. Reports include such species as silkworms, caterpillars, sea urchins, star fish, frogs, fish (including carp), lizards, birds and rabbits. In 1896 R. Hertwig found that sea urchin eggs could be activated by chloroform or strychnine! ["Ueber die Entwicklung des ubefruchteten Seeigeleies", *Festschr. f. gegenbauer*, Leipzig, 1896]. H. Spurway reports experimental parthenogenesis in the guppy, *Lebistes reticulatus* ["Spontaneous Parthenogenesis in a Fish", *Nature*, 171, 1953, p. 437]. In the case of rabbit ova cultivated in vitro, Dr. Chambly in France almost fifty years ago was probably the first to demonstrate that mammals can give birth to viable offspring parthenogenetically [see Gregory Pincus, "Fertilization in Mammals", *Sci. Amer.*, Mar., 1951, p. 47]. There is some evidence of man-induced parthenogenesis in sheep, though I am not sure how dependable this is [Arthur Koestler, *Beyond Reductionism*, London, Hutchinson, 1969, p. 199].

196. "A human egg is a spherical cell . . . . which is one of the largest cells in the body, and when placed against a dark background it is just visible to the naked eye . . . . The large size of the egg cell is due mainly to deposits of yolk in the cytoplasm . . . . In contrast to the egg, the sperm is the smallest cell in the body . . . . The volume of an egg cell is about 85,000 times that of a sperm" [Ursula Mittwoch, *Genetics of Sex Differentiation*, N.Y., Academic Press, 1973, p. 84, 85].

197. It is established that an ovum can be activated without fertilization by the spermatozoon, and in certain cases will go on to full development of a mature female animal, complete with a functioning reproductive system which thus provides the initiating ovum with a mechanism for continuing itself indefinitely. To this extent, the ovum is self-sufficient. The sperm does not appear to be so, under natural conditions.

It was at one time supposed that the limitations imposed upon the spermatozoon was entirely due to lack of energy because of the small amount of cytoplasm surrounding the nucleus. It simply starved before reaching sufficient maturity to extract food from its environment. By reducing its food requirements, at very low temperatures for example, its life can be greatly extended, and certainly in warmblooded animals the temperature of sperm is quite critical to its survival, and unless the testes descend to the scrotum free from the deep body temperature, they are not viable. Excessive use of hot baths in Japan reduced male fertility.

However, there appears to be some other factor limiting sperm life. George Corner observed: "If an ovum is cut into two pieces, one of which has no nucleus, and the latter is then entered by a sperm, it too will divide and become an embryo, though admittedly not as often as in the case of the unfertilized ovum" [*The Hormones in Human Reproduction*, N.Y., Atheneum, 1963, p. 19]. This kind of highly sophisticated manipulation of cells in the laboratory is very different from anything that occurs in Nature whereas the variety of treatments that can lead to parthenogenesis of the ovum is so diverse that at least some of them must probably occur under natural conditions.

Dorthea Rudnick, in her article on *Embryology* in the 1960 edition of the McGraw-Hill *Encyclopedia of Science and Technology* [Vol. IV, p. 573], after pointing out that the sperm itself is by no means essential for the activation of the egg, suggests that the mature egg must be thought of as a system containing all the potential factors for development and the sperm essentially as a trigger that sets off the mechanism. It is, of course, also the source of the paternal set of chromosomes. But it seems clear that it is not at all the same kind of self-contained unicellular organism capable of independent existence that the ovum is. Under natural conditions, by itself it will die, whereas the ovum, left alone, is in no necessity of doing so provided only that it is given a suitable environment and an appropriate though remarkably non-specific stimulation to activate it. If the ovum can thus survive by itself, it can hardly be argued that the sperm contains any absolutely essential component for its activation, since apparently the ovum can be activated without it.

198. The ovum can be activated and developed into a fully mature organism by an amazingly diverse range of stimuli. According to Albert Tyler, "It is clear that there is very little specificity in regard to activating agents. Thus eggs of the sea urchin can be activated by such diverse agents as puncture, heat, cold, ultra-violet radiation, radium emanation, acids, bases, isotonic salt solutions, hypertonic and hypotonic solutions, fat solvents and some alkaloids. This contrasts with the high degree of specificity in fertilization (in nature) . . . ." ["Artificial Parthenogenesis", *Biol. Reviews*, Cambridge Univ., 16, 1941, p. 318].

To these non-specific stimuli have since been added others, including electric shock. The carp eggs mentioned above (ref. # 195) were actually activated by human saliva. Professor Christian P. Raven of the University of Utrecht has added to this growing list of activators such physical treatment as illumination, induction shock and osmotic pressure as well as chemical agents such as urea and saponin [*op. cit.*, (ref. #193), p. 20].

I do not know whether I am reading too much into the evidence, but I think it worth noting that Balinsky observed that most of the agents used are of such a nature that they probably damage the ovum to a greater or lesser degree, and if applied too vigorously they cause the death of the cell. He then adds, "It is reasonable to suppose, then, that activation of the egg involves some kind of sublethal damage to the egg cytoplasm" [*An Introduction to Embryology*, Toronto, Saunders, 1970, p. 127]. Possibly the *human* sperm fertilizes (and so activates) the ovum but at the same time introduces some type of damage to the cytoplasm which is not merely sublethal but lethal. One need only hypothesize that this lethal effect becomes operative only after the original single cell (the ovum) has divided several times into a number of proportionally *smaller* cells, the proportion of cytoplasm to nucleus accordingly being reduced and presumably modified. It is known that with successive divisions there is a progressive change in the amount of cytoplasm as well as in its internal organization and its chemistry. The nucleus meanwhile retains its original size and constitution. Raven remarks: "The local concentration of certain substances will initiate chemical reactions which previously were unable, or almost unable, to take place because of the dilution of the reagents or because of the presence of inhibiting substances" [*op. cit.*, (ref. #193), p. 63]. Transferred to the present context, this observation could very nicely point the way to the actual mechanism whereby some contribution from the cytoplasm of the sperm cell finally becomes lethal in its effect on the growing organism.

A perceptive reader may discern the importance of the finding of the non-specificity of the activating agent. I think the introduction of the word *activate* is significant in the present context because it would be such an appropriate word to apply to the "overshadowing" by the Holy Spirit (Luke 1:35). The preparation of the perfect body that was to be animated for the Lord Himself was truly a miracle in that a *male* child was born. But the stage was clearly already designed for just such a tremendous event, when the event is viewed in its physiological context. Nevertheless, it is important to bear in mind that some *creative* power must still have been at work to supply the Y chromosome in order that a man child might be born, not a female child as would otherwise have been the case.

199. Where birds are concerned, parthenogenesis is always found to result in males. This is because, for some unknown reason, the sex determining roles of the X and Y chromosomes have been reversed. Thus M. W. Olsen and S. J. Marsden, in reporting on "Natural Parthenogenesis in Turkey Eggs", note that in spite of the fact that there had been no male contribution, all the parthenogenetic embryos carried the diploid chromosome number and all the eggs which reached a sufficient stage of maturity to allow for sex determination were found to be male. Seventy-nine turkey hens were involved in this experiment. Males were rigidly excluded. During the eight week period in question, 2537 eggs were laid, of which 568 showed parthenogenetic development. Forty-nine of these differentiated to the extent that blood vessels were clearly visible. In twenty-seven, embryos were identifiable on gross examination. Four of these allowed sex to be determined. All were male [*Science*, 120, 1954, p. 545].

Interestingly, Origen (c. 185 - c. 254) in his *Contra Celsius* [I, 37] mentions that in his time, vultures were reputed to raise parthenogenetic young.

200. B. Bacetti and B. A. Afzelius, in their definitive study of the sperm cell [*op. cit.*, ref. #122], have remarked specifically upon the very high percentage of defective sperm.   See further on this at reference #217.

201. It is often said that Weismann's views have since been proven in error in certain important respects and that it is therefore unwise to quote him in the light of what we now know.   This is unfortunate because the lucidity and insight with which he presented his ideas makes them a most suitable vehicle for communicating some very complex aspects of early embryologic- al events and his contribution to our basic understanding has been tremend- ous in terms of the stimulus of his powers of description.   He appears to have been in error in one of his conclusions, though the error has not other- wise damaged his general thesis regarding the continuity of the germ plasm. In one other matter he was mistaken but only in the sense that he visualized the wrong mechanism for the right results.   Thus his questionable contrib- utions are really limited to the two following points: (1) the role of the second polar body or cell which is cast out by the ovum in its earliest stages of preparation for the admission of the sperm; and (2) the mechanism by which body cells are differentiated from germ cells, and the claim that only the germ plasm retains all the developmental capability of forming a new organism.   [See his "Continuity of the Germ Plasm as the Foundation of a Theory of Heredity", *op. cit.*, ref. #33, Vol. I, p. 214, 225].

With respect to the role of this second polar body, this small cell is ex- pelled from the ovum immediately prior to the penetration of the sperm, removing from the ovum half its chromosomes and thus reducing it to a haploid cell so that the contribution of the sperm nucleus will restore it as a normal diploid cell rather than overburdening it with supernumerary chromosomes.   Weismann surmised that this polar cell probably removed the male component of the heretofore hermaphroditic ovum (no one knew anything at that time about the X and Y chromosomes) and thus opened the way for the sperm's contribution to enter unchallenged.   It is not be- lieved at present that this is so.

Weismann believed that the ovum could conceivably be fertilized by this polar body rejoining the ovum, or possibly even before it had broken away and gained its independence.   In any case, Weismann may not have com- mitted himself altogether to the view that the nucleus of the ovum was hermaphroditic, but was merely stating that this was the opinion of some of his contemporaries.   He had in mind C. S. Minot and F. N. Balfour in part- icular.   The latter had said, "the function of forming polar cells has been acquired by the ovum for the express purpose of preventing parthenogen- esis" [*A treatment of Comparative Embryology*, London, Macmillan, 1880, Vol. I, p. 63].

With respect to his second point, we have already seen that the *nuclei* of some somatic cells, contrary to Weismann's surmise, do apparently contain the whole original complement of the germ cells, but in most animal species the cytoplasm of these somatic cells does not.   There is therefore a real loss of potential *in the cell as a whole*.   Thus Weismann was effectually correct, only he was wrong about the mechanism.

Bernard D. Davis notes in this connection: "Every somatic cell contains all the *genetic* information required for copying the whole organism.   In different cells different subsets of genes are active, while the remainder are inactive.   Accordingly, if it should become possible to reverse the regulatory mechanism responsible for this differentiation, any cell could be used to

start an embryo" ["Prospects for Genetic Intervention in Man", *Science,*
170, 1970, p. 1280]. In some species body cells of some organs do seem to
retain the potential of acting as germ cells for a new organism. In frogs, for
example, it has been demonstrated that some body cells have retained the
totipotency of the germ cells. To this extent therefore Weismann was mistaken in supposing that the *nuclei* of the germ cells lost some of their
character in the formation of somatic cells. The nucleus of the germ cell
loses nothing except *the power to express itself* fully, surrendering this
totipotency in response to changes in cytoplasmic determinants. This cytoplasmic change has been termed 'chemodifferentiation'. As Robert Briggs
and Thomas J. King conclude, the process of organogenesis appears to be
due to the localized development "of certain cytoplasmic materials . . . . The
zygote nuclei play no specific role in this localization" [*op. cit.*, ref. #191,
p. 540]. Thus the nucleus, whatever its potency per se, is evidently subservient to the cytoplasm and will generate what the cytoplasm allows.

Balinsky points out that Weismann has been chiefly criticized for his
observation that it is the "unequal fission of the nuclear material which
introduces differentiation in developing tissues" [*An Introduction to
Embryology,* Toronto, Saudners, 1970, p. 139]. But one only need correct
this to read "unequal fission of the *cytoplasmic* materials" instead of
nuclear materials in order to make it a perfectly valid statement. In the
circumstances, this is a small error and a remarkable tribute to Weismann's
insight. His basic concept of the continuity of the germ plasm remains
essentially unchallenged.

202. Walker, Kenneth, *op. cit.*, ref. #32, p. 63.

203. Pearse, A. S., *General Zoology,* N.Y., Henry Holt, 1930, p. 379.

204. Huettner, Alfred F., *Fundamentals of Comparative Embryology of the Vertebrates,* N.Y., Macmillan, rev. ed., 1968, p. 6, 7.

205. Sherrington, Sir Charles, *Man on His Nature,* Cambridge, 1950, p. 94, 95.

206. The number of cells which initially retain the full potential of the germ
plasm at the moment when the first specialized cells begin to appear as body
cells varies in different species, but thus far it appears that it is remarkably
small. According to M. Fischberg and A. W. Blackler, the beginning of differentiation of cells in the gall midge, *Mayetiola destructor,* must be placed
about the third division when there are only eight cells ["How Cells Specialize", *Sci. Amer.*, Sept., 1961 p. 134].

207. Kuhn, Alfred, *Lectures in Developmental Physiology,* tr. Roger Milkman,
N.Y., Springer-Verlag, 1871, p. 481.

208. Money, John and A. A. Ehrdardt, *Man and Woman, Boy and Girl,* Baltimore,
Johns Hopkins Univ. Press, 1972, p. 37. The once active controversy as to
neogenesis (the origination of oocytes *de novo*) in post-natal life seems to
have been laid to rest by a general consensus of opinion that there is an
un-renewable stock of oocytes at birth. On this point, see P. L. Krohn,
"The Biology of Ageing", *Nature,* 11 Jan., 1958, p. 74; and Gregory Pincus,
"Reproduction" in *Ann. Rev. of Physiol.*, 24, 1962, p. 57. Ursula Mittwoch
observes, "Cell division in human oogonia occurs only during foetal life . . . .
At the time of birth the oogonia have already been transformed into primary
oocytes" [*op. cit.*, ref. #196, p. 87].

209. Michie, Donald, in *A Century of Darwin,* ed. S. A. Barnett, London, Heine-

man, 1958, p. 57.

210. Hardy, Sir Alister, *This Living Stream*, London, Collins, 1965, p. 76.

211. Fischberg, M. and A. W. Blackler, "How Cells Specialize", *Sci. Amer.*, Sept., 1961, p. 134.

212. Kahn, Fritz, *Man in Structure and Function*, N.Y., Knopf, 1960, Vol. II, p. 704,705.

213. McClung, C. E., quoted by Susanne Langer, *Mind: An Essay on Human Feeling*, Baltimore, Johns Hopkins Press, 1967, Vol. I, p. 408 fn.

214. Mottram, V. H., *The Physical Basis of Personality*, London, Penguin, 1949, p. 25.

215. An editorial comment in the world renowned medical journal, *Lancet*, under the heading, "Parthenogenesis in Mammals?", has this observation: "The possibility that a woman might become pregnant without at least one spermatozoon having entered the uterus is not one which 'reasonable men' would likely entertain.   Scientific opinion for several centuries has sided with the reasonable man; but today, biologists and cytogeneticists in particular would be less dogmatic in discussing such a possibility" [5 Nov., 1955, p. 967].

   The writer then notes the number of species of animals in which parthenogenesis has been observed to have occurred in nature or under laboratory conditions, and asks, "In view of this, we may have to re-examine the justification for our belief that spontaneous parthenogenesis is rare in vertebrates and absent in mammals. If it were rare in mammals but *occasionally* present would it in fact be noticed?"

   Subsequently he observes further: "There are sound reasons which might lead biologists, if not to expect parthenogenesis occasionally in mammals, at least to look out for it".   He suggests that "man is clearly the mammal in which parthenogenesis would be least likely to pass unnoticed".   But I submit that this is a questionable assumption.   I think it was Sir Peter Medawar, Director of the Medical Research Council in England, who said that the claim by an unwed mother of a fatherless child would not be believed, and in a married woman would not be noticed.   I think he was correct, human nature being what it is.   But the editorial comment does point out that immunological make-up of a parthenogenetic child would be such that "it could be recognized with absolute certainty" by appropriate medical techniques.   The point is that being so born, such a daughter would theoretically share the genetic constitution of the mother completely, and it should be possible therefore to make a skin graft from the daughter back to the mother with complete success.   There would be other possible tests of a like nature also.

   Subsequent correspondence stirred up enough interest in England at the time that an invitation went out publicly to any woman who believed she had given birth to a parthenogenetic daughter to submit to supervised medical examination along such lines.   Later correspondence in *Lancet* of June 30 of the following year (1956) indicated that nineteen corespondents had presented themselves for examination.

   Dr. Helen Spurway, Lecturer in Biometry and Eugenics at University College, London, was invited to conduct these tests.   And to make a long story short, of these nineteen pairs of mothers and daughters, eleven were eliminated after interview for various reasons, and blood tests eliminated another four.   Of the remaining four, three were eliminated due to such factors as incompatible eye or hair colour, etc.   This left only one mother-daughter pair as a genuine test case.

A battery of tests were conducted between these two which, for the most part favoured the mother's claim. However, a skin graft from the daughter to the mother began to show signs of rejection after six weeks and was later easily wiped off with damp cotton wool. Spurway points out that the daughter would not be completely genetically identical with the mother, since during *meiosis* the ovum would have made a selection of only 50% of the original genes in the mother's body cells and the daughter could not therefore have a completely identical constitution. It is possible, as a consequence, that even this test may not be sufficiently valid by itself.

Spurway concluded, therefore, that "rigorous proof is impossible, though it remains true that all the evidence obtained from serological and special tests is consistent with what would be expected in a case of parthenogenesis". As she noted, the absence of any knowledge on the woman's part of such a possibility "adds to the probability of such a claim being well founded. This mother's claim must not only be considered seriously but it must also be admitted that we have been unable to disprove it".

216. de Beer, Sir Gavin, review appearing in *Sci. Amer.*, Sept., 1962, p. 268.

217. C. L. Prosser observed: "Several types of non-genic inheritance and of indirect effects of environmental selection on the genotype are recognized. Cytoplasmic inheritance is being discovered in more and more groups of organisms, and cytoplasm is more readily influenced by environment than is the nucleus" ["The *Origin* After a Century: Prospects for the Future", *Amer. Scientist*, 47, 1959, p. 545]. He instances cytoplasmic particles which may be transmitted — for example, the granules for the Kappa factor in paramecium or the plastidids of certain plants; also cytoplasmic factors are involved in the inheritance of serotypes in ciliates.

In his small but challenging and lucidly written little book, *Nucleo-Cytoplasmic Relations in MicroOrganisms* [Oxford, 1953], Boris Ephrussi underscored the fact that body cells can be made to "breed true for a practically indefinite time". We have seen this, of course, in connection with Alexis Carrel's chicken heart tissue [see page 10]. We have already noted that Hayflick's apparently contradictory data may have been at fault through cultivation in an inadequate medium [see ref. # 123]. Ephrussi therefore argues that since such cells have precisely the same nuclei that the originating fertilized ovum possessed, these lines of body cells ought to begin to revert to the undifferentiated ovum type of cell if the nucleus alone is providing the blueprint for their development. It has to be concluded, therefore, that these body cells do not revert because some other inheritable blueprint exists in the cell *apart from the information in the nucleus*. Such information must be contained in the cytoplasm. So muscle cells replicate as muscle cells, for example, because the cytoplasm is instructing them to do so and not because of guidance provided by the nucleus. That muscle cells do not replicate suddenly as some other kind of cell, forces us to believe that each kind of tissue is formed of cells with a unique cytoplasm. But this cytoplasm can be acted upon by the environment and changed in its constitution so that a given type of cell may begin to build a new type of tissue. This has a bearing, probably, on the phenomenon mentioned by Sir Peter Medawar in which a completely functioning ball and socket joint may form in an entirely exceptional location [*The Art of the Soluble*, London, Methuen, 1967, p. 26].

In view of the fidelity with which particular tissue cells will go on repliccating themselves, Ephrussi says: "Here we have identical perpetuation, but in this case the inherited differences can hardly be ascribed to nuclear genes, for the different cell types which make up (the organism) are all derived from the egg cell by equational mitosis. They must therefore all possess the same genotype . . . . The differential must have its seat in the cytoplasm" [*op, cit.*, p. 4].

Ephrussi then proceeds to detail the work done with unicellular paramecia which multiply by conjugation, showing clearly that they can pass on certain modifications (in particular, a kind of mortogenic or "killer" factor) not via nuclear genes but via plasmagenes. As he says: "These studies confirm the view that the cytoplasm, like the genes, is endowed with genetic continuity. The genes are therefore no longer to be regarded as the sole cell-constituent endowed with this property" [p. 6].

Ephrussi sums up his conclusions thus: "Considering that embryonic development results in a restriction (and some widening, too) in different cell lineages of the manifold potentialities originally carried by the egg, we may picture the process of differentiation as consisting, for example, in the segregation or sorting out, of an initially mixed population of cytoplasmic particles. Or we may suppose that the egg, to begin with, contains a mixed population of inactive particles, and that development consists in the activation by nuclear genes of different sorts of lineages" [p. 100].

If we assume the former, it is clear that some foreign substance entering the germ cell cytoplasm at some critical stage of its internal organization, could effect a change that in due time will rob it of its power of endless self replication — will, in short, rob it of its potential immortality. This poison may have gained entry in the cytoplasm of the fertilizing spermatozoon. But there is also another possible route.

B. Baccetti and B. A. Afzelius have recently published a work on the *Biology of the Sperm Cell* [see ref. # 122] which reflects the ever growing interest in the cytoplasm, by contrast with the preoccupation with the nucleus which has tended to prevail for some years. They speak of the mitochondria in the sperm cytoplasm which appear to have proteinaceous crystal inclusions that may account for as much as 50% or more of the sperm volume in some species. There is as yet no manifest function for these crystals except possibly as a source of nutrition for the fertilized ovum, somewhat analogous to the yolk granule.

Since the sperm mitochondrion is small compared with the egg volume, and since normally only one sperm, or at the most a few spermatozoa penetrate the egg, the idea seems far-fetched. ᠆On the other hand, the spermatozoa that are *not* taken up by the fertilized ovum perish by the hundred million in the vicinity of it and their cumulative proteinaceous crystal may in the aggregate form a substantial reservoir of nutrient.

We thus have here a situation where the quantity of sperm cytoplasm available to the growing ovum may be quite significant in its influence on the cytoplasm of the ovum, by absorption from its immediate environment. It may well play a significant role in its early stages of development, and it is these early stages of development — the first four or five doublings of the zygote — that the germ line cells are set aside and the body cells begin their differentiation.

There is increasing evidence of the critical importance of the cytoplasm and of changes in its composition after successive cleavages, as soon as the embryo has reached the stage of development which witnesses the initiation of cell differentiation and the formation of body cells as opposed to the mere replication of germ plasm.

A. I. Caplan and C. P. Ordahl have now proposed, as the result of a very elegant series of experiments, that, "The expression of those genes necessary . . . . to give rise to diverse cell types is wholly dependent on exposure of cell nuclei to a small portion of egg cytoplasm . . . . The general state of the cell and the activity of the cell's cytoplasm provide important signals for the developmental programs . . . . The segregation of cytoplasm during cleavage establishes extranuclear environments that are determinants to the developing organism" ["Irreversible Gene Repression Model for Control of Development", *Science*, **120**, 1978, p. 120-130].

It is possible therefore that the poison may remain quiescent and effectively neutralized in the multiplying cells of the fertilized ovum until the cleavage has proceeded to the point of either eliminating a certain *quantity* of cytoplasm by reduction in cell size, or modifying certain cytoplasmic *factors* that had hitherto served as neutralizers. Thereafter, the progressive change in the composition of the cytoplasm subjects the cell increasingly to the original protoplasmic poison which renders all *body* cells mortal as a consequence.

Baccetti and Afzelius point out in their study that many human spermatozoa have bizarre shapes and these are probably the results of faults in the spermiogenesis. For each particular man a sperm sample will show many differently shaped, abnormal spermatozoa, the percentage of which is characteristic of that individual and apparently constant throughout the years. Moreover, a number of diseases such as the common cold can cause a temporary increase in the number of abnormal sperm cells. This demonstrates the fact that the sperm are susceptible to damage from their environment. The authors believe that in spite of the high incidence of defective or abnormal sperm, they actually have little consequence for fertilization itself unless the proportion of normal sperm is exceptionally low. For the defective sperm do not reach the ovum: or they fail to penetrate it. "The many defective spermatozoa are somehow prevented from attaining the fertilizing site" [*op. cit.*, ref. #122, p. 19, 158, 160].

Thus within the developing ovum in its initial stages, two lines of cells soon appear: germ cells and body cells. The determinant that brings about subsequent differentiation of body cells in accordance with their destiny as various organs and their loss of potency as germ cells, appears to reside in the cytoplasm. When the germ line cells are set aside, it is by a kind of quarantine which permits the body cells to be progressively differentiated by factors in their cytoplasm. The process of differentiation evidently exposes them to some mortogenic factor derived perhaps from their source of nourishment. At any rate there seems little doubt that the differentiating body cell lines are established and maintained by cytoplasmic determinants, because the nuclei in all the cells (germ and body alike) remain unchanged.

That unicellular forms (amoeba for example) which are "by nature" immortal may be mortalized by a change in diet has been demonstrated repeatedly. And the mortalized amoeba are now altered in the composition of their cytoplasm, not in the composition of the nucleus. If mortalized amoeba cytoplasm is transferred to immortal amoeba, the latter become mortalized ["How Immortal Are Amoeba?", a note in *Nature*, **217**, 1968, p. 706, 707]. There therefore seem to be now in operation all the mechanisms we require, theoretically, to account for the situation that exists in the human species for whom physical death comes as an *unnatural* termination to life.

It might be thought that if animals die and the process of fertilization is very similar, must we not then suppose that the same poison in their case is having the same effect via a similar route? Then do animals die for the same reason that man does . . . . because they, too, have somehow been poisoned? The answer to this may, I think, lie in one of two directions. First, we do not know for certain that death *is* inevitable for animals, except as a result of "accident". It is statistically certain that every animal will die but it may not be inevitable biologically, as we have seen in Part I; and it is, in my view, certainly not a *penalty*. So that in the sense in which we speak of death as having "entered" (Rom.5:12) for man as a result of the Fall, we have no necessary reason to suppose that death as penalty has "entered" into the stream of *animal* life. The second point is that we do know that Adam and Eve were not subject to death at first. What we may only *surmise* about animals, namely, that they have a potential for physical immortality, we may know with considerable assurance about man from what we are told in Genesis. He was "killed" by ingesting a forbidden fruit. Thus for man we might expect to find, and I believe we should seriously look for, the mechanism whereby mortality as an acquired character has been transmitted. There is no particular reason to assume that such a mechanism exists among other living things: indeed, we know that for millions of living things such a mechanism does *not* exist, for they are truly potentially immortal.

218. Hancock, J. L., "The Sperm Cell", *Science J.*, June, 1970, p. 32.

219. Weismann, August, *op. cit.*, ref. # 33, Vol. I, p. 26.

220. On this see a useful and readily accessible statement by R. L. Watterson, Chairman of Biological Sciences, Northwestern University, in the McGraw Hill *Encyclopedia of Science and Technology*, 1960, Vol. III, p. 168.

    Alfred Kuhn has much to say on this subject: "Only in the germ line through the first germ cell and all the way to mature gametes [the seeds of future generations, ACC] do the chromosomes retain their original integrity. A variety of observations show now that behaviour of the chromosomes depends on the cytoplasm region in which they are found during division . . . . *Even the tiniest inequality within the cytoplasm* reverberates back and forth, resulting in the most extreme disparities among the resulting cells" [emphasis mine; *op. cit.*, ref. # 207, p. 482, 483]. At reference # 192 the reader will find part of his discussion on the importance of the ratio between cytoplasmic and nuclear material and the influence of cleavage upon this ratio.

221. In 1893, James Orr published his *Christian View of God and the World*. In this he laid great stress upon the importance of the body in the constitution of man. He first asked, "Is human death — that crowning evil, which carries so many other sorrows in its train — the result of sin, or is it not?" [N.Y., Scribner, 1893, p. 196 ff]. And then he proceeded to show that physical death was never God's original plan for man: that Redemption "is not a Redemption of the soul only, but of the body as well. It is a Redemption of man in his whole complex personality — body and soul together. It was in the body that Christ rose from the dead, in the body that He has ascended to heaven; in the body that He lives and reigns for ever more".

    His promise to us, Orr observed, "includes a pledge of the resurrection of the body. The truth which underlies this is, that death for man is an effect of sin.   It did not lie in the Creator's original design for man that he should die — that these two component parts of his nature, body and soul, should ever be violently disrupted and severed as death now severs them.   Death is an abnormal fact in the history of the race; and Redemption is, among other things, the undoing of this evil, and the restoration of man to his normal completeness as a personal being . . . .

"It is a false view of the constitution of human nature to regard the body as a mere appendage to the soul, or to suppose that the human being can be equally complete whether he has his body or is deprived of it . . . .   The perfect life for man is a corporeal one; and he is not *pure* spirit, but incorporated spirit" [emphasis his] .

Later he wrote: "It was no part of the Creator's design for man in his ideal constitution that body and soul should ever be separated.   The immortality that man was to enjoy was an immortality in which the body was to have its share . . . .   True immortality is through Redemption, and this Redemption embraces the resurrection of the body".

Orr considered this physical side of the plan of Redemption to be just as fundamental to it as the spiritual.   As he put it [p. 330 f.] : "The aim of God as regards believers is summed up in the simple phrase — conformity to the image of the Son . . . .   This conformity to Christ includes not only moral and spiritual likeness to Christ, but likeness to Him also in his glorious body;   that is, the Redemption of the body, life in a glorified corporeality . . . .

"The doctrine of Redemption of the body is needful for the completion of the Christian view.   It is not an accident, but an essential and integral part of it.   It is essential to a complete Redemption as we saw in speaking of immortality, that not the soul only, but man in his whole complex personality, body and soul together, should be redeemed . . . .

"The doctrine of the Resurrection of the body is not exposed to some of the objections often made to it.   How, it is asked, can the identical body be raised when it is utterly decayed, and the particles of which it is composed are scattered to the winds of heaven . . . .?   But the Resurrection does not involve any such belief.   The solution lies, I think, in a right conception of what it is which constitutes *identity*".

Then he extends his view logically by saying: "The doctrine of the Christian Consummation carries with it, further, the idea that, together with the perfecting of the believer, there will be a perfecting or glorification even of outward nature.   This is implied in the possession of corporeity of any kind, for that (corporeity) stands in relation to an environment, to a general system of things" [p. 333].

If the *body* is essential to truly human existence, and the body is to be raised so that man once again lives in the totality of his complex being, he must live *in* an appropriate environment.   Otherwise he has a part of his being (his body) which is totally foreign to any new universe that does not share its corporeality.   Thus the promise of Scripture is not merely a new heaven but a new *earth* also (Rev.21:1)!

Apropos of the present interest in unidentified flying objects and visitors from outer space, and apropos of the present discussions among biologists about the possibility of other worlds of intelligent beings, it is interesting to read the following words written by Orr so many years ago: "The question still remains even if all these bright worlds were inhabited . . . . by rational beings like to man himself, — are they sinful?   Sin retains its awful significance in the universe, no matter how many worlds there may be.   If this

world alone is sinful, then it is worthy of God to redeem it . . . . The scope
of God's purpose is *not* confined to this little planet but embraces all the
realms of creation" [p. 326, 327].

Because Redemption includes the body, if such intelligences from other
worlds have bodies and are essentially as human as we are, then there can
hardly be any question that they are as redeemable as we. Yet we do not
have any stated evidence in the New Testament that the Lord's sacrifice
extends beyond the human race. We only know that as *in Adam* all die, so
in Christ shall all be made alive (1 Cor.15:22). It might be argued that perhaps there are such intelligences, but they do not need redeeming because,
unlike man, they have not fallen. In which case we have nothing to fear
from them — except that they might be corrupted by us! The only passage
that I can think of which might open the slightest potential in this direction
is in Isaiah 9:7 which reads: "Of the *increase* of his government and peace
there shall be no end". It is not interminability per se that is here promised,
but rather continuous increase: and one has to ask, Increase in what direction? To other worlds than ours?

222. This is a fact of profound theological *and biological* importance. I say *biological* because there is a strong movement, even among evangelicals, to
abandon the doctrine of the creation of Adam's body. The theory is that
so long as he had a specially created spirit (or soul), he had all he needed to
qualify as a human being. His body could have been evolved and it would
make no difference. This volume demonstrates that to surrender to the
demands of evolutionary philosophy would be fatal to evangelical theology.

Many Christians have unthinkingly accepted this "out" — including the
Roman Catholic Church which now officially condones it so long as Adam's
soul is still held to have been a direct creation. The departure began among
evangelicals a long time ago and is to be observed in embryo form in the
works of A. A. Hodge [*Evangelical Theology*, 1890, Banner of Truth
reprint 1976, p. 148, 154, 155], A. H. Strong [*Systematic Theology*, 1906,
Phila, Judson Press, reprint 1974, p. 76], and B. B. Warfield [*Biblical and
Theological Studies*, 1911, Phila, Presbyterian & Reformed Publ. Co., 1968,
p. 238 ff.]. Warfield effectively destroys the chronological framwork of
Scripture in order to accomodate, surreptitiously, an evolutionary interpretation of the origin of man's body. He thus leaves us with a shadowy figure
in some exceedingly remote period of time whom we are called upon to
visualize nevertheless (in his unfallen state at least) as the prototype of the
Second Adam. The foundations of biblical history are almost hopelessly
confused and the rationale of the plan of redemption is accordingly undermined.

The Papal encyclical (*Sui Generis*), already referred to, supplies all the
latitude the orthodox Roman Catholic scholar could ask for in the face of
the implacable offensive of evolutionary philosophy. The encyclical does
emphasize that evolution is still only a theory — but most readers will not
recognize the significance of this cautionary addendum.

223. In some circles there is considerable debate as to whether the Lord's body
was *identical* with ours or only *similar*. It is argued that if his body was
only similar, then He was not a true representative of *man*. Against this
argument it may be said by contrast that we ourselves in our present fallen
state are not *truly* man, and that true Man is to be found only in Adam
before he fell. Since the Fall did irreparable and fatal damage to his body,
a damage shared by all his natural born descendants, then any human being

appearing with such a body as we now have is not a true representative of man-hood as originally constituted by God.

Thus it is appropriate that Romans 8:3 should state very specifically that God sent his Son only "*in the likeness* of sinful flesh" but not actually in the flesh of sin which is ours since the Fall. The Greek is unequivocal. It reads: *en homoiōmati sarkos hamartias* (ἐν ὁμοιώματι σαρκὸς ἁμάρτιας). The crucial word here is *homoiōmati* (ομοιωματι) which means very precisely "similar to" but not "identical with". The first part of this word is *homoi-* (ομοι-) which is to be most careully distinguished from *homo-* (ομο-). The difference lies only in the single letter *i* (iota in Greek) which though seemingly slight makes all the difference in the world. A Greek scholar will not need elaboration of this, but for the reader not acquainted with Greek, here are a number of examples of this prefixed syllable in its two forms and the difference it makes to the words to which they are prefixed.

homoieides	means	"of *like* kind"
homoeides	means	" of the *same* kind"
homoios	means	"*resembling*", "like" (so rendered 47 x in KJV)
homos	means	"one and *the same*"
homonoeō	means	"of *one* mind"
homometrios	means	" of the *same* mother" (i.e., true siblings).

The verb *homoioo* is regularly used to introduce parables: for example, "the Kingdom of heaven is *like* unto . . . ." [see Kittel, *Theological Dictionary of the New Testament*, Vol. V, p. 189].

In the article in Kittel on the word *homoiōma* by Johannes Schneider, emphasis is placed upon the above distinctions, and Romans 8:3 is particlarly referred to. As Schneider says: "Paul is emphasizing that Christ was really man. He bore a physical body, fashioned according to the human body which is infected with sin. *In outward form* He was in no way different from other men. But Paul does not say that He came *en sarki hamartias* [i.e., He did not come in sinful flesh, but only in the *likeness* of sinful flesh, ACC]. With his words *en homoiōmati* Paul is showing that for all the similarity between Christ's physical body and that of [other] men, there is an essential difference between Christ and men . . . . He became man without entering the *nexus* [the actual stream, ACC] of human sin" [p. 195].

The distinction between the two groups of words prefixed by *homo-* and *homoi-* is universally recognized by scholars, and by taking careful note of these distinctive usages in the New Testament many wonderful truths become apparent. For example, that the Lord was tempted in all points *like* we are, means (according to the Greek) "in a similar manner" but not "in an identical manner" (Heb.4:15). The Lord "was made in the likeness of men", but not identical with us as fallen creatures (Phil.2:7). We have been "planted together in the *likeness* of his death" but obviously not in precisely the same way (Rom.6:5). Schneider quotes H. Schlier on this verse as saying "the image (or likeness) of his death is *like* its object but not equivalent" [p. 192]. And he quotes S. Stricker as saying, "It is something similar *in another form*". Again, "It behoved Him to be made *like* unto his brethren in all things that He might be a merciful and faithful high priest" (Heb.2:17) but manifestly not to be made exactly as his brethren are, for then He could never have become our High Priest in the very presence of God.

Students of Church History will recognize the importance of the distinction between the words *homo-ousias* (of the *same* substance) and *homoi-ousias* (of *like* substance) in the formulation of the Nicene Creed (325-374). The Eastern Church favoured the view that the Lord Jesus was only of *like* substance with the Father, whereas the Western Church held the view that He was of the *same* substance ("of *one* substance") with the Father. The result was a final rupture between the Eastern and Western branches of the Church which remains officially to this day. This fundamental division was over an iota, the difference between *homo-* and *homoi-*. Yet this *iota* was crucial to the preservation of the Christian faith! It is interesting that the Lord should have said "not one jot (the Greek iota) . . . . shall pass away from the law till all be fulfilled" (Matt.5:18).

Athanasius himself (c. 296-373), who became a great defender of the *homo-ousias* principle, tells us that in the matter of proving the faith of Christian leaders "*homo-ousias* became the crucial test of orthodoxy" [*The New Schaff-Herzog Encyclopedia of Religious Knowledge*, Grand Rapids, Baker, 1969, Vol. I, p. 345]. And Augustus Neander, in his nine volume *General History of the Christian Religion and Church*, tells us that it was made the "watch-word" as a bulwark in the Nicene Creed against the Arianism favoured by the Eastern Church at that time [Edinburgh, Clark, 1885, Vol. IV, esp. p. 38 ff.].

224. Augustine listed four alternative views regarding the origin of the soul. These four still remain valid today, except that the strict materialist would add that "soul" is a property of matter and appears, not as an addendum but as matter reaches a certain level of organization. These four alternatives are:

(1) All souls are derived (Latin *traducere*, hence the word *traducianism*) from the one given to the first man.

(2) Each individual soul is a direct creation (hence the term *creationism*).

(3) Souls already in existence are sent by divine act into bodies, a form of divinely ordered distribution *(pre-existence)*.

(4) Souls of the departed are reincarnated at their own instigation, or by invitation of the living, or by some ritual manipulation, other than by divine decree *(re-incarnation)*.

The two that have been debated most earnestly by the Church are Traducianism and Creationism. Some form of pre-existence and/or reincarnation has at times been seriously defended. The Jewish rabbis tended towards reincarnation, and this is reflected perhaps in their supposition that Elijah had re-appeared in John the Baptist (Matt.16:14; cf. also Matt.14:2, and also cf. Nicodemus' words in John 3:4). The Alexandrian School under the influence of Origen (185-254 A.D.) was the most forthright defender of pre-existence, but Origen's views were officially condemned by the Catholic Church in 543, by the *Canons Against Origen* [See G. C. Berkouwer, *Man: The Image of God,* Grand Rapids, Eerdmans, 1975, p. 284, fn. 8].

In due time the Roman Catholic theologians settled for *Creationism*, and it is possible that this fact drove Luther to favour *Traducianism*, although in his later years he seems less certain in this respect. Lutheranism, however, has not deviated from this traducianist position. Luther was greatly influenced in his thinking by Augustine. And in this matter Augustine never seems to have quite made up his mind. This is reflected in his correspondence with Jerome. In his letter [No. CLXVI written in 415 A.D.] and titled

"On the Origin of the Human Soul" [chap. IV, § 8] he wrote: "To avoid unnecessary words, let me refer to the opinion which you, I believe, entertain, viz., that God even now makes each soul for each individual at the time of birth".   And then in § 10 he confesses his problem with the opposite view, *Traducianism*, saying that it seems to him strange and unfair that an innocent babe should inherit a soul already guilty along with a body already defective — and be condemned, unless baptized, on that account.

So he comments, "I am willing that the opinion which you hold should be mine also; but I assure you that as yet I have not embraced it".   And it is not clear from his other voluminous works whether he ever did take a firm stand for *Creationism*.

Traducianism is a very ancient view.   From a book now apparently lost, which bore the title *The Two Tables of the Covenant* (author unknown?), we find the following statement quoted as from page 8, col. 2: "The soul of Adam is the root of all souls, and from him all souls were spread out . . . . for all were by his strength" [See F. R. Tennant, *The Sources of the Doctrines of the Fall and Original Sin*, N.Y., Schocken Books, 1968, p. 167].

Traducianism has always seemed the simplest way to explain the universality of man's fallen nature and the explanation for his inheritance of original sin.   The concept of Adam as a Federal Head of the race in whom the whole race sinned has appealed to many as the best explanation of Romans 5:18 and 19.   Charles Hodge in his *Systematic Theology*, though holding firmly to the Creationist position, nevertheless frankly admits that this argument for Traducianism is a powerful one [Grand Rapids, Eerdmans, 1973 reprint, Vol. II, chap. 3, §2, p. 69].

Franz Delitzsch leans strongly towards traducianism [*System of Biblical Psychology*, Grand Rapids, Baker, 1966 reprint, p. 137].   He makes much of the argument that we have a clear precedent in Scripture in Hebrews 7:9, 10 where we are told that Levi paid tithes in Abraham.

Others argue that God is not actively "creating" today: that He ceased his creative activity in Genesis 2:2.   That Jesus in John 5:17 assures us that his Father is still actively at work is not taken to be any contradiction since the reference is assumed to be to his active providence, not *creativity*.   Nevertheless, in the matter of the soul or spirit, we cannot overlook the implication of 2 Corinthians 5:17 where creation of a new spirit is clearly indicated — implying that the old spirit was also created.

W. G. T. Shedd held absolutely to a traducianist position.   He wrote: "The *creation* of the soul subsequently to the conception of the body, and its infusion into it, is contrary to all the analogies of nature" [*Dogmatic Theology*, Grand Rapids, Zondervan, 1969 reprint, Vol. II, p. 76].   By contrast, Calvin was an equally forthright creationist.   A footnote in the McNeill edition of his *Institutes* sums up his position by saying, "Calvin completely rejects the (traducianist) teaching" [Phila., Westminster Press, 1975, Bk. I. i. 7, fn. 20].   Beza and Turrettin both followed Calvin.   In his *Institutio* [IX. xii. 6], Turrettin wrote: "Some are of the opinion that the difficulties pertaining to the propagation of original sin are best resolved by the doctrine of the propagation of the soul *(animae traducem);* a view held by not a few of the Fathers and towards which Augustine seems frequently to incline.   And there is no doubt that by this theory all the difficulties seem to be removed; but since it does not accord with Scripture nor with sound reason, and is exposed to great difficulties, we do not think that recourse should be had to it".

Augustine could not see how a newly created and perfect spirit could be infused into a corrupted body by which it was itself to be corrupted. And yet he could at the same time give examples of a similar nature, where good seed is sown in bad ground.   And he often returned to the question of the justice of condemning innocent children, who had not had the "benefit" of Christian baptism, for a guilt in which they had really never taken any active part personally.

Louis Berkhof asks the pertinent question as to why, if souls are derived *mediately* from Adam and not *immediately* by creation, are they held responsible only for Adam's sin in the Garden and not for all the other and later sins of his life? [*Systematic Theology*, Grand Rapids, Eerdmans, 1969, p. 198].   And, one may ask further, why are we not each of us responsible for all the sins of Adam's *descendants* in the direct line of our own descent? This would have the curious consequence of making each individual soul cumulatively more sinful than all its predecessors as it added its own guilt to theirs!

It is also to be noted that when Eve was brought to Adam he did not exclaim, "This is now flesh of my flesh and spirit of my spirit" but "bone of my bones and flesh of my flesh" (Gen.2:23) as though to emphasize that her body was indeed derived from his but not the spiritual component of her being.   Perhaps one of the commonest arguments against traducianism is the Lord's statement to Nicodemus in John 3:6, a statement which seems almost to refer back to Genesis 2:23, "that which is born of the flesh is flesh; and that which is born of the spirit is spirit".

It is sometimes difficult to know what the Reformed position actually is. Certainly Abraham Kuyper is not a traducianist; yet he held that each man receives his human nature " not *directly* from God but from God through Adam".   Exactly how this is to be understood is not clear, for he statedly chose creationism nevertheless.   He held that God *creates* the soul, in the embryo — the embryo having a predisposition towards a soul predestined for it.   The soul is wholly distinct, and human personality originates in the unity of the body and the soul [See on this, G. C. Berkouwer, *Man: The Image of God*, Grand Rapids, Eerdmans, 1975, p. 289].   Berkouwer states Kuyper's position as being that God "directly and instantly creates" the soul but not in an arbitrary form but specificially for the body it is to indwell.

The issue is clearly one that cannot be resolved to the satisfaction of all parties.   Admittedly both sides can produce "proof texts".   For myself, it seems that the weight of the evidence is strongly in favour of creationism — particularly Genesis 2:23 by implication and in the light of John 3:6; and such passages as Ecclesiastes 12:1, 7.   Genesis 2:2 is counterbalanced by John 5:17 and 2 Corinthians 5:17.   The Fall intervened.   The only difficult passage, to my mind, is Romans 5:18 and 19.   Yet logically, speaking as one with scientific training in a laboratory, I do not think a sound biblical psychology can be built on a traducianist basis, though I acknowledge the work of Franz Delitzsch as a magnificent effort.

225. There is a possibility, though I think it somewhat remote, that the words in Hebrews 2:9, "by the grace of God" ($\H{o}\pi\omega\varsigma$ $\chi\acute{a}\rho\iota\tau\iota$ $\theta\epsilon o\tilde{v}$) may be a transcription error for an original $\H{o}\pi\omega\varsigma$ $\chi\omega\rho\iota\varsigma$ $\theta\epsilon o\tilde{v}$, which would then read "apart from God".   There are a number of New Testament manuscripts and ancient authorities for this alternative.   The meaning would then perhaps be that "He, the Lord Jesus Christ, tasted death *but not as God*".   This is contrary to Scripture (as the following passages show by implication:

Acts 20:28; 1 John 3:16; 1 Timothy 3:16; Luke 17:15, 16; Revelation 1:6, "unto *God*, and his Father").

The problem is to know how to reconcile the idea that God could not die while yet keeping in view the fact that only One who was God could make an atonement sufficient for the sins of the whole world, as 1 John 2:2 seems to require.

226. It has been argued that Heli had at least two daughters, for in John 19:25 reference is made to Mary's *sister*. To have two Marys in the same family seems most unusual unless (as sometimes happens) the later one is named after a sister who has predeceased her. We know this was not true in the present instance for both Marys are spoken of as alive together.   An alternative is to suppose that the Mary of John 19:25 was really only a sister-in-law.   This is fair enough in so far as she would be called Mary's sister in Jewish terminology.   But such a sister-in-law cannot have been the wife of a *brother* of our Mary because it is virtually certain that any brother of Mary would have been mentioned somewhere in the record.   She may have been a sister-in-law by some less direct connection — and this would still account for the wording of John 19:25. There is also the fact that our Mary is called Mariam (Matt.13:55) whereas the Mary of John 19:25 is call- ed Maria. The fact could be made the basis of an argument for the existence of two daughters of Heli, true sisters with variants of a common Jewish name.

227. Repair of DNA. On this subject see A. M. Srb, *Genes, Enzymes and Pop- ulations*, N.Y., Plenum, 1973, p. 223-235. A more readily accessible paper with some excellent diagrammatic illustrations was published by P. C. Han- awalt and R. H. Haynes, "The Repair of DNA", *Sci. Amer.*, Feb., 1967, pp. 36-43. These authors wrote: "Modern industry . . . . involves intensive application of quality-control procedures for the correction of manufactur- ing errors, since even the best assembly lines can introduce faulty parts at an unacceptable rate . . . . Recent studies have demonstrated that living organ- isms employ analogous processes for repairing defective parts in their genetic material: deoxyribonucleic acid (DNA).   This giant molecule must be replicated with extraordinary fidelity if the organism is to survive and make successful copies of itself.   Thus the existence of quality-control mechan- isms in living cells may account in large part for the fact that 'like produces like' over many generations.

"Until recently it has been thought that if the DNA in a living cell were damaged or altered, for example by ionizing radiation, the cell might give rise either to mutant daughter cells or to no daughter cells at all. Now it appears that many cells are equipped to deal with some of the most serious hazards the environment can present . . . .   The ability to recover from injury is a characteristic feature of living organisms".

228. It is an over-simplification to say that the dogma of the Immaculate Con- ception was the Roman Catholic answer to this problem, yet essentially this is the case. This doctrine teaches that Mary herself when she conceived was freed by sanctification from the taint of original sin. It is interesting to note that a precedent was believed to exist by reference to Jeremiah 1:5 which speaks of that prophet being sanctified before he "came out of the womb". Why could this not be true also of Mary?

The doctrine was the result of long and deep reflection upon the problem of how the Lord's body escaped this stain; and it was formulated, of course, in the absence of what is now known about the foetal relationship between mother and child. Since that time, the Roman Catholic theologians have at least officially favoured the position that by reason of the immaculate conception of Mary herself, the sinful but not the human connection between Adam's body and the Lord's body was severed so that the latter was free of original sin but truly human. During prenatal development the Lord's body was preserved or was sanctified in the virgin's womb due to the presence of the divine soul which infused it.

Here are some of the "feelings after the truth" that we find from the writings of the earlier Church Fathers and up to and including Reformation times as men struggled with the problem.

Athanasius (c. 296-373), the great champion of orthodoxy against Arianism, held that Christ's body was first redeemed and then sanctified to become the means of our redemption. As he put it: "Although it was only after He was made man for us and became our brother by similitude of body, still He is called (and is) the 'first-born' of us, because all men being lost according to the transgression of Adam, his flesh before all others was saved and liberated as being the body of the Logos [i.e., the divine Son]. And henceforth we, becoming incorporate with It, are saved after Its pattern" [*Apologia Contra Arianos*, Discourse II. lxi, in *Ante-Nicene Fathers*, N.Y., Scribner, 2nd series, 1913, Vol. IV, p. 381, col. b]. It will be noted that Athanasius did not for one moment suppose that the Lord as Logos needed redemption, but only his body as received from Mary.

Augustine (354-430) wrote: "If the soul of Christ be derived from Adam's soul, He, in assuming it to Himself, *cleansed it* so that when He came into this world He was born of the virgin perfectly free from sin either actual or transmitted. If however the souls of men are *not* derived from that one soul [of Adam] and it is only by the flesh that original sin is transmitted from Adam, then the Son of God created a soul for Himself just as He creates souls for all other men: but He united it not to sinful flesh but only to the 'likeness of sinful flesh' (Rom.8:3)" [Letter No. 164, chap. 7, 19, *Nicene and Post-Nicene Fathers*, N.Y., Scribner, 1st series, 1885, Vol. 1, p. 521].

One observes the influence of Augustine's thought on Roman Catholic theology which also holds that original sin was excluded from the soul of Jesus by the sanctification of it through the divine indwelling presence of the Logos.

In the eighth century, *Felix of Urgellis* (d. 818 in Spain) maintained that the Logos united Himself with a human nature that was *not* sanctified, and that therefore Christ had a corrupted nature although He never actually committed sin. He believed this was a necessary condition of his incarnation in order that He might be tempted in all points like as we are, that is to say, that He might be tempted *from within* also [quoted by W. G. T. Shedd, *Dogmatic Theology*, Grand Rapids, Zondervan, 1969 reprint, Vol. II, p. 302].

It is important, as we have already noted, to keep in mind that the words *like as* (represented in the Greek by *homoi*-otēta) does not mean in exactly the same way — which would have required some such form as *homo*-otēta [see ref. # 223 on this].

Anselm (1033-1109) in his *Cur Deus Homo?* [Bk. II, chap. 17] has his companion in conversation arguing that Christ's mother's body was somehow purified "prospectively" by the power of Jesus' death. With this Anselm seems to agree.

John Calvin (1509-1564) wrestled with the problem.   In his *Institutes* [II. xiii. 4] he wrote: "They betray their ignorance who argue that if Christ is perfectly immaculate and was begotten of the seed of Mary by the secret operation of the Spirit, then it follows that there is no impurity in the seed of the woman, but only in that of the man.   We do not represent Christ as perfectly immaculate merely because He was born of the seed of the woman unconnected with any man, but because He was sanctified by the Spirit in order that the generation might be pure and undefiled as would have been true before Adam's fall".

If only he had known what we now know, he might have seen how near to the truth was that which he firmly denied!

Zacharius Ursinus (1534-1583) in his *Christian Religion* (Question 35) wrote: "Mary was a sinner: but the mass of flesh which was taken out of her substance was by the operation of the Holy Spirit at the same instant sanctified when it was taken".

John Owen (1616-1683) in his *Discourse on the Holy Spirit* [II, published in 1674] wrote: "The human nature of Christ, being thus formed in the womb by a supernatural creative act of the Holy Spirit was in the instant of its conception sanctified and filled with grace . . . . (this) human nature, being not begotten by natural generation, derived no taint of original sin or corruption from Adam".

Francois Turrettin (1623-1687) in his *Institutio Theologae Elencticae* [XIII. xi. 10] wrote: "The Holy Spirit must prepare the substance cut away from the substance of the virgin by a suitable sanctification . . . . by purifying it from all stain of sin . . . . and this in order that Christ may be born without sin.   There is no need of having recourse to the doctrine of the immaculate conception of Mary (herself)".

John Howe (1630-1705), a non-Conformist Puritan theologian, in his *Oracles* [II. xxxvii] wrote: "It is a mighty confirmation of the natural descent of sin with the nature of man in the ordinary way, that when God designed the incarnation of his own Son, in order to avoid the corruption of nature descending to Him, He then steps out of the ordinary course; a consideration that hath weight with it, that, if anyone allow himself to think, it must overbear his mind in that matter, that surely there is some secret profound reason in the council of God — whether obvious to our view or not obvious — that the descent of corrupt nature was in the ordinary way unavoidable; that when God had a design to incarnate his own Son, when it was intended that God should be manifested in the flesh, to avoid that contagion and corruption which in the ordinary course is transmitted, He doth in this single instance recede and go off from the ordinary course. Because the human nature had been corrupted if it had descended in the ordinary way, therefore the ordinary course of procreation is declined and avoided: a most pregnant demonstration that in the ordinary course sin is always naturally transmitted" [quoted by W. G. T. Shedd, *Dogmatic Theology*, Grand Rapids, Zondervan, 1969 reprint, Vol. II, p. 2].   For all the complexity of his sentence structure, it is clear that Howe was nearer than most of his predecessors to recognizing the real significance of the virgin conception.

Throughout these centuries men had struggled with the problem.   How could the Lord Jesus be truly human without a truly human body, and how could He acquire a truly human body without also acquiring the taint of original sin?   Many adopted the view that his body had to be, and indeed was, sanctified either by his own entry into it or by the Holy Spirit before He entered it.   At first the relevance of the virgin conception does not seem to have been clearly perceived.   One of the earliest of the Church Fathers, *Justin Martyr* (110-165), illustrates lack of perceptiveness in this regard when he wrote: "And our Lord Jesus Christ was born of a virgin, *for no other reason* [emphasis mine] than that he might destroy the begetting by lawless desire, and might show to the devil that the formation of man was possible to God without human intervention" [*Fragments of the Lost Works of Justin on the Resurrection*, chap. III, *Ante-Nicene Fathers*, N.Y., Scribner, 1913, Vol. I, p. 295].   To Justin, the virgin birth was a display of God's miraculous power and a rebuke to Satan.   That it could be related to the present issue was not perceived.

It was not until considerably later that it began to be realized such a perfect body was not preserved against the inheritance of original sin by some act of cleansing but by the exclusion of natural generation.   Thus it slowly became apparent that the male seed had to be by-passed.

It is perhaps time now to explore afresh the signficance of the necessity of virginal conception in the light of modern knowledge.

229. Aristotle, quoted by Ashley Montagu, *Human Heredity*, N.Y., World Publ. Co., 1959, p. 19.

230. Wheeler, John A., "Our Universe: the Known and the Unknown", *Amer. Scientist*, Spring, 1968, p. 18.

231. Huxley, Sir Julian, quoted by E. L. Mascall, *The Importance of Being Human*, N.Y., Columbia Univ. Press, 1958, p. 7.

232. For many years until retirement, I served as Head of the Human Physiology Laboratories of the Defense Research Board in Ottawa (Canada).   With highly sophisticated equipment we were engaged in measuring heat stress under various conditions in human volunteer subjects.   One of the most important instruments which was developed in the Laboratories was a Sudorimeter for measuring sweating rates at *exceedingly* low levels, as an index of the body's ability to maintain thermoregulation.   I believe that we would have detected very distinctly a fundamental difference in the functioning of the Lord's body in this respect, since sweating in man is clearly linked (in Genesis 3:19) to certain consequences of man's fallen constitution.

The fact is that sweating (by constrast with perspiration) is directly linked to the circumstance that our appetite for food exceeds the body's needs by approximately 200%, and since this food generates heat that is not needed, a back-up system for the removal of heat has to be set in motion.   If we ate a quarter of what we normally do, this back-up system would not be triggered nearly so soon — but we should be everlastingly hungry.   Appetite and actual need have now been thrown out of adjustment, presumably by the Fall.

This might be considered highly speculative, but we are dealing with what is essentially in this respect a heat-engine that is defective, and the level of its defectiveness is demonstrably related in quantitative terms to its inner state of health when tested under controlled conditions.

233. Gould, G. M. and W. L. Pyle, *Anomalies and Curiosities of Medicine*, N.Y., Julian Press, 6th printing, 1966, p. 698.

234. Gould, G. M. and W. L. Pyle, *ibid*, p. 697.

235. Gould, G. M. and W. L. Pyle, *ibid*, p. 697.

236. F. R. Tennant observed that it was universally taught by the rabbis that our

first parents brought death upon themselves by disobedience. That Adam did not die on the day he ate the forbidden fruit is sometimes explained by the rabbis, as it is in the *Book of Jubilees*, by taking the day to be a thousand years [*Sources of the Doctrines of the Fall and Original Sin*, N.Y., Schocken Books, 1968 reprint, p. 161].

One deviation from this general view, which is found in the *Syriac Baruch-Apocalypse*, is that the penalty was not in death itself but in its prematureness. Adam's death was untimely. The *Book of Enoch, Pseudo-Philo, The Apocalypse of Moses*, most copies of *Baruch-Apocalypse*, and *4 Ezra* all assert physical death was caused by the Fall. The *Slavonic Book of Enoch* attributes the introduction of death to Eve, as does Ecclesiasticus (25:24) which reads: "From a woman sin had its beginning, and because of her we all die". The statement is true in a sense, but a far more precise statement is that made by Paul in Romans 5:12.

Another view found among the Church Fathers and in Jewish literature (*Pirke* di R. Elieser, c. 13) is that Satan was envious of Adam and desired to murder him, by persuading him to poison himself to death. Again, there is a measure of truth here and it is reflected in John 8:44 where the word *murderer* in the Greek is "man-killer".

Many of the Church Fathers explored the relationship between death and Adam's disobedience. Justin Martyr (c. 100-165 A.D.), one of the earliest, wrote: "When God formed man at the beginning, He suspended the things of nature on his [man's] will, and made an experiment by means of one commandment. For He ordained that, if he kept this commandment, he should partake of immortal existence; but if he transgressed it, the contrary should be his lot. Man having thus been made, and immediately looking towards transgression, naturally became subject to corruption. Corruption then becoming *inherent in nature*, it was necessary that He who wished to save should be the One to destroy the efficient cause of corruption". [This is found as a *Fragment of the Lost Writings of Justin*, in *Ante-Nicene Fathers*, N.Y., Scribner, 1913, Vol. I, p. 301]. It is not merely a concise observation: it also shows how it came about that the word *natural* was later applied to man's dying even by those who recognize that it was not part of his original constitution. Augustine sometimes speaks of death as natural for man, in this sense.

Tertullian (c. 160-215) said: "We know what was man's origin and boldly assert and persistently maintain that death happens not by way of natural consequence to man, but owing to a fault and defect which is not itself natural; although it is easy enough, no doubt, to apply the term *natural* to faults and circumstances which seem to have been inseparable to us from our very birth. If man had been directly appointed to die as the condition of his creation, then of course death must be imputed to nature. Now, that he was not thus appointed to die, is proved by the very law which made his condition depend on a warning and made death result from man's arbitrary choice. Indeed if he had not sinned he certainly would not have died. That cannot be nature which happens by the exercise of will after an alternative has been proposed to it, and not by necessity as the result of an inflexible and unalterable condition. Consequently, although death has various forms, in as much as its causes are manifold, we cannot say that the easiest death is so gentle as not to happen by violence to our nature. The very law which produces death, simple though it is, is yet violence. How can it be otherwise, when so close a companionship of soul and body, so inseparable a growth together from their very conception of two sister substances, is surrendered and divided?" ["A Treatise on the Soul", *Ante-Nicene Fathers*, *ibid*, Vol. III, p. 229].

Ambrose (c. 339-397), whose influence on Augustine was tremendous, took the view that death really was imposed as a merciful provision rather than a penalty. He wrote: "The Lord did not inflict death as a penalty but as a remedy. And to Adam when he sinned, one thing was appointed as a penalty, another for a remedy, when it is said: 'Because thou hast hearkened unto the voice of thy wife and hast eaten of the tree of which I commanded thee that of it alone thou should not eat, cursed is the ground in thy labour; in sorrow shalt thou eat of its fruit all thy days of thy life, etc. . . . till thou return to the earth from which thou wast taken'." So here are the two effects according to Ambrose: the burden of life (the penalty), and death (the remedy). Ambrose comments further: "So, then, death is not only an evil, but is even a good thing. So that it is sought as a good, as it is written, 'Men shall seek death and shall not find it. (Rev.9:6). They will seek it who shall say to the mountains, 'Fall on us', and to the hills, 'Cover us'. (Luke 22:30). That soul, too, shall seek it which has sinned. The rich man lying in hell shall seek it, who wishes that his tongue be cooled with the finger of Lazarus (Luke 16:24). We see then, that this death is a gain and life a penalty, so that Paul says, 'To me to live is Christ and to die is gain' (Phil. 1:21)" ["On the Belief in the Resurrection", Bk. II. 37. 3].

Much later, Thomas Aquinas (1224-1274) was to write: "Death is natural considering our material status, but penal considering how we lost the divine endowment of deathlessness" [*Summa Theologica*, 2 a - 2 ae, clxiv, *ad.* 1].

Francois Turrettin (1632-1687) in his *Atonement of Christ* [p. 81] considered that death was an essential remedy. "There are many other weighty reasons", he wrote, "rendering it necessary that all should die; such as that the remains of sin (i.e., the remaining root left in each of us) may be destroyed". Physical death was, in his view, the only way of destroying the seat of the root of sin, and is the answer to Paul's plea in Romans 7:24.

Augustus H. Strong (1836-1921) in his *Systematic Theology* wrote: "The objection that death existed in the animal creation before the Fall may be answered by saying that, but for the fact of man's sin, it would not have existed. We may believe that God arranged even the geological history to correspond with the foreseen fact of human apostasy (cf. Rom.8:20-23, where the creation is said to have been made subject to vanity by reason of man's sin)" [Phila., Judson Press, reprint 1974, p. 658]. Death in the animal world before man was therefore a kind of previsionary paradigm of something which was later to be a *penalty* for man.

Of death for the Christian, A. T. Schofield said, "Death is not an entrance into eternity but an exit from time" ["On Time and Eternity", *Trans. Vict. Inst.*, London, LIX, 1927, p. 284].

237. According to the *Gemarah*, which is a kind of Jewish history book of this period, the scarlet cloth which marked the scapegoat was supposed to turn white as a sign of God's approval in accordance with Isaiah 1:18. But we are told that this never actually happened during the last forty years before the fall of Jerusalem in 70 A.D. Whether the Jewish people were aware of the significance of this tradition, or indeed whether the change of colour had actually occurred in previous years, or was just a Jewish invention, are questions which cannot be answered now. But it is interesting that the tradition survived in their literature, and yet their religious authorities do

not seem to have realized its meaning.   The tradition is referred to by
Alfred Edersheim, *The Temple: Its Ministry and Services*, Grand Rapids,
Eerdmans, 1972 reprint, p. 312.

238. For treatment of the word *Azazel*, see *Smith's Dictionary of the Bible*,
     Grand Rapids, Baker reprint, Vol. I, p.197.   Also *Hastings Dictionary of
     the Bible*, N.Y., Scribners, 1905, Vol. I, p. 207, and *Lange's Commentary*,
     Grand Rapids, Zondervan, 1976 reprint, Vol. I, at Lev.16:8, p. 127.   Also
     L. Feinberg, "The Scapegoat of Leviticus 16", *Bibliotheca Sacra*, 115, Oct.,
     1958, p.320-333; *The Standard Jewish Encyclopedia*, sub. *Azazel*, p. 206;
     Louis Ginsberg, *Legends of the Jews*, Phila., Jewish Publ. Assoc. of Amer.,
     1955, Vol. I, p. 148 (= a fallen angel); G. F. Oehler, *Theology of the Old
     Testament*, N.Y., Funk & Wagnalls, 1883, p. 311; and F. R. Tennant, *The
     Sources of the Doctrines of the Fall and Original Sin*, N.Y., Schocken
     Books, 1968 reprint, p. 182 (connected with "Fallen Angels").

239. Einstein, Albert, quoted by Philipp Frank, *Einstein: His Life and Times*,
     N.Y., Knopf, 1947, p. 178 (chap. 8, § 5).

240. Milne, E. A., *Some Points in the Philosophy of Physics: Time, Evolution,
     and Creation*, Washington Smithsonian Inst. Annual Report, 1933, p. 236.

241. Karl Menninger observed: "The Quakers thought they were acting in a
     humane and Christian way when in 1789 they sought to substitute quiet
     (solitary) incarceration for the floggings, brandings, tongue slicings, ear
     amputations, and the uncomforable and humiliating stocks.   But these
     old-time punishments while painful were public and relatively brief. Intent-
     ionally fearful harships of incarceration were gradually added and the
     duration of the imprisonment became longer and longer.   Six months was
     once considered a very long sentence.   All American sentences are far
     greater than in English and Continental practice.   An adolescent was recent-
     ly sentenced by a Texas judge to thirty years' imprisonment for possessing
     two marihuana cigarettes, presumably for sale" [*Whatever Became of Sin*,
     N.Y., Hawthorne Books, 1975, p. 62] .   This only shows how the substitut-
     ion of duration for intensity can lead to absurdity.

242. Elsewhere in the Bible we seem to be presented with another alternative,
     the alternative of intensity: "few stripes or many" Luke 12:47, 48), accord-
     ing to the offence.   It could be, then, that the biblical term which we have
     rendered *eternal* or sometimes *everlasting* may not really signify duration at
     all.   It could conceivably be a qualitative term which carries rather the idea
     of intensity or depth, as it most certainly does in reference to eternal life.
     Eternal life is a different *kind* of life, a life with a different kind of intensity,
     a life more abundant (John 10:10), a life that does not lack the component
     of endless duration but whose distinguishing character is not so much end-
     lessness as depth.   Perhaps eternal punishment really means punishment
     whose intensity cannot actually be conveyed to our time-bound minds ex-
     cept by saying that it will be experienced as though it were endless.

243. Gould, G. M. and W. L. Pyle, *op. cit.*, (ref. #233), p. 519 f.

244. Tompkins, Peter, *Secrets of the Great Pyramid*, N.Y., Harper and Row,
     1971, p. 257.

245. Reclus, Eli, *Primitive Folk: Studies in Comparative Ethnology*, London,
     Scott, n.d., p. 204, 308.

246. MacIlraith, T., in lectures in the Dept. of Anthropology, University of Tor-

onto, 1954.

247. The Pharisees believed in resurrection but it was a general resurrection which was to occur only at the very end.   This much they were willing to admit, a circumstance which put them in opposition to the Sadducees who did not believe such things.   What the Pharisees were afraid of, in the case of the Lord's body was not so much that He would actually be raised from the dead, but rather that the disciples would steal his body by night and then *claim* that He had been raised from the dead.   For in spite of many things which He had said that they professed not to understand, they do seem to have realized that He was claiming that if He were put to death He would actually raise Himself again the third day (John 2:19).   In point of fact, the Jews seem to have had more fear of his body being removed than his disciples had faith that it might be resurrected!

249. There is an interesting parallel series of resurrections in the Old Testament which seem to be conveying the same message.   The first is found in 1 Kings 17:17-22 which relates the death of the widow of Zarephath's little son. One gathers from the account that this child died while Elijah was present in the house.   Elijah restored the child to his mother alive.

   The second account is found in 2 Kings 4:18-35.   This involved the death of a "grown child", probably due to heat stroke.   The Shunammite woman, his mother, had been hostess to Elisha under particularly dramatic circumstances in a time of general famine.   When the child died, Elisha was away on Mount Carmel some sixteen miles distant.   The Shunammite woman laid the child on Elisha's bed and immediately set out for Carmel.   Even under the best of circumstances, it must have taken her five or six hours to make the journey, and presumably the return journey would occupy another six hours or so.   This means that before Elisha arrived back at the scene of the child's death, some twelve hours had elapsed.   In verses 34 and 35 we learn that by a process perhaps akin to artificial respiration, he restored the child alive to his mother.

   The third instance, in 2 Kings 13:20 and 21, is a rather odd case of resurrection, and the circumstances are not exactly clear except that the young man involved was actually about to be interred in the ground.   It seems that Elisha had died and while he was being buried, a band of Moabite brigands were seen in the neighbourhood, causing those who were burying him to run for their lives.   They had, however, completed the digging of the grave and had laid Elisha's remains in it.   Another party happened at the same time to be on their way to bury the young man.   When they, too, observed the Moabites in the neighbourhood, they fled (as the others had done) but only after rather unceremoniously dropping the young man's body into Elisha's grave.   To their amazement, as soon as the corpse touched the body of Elisha, the young man was instantly restored to life, stood up on his feet, and presumably scrambled out of the grave and joined them in their flight.

   It is difficult to know exactly why the Lord has seen fit to give us this parallel sequence of revivals of the dead after what appears to be an increasing interval of time had passed since death.   But it does seem to be a remarkably similar series of events: revivals being witnessed in one just dead, dead some hours, and dead and effectively buried.

250. Tacitus says of the Christians, whom Nero blamed for the burning of Rome, that their "originator", Christ, had been executed in Tiberias' reign by the Governor of Judea, Pontius Pilate [*Annals of Imperial Rome*, XV. 43, tr. M. Grant, Penguin ed., 1961, p. 354].

251. Suidas: from F. A. Jones, *The Dates of Genesis*, London, Kingsgate Press, 1912, p. 114.

252. Clerke, A. M., *Encyclopedia Britannica*, 1953 ed., article, *Astronomy*.

253. Free, Joseph P., *Archaeology and Bible History*, Wheaton, Ill., Scripture Press, Publ., 1962, p. 32.

254. Pannekoek, Antone, "The Origin of the Saros", *Proc. Roy. Acad.*, Amsterdam, 20, communicated by W. de Sitter, 29 Sept., 1918, pp. 943-955.

255. Sarton, George, *op. cit.*, ref. #110, p. 119.

256. Sarton, George, *op. cit.*, ref. #110, p. 120.

257. Pannekoek, Antone, *op. cit.*, ref. #254, p. 943.

258. Meek, T. J., "Magic Spades in Mesopotamia", *Univ. Toronto Quart.*, 7, 1938, p. 243, 244.

259. Halley, Henry H., *Pocket Bible Handbook*, Chicago, 1951, p. 71.

260. Barton, George, *op. cit.*, ref. #108, p. 325.

261. Pritchard, James B., ed., *Ancient Near Eastern Texts Relating to the Old Testament*, Princeton, 1969, p. 265.

262. 2 Peter 2:5 — It is customary to say that in this passage the phrase "the "eighth" ($\overset{v}{o}\gamma\delta oov$) is a convenient way in the Greek of implying "with seven others", as though the writer really had in mind a phrase such as "he, being the eighth of a party". G. Abbott-Smith, in his *Manual Greek Lexicon*, agrees, but observes that the Greek word $a\dot{v}\tau o$ is usually added. This has not been done in the present instance, though I find that other biblical passages of a similar construction (including 2 Macc.5:27) also omit the $a\dot{v}\tau o$, although the meaning is clearly "with nine others". Young's *Literal Translation* has followed the Authorized Version, as has also the *Concordant Version* and that of Ferrar Fenton. It seems more likely to me that the meaning is strictly "the eighth", the definite article being used (cf. Luke 1:59). Since this is not so in 2 Peter 2:5, it is probable that the meaning is simply "with seven others".

263. Stroud, William, *The Physical Cause of the Death of Christ*, N.Y., Appleton, 1871, 422 pp.

264. Engel, George L., "Sudden and Rapid Death During Psychological Stress", *Ann. Internal Medicine*, 74, 5, 1971, p. 771-783 with extensive bibliography.

265. Valerius Maximus, *Factorum et Dictorum, Memorabilium*, Bk. IX. 12.

266. Titus Livius, *History of Rome*, Bk. XXII. 7.

267. Gaius Pliny, Bk. VII (on *Man*), § 7.

268. Galen: quoted by Gould and Pyle, *op. cit.*, ref. #233, p. 524.

269. Aulus Gellius, *Noctes Atticae*, (130-180 A.D.), Bk. III. 15.

270. Donatus, Marcellus, *De Medica Historia Mirabili*, Libri Sex. 4, Mantua, 1586.

271. Gould, G. M. and W. L. Pyle, *op. cit.*, ref. #233, p. 524.

272. Gould, G. M. and W. L. Pyle, *op. cit.*, ref. #233, p. 625.

273. *MD of Canada*, 14, 10, Oct., 1973, p. 62.

274. O'Rourke, Michael, reporting in *Lancet*, 21 July, 1973, p. 124.

275. Fischer, Daniel, *The London Medical Repository*, Vol. XI, p. 422-427.

276. *The London Medical Repository*, Vol. XII, 1819, p. 164-168.

277. Portal: quoting Dr. Baillie, "Treatise on Morbid Anatomy", *Anatomie des Krankhaften Baues*, etc., Berlin, 1794, tr. by Soemmering.

278. Krumbhaar, E. B. and C. Crowell, "Spontaneous Rupture of the Heart, A Clinical Pathological Study", *Amer. J. Med. Sci.*, **170**, 1928, p. 828 f.

279. Karsner, Howard T., *Human Pathology*, Phila, Lippincott, 1938, p. 379.

280. Zimmerman, J. G., *On Experience in Physic* (tr. from German), London, 1782, Vol. II, p. 268 f.

281. Friedberg, Charles K., *Diseases of the Heart*, Phila, Saunders, 1966, p. 854 f.

282. Friedberg, Charles K., *ibid*, p. 1691f.

283. Burns, Allan, *On Diseases of the Heart*, Edinburgh, 1809, p. 181.

284. Barnes, Albert, *Notes on the New Testament*, Grand Rapids, Kregel Publ., 1962, p. 1260 *loc. sit.*

285. Shelley, W. B. and H. J. Hurley, "Methods of Exploring Human Apocrine Sweat Gland Physiology", *Arch. Dermat. and Syph.*, 66, 1952, p. 156-161.

286. Rothman, Stephen, *Physiology and Biochemistry of the Skin.* Chicago Univ. Press, 1955, p. 187.

287. Bogoras: quoted by Alexander Goldenweiser, *Anthropology*, N.Y., Crofts, 1945, p. 251.

288. Stroud, William, *op. cit.*, ref. #263, p. 97.

289. Maldonatus, Joannes, *Commentary on the Four Gospels*, Paris, 1639, p. 601.

290. Schenck, Joannes, *Rarer Medical Observations* (Observ. Medicae Rariores), Frankfort, 1609, Bk. III, p. 458.

291. Tissot, S. A. D., *Traites des Nerfs*, Avignon, 1800, p. 279, 280.

292. Voltaire, F. M., *Complete Works*, Basle, 1785, Vol. 18, p. 531-532.

293. de Mezeray, *Histoire d'France*, Paris, 1685, Vol. III, p. 306.

294. Gould, G. M. and W. L. Pyle, *op. cit.*, ref. #233, p. 388-391.

INDEXES

It might seem that the making
of any Index is a straightforward
and simple matter.

But does one include *every* name?
Or only the important ones or those
occurring most frequently? And who
decides whether a name is important or not?

Under what headings does one catalogue an idea?

May we suggest to a frustrated reader who has been
searching the subject index fruitlessly that perhaps a
relevant name or biblical reference will provide a clue.

INDEX OF BIBLICAL REFERENCES

INDEX OF NAMES

INDEX OF SUBJECTS